THE MERCHANT OF VENICE

Shakespeare Criticism
Philip C. Kolin, *General Editor*

THE MERCHANT OF VENICE
NEW CRITICAL ESSAYS

EDITED BY

JOHN W. MAHON

AND

ELLEN MACLEOD MAHON

ROUTLEDGE
NEW YORK AND LONDON

Published in 2002 by
Routledge
29 West 35th Street
New York, NY 10001

Published in Great Britain by
Routledge
11 New Fetter Lane
London EC4P 4EE

Routledge is an imprint of the Taylor & Francis Group.

Printed in the United States of America on acid-free paper.

10   9   8   7   6   5   4   3   2   1

Cover photo: Peter Hutt as Antonio in Stratford Festival of Canada production, 2001. Photograph by V. Tony Hauser. Courtesy of the Stratford Festival
of Canada.

Library of Congress Cataloging-in-Publication Data

The merchant of Venice : new critical essays / edited by John W. Mahon and
Ellen Macleod Mahon.
    p. cm.—(Shakespeare criticism ; 26)
  Includes bibliographical references.
  ISBN 0-415-92999-7
    1. Shakespeare, William, 1564–1616. Merchant of Venice. 2. Shakespeare,
William, 1564–1616. Merchant of Venice. 3. Venice (Italy)—In literature.
4. Jews in literature. 5. Comedy. I. Mahon, John W. II. Mahon, Ellen
Macleod. III. Series.

PR2825.M37 2002
822.3'3—dc21   2001058186

For our parents

"How far that little candle throws his beams!"
(5.1.90)

Frank Stone, Study for *Bassanio Receiving the Letter Announcing Antonio's Losses and Peril* (ca. 1850–51). By Permission of the Folger Shakespeare Library.

Contents

List of Illustrations

Acknowledgments

This collection was inspired, in the first instance, by Thomas Pendleton—colleague and fellow-Shakespearean—who alerted us to the need. He has been an important support and model throughout the editing process.

We acknowledge also the inspiration of our Shakespeare teachers in formative years, especially Sr. Loretta Julie Costello, S. F. Johnson, and Erwin Geissman. Our own shared love for Shakespeare was deepened immeasurably by the friendship and support, over the last sixteen years of his life, of Professor Harold Jenkins. As we lost our own parents over the years of our friendship with him, Harold became a father to us both. He felt strongly that *The Merchant of Venice* was best understood as a comic romance, and often argued that one of its principal sources was the playwright's own *The Two Gentlemen of Verona*. Though he could not directly contribute to this volume, his mentoring inspired at least two of the essays as well as a network of good will.

Teachers rejoice to acknowledge the inspiration of their students, and we do. Having taught *Merchant* over many years, we have learned much from our students, including Terence Fitzgerald and Patti (Varol) Fitzgerald about the power and the challenges of Shakespeare's art. Many colleagues at Iona College, especially Joanne Laughlin Steele, Adrianna DiLello, Diana Breen, Kevin Fitzgerald, and Adrienne Franco, helped us to complete this work. We are also grateful for the assistance of several graduate students, including Diane Grecco and Tammyanne Fuller.

We acknowledge the encouragement and support provided by the general editor, Professor Philip Kolin, and by the professionals at Routledge, especially Anne Davidson, Emily Vail, and Henry Bashwiner. And we are grateful for help with the illustrations from a number of institutions and individuals. We have made every effort to identify and acknowledge the copyright holders of all illustrations. Any failure to acknowledge a copyright holder will be rectified in future editions, upon notification from the copyright holder.

Last, but hardly least, we are grateful to our contributors, the eighteen colleagues and friends from around the globe who have provided us with a collection worthy of the play, its author, and the new millennium. Bravo!

NEW ROCHELLE, NEW YORK
19 SEPTEMBER 2001

General Editor's Introduction

The continuing goal of the Shakespeare Criticism Series is to provide the most significant and original contemporary interpretations of Shakespeare's works. Each volume in the series is devoted to a Shakespearean play or poem (e.g., the sonnets, *Venus and Adonis, Othello*) and contains eighteen to twenty-five new essays exploring the text from a variety of critical perspectives.

A major feature of each volume in the series is the editor's introduction. Each volume editor provides a substantial essay identifying the main critical issues and problems the play (or poem) has raised, charting the critical trends in looking at the work over the centuries, and assessing the critical discourse that has linked the play or poem to various ideological concerns. In addition to examining the critical commentary in light of important historical and theatrical events, each introduction functions as a discursive bibliographic essay citing and evaluating significant critical works—books, journal articles, theatre documents, reviews, and interviews—giving readers a guide to the vast amount of research on a particular play or poem.

Each volume showcases the work of leading Shakespeare scholars who participate in and extend the critical discourse on the text. Reflecting the most recent approaches in Shakespeare studies, these essays approach the play from a host of critical positions, including but not limited to feminist, Marxist, new historical, semiotic, mythic, performance/staging, cultural, and/or a combination of these and other methodologies. Some volumes in the series include bibliographic analyses of a Shakespearean text to shed light on its critical history and interpretation. Interviews with directors and/or actors are also part of some volumes in the series.

At least one, sometimes as many as two or three, of the essays in each volume is devoted to the play in performance, beginning with the earliest and most significant productions and proceeding to the most recent. These essays, which ultimately provide a theater history of the play, should not be regarded as different from or rigidly isolated from the critical work on the script. Shakespeare criticism has often been informed by or has significantly influenced productions. Over the last thirty years or so Shakespeare criticism has understandably been labeled "The Age of Performance." Readers will find information in these essays on non-English speaking productions of Shakespeare's plays as well as landmark performances in English. Editors and contributors also include photographs from productions around the world to help readers see and further appreciate the ways a Shakespearean play has taken shape in the theater.

Ultimately, each volume in the Shakespeare Criticism Series strives to give readers a balanced, representative collection of the most engaging and thoroughly researched criticism on the given Shakespearean text. In essence, each volume provides a careful survey of essential materials in the history of criticism of a Shakespearean play or poem as well as cutting edge essays that extend and enliven our understanding of the work in its critical context. In offering readers innovative and fulfilling new essays, volume editors have made invaluable contributions to the literary and theatrical criticism of Shakespeare's greatest legacy, his work.

PHILIP C. KOLIN
UNIVERSITY OF SOUTHERN MISSISSIPPI

The Fortunes of *The Merchant of Venice* from 1596 to 2001

JOHN W. MAHON

Four hundred years after its first performance, *The Merchant of Venice* continues to draw audiences, spark debate, and offer new insights. In 2001 alone, the Stratford Festival in Canada (cover and Figure 3) and the Oregon Shakespeare Festival (Figure 10) both mounted major productions, and more modest productions appeared across the land, as at Boscobel House on the Hudson River. In April, the Seventh World Shakespeare Congress in Valencia, Spain, offered a Spanish-language version of the play, directed by a German. Patrick Stewart, noted for his Shylock with the Royal Shakespeare Company and for his articulate analysis of the character, performed his own one-man show, *Shylock: Shakespeare's Alien,* at the West Yorkshire Playhouse in Leeds in the summer. And in October, for the first time since the BBC version of the play was broadcast in 1980, American television presented *The Merchant of Venice* in a film of the recent Royal National Theatre production. Over the last decade, there have been many productions, not only in English-speaking countries (in 1998 it played simultaneously in Stratford and in London at the new Globe), but around the world, on every continent and in every conceivable language.[1] Among Shakespeare's characters, only Hamlet has inspired more critical commentary than Shylock (Zesmer 116).

Nevertheless, the play's alleged anti-Semitism has inspired some to call for its permanent banning; "perhaps it is time for critics around the world not only to concede the play's pernicious effects," concludes one writer, "but to dare to take the next step and earnestly discourage its perennial production" (Kachuck 72). Virtually every production arouses reaction and counterreaction,[2] and controversy erupts over its appropriateness for school curricula.[3]

This volume offers a collection of original essays on *The Merchant of Venice* from a variety of perspectives, including four essays focused on performance. To provide readers with a full historical and critical context, this essay examines various basic issues surrounding the play and then focuses on a review of four centuries of commentary and performance. It concludes with consideration of the play on the twentieth-century stage and screen, its fortunes outside the English-speaking world, and some allusions and adaptations. For fuller coverage of the extensive critical heritage, readers will wish to consult anthologies of criticism and annotated bibliographies, including those of Sylvan Barnet, Harold Bloom, Martin Coyle, Clifford C. Huffman, Thomas Wheeler, and John Wilders (all listed in "Works Cited" at the end of this essay).

I. Basic Issues

The Genre of the Play and Its Characters

A conundrum in so many ways, *The Merchant of Venice* is, to begin with, a taxonomist's nightmare: even Polonius might quail. Classified from its inception as a comedy, a history (story), or a "comicall historie," it inspired commentators as early as the eighteenth century to regard it as a tragedy, and the Holocaust of World War II has reinforced the idea that Shylock is not only the central character of the play but its tragic hero, who nevertheless leaves the stage, and the play, under his own power.[4]

The Merchant of Venice might, in fact, be best classified as a "problem" play. Indeed "all Shakespeare's plays," observes Lawrence Danson, "are problem plays, but some problem plays are more insistently problematic than others," and *Merchant* is "the most scandalously problematic" (1–2). Although treating the play in the category of "high comedies," Harold Bloom calls *Merchant* an "equivocal comedy" (*Invention* 171), and suggests that the grouping of Antonio-Portia-Shylock could be a "forerunner" of "equivocal groupings" in later "problem" plays: Helena-Bertram-Parolles; Pandarus-Thersites-Ulysses; Duke Vincentio-Isabella-Lucio (177). Yet Kenneth Myrick opens his introduction to the Signet Classic edition by proposing an entirely different set of links: "*The Merchant of Venice* is the earliest of three superb comedies in which Shakespeare has set a generous and clear-sighted woman in sharp contrast to a no less unusual, but markedly unsocial man. From beginning to end, Portia and Shylock—like Rosalind and Jaques in *As You Like It* and Viola and Malvolio in *Twelfth Night*—remain poles apart" (lxiii). Given Shakespeare's apparent determination in *The Merchant of Venice* to avoid definitive judgments or conclusions, useful comparisons could be made with another Shakespearean play of antinomies, *Antony and Cleopatra*.

There has never been agreement on the characters, about either their relative importance in the play or how they are to be regarded. There is even vigorous debate about the meaning of the characters' names, most especially Shylock's, as Grace Tiffany's contribution to this collection attests. Stephen Orgel's enlightening paper on "Shylock's Tribe" at the Seventh World Shakespeare Congress (2001) short circuits the debate by pointing out that *Shylock* is an old English, Saxon name, another form of Whitlock or Whitehead, meaning "white-haired."[5] Like *Romeo*, *Shylock* has entered the language, either as a noun referring to any "hard-hearted moneylender" or as an intransitive verb, "to lend money at extortionate rates of interest," in the definition offered by the *Random House Webster's Unabridged Dictionary* (1998).[6]

Few have proposed Antonio as the central character, although the title is his, and Barbara Lewalski's allegorical interpretation makes him both Everyman and Christ. But is he a selfless and generous friend, loyal unto death, an exemplum of the Gospel command to "Love one another, as I have loved you" (John 15, 12)? Or is he a bigoted, selfish, manipulative conniver and masochist, a raging anti-Semite who kicks Jews and is determined to keep Bassanio for himself, in death if not in life? Or any one of a number of gradations between these extremes? If Antonio is not the central character, the hero, who is? Shylock? Portia? For them, too, the range of interpretation is very broad.

Few would dismiss Shylock as a mere villain, cousin to Aaron the Moor and John the Bastard, yet even in an age highly sensitive to charges of anti-Semitism, he can be booed by an audience at the new Globe on Bankside even as he is cheered in many critical commentaries for his humanity and his witness against hypocritical Christians. Some have argued that he is a caricature of an Elizabethan Puritan. Whatever nuance of interpretation one adopts, Shylock's behavior, far more than his race or religion, makes him a villain.

And Portia, who for centuries was regarded as a heroine in the mold of Rosalind and Viola and Beatrice, and who achieved virtual apotheosis in Victorian commentary, is now sometimes regarded as a spoiled aristocrat who uses tricks to defeat both her father's will and Shylock; or she is judged as a shrewish and clever capitalist whose pretty speeches about Bassanio as lord and master are just that, pretty speeches. The iron hand in the glove taken from Antonio makes certain to retain control in Belmont, even as it has wrested the precious ring from Bassanio's finger, a view Karoline Szatek advances in her essay in this collection. Again, for both Shylock and Portia there are many other appraisals that fall somewhere between the extremes. The same can be said for Bassanio, Jessica, and Lorenzo.

Therefore, in terms of its appropriateness for either stage or curriculum, its genre, and its presentation of characters, *The Merchant of Venice* continues to provoke argument. But in areas that are problematic for other plays—text, date, sources—*Merchant* is relatively uncomplicated.

The Text

Most experts accept the Quarto published in 1600 as the most reliable text, although there are disagreements about how to treat some of the details, as John F. Andrews's essay in this volume demonstrates. Harold Jenkins has asserted that "the most important Shakespeare research in our century . . . is that which has been devoted to his text" (96), and respect for textual issues inspired by such commentators as Jenkins and J. Dover Wilson has prompted the publication of easily accessible editions of the First Folio and of various Quartos. Both versions of *Merchant* have been published in paperback. Applause Books offers the play as it appears in the First Folio, with an introduction that reviews some of the reasons for making this text available (Freeman xxxix–li).

The series "Shakespearean Originals: First Editions" provides the 1600 Quarto of *Merchant*. The importance of this diplomatic text is suggested in just one passage from Annabel Patterson's introduction:

> We can observe Shakespeare making a few mistakes of his own in the naming of characters and places; but we can also detect some of his habits, of orthography, punctuation, and even of thought. And from the special effects of the casket scenes to the rapid and symbolic interchange of the Venice/Belmont plots, more visible here than when sliced and spaced by modern typography, the Quarto gives the reader an intensely *lively* experience of the play's insistence on repetition, balance and ritual action. (14)

Providing such a text reinforces the interpretive insights of many commentators. For example, Myrick, noting that we see much of the play "through Portia's eyes," finds that structure contributes to this perspective, "in the skillful arrangement of contrasting scenes." Thus, Portia's first and second scenes frame Shylock's first, and her third follows Jessica's flight. Portia's fourth scene (2.9) initiates a pattern of alternation between her scenes and Shylock's "with almost complete regularity until their encounter in the courtroom. In this way the playwright silently draws ever more sharply the contrast between the usurer and the wise Renaissance lady, before either has any idea of the other's existence" (lxxiii–iv).[7]

Characteristic of everything to do with this play, the original Quarto text can also modify critical judgments. Thus James Bulman writes:

> If one regards Shylock as evil, then of course [his defeat in the trial scene] must seem good: the devil is exorcised, the Jew turns Christian. Yet Shakespeare endows Shylock with enough integrity to complicate our response to his defeat. This interplay between the individual and the type is interestingly reflected, as Bill Overton observes (pp.28–29), in variations of speech prefixes in the Quarto, where *Jew* precedes those speeches that tend to characterise Shylock as a traditional villain—his nasty aside in I.iii, his harassment of Antonio and the Jailer, and that portion of the trial where he exults in his apparent victory—and *Shylock* precedes those in which he deviates from the type: his domestic conversation with Jessica and Lancelot, his explosions of grief and anger in III.i, and all his speeches at the trial after Portia has defeated him. (21–22)

Bulman concludes that "if these variations originated in Shakespeare's man-uscript (and a scribe, compositor, or theatre official is unlikely to have intro-duced them), they afford us a glimpse of how consciously Shakespeare sought to revise the stage Jew as a credibly complex human being" (22).

Perhaps. Yet Patterson infers from the same Quarto text rather different conclusions about Shakespeare's attitudes:

> It is important to notice that whereas 'Shylock' is the commoner form in the early scenes . . . and is used exclusively in the scene where Tubal torments his kinsman . . . in the later scenes as the catastrophe approaches[,] the Quarto text, like the mood of the play, becomes *more* racially categorical. In the brief scene where Shylock torments Anthonio [*sic*] by his refusal to hear a word of negotiation, his own name has disappeared; and in the great trial scene itself, from 'Enter Shylocke' onwards his name appears fifteen times in the prefixes, whereas 'Jew' has nineteen appearances. . . . Is it possible that the alternation in the playwright's responses deliberately mimics his characters? Or do they think like him? (21)

Where Bulman reads the speech-prefixes to support his point that Shake-speare makes Shylock "credibly complex," Patterson sees a darker possibil-ity, reinforced by a specific textual detail: she asks what it means

> when the Quarto text has Portia . . . asking 'Is your name *Shylocke*?' and when the natural answer, '*Shylocke* is my name', is attributed in the margin only to a '*Jew*'? Of whose consciousness does this silent conflict, never heard on stage, bear witness? Given my assumption of the authorial pres-ence in the 1600 Quarto, there is only one honest reply, and it is not a com-forting one. (22)

Perhaps. Or could the variation in speech-prefixes have little to do with Shakespeare's attitudes and something to do with the availability of type in the printing-house? Jay Halio discusses this possibility in his Textual Intro-duction to the Oxford edition, and his one appendix lists "Speech Prefixes for Shylock (by line number, edition, signature and compositor)" (229–30). After exploring a number of theories, he avoids reading any meaningful pat-tern into the prefixes and implies that definitive conclusions about authorial attitudes are unlikely to emerge from this area of textual investigation (89–90).

The significance of text is again illustrated in Lisa Hopkins's proposed emendation of a line in Bassanio's speech deciding which casket to choose. He describes "ornament" as "the guiled shore / To a most beauteous sea: the beauteous scarf / Veiling an Indian beauty; in a word, / The seeming truth . . ." (3.2.97–100). Editors have questioned the yoking of *Indian* and *beauty*, especially in a play filled with "expressions of racial prejudice" (27).

Hopkins proposes moving the semicolon after *beauty* to follow *Indian*, so that *Indian* becomes a noun and the Elizabethan dislike of dark skin is further emphasized. But the Riverside text just quoted (identical to the Arden) reproduces exactly the punctuation in the Quarto of 1600 and in the First Folio, so the proposed change alters not only what Hopkins calls the "modern punctuation" of the passage, but also the punctuation in the original texts.

Editors of single-volume editions have made a significant contribution to our understanding and appreciation of the play, beginning in 1888 with H. H. Furness's New Variorum and including, in more recent years, the Arden edition of John Russell Brown (1955), the New Cambridge edition of M. M. Mahood (1987), and Halio's Oxford edition (1993). The Arden offers a thorough exploration of technical matters as well as a critical introduction and several appendices that present the texts of all the major sources. The New Cambridge offers helpful illustrations and drawings as well as an extended treatment of the play as romantic comedy, while also surveying what Shakespeare was likely to know about Venice and Jews; an appendix looks at the use of the Bible in the play. The Oxford addresses the issue of anti-Semitism head-on; the introduction is also very helpful on the imagery of the bond, and on allusions in the play to Shrovetide. All three of these texts provide extensive commentary on each page of the script itself. The Cambridge and Oxford texts both survey in some detail the performance history of the play.

Other recent versions include the New Penguin (1967)—W. Moelwyn Merchant's introduction is particularly useful on legal issues; the Folger (1992)—background on Shakespeare's language, Alexander Leggatt's "Modern Perspective" essay, and a brief annotated list for "Further Reading" are helpful; the Everyman (1993)—John Andrews offers a brief but sensitive introductory comment on the play, supplemented by Kelly McGillis's reflections on playing Portia and a section called "Perspectives on *The Merchant of Venice*" in which Andrews reviews some of the most important critical commentary; and the Pelican (2000)—A. R. Braunmuller provides a serviceable introductory essay. The Signet Classic edition (1965, revised in 1987 and 1998) includes a perceptive introduction, as well as samples of critical commentaries ranging from William Hazlitt to Linda Bamber, a useful review of the play on stage and screen, and an extensive bibliography.

The Date

Most editors agree that the play was probably written and first performed between 1596 and 1598. The *terminus ad quem* seems particularly clear, since *Merchant* is listed among Shakespeare's comedies (as the last of six) by Francis Meres in his *Palladis Tamia (Wit's Treasury)* in September of 1598, and the play was entered on the Stationers' Register in July, 1598.

In an apparent reference to a large Spanish galleon captured off Cadiz in June, 1596, Salerio mentions "my wealthy *Andrew* [dock'd] in sand"

(1.1.27).[8] Interestingly, Richard H. Popkin has noted "that there was an actual Jewish merchant from Venice in England from 1596 to 1600, one Alonso Nuñez de Herrera, who was one of the hostages taken in the Earl of Essex's raid on Cadiz" (330), when the *Andrew* was seized. A native of Florence whose family later moved to Venice, Herrera was in Cadiz as an agent of the Sultan of Morocco. Under house arrest in Ware in Hertfordshire, near London, this Jewish merchant of Venice argued against his detention with Spanish hostages, and asked to be allowed to stay with friends in London. Eventually, the Queen herself, in a message to the Sultan, admitted that a mistake had been made, and in 1600 Herrera "was released into the care of an uncle and returned to the Continent."

Comparison with Shakespeare's other work also argues for a date between 1596 and 1598, making such plays as *A Midsummer Night's Dream, Richard II,* and *Romeo and Juliet* its contemporaries, with *Much Ado About Nothing* and the *Henry IV* plays its immediate successors: "The verse, especially in Act 5, strikingly resembles that of the lyric plays [*MND, R2, R&J*], but the prose passages, such as Shylock's 'Hath not a Jew eyes' (3.1.55–69), look forward to Falstaff's" (Halio 28–29).[9] Although the title page of the 1600 Quarto proclaims that "it hath been divers times acted by the Lord Chamberlaine his servants," Brown notes that "the first performance of which there is specific record was by the King's Men at Court on Shrove Sunday, 10 February 1605" (xxxii). There was a second performance on the following Tuesday.

The Sources

The importance of source-study emerges in two essays in this volume: John W. Velz's examination of Portia's Ovidian dimensions and John K. Hale's consideration of sources as guides to understanding Shakespeare's craft. All observers have noted the remarkable resemblances between *Merchant* and a late-fourteenth-century collection of tales (first published in 1558 and available only in Italian) by a Ser Giovanni of Florence, *Il Pecorone* ("the big sheep," or simpleton or dunce). Although the pound of flesh story is quite ancient, the first story of the fourth day uses the motif in a tale of the Lady of Belmonte. In brief, Ansaldo, a rich merchant of Venice, has adopted his godson Giannetto, whose recently-deceased father was a friend of Ansaldo. When the young man wants to join in a trading expedition, Ansaldo provides him with a ship and valuable cargo to sail to Alexandria. But Giannetto is diverted to Belmonte, where the rich Lady, a widow, will marry only the man who succeeds in making love to her; those who fail must pay her all they possess. Like many before him, Giannetto tries and fails, twice, losing two rich ships and cargoes provided by Ansaldo. For a third time, the merchant helps his godson (not knowing the true cause of the two earlier losses), but now must pledge a pound of his own flesh to a Jew in return for a loan of ten thousand ducats.

Giannetto succeeds on his third attempt, because the Lady's maid warns him to avoid the drugged drink offered to suitors as they join the Lady in bed. Meanwhile Ansaldo has defaulted on the loan. Told what has happened, the Lady of Belmonte first sends Giannetto to Venice with sufficient cash to satisfy the loan. Then the Lady herself, disguised as a lawyer at the hearing in Venice, asks the Jew to accept the offered payment; when he refuses, she rescues the merchant by pointing out that precisely one pound, not a bit more nor less, can be cut, and not one drop of blood can be spilled in collecting on the debt. Relenting, the Jew offers to accept the money, but is refused. Infuriated, the Jew tears up the bond and storms off. Still in disguise, the Lady persuades a reluctant Giannetto to give her the ring he had received from her. Back in Belmonte, she taunts him about the lost ring, and his benefactor Ansaldo marries the helpful maid. The similarities between this tale and Shakespeare's plot are many, but so are the differences—for example in the character of the Lady, transformed from a widow who uses frustrated fornication to gain wealth into a maiden heiress bound to her father's will, or in the introduction of Gratiano to pair with Nerissa, leaving Antonio as odd man out. The playwright's adaptation of his sources demonstrates powerfully his mastery of the dramatic craft.

In *Merchant* the story of the caskets, again an ancient folktale, replaces the ribald bed test of *Il Pecorone*. This "lottery" probably derives from the *Gesta Romanorum*, a medieval collection of stories partially published in English translation in 1577 and again, somewhat revised, in 1595. Shakespeare uses the word *insculp'd* only once in his work, in the scene of Morocco's choice (2.7.57), and the word appears in History 32 of the *Gesta* (1595 ed.), where a princess is made to choose among three caskets to determine her suitability as consort to the Roman emperor's son. The gold casket, filled with dead men's bones, carries the motto, "Whoso chooseth me shall find that he deserveth." The silver box, filled with earth and worms, proclaims, "Whoso chooseth me shall find that his nature desireth." The lead casket, filled with precious stones, has "insculped" on it, "Whoso chooseth me, shall find that God hath disposed for him." Choosing lead, the princess wins the emperor's son. Most commentators note that Shakespeare has changed the text of the third motto, which reads in his play, "Who chooseth me must give and hazard all he hath" (2.7.9), but it is also interesting that he adapts for his gold casket—"Who chooseth me shall gain what many men desire" (2.7.37)—the motto on the silver casket in the source, and vice versa (the play's silver casket states, "Who chooseth me shall get as much as he deserves" [2.7.23]).

A third significant source, Christopher Marlowe's *The Jew of Malta,* was originally performed about 1589 and revived in 1594 at the time of the trial and execution of Roderigo Lopez, Queen Elizabeth's Portuguese physician of Jewish birth, who was convicted of attempting to poison both the Queen and a prominent Spanish refugee. Shakespeare clearly knew his colleague's work, and Jessica's role owes something to that of Abigail, daughter of Barabas in Marlowe's play, as Joan Ozark Holmer's essay in this collection makes clear. Barabas and Shylock, however, while similar in some respects, are very different people indeed. Murray Levith's essay here examines Marlowe's "other play," *Doctor Faustus*, for its connections to *Merchant*.

Many other sources have been proposed; indeed Christopher Spencer has published an entire book on the subject,[10] and it is also possible to consider Shakespeare's own earlier comedies, most notably *The Two Gentlemen of Verona*, as sources. Beyond the thematic links between *Two Gentlemen* and *Merchant*, Bruce Boehrer notes the contrast between two dogs in *Two Gentlemen*—the clown Launce's rather disreputable Crab and Proteus's lapdog, referred to as a "little jewel" (4.4.47) and intended as a wooing gift (155). Boehrer suggests that these two very different dogs anticipate the ways in which "dog" Jews are handled in *Merchant*, where no literal dogs appear. The "cur" Shylock—"during Shylock's first appearance onstage, he is associated with the words *dog* and *cur* five times within seventeen lines of blank verse (1.3.11–28)" (161)—is offered a "halter gratis" (4.1.379) by Gratiano, suggesting the image of condemned Jews hanged upside-down between two dogs in medieval prints (165–67). But Jessica, associated with a monkey as a somewhat exotic version of Proteus's lapdog, can be seen as a kind of pampered house pet, a Jew who voluntarily rejects her religion to become a Christian wife (156–60).

In "What Did Shakespeare Read?" Leonard Barkan explores Shakespeare's choice of reading for what it might tell us about his art. He notes that the plots of at least half the plays involve "a cluster of narrative elements including nobly born wives who are entangled for good or ill in their husbands' public lives . . . , calumniated women presumed dead but merely sleeping . . . , and fathers and daughters." These elements all spring from "a relatively small number of originary [*sic*] texts." Barkan infers the creative process: "Shakespeare finds the stories that replicate his personal obsessions; the stories give those obsessions certain shapes; he in turn re-shapes them by producing ever-varying adaptations; in the end he becomes a reader of, and source for, himself" (44).

Barkan's cluster includes, of course, Portia (in two of his categories) and Jessica. His reference to the playwright's "personal obsessions" prompts consideration of another recent discussion, from a different perspective. In "Deaths in the Family: The Loss of a Son and the Rise of Shakespearean Comedy," Richard P. Wheeler notes that Shakespeare lost his only son, Hamnet, a twin to his daughter Judith, in August of 1596. Nineteenth-century criticism tried to link Shakespeare's life to his work, but the anomaly here is that Shakespeare's work in the years following Hamnet's death focused on comedy and history. Nevertheless, Wheeler argues that "it seems entirely implausible that Shakespeare would have been wholly unaffected by the death of his only son" (134). He notes that the histories written at the time (*King John, I* and *II Henry IV,* and *Henry V*), like those that came earlier, very much concern relationships between fathers and sons. But he also notes that the comedies of the period, again like those that preceded them, usually "complete the movement from youth into early adulthood that for the dramatist's son was cut off by death. Do these plays remember the dead boy in their comic actions?" (145). He traces Shakespeare's development of *Merchant, As You Like It,* and *Twelfth Night,* the action in each case turning "on the quasi-magical power of a daughter to transform herself into a young man." Wheeler argues that Shakespeare may have been fantasizing the transformation of his surviving twin daughter into his lost son: "Such a fantasy would be made psychically safe . . . because it preserves the life of the daughter within or beneath the exchange, enabling her never really to disappear, and then to reappear, even while briefly satisfying the wish to bring the male back to life" (146). Wheeler's argument moves on from Portia to examine Rosalind (who assumes the male identity early in the play and maintains it up to the last scene) and Viola (a twin "who appears to have survived the death of her brother" and who is still dressed as a young man when the play ends): "*Twelfth Night* puts right at the center of the action a situation structurally analogous to the death of Hamnet and the survival of Judith in the Shakespeare family. And that action will bring the dead son and brother back" (147). Wheeler's analysis encourages consideration of the broader issue of parent-child relationships in *Merchant,* which offers three such sets, including the father-son relationship of the Gobbos.

The Play as Conundrum

Despite the certainties about text, date, and sources, most who experience the play will agree that it is a conundrum. Why is it such a challenge to audiences and critics alike? Long before the Holocaust further complicated our response to this play, Shakespeare himself initiated the problem: according to one observer, "the materials of *The Merchant of Venice* are in the final analysis not completely integrated" (Zesmer 117). Bulman opens his study of the play for the "Shakespeare in Performance" series by addressing this problem:

> If history is any judge, the crucial problem in staging *The Merchant of Venice* is how to balance its two distinct and seemingly unrelated plots. Although both ultimately derive from folk tales, Shakespeare dramatised them in such disparate styles that they seem to compete with rather than to complement one another. . . . By working such a tonal division between the two plots, Shakespeare made it difficult to bring them into an effective theatrical balance with one another. Venice and Belmont seem to belong to different plays. (1)

As noted already, *Merchant* enters the written record for the first time in the Stationers' Register for 22 July 1598: "the Marchaunt of Venyce or otherwise called the Jewe of Venyce." How are we to read this title? It could suggest that, very early on, Shylock the Jew was recognized as an important character. A nineteenth-century edition of the play depicts Shylock and Jessica on the title page! Could it also suggest that Antonio and Shylock, despite their obvious opposition, have much in common? We know that merchants were frequently moneylenders as well. Questions and potential confusions about genre and interpretation of character are already apparent.

The earliest critical commentary on the play appears on the very title page of the 1600 Quarto:

> The most excellent / Historie of the *Merchant* / *of Venice.* / With the extreame crueltie of *Shylock* the Iewe / towards the sayd Merchant, in cutting a iust pound / of his flesh: and the obtayning of *Portia* / by the choyse of three / chests.

This reference to Shakespeare's two principal sources and their very different plots—Shylock's "merry" (1.3.145) flesh bond and the casket lottery—suggests a tension that has always marked response to the play, as Zesmer and Bulman attest. Yet M. C. Bradbrook would use the term "polyphony" to suggest what she sees as the harmonious development of these apparently opposed plots toward the ultimate comic conclusion (170–79). Indeed, the 1619 second Quarto adds the word "comicall" before "Historie," and in the 1623 Folio the play is again called a "comicall historie" and included among the comedies. One might speak of the "comedy" that revolves around the casket-test and of the "history" that unfolds as a result of the pound of flesh plot. This bifurcation reinforces the sense of conundrum, further heightened by the ambiguous character of Shylock.

Shylock, Usury, and Anti-Semitism

In a seminar paper for the Fourth World Shakespeare Congress in Berlin (1986), I examined the possibility that some of Shakespeare's characters "get away" from him, and the primary example is Shylock. Peter Phialas speaks of the "excessive vitality" of both Falstaff and Shylock, "a vitality which threatens to throw off balance their respective plays" (146). Because the antagonist of *Merchant* is the most forceful character, Phialas finds the comedy "unusual" (142). A contrast seems to lie between what Shakespeare may have intended and what he achieved in creating Shylock.

Many commentators make much of the fact that Shylock appears in *only* five of the twenty scenes, and *yet* manages to dominate the play. But in fact only Portia has more lines (500-plus to Shylock's 300-plus); while she appears in nine scenes, Bassanio (third in number of lines) and Antonio appear in only six (one of Antonio's appearances, in 2.6, consists of six lines urging Gratiano to join Bassanio on the ship departing for Belmont). In other words, Shylock's role is second only to Portia's—appropriately, since they are the mighty opposites of the piece. Shylock, of course, is the only major character missing from act 5, but other comedies present parallel instances. How Shakespeare handles his antagonists at the conclusion of various comedies is discussed further below.

Harley Granville-Barker notes—"it is a near thing"—that Shylock almost overwhelms the play (56). Viewing Shylock as the villain whose values negate the comic spirit of the play's Christians, C. L. Barber nevertheless observes that "about Shylock . . . there is a difficulty which grows on reflection, a difficulty which may be felt too in reading or performance. His part fits perfectly into the design of the play, and yet he is so alive that he raises an interest beyond its design" (190). Depending on who is making the judgment, Shylock either does or does not escape from the playwright's control. Consider John Russell Brown's conclusion to his survey of the play in performance:

> By many devices Shakespeare has ensured that in performance Shylock is the dominating character of the play; none other has such emotional range, such continual development, such stature, force, subtlety, vitality, variety; above all, none other has his intensity, isolation, and apparent depth of motivation. The various interpretations that have become famous are responses to an unmistakable (and unavoidable) invitation to make a strong, adventurous and individual impression in the role. (*Plays* 85)

Traditional commentary sees Shylock as the villain, a descendant of the Vice character in the morality plays, justly defeated in his attempt to murder Antonio; the emphasis is on Shylock's behavior rather than his racial or religious background. In a play shadowed by racism and bigotry, Shylock is as bigoted as anyone: he explicitly tells us in 1.3 that his hatred of Antonio originates in his hatred of Christians.[11] He is defeated because he follows an evil course, whatever the provocations may be. In allegorical interpretations, Shylock represents the Old Law (judgment) opposed to the New (sacrifice).

Springing from its focus on the marginalized "Other," more recent commentary emphasizes Shylock's role as scapegoat and victim. In " 'To Entrap the Wisest,' " René Girard proclaims that "in the city of Venice, no Antonio or Bassanio will ever suffer as long as there is a Shylock to do the suffering for them" (102), and he makes an interesting case for Shylock as two very different kinds of scapegoat. On the one hand, Shakespeare provides the simpletons in the audience with an effective Aristotelian catharsis, as the villain is soundly defeated and sent whimpering away after a particularly thrilling confrontation with the forces of good. On the other hand, more sophisticated members of the audience will recognize the profound irony in Shylock's scapegoating and appreciate that the Christians are the real villains.[12] John Drakakis sees Shylock as "an externalisation, and a demonisation, of a force that Venice finds necessary in order for it to conduct its daily commercial activity, but which it cannot acknowledge as such." He argues that "Shylock is not primarily a realistic representation, not a 'Jew' in the strictly ethnological sense of the term, but both a subject position *and* a rhetorical means of prising open a dominant Christian ideology no longer able to smooth over its own internal contradictions, and therefore a challenge and a threat" (186). Later he declares:

> Shylock is the object upon whom Venetian society vents its own hatred of itself, and in this respect his own dramatic characterisation is made to incorporate those negative social forces, such as puritanism, which challenge the norms of Venetian/Elizabethan society. It is within this complex web of significations, both as an *effect* of Venetian self-hatred, and as the representative of a historically ostracised ethnic group, that Shylock is forced to eke out a precarious existence, marginal, yet symbolically central to Venice's own perception of itself, tolerated, yet repressed. (192)

Therefore, it is only "when [Shylock] is coerced fully into the life of Venice by being forced to become a Christian [that he becomes] a reconstituted subject who can then play a full patriarchal role in its affairs" (198).

Drakakis argues that "if Shylock is the agency through which Venetian institutions are demystified, then Belmont is the place where an attempt is made to reverse that process" (204). As Bassanio makes his choice, "Portia articulates in an 'aside' those very feelings of 'excess' which it is the function of the law of her dead father to constrain":

> At a purely psychological level, Portia's 'fear' here is, surely, the patriarchal fear of 'excess' internalized by the female subject as part of the mechanism of social and emotional regulation. Spoken by a male actor, its parodic potential is foregrounded to the point where it can be made to reinforce patriarchal constraint. To this extent both Portia and her more unruly counterpart, Jessica, are central to an understanding of the normative, regulatory practices of Christian patriarchy as the play represents them. (205)

Drakakis's essay in this volume studies Jessica as "unruly counterpart" to Portia.

Shylock's distinctiveness also surfaces in discussions of the play's language. Analyzing the talk of Antonio's friends in the opening scene, Arthur Humphreys writes of their "flowing and glowing language" (129). He distinguishes three styles in the play: first, the "lyrical and finely ornate" language of Antonio's friends, found also in Portia's "aria-like speech as she heralds

Bassanio's approach to the caskets"; "the finest example is Lorenzo's [poetic elaboration] on the platonic music of the spheres." The second style conveys "the lucidity of goodness," as in Salerio's report of Antonio's farewell to Bassanio, or Bassanio's account of how he yielded the ring. These two styles "preside over the play, just as, in the circles of Antonio and Portia, fineness of display and bearing is the ruling code of life." The third style, of course, is Shylock's: "shrewd, passionate, and accurate." Shylock's motto, "Fast bind, fast find" (2.5.53), is reflected in his style, which offers a powerful counterbalance. It is

> concentrated and purposive. From the first he is businesslike and precise about terms. . . . In all he says, up to his insistence in the trial on the legal exactness of his case, there is a severe, functional reality. He is never expansive or easy-going in idiom, as the Venetians are. (133–34)

Shylock's language is part of his effort to "mark his separateness" from the world around him (134). Danson has observed that Shylock "uses language as he uses money: carefully, and as a weapon. The prodigal Christians may squander their words . . . but Shylock knows the value of a word. . . . The effectiveness of his speaking comes in large part from his canny investment in silence" (139). John Gillies points to "Shylock's mischievous facility with 'voices': his tendency to make debating points by slipping into registers which, while not quite his own, might easily be." He notes "how often Shylock talks at cross-purposes to his Venetian interlocutors, and how uncouth he sounds to the Venetian ear" (128–29).

For John Gross, Shylock's "linguistic idiosyncrasies" help to define his character. Some of the idiosyncrasies are biblical—"words such as *synagogue* and *Nazarite* are not found elsewhere in Shakespeare." Other ticks

> are simply unusual: the plural *moneys* is a famous example. . . . *Equal* (for *exact*) and *estimable* (for *valuable*) are no less odd, while Shylock alone in Shakespeare uses the noun *misbeliever* and the verb to *bane*. His syntax is often irregular, too. He talks of *trifling* time, and says that he has no mind *of* feasting forth (rather than mind *to*). (65)

Gross also notes Shylock's extensive use of prose, which Shakespeare had previously employed for comic characters.[13] Shylock's prose style features repetition and parallelism. He enjoys antithesis and displays a "compulsive verbal pattern-making," quite understandable in a man "with a need to tabulate and enumerate, to keep a tight grip on reality and underline what he means" (65–66).

Mark Van Doren provides a memorable description of Shylock's "music": "The voice of Shylock comes rasping into the play like a file; the edge of it not only cuts but tears, not only slices but saws. He is always repeating phrases, half to himself, as misers do" (84). Seeing Shylock's language in the context of Shakespeare's time, Robert Ornstein assures us that Shylock's "I will feed fat the ancient grudge I bear him" (1.3.47) "is a conventional expression of hatred similar to Beatrice's desire to eat Claudio's heart in the marketplace" (98). Similarly contextual, this time within the psychological dynamic of 4.1 itself, Hugh Short's essay in this volume argues that Shylock's penultimate speech in the play, "I am content" (4.1.394), is a sincere statement of his feelings at that moment.

In a recent essay focused on language, Alan Rosen argues that both Shylock and Morocco use modes of discourse that distinguish them as aliens. If Shylock's dominant tendency as a "plain-speaker" is to insidious repetition, Morocco's style is excessively rhetorical, even in the colorful Venetian setting described by Humphreys. Rosen notes that most observers find Shylock's style congruent with his role as villain, but at least one critic—Sigurd Burckhardt in *Shakespearean Meanings* (1968)—"favors Shylock's plainness," arguing that the play casts suspicion on those who use eloquent language (42). Rosen sees more than extremes of discourse linking the Jew and the Moor, both of whom "claim that what seems different on the surface can be better judged by what is beneath it; that the less favorable exterior they present can be neutralized by reference to an interior dimension: the blood that flows in all people's veins" (46).

Marc Shell's "The Wether and the Ewe: Verbal Usury in *The Merchant of Venice*" offers a difficult, provocative analysis of Shylock as a verbal usurer who employs language to subvert convention. He observes:

> To my knowledge, no one since the medieval era has devoted attention to the category of verbal usury in jurisprudence, rhetoric, and philosophy. . . . Yet "verbal usury" is an important technical term in the Jewish Talmud, in the Christian church fathers, and in the Islamic Traditions. There it refers to the generation of an illegal—the church fathers say unnatural—supplement of verbal meaning by use of methods such as punning and flattering. (108)

According to Shell, Shylock distinguishes between Jewish brothers (such as Tubal, who will not charge interest) and others (such as Antonio, who nevertheless is not asked to pay interest) who are human; Antonio, on the other hand, distinguishes between brothers (all Christians) and others (Jews, Moroccans, all non-Christians) who are not human.[14]

Shylock's language emphasizes his separateness, reinforced by his profession as usurer. Margaret Webster writes that Shylock loves his wife and his daughter "as his, his possessions, like his turquoise and his ducats and his race and his revenge. His, his, his. It is the keynote of the man; the passion of possession raised to demonic power" (146). Although he inspired considerable commentary that sees Shylock as victim, Karl Marx himself condemned Shylock's behavior. Despite an understanding of the human appeal in Shylock's situation, he also saw the moneylender as "an example of the one who, hiding behind the law, dehumanizes others and alienates them into mere property." For Marx, Shylock also represents the difference between law and justice, leading Marx "into a characteristic analysis of the way the law protects private interests and victimizes the poor" (White 96). B. J. Sokol explores in some depth the contention that "legal and social inequality based on prejudice *is* intended to be seen as unjust within the context of *The Merchant of Venice*" (160).

Teaching *Merchant* in a Shakespeare course at the New School in New York in 1946 and 1947, W. H. Auden calls Shylock an outsider partly because of religion and partly because of profession, but "chiefly by character, for which society is partially responsible, though social conditions are never quite enough to determine character" (80). Shylock alienates our sympathy partly because "his revenge is in excess of the injury," but mainly because "he tries to play it safe and use the law, which is universal, to exact a particular, personal revenge" (81).

Different in religion, language, and profession, in language and profession Shylock betrays a need to "play it safe." His caution could also explain why he is the only major character in the play who never leaves Venice: everyone else, including his friend Tubal, travels, at least as far as Belmont.[15] The play may name more places, both real and mythical, than any other in Shakespeare, and this exhaustive naming conveys a sense of an unusually broad canvas, a kind of geographical prodigality. In his evocations of place and in his movement of characters Shakespeare reinforces the play's linguistic and thematic contrasts between the caution of Shylock and the prodigality of everyone else.[16]

But Shylock is also a father, and in "Allegorical Commentary in *The Merchant of Venice*" Judith Rosenheim considers Shylock as a father figure. Although we experience Shylock's villainy, we also have some sense of his "goodness." More or less ignoring Portia's role, Rosenheim argues that Shakespeare's play is an elaborate allegory focused on Shylock and Antonio, who are meant to be father and son. Indeed, the encounter in 2.2 between Old Gobbo and his son Launcelot is "an allegorical representation of the religious conflict represented in Antonio and Shylock" (159). In her analysis, the Gobbos succeed in evolving from power relations to family relations; "[a]nd it is by contrast with this achieved evolution that the settlement between Antonio and Shylock in IV.i will be recognized as minimal and abortive" (160). René Fortin has argued that Launcelot Gobbo's "primary function" in the play is to highlight the theme of filial piety. The Gobbos help to establish an important point: rather than choosing between Jewish law and Christian love, we should recognize the bond of filial piety between the two traditions, even as we know that in an imperfect world the perfection of this filial relationship cannot be realized. Nevill Coghill offers a related insight, as discussed below, and Barbara Lewalski, also discussed below, specifically juxtaposes Shylock (Old Law) to Antonio (New). The essay by John Cunningham and Stephen Slimp in this volume regards the scene between Old Gobbo and Launcelot as emblematic, not just of the Antonio/Shylock relationship, but of the development of the whole play.

Charles Edelman's "Which Is the Jew that Shakespeare Knew?: Shylock on the Elizabethan Stage" (1999) offers a revisionist approach. He observes that "in all that has been written about *The Merchant of Venice*, one point has remained virtually constant: . . . the original Shylock would have conformed to the so-called Elizabethan stereotype of the villainous stage Jew" (99). Edelman concedes that the traditional picture, of Richard Burbage in the earliest performances capering about the stage in a red wig and a false nose, may be accurate, but his research suggests that the original Shylock may have been much more like Edmund Kean's complex villain than Thomas Doggett's buffoon: "my sole object is to challenge the *a priori* assumption that Shakespeare must have conformed to a particular theatrical tradition" (100).

Edelman identifies three variables that could separate the 1590s *Merchant* from those of the nineteenth century and later. First, there are limitations imposed by literary or theatrical tradition. Did Shakespeare in fact have a tradition to adhere to? Edelman notes that three Jewish characters figured in plays in the twelve years leading up to *Merchant*'s presumed earliest performances: Gerontus, in Robert Wilson's *The Three Ladies of London* (1584), is heroic in his efforts to save a Christian from embracing Islam; Barabas, in *The Jew of Malta,* is a parody of the stereotypical Jew, obviously designed to show how un-Christian the Christians are; and Abraham, in Robert Greene's *Selimus* (1594), is a poisoner probably inspired by Barabas. Neither these plays nor what we know in more general terms about Elizabethan attitudes allows us to assume that everyone was an anti-Semite.

Second, there are limitations imposed by audience beliefs, attitudes, and expectations. Documents and literature suggest that Jews were viewed no more harshly than, and probably not as harshly as, Muslims and other "foreigners." And while texts can be produced to demonstrate Elizabethan condemnation of usury, the precise meaning of the term was unclear. In an age that accepted a 10 percent interest rate, both Shakespeare and his father loaned money at high rates, and the playwright took those who defaulted to court (104). Ernst Honigmann writes: "Like his father John, who had lent large sums (£80, £100) at the illegal rate of 20 percent, William seems to have had a sideline as a money-lender, while at the same time Shylock thrilled audiences in London" (7).

Third, there are theatrical limitations upon the range of performance options. Here Edelman notes that the traditionally villainous Shylock seems to spring from the text itself, in the famous "aside," "How like a fawning publican he looks" in 1.3. The term "aside" appears only three times in original texts of Shakespeare, once in the Folio text of *Titus Andronicus*, and twice in the same speech in a Quarto edition of *Pericles* (105). It is difficult, then, to determine how Shylock may have delivered the lines, but, rather than the traditional assumption that he looks conspiratorially at the audience, he may have employed the equivalent of the cinematic voice-over by speaking to himself in a kind of soliloquy, in proximity to characters who don't hear him as they converse with each other. In other words, the traditional villainy could be tempered by the manner in which these crucial lines are delivered.

Shylock's role inevitably raises questions about the play's (and Shakespeare's) attitude toward Jews, although most discussions concede that we cannot definitively determine Shakespeare's personal position. Writing at the beginning of the twentieth century, E. E. Stoll (discussed in detail below) is quite certain about the anti-Semitism of the play, and more recently Derek Cohen has argued that this is "a profoundly and crudely anti-Semitic play" (104). After reviewing the language used against Shylock and Jews in general, Cohen concludes: "It is as though *The Merchant of Venice* is an anti-Semitic play written by an author who is not an anti-Semite—but an author who has been willing to use the cruel stereotypes of that ideology for mercenary and artistic purposes" (118). This position has been asserted yet again, as a foregone conclusion, by Bloom (*Invention* 171). Yet G. L. Kittredge closes his introduction to the play by insisting that it "is no anti-Semitic document; Shakespeare was not attacking the Jewish people when he gave Shylock the villain's role" (x). Webster, in the revised edition (1955) of her book (originally published in 1942), insists that "Shakespeare was not anti-Semitic. Indeed he was not anti-anything in terms of generalizations about races or creeds. He wrote about human beings, each of them an individual and not a 'type' " (147).

William Kerrigan has raised a fundamental point by questioning whether it is reasonable to apply the term "anti-Semitism"—especially with its twentieth-century connotations—to discussion of an Early Modern text (106). James Shapiro in *Shakespeare and the Jews* and Halio in his Oxford edition undercut the certitude of Stoll, Cohen, and Bloom. Shapiro regards the term "anti-Semitism" as one of the "anachronistic . . . inventions of nineteenth-century racial theory" that is "fundamentally ill-suited for gauging what transpired three hundred years earlier" (11). Shapiro's study of the complex relationship between notions of Englishness and Jewishness positions Shakespeare's play within a broad sweep of history: "For Shakespeare's contemporaries, Jews were not identified by their religion alone but by national and racial affiliations as well" (173). Shapiro also observes:

> I am not proposing that Shakespeare is antisemitic (or, for that matter,
> philosemitic). *The Merchant of Venice* is a play, a work of fiction; . . . [the
> play] is thus not "about" ritual murder or a veiled circumcising threat any
> more than it is about usury, or marriage, or homosocial bonding, or
> mercy. . . . Plays, unlike sermons, are not reducible to one lesson or
> another. . . . (121)

Halio begins his introduction to the play by addressing the issue of
"Shakespeare and Semitism." Surveying the unhappy history that extends
into our own time, Halio highlights important details such as the "dual
image" of the Jew—on the one hand, medieval plays represented in such
characters as Judas and the Pharisees the common belief that Jews incarnated
the devil; on the other, the same drama portrays "the patriarchs, Moses,
Daniel, . . . as heroes, symbols or presentiments of patience, constancy, and
other Christian virtues." Halio also points to the theological tenet, based on
Paul's letter to the Romans, that Israel will ultimately be redeemed through
conversion to Christianity: "If Jews were to be shunned as a pariah race, they
also had to be preserved for the ultimate Christian fulfillment" (5). Analyzing
Shakespeare's development of Shylock, especially in contrast to Barabas in
Marlowe's *The Jew of Malta,* Halio concludes that Shakespeare's attitude is
ambivalent and, he writes, "in neither author can we confidently proclaim an
anti-Semitic bias that is more than abstract and traditional" (13). Halio's
effort to find a balanced approach in the play inspires his essay for this collection, in which he argues that the best performances of characters like Shylock are carefully nuanced, capturing both the villainy and the humanity of
the role.

Did Shakespeare know that Shylock is, in fact, a bad Jew, that his oath to
have his bond is in Jewish eyes blasphemous? Familiar with the Bible,
Shakespeare may well have known that Shylock's beliefs and behavior are
merely stereotypes of Jewish belief (promoted and aggravated, it is true, by
the Christian taunts against the "dog Jew," the "Jew," and "devil" Shylock),
that Shylock's behavior is as abhorrent to Jewish teaching as to Christian.
Andrews quotes Shylock's assertion, "What judgment shall I dread, doing no
wrong?" (4.1.89), followed by his "My deeds upon my head! I crave the law"
(4.1.206), and notes: "These words turn out to be a snare, not only in light of
the Christian doctrines that inform the play, but also according to the Hebraic
teachings and rituals that Elizabethans would have seen as prototypes of the
Sacrifice that fulfilled a Divine Law designed primarily to prove everyone
guilty before God (Galatians 2–3)" (xxiii).

Yet Thomas H. Luxon offers an analysis of two distinct phases in the life
of the scriptural Daniel to argue that the play, like Elizabethan society,
regards Jews as "bad" by definition, by virtue of their Jewishness alone; the
only good Jew is a convert to Christianity. Ignorant of this reality when he

praises Portia as "a Daniel come to judgment" (4.1.223), Shylock thinks of one episode in Daniel's story: his cleverness in proving Susanna innocent. Shylock misses the significant fact that Portia's "male" name is Balthazar, the very name given to Daniel by a servant of king Nebuchadnezzar during Daniel's captivity in Babylon (Daniel 1,7); Calvin and other commentators see Daniel in Babylon as "a leader of God's church in captivity" who fore-tells "the exact number of years that would pass before the advent of 'the sonne of man,' or Jesus Christ" (10). Thus Daniel in Babylon represents the "good Jew," able to recognize Christ as Messiah. Hailing "Balthazar" as "a second Daniel" (4.1.333), Gratiano "probably unwittingly calls attention to the differences between the two [Daniels]" (8), the one prophesying in Baby-lon and the one who saves Susanna. Luxon concludes that

> Portia's Daniel represents the Daniel who was crucial to the Reformation notion of the converted or *Christian* Jew as opposed to the blind and stub-born Jew, that Shylock betrays himself as precisely such a blind and stub-born Jew, who effectively misrecognizes Daniel even as he invokes him, and that the play invites its audience therefore to revile Shylock as a typical Jew . . . for whom forced conversion is too good a treatment. (9)

In addressing this issue, Holmer uses the term "anti-Judaic" (religiously biased) in contrast to "anti-Semitic" (racially biased), and asks whether the play is either or both (13). After an extensive discussion, she concludes: "Shakespeare attacks as well as praises both Jews and Christians, less as groups and more as individuals judged according to how truly they live their faith, how well they love God and each other" (28). Laurence Lerner's "Wilhelm S and Shylock" is an ironic consideration of the ways in which the play can be used to advance a variety of political agendas—imagine Shakespeare as a playwright in Nazi Germany, praised for his grasp of racial psychology, and consider Lerner's conclusion that this fantasy, "my 'thought experiment,' was a way of asking how important is the difference between writing an anti-Semitic play, and offering an anti-Semitic interpretation of a play written in 1597" (144). He argues that there is a difference, and that it is important.

Of course anti-Semitism is only one of the bigoted attitudes, albeit the most prominent one, evident in the play. As noted above, Shylock himself is bigoted toward Christians. Extending the insights of Rosen and others, including R. W. Desai in his essay for this volume, Bernard Harris offers in "A Portrait of a Moor" an account of the portrait of Abdul Guahid, the Moroccan who served as an ambassador to the English court in 1600, as the two countries sought—and failed to reach—a strategic alliance. The portrait now hangs in the Shakespeare Institute in Stratford-upon-Avon; there is no suggestion of the clownish Morocco often presented on stage. G. K. Hunter's "Elizabethans and Foreigners" attempts a broader analysis, that could include Spaniards like Arragon in addition to Jews and Moors, but this classic essay must be read with caution, given Shapiro's discussion (83–85) of its weaknesses.

These various, sometimes contradictory, treatments of the issue of anti-Semitism lead to the conclusion that it is difficult to make a definitive determination, especially when the very term may be meaningless in the sixteenth-century context. What is clear, as already noted, is that the play depicts a human Shylock defeated by his own murderous villainy, but it also portrays Christians acting and speaking in violation of the central Gospel command, "Love one another as I have loved you" (John 15, 12).

II. The First Two Hundred Years

After the entry in the Stationers' Register and the early title pages, there is no critical commentary on *Merchant* until 1709, in Nicholas Rowe's pioneering edition of the plays. Similarly, after the two recorded court performances in February 1605, there seems to be no indication of another performance of Shakespeare's script until 1741. Many commentators assume that Richard Burbage played the role of Shylock in the first performances, but we cannot be certain. Did Burbage affect a red wig, beard, and long nose, and wear a gaberdine gown? A poem published in 1664 describes Shylock in this way, but this is hardly a contemporary account (Barnet, "Stage" 162).

Amiel Schotz has argued for John Heminge as the first Shylock. His examination of groups of characters in the plays probably written between 1596 and 1599 suggests that "the actor who played Bassanio was also cast as Prince Hal; he who played Antonio acted Henry IV, and the portrayer of Gratiano also played Hotspur. The logical extension of this parallel casting is that the actor who first played Shylock probably also played Falstaff. According to Edmond Malone, this actor was John Heminge." If this were the case, argues Schotz, we "have a heavy Shylock, played by an actor with comic talents, demanding a pound of flesh from a thin Antonio! Any practicing director would immediately see the comic possibilities in this paradoxical juxtaposition" (14).

Beyond basic information—the bare thrust stage; the proximity of the audience (standing or sitting) to the stage; the absence of scenery and minimal use of props; a variety of sometimes elaborate costumes, usually Elizabethan; performances in broad daylight—we can infer that the actors relied on the audience "to piece out a performance's imperfections with their thoughts. The participation of the audience was necessary to foster any illusion of reality." Bulman discusses the audience's "capacity for multiconsciousness, for adjusting imaginatively to a complex mixture of formal and realistic elements, and losing themselves in the play while remaining aware of its artifice" (6–7). In such a context, actors "could move in and out of their roles more easily than actors do today. They could speak in character yet at the same time signal to the audience their conventionality." The notion of "acting as 'personation' paradoxically involved not only a quest for authenticity of character, but also an element of feigning or self-conscious role-play . . . at odds with modern notions of personality" (7). It is possible that actors addressed the audience directly, even ad-libbing, more often than we realize. The use of boys for women's roles further challenged the audience's imagination, and the cross-dressing of three characters in *Merchant* called attention to the convention, both visually and verbally.

While Venice and Belmont are very different from each other, "on a bare stage, every place is here, every moment is now. Belmont and Venice are the same place because they are undifferentiated by representational sets: the neutral playing space ensures fluid transitions from scene to scene and makes correspondences readily apparent" (11). In act 5, audiences would be watching "Belmont" aware that

> in this very space, and only moments earlier, Antonio came within a hair's breadth of being killed, Bassanio nearly lost a friend, and Portia, quite possibly a happy marriage. The bare stage thus would have reinforced the correspondences between Acts IV and V by serving simultaneously as Belmont and, through imaginative recall, as the court of Venice. The comic artifices by which Act V recreates and resolves the tensions of the trial attest to the suggestive neutrality of Elizabethan staging and to the capacity of Elizabethan audiences to perceive a play on different levels. (Bulman 13)

With regard to performances in the Restoration, Patterson notes in her introduction to the 1600 Quarto that a copy of the 1637 Quarto in the British Library shows names of actors handwritten next to the names of characters in the cast list—"actors not of the period of the first Charles, but of the second." What we find here is that at some point during the Restoration Samuel Sandford played Shylock and Thomas Doggett played Launcelot Gobbo, probably at the Theatre Royal. Sandford "had a reputation as one of the finest tragic villains on the Restoration stage," and Doggett's fame was earned in clown roles. Contrary to the prevailing view, this annotated cast list argues that Shakespeare's own script was performed after the Restoration, and that Thomas Doggett has been "believed incorrectly to have been the first actor recorded as playing Shylock" (24).

Nevertheless, Rowe writes that "though we have seen that play received and acted as a comedy, and the part of the Jew performed by an excellent comedian, yet I cannot but think it was designed tragically by the author" (Myrick 109). Rowe's critical comments are clearly based on experience of the play in performance; what we might now categorize as "performance criticism" dominated commentary in the early years. Rowe notes with special praise the "friendship of Antonio to Bassanio" as "very great, generous, and tender," and he cites two passages worthy of "particular notice: the first is what Portia says of mercy, and the other on the power of music." Rowe's statement that he has "seen that play received and acted as a comedy" probably refers to performances of Shylock by Doggett, "a celebrated clown whose greatest successes had been in the portrayal of low comedy roles" (Wilders 13).

As noted above, however, Doggett probably first performed in the play—Shakespeare's play—as Launcelot Gobbo. Doggett would have performed as Shylock in George Granville's adaptation, *The Jew of Venice*, which held the stage between 1701 and 1741. This adaptation was intended, writes John Russell Brown,

> to make the play acceptable to the taste of the time. . . . a masque of Peleus and Thetis was added, the number of incidents and characters curtailed, and much of the verse omitted or rewritten. The part of Shylock was considerably lightened: he drinks the health of his mistress "Money" at a banquet given by Bassanio, his rage at the flight of Jessica is toned down, and his forced conversion is omitted. (edition xxxiii)

In 1741 Charles Macklin persuaded the management at Drury Lane to permit him to perform Shakespeare's original script. His interpretation of Shylock as a villain but a cunning and complex one, "unyieldingly malignant" (Gross 112), dominated the stage for five decades. "J. T. Kirkman, Macklin's early biographer, reported that Macklin's Shylock exhibited 'the malevolence, the villainy, the diabolical atrocity of the character.' 'Malevolence' seems to be the word most used, and if one gets the impression that Macklin presented not a man but a monster, at least the figure was to be taken seriously" (Barnet, "Stage and Screen" 164). Macklin inspired Francis Gentleman's comments on Shylock as a "most disgraceful picture of human nature." Gentleman praises Macklin by quoting, in 1770, "that very comprehensive, though concise compliment, paid him many years ago, 'This is the Jew, that Shakespeare drew' " (Wilders 26), a bit of doggerel attributed to Alexander Pope that could have two meanings. Pope could mean that Macklin returns to Shakespeare's text, after forty years of Granville's adaptation. Or, Pope could mean that Macklin portrayed Shylock as Shakespeare intended. Such an assertion makes assumptions about Shakespeare's age no longer so readily entertained. Writing about "*The Merchant of Venice* on Stage and Screen," Sylvan Barnet offers a helpful caveat:

> to argue that "the Elizabethans" thought thus-and-so about Jews is scarcely convincing, for although Shakespeare certainly was an Elizabethan, he certainly was not a typical Elizabethan, and he need not have held all the

commonplace views. Moreover, the Shakespeare that interests us is the playwright, not the Elizabethan man who (perhaps) in his routine hours held the prejudices of the period. (161)

In his Valencia paper mentioned above, Stephen Orgel notes that the skullcap often worn by actors playing Shylock is an anachronism, since it was not introduced among Jews until the eighteenth century. Macklin's portrayal was so successful that David Garrick opened his long reign as co-manager of the Drury Lane Theatre with Macklin's performance as Shylock, and Macklin continued in the role for many years. Only in 1789, shortly before his ninetieth birthday, did Macklin retire from his performances as Shylock. Despite the return to Shakespeare's text, performances by Macklin and others included extraneous song and dance, and, as time passed, increasingly elaborate scenery. Thomas Arne, the composer famous for "Rule Britannia," provided a melody for "Tell me where is fancy bred" in 3.2 for Macklin's original 1741 production, but he also wrote a song for Lorenzo to sing under Jessica's window in 2.6, and for Lorenzo again in 5.1, so that Lorenzo became a singing role (Campbell 526). The inclination to "enhance" Shakespeare continued through the nineteenth century, and it was not unusual to make room for the non-Shakespearean elements by trimming the text, occasionally eliminating Morocco and Arragon altogether, as well as act 5; "the action in one production at Drury Lane was punctuated first by a pierrot's dance, then by a pastoral dialogue, then by a hornpipe" (Gross 119).

Meanwhile, the first professional production of a Shakespeare play in the American colonies (in 1752 in Williamsburg, Virginia) staged *The Merchant of Venice*. The date allows us to assume that Shakespeare's text was used, and the casting supports the assumption. Lewis Hallam was both manager and "low comedian" of the company, and he played Launcelot Gobbo, who does not appear in Granville's adaptation (Shattuck, *Hallams* 3, 9).

III. The Nineteenth Century

Edmund Kean's portrayal of Shylock in 1814 was as different from Macklin's as Macklin's had been from Doggett's, and the critical commentary reflects the change. In a review from 1816, William Hazlitt refers to Kean's performance as a revelation: "his Jew is more than half a Christian. Certainly, our sympathies are much oftener with him than with his enemies. He is honest in his vices; they are hypocrites in their virtues" (5:296). In *Characters of Shakespear's Plays* (1817), Hazlitt observes that "Shylock is *a good hater*; 'a man no less sinned against than sinning.' If he carries his revenge too far, yet he has strong grounds." He writes that "there is a strong, quick, and deep sense of justice mixed up with the gall and bitterness of his resentment"

(4:320). Shylock, after all, "has more ideas than any other person in the piece" (324). Hazlitt explicitly distinguishes Kean's portrayal from earlier ones: "When we first went to see Mr. Kean in Shylock, we expected to see, what we had been used to see, a decrepid [*sic*] old man, bent with age and ugly with mental deformity, grinning with deadly malice, with the venom of his heart congealed in the expression of his countenance" (323).

For Hazlitt, "the whole of the trial-scene . . . is a masterpiece of dramatic skill" (4:321). But "Portia is not a very great favorite with us; neither are we in love with her maid Nerissa." He objects to "a certain degree of affectation and pedantry" about Portia. He also objects to Jessica and Lorenzo, but notes that their moonlit conversation in 5.1 is "a collection of classical elegancies." Launcelot is "honest," and Gratiano is "very admirable" (322).

A romantic view of Shylock increasingly dominated nineteenth-century criticism, closely tied to performance. John Gross summarizes Kean's power:

> It was the intensity of his acting that impressed audiences most—the sense of total involvement, the suggestion (though in fact every move was care- fully worked out in advance) of impulsiveness and spontaneity. Coleridge said that watching him was "like reading Shakespeare by flashes of light- ning." . . . His Shylock was still a villain, [but all who saw Kean felt that he gave the character] a large measure of dignity and humanity.
>
> Nothing signaled his intention more clearly than his decision to play the part wearing a black wig and beard. For the first time, the traditional red wig was abandoned, and with it went the most obvious link with the play's medieval origins. Whatever his faults, Shylock was no longer automatically identified as a kinsman of Judas. (128)

Kean's "general conception was that Shylock is not a repulsive beast but a man who has been so unjustly treated that his resentment quite under- standably drives him to acts of destruction" (Barnet, "Stage"165). A gener- ation after Kean's day, George Henry Lewes, who as a child had seen Kean's Shylock, "remained convinced that at his best [Kean] had never been surpassed" (Gross 130). Indeed, the hold Kean's Shylock had on the popular imagination of the time can be traced in a painting J. M. W. Turner exhibited at the Royal Academy in 1837. Now in the possession of the Huntington Library (available for viewing at *www.huntington.org/ ArtDiv/Turner_CanalPict.html*), "The Grand Canal, Venice" is a large can- vas which depicts some kind of religious procession disembarking from gondolas onto a center quay. The Rialto bridge arches the canal in the dis- tance. But at the lower right edge, among the onlookers grouped on the canal bank—yet isolated from the crowd—the figure of Shylock leans out, holding a piece of paper, knife, and scales to confront the viewer. His hair is black. He is an arresting figure. At the 1837 exhibition the painting was accompanied with words from 3.3:

> ANT: Hear me yet, good Shylock.
> SHY: I'll have my bond.

The title on the actual picture frame, when viewed by the editors, was "The Grand Canal, Venice" followed in smaller letters by "with Shylock."

Between them, Kean and Hazlitt set the tone for treatment of the play in the nineteenth century. Hazlitt's emphasis on character remained the critical focus through the ensuing decades, though his hostility to Portia was not the norm, and Kean's Shylock inspired all the actors who followed, including William Charles Macready, who first performed the role in 1823, endowing Shylock "with traces of nobility that later actors developed and emphasized" (Campbell 526).

Macready was as much a manager/director as an actor, who sought "to achieve a harmony in which all the elements in a production, visual no less than verbal, blended together." Macready would not make plays into star vehicles: "every scene was to be given its due weight, and secondary parts were to be cast with as much care as leading roles" (Gross 135).

Not that Shylock automatically became less dominant: reporting in 1839 on a performance of the play in Drury Lane, Heinrich Heine writes that he must include it among the tragedies. Shylock's enemies "are hardly worthy to unlace his shoes. The bankrupt Antonio is a weak creature without energy, without strength of hatred, and as little of love, a melancholy worm-heart whose flesh is really worth nothing save 'to bait fish withal' " (Wilders 29–30).

Charles Kean, Edmund's son, lacked his father's histrionic skill, but he was a gifted producer who mounted elaborate stagings of Shakespeare, most notably at the Princess Theatre in 1858. Kean sought the most authentic sets and costumes, and "the Rialto was thronged with exotic and picturesque figures, among them a small girl carrying a basket of doves—ten-year-old Ellen Terry. . . . There were something like a hundred colorfully outfitted extras in the trial scene" (Gross 137). In the United States, actor-managers like William Evans Burton followed the trend—Burton's own theater on Chambers Street in lower Manhattan boasted of its authentic productions, and in September 1852 Burton "joined the Castle Garden company to celebrate the centenary of the Hallams' first performance in America; the play was *Merchant*, of course, and Burton stood in for Lewis Hallam as Launcelot Gobbo" (Shattuck, *Hallams* 108, 116). At least one hundred professional productions of the play were staged in New York alone during the nineteenth century, featuring such illustrious visitors as both Edmund and Charles Kean and Henry Irving, as well as the native talents of Edwin Forrest, who performed Shylock in New York for the first time in 1826, and Edwin Booth, who had portrayed Shylock in San Francisco, Sydney, and London before he appeared in Boston and New York (1866–67).[17] Edwin's talented father, Junius Brutus Booth, had performed in rivalry with the great Kean before he emigrated to the United States at the age of twenty-five in 1821 and became the leading American Shakespearean of the time; Junius Brutus's son John Wilkes earned notoriety in April of 1865, but several years earlier he, too, had portrayed Shylock in a production that concluded with 4.1. John O'Connor discusses Edwin's conception of the role in his essay in this volume; Edwin regarded Shylock as a lowlife and played him in that way, against the prevailing orthodoxy. Committed to his craft, Booth contributed his own notes on performance to the Furness Variorum edition of the play, and these notes suggest how carefully Booth worked out "bits of business" (Gross 142).

Although Shylock dominated most nineteenth-century productions, Portia attracted talented actors, including Helen Faucit, whose career began in 1836 and included a memorable Portia, a portrayal that emphasized "such values as self-sacrifice in love, obedience to the father's will, and righteousness in pleading the Christian cause" (Bulman 43). She wrote about *Some of Shakespeare's Female Characters* in 1885. Ellen Terry, probably the greatest Portia of the century, first performed the role in 1875. During a brief run in another otherwise disappointing production, Terry recorded: "I knew I had 'got them' at the moment when I spoke the speech beginning, 'You see me, Lord Bassanio, where I stand' " (Gross 153). She realized that she had enthralled the audience and thought, "*Quite* this thing has never come to me before! *This is different.*" She was more demonstrative than Faucit had been—in the 1875 production, after Bassanio made the correct choice of casket and Portia reacted, "Henry James reported that the woman next to him gasped, 'Good heavens, she's touching him!' " (Potter 195). James himself found her "insufficiently the great lady, 'too free and familiar, too osculatory' " (Gross 153), while John Ruskin censured Terry "for failing to achieve the 'majestic humility' " he thought the role required (Bulman 43). But the majority view was expressed by the estimable scholar F. J. Furnivall, who wished that Shakespeare could see her perform: "A lady gracious and graceful, handsome, witty, loving and wise, you are his Portia to the life" (Gross 153).

Terry performed opposite Henry Irving in the landmark 1879 production—it ran for 250 nights, a record never before equalled (Marder 75). After the hundredth performance, "Irving invited 350 guests to a supper on stage, one of whom, the youthful Oscar Wilde, composed a sonnet for Ellen Terry's Portia." Terry and Irving performed together for more than twenty-five years, last appearing together "on July 14, 1907, when they played the roles at Drury Lane" (Thomas Wheeler, *Bibliography* 280). Terry felt that Irving's "heroic saint" (her description) in 4.1 made her role a real challenge. The situation encouraged her "liberationist stance as the 'new woman' who used her wits to get her way and thereby challenged traditional Victorian expectations of female behaviour" (Bulman 43). Ironically, in her lectures on her performances, Terry noted that George Brandes's rather uneasy view of Portia as

Figure 1. John Everett Millais, *Portia (Kate Dolan)* (1886). The Metropolitan Museum of Art, Catharine Lorillard Wolfe Collection, Wolfe Fund, 1906 (06.1328).

"almost masculine" in her behavior (see discussion below) inspired her to maintain a position of authority, not only in the courtroom but in her relationship with Bassanio. Terry argued that this orphan heiress "is used to acting on her own authority" (quoted in Bulman 44). Her attitude as an actress has obvious affinities with the critical commentaries of Anna Jameson and others, as well as with the portrayal of Portia provided in Mary Cowden Clarke's fiction, discussed below. Terry was a beautiful woman, and for many years was thought to be the model for John Everett Millais' "Portia," painted in 1886; in fact, the picture shows actress Kate Dolan dressed in the costume that Terry wore for 4.1 (Figure 1).

Among the Americans, Ada Rehan made a name in various Shakespearean roles, including Portia. Although she played Ophelia to Edwin Booth's Hamlet, her real gift was in comic roles, including Portia in *Merchant* and Katharina in *The Taming of the Shrew*. Between 1879 and 1899, she played over two hundred roles in actor-manager Augustin Daly's company (Campbell 679–80). Daly's "sumptuous" 1898 New York *Merchant,* in fact, was designed to showcase Rehan, and the Shylock was an unknown. The production was "well received" but managed only a short run, probably because the public expected a more impressive Shylock (Gross 170).

In their treatment of the play in *Tales from Shakespeare* (1807), Charles and Mary Lamb emphasize character, beginning with a sketch of Shylock that portrays him as a "hard-hearted man . . . much misliked by all good men," followed immediately by a description of Antonio as "the kindest man that lived, the best conditioned" (71). The Lambs follow Shakespeare's plot fairly closely, quoting from it in some detail. Yet, incredibly in a book meant for children, they eliminate all reference to the casket-test. They write that the "accomplished" Portia, in giving herself to Bassanio, "prettily dispraised herself" (74). According to the Lambs, Bassanio and Portia marry immediately "to give him a legal right to her money" (75). In this version, it is the Duke who demands that Shylock convert to Christianity; Jessica and Lorenzo are first mentioned when Antonio proposes Shylock's deed of gift to them in 4.1; and the Gobbos disappear entirely.

Reprinted frequently, the Lambs' *Tales* enjoyed such success that they "spawned no imitators for nearly three quarters of a century" (Rozmovits 100) and influenced generations of children. The *Tales* were directed primarily at girls, since boys could be expected to read Shakespeare in the original much earlier than their sisters. This "moral protectiveness" (Han 137) characterizes attitudes toward Shakespeare in the nineteenth century, as many popular editions of the plays were produced. 1807 saw publication of the four-volume *Family Shakespeare,* with an introduction by Thomas Bowdler noting the "profanity and obscenity that infest Shakespeare's plays" (Marder 111). That the dangers were real is suggested by the memoir of Charlotte Elizabeth Browne, who recalled in 1845 the impact her reading of *The Merchant of*

Venice "at the age of seven had on her in later years. She described her first experience of Shakespeare as drinking 'a cup of intoxication under which my brain reeled for many a year' and the play as 'the glittering tinsel of unsanctified genius.' Shakespeare was censured for 'ensnaring' her into a life of misanthropic hatred: 'My mind became unnerved, my judgment perverted, my estimate of people and things wholly falsified . . .' " (Han 137).

At the same time, nineteenth-century writers stressed the valuable moral lessons in Shakespeare, if read properly. Mary Cowden Clarke's *The Girlhood of Shakespeare's Heroines* (1850–52) provides a logical follow-up to the Lambs' *Tales*, treating the characters as real people.[18] Clarke provides what we would now call prequels to the stories in the plays. Her very first of fifteen portraits treats Portia, and the imagined details of Portia's upbringing reinforce the impression of a poised, intelligent, generous, and highly moral young woman. Her father studies the law with Bellario at Padua and marries Bellario's sister Portia, who dies in childbirth, sending a heartbroken Guido di Belmonte into voluntary exile for many years. Her loving uncle Bellario raises young Portia, introducing her to the law books in her father's library and engaging with her in discussions of the law, at one point noting that women would not be temperamentally suited to professing the law. Nerissa is a Venetian orphan who joins the household as a companion for the orphan of Belmont. Guido reappears on Portia's eighteenth birthday—she immediately recognizes her father, who throws a big party to celebrate her majority and his return. Guess who comes to the party! It turns out that the Marquis of Montferrat is a particular admirer of Portia and pursues her in several subsequent visits, but Portia dislikes him and his "distasteful assiduity" (13), noting approvingly his constant companion Bassanio. Nerissa comments that the Marquis is not only rather belligerently self-confident but also rather ugly, especially compared to Bassanio, who "surpasses him [Montferrat] in good looks a hundredfold" (12). We also learn that Bassanio has "an exalted sense of honour, and entertain[s] an utter scorn of falsehood in word or deed," while at the same time his love for his friend, kinsman, and benefactor Antonio is "warm and sincere," binding them in an "indestructible attachment" (23).

Meanwhile, Bellario's research discovers that the Marquis is a gambler and womanizer, and Guido, who targeted the Marquis as Portia's ideal husband, decides to set up a marriage lottery in place of his own obviously defective judgment. Father and daughter travel together to Venice, where Guido orders the three caskets. During a Venetian race, Portia is so distracted by Bassanio in his wonderful boat (as they exchange many meaningful glances) that she misses descriptions of the occupants of other boats, including Antonio, Gratiano, Lorenzo, and the Prince of Morocco. She is even too distracted to note "that detestable old jew" (16) when he is pointed out in the crowd of spectators. As Guido and Portia travel home to Belmont, he gives her a ruby ring as a souvenir of their happy time in Venice. When she says she will never part with it, Guido responds, "Nay, you shall give it some day to him who shall possess the hand itself—to your husband" (18). Shortly thereafter, Guido collapses and dies in Portia's arms in the library at Belmont, but not before explaining the casket-test and extracting his daughter's solemn promise to honor his memory in the lottery for her hand. After a year of mourning, Portia prepares to welcome guests once again. She and Nerissa sit "at their embroidery frame in the library" as 1.2 begins.

This focus on character marks the commentary of H. W. Hudson (1872), who declares that in 4.1 Portia "in her gravity and dignity of deportment; her legal knowledge; her moral reflections; and more . . . almost rivals our Chief Justice Marshall [Chief Justice of the United States from 1803 to 1835]" (290). Hudson writes that Portia, "as intelligent as the strongest . . . is at the same time as feminine as the weakest of her sex; she talks like a poet and philosopher, yet, strange to say, she talks, for all the world, just like a woman" (285). But "if Portia is the beauty of this play, Shylock is its strength" (291). According to Hudson, Shylock "is a true representative of his nation": in his pride, his rapacious thrift, his weak hatred of the majority, Shylock is "thoroughly and intensely Jewish," yet "Shylock's character is *essentially tragic* [Hudson's emphasis]; there is none of the proper timber of comedy in him" (295).

Demonstrating Hudson's discomfort with the non-feminine side of the heroine, at least as viewed from a male perspective, Julie Hankey describes his words on Portia as "gender polarities yoked together" (443); in "Victorian Portias: Shakespeare's Borderline Heroine," Hankey notes that Imogen was the Victorians' *real* ideal of a woman, while male commentators betray a certain ambivalence about Portia. None dismisses her as Hazlitt had done, but their superlatives about her try to focus on their ideal Woman, "a haven from the material, an oasis of other-worldiness to restore the battered spirit of commercial Man" (437)—the kind of Portia Helen Faucit represented on stage. Clarke's portrait in *Girlhood* uses all the superlatives but also shows us a Portia gaining a rather sophisticated legal education from her uncle, an education not usually available to Clarke's contemporaries. There is always the risk, from the male point of view, of Portia crossing the boundary, and Clarke seems to enjoy toying with male fears.

"The wit of Portia is like attar of roses," writes Anna Jameson in 1833; among all of Shakespeare's powerful women, "I believe we must assign the first rank to Portia, as uniting in herself in a more eminent degree than the others, all the noblest, most loveable, qualities that ever met together in woman" (quoted in Rozmovits 35–36). This language rivals the most effusive male outbursts about Portia, but Jameson also ventures to suggest that Portia might not be comfortable in Victorian society, as educated and wealthy as she was: "a woman constituted like Portia, and placed in this age and in the actual state of society, would find society armed against her; and instead of being like Portia, a gracious, happy, beloved, and loving creature, would be a victim" (quoted in Hankey 430). Hankey speaks of Victorian women critics (and actors too) wishing for the conditions for women that must have existed in Portia's Italy, at least for women of her class. Lisa Jardine (in an essay discussed below) examines the contradictions inherent in Early Modern attitudes toward education for women, who could become "unruly" if not carefully controlled. In this volume, Penny Gay's essay on Portia in twentieth-century productions opens with a helpful overview of the heroine's uniqueness in the Shakespearean canon.

Linda Rozmovits describes *Merchant* as "a late Victorian obsession" (3), ideal for schools, pulpits, and debates on such issues as feminism and the Jewish question. "For many, *The Merchant of Venice* was a play, first and foremost, about the marriage prospects of a wealthy orphaned young woman with a subplot about a Jewish moneylender hovering in the background" (6). This enthusiasm for the play developed in an atmosphere of unprecedented Bardolatry (a term first used by G. B. Shaw in 1900) which saw the Bible and Shakespeare as "inextricably linked" (25), and which regarded the situations in the plays "as an inventory of moral dilemmas, while his characters were seen to describe the complete range of possible responses to those dilemmas" (26). Louis Marder notes that, after 1858, Shakespeare became a regular subject of instruction in schools, because the Oxford and Cambridge examining board drew up a list of subjects on which students could be tested, and *Merchant* was among about ten Shakespearean plays that appeared on the exams (278). Marder also notes that, when Benjamin Jowett, Master of Balliol College, Oxford, granted students permission to perform Shakespeare, the first play offered, in December 1883, was *Merchant* (280).

Rozmovits sees the treatment of Jessica in Victorian commentary as some indication of the unease surrounding the "Jewish question" at the time, when Jews could be found among the capitalists who were beginning to supplant the landed aristocracy in political power, while at the same time impoverished Jews poured into England as refugees from eastern Europe (6–7). Henry Irving's 1879 production of *Merchant* focuses most of its textual cuts on the role of Jessica:

> Clearly, the difficulty with the story of Jessica was that it presented a litany of what to a late Victorian audience would have been highly charged moral concerns in an uncomfortably complicated set of relations to one another— female disobedience, racial and religious disloyalty, the effects of an unsuitable domestic environment, premeditated deception, conversion, and, of course, miscegenation. (72)

At the same time, the nineteenth century was fascinated with possible links between the Bard's life and his works: "Edward Dowden, in his

Shakspere: A Critical Study of His Mind and Art (1875), but more particularly in his *Shakspere Primer* (1878), popularized a theory . . . that Shakespeare's life was divided into four periods, 'In the workshop,' 'In the world,' 'Out of the depths,' and 'On the heights' " (Marder 164). This biographical interpretation marks the work of Danish critic George Brandes at the turn of the century, who writes that Shakespeare chose to make "a real man and a real Jew out of" Marlowe's Barabas, "this intolerable demon in a man's skin," because "at that moment" his mind was "preoccupied with the ideas of acquisition, property, money-making, wealth" (151). Brandes contends that, when Bassanio chooses the correct casket, Portia's "attitude clearly expresses Shakespeare's ideal of womanhood at this period of his life" (161). Brandes has no use for Bassanio, whom he regards as a "weak spendthrift" whose sole motive in seeking Portia is the clearing of his debts (162). But "Portia's nature is health, its utterance joy. Radiant happiness is her element." Less enthusiastic about Portia in the courtroom, Brandes, like Hudson, suggests that Portia's success in 4.1 is due to "something independent, almost masculine, in her character" (162). As for Shylock, Brandes finds him "the central figure in the play for modern readers and spectators . . . though there can be no doubt that he appeared to Shakespeare's contemporaries as a comic personage, and, since he makes his final exit before the last act, by no means the protagonist" (164). Brandes declares that "the conclusion of *The Merchant of Venice* brings us to the threshold of a term in Shakespeare's life instinct with high-pitched gaiety and gladness. In this, his brightest period, he fervently celebrates strength and wisdom in man, intellect and wit in woman" (168).

For John Wilders, two earlier German critics set the tone for nineteenth-century criticism. Writing in 1839, Hermann Ulrici "was the first critic to regard *The Merchant of Venice* as an examination of human values" (Wilders 16). And Ulrici's work inspired G. G. Gervinus, writing in 1849, to assert that "the intention of the poet . . . was to depict the relation of man to property. To examine the relation of man to property, to money, is to place their intrinsic value on the finest scale, and to separate that which belongs to the unessential, to outward things, from that which in its inward nature relates to a higher destiny" (Wilders 34–35).

Finally, Richard Moulton (1885) emphasizes the way in which what he calls the Story of the Cruel Jew brings out the idea of nemesis: "Antonio's excess of moral confidence suffers a nemesis of reaction in his humiliation, and Shylock's sin of [attempted] judicial murder finds a nemesis of retribution in his ruin by process of law." According to Moulton, "Antonio must be understood as a perfect character: for we must read the play in the light of its age, and intolerance was a medieval virtue. But there is no single good quality that does not carry with it its special temptation, and the sum of them all, or perfection, has its shadow in self-sufficiency. It is so with Antonio" (Wilders 37).

The merchant's defiant response to Shylock's review of the insults he has regularly suffered from Antonio exemplifies this weakness: when Antonio tells Shylock that "I am as like to call thee so again" (1.3.130), Moulton remarks on "the tone of infatuated confidence, the *hybris* in which Greek superstition saw the signal for the descent of Nemesis. . . . So Nemesis [will surprise] Antonio in spite of his perfectness: but the malice of Shylock is such as is perpetually crying for retribution, and the retribution is delayed only that it may descend with accumulated force" (39). In a happy turn of phrase, Moulton judges the outcome of the courtroom scene: "The suitor who rests his case on a whim cannot complain if it is upset by a quibble" (40).

As already noted, Kean's portrayal of Shylock inspired later nineteenth-century actor-managers, most notably Edwin Booth in the United States and Henry Irving in England. Booth actually ended his version of the play with Shylock's departure in act 4. Irving's initial production in 1879 did not do so, but from the spring of 1880 on, he waffled and played it both ways, sometimes lopping off the fifth act, sometimes retaining it (Bulman 50–51). As John O'Connor reminds us in this collection, analyzing Shylock in performance, Irving's interpretation was influenced by seeing the dignity of a Jew in a visit to the Levant. Bulman writes: "By conceiving Shylock in this regal image, Irving transformed him from a seething, malevolent Semite into a natural aristocrat" (31). Yet, as both Julie Hankey and Linda Rozmovits suggest, Portia received a full measure of critical appraisal. Despite Shylock's dominance on the stage, Portia remained a powerful adversary, especially in the work of Ellen Terry and Ada Rehan.

IV. The Twentieth Century

The tragic treatments of the later nineteenth century, featuring elaborately "realistic" sets in addition to sympathetic portrayals of Shylock, inspired William Poel's Elizabethan Stage Society production in 1898, an attempt to restore the play to what he regarded as a sixteenth-century context, complete with himself as Shylock in a red wig and a false nose. This attempt at "authenticity" did not arouse much enthusiasm, but it could have encouraged E. E. Stoll's famous essay on Shylock, which originally appeared in 1911 and was published in its final form in 1927. Gross has noted that "in many respects Stoll can be seen as the academic equivalent of Poel" (181).

According to Stoll,

A villain and a butt. . . . such . . . is the impression which Shylock makes after he has been duly restored to the sixteenth century, an impression in which pathos has no place, and with which our notions of justice and social responsibility, on the one hand, and of ironical art, on the other, have, so far as they are merely modern, nothing to do. (262)

Clearly, irony has no place here. Stoll assumes that the play, and its author, are anti-Semitic, and he offers a prescient observation: "How can we here [at Shylock's exit] for a moment sympathize with Shylock unless at the same time we indignantly turn, not only against Gratiano, but against Portia, the Duke, and all Venice as well?" (260).

From this early start, "controversy and contention arise over the interpretation of the characters and the meaning of the play" (xi): in his 1985 Garland *Bibliography* for the play, Thomas Wheeler identifies a number of strands which emerge in the critical commentaries published between 1940 and 1979. Not surprisingly, Shylock is the center of contention, and the controversy about him necessarily affects the treatment of his nemesis, Portia. Wheeler notes that she attracts polarized responses, as does Antonio, and as do the central scenes of the play, 3.2 and 4.1. In terms of meaning, "the most widely accepted interpretation emphasizes the themes of justice and mercy" and, for Nevill Coghill and Frank Kermode, for example, "the resolution of an apparent conflict between justice and mercy" is the "governing idea" of the play (xvi). The theme of wealth is treated in two broadly contrasting ways, "in purely economic terms" (W. H. Auden, as well as Marxist interpretations), and "as both literal and figurative" (John Russell Brown and C. L. Barber).

Wheeler concludes: "For all its variety, critical response to *The Merchant* tends toward one or another of two opposing positions: either the play is a relatively simple romance which, despite some tension caused by Shylock, succeeds in giving its audience fairly uncomplicated satisfaction [Brown, Barber, Coghill, Kermode], or it is a quite subtle, ironic comedy which tests its audience and its characters severely [Auden and A. D. Moody]."

Moody's analysis emphasizes the difficulty of "simple responses" to the play, Wheeler claims, because Shakespeare here offers "two different and unresolved standards of value" (xviii–xix).[19] "Especially during the last decade of our period [1969–1979]," he observes, "many critics have come to the conclusion that a satisfying interpretation is not possible" (xvii–xviii). In his 1991 introduction to the Garland volume of *Critical Essays* on the play, Wheeler still finds that "taken as a whole, *The Merchant* may be seen as a play which does not resolve the tensions and ambiguities it creates" (xiii). Danson, who entitles his introduction "By Two-Headed Janus," would seem to agree: "there is no single 'established view' of the play" (14).

Psychoanalytic Approaches

Sigmund Freud's analysis (1913) focuses on the caskets. He asserts that Bassanio's speech leading to his choice of the lead casket "has a forced ring about it." Psychoanalysts hearing Bassanio would "suspect concealed motives behind the unsatisfying argument" (59). The source-stories, in which a maiden must make a choice, undergo an inversion in the play, where a man chooses among three caskets. In dream imagery, "it would at once occur to us that caskets are also symbols of women" (60). The lead casket, whose "pale-ness" moves Bassanio "more than eloquence" (3.2.106), is more moving "than the blatant nature of the other two. Gold and silver are 'loud'; lead is dumb, in effect like Cordelia, who loves and is silent" (62).[20] Freud notes that "dumbness is in dreams a familiar representation of death" (63). Indeed, the third casket, the third sister, is the Goddess of Death or, in terms of the classical Fates, Atropos, the inexorable. But Freud asserts that humanity will not accept death; in his theory of "reaction-formation," people "substitute for the terrors of reality a more acceptable version" (Halio 18), and this goddess is, instead, transformed into the goddess of love—not a surprising displacement given the tendency of ancient cultures to regard the same deity as goddess of both birth and death. Thus, Freud concludes,

> Choice stands in the place of necessity, of destiny. Thus man overcomes death, which in thought he has acknowledged. No greater triumph of wish-fulfillment is conceivable. Just where in reality he obeys compulsion, he exercises choice; and that which he chooses is not a thing of horror, but the fairest and most desirable thing in life. (67)

As Halio explains,

> Bassanio's 'choice', then, becomes his fate, and he and Portia, the Aphrodite figure [the goddess of love in the lead casket], are destined for life together in love. But first Shylock, the killjoy, the true spirit of deathliness, must be overcome. Like . . . the clever lady in the flesh-bond tale, Portia accomplishes this deed. Thus the two stories are fused. (19)

Ruth Nevo's chapter on the play in *Comic Transformations in Shakespeare* offers psychoanalytic criticism. Her title, "Jessica's Monkey; or, the Goodwins," expresses Nevo's conviction that Shakespeare does not succeed in reaching the comic resolution typical of his plays in this kind, that the romance of young love (sometimes callous and foolish) sits uneasily with the realities of the flesh bond. Nevo argues that the play is not only "split, sundered, schizoid, but rich in the figuring of the estrangement, alienation and dismembering which are its obsessive themes" (120). She continues:

> The plot Shakespeare is using is . . . at odds with the comic form he characteristically favours and the result is fracture, which he has compounded by an inversion at the level of ordination: the main plot—Portia's and Bassanio's—is subordinated to the plot which is causally dependent upon it. It is Portia's captivity, not Antonio's, which originates the story. (122)

"By throwing upon a scapegoat figure the whole burden of the comic exorcism," she argues, "[Shakespeare] has frustrated his own comic intuitions. . . . What he does with his scapegoat, we find, is to convert him . . . into a quasi-tragic protagonist" (123).

Nevo sees "strangeness and fragmentation" (126) everywhere in the play, not just in Venice. For this reason, Belmont does not function here as the green place of confrontation with folly and ultimate insight that we find in the Athenian wood of *A Midsummer Night's Dream* or in the Forest of Arden in *As You Like It*. Belmont is not a place of transformation but of "uneasy evangelicalism" (137), an idea explored further in Karoline Szatek's contribution to this volume. Meanwhile, the fragmentation evident in the play's settings "is essentialized in Shylock" (126). There are, in fact, two Shylocks, "the burlesque ogre—paradigm of a comic *pharmakos*—and the human being possessing a gloomy and savage dignity. The two alternate bewilderingly and never cohere" (136).

Nevo sees in 4.1 "three wills . . . in asymmetrical conflict," those of Shylock, Antonio, and Portia, and "the wills of Shylock and Antonio are not opposed in the matter of the bond but secretly consonant" (132), since both of them, for very different reasons, would express in the fulfillment of the bond "a desperate act of self-assertion" (135). If Shylock has "a burning need to be recognized as a man more sinned against than sinning," then Antonio "is driven by a positive compulsion to self-immolation" (134).

In "The Counterfeit Order of *The Merchant of Venice*," Leonard Tennenhouse also offers a psychoanalytic perspective:

> By composing a play in terms of geographical, moral, and economic oppositions, Shakespeare obviously sought to make from his material a dramatic world that was finally whole, social, and stable. These oppositions are not simply ideological, however, but reflect psychological tensions as well. The use of two locales, Jessica's betrayal of Shylock, the androgynous characteristics of Portia, the idealization of patronage, the relationship between love and wealth, the ring plot, and the bawdry in the fifth act are all means of resolving oppositions within Shakespeare's culture. At the same time, all signal disturbance, conflict, and anxiety. (197)

In analyzing the two locales, Tennenhouse compares the similar device in other comedies and argues that "at the end of [*Merchant*], Shakespeare does not return or even promise to return his major characters to the world of social and economic reality" (198). Meanwhile, Jessica's "flight . . . establishes the emotionally complex association of betrayal with the spending of a ring, an undoing of a marriage, and a denial of love" (201).

Tennenhouse argues that, for the good of the city, Antonio must be punished as a defaulter on a loan. Although the word *scapegoat* is not used here,

Figure 2. Geraldine James, Leigh Lawson, and Dustin Hoffman in the Peter Hall production, Haymarket Theatre, 1989. Photo credit: Dominic Photography.

Antonio is squarely placed in this position—and so characterizes himself at the start of the trial scene, but Portia saves his day. Antonio's virtues sometimes seem excessively narcissistic, as when he desires to see Bassanio and be seen by him to fulfill the terms of the flesh bond, and in his "exhibitionistic" suffering in 4.1 (204). But, reflecting "the contradictions of the cultural code," the play presents "the belief that selfless charity triumphs over selfish need and [the play presents] the assumption that venture capitalism is more natural than usury . . . in the form of the idealized patron-client relationship . . . the idealization of male love" (207). At the same time, the play leaves Antonio alone at the end. Portia "figuratively" places the merchant, "whom she 'delivered' and to whom he says she gave life, in the position of offspring." Tennenhouse concludes:

> By replacing Shylock with Portia in the triangular relationship with Bassanio and Antonio, Shakespeare has substituted for an orally destructive father a nurturing mother. Fidelity to wife in turn replaces loyalty to

patron-friend. The narcissistic bond between males has been loosened, but Antonio's isolation, like Shylock's punishment—regardless of how we understand either of them morally or thematically—still disturbs the resolution. (210)

In a paper delivered at the Seventh World Shakespeare Congress (2001), Philippa Berry traced Shakespeare's imagery of cutting and incision in the play. If we think of Nevo's concept of the scapegoat as a means for the community to unite, the language of cutting, "cultural incision," is somehow also involved in the community's quest for unity. Thus Medea, cutting into Aeson's flesh to insert her herbal potion to cure him, figures Portia's role as someone who cuts, wounds, in order to heal. Her name is shared with "Brutus' Portia" (1.1.166), renowned for wounding herself in the thigh to demonstrate her worthiness to share her husband's secrets. Jason's Golden Fleece is the skin cut from a sheep. Morocco offers to "make incision for your love, / To prove whose blood is reddest" (2.1.6–7). Bassanio declares that the paper of Antonio's letter is "the body of my friend," and "every word" of the letter is "a gaping wound / Issuing life-blood" (3.2.264–66), anticipating Shylock's knife in the courtroom scene, where he seeks to inscribe himself in Antonio's body (Figure 2). Most remarkably, Berry notes that the biblical manna Lorenzo refers to in describing Shylock's promise of inheritance (5.1.294) is thought to have been produced by an incision in the bark of a tree.

Liberal Humanist Approaches

"*The Merchant of Venice* is a fairy tale"; dating from 1930, Harley Granville-Barker's famous comment on the play appears in the opening sentences of his influential *Preface*: "There is no more reality in Shylock's bond and the Lord of Belmont's will than in Jack and the Beanstalk" (55). As Kenneth Myrick notes, "We may think he made too much of this point, but he reminded us forcibly that the play is set in the realm of high romance. We cannot understand it in terms of modern realism" (lxiv). According to Granville-Barker, Shakespeare's "real problem" is "how to blend two such disparate themes into a dramatically organic whole":

> The stories, linked in the first scene, will, of themselves, soon part company . . . But the difficulty is less that they will not match each other by the clock than that their whole gait so differs, their very nature. How is the flimsy theme of the caskets to be kept in countenance beside its grimly powerful rival? (57–58)

The answer lies in Shakespeare's "contrasting of subjects, scene by scene," a trick that "he never lost his liking for" (58), and in his ability to humanize Portia and Bassanio, both of whom Granville-Barker finds highly attractive.

He contends that Bassanio, despite "the rather poor figure . . . the coercion of the story makes him cut" does measure up "to the stature of sympathetic hero. Shakespeare contrives it in two ways. He endows Bassanio with very noble verse; and whenever he can, throws into strong relief the Bassanio of his own unconvenanted imagination" (60). About Portia Granville-Barker is even more enthusiastic, noting that she comes into her own especially after she is freed from the caskets-plot in 3.2: "To the very end she expands in her fine freedom, growing in authority and dignity" (66).

As for Shylock's role, Granville-Barker sees his final words as characteristic of "the unapproachable Shakespeare. 'I am not well.' It nears banality and achieves perfection in its simplicity. And what a completing of the picture of Shylock!"

> He passes out silently. . . . There can be no greater error than to gerrymander Shylock a strenuously "effective exit"—and most Shylocks commit it. From the character's point of view the significant simplicity of that "I am not well" is spoiled; and from the point of view of the play the technical skill with which Shakespeare abstracts from his comedy this tragic and dominating figure and avoids anticlimax is nullified. (79–80)

Granville-Barker concludes that "the play ends, pleasantly and with formality, as a fairy tale should" (80). And he offers a practical explanation for Shakespeare's decision, "against tradition," to give Gratiano the last word: the other principals "must pace off the stage in their stately Venetian way, while Gratiano's harmless ribaldry is tossed to the audience as an epilogue. Then he and Nerissa, now with less dignity than ever to lose, skip quickly after." Most directors use the play's final "*Exeunt*" as an opportunity to make a summary statement about meaning—one typical recent production, described in this volume by Gayle Gaskill, left Antonio and Jessica alone on stage as the lights went down.[21]

For C. L. Barber, Antonio and Portia are central to the play's exhibition of "the beneficence of civilized wealth, the something-for-nothing which wealth gives to those who use it graciously to live together in a humanly knit group," whereas Shylock suggests human "anxieties about money, and its power to set men at odds" (167). Barber writes that "the whole play dramatizes the conflict between the mechanisms of wealth and the masterful, social use of it" (170):

> [Shylock] stands for what we mean when we say that "money is money." So Shylock makes an ironic comment—and *is* a comment, by virtue of his whole tone and bearing—on the folly in Bassanio which leads him to confuse those two meanings of "good man," to ask Shylock to dine, to use in this business context such social phrases as "Will you *pleasure* me?" (173)

In the world of Bassanio and Antonio,

> [m]oney is not used to get money; that is the usurer's way. . . . Instead Bassanio's purse is invested in life—including such lively things as the "rare new liveries" (II.ii.117) that excite Launcelot. . . . With the money, Bassanio invests *himself*, and so risks losing himself—as has to be the case with love. (Antonio's commitment of his body for his friend is in the background.) It is a limitation of the scene where he makes his choice that the risk has to be conveyed largely by the poetry, since the outward circumstances are not hazardous. (175–76)

When Portia gives herself and all she has to Bassanio at 3.2.149ff, her lines "make explicit, by an elaborate metaphor of accounting, that what is happening sets the accounting principle aside." The speech moves "from possessions, through the paradox about sums, to the person in the midst of them all, 'where I stand,' who cannot be added up" (177). Discussing Portia's "Mercy" speech, Barber concludes: "It has been in giving and taking, beyond the compulsion of accounts, that Portia, Bassanio, Antonio have enjoyed the something-for-nothing that Portia here summarizes in speaking of the gentle rain from heaven" (186).

For Barber, "No other comedy, until the late romances, ends with so full an expression of harmony as that which we get in the opening of the final scene." Given over to their joy, Lorenzo and Jessica "feel the harmony of the universe and its hospitality to life in a quiet moment of idle talk and casual enjoyment of music." And "Jessica is already at ease" in the Christian world, "to the point of being able to recall the pains of famous lovers with equanimity, rally her lover on his vows," (187–88). But Barber also admits to some uneasiness about his analysis when he reflects on the play, rather than seeing it or reading it. Reading or watching the play, he finds that the distinction about the different kinds of wealth works, "but when one thinks about the Portia-Bassanio group, not in opposition to Shylock but alone (as Shakespeare does not show them), one can be troubled by their being so very very far above money" (189–90).

No such shadows exist in the interpretation offered by Nevill Coghill which, appearing in 1950, significantly influenced later writers. Coghill sets up the now almost-clichéd contrast in the play between Old Law and New, and he does so by addressing the problem all directors face: how to deal with a play that "clearly has to do with an enmity between a Jew and a Christian" (108); how to deal with a theme of racial and religious conflict? The background of the play suggests, in fact, that both sides are right. In *The Castle of Perseverance*, an early-fifteenth-century morality play, *Humanum Genus* dies in sin and confronts the four daughters of God: Righteousnesss and Truth demand his damnation, earned by his behavior in life, but Mercy and

Peace point to Christ's redemptive action, and *Humanum Genus* is saved. In this imperfect world Mercy, the focus of the New Law, must win out over Justice, the stress of the Old. The two sides are only in conflict because, "whereas God is held to be absolutely just as He is absolutely merciful, mortal and finite man can only be relatively so, and must arrive at a compromise" (112).[22] To Coghill, act 5 "becomes an intelligible extension of the allegory (in the sense defined), for we return to Belmont to find Lorenzo and Jessica in each other's arms. Christian and Jew, New Law and Old, are visibly united in love. And their talk is of music, Shakespeare's recurrent symbol of harmony" (113).

Coghill's focus on the Old Law confronting the New lies behind Barbara K. Lewalski's 1962 essay on "Biblical Allusion and Allegory in *The Merchant of Venice*." Lewalski argues that in the play "Shakespeare, like Dante, is ultimately concerned with the nature of the Christian life," and that the allegorical significance of the play reflects Dante's four levels of meaning as he expounds them in his letter to Can Grande: literal, allegorical, moral or tropological, and anagogical (34–35). Most importantly, "at what would correspond in medieval terminology to the 'moral' level, the play is concerned to explore and define Christian love and its various antitheses." Antonio embodies Christian love "in all but one respect": his inability to forgive injuries and to love enemies. "Shylock functions as one (but not the only) antithesis to" Christian love. Antonio's practice of Christian love "is indicated throughout the play under the metaphor of 'venturing' " (35).

Shylock's "thrift," completely at odds with "venturing," and his vengefulness, evident from the very start, place him, in the terms of the moral allegory, in the devil's camp. In the trial scene, Antonio "foregoes revenge and rancor, manifesting a genuine spirit of forgiveness. . . . Thus, his chief deficiency surmounted, Antonio becomes finally a perfect embodiment of Christian love." At the allegorical level, the confrontation between Shylock and Antonio "symbolizes the confrontation of Judaism and Christianity as theological systems—the Old Law and the New . . ." (38–39). Similarly, Lewalski sees Bassanio's choice of the lead casket as symbolizing "his acceptance of the self-abnegation, risk, and venture set up throughout the play as characteristics of true Christian love" (44). The casket choice "represents Everyman's choice among values" (45).

A number of biblical passages inform Portia's language in 4.1, not only the Elizabethan translations of the Lord's Prayer ("forgeve us our dettes, as we forgeve our detters"), but several Psalms and Ecclesiasticus 25:19.[23] Lewalski also suggests that there is some sense here "of the trial described in the medieval drama, the *Processus Belial*, in which the Devil claims by justice the souls of mankind due him under the law, and the Virgin Mary intercedes for man by appealing to the Mercy of God" (48). Shylock's forced conversion, then, is logical: having lost his case for legal righteousness, "he is made to accept the only alternative to it, faith in Christ" (50).

Bassanio's surrender of the ring to "Balthazar" is the lover's first real venture in the play: "The ring is the token of his possession of Portia and all Belmont. [Surrendering the ring to "Balthazar,"] Bassanio surrenders his 'claim' to all these gifts, even to Portia's person" (53). Belmont itself "functions chiefly at the anagogical level." As Jessica has suggested in 3.5, Belmont "figures forth the Heavenly City. . . . In Belmont all losses are restored and sorrows end" (53).

Reflecting on such an allegorical analysis, one recalls James Shapiro's observation that a play is not a sermon. In her appendix on Shakespeare's use of the Bible, Mahood refers to Lewalski's interpretation and others before commenting:

> By the end of the sixteenth century the medieval comprehensiveness in drama was giving way to the Renaissance principal of decorum, which can be biblically summed up as "to everything there is a season . . . A time to mourn and a time to dance." There was a time for preaching, and a time for play-acting. A play about Jews and Christians inevitably reflected the Christian beliefs of its writer, but its original audience might have been considerably surprised to be told that it *expounded* them. They were simply there and taken for granted like the air people breathed: the shared cultural environment of writer, watcher, and reader. (188)

It is, nevertheless, true that "*The Merchant of Venice* contains more biblical allusions than any other play by Shakespeare" (Marx 104). Maryellen Keefe's essay in this collection articulates for the modern reader the Biblical ambience "taken for granted" by the play's "original audience." Noting that Christianity, like kingship, is a donnée of Shakespeare's time more treated in some plays than in others, Lawrence Danson singles out Coghill and Lewalski as two writers "who stress the elements of explicitly Christian concern in the play" (16–17).

In *Shakespeare and the Bible,* Steven Marx deliberately juxtaposes Lewalski's interpretation to that of Richard A. Levin in *Love and Society in Shakespearean Comedy* (1985):

> The traditional handsome hero and charming heroine "forfeit our sympathy" . . . because of their calculating ways of courting and their purchase of success by the loss of others. Rather than "figur[ing] forth a Heavenly City" [Lewalski's words] or a romantic fairy-land of music and beauty that contrasts with the self-seeking mercantile world of Venice, Belmont is a country-club suburb which excludes Jews, homosexuals, and foreigners of any complexion, disguising its own cutthroat competition for status and control with surface gentility.

The Christians are just as greedy as the Jews, but more subtle. Although Antonio and Shylock are antagonists, they share exclusion from the celebration in act 5 and from Belmont, one because he is Jewish, the other because he loves a man about to marry (Marx 111–12).

Levin's analysis, so much at odds with Lewalski's, exemplifies the contemporary mood. As John Andrews writes: "Until recently most of the critical commentary on *The Merchant of Venice* has been directed to discovering what the text can tell us about the play's thematic harmonies. But many of today's scholars are more interested in the disturbances and dislocations that lie beneath the surface of a seemingly stable dramatic structure" (211–12). Is it possible that a thematic approach like Lewalski's allows for harmony but that consideration of characters as staged (Shylock's departure after 4.1 and Antonio's isolation in 5.1) undermines thematic harmonies? Modifying somewhat C. L. Barber's sense of uneasiness, can we argue that thematic harmony is possible on the page, in the study, but not on the stage? These questions reinforce the sense of *Merchant* as conundrum.

Taking a thematic approach, Frank Kermode confidently concludes that "*The Merchant of Venice*, then, is 'about' judgment, redemption, and mercy. . . . It begins with usury and corrupt love; it ends with harmony and perfect love. And all the time it tells its audience that this is its subject; only by a determined effort to avoid the obvious can one mistake the theme" (224). Kermode notes the repetition of the word *gentle* in the play—*civility*, *nature improved*, but also, of course, *Gentile*. There is a straightforward contrast between gentleness, the "mind of love," and its opposite, for which Shylock stands (221).

Shakespeare makes the contrast clearer by twice inserting the kind of passage Kermode says he will later learn "to do without," the kind that tells the audience how to interpret specific actions. The first such passage is the debate on Genesis in 1.3. Christian commentators see Jacob as "making a venture. . . . But Shylock sees no difference between the breeding of metal and the breeding of sheep—a constant charge against usurers. . . . Later, in 2.8, we have a pair of almost Spenserian *exempla* to make this point clear. First Solanio describes Shylock's grief at the loss of daughter and ducats; he cannot distinguish properly between them. . . . Then Solario describes the parting of Antonio and Bassanio; . . . [there is no measuring out or calculation in the love displayed here]" (221).

Like others, Kermode regards Bassanio's visit to Belmont as a "venture." In "the central scene of choice . . . Bassanio, rejecting the barren metals which appear to breed, avoids the curse of barrenness on himself (for that is the punishment of failure)"; as the successful Bassanio reads Antonio's letter to Portia, "the conflict between gentleness (Antonio's laying down his life for his friend) and a harsh ungentle legalism becomes the main burden of the plot" (222–23). Peter Phialas regards Shylock as the antagonist in 3.2, physically absent but very much present by implication. Bassanio's choice of lead reminds us of Shylock's love of gold "and his insistence upon receiving instead of giving. . . . [T]he implied conflict with Shylock has a structural as well as thematic significance, for it contributes to considerable unity of impression, [which] can be expressed simply by saying that Bassanio's choice would not be Shylock's" (162–63). Harold C. Goddard (1951) offers a totally opposite view when he describes Bassanio as the gold casket, since he gained what many men desire: a wealthy wife. Portia is also the gold casket because she fails "to be true to her inner self." Antonio is the silver casket. He got as much as he deserved: "material success and a suicidal melancholy." Shylock, "in the supreme irony of this ironical play," is "the leaden casket with the spiritual gold within" (86, 92, 112, 101).

Regarding the final act as a kind of coda to all that precedes (in this respect, he sees *Merchant* as similar in structure to *A Midsummer Night's Dream*), Kermode focuses on the passage about harmonious music that befits a happy ending. It is noteworthy that many commentators, no matter what their sense of the ultimate meaning of the play, see Lorenzo's words on music as crucial to understanding Shakespeare's meaning.

The pendulum of critical judgment swings again as Kermode's conclusion provides A. N. Moody with a point of departure. Moody quotes Kermode's confident declaration that "only by a determined effort to avoid the obvious can one mistake the theme" as "the established view of" the play (100), and then questions it. For Moody, the qualities Kermode considers— judgment, redemption, mercy—are the play's focus, but the "centre of [the play's] meaning" is irony. Thus, argues Moody, the play is about

> the manner in which the Christians succeed in the world by not practising their ideals of love and mercy; . . . it is about their exploitation of an assumed unworldliness to gain the advantage over Shylock; and . . . finally, it is about the essential likeness of Shylock and his judges, whose triumph is even more a matter of mercenary justice than his would have been. In this view the play does not celebrate the Christian virtues so much as expose their absence.

Having thus reversed Kermode's conclusion, Moody next rejects his own conclusion as well because, he says, "no account of the play which offers to see it in terms of simple good and evil can hope to satisfy. It is too subtle and exploratory for that; and also, perhaps, too ironic in its resolution" (101).

Moody regards the worldliness of the Venetian Christians as subversive of their religion. Salerio's speech in 1.1 about the risks Antonio undertakes "is, in effect, a parody of orthodox warnings against putting one's hopes upon worldly fortune, since it echoes them only to reduce them to an occasion for a more anxious concern with the world" (103). In *Merchant* "the

Christian ideal is not deployed as a standard by which the characters are to be judged. The controlling viewpoint is not that of the eye of Heaven, but that of enlightened human feeling." Moody therefore concludes: "The dramatic experience simply does not lead us to judge [the Christians] in relation to the ideal; it leads us to judge them by their treatment of Shylock. Their offence is not against God but against humanity" (104). In the end, he suggests, "we cannot but feel that [Shylock's] humanity is larger in scope and depth than theirs. In consequence his defeat at their hands seems to involve a reversal of the right order of things, the lesser being allowed to put down the greater"(105). The essay in this volume by John Cunningham and Stephen Slimp, in its consideration of the lesser and the greater, could be read as an ironic commentary on Moody's belief that the play is "*essentially* [*sic*] an exposure of Christian hypocrisy" (Danson 8).

In "Brothers and Others," W. H. Auden highlights the play's mercantile atmosphere by showing how very different Venice's commercial emphasis is from that of medieval English society, which focused on a community centered in family or feudal obligation—or, latterly, "united by a common love of impersonal justice" (59–60) where the difference between brothers and aliens is obvious. Such differences are no longer obvious or "givens" in Venice: "Such a mercantile society is international and cosmopolitan; it does not distinguish between the brother and the alien other than on a basis of blood or religion—from the point of view of society, customers are brothers, trade rivals others" (61). In Venice, where wealth is based on money and not land, time itself is not the cyclical time of agricultural society but the forward, linear movement of a contract, which binds the parties and makes people brothers only for a specified period of time.

Just at the point in 4.1 (Figure 3) when Shylock has alienated any sympathy we may have felt for him, Portia invokes the Venetian law against aliens which, incredibly, neither Shylock nor the Duke seems to know about (and which, like the forced conversion of Shylock, is not in the source-story). Shakespeare thus restores some of our sympathy for the villain when we realize that "irrespective of his personal character, [Shylock's] status is one of inferiority. A Jew is not regarded, even in law, as a brother. [Furthermore,] if the wicked Shylock cannot enter the fairy story world of Belmont, neither can the noble Antonio [because he cannot marry]. Had he wished, Shakespeare could have followed the *Pecorone* story in which it is Ansaldo [Antonio], not Gratiano, who marries the equivalent of Nerissa" (71). Shakespeare may well have been aware that Dante links usury and sodomy in canto nine of the *Inferno* (72). Both usurer and (closet?) sodomite are excluded from Lewalski's "Heavenly City."

Concluding his essay, Auden considers the inscription on the leaden casket as applicable to two characters who have indeed given and hazarded all: Shylock ("however unintentionally") and Antonio, but, as noted by Richard

Figure 3. Sarah Dodd (Nerissa), Lucy Peacock (Portia), Donald Carrier (Bassanio), Peter Hutt (Antonio), Nicholas Van Burek (Gratiano), Paul Soles (Shylock) in the Stratford Festival of Canada production, 2001. Photo by V. Tony Hauser. Courtesy of Stratford Festival of Canada.

A. Levin and Auden himself, these men cannot enter Belmont. In Auden's words, "Belmont would like to believe that men and women are either good or bad by nature, but Shylock and Antonio remind us that this is an illusion: in the real world, no hatred is totally without justification, no love totally innocent" (76–77).

Any survey of critical commentaries must at least refer to other works, such as John Russell Brown's essay, "Love's Wealth and the Judgement of *The Merchant of Venice*," which expands on ideas adumbrated in the closing paragraph of his introduction to the Arden edition:

Shall we say it is a play about give and take?—about conundrums such as the more you give, the more you get, or, to him that hath shall be given, and from him that hath not, shall be taken away even that which he hath? The two parts of the play are linked by these problems: Portia is the golden fleece, the merchants venture and hazard as any lover, the caskets deal all in value, the bond and the rings are pledges of possession. In the scramble of give and take, when appearance and reality are hard to distinguish, one thing seems certain: that giving is the most important part—giving prodigally, without thought for the taking. (Arden lviii)

Lawrence Danson's *The Harmonies of "The Merchant of Venice"* proclaims in its very title its relationship to studies like those of Brown and Coghill and Barber which "seek to establish the text more as myth or parable than as a site of conflicting changes in the early modern period"; these writers "argue for an essential unity of idea, usually in terms of 'love's wealth' or the importance of giving and self-sacrifice" (Coyle 11).[24] Again, a thematic approach suppresses conundrum. Danson reads the play in terms of circles that interlock and find ultimate completion in the fifth act: "I begin with the image of things round or circular—ambiguous images, some of them, but suggestive too of harmonious resolutions" (11). He writes that "the major actions of the play reflect in large the circular imagery of the parts. The three delicately interconnected episodes [casket, courtroom, rings] form a series of dramatic paradoxes, in each of which an apparently irresolvable dilemma is revealed at last to be no dilemma at all, as the opposing ends join in a circle of harmony" (20).

Much can also be learned from chapters on the play in books that discuss the comedies in general. In *Shakespeare's Comedies,* Bertrand Evans writes that "Shakespeare's dramatic method relied heavily on arrangements of discrepant awareness" among the various characters and between the characters and the audience (viii). According to Evans, "regularly in the comedies the middle of Act III finds exploitation of [the audience's] margin [of awareness] over the participants approaching a climax" (58). In 3.2 of *Merchant,* for example, the audience shares with Portia the knowledge of the correct casket, denied to Bassanio (54), but we also know more than either she or Bassanio can know about the threat hanging over the scene, because we have just heard Shylock assure his friend Tubal at 3.1.127 that "I will have the heart of him if he forfeit." Evans declares that "the play is rightly named for the merchant, who is its centre; and the centre of Antonio's character is his goodness; and the centre of his goodness is that very heart which Shylock threatens." Shakespeare presents in Antonio "an extraordinary man," and "he does so for the dramatic purpose of requiring us to be deeply concerned for the merchant's safety and welfare" (56–57).

Phialas observes in *Shakespeare's Romantic Comedies:* "Having dealt with the love-friendship conflict in *The Two Gentlemen of Verona* and in a smaller way in *A Midsummer Night's Dream*, Shakespeare proposes here to present the ideal relationship of friendship and love" (134). Placing the play in a context which shows how much it advances on the craft of the earlier comedies, Phialas notes that the two plots come together not in the fifth act, as in some earlier plays, but in the fourth: "As Act IV is laid in Venice and is concerned primarily with the antagonist, so Act V is laid in Belmont and is concerned with the protagonist and what she and Belmont symbolize" (143). Phialas regards the power of the antagonist here as too great, requiring an entire act to dispose of it.

Phialas's analysis leads to the recognition that it is not unusual for the antagonist to be eliminated before the end of the play. In *Love's Labour's Lost*, the men are forsworn in 4.3, thus eliminating the "antagonist"; in *A Midsummer Night's Dream*, the antagonistic father Egeus is silenced in 4.1, and may or may not appear again; in *Much Ado*, Don John is eliminated early in act 5 and does not reappear on stage, while in *As You Like It*, Oliver is converted in 4.3 (and then included in the community) while Duke Frederick is reportedly converted from his wicked intentions but never appears again. On the other hand, the conflict in *Two Gentlemen* is not resolved until the closing moments of the play, and in *Twelfth Night* Malvolio as antagonist is very much present in the closing scene. Clearly, Shylock's disappearance after act 4 is not without precedent in Shakespeare's comedies.

In *Shakespeare's Comedies: From Roman Farce to Romantic Mystery* (1986), Robert Ornstein emphasizes the importance of the women in most of the comedies: "each time Shakespeare adapts an existing story or play in a comedy he amplifies the roles that the women play and enhances their stature. [Thus] he transforms the deceitful mercenary widow of *Il Pecorone* into Portia and places Nerissa by her side" (14). Noting that few plays by Shakespeare's contemporaries give this kind of prominence to women (15), Ornstein also observes that Bassanio is one of the more attractive young men in these plays, second perhaps only to Benedick in his appeal.

The Critical Divide

Conceptually, there is only a short distance from Moody's ironic analysis—a "conventional but acute reading," writes one observer (Coyle 9)—to critics of the last twenty years such as Richard A. Levin, discussed earlier. Although Brian Vickers reminds us that "conventional" readings like Moody's, "not identified with any particular school or ideology, [are] still being produced, indeed perhaps the majority of Shakespeare critics are independents, following no specific line" (ix), we must recognize a chronological and substantive divide. Heather Dubrow's survey in the 1997 Riverside edition makes the break at 1970. In his "Penguin Critical Study" of the play (1993), Graham Holderness distinguishes in his bibliography between "Criticism" (where, for example, he lists James Bulman and John Wilders) and "Theory" (where he includes titles by Walter Cohen and Stephen Greenblatt) (80). Up to about 1975 or 1980, much commentary was "formalist" or "essentialist." The underlying assumption of these writers is that there is a fixed, determinable text of Shakespeare and that we can come to understand its meaning. Yet these critics—such as Harley Granville-Barker, C. L. Barber, and Frank Kermode—are no more likely to offer a definitive interpretation, free of bias and tendentiousness, than such critics of the eighties and nineties as Walter Cohen, John Drakakis, and Karen Newman. The work of recent critics sometimes seems arrogant, and its highly technical language sometimes clouds their arguments. But the perspective of history may show that "liberal humanist" critics who confidently claimed to convey the final meaning of the play were in fact the advance party for the postmodernists, who would themselves assert that there is no escape from ideology.

Terence Hawkes states clearly the contemporary credo in his introduction to *Alternative Shakespeares, Volume 2*:

> The kind of access to the plays which is sought here ultimately depends upon the abandonment of any sense of a 'final' meaning that must necessarily be dug out of them. To accept that they have no once-for-all essential or stable identity is precisely what permits a probing of the plays' unique legacy: it may even help to create it. That they seem to foster these siftings differently from generation to generation as well as from performance to performance is an inescapable—and happy—conclusion. Those who believe that Shakespeare can still engage modern audiences will find their case fully supported by such stratagems, without needing to locate a phantom quality of 'transcendency' in the plays, or to construct ghostly entities vaguely promoted as the plays 'themselves'. (13–14)

Martin Coyle adds that "one of the aims of contemporary criticism is to move beyond the fixed, the predetermined, the set, and to recognise and value difference, plurality, change. In other words, there is no need to stay forever within the bounds of a fixed set of ideas" (3). Coyle provides a context for understanding this criticism:

> Contemporary theory, for all its differences and diversity, does share some common features or propositions: it is oppositional criticism (oppositional in the political sense); it is committed to change; it is opposed to the Enlightenment tradition of liberal humanism; it recognizes that the individual is not the author of meaning but the effect of it; and that the task of the critic is to foreground what is neglected, demonized, rejected, silenced or denied in the text. But, above all . . . contemporary theory has taken up the poststructuralist perspective that meaning is unstable because language is unstable. In other words, contemporary theory, far from regarding meaning as single, sees meaning as always plural. (4)

Many such analyses take one of two perspectives, or a combination of two perspectives; some writers see Shakespeare as subversive, using his drama to question the conventional wisdom of the day, and others view the dramatist as complicitous with his age, quite content with the status quo, but unable to prevent the cracks from showing, so to speak, in his scripts.

Marxism

To Kiernan Ryan, Shakespeare is consciously subversive in portraying Antonio "as the embodiment of the void at the heart of Venice. For it is in the play's rebellion against the expectations of its title, in its conspicuous refusal to project the merchant capitalist as hero, that Shakespeare's anguished rejection of the values invading Elizabethan England finds distorted expression" (40–41). And Ryan is equally clear in another passage:

> To define the play in terms of which party deserves the blame and which the absolution, with readings and productions swinging now to Shylock and now to the Christians, is to miss the point. What is at stake is the deeper recognition that, through the revenge plot and trial, through the ironies and contradictions they lay bare, an apparently civilised society is unmasked as premised on barbarity, on the ruthless priority of money values over human values, of the rights of property over the elementary rights of men and women. The point lies not in the vindication of the Jew at the expense of the Christians, or of the Christians at the expense of the Jew, but in the critique of the structural social forces which have made them both what they are, for better and for worse. (39–40)

Walter Cohen's analysis in *"The Merchant of Venice* and the Possibilities of Historical Criticism"* offers a more complex interpretation, distinguishing between Shakespeare's vision of Venice and his vision of England: "In *The Merchant of Venice* English history evokes fears of capitalism, and Italian history allays those fears. One is the problem, the other the solution, the act of incorporation, of transcendence, toward which the play strives." He continues:

> The fusion in the towns of nobility and bourgeoisie helped generate the Renaissance in Italy and, much later, in England as well. The concluding tripartite unity of Antonio, Bassanio, and Portia enacts precisely this inter-class harmony between aristocratic landed wealth and mercantile capital, with the former dominant. A belief that some such relationship provided much of the social foundation of the English monarchy accounts for Shakespeare's essentially corporatist defence of absolutism in the 1590s. (52)

It follows, then, that the play "is quite obviously pro-capitalist, at least as far as commerce is concerned. . . . Shakespeare is criticizing merely the worst aspects of an emerging economic system, rather than the system itself" (49).

Observing that "the crisis of the play arises not from [Shylock's] insistence on usury, but from his refusal of it" (49), Cohen also notes that Shylock's denunciations of his Christian persecutors in the "Jew" speech and in the comments on slavery in court are meant to "justify his own murderous intentions." His charges about slavery do not apply to most of the Christian characters, as far as we can tell. But such "universalising" denunciations are also not challenged by the Christians, so "they tell us that although Shylock is defeated and then incorporated in the world of the play, in the world beyond the play his values are pervasive."

Cohen concludes that

> if the play revealed that merchants were as exploitative as usurers, that they were in fact usurers, then its entire thrust toward harmonious reconciliation could only be understood as a fiendishly oblique instance of ironic demystification. But if instead Shakespeare intended the movement toward transcendent unity to be taken at least as seriously as the dangers of nascent capitalism, he needed to present the latter in a way that that would not undermine the former. (54)

Therefore, the play's "formal movement—dialectical transcendence—is not adequate to the social conflict that is its main source of inspiration and one of its principal subjects. Some of the merit of *The Merchant of Venice* ironically lies in the failure of its central design to provide a completely satisfying resolution to the dilemmas raised in the course of the action" (55).

Gendered Approaches

In "Portia's Ring: Unruly Women and Structures of Exchange in *The Merchant of Venice*," Karen Newman uses the anthropological analysis of Claude Lévi-Strauss as modified by later writers to demonstrate how the system of exchange found in primitive cultures operates in the play—especially the exchanges among men as they move women from one form of servitude to another, where "women figure as capital, as objects of exchange among men" (121). But while Lévi-Strauss argues that such behaviors are essential to the existence of culture, Newman begs to differ by seeing Portia as an "unruly woman" whose actions interrogate the assumptions of Western culture about relations between women and men, and between man and man. The ring that Portia gives to Bassanio is "a visual sign of her vow of love and submission to Bassanio; it is a representation of Portia's acceptance of Elizabethan marriage which was characterized by women's subjection, their loss of legal rights, and their status as goods or chattel" (124). But, Newman continues, Portia moves away from the exchange system not only by imagining the loss of the ring and the aftermath of that loss, but by giving Bassanio so much more than he can ever reciprocate. Whatever her words of giving may

say, however conventional they may be, "In giving more than can be reciprocated, Portia short-circuits the system of exchange and the male bonds it creates, winning her husband away from the arms of Antonio" (125).

Newman hews close to Shakespeare's text, often providing a careful
line-by-line reading to support her argument. The analysis shows how Bassanio's answer to Portia's gift of herself and all she possesses uses an epic
simile "anomalous in Shakespearean comedy" (126):

> Madam, you have bereft me of all words,
> Only my blood speaks to you in my veins,
> And there is such confusion in my powers,
> As after some oration fairly spoke
> By a beloved prince, there doth appear
> Among the buzzing pleased multitude,
> Where every something, being blent together,
> Turns to a wild of nothing, save of joy
> Express'd and not express'd. (3.2.175–83)

Newman explains that this passage derives from a simile early in the *Aeneid*,
where Neptune's impact in quelling a storm is likened to that of a great leader
before whom the people express their respect through silence: "Bassanio's
comparison figures Portia as dominating and distant—that is, as a prince. . . .
Bassanio's political simile with its Virgilian intertextual exchange 'disguises'
Portia as a man and prefigures her masculine role in the trial scene where she
ensures the Venetian republic by reconciling the principle of equity with the
rigor of the law." Therefore,

> The *Merchant*'s Portia resembles her classical namesake and her figural
> persona ('beloved prince') by entering the male lists of law and politics. Far
> from simply exemplifying the Elizabethan sex/gender system of exchange,
> the *Merchant* short-circuits the exchange, mocking its authorized social
> structure and hierarchical gender relations.
>
> For Portia's ring . . . does not remain on Bassanio's finger, and *his* gift
> of the ring to Balthazar does indeed give Portia 'vantage to exclaim'. The
> gift of Portia's ring shifts the figurative ground of her speech from synec-
> doche to metonymy. Her lines first figure the ring as a part of her which she
> gives as a sign of the whole to Bassanio; in the final lines, however, the pre-
> figured loss of the ring signals not substitution, but contiguity, metonymic
> relations. . . . Portia's ring becomes a sign of hierarchy subverted by estab-
> lishing contiguities in which the constituent parts have shifting sexual and
> syntactic positions. (126–27)

After a careful analysis of the ring's and Portia/Balthazar's travels, Newman
concludes that when the ring is returned to Bassanio via Antonio in 5.1, it has

changed its meaning: "On its figural as well as literal progress, it accumulates other meanings and associations: cuckoldry and thus female unruliness, female genitalia, woman's changeable nature and so-called animal temperament, her deceptiveness and potential subversion of the rules of possession and fidelity that ensure the male line" (130–31). This analysis leads to a final verdict on the play: "The sexual symbolism of transvestism, the transgression of traditional gender roles and the figural transgression of heterosexual relations, the multivalence of linguistic meanings in women's and clowns' speech, all interrogate and reveal contradictions in the Elizabethan sex/gender system in which women were commodities whose exchange both produced and reproduced hierarchical gender relations" (132). Corinne Abate's essay in this volume offers further insight concerning Portia.

In "How To Read *The Merchant of Venice* Without Being Heterosexist,"Alan Sinfield addresses the play as a gay man who finds "mainline" interpretations as exclusionary of gays as of Jews, blacks, and women. His survey of what we know about attitudes toward sexual relations in Shakespeare's day suggests that today's firm boundary lines were unknown then. While it is impossible to reach certitude about the nature of the friendship between Antonio and Bassanio, it seems likely that Elizabethans didn't care much one way or the other about same-sex relationships, whatever their intensity. They seem to have been much more casual than we, perhaps because of the nature of the aristocratic houses where so many people functioned in a variety of roles, where places like Belmont were not uncommon (notice that Launcelot's questionable adventure with the Moor is remarked upon only in passing—imagine his doing such a thing in Shylock's house!). This casual kind of attitude, Sinfield concludes, began to fade later in the seventeenth century as society developed away from the aristocratic house and toward nuclear families. But even in Elizabethan culture, the apparent casualness about same-sex relationships was balanced by the realities of patriarchy and the requirement that men sire more men, in order to keep the hegemony in place: "The role of marriage and child-(son-) bearing in the transmission of property and authority is made to take priority. If (like me) you are inclined to regard this as a failure of nerve, it is interesting that the *Merchant*, itself, offers a comment on boldness and timidity. 'Who chooseth me, must give and hazard all he hath' " (138).

Catherine Belsey's "Love in Venice" offers insights allied to those of Newman and Sinfield in an essay somewhat marred by obscure language: "Riddles too are traditionally dangerous because they exploit the duplicity of the signifier, the secret alterity that subsists in meaning" (143). She also refers at one point to "the disjunction between the two parts of Act V" (150) without clearly delineating the two parts; apparently, the first part—Lorenzo and Jessica on love and the harmony of the spheres—ends with Portia's arrival, so that talk of love and desire moves to talk of marriage and adultery.

Like Newman, Belsey alludes to C. L. Barber's "classic analysis" of act 5 that supports the "conventionally held" view of the act as "dissipat[ing] tension and reconcil[ing] difference" (140). Quoting Barber's words, Belsey disagrees with him by pointing to the unhappy loves of the opening lines of act 5 while paraphrasing Denis de Rougemont's claim in *Love in the Western World* that "happy love has no history" (141). What does have a history is desire, the focus of Shakespeare's sources, but desire is a threat to marriage and is therefore left only as a trace element in the resolution of Shakespeare's plot:

> Love in *The Merchant of Venice* means marriage, concord, consent, and partnership. It means mutual compatibility and sympathy and support. But the older understanding of love leaves traces in the text, with the effect that desire is only imperfectly domesticated, and in consequence the extent to which Venice is superimposed on Belmont becomes visible to the audience. (141)

Bassanio wins the lottery because he alone of the suitors is motivated by desire "and knows that lovers give and hazard all they have" (143).

In the fifth (and penultimate) section of her essay, Belsey offers interesting observations on the relationship between friendship and marriage. Here her argument complements Sinfield's as she notes that "Shakespeare's texts tend to opt, however uneasily, for the nuclear couple" (152). She also agrees with Sinfield's conclusion that the Elizabethans didn't fuss much about homoeroticism, accepting it as a given and not particularly threatening, and, like Sinfield, she alludes approvingly to Stephen Orgel's argument that "homosexual acts were perceived as less dangerous to men than heterosexual love, because it was association with women which was effeminating." Nevertheless, the society was moving away from the chivalric culture, in which "wives do not supplant friends," toward a "new model of marriage in the sixteenth century" which "identified wives precisely as friends" (155).

In "The Bankruptcy of Homoerotic Amity in Shakespeare's *Merchant of Venice*," Steve Patterson complements the analyses of Sinfield and Belsey. He provides extensive background on the popular Renaissance notion of male friendship by examining a number of literary texts on the theme. Patterson concludes that, in *Merchant*, "marriage and amity are squarely at odds because the play questions the possibility of a homoerotic bonding that produces exemplary conduct" (13). The conventions of friendship tales call for friends who are quite similar in fundamental ways, but here Shakespeare rearranges the convention to give us Antonio and Bassanio, "strikingly different in both temperament and demeanor" (14).

Just how complex Elizabethan attitudes must have been comes through in Alan Bray's research into the physical evidence of tombs and funerary monuments. In churches and churchyards across England, Bray has found numerous instances of two men or two women buried in the same grave. Some monuments show two men standing, side by side, hands joined, while extant mottoes state that "Love joined them living. So may the earth join them in their burial." Bray argues that, "in an era where different kinds of kinship overlap, shade into one [an]other, and are not clearly distinguished from friendship," the formal friendships thus memorialized probably did not involve sexual relations. A liturgical ritual apparently recognized such relationships; the two friends would exchange solemn promises outside the church and then ratify their mutual commitment by receiving the Eucharist together during the service. Bray writes that "the vows did not—at least in the Latin West—create expectations of inheritance; nor did they preclude marriage" (1108).

New Historicism/Postcolonialism

In "Guess Who's Coming to Dinner? Colonisation and Miscegenation in *The Merchant of Venice*," Kim F. Hall regards Portia's "unruliness" as merely a cover for her real role as "the focal point of the Venetian economy and its marriage practices: it is through her that money is recirculated to the Christian males and difference is excluded or disempowered" (109). For Hall, "the play's central action [is] a circulation of wealth to an aristocratic, male elite that is predicated on the control of difference. Aliens must be either assimilated into the dominant culture (Shylock's and Jessica's conversions) and/or completely disempowered (Shylock's sentence). Their use as explanations for racial difference allows for the organization of property, kinship, and religion within an emerging national—and imperial—destiny" (106). Hall claims that Morocco, in wooing Portia and losing her, "loses his right to reproduce his own bloodline, a right not explicitly denied the other suitors" (102). But the clearly-stated rules of the lottery also deny Arragon the right to sire legitimate children.[25]

In this context Hall sees the "Negro . . . the Moor" impregnated by Launcelot Gobbo (alluded to in 3.5.28–39), and the conversation among Jessica, Launcelot, and Lorenzo that refers to the incident, as symptomatic: "it may be that this pregnant, unheard, unnamed, and unseen (at least by critics) black woman is a silent symbol for the economic and racial politics of *The Merchant of Venice*. She exposes an intricately wrought nexus of anxieties over gender, race, religion, and economics (fuelled by the push of imperial/mercantile expansion) which surround the various possibilities of miscegenation raised in the play" (94). It is no surprise, therefore, that neither Launcelot nor the pregnant Moor is present in act 5: just as "Portia's originally transgressive act is disarmed and validated by the play's resolution when these 'disorderly' women become pliable wives," so

[t]he only immediately fertile couple presented in the play, Launcelot and the Moor, are excluded from the final scene. Her fecundity exists in threatening contrast to the other Venetians' seeming sterility, particularly as it is created with Launcelot Gobbo, the 'gobbling', prodigal servant whose appetites cannot be controlled. Like Shylock's absence, their exclusion qualifies the expected resolution of the text and reminds us of the ultimate failure to contain difference completely even as the play's aliens are silenced. The Moor, whose presence may be a visible sign for the conflation of economic and erotic union with the Other in the rhetoric of travel, provides a pregnant reminder of the problematic underpinnings of the Venetian economy. (108)

Thus the essay uses a passing reference to the questionable behavior of a minor character (what Coyle calls "an apparently insignificant detail") as key to the meaning of the play, inferring a great deal from a brief exchange, although the precise verbal details of the lines are not analyzed. In his essay for this volume, R. W. Desai also uses a New Historicist approach which explores the cultural implications of the fates of all of Portia's suitors.

In "Cultural Confusion and Shakespeare's Learned Heroines," Lisa Jardine complements the insights of both Newman, with her portrayal of Portia as "unruly woman," and of Alice Benston—who gives us a masterful Portia, very much at the center of the action, as discussed below. Jardine has analyzed Early Modern attitudes toward the education of women and finds in them a fundamental contradiction, or uneasiness; on the one hand, humanists like Thomas More advocated education for women, but on the other, they worried about how such training could make women "unruly," about how knowledge could become "knowingness." Examining this contradiction in reference to both Helena in *All's Well That Ends Well* and Portia in *Merchant,* Jardine observes that *Merchant*'s "ending is dense with sexual punning. Here, I suggest, we have a reminder that Portia's learning/knowledge is always, potentially, culturally translatable into 'knowingness'—into the sexual—and as such has to be bridled by a vigilant husband" (60). Jardine further observes that "it is typical of the ambivalent attitudes circulating in the play that the speech in *The Merchant of Venice* in which Portia offers herself entirely and whole-heartedly as 'vassal' to her new lord and master, the scholar-soldier Bassanio—the speech that culminates in the ring-gift and betrothal [3.2.149–74]—is a speech whose inventory of Portia's womanly deficiencies contradicts everything that the rest of the play tells us about her" (62).

In "Shylock: Why This Usurer Has a Daughter," the conclusion to her study of *The Usurer's Daughter: Male Friendship and Fictions of Women in Sixteenth-Century England,* Lorna Hutson refers several times to *Merchant* as the Shylock play. It is impossible here to do justice to an extended monograph which focuses on the differences between the householder and the husband in Xenephon's *Oeconomicus,* a classical text highly valued and imitated by Renaissance writers because it explores the tensions between *oikonomia* (responsible householding) and *amicitia* (the ideal of male friendship). But Hutson profitably contrasts the world of Antonio and Bassanio, with its willingness "to take decorum, or dramatic effect, into the calculation of costs and returns," to that of Shylock, "who fulfills the tropical function of the good housewife in the humanist discourse of good husbandry, who is defined by the stigma of thrifty anxiety even as Christian 'husbandry' becomes, by her definition, an activity at once more fortunate and more magnanimous" (235).

Geraldo U. de Sousa discusses the play in terms of "Textual Encodings," using the New Historicist technique of thick description to explore in some detail the "written documents [that] govern life in the Venice and Belmont of *The Merchant of Venice,* as they do in other highly literate societies. Through cultural encodings, these texts provide an ideological shield for the Italians and codify the premise of cultural superiority. Aliens who attempt to interpret the Italian texts do so at their own peril" (69). De Sousa demonstrates how the play's aliens fall afoul of cultural encodings they cannot comprehend.

Thus, "choice of the right casket depends not upon valor but rather upon interpretation of texts and culture" (75). Unfortunately for him, Morocco confuses caskets and coffins, not understanding that a coffin was a casket but a casket was not a coffin: he "connects these artifacts. I contend that for him the lead casket becomes an Elizabethan lead coffin. He associates the lead casket and death, bringing his knowledge, though partial and imperfect, of European cultures to bear upon his choice" (78). Rejecting lead, Morocco chooses gold, which he associates with another European artifact, the English gold coin stamped with an image of the Archangel Michael.

Discussing the Golden Fleece legend, de Sousa sees Shakespeare splitting the story into two segments, one related to Portia (the "Golden Fleece" that suitors travel great distances to win), the other to Jessica (the Medea who betrays her father to pursue life with her Jason, Lorenzo). Shylock's own "interaction with Christians hinges upon the interpretation of four texts: the Venetian City Charter [which Shylock refers to explicitly at 4.1.39], Genesis 27–30, the bond, and the decrees against aliens" (91).

De Sousa notes that the play contains seven allusions to Jacob—the name occurs nowhere else in Shakespeare, except in a brief reference in *Measure for Measure.* "Shylock's wife, like Jacob's first wife, was called Leah. The story of Shylock's daughter Jessica and Lorenzo echoes Jacob's" (92). Antonio of course interprets the story of Jacob and Laban's sheep differently from Shylock and identifies Shylock's reading with the devil's.

De Sousa concludes that "both Morocco and Shylock encounter texts that defeat them. Portia's textual negotiations with these aliens, however, expose what the Venetians want to hide: xenophobia and racial and religious prejudice" (96).

Dramatic Structures

Joan Ozark Holmer's study of the play in terms of choice, hazard, and consequence offers a comprehensive thematic and structural analysis. While
acknowledging that there will probably never be "a 'final' interpretation or
any single reading or approach that does justice to the orchestrated *whole* of
The Merchant of Venice" (ix), Holmer argues that the play "derives much of
its powerful dramatic energy from the hard choices for or against wise love
that its characters confront and we experience empathetically. Shakespeare's
emphasis on wise love is probably the most significant addition to the variety
of literary sources he transformed for the invention of his play." Holmer recommends reading Matthew 5–7 juxtaposed with Luke 6, 20–49, "as well as
their attendant glosses in the Geneva Bible," in order to understand "an Elizabethan ethic regarding which choices should be blessed." The blessed are
"those who rightly love God and all others as God has loved them" (7–8).
Holmer concludes:

> For Elizabethans, inner human harmony is established by the rational soul's
> right rule of one's animal or fleshly nature. Humans are all basically bound
> together by the bond of flesh, but unless they are also bound together in the
> spirit of love they can never be truly unbound, truly free. (10)

Holmer also offers a clear analysis of the structure of the play. A "Diagram of structural unity" (50–51) lays out the development of the play
toward its central scene, 3.2 (Figure 4), where Bassanio chooses the correct
casket, and then away from that scene. The diagram shows how scenes in the
first half balance those in the second, and Holmer's analysis provides detail
to justify this schema.

John Lyon also discusses structure, noting that plays "often begin *in
medias res*," and that *The Merchant of Venice* clearly opens in the midst of an
ongoing conversation. He observes that "the world and action of this play are
burdened by their past to an extraordinary degree. Gradually the audience is
explicitly informed, and often invited to make inferences, about that past.
Thus it is often *in retrospect* that the play's actions and characters prove more
troubling than might initially appear" (223). Lyon then enumerates the
details about situations in the play that preexist the action to such an extent
that "the innocence and freedom of new beginnings are not available to the
characters of *The Merchant of Venice*" (224).

Lyon notes that the play is the most sententious of all the comedies
before the problem plays. There are many other literary elements in the play,
but, contrary to the situation that might obtain in a fable or allegory,

> the play's action is not contained by its *sententiae*; instead, these are not
> merely illustrated but tried and tested, by the particularity of the dramatic

Figure 4. *Portia: The Casket Scene from "The Merchant of Venice."* Photo engraving (gravure) by Goupil and Company of painting (1881) by Alexandre Chabanel.

action. The relation between moral generalities and the specifics of dramatic action thus becomes a problem for interpretation. D. J. Palmer
describes the effect as one in which 'our attention is often held by moral
arguments of one kind or another, while a different order of awareness and
response is being solicited by other dramatic means'. (226–27)

Of whatever critical bent, the most impressive studies—like Drakakis's,
Danson's, and Holmer's—offer a reading that takes the entire play into
account. Such is Alice Benston's "Portia, the Law, and the Tripartite Structure of *The Merchant of Venice*," where she argues that the final act is much
more than the coda Frank Kermode sees because it "achieves a synthesis of
the [play's] troublesome antinomies, deepens our understanding of Shylock
and his 'bond,' and incorporates Antonio in the final vision." For Benston, the
play can best be understood as a series of *three* trials:

> The basic form of the play is tripartite: Bassanio's casket scene, Shylock's
> trial, and the ring episode are equal partners in a drama concerned primarily
> not with law versus mercy, but with the law itself and its complex relations
> to vice, virtue, and vicissitude. The play not only has a tripartite structure,
> but is informed throughout by a pattern of triads. There are three trials,
> three caskets, three couples, and, of great importance, three rings. In terms
> of plot structure, however, the sequence of trials forms the significant triad.
> And the play's crucial figure is neither Antonio nor Shylock but Portia,
> since it is her attitude toward the law that is central for these trials.
> (165–66)[26]

To advance her argument, Benston shows that both Antonio and Bassanio tend to excess in their declarations of contracts—thus, Antonio professes no concern about the "merry bond" with Shylock, despite Bassanio's
stated misgivings. And Bassanio is very free with pledges of his life: he
accepts Portia's ring and puts his life on the line as pledge that he will never
give it up, and again during the trial scene he declares that he would give up
his life, as well as his wife's, in order to save Antonio. Part of Portia's mis-
sion is to educate these men in the ways of contracts and oaths. When she
learns in 3.2 for the first time of Antonio's existence, her immediate instinct
is to "incorporate Antonio in the new group formed by the marriage"; as she
explains in an exchange with Lorenzo in 3.4.7ff., "since she is already
'yoked' in equal love to Bassanio, the *three* are united in a bond of love.
Portia does not oppose love to friendship; rather she elides love and friendship" (171).

Benston argues that "it is justice—law—not mercy that prevails under
Portia's direction at the trial" (174). She asks Shylock to show mercy, well
aware that he cannot be compelled to do so. Even as she strives to mitigate
Shylock's murderous intent, she upholds the laws against threats to them by

the Duke (actually, his threat to ignore Venice's laws is made just before
"Balthazar" enters) and, especially, by Bassanio, who urges the Duke "To do
a great right, do a little wrong" (4.1.216), and is severely rebuked by Portia in
turn: "While a debtor may appeal to his bond holder for mercy, a court cannot compel an alteration of the contract prior to adjudication of the rights
involved. This exchange is what first reveals the conflict between Portia's
and Bassanio's values, a conflict which will have to be reconciled later"
(176–77).

But, "just as law and the state would be in jeopardy were Shylock not
allowed his day in court, so both would be equally threatened were Shylock
not punished for the implicit intent of his bond. . . . Portia's role, then, has
been to use the law to save the law" (178–79). After the verdict is finalized,
mercy is allowed "to season justice":

> A new bond is the condition upon which mercy will be shown, a bond
> which ensures two comic adjustments. Since the rancor which led Shylock
> to feel the need for revenge flows from his position as outsider, the first
> remedy is to incorporate him into the community. The second injunction
> forces him to recognize his daughter, the prodigal, whom he had wished
> dead just as he had sought revenge upon Antonio. (180)

Benston notes that the fifth act opens by considering three topics—
betrayals of love, music as temporary escape from the animal side of human
nature, and a "good deed" as light in the darkness of a "naughty world"—
related by a common theme, "the mutability of man, bound as he is to his animal senses and subject as he is to time. Even as Portia speaks, the clouds
have covered the moon, darkening the landscape" (181):

> Were the world and people constant, were the future predictable, there
> would be no risks and no need of contracts. A pledge or vow is that which
> attempts to mitigate the mutability of the human condition. Those who fail
> to perceive this fundamental proposition enter bad contracts in the heat of
> the moment; under a countervailing passion, they tend to abrogate their
> vows. Bassanio and Antonio, whose faults result from an excess of their
> virtues (generosity and love), have both shown a failure to grasp these prin-
> ciples. (183)

Benston argues that Antonio and Bassanio come to understand the principles
through the "rings test." And she contends that the disharmony many commentators see in the concluding moments of the play "is founded on the
assumption that the basic unit is the married couple (of which we have three).
Recalling that the basic 'chord' is a triad, and remembering that the ring
passes through Antonio's hands, we should see this last action as a rebinding
that incorporates rather than rejects him" (186).

Imagine a staging of the play in which no one is left behind or alone—Jessica would exit with Lorenzo, while Antonio-Portia-Bassanio would exit together in just that pattern, with Portia between the men, and—in keeping with Granville-Barker's reading of the final speech as discussed earlier—Gratiano and Nerissa remain long enough for Gratiano to deliver his epilogic lines. Harmony obtains! Such a scenario would presumably suit Alice Benston.

She concludes that three fathers in the play—Shylock, the old Lord of Belmont, and Antonio (understood in a father-son relationship to Bassanio)—give up their control, which they have exercised

> through images of death. Portia's father controls her actions through his death-bed plan of the caskets. (Freud has noted [as discussed above] that the choice of the lead casket is the choice of death.) Interestingly, Antonio manipulates Bassanio only after the threat to his life has occurred. And Shylock's control over Jessica also suggests death. (187–88)

But now Antonio accepts Bassanio's commitment to Portia, indeed he guarantees it and, when Portia restores his argosies, he tells her she has given him "life and living," the very words Shylock used to express his despair at the terms of his defeat in court. So these words link Antonio to Shylock, "but here spoken in an outburst of happiness. For the first time in the play, Antonio has been brought out of his melancholy; he now looks forward to life. [Meanwhile] Portia's protection of the law is complete. . . . [The newlyweds] arc at last free to go about the serious and merry business of generation" (189).

Clearly, Shakespeare's play is so powerful, so much a masterpiece, that it can sustain seemingly endless interpretations, whether the "liberal humanism" of Holmer and Benston or the "theory" of Drakakis and Walter Cohen. Studies based in theory often helpfully restate the debate about the meaning of the play, and they often open up the play to new and enlightening insights. Some patterns certainly emerge from recent work: there is much emphasis on Portia's "excess," the threat she represents to patriarchy. Shylock is almost always the victim in these readings, although he is sometimes seen as participating in the oppressive structures he condemns. Having lost his allegorical significance, Antonio is often dismissed as a member of the oppressive patriarchy, but if Antonio is in love with Bassanio, then he too is Other, a role he plays in Auden as well as in Sinfield and Steve Patterson. Richard A. Levin, like Auden, regards both Shylock and Antonio as Other and therefore unwelcome at the end. While Levin and Hall regard Portia as part of the problem, an attractive front for male/capitalist hegemony, some commentators—by implication, Newman, Belsey, and Jardine—see Portia victimized by patriarchal Venetian attitudes. In various accounts, then, Antonio or Portia or both Antonio and Portia join Shylock as victim and Other. Many recent writers see the play as subversive of Elizabethan values, but there is disagreement about the extent of Shakespeare's conscious participation in such subversion. The varieties of interpretation in twentieth-century criticism, remote and recent, reinforce notions of the play as a conundrum.

V. *The Merchant of Venice* on Stage and Screen

Shakespeare's work always plays a double role, as text for the study or class-room, and as script for performance. The four essays that conclude this col-lection consider *Merchant* as a script: Penny Gay surveys Portias from Ellen Terry to Derbhle Crotty, and John O'Connor does the same for Shylocks from Henry Irving to Henry Goodman, while Gayle Gaskill reviews several contemporary American productions, and Jay Halio offers reflections on the most effective characterizations. This essay has already surveyed the staging of the play from Shakespeare's day to the end of the nineteenth century. Brief consideration of recent productions, as well of the play's presentation on film and television, will be provided here.

Some of the best insights about the play come from those who focus on the work as script, most notably James Bulman in his study of the play for the "Shakespeare in Performance" series. John Gross's survey of Shylock is another important source for details of production, as is Bill Overton's study, while the history of staging in *The Reader's Encyclopedia of Shakespeare* and Sylvan Barnet's brief account in the Signet Classic edition provide help-ful details.

Similarly, such actors and directors as Sinead Cusack, Patrick Stewart, and John Barton have provided valuable perspectives. Dame Judi Dench, who played Portia for the Royal Shakespeare Company in 1971,[27] has com-plained that she loathes the play: "Everybody behaves appallingly, and there's nothing for the *spirit* in the play" (202–204). On the other hand, Patrick Stewart, who played Shylock in Stratford in 1978, writes: "It is said that an actor must love the character he plays—however unpleasant. I loved Shylock and know that it was a privilege to be given an insight into such a life" (quoted in Andrews 218–19).

On the Twentieth-Century American Stage

Some notable productions have been staged in the United States in the twenti-eth century. In 1925, Walter Hampden as Shylock confronted Ethel Barry-more, "an ineffably lovely Portia hailed as magnificent in the trial scene." Hampden's Shylock, "a bitter and lonely man of intellect," dominated the pro-duction. George Arliss was not very successful as Shylock in 1928, but Peggy Wood as Portia "rang true, especially in a casual and winning reading of the mercy speech" (Campbell 528). In 1942 John Carradine portrayed Shylock first in San Francisco and then in repertory on tour around the country.

Bulman notes that "seldom since the Holocaust has a production [in North America] treated Shylock unsympathetically" (144). The 1957 production in Stratford, Connecticut, boasted Morris Carnovsky as Shylock and Katherine Hepburn as Portia. Carnovsky, "a thoroughly human villain, self-loving and without compassion, avoided self-pity and won sympathy for the Jew," while Hepburn portrayed "an intelligent, determined Portia" (Campbell 528). Carnovsky wrote about the role, arguing that "Shylock was a decent man with great nobility and loftiness of character" (Bulman 146) who was "sincere" in claiming that the flesh bond was "merry" (Barnet, "Stage" 171). When he repeated the role at Stratford, Connecticut, in 1967, this time without Hepburn, Carnovsky's "emphasis on revenge made him unsympathetic" (Barnet, "Stage" 171). Yet another interpretation was offered by George C. Scott for the New York Shakespeare Festival's 1962 Central Park production: "Never before was the Jew more intelligent, more sardonic, more terrifying, and, at the same time, more understandable. . . . Here was a Shylock whose intellectual superiority over his shallow Venetian adversaries was unmistakable" (Campbell 528).

The New York Shakespeare Festival offered *Merchant* again in 1995, indoors as part of its Shakespeare Marathon, with "Ron Leibman of *Angels in America* fame as Shylock, but Shylock is no Roy Cohn" (Macdonald 36). Another observer noted that the director "decided that Shakespeare had composed a homosexual tract; [Salerio and Solanio kiss on the lips, and one remains in female dress from Act 2 through the end of the play.] . . . The clincher was the grand finale in which Bassanio gave Antonio that incriminating ring, and the whole crowd left Portia alone on the stage for the fade-out" (Chetta 38).

Some Recent Productions

Experience suggests that no production of the play, however flawed, can be a total failure, so it is helpful to encounter the play on stage as often as possible. Peter Hall's 1988 and 1989 West End and Broadway version, with Dustin Hoffman and Geraldine James as the mighty antagonists (see Figure 2 above), was particularly effective in attempting to balance the two. Viewers who recognized James from the PBS dramatization of *The Jewel in the Crown* found her a strong contender against Hoffman. The Hartford [Connecticut] Stage performance in 1993 distinguished the two locales by lowering the three opulent caskets chandelier-like into the Belmont scenes. Hanging at waist-level, the caskets enabled the suitors making their choices to circle round and engage a theater-in-the-round audience in what director Mark Lamos, alluding to *Merchant*'s pre-Lenten performances in 1605, finds an invitation "to judge, to value and be skeptical about ourselves" (1); he concludes that "it is ultimately we, the audience, whose duty it is to appraise the play's polarities" (45).

The 1998 production in Stratford-upon-Avon was memorable for inter-polating and embroidering a scene originally developed by Henry Irving (Shylock, returning from dinner with the Christians, sees Jessica in the dis-tance among the revelers, but she ignores him, and he approaches his house, knowing that it will be empty).[28] In the Venetian courtroom, Philip Voss enacted the wonderful visual image of Shylock, on his knees to beg mercy, unable to stand up as he slipped and slid on a floor covered with golden ducats. The simultaneous production at the Globe on Bankside reflected director Richard Olivier's effort to recapture an Elizabethan staging. The actor who portrayed Launcelot Gobbo, a founder-member of *Théâtre de Complicité*, recalled the world of *commedia dell'arte* in encouraging the audience to take sides between the warring parties. In *The Stage Clown in Shakespeare's Theatre* Bente Videbaek identifies Shylock and "the clown" as "the characters counterpoised in this play, but only as long as the Jew can be thought of as ridiculous. When we reach the trial scene, Portia has taken over the function of counterweight to the now dangerous Jew. With Launcelot's change of function and style he loses impact" (67).[29]

As Gayle Gaskill indicates, Michael Kahn's 1999 production for the Shakespeare Theatre in Washington, D.C., offered a revisionist view, with Shylock as a dignified victim and hero. New York's Jean Cocteau Repertory followed a similar course in 2000, making certain that Shylock delivered all of his lines, though other roles were severely cut if not eliminated entirely. Old Gobbo disappeared and Launcelot Gobbo appeared only in act 2. Jessica did not cross-dress, and Lorenzo's lines in 5.1 about music were cut. The central casket scene, 3.2, was pruned so that there was neither song nor Portia's words about standing for sacrifice. During a lively question-and-answer session with the director and some of the actors after the performance, the director admit-ted to regret about the decision to cut Portia's "I stand for sacrifice."

The extent to which we live in the age of the director was evident in a Spanish-language version of the play presented in Valencia, Spain, in 2001. In a co-production of Teatro de la Abadía and Ruhrfestspiele Reckling-hausen/Europäisches, director Hans Günther Heyme staged *El Mercader de Venecia* in a bathhouse, where all of the men wore bright pastel skirts evoca-tive of Polynesia, except for Shylock who dressed in a conservative, clerical-style gray suit. To mark their otherness, both Shylock and Jessica wore false noses, anchored by disfiguring black elastic ear loops. When Shylock loses in the courtroom, he is immediately baptized, fully clothed, by submersion in a bathing trough and then voluntarily stands under a shower head reminiscent of those in the Nazi death camps. He very deliberately abandons his "nose" during these proceedings, and Jessica, whom Lorenzo openly abuses and who never surrenders her "nose," discovers Shylock's as act 5 opens and takes it. Portia's three suitors were all portrayed by a single actor;[30] Portia herself reminded some in the audience of the fearsome "bride" Katisha in

The Mikado, while Nerissa, carrying around a screen behind which she tended the three caskets, seemed a veritable Wizard of Oz. Launcelot Gobbo portrays Salerio, Solanio, and all of the messengers in the play, while the Duke, lowered to the stage on a kind of swing, is a little puppet in *commedia dell'arte* style. The director's concept stripped all the characters but Shylock and Jessica of their dignity.

The 2001 production in Stratford, Canada, could not have been more different (Figure 3 above pictures a moment in 4.1). This *Merchant* attempted a balanced approach, symbolized by the curtain call, when Portia and Shylock came out together, equally "stars." Both performances were excellent, as were those of most of the cast. A particularly effective—and appealing— Gratiano clearly showed his kinship with Mercutio. Jessica was charming in her guise as torchbearer, and struck a diffident balance between eager "venture" and awareness of throwing over all she had been socialized to. At times, Antonio seemed too stiff and grim. But most memorable of all, an excessively athletic Morocco traversed the stage like a whirling dervish. As noted already, Muslims objected to certain gestures in the original performance which subsequently were cut; but the hyper behavior of this man still might seem objectionable on religious grounds, while the use of a white actor in blackface might jar the sensibilities of audiences from the United States.

In a generally conservative production, there were some surprises. Klezmer music was used to set the mood as the play began, while the conclusion featured the whole cast reprising "Tell me where is fancy bred" from 3.2. Portia enters strumming on a mandolin and singing John Donne's lyric "Go and catch a falling star." The director chose to move Shylock's penultimate speech, "I am content," so that it became his exit line, in an arrangement that supports Hugh Short's conclusions in his essay below. Gratiano, a rather pleasant fellow before the courtroom scene, is particularly nasty with Shylock, pitching the Jew to the ground when Antonio calls for Shylock's conversion, and tearing off the old man's yarmulke and yellow disc. Antonio is as violently hostile to Shylock in the courtroom as he has been earlier in the play, taking a cross from his own neck and placing it around Shylock's, while all the other performers cross themselves to mark Shylock's conversion.

The director's decision to use two intermissions—one after 2.5, as Shylock leaves Jessica in charge at home, and the other just before 4.1—departed from custom but contributed to good pacing in the production.

Film and Television Versions

Shylock is second only to Hamlet as a subject of critical inquiry, and Mahood reports that *Merchant* "shares with *Hamlet* the distinction of having been more often performed than any other of Shakespeare's plays" (42), but *Merchant* lags far behind in filmed versions. There were nine silent versions of the play, compared to fourteen for the Dane, but once the sound era arrived, not long before the advent of Adolf Hitler, *Hamlet* pulled away. There have been at least sixty-five productions, adaptations, and cinematic allusions to *Hamlet* in the sound era, compared to about ten for *Merchant*. A version of *Hamlet* in Hindi appeared in 1935 (and in Urdu in 1955), and there are films of the tragedy in Japanese, German, Swedish, and Russian, while there seems to be only one non-English version of *Merchant,* a 1952 French/Italian co-production, presumably released in both languages. Such is the conclusion to be drawn from examining Kenneth Rothwell's two comprehensive works on filmed Shakespeare, an "International Filmography and Videography" (1990) and a history (1999). The "Suggested References" in the current editions of the Signet Classic Shakespeare provide a remarkably comprehensive guide to books and essays on this topic. Especially to be noted are the anthology *Shakespeare on Television* (eds. J. C. Bulman and H. R. Coursen, 1988), Coursen's *Watching Shakespeare on Television* (1993), Peter Donaldson's *Shakespearean Films/Shakespearean Directors* (1990), and Susan Willis's *The BBC Shakespeare Plays: Making the Televised Canon* (1992). Both *Shakespeare Bulletin* and *The Shakespeare Newsletter* publish helpful reviews of new works.

The very first *Merchant* film may have been made in France in 1902; but since *Une miroir de Venise: Une mésadventure de Shylock*, probably two minutes long, is now lost, we cannot be certain that it concerns Shakespeare's play. The American Vitagraph Company's 1908 version of *Merchant* ran for ten minutes, while a 1910 Italian version, beautifully tinted and making use of outdoor locations in Venice, runs for eight.[31] *Il Mercante di Venezia* begins with plans for Jessica's elopement; as Rothwell suggests, Shylock becomes a King Lear abandoned by a wicked daughter. But he is also "the Jewish villain, fawning in public, salivating with the pleasure of his scheming in private"; he brings Antonio and Bassanio into his cluttered home, where Antonio signs the bond and Shylock hands over three money bags—dropping one in his enthusiasm. "Antonio and Bassanio go off with him arm in arm to facilitate Jessica's escape" (Coursen 34). When Shylock returns with Tubal, he finds the key that Jessica dropped on the pavement in front of his house. His revenge seems motivated partly by Jessica's departure, but even earlier his gestures suggest eager anticipation of any default by Antonio. We watch Shylock in the courtroom whetting his knife "in a familiar stage tradition" (Rothwell, *History* 15), and the film ends abruptly as he recognizes that Portia has defeated him.

A thirty-three-minute two-reeler from 1913, the French *Shylock, ou le more de Venise,* featured the classical actor Harry Baur as Shylock, "an object of mirth and scorn rather than a victim of bigotry" (Rothwell, *History* 14); sadly Baur, himself Jewish, was later tortured by the Gestapo in prison and died a few days after his release (Rothwell, *Shakespeare* 176). The film's title-cards, Rothwell notes, "suggest how the play's thematic values remain embedded in the film text." An introductory card asks, "Who among us has not in imagination lived with the characters of Shakespeare's immortal drama—portraying as they do, the great elemental qualities of life itself?" There is "no anxiety here that the text may not represent anything but itself." The film refers to the friendship between Bassanio and Antonio as "one of the finest tributes on the loyalty of man to man that has ever been written"; again, "no anxiety here that their relationship might be in some way perverse."

Der Kaufmann von Venedig (1923), sixty-four minutes long, was released in the United States in 1926 as *The Jew of Mestri,* and the English title suggests the film's split personality. Focused primarily on Shylock as portrayed by superstar Werner Krauss (the Portia, Henny Porten, was also a big name), the film emphasizes his victimization, most notably when he discovers Rachela's (Jessica's) betrayal. Emerging from his empty house into crowds of maskers, "he collapses in the street, a lonely discarded bundle of rags" (Rothwell, *Shakespeare* 178). In the courtroom, he whets his knife, "but an unusual twist has Gianetti (Antonio) fainting in fright" (Rothwell, *History* 27). At the end, the film switches rather abruptly from "the horror and desolation on Shylock's face to the careless indifference of the smart young set at Belmont. Comedy swallows tragedy" (Rothwell, *Shakespeare* 178).

The first ever "Shakespeare movie that coordinated sound and image on screen" was "a ten-minute extract from the trial scene" in *Merchant.* The English company De Forest Phonofilms filmed this experiment in 1927, two years earlier than Sam Taylor's first feature-length Shakespearean talkie, the Mary Pickford-Douglas Fairbanks *Taming of the Shrew* (Rothwell, *History* 29). *The Merchant* next appeared twenty years later, on television, in a ninety-minute version from the BBC in 1947; in 1955, Michael Hordern portrayed Shylock in another BBC broadcast, apparently not preserved.

The BBC's 1972 version featured Maggie Smith as Portia, Charles Gray as Antonio, and Frank Finlay as Shylock, performing on sets that imitated Titian for Venice and Botticelli for Belmont. The attention to sets and costumes "emulating the master artists of Shakespeare's own lifetime" continued in the *Merchant* broadcast in 1980 in the BBC's comprehensive series, "The Shakespeare Plays." Here Titian inspired the Belmont sets while Canaletto or Watteau visualized Venice. Produced by Jonathan Miller, directed by Jack Gold, and featuring Warren Mitchell as Shylock (all of them Jewish), the production nevertheless drew fire from some Jewish groups as anti-Semitic, as had the earlier Olivier version. In fact, the film is quite postmodernist in its suggestion that savagery lies just beneath the Venetian surface, notwithstanding, for once, a really persuasive and beguilingly charming Bassanio played by John Nettles. Shylock, "outwardly in no way affable, congenial, agreeable, or sociable, . . . is yet inwardly the man of integrity" (Rothwell, *Shakespeare* 181). In Barnet's words, "such a man, who threatens to expose the corruption beneath the superficially attractive Christian Venetian society, must be crushed . . . to preserve [the Venetians'] pleasures." When Shylock is forced to convert, "Gratiano threatens him with a knife, and Salerio then places a necklace with cross around Shylock's neck—it might as well be a noose—and forces Shylock to kiss the cross" ("Stage" 173).

John O'Connor has discussed at some length the Jonathan Miller production starring Laurence Olivier and Joan Plowright, filmed in 1974 for broadcast on ABC television and based on the stage production for the National Theatre, "surely [in this version] the woefullest but most complicated comedy ever written" (Rothwell, *History* 70).

In 1995, a "schools program" subsidized by the British government presented another film version featuring Bob Peck as Shylock and examining "such contemporary issues as capitalism, feminism, and anti-Semitism" (Rothwell, *Shakespeare* 122). Not one filmed version of the play in the sound era has originated in the United States, although the American actor/director Orson Welles worked on one. Writing in *Theater der Zeit* in 1960, Welles "tells of his boyhood dream of playing Shylock and sees the role in the light of the Nazi attempt to exterminate the Jews" (Wheeler, *Bibliography* 273). Rothwell reports that this film was supposedly completed in 1969, with Welles as Shylock and Charles Gray as Antonio. "In a bold stroke, when Welles's good friend, Oja Kodar, refused to play Portia, the role was eliminated" (*Screen* 93). According to Russell Jackson, Welles left behind

> an editing print of an almost-complete *Merchant of Venice,* set in the eighteenth century: surviving footage includes a striking scene of Shylock confronted in a low-ceilinged chamber by a suavely grinning Antonio and a crowd of masked and cloaked associates. Like the completed Shakespeare films [by Welles], this again shows the hero/victim in oppressive architectural spaces, captured by expressive camera angles and at the mercy of forces, societal and personal, beyond his control. (224)

Shylock is again the hero/victim in the 1999 Royal National Theatre production, which originated in the Cottesloe Theatre, then moved to the Olivier. The director, Trevor Nunn, sets the play in Germany in the *Cabaret* world of the 1930s. A film of this production appeared on American television in October, 2001, as the season premier on *Masterpiece Theatre.* While the original stage production drew rave reviews, as both John O'Connor and Penny Gay note in their essays below, the small screen could not convey the impact of the traverse staging in the Cottesloe auditorium. Robert Smallwood notes that "at one end of the traverse Belmont was a place of chic opulence . . . at the opposite end was the humble, well-locked door to Shylock's house" ("Performances" 268). Reviewing the television broadcast, Mel Gussow echoes earlier critics in his praise for Henry Goodman's Shylock and also notes the director's alterations, designed to emphasize elements of anti-

Semitism and eroticism, which "will prove disconcerting to those who wish to see *The Merchant of Venice* in familiar Shakespearean surroundings. In introducing the television adaptation, Russell Baker discreetly concentrates on the play, not the interpretation, talking about Shylock and anti-Semitism while averting the directorial flourishes" (5).

VI. The Play Outside the English-Speaking World

Avraham Oz has written about the play's fortunes in Israel: "Shakespeare could hardly have anticipated the possibility of his play being performed for a Jewish audience, in Hebrew, in a Jewish state" (218). In his analysis of several Israeli productions, Oz is particularly interested in interpretations of Shylock as a kind of terrorist:

> by temporarily taking hostage the Venetian law, and while the entire audience of the theatre of terrorism hold their breath, Shylock manages to bring forth the very target of political terrorism, exposing the moral fragility of the dominant ideology. His act succeeds in undermining the notion of reality as integrated and rational, as appropriated by the dominant ideology. (230)

"It broke new ground," Geraldo de Sousa says of the first Brazilian production of *Merchant* in 1993, "bringing distinctive cultural elements and Brazilian talents to forge a new national tradition of Shakespearean staging and interpretation" (469). In a society particularly sensitive to racism and anti-Semitism, one of Brazil's most distinguished actors portrayed Shylock "with subtlety and dignity, never allowing his character to deteriorate into caricature or to dominate the play," and "this Shylock grabbed and held the audience's attention and sympathy" (471). The Brazilian Shylock modeled himself on Portuguese Jews of the Renaissance, wearing a period costume and speaking Portuguese with a foreign accent that separated him from the "Venetians": "Seemingly unable to articulate the abundant and difficult Portuguese nasal sounds, Shylock situated himself at the interstices of cultures and left the haunting impression that key words such as *'coração' (heart)* had been hollowed out" (471).

Shylock's "Jew" speech was moved from 3.1 to 4.1, where it became Shylock's initial response to Portia's "Art thou contented, Jew?" Addressing the famous words to the entire Venetian court rather than to just Salerio and Solanio, this

> Brazilian Shylock was empowered at a moment when the text leaves him powerless. The effect was electrifying and the audience cheered. As the Christians proceeded with the forced conversion, the audience gasped in

horror. Portia insisted, "Art thou contented, Jew?" and Shylock replied, "I
become contented" (*"Fico contente"*)—a translation that ironically twists
Shylock's "I am content" to suggest not a state but a process. (471)

To further "accommodate Brazilian sensibilities about racial matters, all
of Portia's foreign suitors were played by the same actor, . . . [and] all of
them seemed unacceptable because of personal eccentricities rather than ethnic or racial difference." At the conclusion, "when all had exited, Antonio
stayed behind, not knowing what to do. Bassanio returned briefly, exchanged
a knowing, perhaps amorous glance with Antonio, and just as quickly exited,
leaving Antonio alone. Obviously, not all of the play's issues had been
resolved" (473).[32]

The play has been performed in many countries and in many languages,
and India of course is a special case, since Shakespeare is familiar in both
English and the various local languages. Although all things English have
been associated with colonial rule, the language is still spoken by a populous
minority. During the 1950s and 60s Geoffrey Kendal and his family-based
Shakespeareana Company traveled the length and breadth of the subconti-
nent performing the plays. Indian actors participated in the company, most
famously Shashi Kapoor, who married Jennifer Kendal and later became a
significant film star. He was in the cast of *Shakespeare Wallah*, the 1964
Merchant-Ivory film that tells a somewhat elegiac version of the Kendals'
story; they all appeared in the film, including Felicity, the younger daughter,
who was starting her own acting career. Her father notes that Felicity's first
stage appearance, at age eight, was the non-speaking role of Morocco's page-
boy in *Merchant* (120).

Twice Kendal mentions that *Merchant* was "one of the favorite plays of
the repertoire in India" (114), and the casket scene was especially popular.
The play has been translated into Hindi twenty times, far more than its near-
est competitors, *Romeo and Juliet* and *Hamlet,* with twelve translations each
(*Bulletin* 26). There are seven versions in Tamil, followed by six each of
Macbeth and *Hamlet*. Both Hindi and Tamil versions present Shylock as a
"Jain moneylender" (*Bulletin 25*). Indian scholarship on Shakespeare com-
plements productions of the plays in its variety and excellence.

In both China and Japan, opinions vary about adapting Shakespeare to
native forms, as opposed to presenting him in Western fashion. One study
traces the movement in nineteenth-century Japan from Kabuki adaptations to
Western forms (Brandon), while another notes that "the fusion of Shakespeare with Noh or Kabuki plays represents a current trend" (Kawachi 67).
One Japanese version of *Merchant* is *Sakuradoki Zeni no Yononaka* ("The
Season of Cherry Blossoms: the World of Money"); produced in 1885, it was
the first performance of Shakespeare in Japan. When the adaptation was published as a book in 1886, the title page said that "the idea is from Shake-

speare's 'Flesh of the Chest' and the style is that of Kabuki script" (quoted by Kawachi 52). Indeed, the first production was all male, making use of Kabuki actors (65). In the seventeenth century, boys played female roles in Kabuki. In a prologue to this version, a college student says that *Eigaku* (English education [as represented in a Shakespearean play]) is the best way to "civilize and enlighten Japan" (Yukari Yoshihara 11). So the adaptation seems to blend Japanese dramatic traditions with a pursuit of westernization.

In addition to *Sakuradoki*, there are earlier non-dramatic adaptations of the story. In *A Strange Litigation about Flesh of the Chest* (1877), Portia becomes Kiyoka, "odor of purity," and Shylock is Yokubari Ganpachi, "stubborn close-fisted." In an 1883 version, *A Western Strange Story of the Trial of Pawned Flesh*, Shylock is compared to the *eta-hinin*, "the humble people of the lowest caste in Japan who lived in a limited area" (Kawachi 48). Unfortunately, "as minorities both the Jews and the *eta-hinin* (or outcasts) suffered the sting of discrimination" (50). In this version the characters travel by train, reflecting the new enthusiasm in Japan for all things modern and Western.

Japanese versions usually omit the Lorenzo/Jessica subplot, perhaps because Japanese girls were expected to marry someone approved by their families. The 1885 production (*Sakuradoki*) is set in Osaka of the Tokugawa period (1603–1867) when Japan was closed to most foreign influence. Osaka is an old commercial city with a topography that includes canals, "the city built on water" (54). In this production, the caskets are gold, silver, and iron, and iron is the correct choice, not because of its humble status but because the Japanese regarded iron as "the most valuable treasure" (53).

The subtitle of this adaptation, *The World of Money*, appealed to people of the time, who associated Western civilization with finance and believed that "finance was most important for Japanese modernization" (54). The courtroom scene was so popular that it was sometimes staged as an independent production, probably because the Japanese were revamping their own legal system at the time. One of the speakers in the prologue says that "the novel [was] written to let the people know the relationship between morality and law" (52). The pound of flesh motif would remind audiences of the 1695 Kabuki play by Chikamatsu, *The Picture of the Birth of Buddha*, where "the servant of Davedatta, a disciple of Buddha, is going to cut someone's flesh" (54).

Until World War II, *Merchant* was the play most frequently performed in Japan; *Hamlet* has dominated since 1945 (51). In 1903, a Japanese production imitated that of Henry Irving (65). Shylock is usually treated sympathetically in the productions Kawachi describes, whatever the style or setting chosen by the directors.

Staged in Shanghai in 1913, *Merchant* was the first professional Shakespearean production in China (Ruru 355). Spanning the century, *Merchant* was also performed during the 1994 Shanghai International Shakespeare Festival in a fairy-tale mode, the first Shakespeare production of the Shanghai

Children's Theater. Performed by adult professionals for youngsters, the production eliminated act 5, as well as all references to race and religion in order to focus on the moral issue of greed as a lesson for Chinese youth. According to Audrey Stanley, Shylock "was dressed as a commedia dell'arte Pantalone with a hooked nose and long gray hair." A grasping old man, "both comic and sinister, [he] performed a darkly comic routine of repeatedly withholding the keys from Jessica and ominously stabbing his contract to the wall of the court with a sharp dagger." The many set changes were accompanied by a group of teenage dancers performing various European dances along the front of the stage. "Actors declaimed many of the speeches facing front, the women using graceful gestures and the men using warriorlike motions" (76–77).

When Inga-Stina Ewbank saw a production in Cantonese at an outdoor theater in Hong Kong in the early nineties, "the play was received as a glorious comedy. In a society honestly and unashamedly materialistic there is nothing suspect about the commercial values which prevail in Venice, . . . nothing to problematize the ending. And above all, Shylock, the speculator who misjudged the rate of exchange, was to this audience the uncontested clown of the piece. He was a creation for a culture which does not know anti-Semitism" (2). The *Chinese Shakespeare Yearbook for 1994* includes articles in Chinese on "Shylock: A Challenging Character" and "Why Portia Changes Costume: Exploration of Misidentity of Female Characters in Shakespeare's Plays." In an article in English on "The Adventurers" in the play, we learn that "nearly every character turns out to be an adventurer, with a particular gamblesome [*sic*] tendency of his own" (30). The author, identified only in Chinese characters, argues that even Shylock can be seen as an adventurer, since he proposes the bond trusting, against all common sense, that Antonio will fail to pay on time. The Jew's hatred for Antonio is so intense that "he almost loses his senses in finding a more effective means to revenge himself" (39). While the other characters venture for their own happiness, Shylock acts for others' misfortune "as well as his own comforts" (40), but all the characters' adventures are concerned with money, appropriately enough in the developing bourgeois world of the Renaissance.

Shakespeare's works are regularly performed in Europe. He has long been a special favorite in Germany, where the world wars of the twentieth century posed a problem, for *unser Shakespeare*, after all, was English. Like many translations of Shakespeare into other languages, A. W. von Schlegel's has earned classic status on its own merits, and German scholarship on Shakespeare has long been highly regarded. Predictably, the Nazis tried to use Shylock to advance their murderous racism, but a more balanced German attitude is evident in a film like *Der Kaufmann von Venedig* discussed above.

Nico Kiasashvili notes that "Colchis' strond" (1.1.171) is western Georgia (Cholchis) in the modern country of Georgia, and Jason's quest introduces him to the Georgian princess Medea. Shakespeare was performed for the first time in Georgia in 1873, in Bandza, in Cholchis, and *The Merchant of Venice* was the selection (185).

Shakespeare Quarterly's Annual Bibliography provides helpful brief summaries of articles by Japanese, Chinese, Spanish, German, Italian, Romanian, and other scholars. For example, the Mexican writer Jaime Cardeña argued in 1994 that *Merchant* displays Shakespeare's psychoanalytic genius, with emphasis on the name "Shylock" as an index to the character's anal retentive personality, and on the play's connections to the fourth circle of Dante's *Inferno*. In 1995 Guido Castelli writes in an Italian journal on Antonio as the central character of the play, who signifies greatness of moral and spiritual character; his sadness, for Castelli, arises from pondering the meaning of life.

Italian Studies in Shakespeare and His Contemporaries (1999) includes two essays on *Merchant*. In "Bonds of Love and Death in *The Merchant of Venice*," Alessandro Serpieri suggests that "the ambiguity of the text" could be caused by a "discrepancy between forms of expression and forms of content" (49). But the heart of the play is the reality of bonds: *bond A*, the flesh bond (a contract of death), forces suspension of *bond B*, the love bond. The conditions imposed on Shylock in 4.1 constitute *bond C*—"a bond which would appear to be a bond of Christian love but which, in fact, is clearly a violent bond of coercion of the outsider: yet another bond of 'death,' then, produced by the false conscience of European ethnocentrism." The understanding reached between the lovers in 5.1 after the rings episode, brokered by Antonio, is *bond D,* to which Antonio commits his soul. "Antonio's *bond D* and Shylock's *bond C* correspond, albeit secretly," writes Serpieri. "The Jew was obliged to suffer an ironic-tragic inclusion (exclusion) in the Christians' community, while now the homosexual Antonio has to accept his own ironic—and, in its way, tragic—inclusion (exclusion) in the lovers' community" (53–54).

In "'Now I play a merchant's part': The Space of the Merchant in Shakespeare's Early Comedies," Mariangela Tempera characterizes *Merchant* as "the bitterest of Shakespeare's comedies" (159). Focusing on Antonio, who occupies "the most ambiguous zone of the play" (160), Tempera notes that his social status is uncertain. He is not in the same class as Bassanio and Portia: "even without money, Bassanio remains an aristocrat, while, without money, Antonio is nothing" (161). In fact, the merchant (often referred to in 4.1 as "the merchant" rather than as "Antonio") is more nearly Shylock's social equal than Bassanio's: "Antonio represents the ambition of a new class to enter the theater in the protagonist's role. His failure demonstrates how this process, at the end of the 1590s, is still far from complete. Only Bassanio, like Petruchio, can move from one social group to the other with absolute ease" (163).

This conclusion can be contrasted to that of Joo-Hyon Kim, a Korean scholar who has published, in English, *Bi-Cultural Critical Essays on*

Shakespeare (1995). In "A Religious Approach to Shakespeare," he describes Antonio as "a sacrificial figure of Christ, who willingly commits himself to the danger of shedding his blood in order that his friend may live." Antonio's conditions in 4.1 for Shylock's release demonstrate "the power of the Christian love that can redeem the Jew" (115). Again we see the response of a culture innocent of anti-Semitism.

VII. Adaptations and Allusions

Much may be learned from the way that the play has been adapted to suit different tastes. Granville's eighteenth-century adaptation has inspired later ones, most notably Arnold Wesker's *The Merchant* (1977). In this version,

> Shylock and Antonio are friends. The bond is in truth merely a jest, but when Antonio cannot pay it, Shylock cannot release him because the Jews so desperately need the law to protect them in their dealings with Gentiles. Portia saves Antonio and, at the end of the play, makes it possible for Jessica to join her father in his pilgrimage to Jerusalem. (Wheeler, *Bibliography* xx)

In the summer of 2000, the Washington Shakespeare Festival in Olympia produced Mark Leiren-Young's play *Shylock*, performed by an actor who had previously played Shakespeare's Jew. The company's press release explains that "in *Shylock*, a Jewish actor named Jon Davies finds himself condemned by his own community" because he portrays the character as a total villain. The controversy forces the production to close early. On closing night, Davies participates in a "talk-back" with the audience, "where he explores his conflict over the role and makes his feelings, motives and ideas known. The play deals with weighty issues of racial identity, censorship, the nature of art and the power of theatre."

A. R. Gurney, long regarded as the playwright of white, Anglo-Saxon, Protestant America, ventures beyond the pattern in *Overtime: A Modern Sequel to "The Merchant of Venice"* (1997). Built around act 5, the scene is Belmont after the trial; Portia and Lorenzo represent the WASP ethic on stage, surrounded by an Irish Bassanio, a Latino Nerissa, a Black Gratiano, and characters of other backgrounds. Though Gurney's occasion is allegedly a wedding celebration for Portia and Bassanio—Shylock has been invited and arrives in tuxedo—reviewer William Green finds a traumatic reaction to the trial "because the characters suddenly begin to examine their own identities and their ideas about ethnicity" (16). Antonio reveals that he is gay, while Jessica ends up paired with Nerissa. Portia and Shylock, "the two individuals who most understand themselves," work together to resolve the various tensions and move toward a Venice much more open to diversity. Green notes that the title comes from Shylock's line telling "Portia that women 'keep the whole game going even in overtime'—and over time from Renaissance Venice to present-day New York and beyond." Finding affirmation in this adaptation, Green concludes with a genre judgment:

> Gurney has succeeded in combining high comedy—with its depiction of upper-class society, its focus on love, and its employment of witty dia- logue—with comedy in the traditional sense of the form, for at its heart the characters go through a learning process. (16)

The play has also inspired various musical compositions, including an opera in two acts, *Il Mercante di Venezia*, by Mario Castelnuovo-Tedesco (1961). In 1981 it was transformed into a full-length musical comedy. Hector Berlioz "drew on the words of Lorenzo's 'In such a night' for the ravishing love-duet between Dido and Aeneas in *The Trojans* (*"O nuit d'ivresse"*)" (1856/58) (Gross 99). First performed in 1938, Ralph Vaughan Williams's *Serenade to Music* is a setting for chorus and orchestra of lines from act 5, while Virgil Thomson provided a setting of "Look, How the Floor of Heaven" from act 5 for the American Shakespeare Festival production with Carnovsky and Hepburn (1957). Wheeler reports that there is "no concord in this setting," where the "harmony is insistently dissonant" (*Bibliography* 336). Written for high voice, the piece concludes with "we cannot hear it" (5.1.65).

Performed widely in Europe and North America between 1957 and 1967 and recorded by Columbia Records, John Gielgud's one-man show, *Shake- speare's Ages of Man*, opens with Jaques's disquisition on the "seven ages" in *As You Like It* and includes, as the second of six passages illustrating youth, a carefully edited version of Lorenzo's speeches in 5.1. Gielgud declaimed:

> The moon shines bright!—In such a night as this
> When the sweet wind did gently kiss the trees,
> And they did make no noise;
>   ... in such a night
> Stood Dido with a willow in her hand
> Upon the wild sea-banks, and wav'd her love
> To come again to Carthage. [*Gielgud then jumps to*]
> How sweet the moonlight shines upon this bank!
> [*and continues through to*]
> But whilst this muddy vesture of decay
> Doth close it in, we cannot hear it. (5.1.1–3, 9–12, 54–65)

In his prime, Gielgud both directed and starred in the play, most notably with Peggy Ashcroft in 1937, when, by his own report, he "tried to make [Shylock] a squalid little guttersnipe." The critics did not like his portrayal and "of course it was the time of Hitler, which did not help matters." Perhaps, he writes, "I would have satisfied more people if I had created a haughty Irvingesque character rather than a cringing Fagin-figure—though Olivier told me he liked me in it better than almost anything else I did in Shakespeare." But Gielgud concludes, "I think I did good work on the play because I loved all the Belmont scenes, which are often considered very silly" (61).

In recent years, Steven Berkoff has designed and performed the one-man show *Shakespeare's Villains: A Master Class in Evil*. Having seen Gielgud's *Ages of Man* as a student, he notes that he was impressed by "its clarity and drama." In his own show, Berkoff features only two characters from the comedies, Oberon and Shylock, who "is denied the love of an entire nation and thus seeks revenge." According to Berkoff, Shylock "defends his villainy by crying that he has been sorely wronged and, therefore, is not his anger justified by the abuses he has been made to suffer?" (5).

Reviewing a New Delhi performance, Poonam Trivedi writes that "Berkoff was pushing a simple thesis, of Shakespeare's villains as unloved men, their evil engendered by society." Trivedi describes the performance:

> Shylock came off the best: a man deranged through being hated by society. Berkoff played him alternately raving and cringing, flaying his arms, shaking his head, slouching and twisting his torso and twitching his mouth, till in a crescendo of cunning he came to the business of the bond, when "an equal pound / Of your fair flesh" was uttered almost *sotto voce*, slyly, with a controlled satanic glee and relish which could easily be mistaken as deferential! Interspersed were his witty and often incisive ad lib comments: on how Shylock, who was traditionally imaged with a long beaked nose, was now finding his nose getting shorter and shorter! And how Olivier's Shylock got by only with a "nose-bump!" Berkoff's patter, comic, bawdy and subversive, and dexterously interwoven with his act, kept a hold on the audience. (21)

Like most of Shakespeare's plays, *Merchant* appears in various forms in subsequent literature; the story is so well known that writers can refer to it confident that their allusions will be recognized. In a 1993 article, Michel Pousse notes similarities in plot, characterization, and thematic structure between Shakespeare's play and the late R. K. Narayan's novel *The Man-Eater of Malgudi*. Intertextuality flourishes in English literature, early and late. In "Sweet, Savage Shakespeare," Laurie Osborne examines Shakespeare's appropriation in romance novels, especially Regency romances and historical romances, where Shakespeare's work helps in "mapping out class and gender hierarchies that are envisaged as historically specific obstacles to the love story. At the same time, his works help to resolve and dissolve those boundaries . . . because [his works] are appropriable and revisable" (141). Osborne cites as an example

Alicia Rasley's romance *Poetic Justice* (1994). Here the plot "uses and reworks *The Merchant of Venice*'s 'the will of a living daughter curb'd by the will of a dead father' (1.2.23–25)." The heroine, Jessica Seton, on the one hand obeys her father's will; on the other, she seems to run off with an "inappropriate suitor," thus combining "Portia's and Jessica's experiences" (140).

Gross cites Maria Edgeworth's novel *Harrington* (1817), one of her last, written in reparation for the unpleasant Jews that figure in her earlier works. The eponymous hero, whose casually anti-Semitic upbringing has been modified by his actual experience of several Jews at school and at Cambridge, is introduced to "the most famous Jew in England," Charles Macklin, and then attends a performance of Macklin's *Merchant.* Berenice Montenero, the daughter of a wealthy Jewish banker, sits in an adjoining box, and Harrington suffers with her at every anti-Semitic remark in the play. The next day he visits her father, and Edgeworth gives us "the first full-length portrait of a sympathetic Jew in English fiction" (116–18).

In *Major Barbara* near the end of act 2, George Bernard Shaw's Sir Andrew Undershaft, an arms manufacturer, writes a check for £5,000 to the Salvation Army, thereby helping to disillusion his daughter Barbara about the militant Christian group. As Undershaft marches off to an Army celebration, he cries out in possessive triumph, "My ducats and my daughter!"—quoting Shylock in an utterly different context (266).

Another Irish writer incorporates themes from many of Shakespeare's plays into *Ulysses* (1922). James Joyce refers to *Merchant* twelve times, and alludes to only three plays more frequently: *Hamlet* (more than one hundred references), *Macbeth* (fifteen), and *Othello* (fourteen) (Gifford "Index"). Given the nature of his novel, it is not surprising that Joyce alludes three times to Launcelot Gobbo's reversal of the traditional proverb into "it is a wise father that knows his own child" (2.2.76). Not only is the protagonist Leopold Bloom a father, but he is, even more significantly, a Jew, an outsider in Dublin. Joyce's references demonstrate that he knew the play well, making certain that both Bloom and Stephen Dedalus are familiar with it. Dedalus, for example, says that Shakespeare "drew Shylock out of his own long pocket" (168), alluding to the likelihood that the playwright was himself a moneylender. In Episode 16, Bloom refers to "the harmless necessary animal of the feline persuasion" (520), recalling Shylock's "harmless necessary cat" (4.1.55). Jennifer Levine has argued in "James Joyce, Tattoo Artist: Tracing the Outlines of Homosocial Desire" that the sailor in this episode of the novel is homosexual and associated in several ways with Shakespeare's Antonio. In *Shakespeare among the Moderns*, Richard Halpern focuses his interesting, sometimes confusing, chapter "The Jewish Question: Shakespeare and Anti-Semitism" on Shylock and Leopold Bloom.

From the sublime to the ridiculous, the Reduced Shakespeare Company has for some years staged *The Complete Works of William Shakespeare*

Abridged; the current video version features a short segment reducing the sixteen comedies to one! Long-lost sons of the Spanish Duke's brother, three sets of identical twins, are cast up destitute on the Italian coast. In the utmost extremity, they are forced to borrow money from an old Jew who deceives them into putting up their brains for collateral. Ultimately unable to repay the loan, they administer themselves lobotomies.

Similarly silly but more subtle, Cole Porter in his 1948 musical *Kiss Me, Kate* manages to name thirteen of Shakespeare's plays in "Brush Up Your Shakespeare":

> Brush up your Shakespeare,
> Start quoting him now,
> Brush up your Shakespeare
> And the women you will wow.
> Better mention "The Merchant of Venice"
> When her sweet pound o'flesh you would menace.

I conclude with *Theater of Blood,* the 1973 film in which Vincent Price plays an embittered, has-been actor, Edward Lionheart, who recruits his faithful, and somewhat mad, daughter (Diana Rigg) to help him take revenge on all the critics who have made his professional career such a misery. According to Thomas Pendleton, "Shylock is Price at his most impressive. He performs in full costume at what the victim, Trevor Dickman (Harry Andrews), thinks is a dress rehearsal." This Shylock remembers being spat upon and called *dog* "with a remarkable false geniality, with just the right hint of repressed menace." Here is "a man of power, dignity, and resource." Rigg as Edwina Lionheart plays Portia, and "her final exchange with her father—'Are you content?' 'I am content.'—is beautifully done by both performers" (144). As portrayed by Price's Edward Lionheart in this film, Shylock finally succeeds in collecting on his debt.

VIII. In Conclusion

riverrun, past Eve and Adam's, from swerve of shore to bend of bay, brings us by a commodius vicus of recirculation back to Howth Castle and Environs.

James Joyce's last book begins with the end of its final sentence, a wonderful evocation of the circular course of the River Liffey as it emerges from the Irish hills toward the sea. Returning to concerns that have occupied this survey from the beginning, we invoke yet again the image of conundrum to explain the elusiveness of *The Merchant of Venice*. Surely Shakespeare's play is less dense than *Finnegans Wake*, but every experience of the play reinforces a sense of its infinite wealth of meaning.

In *Shakespeare's Comic Sequence*, Kenneth Muir stimulates reflection by enumerating some "perverse interpretations" he associates with readings of the play. Among other "misreadings," he rejects arguments for Shylock as the tragic hero (57–58) and the claim that Portia tells Bassanio which casket to choose (59–60); and he questions assertions that Antonio's opening melancholy, suicidal attitude in the courtroom, and isolation in Belmont are based on a homosexual passion for Bassanio (60).

Muir also rejects arguments that Shakespeare is anti-Semitic: "What he thought of racial intolerance" (55) seems clear enough in a scene Shakespeare inserted in the play of *Sir Thomas More* at about the same time he was working on *Merchant*. More is trying to calm a mob rioting against foreigners and, particularly in two passages, he appeals to a sense of fair play, first by imagining the crowd of deported refugees streaming toward the ports (lines 72–87), then by asking the mob to consider an alternative scenario, in which the mob itself becomes the victim of people of "barbarous temper" who

> Spurn you like dogs, and like as if that God
> Owned not nor made not you, nor that the elements
> Were not all appropriate to your comforts
> But chartered unto them, what would you think
> To be thus used? This is the strangers' case
> And this your mountainish inhumanity. (135–40)

Muir's point is clear, that some critics are too ready to deliver judgment despite the complexities of the play. In later comments, Muir argues that the element of fantasy must be accepted as a defining characteristic of the play, and he sees both the rings plot and the caskets plot as linked to the pound of flesh plot, connecting his ideas to those of Alice Benston and others cited above.

Kenneth Muir writes that the interpretations he rejects are "not so much wrong as selective and partial" (67). And he concludes: "*The Merchant of Venice* is in some ways one of the simplest of Shakespeare's plays, but, as with all the others, we ignore its complexities at our peril" (68). Again, the most effective readings, of whatever "school," take the entire play into account. The essays in this volume will contribute to further fruitful reflection on the play.

Notes

1. Including Austria, Brazil, Bulgaria, China, the Czech Republic, Denmark, Finland, France, Georgia, Germany, Greece, India, Israel, Italy, Japan, Lithuania, Norway, Slovakia, South Africa, Spain, Switzerland, and so on. See *The Shakespeare Newsletter* 48:2 (Summer 1998): 29, 34, 36, 43 for a review of the two major British productions in 1998, including an interview with the director of the Globe version, Richard Olivier.

2. In March of 1974, Lawrence Danson notes, *The New York Times* ran a column
    by a member of its editorial board on "Why Shylock Should Not Be Cen-
    sored," responding to concerns about a televised presentation of the National
    Theatre Company's production, with Laurence Olivier as Shylock and Joan
    Plowright as Portia. Fred Hechinger's argument makes the play "deeply
    ironic" because it condemns "the hypocrisy of predatory Christians" (Danson
    3–4). Consider, in contrast, Professor Thomas Pendleton's comments in a let-
    ter to *The New York Times* in 1981, in response to calls for banning the tele-
    vising of what some viewers saw as the "anti-Semitic" BBC version:

    > Even allowing that Shakespeare, through Shylock, continually insists
    > that one cannot deal with Shylock's inhuman ferocity without also deal-
    > ing with the lifetime of contempt and discrimination that begets it, Shy-
    > lock is the villain, and the trial scene is clearly the triumph of the
    > Christian ethic over the Jewish ethic. (D6)

    Nor is the disagreement only about Shylock. As recently as June, 2001, the
    Stratford Festival changed its production of the play in response to protests
    by the Canadian division of the Council on American-Islamic Relations,
    which objected to details in a broadly comic portrayal of the Prince of
    Morocco. The character fell on his face while prostrating himself to Allah and
    also prostrated himself before a woman. Since Muslims are forbidden to
    prostrate themselves before anyone but Allah, Stratford's Morocco discontin-
    ued prostrations, according to the report in the *Globe and Mail* of Toronto.
    But Americans who saw the production were more likely to be offended by
    the decision to assign to the role of Morocco a white actor in blackface!
3. A school district in suburban New York removed the play from its curriculum
    between 1988 and 1995 after a substitute teacher objected to its use and com-
    plained specifically about the showing of the 1981 BBC film. Robert J. Wil-
    son, the regular teacher of the high school sophomore class, argues that the
    play "with its enticing moral complexities has been for centuries part of the
    critical canon" (44) and should be taught. Eventually he and others persuaded
    the Suffern school district to reinstate the play, but all copies of the play had
    disappeared from the book room and the budget did not allow for the pur-
    chase of new textbooks.
4. In a recent catalog incorporating the Signet Classic Shakespeare (*Literature
    and Language*, "Books for Courses 2000/2001"), Penguin Putnam classifies
    the play as a tragedy.
5. Joan Ozark Holmer writes: "Some critics have also noted that 'Shylock'
    might possibly be derived from a British surname" (84), and in a note she
    points to John Russell Brown's discussion in the Arden edition, crediting M.
    A. Lower who, in 1850, reported "Richard Shylok" as a proper name in Hoo,
    Sussex, in 1435 (Brown, *Arden* 3). Holmer also refers to Robert Fleissner's
    1966 discussion of a "Richard Shacklock."
6. Elmore Leonard's recent novel, *Pagan Babies*, quotes an enforcer for a mob
    boss in Detroit: "[The mob] put me on the street. You know, lean on the book-
    ies, make sure they pay their street tax. I'd do a shylock collection if the guy

fell behind." Asked to explain, "Mutt" says that he would visit the delinquent's home, "meet his wife, talk to him. If there was a second time I'd catch him away from home and body-punch him good, break a couple of ribs" (138).

7.   James Bulman uses the same structure to pursue a different thrust:

> Shakespeare allowed the bond plot . . . to keep subverting the romance plot. The juxtaposition of the play's twin climaxes illustrates this sub-version. Bassanio's winning of the lottery and Portia in III.ii, a scene full of romantic hyperbole, is immediately preceded by the passionately col-loquial scene in which Shylock vows to take revenge on Antonio. Our knowledge of this sober turn of events invariably colours our response to Bassanio's victory, just as the power of Shylock's idiolect, with its unconventional rhythms and Biblical repetitions . . . sets in arch relief the artifice of the verse spoken by Portia and Bassanio. When, therefore, a letter from Antonio interrupts the festivities in III.ii, . . . the bond plot intrudes on and threatens to overwhelm the comic romance. (1–2)

8.   Quotations from Shakespeare's plays in this essay use *The Riverside Shake-speare*, ed. G. Blakemore Evans (Boston: Houghton Mifflin, 1997). Quota-tions from Shakespeare in extracts from critical commentators use a variety of texts (most often, by rough count, John Russell Brown's Arden edition), but the act-scene-line references are usually similar to those in the Riverside edition.

9.   It is also interesting to note that the five comedies listed by Meres preceding *Merchant* are predictable in terms of this dating: "his *Gentlemen of Verona*, his *Errors*, his *Love labors lost*, his *Love labours wonne*, his *Midsummers night dreame*" (*Riverside* 1970).

10. *The Genesis of Shakespeare's "The Merchant of Venice."* Lewiston, ME: Mellen, 1988. Generous extracts from *Il Pecorone*, the caskets story in the *Gesta Romanorum*, and other likely sources are readily available in John Rus-sell Brown's Arden edition of the play. Extensive selections from sources and analogues are published in Geoffrey Bullough's *Narrative and Dramatic Sources of Shakespeare*. 8 vols. London and New York: Routledge & Kegan Paul and Columbia University Press, 1957–75. Volume 1 covers *The Mer-chant of Venice.*

11. Beyond his clear statement in 1.3, Shylock displays his anti-Christian feeling throughout in his routinely patronizing dismissal of Christians, their "prophet" (1.3.34), and their professed (as painfully opposed to their practiced) values. He contemns notions of charity and hazard, and the fact that the Christians do not always practice what they preach merely reinforces Shylock's own meanness and vengefulness; a good person would not model himself on hypocrites.

12. Girard applies the same logic to *Richard III*, where Shakespeare makes cer-tain to provide the "good" ending most of the dolts in the audience would expect while at the same time he shows that Richard is only the most clever of a group of characters, *all* of whom have been implicated in murder and are only too willing to make Richard the scapegoat for their own crimes. *Pace* Girard, it could be argued that Shylock is "saved" by conversion: no longer

"castrated," he is christened and becomes a "lifegiver," providing manna to his son-in-law and daughter.

13. Portia also uses prose. Shakespeare seems to be preparing for *Much Ado About Nothing* and the *Henry IV* plays, where both Falstaff and Hal use prose. See the discussion above on the play's date.

14. But Shell's insights are marred by curious errors in reading the text of the play. He understands a line in the message Arragon finds in the silver casket ("take what wife he will to bed") as declarative when it is in fact conditional, leading Shell to the same error Kim Hall makes in the article discussed below: "Unlike the black Muslim, the white Christian is allowed to try to generate kin in wedlock" (113). Such a reading contradicts the text, especially since Arragon begins his scene of choice by restating the rules of the game and explicitly agreeing to them. In discussing Bassanio's casket choice, not only does Shell insist that Portia tells Bassanio which is the correct casket (a position also taken by other commentators), but, after Antonio's letter arrives, Shell writes: "Portia wanted to marry Bassanio right away, as her father required (2.9.5–6), but now she may fear that her interference in the trial by caskets resulted in her getting a suitor who is (as yet) unsuitable. She encourages him to leave before they marry" (115). Yet in 4.1, both Bassanio and Antonio refer to Portia as Bassanio's wife.

15. It should be noted that Shylock's current rootedness may not characterize his entire experience: when he is lamenting the loss of his daughter and his ducats, he refers to "A diamond gone, cost me two thousand ducats in Frankford" (3.1.83–85), implying at least the possibility that in earlier days he traveled to Germany.

    Readers interested in more detail about the Italian setting of the play will find relevant essays in *Shakespeare's Italy: Functions of Italian Locations in Renaissance Drama*, edited by Michele Marrapodi and others. In *Shakespeare and the Geography of Difference*, John Gillies explores the play's ambiguities about Venice and its double role, as "constitutional heir of the ancient city-state" and as an "open or cosmopolitan city," a multicultural center (123): "The merchant adventurers of Shakespeare's Venice are at once triumphant and problematic. Shakespeare clearly has reservations about Antonio and the young Venetian 'Jasons' but is unable to express them fully" (135). In *Sea-Mark: The Metaphorical Voyage, Spenser to Milton,* Philip Edwards notes that *Merchant*, like *The Comedy of Errors* and *Twelfth Night*, opens with a shipwreck, an imaginary one, in Salerio's description (1.1.8ff.). Edwards writes that "shipwreck symbolizes loss, deprivation, separation—the condition towards which tragedies work, and from which comedies start" (147).

16. Claiming that the word *prodigal* appears more often in *Merchant* than in any other play, Susan McLean observes:

    The motif of the Prodigal Son not only links several plots and subplots of the play, but also should serve to moderate the current critical tendency to sympathize with Shylock and to judge the Christians harshly for not living up to the merciful ideals that they profess. The basic premise of Christianity—that the sinner who believes and begs forgiveness will find mercy, while the self-righteous and the non-believer will not—may seem unfair, as the parable of the Prodigal Son presumably did to the Pharisees to whom Jesus told it when they objected to his eating with sinners. Yet according to that premise, even such feckless or unfilial prodigals as Launcelot, Jessica, Gratiano . . . and Bassanio must be forgiven, along with the more virtuous Portia and Antonio, while Shylock the Jew, the arrogant pagan Prince of Morocco, and the self-regarding Prince of Arragon may not. (7)

17. Edelman notes that, contrary to accounts in Gross and elsewhere, Booth first acted Shylock in San Francisco in 1854, before he went to Sydney. A reviewer in San Francisco pronounced Booth "highly successful in the difficult delineation of character, giving promise of great future excellence in" the role (Edelman, "Booth" 78). Booth's one Australian performance as Shylock was not reviewed by the local press (79).

18. Charles and Mary Cowden Clarke devoted their life as a married couple to Shakespeare. While Charles delivered lectures and published articles, Mary not only wrote *The Girlhood of Shakespeare's Heroines* but also prepared the first concordance to Shakespeare's works; as sacred scripture for the intellectual world, the plays demanded such a work (Rozmovits 43).

19. Wheeler also notes that "Freudians and Marxists have studied the play from their own particular points of view, and there are many critics for whom the Christian religion is essential to an understanding of *The Merchant*" (xix–xx). But his bibliography could not anticipate the flood of theory-based analysis that has appeared since 1980.

20. An interesting parallel might be drawn to the idea, developed in postcolonial criticism, of the inability of the subaltern to speak. In such a context, statements can be eloquently made by what is *not* said. See the discussion below of Kim Hall's essay and Launcelot's unseen and unheard Moor.

21. In "Directors' Shakespeare," Robert Smallwood discusses how four recent directors have handled this *"Exeunt"* (193–94). The relevant pages are reprinted in the 1998 Signet Classic edition.

22. Commenting on this insight, Lawrence Danson notes that "insistence upon the inherent rightness of both parties to the thematic conflict" makes that conflict "eternally interesting, rather than merely a matter of an obvious right versus an obvious wrong" (17).

23. M. C. Bradbrook notes that "Portia's famous speech is the most purely religious utterance in the canon—the most directly based upon Christian teaching . . ." (172).

24. In his introduction to *Twentieth Century Interpretations* of the play, Sylvan Barnet feels "it is reasonable to say, for a start, that [the play] is about giving" (3) and that "the broad contrast between lavish giving and cautious getting is set forth in many ways" (5).

25. Hall's endnote quotation from Edmund Spenser's *View of the Present State of Ireland* suggests that Spenser, at any rate, was at least as hostile toward what he regarded as the mongrel and bastardized Spanish (whose bloodlines are so confused, God knows where they come from) as toward Moors. Hall's essay could consider yet another Elizabethan Other.

26. In an endnote, Benston argues that Shakespeare allots about the same amount of stage time to each of the three trials. Her focus on three significant movements in the play is similar to the analyses in the work of Danson and Holmer.

27. Directed by Terry Hands, the production also featured Emrys James as Shylock, Tony Church as Antonio, and Michael Williams as Bassanio. Of this production Alexander Leggatt observes: "an attempt was made to present the ring sequence as a serious emotional dilemma (for example, when Bassanio parted with the ring, Portia burst into tears). But all through the last scene, there was a distinct feeling that the actors were fighting the natural rhythm of the dialogue, and I think the experiment, interesting though it was, demonstrates that the normal comic reading, which usually works so well, is in fact the right one" (147).

28. In a famous story, Herbert Beerbohm Tree, Irving's successor as leading actor-manager on the London stage, elaborated on Irving's interpolated action of Shylock's return to his empty house—in Irving's production, as Shylock knocked on his door, realizing that Jessica was gone, the curtain descended for the interval. In 1908 Beerbohm Tree as Shylock called out "Jessica" at the door, then "raged through the house, emerged, hurled himself to the ground, tore his clothes, and poured ashes over his head" (Barnet, "Stage" 169).

29. In fact, Videbaek claims "that Launcelot's whole function changes radically when he leaves Shylock's household. The Folio has the suggestive stage direction, *Enter the Iew, and his man that was the clown* . . . a typical rustic clown"; Videbaek notes that "after he is employed by Bassanio," Launcelot "becomes more polished. Even his language changes, leaving out the malapropisms and adding elaborate puns, and his propensity for practical jokes disappears." As "Launcelot's relationship with both his fellow characters and the audience is altered," he "becomes more of an equal to his betters, and in this context the jokes about the Moor's pregnancy . . . do not have to mean anything but banter" (67).

30. The German director may have been aware of a 1993 Brazilian production, discussed below, that used the same tactic.

31. This version of the play, *Il mercante di Venezia,* is available on the VHS video *Silent Shakespeare*, released by Milestone Film and Video in 2000.

32. An interesting shift in perspective occurs between de Sousa's 1994 review of the Brazilian production, positive in its evaluation, and his comments on the production in the 1999 essay, "Textual Encodings in *The Merchant of Venice,*" where he writes that "the characters refused to confront the real issue of racial and religious prejudice" (69). Alluding to an element in the production absent from his 1994 review, de Sousa notes that "the producers sought to transform the play into a comedy of humors to explain and justify the characters' prejudice: the focus on humors oversimplifies the dynamics of racial and religious interaction in the play; it masks Portia's racism, Antonio's religious prejudice, and Shylock's resentment; consequently, it distracts from the real issues, which neither the characters in the play nor the Brazilian producers want to confront" (70).

Works Cited

Alexander, Catherine M. S. and Stanley Wells, eds. *Shakespeare and Race.* Cambridge: Cambridge University Press, 2000.

Andrews, John, ed. *The Merchant of Venice.* London: Dent, 1993.

Auden, W. H. "Brothers and Others." From *The Dyer's Hand.* 1962. Wheeler, *Essays* 59–78.

———. *Lectures on Shakespeare.* Ed. Arthur Kirsch. Princeton, NJ: Princeton University Press, 2000.

Barber, C. L. *Shakespeare's Festive Comedy.* Cleveland and New York: World, 1963.

Barkan, Leonard. "What Did Shakespeare Read?" 2001. De Grazia 31–48.

Barnet, Sylvan. "*The Merchant of Venice* on Stage and Screen." Myrick 160–73.

———, ed. *Twentieth Century Interpretations of "The Merchant of Venice."* Englewood Cliffs, NJ: Prentice-Hall, 1970.

Bate, Jonathan and Russell Jackson, eds. *Shakespeare: An Illustrated Stage History.* Oxford: Oxford University Press, 1996.

Belsey, Catherine. "Love in Venice." 1991. Coyle 139–60.

Benston, Alice N. "Portia, the Law, and the Tripartite Structure of *The Merchant of Venice.*" 1979. Wheeler, *Essays* 163–94.

Berkoff, Steven. "Shakespeare Wrote Arias for Villains." *The New York Times*, 14 January 2001, section 2, 5.

Berry, Philippa. "Cultural Incision in Venice." Paper delivered at the Seventh World Shakespeare Congress, Valencia, Spain, 19 April 2001.

Bloom, Harold. *Shakespeare: The Invention of the Human.* New York: Riverhead, 1998.

———, ed. *William Shakespeare's "The Merchant of Venice": Modern Critical Interpretations.* New York: Chelsea House, 1986.

Boehrer, Bruce. "Shylock and the Rise of the Household Pet." *Shakespeare Quarterly* 50 (1999): 152–70.

Bradbrook, Muriel. *Shakespeare and Elizabethan Poetry.* London: Chatto and Windus, 1965.

Brandes, George. *William Shakespeare, A Critical Study.* New York: Macmillan, 1911.

Brandon, James. "Kabuki and Shakespeare: Balancing Yin and Yang." *The Drama Review* 43:2 (Summer 1999): 15–53.

Bray, Alan. "Wedded Friendships." *The Tablet* (London), 4 August 2001, 1108–109.

Brown, John Russell, ed. *The Merchant of Venice.* London and New York: Methuen, 1955.

———. "Love's Wealth and the Judgement of *The Merchant of Venice.*" *Shakespeare and His Comedies.* London: Methuen, 1957.

———. *Shakespeare's Plays in Performance.* New York: Applause, 1993.

Bulletin of the Shakespeare Society of India, 1997–99.

Bulman, James C. *"The Merchant of Venice." Shakespeare in Performance.* Manchester: Manchester University Press, 1991.

Burckhardt, Sigurd. *Shakespearean Meanings.* Princeton, NJ: Princeton University Press, 1968.

Campbell, Oscar James and Edward Quinn, eds. *The Reader's Encyclopedia of Shakespeare.* New York: Crowell, 1966.

Chetta, Peter N. "The Shakespeare Marathon: A Personal Perspective." *The Shakespeare Newsletter* 47 (1997): 25,32,38,42.

Chinese Shakespeare Yearbook 1994. Ed. Meng Xianqiang. Changchun: Northeast Normal University Press, 1995.

Clarke, Mary Cowden. *The Girlhood of Shakespeare's Heroines*. London: Bickers, 1884.

Coghill, Nevill. "The Theme of *The Merchant of Venice*." Barnet, *Twentieth Century Interpretations* 108–13.

Cohen, Derek. *Shakespearean Motives*. New York: St. Martin's Press, 1988.

Cohen, Walter. "*The Merchant of Venice* and the Possibilities of Historical Criticism." 1982. Coyle 45–72.

Coursen, H. R. "Responding to Shakespeare in Silent Film." *Shakespeare Bulletin* 19 (2, Spring 2001): 32–36.

Coyle, Martin, ed. *New Casebooks: "The Merchant of Venice."* New York: St. Martin's Press, 1998.

Danson, Lawrence. *The Harmonies of "The Merchant of Venice."* New Haven and London: Yale University Press, 1978.

De Grazia, Margreta and Stanley Wells, eds. *The Cambridge Companion to Shakespeare*. Cambridge: Cambridge University Press, 2001.

De Sousa, Geraldo U. "*The Merchant of Venice:* Brazil and Cultural Icons." *Shakespeare Quarterly* 45 (1994): 469–74.

———. *Shakespeare's Cross-Cultural Encounters*. New York: St. Martin's, 1999.

Dench, Judi. "A Career in Shakespeare." 1996. Bate 197–210.

Drakakis, John. "Historical Difference and Venetian Patriarchy." 1996. Coyle 181–213.

Dubrow, Heather. "Twentieth Century Shakespeare Criticism." *The Riverside Shakespeare,* 2nd edition. 27–54.

Edelman, Charles. "Edwin Booth's First Attempt at Shylock." *Theatre Journal* 55 (2001): 78–79.

———. "Which Is the Jew that Shakespeare Knew?: Shylock on the Elizabethan Stage." *Shakespeare Survey* 52 (1999): 99–106.

Edwards, Philip. *Sea-Mark: The Metaphorical Voyage, Spenser to Milton*. Liverpool: Liverpool University Press, 1997.

Evans, Bertrand. *Shakespeare's Comedies*. Oxford: Clarendon Press, 1960.

Ewbank, Inga-Stina. "Shakespeare Translation as Cultural Exchange." *Shakespeare Survey* 48 (1995): 1–12.

Fortin, René. "Launcelot and the Uses of Allegory in *The Merchant of Venice*." *Studies in English Literature 1500–1900* 14 (1974): 259–70.

Freeman, Neil, ed. *The Merchant of Venice*. First Folio Edition. New York: Applause, 1998.

Freud, Sigmund. "The Theme of the Three Caskets." Wilders 59–68.

Furness, Horace Howard, ed. *A New Variorum Edition of Shakespeare: "The Merchant of Venice."* Philadelphia: Lippincott, 1888.

Gielgud, John. *Acting Shakespeare*. New York: Applause, 1999.

Gifford, Don. *"Ulysses" Annotated*. 2nd ed. Berkeley: University of California Press, 1989.

Gillies, John. *Shakespeare and the Geography of Difference*. Cambridge: Cambridge University Press, 1994.

Girard, René. "'To Entrap the Wisest.' " 1980. Bloom, *Interpretations* 91–105.

Goddard, Harold C. *The Meaning of Shakespeare.* Chicago: University of Chicago Press, 1951 (rpt.1960).

Granville-Barker, Harley. *The Merchant of Venice.* 1946. Barnet, *Interpretations* 55–80.

Green, William. *"Overtime." Shakespeare Bulletin* 14 (3, Summer 1996): 16.

Gross, John. *Shylock: A Legend and Its Legacy.* New York: Simon and Schuster, 1992.

Gurney, A. R. *Overtime: A Modern Sequel to "The Merchant of Venice."* New York: Dramatists Play Service, 1997.

Gussow, Mel. "What News on the Rialto? Decadence and Injustice." *The New York Times,* 7 October 2001, section 13: 4–5.

Halio, Jay, ed. *The Merchant of Venice.* Oxford and New York: Oxford University Press, 1994.

Hall, Kim F. "Guess Who's Coming to Dinner? Colonisation and Miscegenation in *The Merchant of Venice.*" 1992. Coyle 92–116.

Halpern, Richard. *Shakespeare Among the Moderns.* Ithaca, NY: Cornell University Press, 1997.

Han, Younglim. *Romantic Shakespeare: From Page to Stage.* Madison, NJ: Fairleigh Dickinson University Press, 2001.

Hankey, Julie. "Victorian Portias: Shakespeare's Borderline Heroine." *Shakespeare Quarterly* 45 (1994): 426–48.

Harris, Bernard. "A Portrait of a Man." 1958. Alexander 23–36.

Hawkes, Terence. *Alternative Shakespeares. Volume 2.* London and New York: Routledge, 1996.

Hazlitt, William. *The Complete Works.* Ed. P. P. Howe. 1930. New York: AMS Press, 1967.

Holderness, Graham. *William Shakespeare: "The Merchant of Venice."* Penguin Critical Studies. Harmondsworth: Penguin, 1993.

Holmer, Joan Ozark. *"The Merchant of Venice": Choice, Hazard and Consequence.* New York: St. Martin's Press, 1995.

Honigmann, Ernst. "Shakespeare's Life." 2001. De Grazia 1–12.

Hopkins, Lisa. "'An Indian Beauty?': A Proposed Emendation to *The Merchant of Venice.*" *The Shakespeare Newsletter* 50 (2000): 27.

Hudson, H. N. *Shakespeare: His Life, Art, and Characters.* Vol. I. Boston: Ginn, 1872.

Huffman, Clifford Chalmers, ed. *Pegasus Shakespeare Bibliographies: "Love's Labour's Lost," "A Midsummer Night's Dream," "The Merchant of Venice."* Binghamton, NY: Medieval and Renaissance Texts and Studies, 1995.

Humphreys, A. R. "Style and Assessment." 1973. Wheeler, *Essays* 127–38.

Hunter, G. K. "Elizabethans and Foreigners." 1964. Alexander, 37–63.

Hutson, Lorna. *The Usurer's Daughter: Male Friendship and Fictions of Women in Sixteenth-Century England.* London: Routledge, 1994.

Jackson, Russell. "Shakespeare and the Cinema." 2001. De Grazia 217–34.

Jardine, Lisa. *Reading Shakespeare Historically.* London and New York: Routledge, 1996.

Jenkins, Harold. "Address to the Honors Convocation of Iona College, 16 October 1983." *The Shakespeare Newsletter* 49:4 (Winter 1999/2000): 95–98.

Joyce, James. *Finnegans Wake*. New York: Viking, 1939.

————. *Ulysses*. Ed. Hans W. Gabler. New York: Random House, 1986.

Kachuck, Rhoda S. "Yiddish Journals and Shylock." *The Shakespeare Newsletter* 46:3 (Fall, 1996): 61 and 72.

Kawachi, Yoshiko. "*The Merchant of Venice* and Japanese Culture." *Japanese Studies in Shakespeare and His Contemporaries*. Ed. Yoshiko Kawachi. Newark: University of Delaware Press, 1998. 46–69.

Kendal, Geoffrey. *The Shakespeare Wallah*. London: Penguin, 1987.

Kerrigan, William. *Shakespeare's Promises*. Baltimore: Johns Hopkins University Press, 1999.

Kermode, Frank. "The Mature Comedies." *Stratford-upon-Avon Studies 3: Early Shakespeare*. Eds. John Russell Brown and Bernard Harris. London: Edward Arnold, 1961. 211–27.

Kiasashvili, Nico. "The Martyred Knights of Georgian Shakespeariana." *Shakespeare Survey* 48 (1995): 185–90.

Kim, Joo-Hyon. *Bi-Cultural Critical Essays on Shakespeare*. Cambridge: D.S. Brewer, 1995.

Kittredge, George Lyman, ed. *The Merchant of Venice*. Boston: Ginn, 1945.

Lamb, Charles and Mary. *Tales from Shakespeare*. 1807. Ed. Elizabeth Story Donno. New York: Bantam, 1962.

Lamos, Mark. "Reflections." Program for 1993 Hartford Stage production of *The Merchant of Venice*. 2, 45.

Leggatt, Alexander. *Shakespeare's Comedy of Love*. London: Methuen, 1974.

Leonard, Elmore. *Pagan Babies*. New York: Delacorte Press, 2000.

Lerner, Laurence. "Wilhelm S and Shylock." 1995. Alexander 139–50.

Levin, Richard A. *Love and Society in Shakespearean Comedy*. Newark: University of Delaware Press, 1985.

Levine, Jennifer. "James Joyce, Tattoo Artist: Tracing the Outlines of Homosocial Desire." *James Joyce Quarterly* 31 (1993–94): 277–99.

Lewalski, Barbara. "Biblical Allusion and Allegory in *The Merchant of Venice*." Barnet, *Interpretations* 33–54.

Luxon, Thomas H. "A Second Daniel: the Jew and the 'True Jew' in *The Merchant of Venice*." *Early Modern Literary Studies*, 4.3 (January, 1999): 3.1–37.

Lyon, John. "Beginning in the Middle." 1988. Wheeler, *Essays* 217–40.

Macdonald, Robert. "All 36: A Marathon Journal." *The Shakespeare Newsletter* 47 (1997): 33–34, 36.

Mahon, John W. "Peripatetic Shakespeare." *The Shakespeare Newsletter* 48 (1998): 29, 34, 36, 43.

————. "Richard Olivier Directs *The Merchant of Venice*." *The Shakespeare Newsletter* 48 (1998): 36.

Mahood, M. M., ed. *The Merchant of Venice*. Cambridge: Cambridge University Press, 1987.

Marder, Louis. *His Exits and His Entrances: The Story of Shakespeare's Reputation*. London: John Murray, 1963.

Marlowe, Christopher. *The Jew of Malta*. Ed. N. W. Bawcutt. Manchester: Manchester University Press, 1978.

Marrapodi, Michele et al., eds. *Shakespeare's Italy: Functions of Italian Locations in Renaissance Drama*. Manchester: Manchester University Press, 1997.

———— and Giorgio Melchiori, eds. *Italian Studies in Shakespeare and His Contemporaries.* Newark: University of Delaware Press, 1999.

Marx, Steven. *Shakespeare and the Bible.* Oxford: Oxford University Press, 2000.

McLean, Susan. "Prodigal Sons and Daughters: Transgression and Forgiveness in *The Merchant of Venice.*" *Papers on Language and Literature* 32 (1996): 45–63. Rpt. *Infotrac Expanded Academic* A18167168 (1999): 1–10. 11/18/99.

Merchant, W. Moelwyn, ed. *The Merchant of Venice.* Harmondsworth: Penguin, 1967.

Muir, Kenneth. *Shakespeare's Comic Sequence.* New York: Barnes and Noble, 1979.

Myrick, Kenneth, ed. *The Merchant of Venice.* Signet Classic Shakespeare. New York: Penguin, 1998.

Nevo, Ruth. *Comic Transformations in Shakespeare.* London and New York: Methuen, 1980.

Newman, Karen. "Portia's Ring: Unruly Women and Structures of Exchange in *The Merchant of Venice.*" 1987. Coyle 117–38.

Orgel, Stephen. "Shylock's Tribe." Address to Plenary Session, Seventh World Shakespeare Congress, Valencia, Spain, 22 April 2001.

Ornstein, Robert. *Shakespeare's Comedies: From Roman Farce to Romantic Mystery.* Newark: University of Delaware Press, 1986.

Osborne, Laurie. "Sweet, Savage Shakespeare." *Shakespeare Without Class: Misappropriations of Cultural Capital.* Eds. Donald Hedrick and Bryan Reynolds. New York: Palgrave, 2000. 135–51.

Overton, Bill. *Text and Performance: "The Merchant of Venice."* London: Macmillan, 1987.

Oz, Avraham. "Transformations of Authenticity: *The Merchant of Venice* in Israel." 1998. Coyle 214–33.

Palmer, D. J. *"The Merchant of Venice,* or the Importance of Being Earnest." *Shakespearian Comedy,* eds. Malcolm Bradbury and D. J. Palmer. New York: Crane, Russak, 1972. 97–120.

Patterson, Annabel, ed. *The Most Excellent Historie of the Merchant of Venice.* Hemel Hempstead, Herts: Prentice-Hall, 1995.

Patterson, Steve. "The Bankruptcy of Homoerotic Amity in Shakespeare's *Merchant of Venice.*" *Shakespeare Quarterly* 50 (1999): 9–32.

Pendleton, Thomas. "To the Editor." *New York Times,* 8 March 1981, D6.

————. "What [?] Price [?] Shakespeare [?]." *Literature/Film Quarterly* 29: 2 (2001): 135–46.

Phialas, Peter. *Shakespeare's Romantic Comedies.* Chapel Hill: University of North Carolina Press, 1966.

Popkin, Richard. "A Jewish Merchant of Venice." *Shakespeare Quarterly* 40 (1989): 329–31.

Potter, Lois. "Shakespeare in the Theatre, 1660–1900." 2001. De Grazia 183–98.

Pousse, Michel. "From Venice to Malgudi: Eternal Themes, Eternal Devices." *The Quest* 7, nos. 1–2 (1993): 5–10.

Rosen, Alan. "The Rhetoric of Exclusion: Jew, Moor, and the Boundaries of Discourse in *The Merchant of Venice.*" *Strands Afar Remote: Israeli Perspectives on Shakespeare.* Ed. Avraham Oz. Newark: University of Delaware Press, 1998. 38–50.

Rosenheim, Judith. "Allegorical Commentary in *The Merchant of Venice.*" *Shakespeare Studies* XXIV (1996): 156–210.

Rothwell, Kenneth S. *A History of Shakespeare on Screen.* Cambridge: Cambridge University Press, 1999.

———— and Annabelle Henkin Melzer. *Shakespeare on Screen.* New York: Neal-Schuman, 1990.

Rozmovits, Linda. *Shakespeare and the Politics of Culture in Late Victorian England.* Baltimore: Johns Hopkins University Press, 1998.

Ruru, Li. "Shakespeare on the Chinese Stage in the 1990s." *Shakespeare Quarterly* 50 (1999): 355–67.

Ryan, Kiernan. "Re-reading *The Merchant of Venice.*" 1995. Coyle 36–44.

Schotz, Amiel. "Who Played Shylock?" *The Shakespeare Newsletter* 49 (1999): 13–14.

Serpieri, Alessandro. "Bonds of Love and Death in *The Merchant of Venice.*" 1999. Marrapodi, *Italian* 44–56.

Shakespeare, William. *The Riverside Shakespeare.* Ed. G. B. Evans. Boston: Houghton Mifflin, 1997.

Shapiro, James. *Shakespeare and the Jews.* New York: Columbia University Press, 1996.

Shattuck, Charles H. *Shakespeare on the American Stage, from the Hallams to Edwin Booth.* Washington, DC: Folger Library, 1976.

————. *Shakespeare on the American Stage, from Booth and Barrett to Sothern and Marlowe.* Washington, DC: Folger Library, 1987.

Shaw, George Bernard. *John Bell's Other Island and Major Barbara.* New York: Brentano's, 1907.

Shell, Marc. "The Wether and the Ewe: Verbal Usury." Bloom, *Modern Critical Interpretations* 107–20.

Sinfield, Alan. "How To Read *The Merchant of Venice* Without Being Heterosexist." 1996. Hawkes 122–39.

Smallwood, Robert. "Directors' Shakespeare." 1996. Bate 176–96.

————. "Shakespeare Performances in England, 1999." *Shakespeare Survey* 53 (2000): 244–73.

Sokol, B. J. "Prejudice and Law in *The Merchant of Venice.*" *Shakespeare Survey* 51 (1998): 159–74.

Stanley, Audrey. "The 1994 Shanghai International Shakespeare Festival." *Shakespeare Quarterly* 47 (1996): 72–80.

Stoll, E. E. "Shylock." 1911, 1927. Wheeler, *Essays* 247–62.

Tempera, Mariangela. "'Now I play a merchant's part': the Space of the Merchant in Shakespeare's Early Comedies." 1999. Marrapodi, *Italian* 152–64.

Tennenhouse, Leonard. "The Counterfeit Order of *The Merchant of Venice.*" 1980. Wheeler, *Essays* 195–215.

Trivedi, Poonan. "The Year of *Othello.*" *Bulletin of the Shakespeare Society of India,* 1997–99, 21.

Van Doren, Mark. *Shakespeare.* 1939. New York: Doubleday Anchor, n.d.

Vickers, Brian. *Appropriating Shakespeare.* New Haven and London: Yale, 1993.

Videbaek, Bente A. *The Stage Clown in Shakespeare's Theatre.* Westport, CT and London: Greenwood Press, 1996.

Webster, Margaret. *Shakespeare Without Tears.* 1942, 1955. Greenwich, CT: Fawcett, 1963.

Wheeler, Richard P. "The Loss of a Son and the Rise of Shakespearean Comedy." *Shakespeare Quarterly* 51 (2000): 127–53.

Wheeler, Thomas. *"The Merchant of Venice": An Annotated Bibliography.* New York and London: Garland, 1985.

——, ed. *"The Merchant of Venice": Critical Essays.* New York and London: Garland, 1991.

White, R. S. "Marx and Shakespeare." *Shakespeare Survey* 45 (1992): 89–100.

Wilders, John, ed. *"The Merchant of Venice": A Casebook.* London: Macmillan, 1969.

Wilson, Robert J. "Censorship, Anti-Semitism, and *The Merchant of Venice.*" *English Journal* 86:2 (February 1997): 43–45.

Yoshihara, Yukari. "Japan as 'Half-Civilized': An Early Japanese Adaptation of Shakespeare's *The Merchant of Venice.*" *Bulletin of the Shakespeare Society of India, 1997–1999.* 11.

Zesmer, David. *Guide to Shakespeare.* New York: Barnes and Noble, 1976.

Shakespeare's *Merchant* and Marlowe's Other Play

MURRAY J. LEVITH

Launcelot Gobbo's confused but colorful monologue in *The Merchant of Venice* (2.2.1–30) is an important clue to the dynamics of Shakespeare's Faustian comedy.[1] We recall that the clown is contemplating breaking his servile bond with the Jew Shylock, "the very devil incarnation," in order to cast his lot with the Christian Bassanio, who has "the grace of God" (2.2.143–44). Launcelot imagines himself at the center of a morality struggle, a Faust character with a good angel, his "conscience," at one elbow and a bad angel, the "fiend," at the other. Of course, he gets things comically confused, but ultimately decides to "run" from the Jew.

Christopher Marlowe's *Doctor Faustus* and Shakespeare's *The Merchant of Venice* were written within a few years of each other. Although the precise dates of their composition are not known, *Doctor Faustus* was likely written in 1593, the year of Marlowe's death, and *The Merchant of Venice* in 1596–1597.[2] Further to the point, *Doctor Faustus* was acted twenty-plus times between late September or early October of 1594 and January 5, 1597 (Bowers 123); that is, it was on the boards during the very time Shakespeare was writing his *Merchant*.

It is clear that *The Merchant of Venice* not only owes something to Marlowe's usually acknowledged *The Jew of Malta* (see Brown xxxi, and Bullough 454–57), but also, and importantly, to his Faust play as well. The plot details are different, but the ideational structure is recognizably similar. In both plays, for example, there is a singular bond with a devil-associated character, a central "Faust" protagonist to be tested, "correct" and "incorrect" character choices, and specific place settings associated with "good" and "bad" values. Moreover, both plays can be seen as being about the nature of the good Christian life in the face of worldly temptations. As T. S. Eliot avers in his 1919 essay on Marlowe, ". . . when Shakespeare borrowed from him, which was pretty often at the beginning, Shakespeare either made something

95

inferior or something different" (56). In the case of *The Merchant of Venice*, it was nothing "inferior."

Marlowe's main source for *Doctor Faustus* is the so-called *English Faust Book* [*The History of the Damnable Life and Deserved Death of Doctor John Faustus*] (1592), translated by one P. F. *Gent.* from the German *Historia von D. Johan Fausten* (1587). Shakespeare's *Merchant* may owe something to this *English Faust Book* as well. In it there is an episode about a Jew that is conflated in Marlowe's *Doctor Faustus* with the "Horse-courser" episode (4, 5–6). The *Faust Book* chapter is titled "How Doctor Faustus borrowed money of a Jew and laid his own leg to pawn for it" (Chapter 33). The tale begins with Faustus' "merry jest to deceive a Jew," echoing Shylock's "merry bond" (1.3.169) to deceive Antonio (see Laroque 117–18). The magician borrows "threescore dollars," similar to the "three thousand ducats" in Shakespeare's play. As surety for the Jew, Faustus "cuts off" his leg, his "pawn of flesh," to be reclaimed and sewn back upon repayment of the loan. "Thinking it would stink and so infect my house," the Jew discards the severed limb; besides, he says, "it is too hard a piece of work to set it on again" (Jones 153). Of course, the loan is repaid in time and Faustus demands his leg or, if the Jew cannot produce it, the Jew's own limb![3] As in *The Merchant*, the *Faust Book* Jew is tricked, defeated, and made to look foolish. After pleading to save his leg, he is forced to pay additional money beyond the loan to satisfy the magician.

The Merchant of Venice, like *Doctor Faustus*, is a play about choice.[4] The words "choice," "choose," "chooses," "chooseth," "choosing," "chose," and "chosen" occur more than fifty times in Shakespeare's play. We have already noted that Launcelot Gobbo chooses to leave the Jew's service. So too does Jessica leave her father's house, to elope with Lorenzo and "Become a Christian" (2.3.21). The presumably Muslim Morocco and the outsider Arragon cannot choose the proper casket and so win Portia because they are dazzled by external show and egotistical pride, rather than understanding the Christian message that least is most and "All that glisters is not gold" (2.7.65). Additionally, as Barbara Lewalski argues, "the defeat and lessoning of Morocco and Aragon [*sic*] foreshadows the defeat and conversion of Shylock, for he represents in somewhat different guise these same antichristian values of worldliness and self-righteousness" (337). The three alien characters are without mates at the end, doomed to the sterile life their world views suggest.[5] Indeed, Arragon reminds the audience of the consequences of an improper choice in the lottery: "I am enjoin'd by oath . . . never in my life to woo a maid in way of marriage" (2.9.9–13). So too does Portia remind Morocco: "You must take your chance, / And either not attempt to choose at all, / Or swear before you choose, if you choose wrong / Never to speak to lady afterward / In way of marriage" (2.1.38–42).[6]

On the other hand, Bassanio, when given a choice to make, chooses correctly: the humble leaden casket that nonetheless promises a golden future of

love and marriage. He comments, "The world is still deceiv'd with ornament" (3.2.74), a slur at those we have seen choose before him. Lewalski
contends, "At the allegorical level, the caskets signify everyman's choice of
the paths to spiritual life or death" (336). Thus, the selection of the leaden
casket by Bassanio is understood as life affirming. As Jessica notes, "For
having such a blessing in his lady, / He finds the joys of heaven here on
earth" (3.5.69–70). The lover's name comes from *basanite*, the touchstone
used to test for true gold (Levith, *Names* 79, 89).[7] Bassanio seems intuitively
to understand not only which casket to choose, but also the difference
between the letter and spirit of a bond: when he is faced with surrendering his
wedding ring, he again makes the appropriate Christian choice.

Despite Launcelot's "good angel/bad angel" monologue and Bassanio's
proper choices, Antonio is clearly the central Faustian character in *The Merchant of Venice*. However, Antonio differs significantly from Marlowe's
magician. Whereas Dr. Faustus signs over his eternal *soul* to the devil, Antonio secures his loan from the vengeful Shylock pledging only "an equal
pound / Of . . . fair *flesh*" from his *body* (1.3.145–46; emphasis mine). As the
devil Mephistopheles concedes in Marlowe's play, the body ". . . is but little
worth" (5.1.86). The magician, when sealing his bond, has clear warnings
that he is doing something damnable: his blood only "trickles" from his arm
and then "congeals" (2.1.57, 62), so that fire must be brought to liquify it.
Signing the "bill" turns out to be a laborious process, also underlining its
tragic seriousness. "What might the staying of my blood portend?" Dr. Faustus asks rhetorically (2.1.65). Conversely, and despite Bassanio's repeated
misgivings—"You shall not seal to such a bond for me, / I'll rather dwell in
my necessity," or "I like not fair terms, and a villain's mind" (1.3.150–51,
175)—Antonio readily agrees to Shylock's not-so-"merry bond." The magician signs over his soul for self-serving knowledge, worldly power, and
fame, while Antonio pledges his pound of flesh only to help his good friend.
The merchant thus suggests the New Testament teaching: "Greater loue then
this hathe no man, when any man bestoweth his life for his friends" (Geneva
Bible, *John* 15:13).

At the beginning of their plays both the magician and the merchant are
unhappy. Dr. Faustus, though, thinks he understands the cause of his disquiet.
Although favored with deep learning, he is frustrated by human limitations
and thus seeks to go beyond what he has and knows. What "Faustus most
desires . . . [is] a world of profit and delight, / Of power, of honor, of omnipo-
tence" (1.1.50–52). Such earthly rewards seem at first grand and worth a
hellish contract, but ultimately they are shown to be small payment in
exchange for eternal damnation after a mere twenty-four years.[8] Moreover,
many of the things the magician desires he does not get: a wife, straight
answers to important questions (e.g. "who made the world?" [2.2.71–72]),
and so on. What he does receive are various diversions, including the lavish

masque of the Seven Deadly Sins. These entertainments, to be sure, are fleeting and are meant to shift attention away from his fearsome bargain with Lucifer.

The magician, most of all, would have the power of God or Jesus Christ. At the beginning of his play he complains, "thou are still but Faustus and a man. / Coulds't thou make men to live eternally / Or being dead raise them to life again / Then this profession [i.e. philosophy] were to be esteemed" (1.1.21–24). While Antonio cannot raise the dead, his willingness to place his corporeal body in bond for love of his fellowman aligns him with Christ. Antonio demonstrates Christ-like patience in the face of threat from the devil-associated character Shylock who harrows him: "I do oppose / My patience to his fury and am arm'd / To suffer with a quietness of spirit, / The very tyranny and rage of his" (4.1.10–13). Lewalski observes, "Antonio baring his breast to shed his blood for the debt of another, [makes plain] . . . the identification with Christ" (339). Just as Dr. Faustus' devilish bond must be signed in blood, Antonio's would-be sacrifice for love is also a potential blood rite. Antonio is, again in Lewalski's words, "a perfect embodiment of Christian love" (331).

Antonio's melancholy at the start of *The Merchant of Venice* is something that he himself does not understand: "In sooth I know not why I am so sad" (1.1.1). He is neither in love with a woman nor overly worried about his ships. Yet his merchant's life in commercial Venice and his obvious wealth do not give him fulfillment and ease. Unlike the overweening magician, however, Antonio senses that his true "estate" is not *this world* or *this life*. He explains, "My ventures are not in one bottom trusted, / Nor to one place; nor is my whole estate / Upon the fortune of this present year" (1.1.42–44). He is aware of a promised future. Antonio goes on to say that because the world is transitory, "I hold the world *but as the world*" (1.1.77; emphasis mine). His words recall *Matthew* 6:19–20: "Lay not up treasures for your selves upon the earth, where the mothe & canker corrupt, & where theves digge through, and steale. But lay up treasures for your selves in heaven." The merchant is willing, therefore, to pledge his earthly body as a Christian saint might do. Cynthia Lewis contends that "the very name *Antonio*," with its saintly associations, "suggested to audiences of high English Renaissance drama a willingness to compromise one's own well being for a person or principle seen as more important—or higher—than the self." [9]

Like Antonio, Portia is melancholy too. The reason for her weariness "of this great world" (1.2.1–2) is that she is denied choice of a husband. Portia complains, "O me, the word 'choose.' I may neither choose who I would, nor refuse whom I dislike, so is the will of a living daughter curb'd by the will of a dead father: . . . I cannot choose one, nor refuse none" (1.2.22–26). She later adds, "In terms of choice I am not solely led / By nice direction of a maiden's eyes: . . . the lottery of my destiny / Bars me the right of voluntary choosing" (2.1.13–16). Portia has no choice because she functions in part as the allegorical "portion," the symbolic prize her heavenly father offers as reward to the Christian Everyman. In Shakespeare's allegory, Portia is a kind of Fairy Queen or Queen Elizabeth, presiding over a special and clearly otherworldly place. Belmont is a "beautiful mountain," as its name suggests. It can be seen as fairyland England, much in the manner of Edmund Spenser's *The Faerie Queene*, another text from the 1590s. Like Queen Elizabeth herself, Portia rejects various inappropriate suitors despite their pedigrees. Identified with the True Church, she will wed only the true-born English Everyman, represented by Bassanio. The lover is like Prince Arthur who is to be united ultimately with The Fairy Queen and all she represents. She offers the prospect of salvation through spiritual love and marriage to the True— that is, Anglican—Church, and so contrasts with Marlowe's Helen.

Dr. Faustus at first asks Mephistopheles for a wife, but when confronted with a woman devil, a "hot whore" (2.1.152), he changes his mind. Mephistopheles agrees: "Marriage is but a ceremonial toy" (2.1.153). However, late in Marlowe's play Faustus demands that Helen appear, "To glut the longing of my heart's desire" (5.1.88). But Helen does not have the power to make the magician "immortal with a kiss"; indeed, the woman whose "face . . . launched a thousand ships" to war has "lips [that] suck forth [Faustus'] soul" (5.1.96,99). "Helen," in Jan Kott's view, is the "sign and omen of doom" (17), just as Portia represents fulfillment in Shakespeare's play.

Portia is also, just as Antonio, a Christ-like figure. She obeys her father's will, and rescues the merchant, a would-be Christian martyr. When Bassanio is ready to choose from among the caskets, she affirms, "I stand for sacrifice" (3.2.57). Her statement sharply contrasts with Shylock's, "I stand for judgment" (4.1.103) or "I stand here for law" (4.1.142), later in the trial scene. Coming down from heavenly Belmont to earthly Venice, she assumes the role of Balthazar (a name associated with one of the three Magi [scc *Matt.* 2]), arguing eloquently that mercy is necessary for sinful man, as against Shylock's prideful Hebrew notion of self-righteousness. Her text comes from John's *First Epistle* (1:8): "If we say that we have no sinne, we deceive our selves, and trueth is not in us," a passage quoted by Dr. Faustus in his first speech.

Shylock has made Dr. Faustus' selfish choice of the superficial temporal world before Shakespeare's play begins. G. K. Hunter cites the tradition of ". . . seeing Jewishness as a moral condition, the climactic 'Jewish choice' being that which rejected Christ and chose Barabbas, rejected the Saviour and chose the robber, rejected the spirit and chose the flesh, rejected the treasure that is in heaven and chose the treasure that is on earth" (214). Shylock is concerned with profit, ducats, and revenge. The Jew despises the merchant because he is a Christian, and also for lending "out money gratis" (1.3.39). Shylock has aligned himself with the "bad angel" or devil character in

Shakespeare's Faustian comedy. When asked why he wants Antonio's pound
of flesh he replies, "To bait fish withal" (3.1.47). Perhaps his meaning is: to
catch other Christians "upon the hip" (1.3.41). If Jesus would be a fisher of
men to save them, Shylock would fish to ensnare. Marlowe's magician asks
Mephistopheles, "What good will my soul do thy lord [Lucifer]?" (2.1.40),
and the devil replies, "Enlarge his kingdom" (2.1.41).

The Jew is associated explicitly with the devil many times in *Merchant*,
and Jessica describes their house as "hell" (2.3.2). The biblical allusion is to
John (8:44), where Jesus chides the doubting Jews: "Ye are of your father the
devil." Like the devil, Shylock "can cite Scripture for his purpose. / [He is]
An evil soul producing holy witness" (1.3.94–95). He gives a twisted reading
of the Jacob and Laban's sheep story (see *Genesis* 30:31–43) as a way of justifying his usury, and perhaps his exegesis is meant to satirize Hebrew
midrashic interpretation. Bassanio remarks, "In religion, / What damned
error, but some sober brow / Will bless it, and approve it with a text, / Hiding
the grossness with fair ornament?" (3.2.77–80). The devil is a Jew because,
as Kott affirms, "The devil always appears in disguise; . . . otherwise he
could frighten but not tempt" (6).

Shylock's hellish world is without harmony, vengeful, grimly austere,
and humorless. The Jew tells his daughter, "Let not the sound of shallow fop-
p'ry enter / My sober house" (2.5.35–36); he orders, "Lock up my doors, and
when you hear the drum / And the vile squealing of the wry-neck'd fife /
Clamber not you up to the casements then / . . . But stop my house's ears"
(2.5.29–34). Shylock has no time for masques and music. However, as
Lorenzo reminds us, "The man that hath no music in himself . . . / Is fit for
treasons, stratagems, and spoils, / . . . his affections dark as Erebus [i.e. hell]:
/ Let no such man be trusted" (5.1.83–88). When Shylock is "bid forth to
supper" by Antonio and his fellows, he goes "in hate, to feed upon / The
prodigal Christian" (2.5.11,14–15); that is, to "spend" or waste their generous offer of food and hospitality. The Jew is hateful and his focus is on
revenge and ducats. Lewalski contends, "This concern for the world poisons
all his relations with others, and even his love for Jessica" (330). Shylock's
comment about his only child who has run away is chilling: "I would my
daughter were dead at my foot, and the jewels in her ear; would she were
hears'd at my foot, and the ducats in her coffin" (3.1.80–82).

Venice, the title setting for *Merchant*, is among the places Dr. Faustus
visits during his travels. The magician describes the city's cathedral as "a
sumptuous temple . . . / That threats the stars with her aspiring top, / Whose
frame is pav'd with sundry colour'd stones / And roof'd aloft with curious
work in gold" (3.1.17–20). This description of St. Mark's is in the tradition of
Spenser's view of St. Peter's in Rome, which the poet sees as a "House of
Pride" (*The Faerie Queene* 1.4.4), and was common contemporary Protestant
cant against the perceived wealth, extravagance, and ostentation of the

Catholic Church. The Revels' editor of Marlowe's play points out that St. Mark's does not have (and never did have) an "aspiring top" (Jump 48n).

Protestant schoolmaster Roger Ascham reported that he witnessed more sin in nine days in Venice than he saw in nine years in London (83). After his brief visit, the queen's tutor describes Venice as home to the "*diabolo incarnato*," the "Englishman Italianated":

> He, that by living, and traveling in *Italie*, bringeth home into England out of *Italie*, the Religion, the learning, the policie, the experience, the maners of *Italie*. That is to say, for Religion, Papistrie or worse: for policie, a factious hart, a discoursing head, a mynde to medle in all mens matters: for experience, plentie of new mischieves never knowne in England before: for maners, varietie of vanities, and chaunge of filthy lyving. (78)

Ascham believed that Venetian courtesan bastards were so numerous that they could supply the Catholic Church! Yet Venice was a magnet for the relatively provincial English despite its perceived dangers. The city was sophisticated and stylish, and represented, perhaps more than any other single place, alluring worldly temptations of all sorts—licentiousness, salacious books, and "false" religion.

Thus, Venice is not only Shylock's Jewish world of getting and spending, but also by extension the Pope's Catholic "Rome" as well. If Portia can be seen as the nubile "queen" in fairyland Belmont, the Jew in turn is the "Pope" in Venetian Rome. Shylock, that is, is symbolically more than a Jew: he is the composite "bad angel," alien-outsider, the "other," who represents the one in league with the devil, who is the tempter in Shakespeare's Anglican Protestant setting. The late sixteenth century was a time, we are told by James Shapiro and others, when England was trying to locate and define its national, racial, and cultural identity, as well as continuing to insist on its uniquely religious one. One way to do this was to consider what the English were not. Jews, who had been banished in 1290 and were relatively few in number in Early Modern England (Shapiro estimates "never more than a couple of hundred at any given time" [76]), obviously were not. Shapiro writes, ". . . Elizabethans considered Jews to be unlike themselves in terms of religion, race, nationality, and even sexuality" (3). Catholics, a constant challenge to Anglican and monarchical authority at home and from abroad, were also thought of by the orthodox at this time as not truly "English." Pope Pius V excommunicated the queen in 1570, dissolving her subjects' allegiance, and in turn Papistry was deemed treasonable.

English Protestants often accused Catholics of exhibiting Jewish tendencies. "The Elizabethan word 'Jew,' " according to Hunter, "was a word of general abuse" (215). Shapiro notes Martin Luther's commentary on *Galatians* (published in 1575), that the "Papists are our Jews which molest us no less than the Jews did Paul" (quoted in Shapiro 21). There was ongoing and justifiable fear that Catholics from Portugal, Spain, Italy, and Rome were infiltrating Protestant England, sometimes masquerading as Jews, in order to convert the queen's subjects and subvert the crown (Shapiro 27–28). Before the century's turn, England and, therefore, the Established Church could be easily perceived by its enemies as fragile and vulnerable. The queen was still unmarried, in her sixties, and long past childbearing age. It is no wonder then that late-sixteenth-century English literature is replete with nervous anti-Catholic propaganda and satire.

Marlowe devotes two scenes in act 3 of *Doctor Faustus* to satirizing the Pope and the ceremonies of Catholicism. Dr. Faustus "long[s] to see the monuments / And situation of bright-splendent Rome" (3.1.50–51), and Mephistopheles obliges him with a tour of the city in recognizably tour-guide language (3.1.31–46). The two mischievously disrupt the Pope's "solemnity," and hear statements that the Pope "cannot err" and "all power on earth" is his (3.1.153,152). The action dissolves into low comedy with the invisible Dr. Faustus speaking insults, snatching dishes and goblets, striking the Pope and friars, and climactically setting off firecrackers (3.2).

But Catholics and Jews were not the only perceived alien-devils. Any religious group outside the Established Church was suspect and at times labeled "Judaizers," to associate it with Judaism (Shapiro 21). In Elizabethan times, Protestant exiles who had come into contact with Calvinism, and other more local sects, developed the sober values associated with both Shylock and the Puritans. One John Traske was detained with his followers for Jewish leanings: he is described as "first a puritan, then a separatist, and now is become a Jewish Christian" (quoted in Shapiro 23). The Scottish intellectual George Buchanan, tutor to the future King James I, was imprisoned by the Portuguese Inquisition "on suspicion of Judaizing" (Shapiro 21). And Luther accused John Calvin himself of "Judaizing" for denying the prophecy of the virgin birth (Shapiro 22).

Austere Protestant groups were particularly targeted. Some, in fact, invited their own trouble. Puritans, for example, considered themselves God's newly "chosen people." They self-consciously attempted to emulate Jewish ways and customs, giving themselves and their children Old Testament names, keeping kosher, observing a strict Sabbath, and even undergoing circumcision in some cases. Such activities were eagerly noticed and exploited by Catholics and Anglicans alike. But, in turn, the Puritans "looked upon the Anglican Church [as well as the Catholics] as idolatrous" (Siegel, *Shylock* 15).

The established clergy and court advisors rightly understood that the Puritans posed a challenge and threat to the queen's authority. Their belief in and strict adherence to the Mosaic Code, for example, which included death for blasphemy or adultery, did not permit a merciful pardon by a temporal queen (Siegel, *Shylock* 16–17). Indeed, "Puritans as well as Jews were called devils in

Shakespeare's time. ... The pious exterior of the Puritans, it was charged, concealed the spirit of the Devil" (Siegel, *Usurers* 135). According to Wilhelm Creizenach, Jews and Puritans were afforded much the same treatment (109).

Like Jews, Puritans were also usurers. According to Paul Siegel, "Many of Shylock's traits would have reminded Shakespeare's audience of the Puritan usurers of its own time" (Siegel, *Usurers* 130). Shakespeare depended on them "to associate Judaism, Puritanism, and usury" (Siegel, *Shylock* 15). Playwright John Marston's *Satire II* (published in 1598 but in circulation before) describes a Puritan moneylender who is worse than a Jew: "No Jew, no Turk, would use a Christian / So inhumanely as this Puritan" (Bullen 271).

In his recent book, Harold Bloom admits to being troubled most of all by Shylock's forced conversion in *The Merchant of Venice*. Yet like Portia, the Jew seems another character in the play who functions in part symbolically and thus is without choice. Bloom asks, "Why did Shakespeare allow Antonio this final turn of the torturer's screw?" (175). Shylock's conversion, however, probably was perceived by Elizabethan audiences as a mercy, in that it offered the Jew the possibility of salvation. Additionally, the conversion might also have to do with when *Merchant* was written. Shakespeare composed his play just a few years before the turn of the seventeenth century. At this centennial time there was excited anticipation by Christians of all stripes, but especially Baptists, Quakers, and other fundamentalist Protestant groups, of the imminent conversion of the Jews (Shapiro 28). Shylock's agreeing to conversion, therefore, might have been seen as a symbolic fulfillment of the long-awaited and now imminent mass Jewish conversion. Too, Shylock is gone before the last act, a scene of poetry, music, harmony, playfulness, and love in heavenly and Christian Belmont.

So then, the bad angel-devil Shylock can be seen as Pope and Puritan. Well, what about a Jewish Dr. Faustus? Shakespeare may have known the tradition of associating the Jewish Johan Fust, Johannes Gutenberg's financial backer and subsequent legal antagonist, with Dr. Faustus. Fust was thought to have stolen the Christian Bible printer's invention of moveable type. Additionally, Frances Yates calls attention to a Rembrandt etching, sometimes titled "The Inspired Scholar" (c. 1652), that is often interpreted to represent "Faust and is depicting a profound search for forbidden knowledge" (187). Indeed, the composition has come to be called "Faust in His Study, Watching a Magic Disc." Although Yates discredits this identification, Kott views the pensive scholar as both Faust and Jew: "Faust wears a wide, loose coat and has a nightcap or white turban on his head, much like those worn by the Jewish elders of Amsterdam in other paintings" (1). The bright "magic disc" shining through the window contains the letters I N R I, the monogram of Christ, as well as a Hebrew anagram in the outer ring (Yates 187). Thus, the scholar's mystical vision might suggest an understanding of the limitations of his "book," and spiritual knowledge offered through conversion.

Shakespeare's Prospero is, of course, the scholar who ultimately drowns his "book" (5.1.57). He is the "white" magician teaching reconciliation and forgiveness, as opposed to Dr. Faustus' self-serving "black" magic. Roger Shattuck points out that "The Latin Faustus means 'the favored one,' a form that can yield Prospero in English." And he adds, "It is instructive to read *The Tempest* as a modified Faust play" (80n). Indeed, *The Tempest* and not *The Merchant of Venice* is the Shakespeare play most often compared with Marlowe's *Doctor Faustus* (the *English Faust Book* editor notes four parallels with the romance from Marlowe's source [Jones 258].) Both dramas contain banquet scenes, "echo" scenes, plays-within-plays, and low comic actions that reflect events of high seriousness. Both also have central magician characters with spirit servants aiding them.

However, so too can we read *The Merchant of Venice* as a Faust play. We have shown that *Doctor Faustus* has much in common with Shakespeare's comedy, a play composed when Marlowe's tragedy was popular on the stage. The Faust motif is clearly observable in *Merchant*, placing characters with choices to make between two worlds, at times exhorted by good and bad angels, or identified with one or another of these worlds and its values. The hellish choice or identification involves over-concern with the here-and-now, suggested by the vengeful and profit-driven values of Shylock the Jew, who generalizes to all the "alien-others" despised by the Elizabethan English. The Christian choice or identification, on the other hand, affirms the supposedly Anglican message, that the soul and eternity are more important than the body and this life, and that generosity, friendship, love, mercy, and sacrifice are the correct values to have on this earth. Shakespeare, then, not only borrowed from Christopher Marlowe's *The Jew of Malta* for his Shylock play, but also, and significantly, from *Doctor Faustus* as well.

Notes

1. All references to play texts are as follows:
    Barnet, Sylvan, ed. *Doctor Faustus by Christopher Marlowe.* New York: New American Library (Signet Classic), 1969. [An edition based on the B text but incorporating relevant A text passages. See pp. 103–109.]
    Brown, John Russell, ed. *The Arden Shakespeare: The Merchant of Venice.* New York: Random House (paper), 1964.
    Lothian, J. M. and T. W. Craik, eds. *The Arden Shakespeare: Twelfth Night.* London: Methuen (paper), 1975.
2. For the Marlowe dating see John D. Jump, pp. xxv–vi, and Fredson Bowers, pp. 123–24; John Henry Jones argues for a somewhat earlier date, pp. 54–72. For the Shakespeare dating see Jay L. Halio, pp. 27–29, and John Russell Brown, p. xxvii.
3. One wonders here if there isn't some comic circumcision allusion, as this Jewish ritual fascinated early modern England (see Levith, *Italian* 28).
4. See Richard Horwich, "Riddle and Dilemma in *The Merchant of Venice.*" *Studies in English Literature* 17 (1977): 191–200.

5. Although Antonio also remains unmarried, he is understood to be the saintly, Christ-like Christian, as we shall see below.

6. But, as Dr. Johnson points out, Shakespeare seems to have forgotten this condition at II,ix,70 (Brown 67n).

7. Cynthia Lewis suggests that *Bastinao*, close to *Bassanio*, is an Italian diminutive for Sebastian, and might suggest that Bassanio is meant to be associated with the saint (28).

8. To be sure, some critics and especially Romantic writers like Goethe see a subtext here: Faustus as the Renaissance man of integrity who makes a tragic but ultimately heroic choice.

9. Antonio's name recalls two important saints, St. Anthony the Great (also known as St. Anthony of Egypt, St. Anthony the Hermit, and St. Anthony Abbot), and St. Anthony of Padua, both models of Christian forbearance. St. Anthony the Great lived from 250 to 356 C.E., and his reputation came to the West during the time of the Crusades (see St. Athanasius' "Life"). One of the frequently rendered subjects in Medieval and Renaissance art, this St. Anthony is remembered as an ascetic who distributed his wealth among the poor and struggled against and resisted various evil demons. His "Life" contains a sermon on temptation (15–29). Among his own temptations is an instance of silver and gold placed in his path by the devil, but St. Anthony ignored them. He is often pictured with a pig, symbolizing his triumph over gluttony and sensuality, and he is the patron of swineherds. A "Tantony pig" is the smallest of a litter, a detail that might recall Antonio's description of himself in Shakespeare's play as the "tainted wether of the flock" (4.1.114). St. Anthony the Great is also remembered for combating heresy and offering himself as a victim for martyrdom, again similar to Antonio's role in Shakespeare's *The Merchant* (see Lewis 45, 30, 53).

    St. Anthony of Padua, who lived a brief life from 1195 to 1231, is the patron of lost property, suggesting Bassanio's appeal to Antonio in the first scene of the play: "In my school days, when I had lost one shaft / I shot his fellow of the selfsame flight / The selfsame way, with more advised watch / To find the other forth, and by adventuring both, / I oft found both" (1.1.140–44). This St. Anthony is also the apostle of charity, invoked for both spiritual and temporal needs, and the patron of lovers and of marriage as well. Also to the point of *Merchant* is the episode in St. Anthony's life of the heretic (in some versions Jewish) who refused to believe in the presence of Christ in the Eucharist unless his mule knelt before the Sacrament. This happened, and many were converted (see Purcell 87–89, 112; and Lewis 17, 15).

Works Cited

Ascham, Roger. *The Scholemaster.* Ed. Edward Arber. London: Constable, 1920.

Athanasius, St. "The Life of St. Anthony the Great." *The Life of St. Anthony the Great, The Life of St. Hilarion, and Life of St. Paul the First Hermit.* Willits, Calif.: Eastern Orthodox Books, 1976. 5–50.

Bloom, Harold. *Shakespeare: The Invention of the Human.* New York: Riverhead, 1998.

Bowers, Fredson, ed. *The Complete Works of Christopher Marlowe.* Vol. 2. Cambridge: Cambridge University Press, 1973.

Brooks-Davies, Douglas, ed. *Edmund Spenser: The Fairy Queen.* London: J. M. Dent, 1996.

Bullen, A. H., ed. *The Works of John Marston.* Vol. 3. London: John C. Nimmo, 1887.

Bullough, Geoffrey. *Narrative and Dramatic Sources of Shakespeare.* Vol. 1. London: Routledge and Kegan Paul, 1957.

Creizenach, Wilhelm. *The English Drama in the Age of Shakespeare.* Philadelphia: Lippincott, 1916.

Eliot, T. S. *Essays on Elizabethan Drama.* New York: Harcourt, Brace, and World (Harvest), 1956.

Geneva Bible: A Facsimile of the 1560 Edition. Madison: University of Wisconsin Press, 1969.

Halio, Jay L., ed. *The Oxford Shakespeare: The Merchant of Venice.* Oxford: Clarendon Press, 1993.

Horwich, Richard. "Riddle and Dilemma in *The Merchant of Venice.*" *Studies in English Literature* 17 (1977): 191–200.

Hunter, G. K. "The Theology of Marlowe's *The Jew of Malta.*" *Journal of the Warburg and Courtauld Institute* 27 (1964): 211–40.

Jones, John Henry, ed. *The English Faust Book.* Cambridge: Cambridge University Press, 1994.

Jump, John D., ed. *The Revels Plays: Doctor Faustus by Christopher Marlowe.* London: Methuen, 1962.

Kott, Jan. *The Bottom Translation: Marlowe and Shakespeare and the Carnival Tradition.* Trans. Daniela Miedzyrzecka and Lillian Vallee. Evanston: Northwestern University Press, 1987.

Laroque, François. "An Analogue and Possible Secondary Source to the Pound-of-Flesh Story in *The Merchant of Venice.*" *Notes and Queries* (New Series) 30 (April 1983): 117–18.

Levith, Murray J. *Shakespeare's Italian Settings and Plays.* New York: St. Martin's, 1989.

———. *What's in Shakespeare's Names.* London: George Allen and Unwin, 1978.

Lewalski, Barbara. "Biblical Allusion and Allegory in *The Merchant of Venice.*" *Shakespeare Quarterly* 13 (1962): 327–43.

Lewis, Cynthia. *Particular Saints: Shakespeare's Four Antonios, Their Contexts, and Their Plays.* Newark: University of Delaware Press, 1997.

Purcell, Mary. *St. Anthony and His Times.* Dublin: M. H. Gill, 1960.

Shapiro, James. *Shakespeare and the Jews.* New York: Columbia University Press, 1996.

Shattuck, Roger. *Forbidden Knowledge.* New York: St. Martin's, 1996.

Siegel, Paul. "Shylock the Puritan." *Columbia University Forum* 5 (Fall 1962): 14–19.

———. "Shylock and the Puritan Usurers." *Studies in Shakespeare.* Eds. Arthur D. Matthews and Clark M. Emery. Coral Gables: University of Miami Press, 1953. 129–38.

Yates, Frances A. *The Occult Philosophy in the Elizabethan Age.* London: Ark Paperbacks, 1983.

Jewish Daughters

The Question of Philo-Semitism in Elizabethan Drama

JOAN OZARK HOLMER

In an age rife with intolerance, why do two Elizabethan playwrights approvingly feature "the other"—a Jewish daughter—as a heroine who is loved and admired by Christians surprisingly *before* as well as perhaps less surprisingly *after* she actually converts to Christianity? Much has been written about the problem of anti-Semitism and the demonization of the Jew in relation to Marlowe's *The Jew of Malta* and Shakespeare's *The Merchant of Venice*, but these plays also include a contrary, and perhaps quite remarkable and complicating, element of philo-Semitism embodied in the Christian love and admiration that the two Jewish daughters inspire in their respective dramatic worlds. Marlowe's Abigail, who is the daughter of Barabas, a rich Jewish merchant living in Malta, has two Christian suitors: Lodowick, the son of the Christian governor of Malta, and Don Mathias, the son of a Christian widow and the gentleman whom Abigail truly loves. Shakespeare's Jessica, who is the daughter of Shylock, a rich Jewish usurer living in Venice, enjoys a mutual friendship with the Christian servant Lancelot Gobbo and is loved by Lorenzo, the Venetian gentleman whom she marries. Marlowe proves Shakespeare's theatrical prompter in many ways, ranging from minor (verbal echoes) to major (ideas and characterization) elements, and Elizabethan audiences familiar with Marlowe's play would be eager to remark what Shakespeare does with another cast of Jews and Christians in exotic locales. M. M. Mahood sees Marlowe's play less as "a source" and more as "a challenge" to Shakespeare (8).[1] I would suggest it is a challenging source to which Shakespeare rises, not so much from the anxiety of influence as from the confidence of a different vision, one that is generically shaped by his choice of comic emphasis over tragic.

Both plays feature good and bad Christians, as well as good and bad Jews, while spiritual enlightenment and reformation attend some but not all characters. Both plays pit love against hate, but the former prevails in

Shakespeare's "naughty world" (5.1.91), while the latter predominates in Marlowe's Machiavellian Malta. Hate crimes are actualized in Malta but attempted in Venice. What are some of the ways in which Marlowe cues Shakespeare's imagination so that he takes similar metal, such as a Jewish daughter, but recasts it for different dramatic mettle? What perspectives might such a comparison reveal about these plays in their contexts and for ours? For example, a striking difference between then and now can be glimpsed in the comparison between Lorenzo's marriage of Jessica and a Nazi's racially forbidden attraction to a beautiful Jewess in Steven Spielberg's modern Holocaust film, *Schindler's List* (1993). Unlike Lorenzo whose love crosses all putative barriers and places Jessica in his "constant soul" (2.6.58), Commandant Amon Goeth cannot bring himself to cross the supposed racial barrier. After the intoxicated Goeth stares longingly at his Jewish maid, Helen Hirsch, while simultaneously reciting Shylock's line on the bond of shared humanity ("Hath not a Jew eyes?" 3.1.46), he physically beats Helen, violence denying desire. How might we explain the possibility of marital love in Shakespeare's sixteenth-century play and its impossibility in Spielberg's twentieth-century film?

I

First of all, we should highlight the often underestimated *originality* of Marlowe and Shakespeare in creating for the stage essentially good contemporary Jewesses, women whose motive for eternal salvation outweighs their human frailty. Some critics, like Edgar Rosenburg, have claimed that the Early Modern English could not conceive of good contemporary Jews, that "the notion of a `good Jew' would have struck all these people as a fundamental absurdity" (456). However, a dramatic precedent for just such a Jew is set by Robert Wilson in *The Three Ladies of London* (1584), a half decade before Marlowe's play. Although the play is set in London, Wilson transports his audience to Turkey for his good Jew/ bad Christian trial scene. His Gerontus stuns typical Elizabethan expectations by being virtuous as a Jewish man and a moneylender. This practicing Jew does not convert to Christianity. Instead, he attempts to save a despicable Christian merchant from a feigned conversion intended as a trick to escape legal consequences for failure to repay a loan; therefore, Gerontus's morality is praised by the judge. In *The Jew of Malta* Barabas's feigned desire for conversion (4.1.48–112) may emulate the use of conversion as an escape from just legal consequences, as it is presented in Wilson's play, but Marlowe charts a new direction when he presents a Jewish *family* of villainous father and virtuous daughter, stimulating Shakespeare's own imitative innovations in *The Merchant of Venice*.[2] Moreover, Marlowe and Shakespeare add a focus on female gender as well as voluntary and genuine conversion of the beautiful Jewess. No matter how

Jewish Daughters					109

morally good these lovely Jewish women are on earth, post-Reformation audiences in sixteenth-century England would tend to believe that they could not be saved in heaven without a conversion of faith. Given the gradual advent of religious toleration and the decrease in wars of religion, an almost exact reversal in emphasis tends to prevail in the twentieth century: individual goodness is now held to outweigh religious allegiance. Marlowe's and Shakespeare's artistic choices are all the more noteworthy because nothing similar precedes them in extant English drama nor follows them in the subsequent century. In other words, Marlowe's example of the Jewish daughter is short-lived for the stage, expiring with his rival's emulation. Why does such a theoretically attractive motif for sixteenth and seventeenth century audiences exit so quickly from their drama's national scene? Were Marlowe and Shakespeare too original or too "progressive" for their general audiences? Or did other dramatists despair about improving on the masters? Or what?

Although James Shapiro in his wide-ranging *Shakespeare and the Jews* maintains that in fiction "the marriage and conversion of Jewish women usually go hand in hand," and "the exception that seems to prove the rule is Abigail" (132), one is tempted to ask, "What rule?" For example, in nineteenth-century English fiction, David Katz explains that despite Sir Walter Scott's attempt to make "Jews respectable in English literature," the beautiful Jewess Rebecca is denied intermarriage in *Ivanhoe* (1819) because, as Scott explains, " 'the prejudice of the age rendered such a union almost impossible' " (*Jews* 350).[3] Shapiro's assertion about Jewish women obfuscates the innovative dramatic practice of Marlowe and Shakespeare. In extant drama Marlowe appears to be original in introducing to the Elizabethan stage the very *alliance* of love between a chaste Jewess and her Christian suitor, but Shakespeare is equally original in celebrating the *marriage*, not the demise, of such a pair and incorporating that union into the greater variety of bonds his play dramatizes. Given the preoccupation of recent scholarship with the problem of "difference" and the categories of race, gender, and nation, Marlowe's and Shakespeare's individual scenarios of mutually desired marriage between Jew and Christian should capture our attention more than they have. Shapiro's extensive research instructively exposes the possibilities of racial thinking in Early Modern England (83–85), and thereby tempers G. K. Hunter's emphasis on prejudice against Jews as being solely religious in nature (215–16), although Elizabethan drama, in my view, reveals that religious bias is still the more crucial emphasis.

Despite Shapiro's work on the definitional instability of the Jews and the seemingly hopeless entanglement of racial, national, and religious identities, the lovers' goal of intermarriage, as figured forth in both Marlowe's and Shakespeare's plays, tends to downplay racial or somatic difference in order to prioritize the importance of all-conquering love, such as "soul to soul affordeth" (*Othello* 1.3.114). Such marriage might be seen as anti-racist because through it "the other" becomes "us." Intermarriage attempts to cross boundaries and to defy difference through the triumph of honorable human love that, for Elizabethans, should be modeled ideally on the example of divine love. The idea and the act of marriage itself signifies the paradoxical union of opposites (man and woman), and its engrafting mystery (two shall become one flesh) celebrates the conversion of two different entities into one new being. In medieval-Renaissance discourse the marriage metaphor has a venerable history, allegorically signifying a variety of social, political, and personal unions based on the spiritual model of Christ and the Church: as Christ is wedded to the Church, so should the husband be married to the wife, the ruler to the nation, and the spirit to the flesh. This marriage model of Christ and the Church would be well-known to Elizabethans since its articulation occurs prominently at the beginning as well as the end of the rite of matrimony in the Book of Common Prayer (1559):

> O God, which hast consecrated the state of matrimony to such an excellent mystery, that in it is signified and represented the spiritual marriage and unity betwixt Christ and his Church, look mercifully upon these thy servants, that both this man may love his wife, according to thy Word (as Christ did love thy spouse the Church, who gave himself for it, loving and cherishing it even as his own flesh), and also that this woman may be loving and amiable to her husband as Rachel, wise as Rebecca, faithful and obedient as Sarah, and in all quietness, sobriety, and peace be a follower of holy and godly matrons. O Lord, bless them both, and grant them to inherit thy everlasting kingdom; through Jesus Christ our Lord. Amen. (296–97; cf. 290)

Marriage might be seen as symbolizing the ideal union of love in terms of mutual assistance to eternal salvation.

In the Elizabethan era of widespread religious intolerance, Christian love of Jews and Judaism proves a complex affair. Since Christianity is supposed to be a religion of love—love of God and His human creations, or as Paul puts it, a religion in which faith ideally operates through love (Gal. 5.6)—Elizabethans should love the Jewish believer as a person created by God and capable of salvation. The question of belief as opposed to the believer, however, produces a divided position. Elizabethan Christians appreciate the true belief of ancient Judaism (the Hebrew Bible) which made possible the advent of their Messiah (hence the Old Testament is bound with the New in their Bible), but they reject as false the belief of contemporary Judaism which denies Christ and the New Testament. Solomon Rappaport observes that "the system and ideas leading to philo-Semitism, a notable tendency existing throughout the history of Gentile-Jewish relations, has attracted scant attention"; however, "one of the strongest motives in philo-

Semitic feeling is the consciousness of the Jewish origin and Jewish background of Jesus and the Apostles" (1, 99).

Although David Katz tends to mention only "the stock references from
Marlowe and Shakespeare to demonstrate . . . the demonic aspect of the
Jew," he stresses primarily scholarly and religious motives for the English
philo-Semitic movement, visible from at least the early part of the Jacobean
era, especially the growth of Hebrew and Old Testament studies and the
belief that the Jews would play a major role in English history, as in the
eschatological view of the millenarians supporting the conversion of the Jews
before the End of Days (*Philo-Semitism* 4, 6, 10, 244). Between Rappaport
and Katz we encounter what might be described as an alpha and omega tra-
jectory for Christian relations with Jews, in which Jews seem to be valued
primarily not for themselves but as a means to an end, whether at the beginning of Christian salvation history or at its end. Such philo-Semitic views can
well be seen as a disenfranchisement of the Jews, views that do not measure
up to our modern standards of religious toleration and equality. However,
given the developmental history of ideas, our standards for toleration,
whether religious, racial, national, or sexual, had not yet evolved for the general Elizabethan populace.[4] Therefore, we best approximate an understanding of this foreign time and culture insofar as we can discover some of their
ideas and values within specific contexts. One illuminating context for our
plays is the Bible.

Given the relative novelty of Jewish characters in Elizabethan drama,
Marlowe's use of biblical names, Barabas and Abigail, suggests a direction
which Shakespeare will develop further in his fuller and more complex incorporation of biblical allusion throughout his play. The English Bibles of the
sixteenth century cherish a view of the Jews as God's Chosen People from
whose flesh and faith comes Christ. A keen interest in the Old Testament and
the Hebrews is made abundantly clear, for example, in the prefatory matter to
the Bishops' and the Geneva Bibles. Marlowe names Barabas's daughter
"Abigail," which means "the father's joy," according to the Table of Names
appended to the Geneva Bible (sig. HHh.iii). Barabas says as much, and
much more, when he hugs his bags of gold retrieved for him by Abigail: "O
girl, O gold, O beauty, O my bliss! / . . . Farewell, *my joy*, and by my fingers
take / A kiss from him that sends it from his soul" (2.1.54, 59–60, my italics).
Many in a biblically astute Elizabethan audience would also know that the
name "Abigail" could refer to two different women in the Old Testament.
Both, however, were linked to David and the Messianic line; the chapter
headings as well as glosses in the Geneva Bible emphasize this genealogy.
One is the beautiful, wise, and godly wife who saves her foolish husband
Nabal and later marries David, bearing him a son named Daniel or Chileab (1
Sam. 25.2–42, esp. 39 gloss; 2 Sam. 3.3; 1 Chron. 3.1 and gloss). She resem-
bles Marlowe's Abigail in beauty, in her wise aversion to bloodshed, and in

godliness (once Abigail converts from doing the will of her earthly father to that of her Heavenly Father); however, her role as a precious wife contrasts with the tragic loss of such fulfillment for the Marlovian Abigail who loses her beloved and dies a virgin. The other Abigail is the daughter of Jesse and therefore David's sister; she is biblically introduced in terms of the genealogy of Judah through Jesse, the father of David, and from whose root comes Christ, the Messiah promised to Abraham and his stock, according to Christian theology (1 Sam. 16.11–13; Matt. 1, 5; Luke 3.32).

Marlowe and Shakespeare play on the etymological significance of names, but Shakespeare develops more the genealogical significance. Marlowe's Abigail and Shakespeare's Jessica, both of whom willingly convert to Christianity, interestingly share an allusion to Jesse's and David's Messianic line in their biblically derived names. The most likely explanation, thus far, of how Shakespeare apparently created the name Jessica is that Jessica is a feminization of Jesse, a very familiar biblical name with associations that are meaningful for the Judaeo-Christian lineage of the Church of God mentioned repeatedly in the Geneva Bible's glosses and illustrated prominently in the Bishops' Bible.[5] Shylock's wife's name is Leah, not Rachel, although his favorite patriarch with whom he seeks to identify is Jacob, and Jacob's preferred wife was Rachel. But it is from the genealogical line of Leah and Jacob that Jesse comes. Isaiah's well-known prophecy about the "root of Ishai [Jesse]" (11.1; 11.10) is explained by Paul as Christ who reigns over the Gentiles as their salvific hope, and the striking gloss on that passage further demonstrates why these Jewish daughters are so aptly named:

> Then seing [Christ] toke bothe the Iewes and Gentiles to his Fathers glorie,
> they oght by his example to loue together (Rom. 15.12).[6]

Jessica, a Venetian Jewess, and Lorenzo, a Venetian Christian, do just that—love together. And so would Marlowe's Abigail and Don Mathias were it not for Barabas's physically based discrimination against all Christians as "heretics" (2.3.313) because he claims they are misbegotten or "not of the seed of Abraham" (2.3.232). Although Barabas's ancestral indictment aptly applies to Gentiles, the irony of his birthright bias would not be lost on an Elizabethan audience fully aware that many of the first Christians as well as their leader were indeed Jews of Abraham's seed, as is Barabas's own daughter Abigail who, despite her later Christian conversion, should not be judged a "heretic" by her father given his own flesh-based conception of faith. Is it merely coincidence that Abigail's beloved is named "Mathias," a name glossed in the Geneva Bible as meaning "a gift of the Lord" (sig. IIi.i)? The adults in this play do not set a good example, because they are less love-oriented than their children. Katherine as the Christian mother of Don Mathias is also prejudiced, but her bias is more spiritually articulated: "Con-

Figure 5. Peter Paul Rubens, *The Meeting of David and Abigail* (ca. 1660). Bequest of Lore Heinemann in memory of her husband, Dr. Rudolf J. Heinemann. Photograph © 2001, Board of Trustees, National Gallery of Art, Washington, D.C.

verse not with him [Barabas]; he is cast off from heaven" (2.3.156). Barabas's own description of his "one sole daughter, whom [he] hold[s] as dear / As Agamemnon did his Iphigen" (1.1.136–37) is a "dear" description indeed because he will "*sacrifice her on a pile of wood*" before he will let a Christian have her (2.3.53).[7] Shakespeare's decision to use the "root" name of "Jesse" for his Jessica may also owe something to the idea of "sacrifice" or "oblation" that Marlowe develops for his Abigail. The Geneva Bible glosses the name "Jesse" (frequently spelled "Ishai") as meaning "a gift or oblation"; Robert F. Herrey's concordance for the Geneva Bible elaborates: "*a gift or an oblation*, or a *debitour*, or *being*," and also explains Jesse's importance— "Christ promised to come of his stock. Isa.11.1."[8] Elizabethans might also contextualize the idea of giving in religious terms, believing that God's ulti-mate gift is His Son who became the oblation to appease justice and grant mercy in the potential salvation of the entire human race. Unlike Abigail's first action of sympathetic tears for her father's loss of money, Jessica's first action is one of giving money to servant Lancelot, thereby linking her to the idea of love as giving that is associated with the leaden casket choice: "There is a ducat for thee" (2.3.4). This action contrasts with the "manners" (2.3.18), meaning "morals" or "character," of her father who dislikes giving in general and to Lancelot in particular. Lancelot claims he is "famished" in Shylock's service, and therefore suggests Shylock not be given his father's intended gift of food, a dish of doves, but instead, as the "merry devil" (2.3.2) he is, Lancelot professes an un-Christian spirit by suggesting a more appropriate "present": "Give him a halter!" (2.2.86–89).

Why do Marlowe and Shakespeare opt for Jewish daughters instead of sons, given the dominance of male Jewish characters in medieval-Renaissance literature? Why women? Possible reasons abound, and doubtless more will be forthcoming with the escalation of gender studies. Aside from "humanizing" Barabas and Shylock as family men with children, dramatic interest is enhanced through the contrasting genders of father and daughter, while also serving the practical purpose of giving boys in the company female parts to play. Since beauty is typically associated with women, and beauty in the eye of the beholder inspires love, attractive women seem logical choices for gen-erating romance plots. Perhaps correspondence between inner and outer com-plexion is another reason for the acclaimed beauty of Abigail and Jessica. But the women in the plays could just as easily have been pretty daughters of Christians who attracted the sons of Jewish fathers. John Gross offers a help-ful theory when he observes that the Christian binding of the Old Testament with the New came about through the birth of Christ to a Jewish mother who, from a Christian viewpoint, "was both Jewish and profoundly non-Jewish," and he queries: "What more natural than to think of the salvageable, redeemable part of Judaism as being embodied in a woman rather than a man?" (71). But countering this thought, we must remember that Christ was also Jewish and non-Jewish, and "the redeemable part of Judaism" in English drama prior to Marlowe's and Shakespeare's plays includes males who freely convert after witnessing miracles, such as Jonathas and his four fellow Jews in the late-fifteenth-century play, the Croxton *Play of the Sacrament*.[9] Another obvious explanation might be that women have been described in the New Testament as "the weaker vessels" (1 Pet. 3.7). They, therefore, could be seen as most in need of conversion, either easier conquests because less physically strong to resist, or more desperate conquests because supposedly less spiritually virtuous than men. However, Abigail and Jessica demonstrate a surprising degree of courageous agency and spiritual insight in their rebellions against their fathers, so that we might conclude with Robert Greene's *Mamillia* (1583): "They say, a woman is the weaker vessel, but sure in my iudgement, it is in the strength of her body, and not the force of her minde" (95).

I suggest one possible reason for the use of Jewish daughters, who love Christian gentlemen and who ultimately convert, concerns the thematically significant wordplay both Marlowe and Shakespeare deploy with the "gentle/gentile" pun, a pun that interestingly does not appear in Wilson's earlier play lacking a woman in its Jew/Christian conflict. Precisely when women become identified as "the gentle sex," and not simply "the weaker sex," is unclear. In the *Oxford English Dictionary* 1583 is the date of the first citation demonstrating the use of this phrase to describe women as mild, kind, or tender ("Gentle," a. and sb., 8). Women as "the gentle sex" embody well one defining idea of Christianity that is not readily related to the male sex. Christians are supposed to imitate the example of gentleness set by the Sacrificial Lamb. This particular conception of women as "gentle" renders all the more monstrous, therefore, ancient ballads like "The Jew's Daughter" in which a Jewish daughter, and not a conspiracy of Jewish men, is represented as the vicious murderer in a later medieval adaptation of the alleged ritual murder of Hugh of Lincoln (1255), a story recounted by Chaucer's Prioress in *The Canterbury Tales*.[10] If members of the Elizabethan audiences were familiar with this ballad or its variants, Marlowe's and Shakespeare's choice of a gentle Jewess would seem all the more radical.

"Gentle" also signifies a range of good meanings, referring to persons of good character as well as of good birth (*OED* 2; 3). As persons of basically good character, both "gentle Abigail" (2.3.317) and "gentle Jessica" (2.4.19) possess generous and loving natures, and unlike their suitors who appear socially to be of good breeding as gentle folk, these daughters of a Jewish merchant and a Jewish usurer are not gentlewomen by class but can claim, from a theological perspective, ancient good breeding because they derive from the stock of God's Chosen People, the Jews, who made possible the birth of Christ and the salvation of the Gentiles, or non-Jews. Salo W. Baron suggests that for the English "Shakespeare's *Merchant* may indeed have proposed a solution for the alien problem in Shylock's ultimate conversion to Christianity and Jessica's marriage to Lorenzo; in other words, in the speedy absorption of alien groups by the native majority"; he also postulates that this sentiment may account for why "Shakespeare and Marlowe present very attractive Jewesses" (15:135). Marlowe's Abigail, like Shakespeare's Jessica, converts deliberately, but unlike Jessica, she does not get absorbed by marriage, rather only by conversion.

Shapiro argues that gender affects conversion so that Jewish women are favored over Jewish men, whether in fiction or life: "To early modern Englishmen, the fantasy of Christian men marrying converting Jewesses was far more appealing than the idea of Jewish men, even converted ones, marrying Christian women," or "Jewish men who convert to Christianity are never married off to Christian women" (132). For fiction, these statements seem apropos, but for history, the Portuguese Marrano community in London provides contradictory evidence because Gomes Davila, a member of this community who was observed celebrating Passover in 1605, married an Englishwoman (Shapiro 72). For the same period, the reversed alliance of Jewish wife/Christian husband receives no historical documentation. Shapiro also contends that the absence of the sign of fleshly circumcision "helps explain why Jewish daughters like Jessica . . . and Abigail . . . can so easily cross the religious boundaries that divide their stigmatized fathers from the dominant community" (120). But this sign is not publicly visible, and if such a theory is true, how do we explain the historical Gomes Davila or the fictional Gerontus who "excell[s] in Christianitie" (Wilson 39)? Quite contrary to Shapiro's notion, in Marlowe's play it is the Jew who bonds with a Turk in their shared fleshly circumcision and who ridicules Christians for not being so circumcised (2.3.8, 217); on the other hand, Christians in Marlowe's and Shakespeare's plays do not criticize Jews for their circumcision.

The emphasis on "physical stigmatization" may be more representative of a twentieth-century perspective than the greater emphasis on spiritual difference which may be more characteristic of Early Modern England. For example, in his ballad "The Forfeiture, A Romance" (1664), Thomas Jordan plagiarizes and adapts Shakespeare's play, deleting all personal names while giving to the Jewish daughter Portia's role as sole/soul heroine. Revealing religious bias, he makes this choice not because the daughter lacks any physical stigma but because she has "a Christian soul / Lodg'd in a Jewish body" (462), long before she is actually baptized, an event that occurs only after she defeats her father in court, weds the beloved merchant she saves, and receives her father's forfeited estate. Jordan declares any one who calls this Jewish lady "foul" has to be "a purblinde noddy" because she is "so sweet a virgin," "wise," and a "true heart" (462). He hopes, however, the likes of her Jewish father may never come to England, not because he is fleshly circumcised but because he attempted "slaughter" (463).[11] Recent scholarship, such as Shapiro's exhaustive work,[12] has helped us better understand the roots of racial and national thinking regarding perceived Jewish and Christian identities, but the emphasis on critical difference pertains primarily to the individual's spirit in Marlowe's and Shakespeare's plays.

Like Shapiro's overstatement of fleshly circumcision as the chief stigma for Jewish men in Christian nations that alienates them more than physically unmarked Jewish women, his influential argument about "the presence of circumcision in *The Merchant of Venice* and its sources" (114) appears unwittingly erroneous, despite the wealth of information he provides regarding this subject (113–30). Shapiro argues "an occluded threat of circumcision informs Shylock's desire to cut a pound of Antonio's flesh" (114). But "what Shylock had in mind for [Antonio]" (130) was never circumcision or castration, either or both of which could have left Antonio alive. On the very day the bond was written, signed, and notarized, Shylock stipulated that he wanted to cut a pound of flesh nearest Antonio's heart. From the start, then, Shylock's knockout punch for Antonio has been directed above, not below, the belt. Thus, Shylock attempts not so much a ritual murder as paradoxically a "lawful murder" with no legal risk (or so he thinks) to himself. However, the audience, as opposed to Shylock, does not know for certain the intended location of Shylock's incision until the trial scene when the precise wording of the bond is announced, although Shakespeare does provide clues that Shylock "will have the heart" of Antonio (3.1.100–102), and that Antonio eventually discovers his life is at stake (3.3.21). For the language of "having one's heart" as a death threat, Shakespeare may be indebted to Marlowe's play (2.3.16; 2.3.346).[13] However, Shapiro (126) rightly alerts us to the possibility that some audience members might have feared castration, especially because Silvayn's *The Orator*, one of Shakespeare's sources, suggests castration as one option among others for obtaining a pound of flesh that does not result in death.[14] But this purpose, unlike Shylock's motive, is life-oriented: the victim must choose the location for the loss of flesh in order to live, albeit maimed. Thus, Shapiro confuses one posssible and legitimate *audience* expectation (castration) with the *antagonist's* very different expectation (lethal heart surgery). This source, moreover, does not introduce the idea of circumcision; Shapiro does.[15] Although Shakespeare's play does not include allusions to literal circumcision, as Marlowe's does, Shakespeare does add a specifically Hebraic moment for Jessica that Marlowe lacks for Abigail. Jessica's embarrassment, so unlike Portia's eagerness (3.4.60–78), regarding transvestite attire reflects her apologetic awareness of how her disguise as a male violates Judaic precept (Deut. 22.5).[16] Although conscious of lovers' "pretty follies"

(2.6.38), Jessica compounds her transgression by becoming also a torch-bearer at Lorenzo's request, thus holding "a candle to [her] shames" (2.6.42), with her inner rebellion against her father signified by the outer rebellion of her apparel.

II

Conversion complicates both plays. Marlowe's quadruple use of literal conversion to Christianity—whether refused, as in Barabas's defiance (1.2.83), or feigned, as in Abigail's first conversion (1.2.279–95) and Barabas's dissembling (4.1.48–112), or genuine, as in Abigail's second conversion (3.3.59–64)—challenges Shakespeare to develop his own double use of this motif in Jessica's voluntary act and her father's constrained commitment. However, there is a notable difference between Marlowe's and Shakespeare's use of the conversion trope for the heroine.[17] Unlike Jessica, who apparently only the audience knows for certain intends to convert to Christianity through her marriage to Lorenzo, Abigail's love for Don Mathias does not include any mention of a desire to convert. Not until it is tragically too late for these lovers does Abigail realize her father's perfidy and how he has sacrificed her in obtaining his "extreme revenge" (3.3.45); only then does Abigail choose to convert. Unlike her biblical namesake who wisely interprets the meaning of her husband's name (Nabal means "fool," 1 Sam. 25.3) in time to prevent bloodshed, Abigail implicitly discovers the hard way that her father's name means "son of confusion" (Matt. 27.16). From Barabas's perspective, however, Abigail's fake conversion to retrieve her father's gold makes her his "joy." As a false nun but a true daughter, Abigail "steals" back for her father his hidden wealth, which he justly earned through the mercantile adventures celebrated in his opening soliloquy (1.1.1–45). The rest of his accessible wealth is "stolen" by the hypocritical Maltese Christians to pay the Turkish tribute. Unlike Shakespeare's play in which the Venetian court conditionally returns at least half of Shylock's wealth (4.1.364–86), none of Barabas's wealth is returned to him even though the gold is never used for its originally stipulated purpose.[18] Stealing *for* and not *from* her father, Abigail tosses down moneybags to him (not to her Christian beloved), and her vigil at the window is probably parodied and changed in Shakespeare's scene of Jessica's elopement (2.6). Perhaps less obvious is Shakespeare's possible reworking of Abigail's happy wish for her father to have "a golden dream" (2.1.37) as Shylock's unhappy "dream of money-bags" (2.5.17–18). Abigail genuinely loves her father, and he, like many Renaissance patriarchs, loves her *if* she doesn't cross him. Their opening scene together appears tenderly touching as each sympathizes with the grief of the other. Barabas pleads: "But whither wends my beauteous Abigail? / O what has made my lovely daughter sad?"

(1.2.226–27). Abigail explains: "Not for myself, but agèd Barabas, / Father, for thee lamenteth Abigail" (1.2.230–31). Their shared language of mutual affection is markedly different from the almost master-servant discourse Shakespeare writes for his Jewish father and daughter in their only scene together (2.5), staged mostly in the presence of the servant figure, Lancelot.

Unlike the unruly Jessica, the obedient Abigail denies her heart in order to fulfill her father's command that she dissemble love for Lodowick: "*I cannot choose, seeing my father bids*" (2.3.318). Marlowe's brilliant wordplay on Barabas's diamond as both a tangible gem and a figurative gem, namely his daughter Abigail (2.3.49–94, 138–40, 221–23, 294), reminds us that not only is the daughter her father's property, but also she is his true wealth if he treasures her wisely. Shakespeare adopts this same motif for Portia and Jessica. Before Barabas turns against Abigail, he proclaims in soliloquy that all his wealth is hers—"And all I have is hers" (1.1.138)—and during his lethal deception of Lodowick, Barabas claims that Lodowick would "disdain / To marry with the daughter of a Jew" (2.3.296–97), so he feigns that he will financially compensate him, even make Lodowick his "heir" (2.3.330). Lodowick, however, asserts, "'Tis not thy wealth, but her that I esteem" (2.3.300), suggesting he does appreciate Abigail herself. In an aside responding to Lodowick's claim, Barabas rejects him because he hates Christians (2.3.212), identifying Lodowick as "*this offspring of Cain, this Jebusite, / That never tasted of the Passover,*" one who shall never "*see the land of Canaan, / Nor our Messias that is yet to come*" (2.3.303–306). Lodowick as the son of Governor Ferneze, Barabas's "chiefest enemy" (2.3.252) in being the thief of his diamonds (2.3.50), becomes a self-destructive tool in Barabas's plan to destroy Abigail's Christian beloved. Ignorant about her father's policy but alarmed at the animosity sparked between these two young men, Abigail vows to make them "friends again" (2.3.359). She also insists, "I will have Don Mathias; he is my love" (2.3.363). Barabas lies and says she shall, while commanding his Turkish slave Ithamore "to put her in" the house (2.3.364), forcibly preventing her from marring his stratagem.

After the "trusty Turk" (4.1.129) Ithamore reveals that Barabas villainously murdered Abigail's beloved, who "*ne'er offended*" Barabas (3.3.44, my italics), Abigail leaves her "hard-hearted, unkind" father (3.3.39) to convert sincerely to Christianity and become a true nun in her father's former "mansion," confiscated by Ferneze and "convert[ed]" to a nunnery (1.2.130). Abigail, now fully aware how her "favor" was the bait used in deadly "policy" (3.3.37–39), sees the murder of her beloved as a figurative murder of herself through heartbreak (3.3.46). With youthful hyperbole, she generalizes on the basis of her closest exemplars—Barabas and Ithamore—to conclude that "there is no love on earth, / Pity in Jews, nor piety in Turks" (3.3.49–51). Despite Abigail's earlier demonstrations of devoted loyalty to him, Barabas now claims she has "lost" him (3.4.20). He views her conversion as "false

and unkind," suspects her request that he repent, and concludes that her vari-
ance from him "in belief" suggests she either does not love him, or if she
does, she dislikes something he has done (3.4.2–12). No longer perceiving
Abigail as his joy, he kills her, as well as the entire convent of nuns, through
a pot of poisoned porridge sent ironically as an alms gift to the nunnery.
Barabas's spiritual tragedy is underscored with the replacement of Abigail by
Ithamore (whose name means "woe to the change") whom Barabas embraces
as his "trusty servant, nay, [his] second self," as "no servant, but [his] friend,"
and as his adopted "heir" (3.4.15, 39)—or so Barabas feigns (3.4.51–52)—
only to discover later that Ithamore, unlike Abigail, is as greedily treacherous
as himself.

Although Abigail is the only morally admirable character in Marlowe's
play, the only one, as N. W. Bawcutt notes, who enacts "genuine and disinterested love" (28), Marlowe makes her learn through tragic experience that
her father is not to be trusted, that he puts his own interests first (1.1.188).
Although Abigail is also cognizant of the discrepancy between what some
Christians in Malta do and what their faith prescribes for them to do, she uses
powerful language to correct the pretense of her earlier feigned conversion:

> Then were my thoughts so frail and unconfirmed
> And I was chained to follies of the world,
> But now experience, purchasèd with grief,
> Has made me *see the difference of things.*
> My sinful soul, alas, hath paced too long
> The fatal labyrinth of misbelief,
> Far from the Son that gives eternal life. (3.3.62–68, my italics)

Her conversion is so genuine that as she dies (a death the audience
knows is her father's doing, as she does not), she begs Friar Bernardine, after
her own confession of sin, "Convert my father that he may be saved, / And
witness that I die a Christian" (3.6.39–40). Through Friar Bernardine's crass
rejoinder, "Ay, and a virgin, too, that grieves me most" (3.3.41), Marlowe
continues his savage satire on human vice, whether of Christian, Turk, or
Jew. As N. W. Bawcutt argues, "What subtlety there is in the play does not
come from patient introspection and self-discovery but from ironic clashes
and juxtapositions"; therefore, the "complex response" generated by "the
brutality" of the friar's reply does not "merely make Abigail ridiculous, but
intensifies the pathos and difficulty of her attempt to live decently" (35).
Although Christians may be foul in practice, the faith itself is not condemned
in the play. Whatever may have been Marlowe's personal beliefs, his play,
not surprisingly given Elizabethan censorship and the dominant Christian
culture, upholds Christian faith, not necessarily practice, as the path to eternal life. Given the Reformation's emphasis on salvation by faith, it is not

coincidental that both Abigail and Jessica emphasize the idea of salvation through conversion to Christian faith.

Abigail's genuine request midpoint in the play provides a stark contrast to the opening "Christian" command for conversion that precipitates the course of tragic consequences. These corrupt Christians in power disregard the spiritual status of the Jews and value only their financial status, hypocritically demanding that each Jew pay half his wealth to satisfy the overdue Turkish tribute, or "straight become a Christian" (1.2.73). Abigail's conversion request for Barabas is as well-intentioned as it is extraordinary, and it probably influences Shakespeare's addition of the conversion stipulation for Shylock (not found in his literary sources), which he adapts to suit his play. He transfers the request from the Jewish daughter/Christian convert to the Jew's most hated Christian enemy, Antonio, while also amending for the Duke the line on differential insight regarding "things" to seeing "the difference of our spirit" (4.1.364). When Abigail sought true conversion but was suspected of apostasy (3.4.70–71), she was careful to keep her father's criminal secret after her admission that her former feigned conversion was her "father's fault" (3.4.75); she explains in an aside to the audience her mercy, despite her father's deserts: "*O, Barabas, / Though thou deservest hardly at my hands, / Yet never shall these lips bewray thy life*" (3.4.76–78).

Now converted to "see the difference of things," Abigail no longer adopts her father's ethos of worldliness or revenge as she formerly did, for example, "Father, whate'er it be to injure them / That have so manifestly wrongèd us, / What will not Abigail attempt?" (1.2.274–76). Despite having a motive for personal revenge—her father's ill use of her to accomplish the murder of her beloved—Abigail does not seek to repay death with death but rather generously protects her father's physical life from the penalty of civil law. When she knows she is dying, only then does she confess her involvement in her father's murderous policy: "To work my peace, this I confess to thee; / Reveal it not, for then my father dies" (3.6.31–32). Abigail knows the death penalty for a priest's violation of the secrecy of confession, and the friar verbally affirms this to her, although he willfully violates it after her death (3.6.33–37), once again demonstrating the difference between theory and practice. Abigail can not reasonably expect that Barabas would desire conversion to Christianity. Yet she begs his conversion so that he might be spiritually saved, complementing her concern for his physical life with the greater concern for his eternal life. Although her father has proven himself a malefactor to her, she tries to be his benefactor. Contrary to Barabas's earth-bound view as the son of confusion, from an Elizabethan perspective Abigail becomes the incarnation of her name as "the f[F]ather's joy."

Unlike the tragic ending for Abigail, Jessica (like Portia and Nerissa) achieves a comedic resolution—marriage to the man she loves. Like Portia, she is "curbed" (1.2.21) by her father's will, but unlike Portia, Jessica becomes the mastermind of her own marriage plans, partly because her father has overlooked such provision for her. Like Abigail, she, not her father, is in control of their parting. Shakespeare, however, rewrites Barabas's fatal line, namely that Abigail has "lost" him, for Jessica's comically controlled anticipated escape: "I have a father, you a daughter, lost" (2.5.55). Jessica thrives, whereas Abigail dies, not solely because Shakespeare's play is primarily a romantic comedy and Marlowe's is chiefly a farcical tragedy, but also because Shakespeare departs from Marlowe's influence by investing his character with a discerning wisdom about her father that her prototype lacks until it is too late. The proverb, "It is a wise child that knows its own father," applies literally and spiritually to Jessica, and given Lancelot's comic reversal of this proverb (2.2.63), we are invited to compare the play's three parent-child relationships in terms of how wisely one knows the other.[19] In the description of Jessica as "wise, fair, and true" (2.6.57) Shakespeare significantly substitutes "wise" for the word "kind" that appears in the conventional phrasing—"fair, kind, and true."[20] Jessica proves herself wise in motivation and execution of her successful flight, but she also is unkind in her departure. Like Abigail, she may be seen as "unnatural" in rebelling against her father, but unlike Abigail, she writes no letter of compassionate explanation, and she also steals some of her father's wealth. Shakespeare follows Marlowe in palliating the "unnatural" course of the daughter's rebellion by establishing the father as provocatively unnatural in his treatment of his daughter. Jessica, seconded by Lancelot, finds her house a hellish existence (2.3.2), whereas Abigail, after being used as a pawn, is figuratively and then literally killed by her father. Both Marlowe and Shakespeare also elevate the daughter's motivation for escape to emphasize the desire for *spiritual salvation*. However, Shakespeare complicates Marlowe's thievery motif, integrating it more sophisticatedly within his dramatic interplay of money and love, living and life, and justice and mercy.

Abigail eventually realizes what the wiser Jessica already knows when she first enters the play, namely that spiritual morals should have a higher value in human relationships than physical "blood" (2.3.17–18). However, Jessica is not insensitive but tormented by inner strife in her conflict over filial duty: "Alack, what heinous sin is it in me / To be ashamed to be my father's child!" (2.3.15–16). It deeply disturbs her to be ashamed of her father's character when she owes her life to him. Regarding Shylock, she experiences a conflict of conscience on a much more serious level than Lancelot's in his self-debate whether to leave or stay (2.2.1–23). But Lorenzo's "promise" to Jessica (2.3.19), which he does faithfully keep, enables her to transfer her allegiance to a husband whose morality of love she is happy to adopt; he proclaims, "Beshrew me but I love her heartily" (2.6.53) and vows to place her in his "constant soul" (2.6.58). The higher value of the spirit permits Jessica and Lorenzo to transcend through inter-

Figure 6. Sir Samuel Luke Fildes, *Jessica,* from *The Graphic Gallery of Shakespeare's Heroines* (1896). By Permission of the Folger Shakespeare Library.

marriage the boundaries of flesh (tribe and nation), whereas Shylock would insist on those boundaries, preferring for Jessica's husband a native son ("any of the stock of Barabbas," 4.1.292) over a loving alien like Lorenzo. So also would Barabas who reprimands Abigail: "Are there not Jews enow in Malta, / But thou must dote upon a Christian?" (2.3.361–62).

Shylock gives no indication of being interested in finding Jessica a husband, let alone a worthy husband. Unlike the deceased Lord of Belmont who was attuned to his child's needs and wisely knew her well enough to devise a test of ensuring true and mutual love, old Shylock resembles more the half-blind, old Gobbo whose recognition of his "own flesh and blood" (2.2.76) depends on physical or nominal identification (2.2.75–78). If Jessica was "fledged," as Solanio asserts (3.1.24), Shylock neglects what Elizabethans perceived as his patriarchal duty, namely to find a suitable husband, as Portia's father does for her.[21] Unlike Portia's "virtuous" father (1.2.23), who locks up a picture of his daughter in a casket so that he can give her away to the man with the right key who unlocks their future, Shylock hoards his daughter herself in his house, under lock and key, as the keeper of his earthly treasure: "There are my keys . . . / Fast bind, fast find" (2.6.52).[22] Small wonder that Jessica finds the generous Portia "a blessing" who has no match in "the poor rude world" (3.5.63–71). The friendly chorus of mutual good wishes—"all heart's content"—when Portia graciously entrusts Belmont to "[Lorenzo] and Jessica / In place of Lord Bassanio and [herself]" (3.4.37–44) contrasts sharply with Jessica's last similar opportunity, Shylock's command to lock herself up in his house. The image of Jessica as incarcerated in her rich father's house anticipates her father's distraught wish, once she disappoints him, that he have her hearsed at his foot with his ducats in her coffin (3.1.70–71).

Unlike Barabas before he converts to hating Abigail, Shylock appears to treat Jessica less as daughter and more as servant. Such a relationship imitates the depiction of a young heroine as her miserly father's "hireling" (1: 504) in Masuccio Salernitano's fifteenth-century *Il Novellino*, the likely Italian source for some aspects of the Jessica-Lorenzo plot. Unlike Barabas's initially kind words to Abigail, Shylock uses many more imperatives in his dialogue with Jessica: "Do as I bid you" (2.6.51). There is no gentle calling for his daughter ("What, Jessica!"), and when he does speak to her his language is abrupt, commanding, devoid of tender expression, except for the possible intonation of "Jessica my girl," which tends to be undercut by his subsequent order, "Look to my house" (2.5.15–16). In his only domestic scene with his daughter, Shylock the patriarch shows how little he shares with Jessica, because there is no room in his vocabulary for "our": "my keys," "my girl," "my doors," "my house's ears," "my casements," and "my sober house" (2.5.12–35). When Barabas's wealth is stolen, he tries to comfort Abigail, "Thy father has enough in store for thee" (1.2.229). If Shylock loves Jessica more than his material wealth, he does not seem to have communicated that to her. Shylock's later agonized confusion of his daughter and his ducats parodies the idea, but not the tone, of Barabas's joyful equation of his girl and his gold (J. R. Brown 2.8.15n.), and as Mahood notes, Shylock resembles the miserly father in Masuccio's story: " 'for the last-named loss [his money and jewels] he felt no less grief than for the first [his daughter]' " (2.8.15n.). Shylock may lament even more the loss of his ducats, given his "coffin" metaphor and his regret over having to spend so much money to find Jessica (3.1.70–74). Jessica flies far enough to escape her father's reach, as Abigail does not, but it is to Shylock's credit that he, unlike Barabas, does not even attempt to enact his deathwish for his daughter (Tubal is sent to search for Jessica, not to poison her).

Particularly for a modern audience, Jessica's departure from her house of "hell" (2.3.2) is not so disturbing as the manner of her departure—her deceptive elopement and her stealing from her father's treasure two sealed bags of ducats and two precious stones. For this, some would agree with Shylock's interpretation: "She is damned for it" (3.1.26). However, such a view does not take into account the self-imposed limits on the amount taken, the probable purpose of the theft, and the fact that in the process of gilding herself with more ducats, Jessica is careful to preserve her father's estate for him, making "fast the doors" (2.6.50), or locking up to prevent further theft. Some literary and historical perspectives help us put the nature of Jessica's unkind flight in a broader Elizabethan context of rough justice rendered to the unkind father, who is both usurer and miser. Similar imagery of theft bonds the family of Shylock, Jessica, and Lorenzo. Even Lancelot is so described: "thou a merry devil / Didst *rob* [Shylock's house] of some taste of tediousness" (2.3.2–3, my italics). For conservative Elizabethans, usury is seen as theft, not "thrift" (1.3.82), and, therefore, the usurer is commonly seen as a thief in taking "excess" on a loan. This "excess" is believed to violate friendship or brotherly love, commutative justice, and natural process.[23] The development of the idea of usury constitutes Shakespeare's significant addition to Ser Giovanni's *Il Pecorone*, his main source for the flesh-bond story. Shakespeare also contemporizes the old medieval legend for his Elizabethan audience by incorporating some of the most recent ideas debated on this important but vexed issue. However, for modern audiences, Shakespeare's use of usury remains the play's most underestimated and least understood element, often resulting in the erroneous assumption that Antonio hates Shylock simply for who he is (a Jew), and not primarily for what he does, cruel usury that makes his victims "moan" (3.3.23) so piteously that Antonio rescues them with his own money.

Jessica's theft turns the tables: the usurer now has the theft done unto him that he has done unto others. Enacting the Elizabethan comic trait of turnabout as fair play, Jessica steals some of her father's wealth as a self-appointed dowry, imitating the stolen "dowry" (1: 503) of Masuccio's heroine, and Lorenzo plays the thief in order to get his wife (2.6.24). Although

Jessica earlier distinguishes herself from her father's manners, she seems to emulate them here. However, Shylock's usurious thievery for self-love's gain contrasts motivationally with Jessica's and Lorenzo's thefts for love of another; their liberal natures counterpoint Shylock's parsimony: "In such a night / Did Jessica steal from the wealthy Jew, / And with an unthrift love did run from Venice / As far as Belmont" (5.1.14–17). Shakespeare reinscribes Marlowe's motif of stolen Jewish wealth, linking it to his added emphasis on usury, his concern with how wealth is obtained, used, and viewed, and his comedic resolution of romantic marriage for true lovers who hazard for each other.[24] Elopement, as a stock convention in romantic comedy, necessarily involves the theft of a father's property in stealing his daughter. For example, Masuccio, in an appended note, predicts his readers will praise his heroine's "sagacity" because she managed to escape her "wretched plight" and "to obtain out of the hoard of her miserly old father a greater sum of money than would have been given to her as a dower"; he asserts that the vices of the father are "the real causes of the flout that was put upon him" (1:504–505).[25] But does Lorenzo "steal" Jessica for her "stolen wealth" as some productions sinisterly suggest by portraying Lorenzo as obsessed with the "casket . . . worth the pains" (2.6.34) that she tosses to him? Probably not, because Lorenzo doesn't lead Jessica into a fool's paradise. He never attempts to abscond with the money, nor does he desert Jessica after she spends much of it enroute to Belmont; in his final lines, Lorenzo admits that together they are greatly in need of wealth (5.1.294–95).

What most disturbs modern audiences is Jessica's handling of her father's turquoise ring. She takes two stones, a diamond and a turquoise. In addition to the Elizabethan association of diamonds with what is heavenly,[26] Shakespeare is probably influenced by Marlowe's figurative use of the diamond as the recurrent metaphor for Abigail in his similar distinction between literal and figurative wealth. Unlike Shylock's reaction to the loss of his Frankfurt diamond, his reaction to the turquoise ring hints of nobler possibilities in his character: he values the turquoise not for its price but for its meaning as his betrothal ring from Leah. In Marlowe's play Abigail remains a motherless maid, and Barabas receives no similar spousal line of affection but rather mentions only his past "fornication" (4.1.40–42). But Shakespeare "fleshes out" his Jewish family by including a significant name for its wife and mother that clarifies his use of biblical allusions for this Jewish family in which desired and undesired conversions occur. Although the audience knows the personal significance of this ring, Jessica probably does not. It seems likely that Jessica would not know the history of this ring, not only because Shylock shares so little with her, but especially because her father no longer wears the ring, suggesting to the uninitiated that it has no more particular value than his other jewels. Whatever may be Shylock's reasons for no longer wearing this ring, he nonetheless stashes it among his other precious stones from which Jessica helps herself on the eve of her elopement. And Jessica has to steal quickly because Shylock's parting words threatened that he might change his mind and "return immediately" (2.5.50).

A costly diamond seems an obvious choice, but why a turquoise? The turquoise, derived chiefly from Persia and Turkestan, has no particular Hebraic associations and does not appear in the Bible; however, it is one of the precious stones English gentlewomen want to have imported.[27] Jessica might take this stone for its well-known quality to monitor and preserve the well-being of its wearer.[28] Once safe in Genoa where she has escaped Shylock's reach, she may feel she no longer needs such a talisman for personal protection. She parts with the turquoise of earthly significance but apparently keeps the diamond of heavenly significance. Perhaps in the joyous relief of physical safety, she rids herself of lapidary superstition by selling the turquoise for a monkey, an inanimate stone for an animate pet. Monkeys were popular pets, kept for the laughter they provoked by their mimicry and giddy behavior, and a monkey could be seen as an animal version of the human fool that noblemen also kept for their entertainment.[29] Jessica, having lost her former fool Lancelot, has just escaped Shylock's "sober house" (2.5.35) and should be in a carnival mood to celebrate with exuberant laughter and freespending, especially after such long confinement. While we can sympathize with Jessica's honeymoon indulgences, we simultaneously sympathize with Shylock's lament over his turquoise, especially because its sentimental value is conveyed to us firsthand through his pained perspective of losing a ring symbolic of Jessica's parental ancestry. With its greater awareness of the whole play, the audience is privileged to find more meanings in the selling of this symbolic ring as generally part of the play's use of betrothal rings, as well as specifically a parodic precursor to Portia's giving of her symbolic ring to Bassanio in the next scene (3.2.171). Their juxtaposed actions link these two heroines in parallel matters of money and marriage, yet also contrast their filial behavior given the quality of their respective fathers, enhancing Portia as the play's chief heroine who deserves Jessica's high praise (3.5.61–71).[30]

Whereas Marlowe climaxes Abigail's life onstage with conversion outside of marriage, Shakespeare begins Jessica's with the intention to convert through marriage, and later reveals her motive of spiritual salvation. In her first appearance Jessica informs the audience that she intends to end her personal strife over blood alliance versus moral non-alliance with her father by becoming Lorenzo's "loving wife" and "a Christian" (2.3.15–29). Perhaps Lorenzo knows of her intention, although his recital of the gist of her love letter provides no clear evidence (2.4.29–39), and we are given no evidence that anyone else knows, including Shylock, who comments only on her flight with a Christian and his transfer of wealth. Unlike Abigail who directly communicates her conversion to her father by a letter (3.4.S.D.), Jessica uses secrecy to cloak her designs and thereby escapes. Gratiano, who helps Lorenzo steal Jessica, greets her in Belmont as Lorenzo's "infidel" (3.2.317), an example of Gratiano's crude but also ignorant humor. He reiterates this view when he urges Nerissa to "cheer *yond stranger*, bid her welcome" (3.2.236, my italics), kindly observing that Jessica stayed back when Lorenzo and Salerio came forward to be greeted as Bassanio's "very friends and countrymen" (3.2.222).[31] Not even her confidant Lancelot seems to have known about her intention to convert, because she has to announce it to him in Belmont (3.5.15). Their scene opens with Lancelot's belief that Jessica is "truly . . . damned," and he presents his fleshly theory that Jessica's best hope for Christian salvation lies in a "bastard hope," the off chance that one of her parents could have been a Christian (3.5.4–10).[32] Salvation is a matter of birthright for the comically literalistic Lancelot. In her teasing debate with Lancelot, Jessica reveals both her conversion by marriage and her reason for it: "I shall be saved by my husband; he hath made me a Christian" (3.5.15).

Lancelot, however, expostulates on Jessica's damnation because "the sins of the father are to be laid upon the children," according to Exodus 20.5 and the Second Commandment in the Catechism for Confirmation in the Book of Common Prayer (285). But Lorenzo's earlier optimistic line, the hypothesis that Shylock as "a faithless Jew" could come to heaven for "his gentle daughter's sake" (2.4.33–37), may recall Marlowe's use of the daughter to save the father. This hopeful view accords well with Jessica's Pauline version of salvation by marriage (1 Cor. 7.14) and comedically opposes Lancelot's darker view of humans as agents of damnation. For Lancelot damnation, like salvation, is a matter merely of regeneration by the flesh, as it is in Shylock's literal view when he declares Jessica "is damned" for rebelling against her "own flesh and blood" (3.1.26–28), or in Salarino's misprioritization of hypothetical differences in flesh and blood over genuine differences in spirit (3.1.31–34). But Jessica understands Paul's explanation that regeneration by the spirit is more significant than regeneration by the flesh. Salvation is not a matter of physical birthright but of spiritual birthright— being born again through baptism or conversion—so that the way to salvation lies open to all peoples in the world, regardless of parentage. Elizabethan religious bias, of course, undergirds this apparently liberal view because salvation, as advocated by Paul, depends on faith in Christ who is presented as "the end [the fulfillment, as the gloss clarifies] of the Law for righteousness":

> For there is no difference between the Jew and the Grecian: for he that is Lord over all, is rich unto all, that call on him. / For whosoever shall call upon the Name of the Lord, shall be saved" (Rom. 10.4,12–13).[33]

Therefore, Lancelot loses the quarrel when he claims "there's no mercy for [Jessica] in heaven because [she is] a Jew's daughter" (3.5.26–27).

Lancelot's literalistic humor about the rising price of pork comically perverts the value of conversion because he elevates the physical over the spiritual, esteeming flesh more than souls, as Jessica and Lorenzo do not. This playful but important scene reemphasizes conversion and anticipates the following scene in which the conversion stipulation for Shylock appears, a condition that outrages modern audiences because we, unlike most Elizabethan audiences, are more enlightened about religious freedom and human rights. Although conversion could be, and often was, influenced by economics, as is especially the case in Marlowe's play (1.2), Bishop Lancelot Andrewes provides an Elizabethan corrective to clown Lancelot's facetious claim: " 'It is a good work to make a Jew a Christian' " (quoted in Katz, *Philo-Semitism* 24).[34] The economy of souls should excel the economy of flesh. Lancelot's porcine fleshly accusation is rebutted by Lorenzo's human fleshly counteraccusation, that Lancelot's begetting an illegitimate child with "the Moor" (3.5.35) constitutes a graver concern for the commonwealth.[35] Lancelot's vice bears economic consequences because if he does not marry the Moor, the burden for raising a bastard weighs heavily on society. As Lawrence Stone observes for Early Modern England, "The production of a bastard child was likely to result in a drain on the financial resources of the parish and was, therefore, treated with exceptional severity" (520). Unlike Jessica, Lancelot humorously doesn't escape his threat about the father's sins being laid upon the children because like his father (2.2.15–17), he has a lusty appetite (2.2.135–36), although he may hopefully follow his father's style of becoming an "honest man" and make an "honest woman" of the Moor (2.2.15). Illegitimate versus legitimate hopes inform some of the witsnapping in this scene. Lancelot generates a "bastard hope" (3.5.6) for Jessica as well as his own. Such illegitimacy contrasts with Jessica's legitimate Jewish ancestry and her legitimate hope for salvific marriage, whether for herself (3.5.15), or for Bassanio and Portia (3.5.61–66).

By comparison, Abigail's fate illuminates Jessica's much happier outcome. However, some critics see Jessica as "a nice worldly tart, highly sexed, dying to get on with it, who turns her defection into an escapade" (Rosenburg 458), and some suspect "the darker side of the female Jewish convert" who will eventually reveal an ugly interior masked by a beautiful exterior (Shapiro 159–60). Jonathan Miller's 1970 production of *The Merchant of Venice* at the National Theatre inaugurated a bleak ending of tragic isolation for Jessica who is left alone and distraught on stage, thereby precipitating a performance trend that influenced the BBC production (1981), and that is recently recalled in Michael Kahn's production (1999) at the Shakespeare Theatre in Washington, D.C., in which a "mournful, dismayed Jessica" is left on stage alone with Antonio (Mahon 15). Despite the hearing of sweet music for the "not merry" because "attentive" (5.1.69–70) Jessica, whom Lorenzo addresses as his "sweet soul" (5.1.47–48), and despite Lorenzo's meditation on the unheard but essential harmony in heavenly spheres and human souls, some prefer to stress the tragic fates of the lovers cited in Jessica and Lorenzo's mythological allusions (5.1.1–14) as ominously foreboding. I think, however, these tragic endings may be better understood as ominously reflexive, suggesting what might have been when Jessica and Lorenzo describe that on just such a night some three months ago they hazarded their stealthy elopement. In such a night in Venice these present Christian lovers, unlike the past pagan lovers to whom they allude, escaped tragedy so that they now enjoy together such another night in Belmont. The inclusion of tragic notes in their lyrical scene heightens by contrast the comedic conclusion of their risky venture for love while simultaneously striking a minor discord that anticipates the upcoming quarrel over the rings. Negative innuendo, moreover, is fundamental to lovers' teasing in which false accusation has an edge to provoke a fuller profession of love. Lorenzo and Jessica's discourse picks up where they left off when last onstage, bantering about Jessica's praise for Lorenzo as a husband (3.5.71–78), after having extolled Portia as the ideal wife, or "the joys of heaven on earth" (3.5.64). Such tonality also characterizes the witty exchanges on "the rack" and "treason" between Portia and Bassanio before he faces the casket test (3.2.26–33), just as Miranda in a game of chess lovingly teases her betrothed Ferdinand in *The Tempest*: "Sweet lord, you play me false" (5.1.172).

Within the flesh and soul bond of marriage, Jessica and Lorenzo have already proved their mutual love by keeping faith with one another. The lovers' feigned quarrel in which "pretty Jessica" "did . . . slander her love" about false vows but "he forgave it her" (5.1.21–22) sets the stage for the more serious (yet masterminded by Portia and Nerissa) quarrel over the other lovers' actually broken vows. Neither "quarrel" ends in divorce or death but rather the reaffirmation of love through forgiveness. Given our "muddy vesture of decay" (5.1.64), love can convert to hate if forgiveness of human error does not prevail. Whatever darker undercurrents might be discovered in this scene contribute to the patterning of chiaroscuro Shakespeare has cultivated throughout this play by allowing tragic potential to jostle comic structure, just as the presence and absence of music and moonlight alternate in this well-constructed finale that ends reflooded with moonlight, two hours before dawn, in anticipation of Portia's forthcoming enlightenment of her "amazed" (5.1.266) audience. Charged "upon inter'gatories," she "will answer all things faithfully" (5.1.298–99).

Marlowe, however, provides another overlooked clue for how Shakespeare has crafted a positive emphasis for Jessica and Lorenzo's marriage. Both playwrights use the word "manna" only once in their respective canons and in their only plays featuring Jews. Barabas cruelly vows his murderous intent: "As sure as heaven rained manna for the Jews, / So sure shall [Don Lodowick] and Don Mathias die" (2.3.250–51). His vengeful use of this biblical allusion ironically perverts the significance of manna. Manna was the miraculous yet material food God mercifully provided in the wilderness in order to sustain the physical lives of the Jews, but Barabas swears by manna to destroy the physical lives of two young, innocent Christian sons/suitors. In Shakespeare's play, Portia analogizes the free and godly gift of mercy with "the gentle rain from heaven" (4.1.181), but Barabas perversely links heaven's mercy to his own deadly revenge, visiting the sins of the father (the Governor) upon the son Lodowick as well as his own sins upon his daughter. In his representation of a Jew, Marlowe's use of "manna" amounts to little more than biblical coloring for strikingly ironic effect.

Shakespeare, however, more dextrously integrates his use of manna. Earlier in his play Lorenzo specifically refers to Shylock as his "father Jew" (2.6.26), meaning his expectation to have Shylock as a father-in-law, and likewise in the trial scene, Antonio stresses familial bonds when he refers to the newlyweds as Shylock's "son Lorenzo and his daughter" (4.1.386). But in the broader context of Judaeo-Christian biblical salvation history and Shakespeare's specific choice of Jewish names for his play, he has developed the idea of the Jew as the father to the Christian, and hence Christ's lineage is traced back through the Jewish patriarchal line to Abraham in the genealogical charts of such sixteenth-century Bibles as the Bishops' version (1568). Lorenzo appropriately chooses the Old Testament idea of "manna," perhaps out of respect for this gift as a Jewish inheritance, to describe how he and his newly converted wife might perceive this very surprising and "*special* deed of *gift*" from "the rich Jew" (5.1.292, my italics), now at Portia's instruction given freely ("without a fee") by Nerissa to both Lorenzo "and Jessica" (5.1.290–91).[36] The whiteness of the scroll that Nerissa hands to the couple, as well as the fact that "it is almost morning" (5.1.295), might reinforce the idea of manna which was white and found in the morning. But far more important are manna's characteristics as miraculous, heaven-sent food to support physical life but which like all matter is fragile and subject to loss (Exod. 16.1–35). As an Elizabethan audience would know, manna disappeared quickly and needed to be renewed daily. So also can material wealth be lost and need to be refunded. Jessica and Lorenzo have already spent much of her stolen dowry, and like Bassanio who describes his own fault as being "something too prodigal" (1.1.128), they seem to be incorporated into the play's thematic discrimination between wise and foolish uses of wealth. They now find themselves as "starvèd people" (5.1.295), desperately in need of wealth seen as analogous to food in order to sustain physical life. Earlier both Antonio (4.1.262–68) and Shylock (4.1.370–73) voiced similar speeches about the need for wealth as the prop to sustain life, and the play's appetitive imagery takes a comedic turn away from feeding revenge toward feeding life. During the remainder of his life Shylock will independently possess half his estate and may receive the profits from the other half held in trust by Antonio (4.1.376–82).[37] Life is ultimately prioritized over livelihood, but Shakespeare elaborates much more sensitively the importance of living to sustaining life that he finds articulated in Marlowe's play where Barabas refers to his wealth as "the comfort of mine age, my children's hope" (1.2.147–52).

How might Jessica respond now? Since Jessica has no lines at this point in the play, multiple possibilities for body language present themselves. As yet, Lorenzo and Jessica know none of the details of the trial in Venice and probably marvel over this seemingly miraculous gift from Shylock, just as Antonio is amazed or struck "dumb" (5.1.279) to receive "life and living" from the "sweet lady" (5.1.286) Portia who provides "good comforts" (5.1.289) to him through the letter verifying the safety of three of his ships. Some modern productions darken the ending by having Jessica linger sadly on stage (despite the final textual stage direction, *"Exeunt"*). Wouldn't it be more likely that Jessica would eagerly follow Portia and Nerissa into the house in order to satisfy her wonderment about *how* Shylock's "manna" materialized? What she will discover is how Antonio played surrogate father in establishing a trust for her and Lorenzo with his awarded half of Shylock's wealth, as well as in prompting Shylock to assume the natural role of fatherly providence by signing a deed of gift that grants all inheritance to the "children" after he dies. Perhaps Antonio's providence was partially sparked by Shylock's remark, "I *have* a daughter" (4.1.291, my italics), in which he now contemplates Jessica in marriageable terms, though harshly to "any of the stock of Barabbas . . . rather than a Christian!" (4.1.292–3). Jessica may discover that her father still thinks of her in the present tense. She—and he—face what this play presents as the most difficult human choice—forgiveness. She will learn about his conversion, not martyrdom, and will have to ponder how and why he agreed to the Duke's and Antonio's conditional mercy rather than undergoing the law's strict penalty for attempted murder, loss of life and wealth.

Although John Gross sees *The Merchant of Venice* as "still a masterpiece," to what extent "there is a permanent chill in the air, even in the gardens of Belmont" (352), depends ultimately on the perspectives of individuals and their awareness as well as interpretation of Elizabethan contexts germane to this play. But one historical context of possible influence regards a criminal's wealth being awarded his family, and concerns Dr. Roderigo Lopez, the converted Portuguese Jewish physician who enjoyed thirty-five years of significant success in England before he ran afoul of the law and who has been thought to influence Shakespeare's characterization of Shylock. Like Shylock, Lopez was judged guilty of *attempted* murder, but unlike Shylock's fictional case in which his life and at least half his wealth will be spared if he agrees to several conditions, no one in the court judging Lopez's real-life case alleviated strict justice with any mercy; therefore, in

1594 Lopez was executed and all his wealth was confiscated by the state. The idea of mercy is often overlooked as Shakespeare's significant *addition* to the trial in *Il Pecorone*.[38] Queen Elizabeth, however, did set an example of monarchical mercy, "mercy . . . enthronèd in the hearts of kings" (4.1.190). Although Lopez's alleged crime of attempted murder by poison was to be directed against the Queen herself, Lopez's wife, Sarah, nonetheless begged mercy of the Queen that she be allowed to retain much of her executed husband's property for the necessary support of herself and their five children because they were innocent, and in a rare exercise of her royal power Elizabeth granted this request a year later.[39] If Shakespeare knew about Elizabeth's act of exemplary generosity in 1595, which predates the *terminus a quo* for his play's composition, it could have influenced his portrayal of another target of attempted murder who also provides financially for the perpetrator's family even though he himself is now a "bankrupt" (3.1.35), desperately in need of money as the Queen, of course, was not.

III

Although Marlowe's mighty line haunts Shakespeare, he experiments with much more than merely the containment of Marlowe. In his creation of Jessica he highlights her comedic potential by opposing Marlowe's tragic death for Abigail. Jessica possesses a sense of humor that the earnest Abigail lacks; contrary to Abigail's discovery that there may be "no love on earth" (3.3.49), Jessica believes she finds an earthly love that leads to heavenly salvation. Jessica is granted a trusty servant/friend in Lancelot, a devoted spouse in Lorenzo, new female friends in Portia and Nerissa, and perhaps the possibility of rapprochement with her father. In his interplay of comic and tragic tonalities, Shakespeare consistently converts Marlowe's tragic bent to comic. Abigail's deceptions are all motivated by love for a father who ends up killing her. Jessica's deceptions are all motivated by love for a husband who saves her. Tragic irony even pervades Abigail's kind "stealing" of her father's wealth for him because with some of this recovered wealth Barabas is able to purchase his villainous slave, Ithamore, who is instrumental in causing Abigail's grief and death, and who even nominally displaces the disowned Abigail when Barabas cleverly feigns to adopt him as his "heir" (3.4.43). Ithamore, not Abigail, expends dying breath to ensure Barabas's physical death by civil law (5.1.29–34). Barabas's wealth ends up in the state's coffers while he exits this life cursing, trapped in his own trap, the hellish boiling cauldron.

Jessica's unkind stealing of some of her father's wealth enables her to give a dowry to her husband and to finance her escape to new life and love that eventually will be crowned with the inheritance of her family's wealth after Shylock's natural decease. Shakespeare reinstates half of Shylock's estate to him and keeps his wealth within his family, but not his tribe. According to Mosaic Law, a daughter was entitled to inherit a father's possessions if he had no son (Num. 27.1–8); however, such a daughter had to marry within her father's tribe to prevent the paternal inheritance from passing to another tribe (Num. 36). From a Jewish perspective, Jessica violates this rule, but from an Elizabethan perspective, the rule is overruled through conversion to Christ in whose Mystical Body all are believed to be made one, many members but one body. For a sixteenth-century audience, Shakespeare weds prosperity to posterity through the true alms gift of Shylock's deed; through Barabas's false alms gift of poison, Marlowe liquidates the natural order of inheritance.

Both plays feature a matrix of comic and tragic effects, but the generic predisposition chosen by each playwright determines the dominant emphasis. Literal death is avoided in *The Merchant of Venice*, as it is not in *The Jew of Malta*. Shakespeare's characters enjoy the gift of more time for life and another chance for better living, perhaps even reconciliation. Masuccio ends his tale with a reconciliation of the flouters and the flouted. Such an ending lies outside the confines of Shakespeare's text, but suggestive new bonds of shared faith and wealth reunite the divided family of Shylock and his "son Lorenzo and his daughter" (4.1.386). Whether these bonds foster hate or love will depend on the future choices of those so bonded. Shakespeare remains specifically indebted to his predecessor's play in many matters, such as pervasive biblical allusion, the love alliance between a Jewish father's good daughter and her Christian suitor, the father-child-servant relationship, fidelity and infidelity, earthly and heavenly inheritance, literal and figurative wealth, secular and spiritual salvation, and the act and image of conversion.

These plays will undoubtedly continue to challenge us, but a comparison of Marlowe's Abigail and Shakespeare's Jessica opens a window to many issues, especially illuminating a philo-Semitic, or at least less Judeophobic, emphasis than usually imagined. Shakespeare, moreover, seems to find Marlowe's voice less a source of threatening influence than an important catalyst for his own revisionist approach, which features his remarkable reversals of Marlowe's generic expectations and his characters' final fates as well as his confident adaptation of Marlovian material to suit the highly integrated design of his own richly problematic play. Marlowe emphasizes bold juxtapositions and divisiveness; Shakespeare prefers multiple interconnections and wholeness. Although both plays present physical and spiritual conflicts in light of Jewish and Christian representations, Shakespeare manifests greater subtle fusion in binding together these differences through his development of the idea of the family of man. His play suggests that though all humans share the bond of flesh, unless they are also bound together in the spirit of love, they can never be truly unbound, truly free.

Notes

1. All quotations from Shakespeare's play are from M. M. Mahood's New Cambridge Shakespeare edition of *The Merchant of Venice*. This essay adapts some material in my book, *The Merchant of Venice: Choice, Hazard and Consequence*, in order to explore new issues and arguments. All citations to the rest of Shakespeare's canon are to *The Riverside Shakespeare* (second edition).

2. All quotations from Marlowe's play are from N. W. Bawcutt's edition of *The Jew of Malta*.

3. Katz also cites Maria Edgeworth's novel *Harrington* (1817), which presents a good Sephardi Jewess who is to marry the eponymous English hero, but Katz suggests that "would be unrealistic and perhaps indecent," so Edgeworth makes the Jewess turn out to be Christian on her mother's side (*Jews* 350). This half-Jew and half-Christian "solution" ironically approximates the clown Lancelot's "bastard hope" for Jessica (3.5.1–14), but Shakespeare more tolerantly avoids it by keeping both her parents Jewish.

4. For the difficult progress of religious toleration, see, for example, the work of Elizabeth Labrousse, Joseph Lecler, William Monter, and Nederman's and Laursen's collection of essays, *Difference and Dissent* (1996). Two opposed but interesting examples regarding coerced conversion might be added here. Some medieval Jews sought the aid of King William Rufus to have Christian converts from their nation enforced to return to the Jewish religion (see Holinshed 2:45–46). In his sixteenth-century defense of English Catholics against religious compulsion, Robert Parsons (a Jesuit) also argued on behalf of Jews: "Surely, as I am now minded I would not for ten thousand worlds, compel a Jew to swear that there were a blessed Trinity. For albeit the thing be never so true, yet should he be damned for swearing against his conscience, and I, for compelling him to commit so heinous and grievous a sin" (Baron 15: 128).

5. Shakespeare may also play on the name "Iscah" or "Jesca" as it is rendered in some earlier English Bibles. For the etymological and functional significance of Shakespeare's names for Jewish characters, see Holmer 69–93.

6. All quotations are from Lloyd E. Berry's facsimile of the 1560 edition of *The Geneva Bible* and will be documented parenthetically in the text.

7. The motif of the sacrificed daughter may be classical in origin, but to the best of my knowledge, it has not been suggested that Marlowe's Abigail probably influences some aspects of Shakespeare's characterization of Ophelia in *Hamlet* as a sacrificed daughter, one who like Abigail denies her heart to obey her father and dies a virgin (Hamlet refers to Ophelia as the daughter of "Jephthah" [2.2.403–12], the biblical virgin sacrificed by her father). However, Ophelia is more passive than Abigail; she never gets to a "nunnery" (3.1.136), nor does she rebel against her father on behalf of her beloved. The tragic cause and effect of Ophelia's situation reverses Abigail's because her beloved kills her father.

8. See *The Bible* (Geneva version), [bound with] *Two . . . Concordances* (trans. Robert F. Herrey, 1578), published in 1590, sig. C5^v. When the Geneva Bible was first published in 1560, it included an appendix of two tables, the first

being the interpretation of the proper names in the Old Testament. From 1580 to 1615 Herrey's concordance was bound with all the quarto Geneva Bibles, except those with Tomson's version of the New Testament.

9. Jonathas is a Jewish merchant whose opening boast about his wealth may influence Barabas's opening panegyric to wealth (Bawcutt 9). Unlike the older emphasis on supernatural causes for conversions, natural or human causes prompt conversions in Marlowe's and Shakespeare's Renaissance plays.

10. For this ballad, see "The Jew's Daughter, A Scottish Ballad," in Percy I:29–31. This undated ballad exists in twenty-one versions, the oldest of which were recovered in the mid-eighteenth century (Sargent and Kittredge 368). Cf. also, Jacobs 41–66.

11. Unlike Shakespeare, Jordan depicts the Jewish father as physically ugly or "deformed" (462). Whatever may have been the precise staging practices in the 1590's, Shakespeare's script avoids mentioning any physical traits for Shylock, other than to indicate six times in the play that he is "old." The only other character in the play described as old is Father Gobbo, and I wonder if the actor who played that role also played old father Shylock. There would have been sufficient time for costume changes because Shylock first appears in 1.3, and "Old Gobbo" (2.2 SD) doesn't appear until 75 lines after Shylock exits; after Old Gobbo exits from the play, 95 lines transpire before Shylock reenters (2.5). I do not know if any modern productions have ever tried this doubling for the play's designated two old men/fathers, but significant visual and thematic connections are obvious in such a casting for a play that develops the father-child-servant relationship (for the biblical significance of "old," see Holmer 193). Shakespeare does mention apparel, Shylock's "Jewish gaberdine" (1.3.104), but no hat; Marlowe mentions the Jew's elegant hat (4.4.67) but no gaberdine. If Shakespeare's company did deemphasize somatic differences and relied more on costume to signify identity, this practice would concur with the Elizabethan theater's typical use of clothing for semiotics. But it would also parallel the same emphasis that Shapiro has discovered for Renaissance pictures of Jews which do not clearly define a physical image of the Jew (unlike the eighteenth-century images of Jewish men with large noses to denote their race), and which do use clothes as distinguishing signifiers. Indeed, early modern woodcuts were often reused with new captions so that images of Christians could be reused to portray Jews (Shapiro 12, 233 n.28). Marlowe, however, does use a large nose for Barabas (2.3.173; 3.310; 4.1.23), but Shakespeare avoids any such mention for his Jew. All of this may also shed some new light on Portia's initial inquiry in the trial: "Which is the merchant here and which the Jew?" (4.1.170), a line that can be played a number of ways, including for laughs. Although Portia is not impartial, her question may be genuine; she has not met, and therefore can not certainly identify any of the Venetian men, other than Bassanio, Gratiano, and Salerio who came to Belmont (3.2). However, the Duke provides a verbal clue for visual identification when he answers by asking "Antonio and *old* Shylock" (4.1.171, my italics) to stand forth. Portia then immediately addresses the "old" one of these two men and asks correctly, "Is your name

Shylock?" (4.1.172). From the audience's perspective, Portia's question is thematically significant in terms of the playwright's deliberate blurring of identities at different moments through characters who can behave like "Jewish Christians" or like "Christian Jews," a strategy of "doubleplay" encountered elsewhere in Wilson's and Marlowe's plays as well as in the sixteenth-century usury treatises of Thomas Wilson (204, 222, 232, 283) and Miles Mosse (sig. B2). Was Shylock meant to be not too physically different, and therefore not so conspicuously identifiable as is the Jew in Jordan's ballad or even Marlowe's Jew? If so, the focus of difference shifts from body to spirit.

12.   Shapiro, however, claims that Marlowe seriously uses the *foetor Judaicus* myth (36), but as Bawcutt's note on the passage in question (2.3.45n.) reveals, the meaning of the myth is comically reversed: it is the Jew who implies that Christians stink. See also Barabas's ability to "smell" the approach of Christians (4.1.22). Shakespeare does not refer to this myth.

13.   Marlowe can use this phrase in the opposite context to signify love (2.3.289; 2.3.309). Shakespeare (3.1.56–57) also parallels Marlowe (2.3.17; 2.3.95) in the use of the threatening phrase "it shall go hard."

14.   See Silvayn, quoted in Bullough 1: 484; quoted in J. R. Brown 170. Those audience members familiar with the flesh bond story in *Il Pecorone* (see Bullough 1: 472), or the *Ballad of Gernutus*, if the ballad predates the play (see J. R. Brown 155, stanzas 26–30), would anticipate a pound of flesh to cause death, not merely mutilation.

15.   Does Shapiro's attempt (114) to predate the twentieth-century psychoanalytic notion of circumcision as a symbolic form of castration work well for either Marlowe's or Shakespeare's plays? In setting up his argument that "circumcision could easily slide into the more definitive cut of castration . . . in English culture" (114), Shapiro himself seems to slide a little too easily between these two different concepts in both his leading examples. The example from King John's reign (114) legally distinguishes (not conflates) castration from circumcision. Gabriel Harvey is then cited for his use of circumcision "as a metaphor for castration" (114), but what Harvey intends here is not figurative castration (mutilation) but rather figurative circumcision (purification), especially because he asks God "to increase the best and to pardon the worst" (1: 205) in his enemies while he patiently suffers the injury done by their slander. If Harvey's quotation is read in its full context (1: 203–205) "circumcise" means not "castrate" but "reform" (1: 204) or spiritually purify, a sense available in both the Old (Deut. 10.16; 30.6; Jer. 4.4) and New Testaments (Rom. 2.28–29). Other contemporaries cited, such as Andrew Willet and John Donne, also do not equate circumcision with castration, and Shapiro comes close to articulating this (120). Shapiro's stimulating work on this vexed and vexing subject suggests we still have more to understand.

16.   Jessica's choice to disguise herself as a page not only suits the Elizabethan transvestite stage but also seems an astute choice to prevent her discovery. In response to Queen Elizabeth's desire to see Mary, Queen of Scotland, Sir James Melville, a Scottish envoy in 1564 to Elizabeth's court, suggested that he could " 'convey [Elizabeth] secretly to Scotland by post, *clothed like a*

page; so that under this disguise she might see the Queen' " (quoted in Pringle 63, my italics). For an illuminating discussion of the biblical injunction against cross-dressing for theatrical practice, see Rosenblatt and Schleiner 44–74.

17. For some medieval exempla of relations between Jewish women and Christian men, see B. D. Brown 227–32. The exemplum closest to Shakespeare's story, however, presents no conversion or marriage of the Jewish daughter, but rather the voluntary conversion of the Jewish father. The father asks his personal demon to discover the identity of his daughter's Christian lover in order to kill him; however, the father converts because he is impressed that even his demon cannot penetrate the secrecy of sacramental confession. The exemplum perhaps closest to Marlowe's story differs with its emphasis on fornication and the absence of deaths. If Marlowe and Shakespeare are indebted to this narrative tradition, they both ennoble the purity of their lovers by avoiding premarital sex, a choice also especially notable in Shakespeare's adaptation of Masuccio's *Il Novellino* for elements in his Jessica-Lorenzo plot.

18. Barabas is introduced to the audience as a fabulously wealthy merchant, "a merchant, and a moneyed man" (1.2.53). Although Barabas later admits he has practiced cruel usury, this admission is merely one in a list of vices about which he boasts to Ithamore (2.3.169–203), and later pretends to confess to Friar Bernardine (4.1.30–58). It is Shakespeare who foregrounds the problem of usury, especially in specific ways that would capture the interest of his audience, but which necessitate recovery for modern audiences.

19. For this proverb in both its forms, see Tilley C309.

20. For examples of this conventional figure, see Mahood 2.6.53–58n.

21. Munday's *Zelauto* (1580) underscores the mutuality of familial obligations in presenting a daughter who contends that if the father violates his duty to provide a good husband and have his daughter "meetely matched," then the daughter need not fulfill her duty of obedience; this virtuous young woman objects strenuously to a false match with a lusty, old usurer: "Shall I for paltrie pride run headlong to hell? Shall I for mortall muck, forsake immortality?" (quoted in J. R. Brown 159; Brown reprints the entire text).

22. Keys are also important in *The Jew of Malta* (e.g., 3.4.46; 4.3.33) as well as in Ben Jonson's *Volpone* when Volpone unwittingly digs his own grave by giving his keys to his parasite Mosca (5.5). For an analysis of the theatrical significance of visible keys in *The Merchant of Venice*, see Dessen 170–74.

23. For a summary of Elizabethan views on usury, see Holmer 29–39. Cf. also, Jones, *God and the Moneylenders*, especially pp. 3–5, 6–46, 172–4, 194–205.

24. All the emphasis on the need for secrecy regarding the intended elopement of Jessica and Lorenzo underscores the hazard of being caught. Such an emphasis is also found in Masuccio's tale where this "dangerous adventure" (1: 502) requires the lovers' "greatest courage" (1: 505). A severe penalty for attempted elopement (exile for Valentine) occurs in Shakespeare's *The Two Gentlemen of Verona* (3.1.157–69).

25. Without referring to Masuccio, two critics also see Jessica's stealing as the taking of dowry; see Ranald 69–70 and Cook 136–37.

26. See, e.g., Edmund Spenser, *The Faerie Queene*, ed. Roche, 1.7.33 and p. 1096 (notes).
27. See, e.g., Wilson, *The Three Ladies of London*, in Bullough 1: 479.
28. See Steevens's commentary, quoted in Furness's Variorum edition of *The Merchant of Venice*, 132; cf. Charney 40. For the positive and negative as well as Eastern and European associations of the turquoise, see Boswell 481–83; however, if Jessica knew the possession of the turquoise was thought to cause sterility (Boswell 483), she probably would not have taken it in the first place.
29. See, e.g., Nashe 2: 269; Janson 199–237. Cf. the Italian emphasis on foolishness in derivatives ("sciminésco," "scimionáte") of the word for monkey or ape, "scímia"; see Florio 477. For a different view of the monkey as associated with lechery or human derogation, see Charney 39.
30. Wordplay and number symbolism for the goods Jessica steals, as well as the allegorical significance of the turquoise ring, are matters too lengthy for treatment here. See Holmer 123–27. Shakespeare does not derive the ring prop from Marlowe's play but rather from *Il Pecorone*; however, Shakespeare pluralizes this prop and invests it with symbolic significance absent from his source.
31. The identity of Jews as a "nation" occurs several times in both plays, and Barabas even refers to Christians as the "Unchosen nation" (2.3.8). Although Abigail has no similar line, Jessica hints that religious conversion can involve national consequences when she refers now to Tubal and Chus as Shylock's countrymen (3.2.284). Jessica's language parallels a similar emphasis in Wilson's play where conversion to Turkish Mohammedanism requires the renunciation of one's "countrie" and even "honour" to one's "parents" (1: 481).
32. Some knowledgeable members of an Elizabethan audience might have found additional ironic humor in Gobbo's fleshly "solution" which backfires from the perspective of rabbinic law. Gobbo bases his definition of identity for Jessica on the patrilinear model in order to "save" Jessica through a fleshly descent from a Christian father. However, Gobbo is ironically ignorant of the opposite matrilinear model which would identify Jessica as Jewish through her mother Leah if she is fathered by a Gentile. This rabbinic law could have been known in Elizabethan England through the writings of Ambrosiaster (an older contemporary of Jerome and Augustine) and his medieval followers, or even perhaps through members of the London Marrano community. For this law, see Cohen 261–68. I am indebted to Father James P. Walsh for this reference.
33. The gloss defines "the worde of faith" that Paul preaches: "that is, the promes & the Gospel which agreeth with the Lawe" (Rom. 10.8 and gloss).
34. Economic, as well as spiritual, consequences also attend Antonio's stipulation for Shylock's conversion. Antonio believes he is now penniless and can no longer befriend Venice by financially rescuing Shylock's victims of exorbitant usury. Because only Jews in Venice could lawfully practice usury, requiring Shylock to become a Christian limits his ability to inflict financial damage. As a "Christian," Shylock could practice usury illicitly or use his wealth licitly in an occupation such as merchantry. In the latter case, the court's restoration of half of Shylock's wealth enables him to be in league or

in competition with other merchants, including Antonio. In 1552 Venice had a population of about nine-hundred Jews, many of whom were merchants, and a number of these established partnerships with Christian merchants (*Encyclopedia Judaica* 16: 98). Therefore, despite the potential fiscal benefit of Shylock's "conversion" for the general population of Venice, Shylock and Antonio could continue to confront the personal choice of whether to be financial foes or friends.

35.   Shapiro suggests that miscegenation provokes the anxiety here because Lorenzo with a Jew and Lancelot with a Moor "threaten to sully their white, Christian commonwealth" (173). But in Shakespeare's fictional Belmont, the marriage between Portia and Morocco (a tawny Moor), that would necessarily occur if he had been successful, provokes no such political objection. Although Portia is not Desdemona in her choice of a husband, the marriage between Desdemona and Othello, the Moor, is affirmed as lawful by the Duke of Venice, and during their trial the Senate does not raise miscegenation as a possible impediment (*Othello* 1.3). For a reading of Jessica that stresses the importance of skin color as a prerequisite for integrating Jews into Christian society, see Metzger 52–63. Despite Solanio's claims of difference (3.1.31–33), Jessica is Shylock's genuine flesh and blood; she is never depicted in the play as a "dark infidel" (57), nor is she, her father, or Tubal represented as "blackened" (53) even though their countryman Chus bears the name of "the mythical originary black African" (55). Neither Wilson's nor Marlowe's plays privilege skin color as a meaningful condition for the assimilation of converts.

36.   In Kahn's more cynical 1999 production, "Portia hands [Lorenzo] Shylock's deed of gift, Lorenzo dances for joy, pointedly ignoring his wife as he prances off in self-satisfied glee" (Mahon 15).

37.   Jordan's ballad (1664) changes Shakespeare's play by deleting fiscal mercy to the Jewish father; he is consigned to a living death ("The Jew cryes out he's undone") because all his wealth is immediately forfeited to his daughter (463). Omitting also the conversion condition, Jordan wishes to keep this Venetian Jew spiritually as well as physically excluded from his community of London and homeland of England (463), a contrast to what may be seen as a more inclusionary bent in the play.

38.   The tension between justice and mercy is not a given in Shakespeare's literary sources, but rather a theme he chooses to develop by using the Bible for inspiration as well as capitalizing on hints found chiefly in Anthony Munday's *Zelauto* (1580), where all the characters are Christians, so an appeal to the cruel usurer is based on love of neighbor and the golden rule (see J. R. Brown 164–65; Bullough 1: 487). Shakespeare's play complicates these hints by expanding the definition of neighbor to include Jew as well as Christian.

39.   See Holmer 24–27. Cf. Katz who argues that although it used to be "tantamount to a declaration of anti-Semitism" for moderns to proclaim Lopez guilty, Lopez clearly violated the contemporary laws against treason "enough to hang him many times over" (*Jews* 49, 105–106). Despite her largesse to Lopez's family, the Queen refused to return a particular ring sent to Lopez by a minister of the King of Spain, but instead wore it at her girdle

" 'in Triumph' " over " 'the price of her blood' " (Katz, *Jews* 100–101). Katz also surprisingly demonstrates that "Lopez's Jewish origin was not a key element in his prosecution" (106). In Shakespeare's Venice, it is important to note that Shylock is the only Jew prosecuted by the law for attempted murder; although Tubal or Chus may have known about Shylock's intent, neither Jew is called to "this strict court of Venice" (4.1.200).

Works Cited

The Ballad of Gernutus (undated). *The Merchant of Venice*. Ed. John Russell Brown. New Arden Shakespeare. 1955. London: Methuen, 1969.

Baron, Salo W. *A Social and Religious History of the Jews*. 2nd ed. 16 vols. New York: Columbia University Press, 1952–76.

The Bible (Bishops' version). London: Richard Jugge, 1568.

The Bible (Geneva version), [bound with] *Two . . . Concordances*. Trans. Robert F. Herrey (1578). London: Deputies of Christopher Barker, 1590.

The Book of Common Prayer 1559: The Elizabethan Prayer Book. Ed. John E. Booty. Washington: The Folger Shakespeare Library, 1976.

Boswell, J. C. "Shylock's Turquoise Ring." *Shakespeare Quarterly* 14 (1963): 481–83.

Brown, Beatrice D. "Mediaeval Prototypes of Lorenzo and Jessica." *MLN* 44 (1929): 227–32.

Brown, John Russell, ed. *The Merchant of Venice*. New Arden Shakespeare, 1955. London: Methuen, 1969.

Charney, Maurice. "Jessica's Turquoise Ring and Abigail's Poisoned Porridge: Shakespeare and Marlowe as Rivals and Imitators." *Renaissance Drama* 10 (1979): 33–44.

Cohen, Shaye J. D. "Was Timothy Jewish (Acts 16:1–3)? Patristic Exegesis, Rabbinic Law, and Matrilineal Descent." *Journal of Biblical Literature* 105.2 (1986): 251–68.

Cook, Ann Jennalie. *Making a Match: Courtship in Shakespeare and His Society*. Princeton: Princeton University Press, 1991.

Dessen, Alan C. *Recovering Shakespeare's Theatrical Vocabulary*. Cambridge: Cambridge University Press, 1995.

Encyclopaedia Judaica. Ed. Cecil Roth and Geoffrey Wigoder. 16 vols. Jerusalem: Encyclopaedia Judaica, 1972.

Florio, John. *Queen Anna's New World of Words*. 1611. Menston: Scolar Press, 1968.

The Geneva Bible (a facsimile of the 1560 edition). Intro. Lloyd E. Berry. Madison: University of Wisconsin Press, 1969.

Giovanni, Fiorentino. *Il Pecorone* (1558) (Day 4, Story 1). Trans. Geoffrey Bullough. *The Narrative and Dramatic Sources of Shakespeare*. Ed. Geoffrey Bullough. 8 vols. 5th imp. London: Routledge and Kegan Paul, 1977.

Greene, Robert. *Mamillia. The Life and Complete Works in Prose and Verse of Robert Greene*. Ed. Alexander B. Grosart. 15 vols. London: Huth Library, 1881–86.

Gross, John. *Shylock: A Legend and Its Legacy*. New York: Simon & Schuster, 1992.

Holinshed, Raphael. *Holinshed's Chronicles: England, Scotland, and Ireland*. 6 vols. 1807. New York: AMS, 1965.

Holmer, Joan Ozark. *"The Merchant of Venice": Choice, Hazard and Consequence.* London: Macmillan, 1995.

Hunter, G. K. "The Theology of Marlowe's *The Jew of Malta.*" *Journal of the Warburg and Courtauld Institute* 17 (1964): 211–40.

Jacobs, Joseph. "Little St. Hugh of Lincoln: Researches in History, Archeology, and Legend." *The Blood Libel Legend: A Casebook in Anti-Semitic Folklore.* Ed. Alan Dundes. Madison: University of Wisconsin Press, 1991. 41–66.

Janson, Horst Noldemar. *Apes and Ape Lore in the Middle Ages and the Renaissance.* London: The Warburg Institute, University of London, 1952.

Jones, Norman. *God and the Moneylenders: Usury and Law in Early Modern England.* Oxford: Basil Blackwell, 1989.

Jordan, Thomas. "The Forfeiture, A Romance" (1664). *The Merchant of Venice.* Ed. H. H. Furness. The Variorum Shakespeare. Philadelphia: J. B. Lippincott, 1888.

Katz, David. *The Jews in the History of England.* Oxford: Clarendon, 1994.

———. *Philo-Semitism and the Readmission of the Jews to England 1603–1655.* Oxford: Clarendon, 1982.

Labrousse, Elisabeth. "Religious Toleration." *Dictionary of the History of Ideas: Studies of Selected Pivotal Ideas.* Ed. Philip P. Wiener. 4 vols. New York: Charles Scribner's Sons, 1968–73.

Lecler, Joseph, S. J. *Toleration and Reformation.* London: Association, 1960.

Mahon, John W. "Holbrook Triumphs as Shylock." *The Shakespeare Newsletter* 49.1 (Spring 1999): 15, 24.

Marlowe, Christopher. *The Jew of Malta.* Ed. N. W. Bawcutt. The Revels Plays. Manchester: Manchester University Press and Johns Hopkins University Press, 1978.

Masuccio, Salernitano. *Il Novellino* (The Fourteenth Story). Trans. W. G. Waters. *The Narrative and Dramatic Sources of Shakespeare.* Ed. Geoffrey Bullough. 8 vols. 5th imp. London: Routledge and Kegan Paul, 1977.

Metzger, Mary Janell. " 'Now by My Hood, a Gentle and No Jew' ": Jessica, *The Merchant of Venice*, and the Discourse of Early Modern English Identity." *PMLA* 113 (1998): 52–63.

Monter, William. *Ritual, Myth and Magic in Early Modern Europe.* Athens: Ohio University Press, 1984.

Mosse, Miles. *The Arraignment and Conviction of Usury. That is, The iniquity and unlawfulness of usury, displayed in six Sermons, preached at Saint Edmunds Burie in Suffolke, upon Proverb 28.8.* London: Widow Orwin, 1595.

Munday, Anthony. *Zelauto or The Fountain of Fame* (Book III) (1580). *The Merchant of Venice.* Ed. John Russell Brown. New Arden Shakespeare. 1955. London: Methuen, 1969.

Nashe, Thomas. *The Works of Thomas Nashe.* Ed. R. B. McKerrow. 5 vols. 1904–1910. Oxford: Basil Blackwell, 1958.

Nederman, Cary J. and John Christian Laursen, eds. *Difference and Dissent: Theories of Tolerance in Medieval and Early Modern Europe.* Lanham: Rowman and Littlefield, 1996.

Percy, Thomas. *Reliques of Ancient English Poetry.* 3 vols. Edinburgh: James Nichol, 1858.

Play of the Sacrament (Croxton). Non-cycle Plays and Fragments. Ed. Norman Davis. London: Oxford, 1970.

Pringle, Roger, ed. *A Portrait of Elizabeth I in the Words of the Queen and her Contemporaries.* Totowa, NJ: Barnes & Noble, 1980.

Ranald, Margaret Loftus. *Shakespeare and His Social Context.* New York: AMS, 1987.

Rappaport, Solomon. *Jew and Gentile: The Philo-Semitic Aspect.* New York: Philosophical Library, 1980.

Rosenblatt, Jason P. and Winfried Schleiner. "John Selden's Letter to Ben Jonson on Cross-Dressing and Bisexual Gods [with text]." *English Literary Renaissance* 29 (1999): 44–74.

Rosenburg, Edgar. "The Jew in Western Drama: An Essay and a Checklist." *Bulletin of the New York Public Library* 72 (1968): 442–91.

Sargent, Helen Child and George Lyman Kittredge. *English and Scottish Ballads.* 1904. Cambridge: Riverside Press, 1932.

Shakespeare, William. *The Merchant of Venice.* Ed. H. H. Furness. The Variorum Shakespeare. Philadelphia: J. B. Lippincott, 1888.

———. *The Merchant of Venice.* Ed. M. M. Mahood. New Cambridge Shakespeare. Cambridge: Cambridge University Press, 1987.

———. *The Riverside Shakespeare.* Eds. G. Blakemore Evans, et al. 2nd ed. Boston: Houghton Mifflin, 1997.

Shapiro, James. *Shakespeare and the Jews.* New York: Columbia University Press, 1996.

Silvayn, Alexander. *The Orator.* Trans. L. P. (1596). *The Narrative and Dramatic Sources of Shakespeare.* Ed. Geoffrey Bullough. 8 vols. 5th imp. London: Routledge and Kegan Paul, 1977.

Spenser, Edmund. *The Faerie Queene.* Ed. Thomas P. Roche, Jr. Harmondsworth: Penguin, 1978.

Stone, Lawrence. *The Family, Sex and Marriage in England, 1500–1800.* London: Weidenfeld & Nicolson, 1977.

Tilley, Morris Palmer. *A Dictionary of Proverbs in England in the Sixteenth and Seventeenth Centuries.* Ann Arbor: University of Michigan Press, 1950.

Wilson, Robert. *The Three Ladies of London. The Narrative and Dramatic Sources of Shakespeare.* Ed. Geoffrey Bullough. 8 vols. 5th imp. London: Routledge and Kegan Paul, 1977.

Wilson, Thomas. *A Discourse upon Usury* (1572). Ed. R. H. Tawney. New York: Harcourt Brace, 1925.

Jessica

JOHN DRAKAKIS

In Jonathan Miller's 1970 National Theatre production of *The Merchant of Venice* (filmed in 1973) the final scene is played with Jessica, formerly the daughter of Shylock the Jew, and now the wife of Lorenzo, reflecting silently on the enormity of her elopement. In James Bulman's account of the performance, Olivier's "tragic" reading of Shylock's demise is paralleled in act 5 by a questioning of Jessica's newfound Christianity that serves to transform her situation "into a tragedy to parallel—and extend—her father's" (Bulman 96), and the performance ends with a singing of the Jewish *Kaddish*, "a dirge for the father who is now dead to her"(98). In a much more recent performance, that of the Sheffield-based Compass Theatre in 1997, directed by Neil Sissons, the roles of Jessica, Nerissa, and the Duke of Venice are doubled by the actress Carolyn Bazely, and although this makes for a severely truncated final act of the play, the effect serves to contrast the positions of Portia and Jessica. In Sissons' production the Christians retired to Portia's house at Belmont, closed the gates, and left Jessica outside sobbing. The powerful effect was to suggest that once having secured both the money that she stole from her father, and the wealth to which Lorenzo, by virtue of his marriage to her, has now become heir, she can be excluded from the exclusively Christian festivity of Belmont.[1]

Both these productions, widely separated in time, indicate that in the theatre the figure of Jessica is a troubled and a troubling one. Lawrence Danson, for example, cites Sir Arthur Quiller-Couch's sense of outrage at her unfilial treatment of her father: "bad and disloyal, unfilial, a thief; frivolous, greedy, without any more conscience than a cat and without even a cat's redeeming love of home" (Danson 132), and counsels against taking so extreme a view since it might upset the dramatic balance of the play. In the acknowledged sources for *The Merchant of Venice*, Ser Giovanni's *Il Pecorone*, and *The Ballad of Gernutus*, neither Jessica, nor, indeed, any daughter appears. The curious and volatile relationship between Barabas and his daughter Abigail in Marlowe's *The Jew of Malta* (c.1590) may well have provided a model that Shakespeare went on to develop; the echoes to be found in lines such as Barabas's "O my girl, / My gold, my fortune, my felicity" (2.1.47–48; Bawcutt 101), and in his later rejection of her because she has become a Christian (3.4.1–11), are conflated in *The Merchant of Venice*. But ever since Ellen Terry's version of Portia as a figure who, in the words of George Brandes, is "independent, almost masculine in her attitude towards life," who is "an orphan heiress [who] has been in a position of authority from childhood" (Terry 197), the critical focus has been very much upon her empowerment in the play to the exclusion of anyone else's.

To take a recent example, Karen Newman's essay, "Portia's Ring: Unruly Women and the Structures of Exchange in *The Merchant of Venice*," barely mentions Jessica, and is content to rehearse a familiar reading of the final act in which "even the idyllic dialogue between Jessica and Lorenzo is troubled by allusions to unhappy love and broken vows"(131). Similarly, Catherine Belsey acknowledges that "Love in Venice generally has a poor record" (139–160), but, following a familiar critical line (Fortin 268–69), is content simply to record the incongruousness of Lorenzo's lyrical invocation of love stories that are fundamentally tragic in their general contours (140–41). Belsey provocatively mentions the case of Desdemona and Othello, but does not pursue its antecedents in *The Merchant of Venice*. Indeed, the figure of Jessica is usually invoked by critics of the play as a means of revealing the inner life of what might otherwise be little more than the stereotype of the Jew. This seems to have been the cue for Sigurd Burckhardt's speculation that "the union of Jessica and Lorenzo would have offered a more harmonious means of conversion" for her father, and that there "should" have been a further scene, replete with "the satisfying, conciliatory finality and completeness we expect in comedies" in which Shylock "embraces Christianity and his new-found children" and "Antonio magnanimously renounces his claim to half of Shylock's property in favour of the lovers" (251). Similarly, Katharine Eisaman Mauss's introduction to the play in the *Norton* edition emphasizes this general ethos in her comment that "Shylock pretends that he thinks of people in purely materialistic, economic terms; but he becomes a moving character at precisely those moments when he admits another kind of value" (Greenblatt 1085). Such moments include his lamenting the flight of Jessica and her subsequent parting with her mother's ring (3.1.110ff), following the Jew's equation of "daughter" and "ducats" (2.8.15ff), and its apparent reduction of the human to the material. Mauss comments: "Insisting upon the sentimental value of the turquoise ring, Shylock seems directly to deny the convertibility of human into monetary relations" (Greenblatt 1085).

The role Jessica plays in the structure of *The Merchant of Venice* is a crucial one, insofar as it provides, at one level, a mirror for the romantic plot involving Portia and Bassanio. Burckhardt, for example, in a more extreme version of this thesis, regards the Jessica-Lorenzo subplot as the sharpest possible contrast to the Portia-Bassanio plot on the grounds that "Their love is lawless, financed by theft and engineered through a gross breach of trust," and he goes on to argue that "They are spendthrift rather than liberal, thoughtless squanderers of stolen substance; they are aimless, drifting by chance from Venice to Genoa to Belmont" (253).

The relationship, however, rather than acting as the stark contrast that Burckhardt proposes, is one of a number of mirrors in the play, each of which refracts the dominant values of Venice. It is neither direct contrast nor a mimetic double. One of the most crucial issues with which the play deals involves *two* fathers, the one dead and the other living, the one Venetian, and hence Christian, and the other a Jew, the one able to control the behavior of his daughter, even from beyond the grave, while the other is unable to control his daughter's behavior at all. A third father, Old Gobbo, offers in some respects a comic perspective that extends the concerns of the other two, and introduces yet another dimension to the play involving the suffering of old age, its propensity to duping, and the filial consideration that patriarchy is entitled to demand. At issue is the power of patriarchy to impose limits and obligations upon its subjects, particularly its female subjects, and this is a tension that informs a number of Shakespeare's comedies. Significantly it is the relationship between Jessica and Lorenzo that is projected into the later play *Othello* (c.1604), and given a decidedly tragic inflection. But before approaching Jessica directly, we need first to investigate what might be considered the female "norm" in Venice as represented by the figure of Portia.

Portia first appears in the second scene of the play, and immediately confesses that she is "aweary of this great world" (1.2.1–2). It is now a critical commonplace to notice the connection between Portia's world-weariness and that of Antonio in the previous scene (1.1.1–2), although the causes of Antonio's "sadness" are less easy to determine. The cause of Portia's lassitude is a frustration consequent upon living within the parameters of a balanced existence; Nerissa makes the point: "it is no mean happiness therefore to be seated in the mean" (1.2.6–8), but Portia languishes in the gulf between her own reason and her emotions:

I can easier teach twenty what were good to be done, than be one of the twenty to follow mine own teaching: the brain may devise laws for the blood, but a hot temper leaps o'er a cold decree,—such a hare is madness the youth, to skip o'er the meshes of good counsel the cripple; but this reasoning is not in the fashion to choose me a husband, O me the word 'choose'! I may neither choose who I would, nor refuse who I dislike, so is

the will of a living daughter curb'd by the will of a dead father: is it not hard
Nerissa, that I cannot choose one, nor refuse none? (1.2.15–26)[2]

She desires to be free to choose a husband, but she is prevented from
doing so by a "will" much stronger than her own, that of her dead father.
Indeed, Portia is the only Shakespearean heroine to be constrained in this
way and this leads directly to the question of why this should be so. What
danger does the freedom that Portia craves represent? She is an heiress, and
as such she is in possession of material power, but her wealth is circumscribed. She is "richly left" (1.1.161), and Belmont is "Colchos' strond"
(1.1.171) with Portia as the "golden fleece" for whom suitors come in quest.
And yet, despite the provision that her dead father has made for her against
masculine unscrupulousness, her impulse is to rebel. Not only that, but her
rebellion would take a particular form, one articulated shrewdly, and appropriately, by the maid Nerissa:

> Your father was ever virtuous, and holy men at their death have good inspi-
> rations,—therefore the lott'ry that he hath devised in these three chests of
> gold, silver, and lead, whereof who chooses his meaning chooses you, will
> no doubt never be chosen by any rightly, but one who you shall rightly love.
> (1.2.27–32)

Portia is, curiously, her father's *meaning*; he has both authorized her and
is the origin of her legitimacy; her every action is circumscribed within the
semantic field of the Law of the Father and continues to be so. To refuse to
accept this "curb" would be to give her own "blood" free rein with the risk of
challenging fundamentally the very source of authority, legitimacy, *and*
meaning. Clearly, however, to accept this restraint is to forego the possibility
of an independent identity.

But there is another angle from which we need to view this problem. In
the game that originates in the will of her father, Portia becomes an object of
choice whose qualities, as Freud noted, are displaced into the three caskets
(244–45). In a play where financial success is dependent upon forces outside
human control, choice becomes a means of subverting destiny. Freud puts the
matter thus: "Choice stands in the place of necessity, of destiny. In this way
man overcomes death, which he has recognized intellectually. No greater triumph of wish-fulfilment is conceivable." It is Freud's claim that the mythological goddess of Death is transformed in a play such as *The Merchant of
Venice* into "the fairest and most desirable of women" but that she retains
"certain characteristics that border on the uncanny" (244–45). "The Theme
of the Three Caskets" does not offer a *reading* of *The Merchant of Venice*
since Freud is much more eager to engage with a transformation of the theme
as it is represented in the later play, *King Lear*. But the argument is suggestive with regard both to the conduct of Portia's suitors, and to the matter of

her own self-perception. On the crucial matter of the choice of suitors, Portia is constrained to remain silent, and the reason *she* gives for this is the fear that her "blood" and her "hot temper" require to be curbed. Moreover, if she were to speak in a voice other than that prescribed by her father—in other words, if she were to take full responsibility for her own *meaning*— then his death will have been both assured and final. To this extent Portia embodies what Freud calls "the three inevitable relations that a man has with a woman—the woman who bears him, the woman who is his mate and the woman who destroys him" (247). Portia's "blood" is the sexual urge to procreate that requires control; she is the mate that requires to be "chosen" in man's attempt to outwit destiny; and she is also the symbol of mutability that signals Death itself.

If we view Portia in this way, then we can begin to understand what Freud meant by his suggestion that although "the fairest and best of women" stands in the place of the Death-goddess, she "has kept certain characteristics of the uncanny." That threat is precisely what fuels patriarchal constraint in the play, while at the same time it constructs an identity for Portia as the dutiful female subject. But, as we have seen from Portia's complaints, the dutiful subject both perceives and *feels* the effects of a structure of oppression that is mapped across the axis of gender difference. In short the play describes an interiority for Portia that allows her to live the ideology of patriarchy at the same time as it permits her a glimpse of the contradiction of her own position. And yet, that ideology can allow her to represent to herself her own radical alterity as the "madness" or irrationality of "youth." The casket scenes in the play are a severe test of Portia's faith in that ideology, since throughout, whatever her opinion of her suitors, she must remain silent. However, although the contest has all of the appearance of a lottery, the end is a foregone conclusion, both in terms of the status of her suitor and his ethnic origin. The natural order thus finds a way of articulating human uncertainty in such a way that it can reinforce its exclusive categories. Portia and Bassanio are thus "natural" partners, while others, of different races or nationalities, are rejected as unsuitable. Here we might say that Venetian supremacy defines itself through a process of naturalization of its own social categories.[3] It is for this reason that Portia is able to (apparently) shift identities at the moment of Bassanio's success. What at the beginning of the play appeared as a reluctant submission to a transcendental parental will becomes, at the moment when the appropriate suitor presents himself, an act of choice: Portia gives herself away:

> You see me Lord Bassanio where I stand,
> Such as I am; though for myself alone ,
> I would not be ambitious in my wish
> To wish myself much better, yet for you,

> I would be trebled twenty times myself,
> A thousand times more fair, ten thousand times more rich,
> That only to stand high in your account,
> I might in virtues, beauties, livings, friends
> Exceed account: but the full sum of me
> Is sum of something: which to term in gross,
> Is an unlesson'd girl, unschool'd, unpractised.
> Happy in this, she is not yet so old
> But she may learn: happier than this,
> She is not bred so dull but she can learn;
> Happiest of all, is that her gentle spirit
> Commits itself to yours to be directed,
> As from her lord, her governor, her king.
> Myself, and what is mine, to you and yours
> Is now converted. (3.2.149–67)

This is a long and complex speech in which, paradoxically, the dependent daughter asserts independently her dependence upon her new "lord." Moreover, the convoluted fiscal metaphors simply reinforce the material nature of the exchange that is both taking place and that now requires to be mystified or spiritualized. Fiscal increase and the wish for it, itself a topic of serious discussion in the play, is now authorized as a metaphor for the prospect of "breeding," an activity that the institution of Christian marriage legitimates. For Portia, marriage to Bassanio effectively performs a restatement of submission to the will of the Father; her "blood" and her "hot temper" now have a legitimate outlet, but at the same time the "self" that emerges is one that continues to articulate patriarchal meaning. Portia's transformation in act 4 to the masculine Dr. Balthazar is, in this context, only the most superficial act of cross-dressing, since her interior life has become gradually masculine up to this point. Nor is it any accident that her field of representation is the Law and its meaning. And it is fidelity to meaning that becomes one of the issues in the final scene of the play where Bassanio and Gratiano are accused of a "female" inconstancy, while—in a curious inversion that parades the threats of infidelity, cuckoldry, and more sensationally, pederasty, before the defensive patriarchs—the women, Portia and Nerissa, occupy the "masculine" high ground.

Portia's unruliness, then, is of very limited efficacy since her potentially subversive energies can easily be turned back into the very ideology that positions her identity as a woman, and that identity itself permits her to make certain demands upon her newfound husband. Portia, in other words, lives her subjection as a freedom within the patronizing Law that provides, precariously, for her every wish. She is permitted some room for negotiation, but ideologically and aesthetically she is only ever allowed to speak from within the boundaries circumscribed by the will of her dead Father.

The case of Jessica is different, in part because the familial context within which she is inscribed as "daughter" is different. When she first appears at 2.3 she describes her father's house as "hell" (2.3.2), and asks "what heinous sin is it in me / To be asham'd to be my father's child!" (2.3.16–17). Moreover, she even refutes the claim that she is her father's daughter by drawing a distinction between ties of "blood" and "manners": "But though I am a daughter to his blood / I am not to his manners" (2.3.18–19). In short, her resistance to a patriarchal law that is restrictively puritanical, is, in its effects, much more radical than that suggested by the youthful frustrations of Portia. Later, at 2.5.10ff we see more precisely the nature of the constraints under which she lives. Shylock begins this formative exchange by giving his daughter the keys to his "house": "There are my keys" (2.5.12), and he exhorts her to "Look to my house" (2.5.16). Moreover he is only willing to yield to the outward form of Christian festivity, seeking secretly and usuriously "to feed upon / The prodigal Christian" (2.5.14–15).[4] His anti-festive sentiments are, in fact, given much fuller restrictive force than the patriarchal "will" to which Portia reluctantly submits herself, in the instructions that he gives to Jessica:

Figure 7. Jessica (Deborah Goodman) and Shylock (Anthony Sher) in the 1987 Royal Shakespeare Company production. Joe Cocks, The Shakespeare Centre Library, Stratford-upon-Avon.

> Hear you me Jessica,
> Lock up my doors, and when you hear the drum
> And the vile squeaking of the wry-neck'd fife
> Clamber not you up to the casements then
> Nor thrust your head into the public street
> To gaze upon the Christian fools with varnish'd faces:
> But stop my house's ears, I mean my casements,
> Let not the sound of shallow fopp'ry enter
> My sober house. (2.5.28–36)

This repeats, although in a rather different register, the earlier exchange between Portia and Nerissa; Shylock is caught in the very act of devising "laws for the blood" (1.2.17–18) that will prevent what he fears to be his daughter's "hot temper" from leaping "o'er a cold decree,—such a hare is madness the youth, to skip o'er the meshes of good counsel the cripple" (1.2.18–20). What for Portia is proverbial wisdom that it is ultimately in the interests of "youth" to be bound by, becomes for Jessica an oppressive material constraint to be resisted at the earliest opportunity; what for Portia is a temporary bar to ultimate happiness is, for Jessica, the source of "strife" that she proposes actively to end by becoming "a Christian and thy [Lorenzo's] loving wife" (2.3.20–21). Moreover, the path for her filial rebellion is further prepared by Lorenzo's unusual justification for her behavior in his exchange with Gratiano at the end of 2.4:

> If e'er the Jew her father come to heaven,
> It will be for his gentle daughter's sake,
> And never dare misfortune cross her foot,
> Unless she do it under this excuse,
> That she is issue to a faithless Jew. (2.4.33–37)

Whereas Portia ultimately *trusts* in the rightness of her dead father's provision for her, no matter what anxiety it might provoke, Jessica can have no such confidence in the law of a father whose own constitutive infidelity (literally his "want of faith") provides the justification for rebellion. Here social and religious contexts overlap in a mutually validating prejudice; it is what Albert Memmi, in another context altogether, calls "a behaviour of refusal" that betrays the structure of a racism that is "a real though destructive relation between two individuals who emerge from their own particular socially given contexts" (32). What both Jessica and Lorenzo contrive to do in these scenes that precede Jessica's exchange with her father is to establish a *difference* to which is ascribed a series of particular significations, designed specifically, in Memmi's words, "to denigrate the other, to the end of gaining privilege or benefit through that stigmatisation" (37–38). Such a reading of

Jessica's role in this process, combined with the general Venetian stigmatization of the Jew, provides a critical context for Shylock's later appeal at 3.1.47ff to "sameness." It is part of the complexity of *The Merchant of Venice* that what appears to be a mirroring of Christian characteristics as articulated by the imitative Jew should disclose a face that no Christian in the play is prepared to acknowledge. Confronted with the loss of his daughter and his money, Shylock will use the law in order to be "revenged" upon his Christian adversaries (3.1.60). Such a view of Christian justice threatens to strip its procedures of a mystifying veneer, but also to position the Jew paradoxically as both the coercively restraining father *and* the energy that perverts and threatens the order of the Venetian state. What makes the play so disturbing is that these textualizations are far from stable, and that what under normal circumstances would result in the apportionment of blame to a wayward daughter, is now displaced onto an alien, and alienated, father.

Having said that, Shylock is still a father and, for late Elizabethan culture, the theatrical representation of a thwarted or deceived father demands careful negotiation. To this extent Burckhardt's claim that "Wherever we look, the Jessica-Lorenzo affair appears as an inversion of true, bonded love"(253) is exaggerated, since a great deal of attention is given to providing some justification for this elopement. Moreover, the statement that "The ring, which ought to seal their love, is traded for a monkey" (253) reads Jessica's behavior exclusively through the eyes of a father who has already been the subject of intense criticism from the point of view of both his domestic affairs and his public dealings.

It is difficult to know at this point in the action precisely how much of this criticism should carry over to what is an unusually intimate revelation that appears to offer "otherness" in the play a momentarily resistant voice. Tubal tells Shylock that Jessica has exchanged a ring with one of Antonio's creditors in return for a monkey, and this is often thought by critics and directors alike to be the motive for transforming the erstwhile "merry bond" into a single-minded pursuit for justice. The motive for Jessica's exchange is, however, unclear even though it provides the occasion for an unusual glimpse into her father's own marital history. Here the question that Burckhardt eschews, "Why" in favor of "What" (253), appears to be of some direct relevance. Why would Jessica exchange a ring for a monkey with one of Antonio's creditors, unless it is to establish some connection with the Venetian counterpart to her father? Moreover, the transfer of Shylock's ring to a Christian adversary in return for an animal noted for its capacity to mimic human behavior—the "What" of Burckhardt's question—recalls Shylock's own strategy of imitating through mimicry the form of Christian conduct. Jessica's exchange of her father's ring heralds the later gift of rings effected by Portia and Nerissa to their respective husbands, and her gesture effectively recuperates this symbol for the Christian ritual of betrothal.

The irony is that this episode lays open to question the very form of Shylock's "marriage" in that his own behavior is shown, like a monkey, to mimic some aspect of Venice's "human" behavior. And yet, attached to this mimicry is a structure of feeling that qualifies the Jew's alienation in its privileging of the terms of both "husband" and "father." To this extent Jessica's gesture deconstructs at the most intimate of levels the symbolic capital of her father's domestic life, which borrows its authority from Venetian (and Elizabethan) standards of legitimation, and in a way that anticipates a modern liberal perspective that would have no difficulty in identifying with Shylock's anguish at this point in the play. In this crucial respect, Jessica and Lorenzo do not "stand in the sharpest imaginable contrast to Portia and Bassanio"(253), as Burckhardt would have us believe. Rather, Jessica functions at this moment in the play to effect a double deconstruction, both of Shylock's imitative behavior that is asserted by implication to be "monkey-like" (hence the harmonization of the details of this exchange with the dominant racist idiom of the play), and of the fiscal nature of the monetary exchange that underpins the romantic discourse associated with Belmont. In Derridean terms Jessica is a kind of *pharmakon*, an ambivalent figure, "the medium in which opposites are opposed, the movement and the play that links them among themselves, reverses them or makes one side cross over into the other," capable of effecting both a poison and a cure (Derrida 127). Jessica can "poison" her father's life through her willful violation of his own commitments, and yet, by literally "crossing over into the other" she can effect a cure for the very infidelity that ostracizes him as the "other" of Christianity in the play. In fact it would not be inaccurate to say that Jessica is not anything in herself, but rather an effect of the structures within which she is variously inscribed. Although she is, as we have seen, "a daughter to his [Shylock's] blood / I am not to his manners" (2.3.18–19), as a consequence of her plan to disguise herself "even in the lovely garnish of a boy" (2.6.45), she "loses" her father just as he "loses" a daughter (2.5.56).

This loss—or to put it more accurately, this ambivalence—of identity is shown, paradoxically, to be both a direct consequence of a divided household and the ultimate cause of its unification. In this Jessica's disguise is unlike that of Portia and Nerissa later in the play since their functions as Balthazar and the Lawyer's Clerk serve to uphold the laws of Venice rather than to shift from one ideologico-religious regime to another. Where Portia and Nerissa can combine androgynously the roles of male and female but without posing a serious threat to their own subjectivities, Jessica's transformation effects an ideological shift that is retrospective in its capacity to transform the full gamut of domestic relations within her father's household.

By her action in eloping with Lorenzo Jessica is "translated": temporarily she becomes a "boy." Whereas before, the actor impersonated a woman, through a series of transformations of identity she now becomes a wife where before she was a daughter, and she becomes a Christian, where before she was a "Jewess." All of this exposes the actor's investment in the role, while at the same time "alienating" Jessica from an already marginalized and demonized patriarch. At a purely mimetic level her translations elicit some sympathy in that she is the downtrodden daughter of an oppressively puritanical father and her rebellion, therefore, appears to be *politically* justified in that it demystifies for the spectator the foundations of an oppositional politics. This, in itself, makes it surprising that feminists have paid scant attention to Jessica whose plight is, therefore, *structural*. But even more interesting is the fact that its politics echo the deeper racial structure of the play and repeat at a slightly different discursive level the very relations that bind Shylock to his Christian adversaries in a state of mutual enmity. And yet, Jessica herself, in a moment of introspection that echoes those introspective moments of her father, is uncomfortable with the process of elopement:

> Here, catch this casket, it is worth the pains.
> I am glad 'tis night—you do not look on me,
> For I am much asham'd of my exchange:
> But love is blind, and lovers cannot see
> The pretty follies that themselves commit,
> For if they could, Cupid himself would blush
> To see me thus transformed to a boy. (2.6.33–39)

We may, of course, read this admission literally in that Jessica expresses embarrassment that she is forced to disguise herself, but there appears to be a little more at stake in her "shame." The casket that Jessica steals from her father contains his "meaning"; it will be given in "exchange" for a Christian husband, and its contents are in no sense mysterious, unlike those of the caskets that will determine Portia's future. Portia remains within the rules set down by her dead father *even though* she must know by the time Bassanio comes to choose what, in general terms, the contents of the leaden casket are. By contrast, the contents of Jessica's casket are manifest—that is to say, they are entirely demystified—and she consequently displaces the anxiety she feels for her having violated the domestic regime of her father onto her disguise itself, which now becomes the symbol of a dislocated subjectivity. By invoking the figure of blind Cupid as an analogue of her own situation, the actor playing Jessica effectively comments on the process whereby a transgressive act can be brought within a discursive field that ameliorates the transgression. But not completely, since the dramatic character cannot expunge the emotional consequences of a serious domestic violation. Jessica may be able to remover her/himself physically from the "hell" that is Shylock's house, but the "shame" associated with her rebellion remains, even if it appears to be treated lightly: "What, must I hold a candle to my shames? /

They in themselves (goodsooth) are too too light" (2.6.41–42). Jessica's anxiety, at the very point of departure, undercuts the pleasure that her engaging appeal to the "follies" of lovers appears to legitimate. In other words, Jessica is never allowed in the play to indulge fully the positive consequences of her action, since what is put at risk in her elopement are, precisely, those regulatory practices that govern marital exchange in the play, and that the discourses of "love" seek imperfectly to mystify. Moreover, as if to underscore the process, Jessica is caught in the act of *undoing* her father's meanings as she appropriates both his material wealth and his idiom in her desire to "make fast the doors," and in gilding herself "with some moe ducats" (2.6.49–50). Of course, the process of "gilding," as we shall see shortly, here comments proleptically upon Bassanio's later caution in which "crisped snaky golden locks" materially manifest "the guiled shore to a most dangerous sea" (3.2.92, 97–98) and is emblematic of "thou gaudy gold, / Hard food for Midas" (3.2.101–102). Gratiano's approval of Jessica's appropriation of her father's gold, "Now (by my hood) a gentle, and no Jew" (2.6.51), and Lorenzo's acquiescence in the ruse are the antithesis of Bassanio's strategy, almost to the point where we can accuse the latter of being in denial of the motive for his own quest. Nor should we miss the play of meaning that can transmute "gild" into "guiled." Given this context, Jessica's elopement is made to resonate throughout the play, and the net effect, apart from the stripping of her female subjectivity, is the furthering of an uncomfortable linguistic play that focuses upon the discomfort surrounding the question of the material exchanges that take place as part of the ritual of marriage. Moreover, her embarkation upon a path of disguise subsumes linguistically the "mythical" Cupid into a web of deception that exposes the fictionality of those ideological constraints that would bind daughter to father in the play.

The more we peel off the layers of signification that inscribe Jessica within the action, the more we come to realize that her role, and hence that of her father, is unique in Shakespearean comedy. We are used to initially rebellious daughters whose futures are consolidated as paternal opposition to their marriage choices melts miraculously away. But where fathers are not ultimately persuaded of the rightness of their daughters' choices then the conclusions are tragic, as evidenced in the earlier *Romeo and Juliet* and the later, much more pertinent, *Othello*.

It is no accident that the news of Jessica's elopement and Antonio's demise immediately precedes the successful outcome of Bassanio's Jason-like quest for Portia. Jessica's elopement both violates and subverts in a very radical way the "law" of the father, whereas, as we have seen, the risks that Portia faces are circumscribed by the conditions of her dead father's "will." Bassanio chooses what Freud, in his essay on "The Theme of The Three Caskets," calls "the fairest and best of women" (245), but he is not unaware of the "death" that beauty masks, and of which Jessica is a complex harbinger:

> Look on beauty,
> And you shall see 'tis purchas'd by the weight,
> Which therein works a miracle in nature,
> Making them lightest that wear most of it:
> So are those crisped snaky golden locks
> Which make such wanton gambols with the wind
> Upon supposed fairness, often known
> To be the dowry of a second head,
> The skull that bred them in the sepulchre. (3.2.88–96)

The dowry he seeks is Portia's material wealth, mystified in the discourse of romantic love, but he is aware of another, less attractive alternative that is a harbinger of death. Portia's "dowry" left by her father to be disposed of in the choice of the caskets (and hence left to chance) is of a radically different kind from the "dowry" that Jessica steals from her father. In the latter case the entry into the society of Christian Venice depends, as we have seen, upon a filial violation that is the metaphorical equivalent of death itself. Jessica, then, stands in a strange and uncanny relation to Portia, and she draws to herself a number of the negative aspects surrounding the transaction of marriage itself. She is referred to as an "infidel" (3.2.217), and she is briefly acknowledged by Gratiano, who had earlier transformed her into a "gentle," with the words "Nerissa, cheer yond stranger, bid her welcome" (3.2.236). Jessica is, at this point in the play, in every sense a stranger to herself, a complex image of the very materiality that Venice seeks, almost desperately in the play, to marginalize.

I have suggested that Jessica is the means whereby the play interrogates those details of the marriage contract that the play's preoccupation with money renders uncomfortable and difficult to negotiate. In every other Shakespearean context her elopement would be regarded with ambivalence, but because of her association with Shylock it elicits sympathy. Indeed, the episode in which a ring is exchanged for a monkey returns in this scene as the inhuman "ape-like" Shylock who becomes the object of Salerio's scorn:

> never did I know
> A creature that did bear the shape of man
> So keen and greedy to confound a man. (3.2.273–75)

This is also the moment for yet another intimate revelation from the unrepresented life of Shylock, an insight into the outsider's "self" and into the symbolic exchanges that validate his own subjectivity, in which Jessica opposes his now inhuman quest to the just and merciful "law" of Venice:

> When I was with him I have heard him swear
> To Tubal and to Chus, his countrymen,

> That he would rather have Antonio's flesh
> Than twenty times the value of the sum
> That he did owe him: and I know my lord,
> If law, authority, and power deny not,
> It will go hard with poor Antonio. (3.2.283–89)

Ironically, however, in prising open the private motives of her father she also draws attention to her own "strange" position and to her actions that are partially justified insofar as they appear to be motivated, but which are still, in the final analysis, dangerous.

Jessica's multiple identity in the play is, as we have argued, overdetermined by a number of forces. She is, first and foremost, the daughter of a Jew and as such is an "outsider." Her defection to Christianity through her elopement with Lorenzo draws her into Venice that is the structure-in-dominance of the play. But her defection threatens the organization of the "family" that is the mimetic "other" of its Venetian counterpart. To this extent Venice and Belmont function as two sides of an ideology that seeks to harmonize fiscal dealing and romantic entanglement. Although Portia is the only surviving member of her "family" (her father is dead, and, we presume, so is her mother), the structure within which she is inscribed is identical to that of Jessica, but with one exception: the "law" that remains in place, even after the death of her father, is a Christian law. In the case of Jessica she is subject to the law of her father, which is Jewish law. Notwithstanding this important difference, what is crucial for the purposes of this argument is the recognition of the fact that Jessica's violation of a *family* obligation—irrespective of the nature of that family and of the motivation for her action—cannot entirely be separated from the ideological commitment to what the play asserts is the universal principle of family order. In taking her future into her own hands Jessica manages what Portia effectively refuses to do, even though she recognizes the libidinal impulse that might urge her to challenge the law of her dead father: Jessica makes her own law that effectively detaches her from the network of constraints designed to check her impulsiveness.

By its evocation of a degree of sympathy for the domestic plight of Shylock (whose own wife Leah is also absent) the play points up the danger of Jessica's elopement. She has become the unruly woman who refuses parental control and who violates the order of the family. Thus, her action is both condoned and criticized in the play; it is condoned through the motivation to escape which she shares with Lancelet, but her actions are subsequently placed in contexts that emphasize violation and uncertainty, and she effectively acknowledges this. Her parting with her absent mother's gift to her father aligns Shylock momentarily with the later Christian exchange of rings and serves to suggest something other than a purely parodic version of Christian marriage. Whereas the Jew stands, generally, in a mimetic relation to the domestic practices of Venice, in this instance he appears, uncomfortably, perhaps, simply to replicate them both in terms of actions and emotions. Whereas elsewhere in the play we might recognize, but not sympathize with, the strength of his enmity towards his Venetian adversaries, at this crucial moment the focus is upon an intensity of feeling from which spectators cannot easily detach themselves. It is the emotion of a father faced with the actions of a wayward and unruly daughter. Jessica's action is one that in the later play, *Othello,* will be the death of the disillusioned father Brabantio whose daughter, Desdemona, elopes with a "stranger." It is the one gesture that is designed to expose the vulnerability of patriarchy itself, and it signals the deaths of fathers. Moreover, to a society politically committed to the organization of the family as a "commonwealth," as a replication of the order of the state, elopement was tantamount to a form of domestic treason in its capacity to undermine the established hierarchy. The context of Jessica's elopement does something to mitigate the extremity of her action but it does not, indeed it cannot, as we have already seen, justify it entirely.

Having allowed the danger that Jessica represents to articulate itself, the play then takes an interesting and quite unusual turn. The daughter becomes the instrument whereby the "strange" father is brought within the bounds of Christian law and Christian domestic practice. To this extent Jessica is the term in the play that both deconstructs *and* reconstitutes the very order that Shylock threatens. Here what is throughout the play a fraught and anxious wisdom is displaced from the father onto the child and, through the acquisition of a Christian son, his "children" become the instrument of his salvation. Of course, that salvation itself is not unproblematical since the agony of the Jew's metaphorical death initiates him into a society, some of whose members confess, as did Antonio at the beginning of the play, to an inexplicable sadness. Everywhere we look in the play there is disunity and dislocation, radical disharmonies that the action is now required to negotiate. The only way in which Venice can cope with the self-alienation that inheres in its fiscal dealings is to project (in both senses of the word) its fantasies onto the world of Belmont. Belmont is, in other words, Venice's fantasy of itself, a place where the world of fiscal exchange can be transmuted into the mystifying romantic discourses of social harmony. But those romantic discourses themselves are fraught (much like the merchant venturing of Antonio) with peril, and the dangers are never far from the surface. Even in Belmont appearances can be deceptive: under the "crisped snaky golden locks" there may be "the skull that bred them in the sepulchre," while the unruly female "will of a living daughter" (1.2.24), notwithstanding the later exchange of rings between Portia and Bassanio, may threaten the ecstasy of marital union that he later fails to express:

> Madam, you have bereft me of all words,
> Only my blood speaks to you in my veins,
> And there is such confusion in my powers,

> As after some oration fairly spoke
> By a beloved prince, there doth appear
> Among the buzzing pleased multitude,
> Where every something being blent together,
> Turns to a wild of nothing, save of joy
> Express'd and not express'd: but when this ring
> Parts from this finger, then parts life from hence,—
> O then be bold to say Bassanio's dead! (3.2.175–85)

What keeps the unruly "blood" in check here—and we may recall that Shylock is accused earlier of an incestuously venal unruliness—is the ring as a symbol of union. This is, in effect, a "hiding of the grossness with fair ornament" (3.2.80) indeed.

It is in passages such as this that the play can be seen to be negotiating some of the intractable material that the comedy has unearthed. Indeed we can detect in such moments, and there are many in the play, the ideological force of a laughter that seeks to distance those anxieties that are generated from within a series of linked institutions whose overlapping concerns render them increasingly problematical. Bassanio's vow invites consideration of death; the articulation of his vow is predicated upon a premise whose own conditionality mocks the speaker. We know that Bassanio will be persuaded to part with Portia's ring but the question is: to whom will he give it, and for what reasons?

In the play moments of transition serve to demarcate boundaries, but once identified, the histories of their traversing return to haunt the narrative. It is in this context that we need to view the exchange between Lorenzo and Jessica that opens the final act of the play. Their dual recounting of the types of thwarted love offers a verbal analogue of the contrasting brightness of the moon and the surrounding darkness of night. Lorenzo also suggests this as a context for Jessica's elopement:

> In such a night
> Did Jessica steal from the wealthy Jew,
> And with an unthrift love did run from Venice
> As far as Belmont. (5.1.14–17)

And she, for her part, repeats the formula but transforms the transgression into the familiar domestic discourse of playfully uncertain love:

> In such a night
> Did young Lorenzo swear he loved her well,
> Stealing her soul with many vows of faith,
> And ne'er a true one. (5.1.17–20)

Again this episode anticipates the dilemma that Bassanio and Gratiano later find themselves in when they are accused of infidelity by their respective spouses. The Lorenzo-Jessica prolepsis serves to draw off the potentially serious consequences of human inconstancy that are tied up in the process of courtship, and where infidelity here becomes a symptom of a more general infidelity whose consequences are potentially deadly. In this respect *The Merchant of Venice* anticipates the sentiment of the thwarted patriarch Brabantio whose warning to his son-in-law echoes throughout the later play, *Othello*:

> Look to her, Moor, if thou hast eyes to see:
> She hath deceived her father, and may thee. (1.3.293–94)

The emphasis at this point in *The Merchant of Venice*, however, is upon "harmony" and the transformation of jarring discord into a concord that, ideologically speaking, draws together music and religion as the stabilizing elements in an otherwise riven human society. Now the night is associated, not with what Jessica earlier calls the rather more negative business of "outnighting" (5.1.23), but with stillness and "the touches of sweet harmony" (5.1.56–57). In this ideologically reconstituted night the order of "heaven" is disclosed: "Sit Jessica,—look how the floor of heaven / Is thick inlaid with patens of bright gold" (5.1.58–59). The "paten" is, of course, the ceremonial dish on which the host, the symbolic representation of the body of Christ, is presented to the communicant. Clearly, at this moment in the play the husband Lorenzo seeks to explain what are, in effect, the implicitly political rituals of Christian society to a wife who has become a recent convert. Her conversion heralds the conversion of her father, who is forced by Venetian law to relinquish his "Jewish" faith, but the description of the stars as "patens of bright gold" also effectively transubstantiates the night in precisely the same way in which the romantic poetry of seduction transforms the libidinal energies of the lovers into a spiritual jouissance. What makes the process incomplete is that physical excess that stubbornly resists transubstantiation.

Nevertheless, it is the figure of Jessica that persistently brings this rhetoric down to earth, so to speak, and in a much more protracted way than either Portia or Nerissa is capable of doing. In the same way that she undoes the patriarchal ordering of courtship procedures, she stands now in Belmont as a material challenge to the orthodoxy that Portia and Nerissa represent. She inhabits the hierarchy of Belmont strangely, not as a figure lamenting the death of her father's religion, as had been the case in the Jonathan Miller production of the play in 1970, nor as the excluded outsider of the more recent Compass Theatre production, but as a defiant rebuke to the supinely confident Portia. This is perhaps the reason why she confides to Lorenzo, "I am never merry when I hear sweet music" (5.1.69), and it is also, perhaps, the reason why Lorenzo then proceeds to lecture her on the politics of music:

therefore the poet
Did feign that Orpheus drew trees, stones, and floods,
Since naught so stockish, hard and full of rage,
But music for the time doth change his nature,—
The man that hath no music in himself,
Nor is not moved with the concord of sweet sounds,
Is fit for treasons, stratagems, and spoils,
The motions of his spirit are dull as night,
And his affections dark as Erebus:
Let no such man be trusted:—mark the music. (5.2.79–88)

These lines are part of the ensemble of "gorgeous lines about night and music at the opening of the last act"(Burckhardt 254) to which most critics of the play respond positively. But they have a dual frame of reference, reminding us firstly of Shylock's earlier dismissal of "the vile squealing of the wryneck'd fife" (2.5.30), and secondly of Jessica's own admission and her propensity for "treasons, stratagems, and spoils." Where the potential unruliness associated with the partners in Christian marriage is either obviated by the continuing force of marriage vows, or by the fear of a human propensity to err, Jessica's capacity for subversion moves beyond these containing discourses. Apart from Portia's perfunctory enlisting of her and Lorenzo in the plot to humiliate Bassanio, Jessica remains a silent and multiform presence onstage until the ending of the play. The deed of gift "From the rich Jew" (5.1.292) comes hard on the heels of the news that Antonio's argosies are safe, and is the material evidence of the newly constituted Christian family that Jessica's defection has brought to birth. Moreover, at the end of the play she is, in effect, the means through which caskets, rings, and argosies are reprised: she has seized her father's casket, exchanged his ring for a monkey, and is now in receipt of a metaphorical argosy through the gift of her father. Significantly she never gives herself to Lorenzo in quite the way that Portia relinquishes her independent power to her "lord" Bassanio, and at the end of the play there is a clear sense that the safekeeping of her "ring" is likely to be a very different matter compared with Gratiano's lighthearted dismissal of his "fear." If woman in the play retains a degree of sexual power that it is the purpose of marriage to harness completely, then Jessica is, much more substantially than the other female characters in the play, that symbol of excess that patriarchy will always fear. Her shape-changing is strategic but, unlike Portia's, it augments her breaking of the bonds of patriarchy; her subsequent "incorporation" into the structures of Venice presents a much more wide-ranging radical challenge to its harmony. Venice may transform Jessica into a Christian wife, and her father into a Christian patriarch, but the exposure of that ideological process means that it cannot erase the history of their transformation. What will bind the dead Shylock to his daughter is not a restrictive law that will guarantee the control of her "will," but a deed of gift that will release the very material substance that is the root cause of Venice's anxieties, money and possessions.

For the moment Jessica remains silent, but it is the silence of repression that always threatens to return. She apes Portia, but her condition as the receiver of unexpected wealth also apes Antonio, and in this play mimicry distorts the object of imitation rather than confirms its authority. In this respect the focus at the end of the play is not so much upon the alleged loneliness of Antonio, but rather upon the silent threat that Venice has blindly, but of economic necessity, incorporated into itself. This is the danger that Jessica represents in *The Merchant of Venice*.

Notes

1. I am grateful to Samantha Richardson of Compass Theatre Company for providing me with details of this performance including a range of reviews of the production.
2. All references to *The Merchant of Venice* are from John Russell Brown ed., *The Merchant of Venice*, Arden Shakespeare Series (London, 1955).
3. See Albert Memmi, *Racism*, trans. Steve Martinot (Minneapolis & London, 2000), p.xxiii. I have borrowed this formulation from Martinot's excellent introduction.
4. Cf. Philip Caesar, *A Generall Discourse Against the Damnable Sect of Usurers* (London 1578), p. 4, where usurers are described as "likened to poysoned serpentes, to madde Dogges, to greedie Womes, to Wolues, Beares, and to other such rauening beastes." See also John Drakakis, "Violence in Venice" (University of Passau, forthcoming).

Works Cited

Bawcutt, N.W., ed. *Christopher Marlowe: The Jew of Malta.* Manchester: Manchester University Press, 1978.

Belsey, Catherine. "Love in Venice." 1991. Coyle 139–60.

Bulman, James C. *The Merchant of Venice.* Manchester: Manchester University Press, 1991.

Burckhardt, Sigurd. "*The Merchant of Venice*: The Gentle Bond." *English Literary History* 29 (1962): 239–62.

Coyle, Martin, ed. "*The Merchant of Venice*": *New Casebooks.* New York: St. Martin's Press, 1998.

Danson, Lawrence. *The Harmonies of "The Merchant of Venice."* New Haven and London: Yale University Press, 1978.

Derrida, Jacques. "Plato's Pharmacy." *Dissemination.* Trans. Barbara Johnson. Chicago and London: University of Chicago Press, 1981.

Fortin, René. "Launcelot and the Uses of Allegory in *The Merchant of Venice*." *Studies in English Literature 1500–1900* 14 (1974): 259–70.

Freud, Sigmund. "The Theme of The Three Caskets." *The Pelican Freud Library, vol.14: Art and Literature*. Harmondsworth: Penguin, 1985.

Greenblatt, Stephen, Walter Cohen, Katherine Eisaman Mauss, eds. *The Norton Shakespeare*. New York and London: Norton, 1997.

Memmi, Albert. *Racism*. Trans. Steve Martinot. Minneapolis and London: University of Minnesota Press, 2000.

Newman, Karen. "Portia's Ring: Unruly Women and the Structures of Exchange in *The Merchant of Venice*." 1987. Coyle 117–38.

Shakespeare, William. *The Merchant of Venice*. Ed. John Russell Brown. London: Methuen, 1998.

Terry, Ellen. *Lectures on Shakespeare*. London: Chatto and Windus, 1932.

Textual Deviancy in
The Merchant of Venice

JOHN F. ANDREWS

Although the thematic issues it poses have made *The Merchant of Venice* increasingly problematic in recent decades, so much so that any company that sets out to produce the comedy must weigh the effect it might have upon impressionable playgoers, the text of the work is rightly regarded as one that confronts us with, at most, minor difficulties. Modern printings are based essentially upon the 1600 First Quarto, which seems to have been set into type with great care by methodical compositors, and which is generally thought to derive either from a reasonably clean authorial manuscript or from a conscientious scribal copy of one. As a result, anyone who collates today's most popular and widely employed editions will discover no more than a handful of minor discrepancies between one rendering of the play's dramatic blueprint and another.[1]

This kind of editorial consensus is, of course, reassuring, particularly when it relates to a title that has generated so much controversy in other respects. Owing to the premium such concord places on uniformity, however, especially with regard to the maintenance of current conventions in orthography, grammar, and lexicology, the usual approach to *The Merchant of Venice* will often deprive twenty-first-century readers of the opportunity to experience nuances of sound and sense which emanate from inconsistencies in its original text—subtle variations in spelling and punctuation, for example—and which appear to have been integral to the writer's conceptual process.

I would argue that a close look at the publication in which this work was initially made available to the Elizabethan public will disclose a number of characteristics that provide helpful clues to Shakespeare's artistry. As such they merit our attention, not merely because of their intrinsic interest, which is incalculable, but because of the questions they compel us to ponder about linguistic criteria and hermeneutic procedures that continue to be applied to this and similar texts despite a growing body of evidence that post-Jacobean "normalizing" practices, which by definition are alien to any archaic features they modify, have systematically obscured significant distinctions between Shakespeare's orientation to language and our own. By imposing twentieth- and twenty-first-century standards on all the discourse in sixteenth- and seventeenth-century works such as *The Merchant of Venice*, we have largely incapacitated ourselves from noticing, let alone appreciating, many of the advantages a comparatively flexible and unfettered medium, with its amenability to deviations that would have been precluded by later canons of semantic rectitude, supplied a Renaissance wordsmith of peerless genius.[2]

With an admiring nod to poet Henry Reid, I propose to launch these explorations with the "Naming of Parts." In the typical twentieth-century edition of *The Merchant of Venice*, the young apprentice who abandons Shylock to join Bassanio's retinue is presented to us as *Lancelot*, an appellation that never occurs either in the 1600 First Quarto or in the primarily derivative 1623 First Folio printing. For the playwright, and for his earliest theatergoers and readers, this Clown appears to have been known solely as *Launcelet*, a name that can be translated "little lance" or "small knife." In all probability Shakespeare was amusing his theater patrons with a variation on *Launce*, the moniker that Will Kempe, the comic virtuoso who is believed to have been the first actor to inhabit both roles, carried as Launcelet's predecessor in *The Two Gentlemen of Verona*. Like *Launce*, *Launcelet* is a handle with phallic implications,[3] and those implications manifest themselves not only in the scene (2.2) in which the Clown depicts himself as something other than "an honest mans sonne"—since, as he says, "my Father did something smacke, something grow to"—but during a later colloquy (3.5) in which Lorenzo, reacting to Jessica's report that Launcelet has cast aspersions on her husband's credentials as an upright "member of the common-wealth," reminds a feisty servant that "the Moore is with child" by him.[4]

Only once in the earliest texts—in a single passage of the unauthoritative 1619 Second Quarto—does the form *Lancelot* emerge.[5] There is every reason to infer, in short, that the playwright who devised this character went out of his way to eschew a precise orthographic equivalence between Launcelet's name and that of the Arthurian knight it calls to mind. So why have editors since the fourth decade of the seventeenth century presumed to bestow upon Shakespeare's Clown a mock-heroic dignity his author evidently declined to accord him? As Falstaff might put it, a question to be ask'd.

And speaking of Launcelet, how should we render the Clown's surname? Before "*old Gobbo*" enters with his basket in 2.2, his loquacious offspring refers to himself several times as "*Launcelet Iobbe.*" This, it may surprise us to learn, is the only spoken form in which the Clown's patronymic occurs in Q1, and it is limited to the soliloquy with which the scene commences. Like *Claudius*, in other words (an identity which is provided for the usurping King in the opening stage direction of *Hamlet* and in the immedi-

ately succeeding speech heading of the 1604/5 Second Quarto printing of
1.2, but which is never voiced in the tragedy's spoken text), *Gobbo* (which
means "lump" or "humpback," and which would carry a hard-g sound in
modern Italian) occurs only in the original stage directions and speech headings. It is a purely literary version of Launcelet's family name, and so far as
we can determine it was never enunciated from any stage during the playwright's lifetime.

What's more, the Clown's wordplay on what the dramatic context—a
delightful, and often brilliant, parody of tropes from the medieval *psychomachia*—shows to be a variation of *Job* can be construed as an indication
that, whether rightly or wrongly, Shakespeare thought of both *Iobbe* and
Gobbo as proper nouns to be articulated with a soft-g sound.[6]

During a fascinating comment on this passage in her meticulous and
thought-provoking edition of *The Merchant of Venice*, M. M. Mahood
informs us that "A famous Venetian church is dedicated to S. Giobbe, i.e.
Job."[7] Professor Mahood goes on to observe that in the 1663 Third Folio,
"*Iobbe*" becomes "*Job*." But even if she is on firm ground to infer that "The
name 'Gobbo' may derive from *il Gobbo di Rialto*" (a "crouching stone figure" who supported "the platform from which laws were promulgated" in
Venice), it may well be that what Mahood ascribes to Shakespeare's "initial
uncertainty about how to spell" the Clown's name in *The Merchant of Venice*
can be explained with equal persuasiveness in a less condescending fashion.
To my mind, the shift from *Iobbe* in Launcelet's soliloquy to the *Gobbo* to be
found in the stage directions and speech headings of 2.2 and subsequent
scenes is more plausibly accounted for as an example of the dramatist's
habitual propensity to have things both ways. To be strictly correct, Shakespeare would have needed to go with either *Giobbe* or *Gobbo*. What he
seems to have opted for instead was a witty, if solecistic, conflation of two
Italian words, to yield a coinage that sophisticated but tolerant readers of the
First Quarto might have silently adjusted to *Giobbo*, and one that would have
revealed the author's quintessentially eclectic imagination to be oscillating
between such disparate (though, upon reflection, amusingly compatible)
archetypes as the proverbially afflicted Job and the dwarfish hunchback of *il
Gobbo di Rialto*.

Now let's turn to other portions of the text in which the phrasing a contemporary reader encountered in the 1600 printing of *The Merchant of Venice*
would have differed from that to be apprehended by anyone in our own era
who comes to the play exclusively through the medium of a representative
late twentieth- or early twenty-first-century edition.

In the speech that opens the play in Q1, Anthonio[8] says

> In sooth I know not why I am so sad,
> It wearies me, you say it wearies you;

> But how I caught it, found it, or came by it,
> What stuff 'tis made of, whereof it is borne,
> I am to learne.

Here the word that is most likely to elicit our curiosity is *borne*, a form that antedates the distinction we have long made between *borne* and *born*, the two phonemes which descend from it.[9] Practically all recent editions select the latter in this instance. But surely the expression in which the word occurs could logically be paraphrased either "whence it is born" (i.e., "what gave birth to it") or "by what means it is borne" (i.e., "what there is in my nature which makes me carry, and thereby be susceptible to the influence of, this malady"). If today's reader of *The Merchant of Venice* happens upon an unannotated *born* in this passage, only the first set of possibilities will be available for appropriation. If, on the other hand, that person's initial exposure to Anthonio's meditation is an auditory one (i.e., one that takes place as the sounds the author called for are being executed by performers), he or she may be disposed to wonder whether the merchant means "born" or "borne." I'm persuaded that a vigilant awareness of the potential for ambiguity should continually guide our response to moments such as this. We should remember, whenever we deal with a Shakespearean playscript which has made its way into print, that all of its words were designed to be transmitted through our ears before they were to be taken in as the ink-born(e) alphabetic symbols on a page that we process through our eyes and brains.[10]

   An apt reminder of the applicability of this principle occurs in 1.1 where Gratiano says

> O my *Anthonio* I doe know of these
> That therefore onely are reputed wise
> For saying nothing; when I am very sure
> If they should speake, would almost dam those eares
> Which hearing them would call their brothers fooles,
> Ile tell thee more of this another time. (94–98)

In the fourth line of this passage modern editions ordinarily follow the 1685 Fourth Folio and emend *dam* to *damn*. That yields an acceptable meaning, of course, and one that looks forward to the remarks that introduce 3.5, where Launcelet tells Jessica that he fears she's doomed to perdition. But in the absence of a helpful note such as the one that Jay Halio includes in his 1993 Oxford World Classics edition[11] of the play, this alteration closes off a sense of *dam* (plug up, and thus block, a passage) that is at least equally suited to the immediate context. Most of today's editions do nothing to alert a reader to the potential for wordplay on the homonyms *dam* and *damn*. Nor do they prepare the way for 3.1.31–34, where Solanio's reference to Jessica's "dam"

(mother) prompts Shylock to swear that "She is damnd" for her disrespectful
behavior.

In the following scene, 1.2, we meet Portia, who tells her "wayting
woman" that she is "awearie of this great world." The sympathetic Nerissa
replies:

> You would be sweet Madam, if your miseries were in the same aboundance
> as your good fortunes are: and yet for ought I see, they are as sicke that sur-
> feite with too much, as they that starue with nothing; it is no meane happi-
> ness therfore to be seated in the meane, superfluitie comes sooner by white
> haires, but competencie liues longer.

In this passage, so far as I know, the Guild and Everyman volumes are the
only twentieth-century editions to retain the Quarto's *aboundance*, which is
normally modernized to *abundance*. For most scholars, a tiny disparity
between an obsolete form in the control text and the familiar spelling that
readers glide by in virtually every current edition appears to be a matter of
complete indifference. Inasmuch as *aboundance* would appear to be an
option that Shakespeare employed with some frequency, however (it turns up
in five of the fourteen instances in which the word occurs in the early printings of his works, a number that includes both of its uses in *2 Henry IV* and
two of its four uses in the *Sonnets*), the original texts may indicate either how
he customarily pronounced the noun or how he preferred to have it treated in
certain dramatic situations. If so, I suspect that his choice in this case was
conditioned by a desire to foreshadow the many iterations of *bound*, a word
that will acquire considerable thematic resonance in subsequent portions of
The Merchant of Venice. Bound occurs no fewer than four times in the first
twenty lines of the succeeding scene, for example, and seven times more in
acts 4 and 5.

In their comments on 1.3, editors and critics frequently allude to the wit
with which Shylock puns on *rats*, *rates*, and *pirates* in lines 15–28. But practically no one calls attention to the plangent echo of *curre* (cur) in what is
undoubtedly the most emotion-packed clause of a memorable indictment:

> What should I say to you? Should I not say
> Hath a dog money? Is it possible
> A curre can lend three thousand ducats? Or
> Shall I bend low, and in a bond-mans key
> With bated breath, and whispring humbleness
> Say this: Faire sir, you spet on me on Wednesday last,
> You spurnd me such a day another time,
> You calld me dogge: and for these curtesies
> Ile lend you thus much moneyes.

Here, of course, the spelling in the original text—*curtesies*, rather than the *courtesies* a reader's eye will encounter in modern editions—makes it easier to discern a relationship that any actor who plays Shylock with insight and sensitivity will want to emphasize with a telling stress upon the bitter ironies of the first syllable.[12]

From this passage let's proceed to others in which First Quarto spellings in *The Merchant of Venice* carry the potential for implications that get excised by today's editorial operations and thus fall prey to the dark backward and abysm of time.

In the speech with which she conducts Arragon to the chamber in which he will make his fatal choice (2.9.4–8), Portia says

> Behold, there stand the caskets noble Prince,
> yf you choose that wherein I am containd
> straight shall our nuptiall rights be solemniz'd:
> but if you faile, without more speech my Lord
> you must be gone from hence immediatly.

Here not only do almost all modern editions change *rights* to *rites*. They do so without acknowledging that in a drama for which legal issues can be matters of life and death, *rights* (contractual provisions and privileges) are at least as important to the heroine's suitors as are the *rites* (ritual ceremonies) by which the victorious competitor's choice will be "solemniz'd" (publicly ratified and celebrated).

Bassanio will be that winning competitor, of course, and it may be worth listening to some of what he says as he meditates upon the caskets in 3.2.74–88:

> The world is still deceau'd with ornament
> In Law, what plea so tainted and corrupt,
> But being season'd with a gracious voyce,
> Obscures the show of euill. In religion
> What damned error but some sober brow
> will bless it, and approue it with a text,
> Hiding the grosnes with faire ornament:
> There is no voyce[13] so simple, but assumes
> Some marke of vertue on his outward parts;
> How many cowards whose harts are all as false
> As stayers of sand, weare yet vpon their chins
> The beards of Hercules and frowning Mars,
> who inward searcht, haue lyuers white as milk,
> And these assume but valours excrement
> To render them redoubted.

In this speech it is the word *stayers* upon which I wish to focus. With one noteworthy exception (M. M. Mahood's Cambridge text), modern editions invariably substitute *stairs* here. Some point out, while doing so, that *stayers* is a variant spelling of *stairs* that may allude to *stays* in a sense that means "props" or "supports." Professor Mahood defends her decision to retain the Quarto reading by explaining that "A coward's support is unreliable, like an untrustworthy 'stay' or rope in the rigging of a ship."[14] What no one[15] seems to have considered, however (even so judicious a critic as Professor Mahood), is the possibility that *stayers of sand* is a phrase the playwright devised to suggest both (a) "stairs composed of sand" and (b) "cowards" who "stay" away from danger because their valor is as soft, shifting, and insubstantial as "sand."

After Bassanio has selected the proper casket, his friend Gratiano announces (in 3.2.191–208) that he too has been successfully engaged in matrimonial overtures:

> For wooing heere vntill I swet again,
> and swearing till my very rough was dry
> with oathes of loue, at last, if promise last
> I got a promise of this fair one heere
> to haue her loue: prouided that your fortune
> atchiu'd her mistres.

In the second line of this speech the 1619 Second Quarto replaced *rough* with *roof*, and modern editors have traditionally followed suit, occasionally observing while doing so that *rough* is a dialectal form of *roof*. Here again it would seem to be entirely in keeping with Shakespeare's customary practice to adopt a spelling—and thereby encourage, in the actors who would deliver these lines, a pronunciation—that can accomplish a pair of overlapping objectives simultaneously: (a) conjure up an image of the roof of Gratiano's mouth, and (b) convey the texture that that granular surface would have in the "dry" condition he describes when he refers to it.

As Anthonio is being arrested for his failure to comply with the repayment schedule to which he has committed himself, Solanio describes the merchant's enemy as "the most impenitrable curre / that euer kept with men" (3.3.18–19). Here today's editors silently emend *impenitrable* to *impenetrable*, and those few who indicate the change in their textual collations tend to do so without evincing any awareness of a need to comment on so minuscule a correction. But can we be sure that the spelling in the Second Quarto is not a Shakespearean coinage? To me it has every sign of a nonce-word that combines two contextually relevant senses: (a) so hard-hearted as to be invulnerable to penetration by what the protagonist's Lady calls "the compunctious visitings of Nature" in *Macbeth*, I.5.47, and, as a consequence, (b) incapable of the pangs of guilt and remorse that must be present before a sinner can become a penitent.

In a thematically related passage (4.1.3–6) at the beginning of the Trial Scene, the Duke tells Anthonio

> I am sorry for thee, thou art come to aunswere
> a stonie aduersarie, an inhumaine wretch,
> vncapable of pitty, voyd, and empty
> from any dram of mercie.

Those who come upon these lines in current editions will ordinarily find *inhuman* rather than *inhumaine* or *inhumane* in the phrase which describes the kind of "wretch" a vengeful Shylock has become. Even if they consult the textual notes and collations, they will probably remain uninformed that what a sixteenth-century audience heard, and inferred from, the Duke's phrasing was almost certainly different from, and more profoundly ominous than, what anyone who hears or reads this passage in our day is likely to extract from a post-Renaissance redaction of it.[16]

A bit later in the Trial Scene (4.1.59–62), Shylock tells the Duke he feels no compulsion to justify his behavior in any manner that will satisfy his victim's advocates.

> So can I giue no reason, nor I will not,
> more then a lodgd hate, and a certain loathing
> I beare *Anthonio*, that I follow thus
> a loosing sute against him? are you aunswered?

Here the word most of us will zoom in upon is *loosing*, another multivalent pre-modern form, and one that can be rendered either "losing" or "loosing." As one might expect, it is characteristically normalized to *losing* in today's texts. There can be little doubt that the standard editorial procedure conforms to the intent an imprudent, and increasingly hubristic, speaker expresses. But does it also capture all the proleptic possibilities the playwright wanted those with "judgements in such matters" (*Hamlet*, 2.2.470–71) to register at this moment in a well-conceived production of the play? We have no means of resolving an issue such as this, of course, but it seems vital to recognize that a shift from *loosing* to *losing* erases most, if not all, of the equivocal potential in the original Elizabethan form. It thus shortchanges the audience by eliminating any chance that even the most perceptive observers will foresee that Shylock's implacable pursuit of Anthonio is likely to lead, not only to the plaintiff's forfeit of far more than he appears capable of imagining to be at risk, but to his "loosing" (releasing, and thereby setting at liberty to retaliate)

a defendant who will eventually be granted an opportunity to exact an excru-
ciating fine from his relentless creditor.[17]

When a concerned Bassanio implores "the learned Iudge" to "Wrest
once the Law" to his "Authority," the disguised Portia replies with another
statement (4.1.221–25) which proves susceptible to the kind of "double
sense" (*Macbeth*, 5.7.49) that figures so pervasively in other Shakespearean
masterworks. "It must not be," the Trial Scene's surrogate magistrate insists,
because

> there is no power in Venice
> can altar a decree established:
> twill be recorded for a precedent,
> and many an errour by the same example
> will rush into the state, it cannot be.

In this instance the intriguing word is *altar*, which the spell-checkers who
regulate modern editions automatically replace with *alter*. Once again, the
impact of what would seem to be an obvious correction is to give priority to
a sense that fits the present context, and surely the sense a clever Portia
expects her hearers to assume that her statement is meant to convey. But in
the event that a listener has failed to take in what will turn out to be a pertinent homonym, the Quarto spelling makes it accessible to the eye of an attentive reader. Not only does the sound of Portia's word anticipate Gratiano's
plea that Shylock be granted "A halter gratis" (4.1.382); it foreshadows the
disposition that Anthonio will recommend in the speech that follows, when
he asks the Duke to order that Shylock—if he wishes to avoid the penalty he
would otherwise be forced to suffer by virtue of "a decree established"—be
brought to the altar and there be altered from a Jew to a Christian.[18]

Let's draw this brief survey to a close with a few illustrations of the
potential for ambiguity in the letter *I*.[19] Early in the Trial Scene, when "Balt-
hazer" enters to preside as a deputy for "the learnd Bellario," the resourceful
Portia begins by asking the plaintiff and the defendant to identify themselves.
After being introduced to Shylock, she turns to Anthonio with the question
"You stand within his danger, doe you not," to which he replies "I, so he
sayes" (4.1.183–84). Here most of today's editions substitute *Ay* for the *I* to
be found in the early printings. But the more restricted modern sense of "I"—
for "[Yes, it is] I" or "I [do]"—could function equally well in this setting.

So also in the fifth line of a later passage (4.1.286–91) of the same scene,
where Bassanio tells his friend,

> *Anthonio*, I am married to a wife
> which is as deere to me as life it selfe,
> but life it selfe, my wife, and all the world,

> are not with me esteemd aboue thy life.
> I would loose all, I sacrifize them all
> heere to this deuill, to deliuer you.

The conclusion of this fervent testimony is normally rendered "I would lose all, ay, sacrifice them all, / Here to this devil, to deliver you." But here, as in the instance cited at 4.1.59–62 above, *loose* (release, surrender) is just as relevant as *lose*, and "I sacrifice them all / Here to this devil" yields a reading that is as natural, and at least as sensible, as the one usually found in today's editions.

In the concluding Belmont scene that transposes the mood of the play's action to a more conventionally comic key, Nerissa mocks Gratiano's claim that he gave her bridal ring to "a Iudges Clarke." No, she says, "Gods my Iudge / the Clarke will nere weare haire ons face that had it." That exclamation prompts the following couplet (5.1.179–80):

> *Gra.* He will, and if he liue to be a man.
> *Nerissa.* I, if a woman liue to be a man.

Modern editions almost invariably replace *I* with *Ay*. By doing so, they give precedence to the surface potential in Nerissa's enigmatic utterance, the only sense that Gratiano will have any basis for considering. What the practice of today's editors will obscure, unfortunately, is the irony an alert audience, cued in to the game the newly returned women are playing, will relish as listeners note that Nerissa's statement can also mean "I [will], if a woman live to be a man."

Similar deprivations for today's readers occur when modern editions change *I* to *Ay* in the dialogue with which Portia and Nerissa draw their second trial scene to its frolicsome consummation in 5.1.281–83, 289–90:

> *Gra.* Were you the Clark that is to make me cuckold.
> *Ner.* I but the Clarke that neuer meanes to doe it,
>   vnlesse he liue vntill he be a man.
>
> . . . .
> *Por.* How now, Lorenzo?
>   My Clarke hath some good comforts to for you.
> *Ner.* I, and ile giue them him without a fee.

In both of these passages the "I" in Nerissa's reply will be just as salient a factor in a with-it audience's full participation in her jest as will the "Ay" that ordinarily supplants the Quarto's rendering of this sound when *The Merchant of Venice* is reproduced in twentieth- and twenty-first-century editions.

Here as elsewhere, those who experience Shakespeare's dramaturgy solely as readers of modern texts are severely handicapped. They are unequipped to savor all the jokes upon which the final moments of the play depend for their erotic *double entendre*. With insufficient background to enter into the full spirit of the banter that dominates act 5, they are deprived of an ability with analogies to the instrument a bawdy Gratiano knows a male newlywed will sorely need if he pledges to do his part in "keeping safe *Nerissas* ring" (5.1.306–307).

Notes

1. The editions examined for purposes of this article include John Russell Brown's text of *The Merchant of Venice* for *The Arden Shakespeare*, general editors Harold F. Brooks and Harold Jenkins (London: Methuen & Co., 1955); Kenneth Myrick's text of *The Merchant of Venice* for *The Complete Signet Classic Shakespeare* (New York: Harcourt Brace Jovanovich, 1963); W. Moelwyn Merchant's text of *The Merchant of Venice* for *The New Penguin Shakespeare*, general editors T. J. B. Spencer and Stanley Wells (Penguin Books: Harmondsworth, Middlesex, 1967); Brents Stirling's text of *The Merchant of Venice* for *William Shakespeare: The Complete Works*, general editor Alfred Harbage (Baltimore: Penguin Books, 1969); Irving Ribner's *The Complete Works of Shakespeare* (Waltham, Mass.: Ginn and Company, 1971, a revision of the 1936 text by George Lyman Kittredge); G. Blakemore Evans' *The Riverside Shakespeare* (Boston: Houghton Mifflin Co., 1974); David Bevington's *Complete Works of Shakespeare*, third edition (Glenview, Ill.: Scott, Foresman and Co., 1980); Stanley Wells and Gary Taylor's *William Shakespeare: The Complete Works* (Oxford: Clarendon Press, 1986); M. M. Mahood's text of *The Merchant of Venice* for *The New Cambridge Shakespeare*, general editor Brian Gibbons (Cambridge: Cambridge University Press, 1987); Barbara Mowat and Paul Werstine's text of *The Merchant of Venice* for *The New Folger Library Shakespeare* (New York: Washington Square Press, 1992); and Jay L. Halio's text of *The Merchant of Venice* for the *Oxford World Classics* set of *The Oxford Shakespeare*, general editor Stanley Wells (Oxford and New York: Oxford University Press, 1993).

2. For a more extended discussion of the issues touched upon here, see "Site-Reading Shakespeare's Dramatic Scores," an article (referred to hereafter as "Site-Reading") that I contributed to *Shakespearean Illuminations: Essays in Honor of Marvin Rosenberg*, edited by Jay L. Halio and Hugh Richmond (Newark, Del.: University of Delaware Press, 1998), pp. 183–202. That essay drew heavily upon the research that went into the sixteen volumes that have now been completed for *The Everyman Shakespeare*, a paperback set I have been editing since 1993 for J. M. Dent Publishers in London. That collection is an outgrowth of *The Guild Shakespeare* (Garden City, N.Y.: GuildAmerica Books, 1989–92), a nineteen-volume clothbound collection for the Doubleday Book and Music Clubs.

3. For a discussion of other names in the original texts that have been effectively obliterated in today's editions of Shakespeare—among them Fortinbrasse and Ostricke in *Hamlet*, Mountague in *Romeo and Juliet*, and the Weyward/Weyard Sisters in *Macbeth*—see pages 185–86 of "Site-Reading."

4. Unless otherwise noted, all quotations from *The Merchant of Venice* are reproduced as they appear in the 1600 First Quarto edition of the play. The line numbers provided are those to be found in my Everyman text (London: J. M. Dent, 1993). I have made no attempt to replicate forms such as the long *s*, but I have retained the Quarto's *u* and *v* characters, its use of italics, and its occasionally anomalous handling of capital and lowercase letters.

5. For this information, as well as for that about the names *Giobbe* and *Gobbo* three paragraphs hence, I'm indebted to the footnotes on page 82 of Molly Mahood's New Cambridge edition of *The Merchant of Venice*. Professor Mahood points out that the Clown's "name is always 'Launcelet' in Q1 (*au* being a typical Shakespearean spelling for nasalised *a*), and usually 'Lancelet' in Q2 and F. 'Lancelot' occurs only once in Q2 (2.2.70), but it is the form throughout Q3" (a post-Folio text that appeared in 1637).

6. Two I[J]/G parallels that may be pertinent to this discussion are the Quarto's *Iem* at 2.7.54 (for "gem"), and its *Iaylor* in 3.3 (for an officer who would now be called a "jailer" in the United States and a "gaoler" in Great Britain).

7. Mahood, p. 82.

8. *Anthonio* is the form in which this name appears throughout the First Quarto. In all likelihood it was pronounced either "Ant-hon-io" or "An-ton-io." As evidence we need look no farther than the First Folio text of *Julius Caesar*, which uses *Antony* as its spelling for the same name that is consistently rendered *Anthony* in the play the Folio titles *Anthony and Cleopatra*. Compare *Protheus* (for "Proteus") in the Folio printing of *The Two Gentlemen of Verona*. We've long known that *noting* and *nothing* were homonyms or near-homonyms; so also with *moth* and *mote*. So how, we may ask, was *Othello* pronounced on the Globe stage? The answer, I suspect, was either "Ot-hel-lo" or "O-tel-lo," as in Giuseppi Verdi's operatic treatment of the tragedy.

9. For a discussion of the importance of retaining *borne* (in a modern edition's notes and commentary, if not in its text) in *Macbeth*, see note 22 in "Site-Reading."

10. See the section on "Recapturing the Ability to Hear with our Eyes" (pages xxvii–xxix) in the Everyman edition of *The Merchant of Venice*, cited in note 4.

11. See page 108, where Halio observes that "Kittredge sees a pun, dam-damn, and in fact follows the Q1–2 spelling (see Collation). The primary sense then = 'cause their hearers to stop up their ears against the foolishness they are hearing'." In his 1966 revision of Kittredge's text (see the citation in note 1), Irving Ribner retains *dam* too.

12. Anyone who doubts that Shakespeare expected his audiences to pick up on the associations to which Shylock alludes should compare the play on *curs*, *courtesies*, and *curtsies* in the First Folio printing of one of the title figure's last speeches (3.1.35–48) in *Julius Caesar*:

> I must preuent thee *Cymber*:
> These couchings, and these lowly courtesies
> Might fire the blood of ordinary men,
> And turne pre-Ordinance, and first Decree,

> Into the lane of Children. Be not fond,
> To thinke that *Caesar* bears such Rebell blood
> That will be thaw'd from the true quality
> With that which melteth Fooles, I meane sweet words,
> Low-crooked-curtsies, and base Spaniell fawning:
> Thy Brother by decree is banished:
> If thou doest bend, and pray, and fawne for him,
> I spurne thee like a Curre out of my way:
> Know, *Caesar* doth not wrong, nor without cause
> Will he be satisfied.

13. Most of today's editions follow the Second Folio (1632) and emend *voyce* to *vice*. But in a note on this passage in his Oxford Shakespeare edition of the play, Jay Halio comments that " 'voyce' (like 'smoyle' for *smile* in Q *Lear* 7.80) is apparently an inverted spelling on the analogy of words like *voyage* spelled 'viage', *Hamlet* 3.3.24 (Cercignani, 247)." But why can't *voyce*, which, as Halio implies, is a dialectal form of *vice*, serve here to convey *both* "voice" and "vice"? It was surely employed at this point to echo the same sound five lines earlier in Anthonio's speech. Like its predecessor in *The Guild Shakespeare* (1991), the Everyman edition of *The Merchant of Venice* (1993) prints "Voice," thereby preserving the reading to be found in Q1 (1600), Q2 (1619), and F (1623).

14. Molly Mahood's note on this passage (page 116) begins as follows: "Usually modernised to 'stairs', which is what we hear in the theatre, but an expression similar to Herbert's 'ropes of sands' in 'The Collar' could have been in Shakespeare's mind."

15. I confess to my chagrin that it didn't occur to me to retain *stayers*, or even refer to it in a note, in my Guild and Everyman texts. I hope to remedy these embarrassing oversights in a revised Everyman edition of the play.

16. *Humane* and *inhumane* are the normal Renaissance forms for both of the modern words that branch out from each of them; to be fully *human* or *inhuman*, then, was *ipso facto* to be *humane* or *inhumane*. See the discussion of "too full o'th' Milke of humane kindnesse" on pages 186–87 of "Site-Reading"; also see note 11 of that article.

17. For other instances of "loose/lose," see page 187 of "Site-Reading."

18. Compare the wordplay in Escalus' statement that "my brother Angelo will not be alter'd" in *Measure for Measure*, 3.1.504–505, as well as in the Countess' description of the recalcitrant Bertram as an "unbridl'd boy" in *All's Well That Ends Well*, 3.2.30.

19. See my observations about *I/ay* on pages 189–90 of "Site-Reading."

Portia and the Ovidian Grotesque

JOHN W. VELZ

What every actress who has played Portia of Belmont knows is that this lady has two apparently incompatible identities. On the one hand she is, as we first see her in 1.2, a young virgin and orphan who is very anxious about her future which has been mysteriously circumscribed (though not guaranteed happy) by her father's will:

> O me, the word "choose"! I may neither choose who I would nor refuse who I dislike; so is the will of a living daughter curbed by the will of a dead father. Is it not hard, Nerissa, that I cannot choose one nor refuse none? (1.2.22–26)[1]

This is the Portia who describes herself in 3.2 to Bassanio as an

> unlessoned girl, unschooled, unpracticèd;
> Happy in this, she is not yet so old
> But she may learn; happier than this,
> She is not bred so dull but she can learn;
> Happiest of all is that her gentle spirit
> Commits itself to yours to be directed
> As from her lord, her governor, her king. (3.2.159–66)

On the other hand, Portia is a shrewd counterfeit lawyer, capable of finding a loophole no one else can find in Shylock's airtight case against Antonio. And she manages this triumph over Shylock with a dramatic flair that clearly implies inventive self-possession:

> Tarry a little; there is something else.
> This bond doth give thee here no jot of blood;
> The words expressly are "a pound of flesh." (4.1.302–304)

It is Shylock himself who has just put emphasis on what the bond says and does not say about blood:

POR: Have by some surgeon, Shylock, on your charge,
        To stop his wounds lest he do bleed to death.
SHY: Is it so nominated in the bond?
        . . . .
        I cannot find it. 'Tis not in the bond. (255–60)

Portia allows Shylock himself to set the technicality trap that she springs on him.

This is also the Portia who later in 4.1 lures Antonio into persuading Bassanio to give away the engagement ring that Portia has told Bassanio will, if given away, "presage the ruin of your love / And be my vantage to exclaim on you" (3.2.172–74). And this is the Portia as well who can produce argosies safely and richly come to harbor when all indications are that they have foundered. It is a mystification: "You shall not know by what strange accident / I chancèd on this letter." (5.1.277–79). Portia's mystifications have a vaguely supernal quality; Lorenzo exclaims when Portia produces the deed of gift Shylock has signed over to Jessica and him, "you drop manna in the way / Of starvèd people" (5.2.294–95), as if she were some God of the Israelites.

Ask the actress who has played the lady of Belmont and she may give you any one of a number of answers to this conundrum; but she will readily admit that coping with this strange conflict in Portia's character onstage was a major challenge for her. We will not be able to make it easier for an actress to play her next Portia, but we can at least tell her where Shakespeare got the strange disjunction between the two discrete identities in one Portia.

It is to be found in an important mythological substructure that underpins the role and the action: the Medea legend, which is referred to more than once in the play. From the first description of Portia we learn that her hair is a

golden fleece,
Which makes her seat of Belmont Colchis' strand,
And many Jasons come in quest of her. (1.1.170–72)

As if remembering this metaphor of Bassanio's (which he has not heard), Gratiano exclaims to Salerio when Bassanio has succeeded in the casket test, "We are the Jasons; we have won the fleece" (3.2.241). To underscore the allusion, Shakespeare has Salerio make a sardonic pun on it. "I would you had won the fleece [fleets] that he [Antonio] hath lost" (242). Much later, in 5.1, Medea appears again, in Jessica's lines, as the fourth in a quartet of mythological ladies who did important things by night:

> In such a night
> Medea gathered the enchanted herbs
> That did renew old Aeson. (12–14)

As the first of these three allusions suggests, Portia is based in part on Medea; they are both the ultimate in prize ladies to be won by a bold young suitor willing to risk all for the prize. Shakespeare knew about Medea from Ovid's *Metamorphoses* Book 7; Jason and Medea was one of his favorite myths. The herbs that did renew old Aeson reappear much later in the canon where Prospero's invocation of the "elves of hills, brooks, standing lakes, and groves" and the details that follow (*Tempest* 5.1.33–50) are quite precisely based on Arthur Golding's translation of the passage in Book 7 of the *Metamorphoses* in which Medea intones incantations as she gathers those herbs. Interestingly, Golding gets one detail ("trees" 5.272) only partly right and Shakespeare has it entirely right ("Jove's stout oak," 5.1.45), showing that he conflated in his creative imagination the original Latin that he would have worked through in grammar school with the Golding that surely was the trot for the boys at King Edward VI Grammar School, Stratford-upon-Avon. He knew the story virtually letter perfect in both Ovid's Latin and Golding's English and had stored it in his memory for most of a lifetime.

Medea is an innocent virgin in love for the first time, yet she is a witch with supernal powers. She is, in this almost absurd amalgam of innocence and extraordinary competence, an Ovidian grotesque of the first order. Ovid in the *Metamorphoses* is over and over again inherently grotesque: disjunctive, indecorous, sometimes ludicrous, even when the story is a drama of disaster like the Jason/Medea story. By blending incompatibles, a kind of syneciosis of disparate elements, Ovid conveys a tone that hovers equally on the sentimental and pathetic on the one hand, and on the absurd and ironic on the other.

The Ovidian grotesque stretches throughout the *Metamorphoses*, taking several forms of which this disjunction of character is but one. In some other contexts, Ovid conveys gruesome physical details in elaborate rhetoric that paradoxically screens the horror from us as it pruriently conveys that horror. Philomela's excised tongue in Book 6 twitching horridly on the ground as if trying to speak is gracefully described. Ovid is startlingly lurid at times; the battle of the Lapiths and the Centaurs in Book 12 is a fair example, as blood and brains spout together from one centaur's head and another's eyeballs are described as removed, one of them stuck to the antler that blinded it. And all of this is described eloquently. Such gruesome details couched in fluent and sculpted poetry are ultimately Homeric in character (one thinks of details from the battle scenes in the *Iliad* and of the great slaughter in the hall in Book 22 of the *Odyssey*, always gory, always eloquently described). Shakespeare was enthralled by Ovid's lurid-ness in the presence of the poetic, which he adapts for *Titus Andronicus* and the second and third *Henry VI* plays. We get some of it in *Macbeth*, when the slaughtered King is described by his murderer:

>   Here lay Duncan,
> His silver skin lac'd with his golden blood,
> And his gash'd stabs look'd like a breach in nature
> For ruin's wasteful entrance . . . (2.3.111–14).

We might say that *The Merchant of Venice* has a variation on this special kind of Ovidian grotesque in the insistent references to the pound of flesh to be cut from the breast of Antonio; eloquence is displaced from this special grue-some context by the legalistic language of the bond, a suitable substitute.

Another sort of Ovidian grotesque occurs when a character speaks in elaborately articulated formal rhetoric when what is being expressed is a pas-sion out of control. Apollo speaks a fulsome suasorian rhetorical formula from the Roman law courts while running at top speed to catch and ravish Daphne—the dislocation of utterance from mental state is so grotesque as to be nearly comic. The effect is just that of Andrew Marvell's "To His Coy Mistress" where the impassioned lover uses a schema of formal logic to try to persuade his reluctant lady to yield to him. It is comic precisely because we readers know that never was fair lady won by mere logic. There are many other such passages in the *Metamorphoses*. Ovid does particularly well with a succession of young women in the middle books of the poem, each of whom is overwhelmed by an amatory passion that is a sexual taboo. Medea is the first of these. The most memorable of these young women is Byblis, who writes an elaborate if jerky letter to her brother Caunus proposing incest, though she is so overwhelmed with desire for him that we marvel at or smirk at her extended rhetoric where mindless passion is dominant. Ovid makes a joke of the whole thing when poor Byblis' elaborate letter, complete with an addendum in the margin of the tablet, is thrown away by the horrified Caunus, most of it unread.

And there are other disjunctions in Ovid—at every turn, nearly. We are inclined by some of them to smile wryly at the paradoxes involved and by others to wince in near pain, by yet others to feel the pathos of the situation Ovid has contrived for us. But the grotesques in Ovid animate the entire experience of the poem.

Medea's girlish infatuation with Jason is vividly conveyed in a long soliloquy early in Book 7. She agonizes over her divided loyalties—to the heroic Jason she is in the process of falling in love with, and to her royal father and his nation. Medea soliloquizes about her conflict at length:

> Medea,
> You fight in vain; there is some god or other
> Against you. . . .
> Why should my father's orders seem too cruel?
> They are too cruel! A fellow I have hardly
> Much more than seen may die, and I am fearful!
>
> . . . .
>
> Why do you burn for a stranger, royal maiden?
>
> . . . .
>
> Only the cruel-hearted
> Would not be moved by Jason's youth, his manhood,
> His noble birth. And even if these were lacking,
> His beauty would move a heart of stone—at least
> It has moved mine. (7:12–34 in the Rolfe Humphries translation)

Shakespeare could be attracted by such a speech as this, a speech in which a young person is tempted by passion and tries to rationalize the temptation; I once argued the matter in "The Ovidian Soliloquy in Shakespeare"(*Shakespeare Studies* 1986). Indeed this Medea story seems to have been seminal in Shakespeare's creative imagination, as it was in Ovid's. Ovid imitated the disjunction between the tortured psyche and the rhetoric of Medea's speech in a series of other stories spread across several books of the *Metamorphoses*; as mentioned above, in each case in a serio-comic soliloquy a young woman contemplates breaking a sexual taboo—in Medea's case it is uniting herself to a foreigner despite her father's contrivance to prevent that union.

But Medea is not just the amusingly and touchingly muddled thinker of this soliloquy. Once she commits herself to Jason, she shows supernal powers beyond even those of Portia. She is a cross between an ingenue and a fairy godmother.

It is easy enough to see why Shakespeare might find Medea an interesting model for a character in a fairy-tale-like play. (Even the germ of the ring plot is to be found in Medea's fleeting reflection in this speech that Jason might at some future time prefer another woman to her.) The disparity within a single personality of innocence and competence was surely an attraction, because it can potentially convey that enigmatic mixed tone that Ovid conveys with Medea.

But Shakespeare was misguided in making the choice, because what Medea is tempted to do and does do in her story is to help Jason to escape the fatal traps of her father's obstacle course by telling Jason how to defeat them. If Shakespeare were to follow Medea closely, he would have Portia tell Bassanio how to succeed in her father's casket test. Many postmodern cynics think he did have her do so; "a scheming vixen" is what one of them once called her. I have not encountered any that used the Medea story as a justification for the assumption. A spirited discussion that took place in SHAKSPER ("The Electronic Shakespeare Conference") in May of 1999 is exemplary of contemporary assumptions; a point of focus was: whether Portia gives a hint to Bassanio, especially through the song sung as Bassanio makes his choice among the caskets, a song in which key words rhyme with "lead."

Shakespeare sensed the danger in his symbolism, because he twice in *The Merchant of Venice* has Portia protest that she will never choose a spouse by other means than the stipulations of her father's will. In 1.2, early in the play, when Nerissa tells her that a group of suitors have given up their suits to her "unless you may be won by some other sort than your father's imposition depending on the caskets," we hear her reply categorically:

> If I live to be as old as Sibylla, I will die as chaste as Diana,
> unless I be obtained by the manner of my father's will. (1.2.104–106)

Later she is very direct with Bassanio, affirming that she will never help him (as Medea helped Jason) though she is deeply in love with him (as Medea was with Jason):

> .... I could teach you
> How to choose right, but then I am forsworn.
> So will I never be. So you may miss me.
> But if you do, you'll make me wish a sin,
> That I had been forsworn. .... (3.2.10–14)

Through Ovid, we can understand not only *The Merchant of Venice* but also Shakespeare's mindset as he was writing it: cover your sources up by denying them, but use them all the same. We come close in such a scholarly/critical exercise to looking over Shakespeare's shoulder while he writes.

The Merchant of Venice is Portia's play, more than Shylock's or Bassanio's or Antonio's—she has more than one-fifth of the lines. Therefore, her divided nature, ingenue and fairy godmother, is indicative of the divided nature of the play itself: her play is part mimetic (holding "a mirror up" to life) and part mythic (idealizing and exceeding life). The problem for critics of *The Merchant of Venice* in the late twentieth century was that they ignored the mythic dimension. The play asks us to believe things that realism would say are impossible. If we do not accept the mythic/symbolic dimension, the play is a chaotic welter of meaningless contradictions of plausibility. Seeing her in light of the Ovidian grotesque in personal identity saves Portia from mere "defective characterization," as some frustrated actress might put it.

There is another sense in which the Ovidian grotesque bears upon Portia. She is both a young female yearning for marriage to the man of her choice and a complete and confident young male, an astute professional learned in the law and entirely in command of a courtroom proceeding of the most dire implications. In donning male garb she puts on an impenetrable façade of maleness; she is figuratively metamorphosed in a quasi-Ovidian manner; no one penetrates her new appearance until she herself reveals the true state of affairs *ex post facto* back at Belmont in act 5. Yet all this time she is very much still the sensitive, intelligent, articulate young woman we have come to know earlier in the play. She confides in the audience about her disguise while she is confiding in Nerissa about it, so that we are aware of the true nature of the new identity from the first. And then she makes the sort of jokes about her femaleness-within-maleness that other cross-dressed young women (Rosalind and Viola, especially) do in the four other plays that feature this ultimately Ovidian set of ironies. Jokes or no jokes, however, the toying with gender in Shakespeare can have serious implications, as Ellen Mahon reminds me in citing Julia's observation at 5.4.108–109 of The *Two Gentlemen of Verona*: "It is the lesser blot, modesty finds, / Women to change their shapes than men their minds." Julia's comment is apt to the world of *The Merchant of Venice*: Jessica is ashamed at her appearance as a male torchbearer to Lorenzo, but the greatest shame in the play is when Bassanio and Gratiano are found to have given away their rings.

A special case of the Ovidian grotesque occurs frequently in the *Metamorphoses* when the identity of a person remains the same though his/her shape is altered. Daphne takes on the shape of a laurel tree, yet remains a girl inside that emblematically impenetrable bark and wood. Io remains Io, raped by Jupiter, though he imposes the disguise of a heifer on her. She writes her name in the dust with her hoof when her father fails to recognize her under her metamorphosis (this episode is Shakespeare's source for Lavinia's use of a stick held in her mouth to write her rapists' names in sand in *Titus Andronicus* 4.1). The hyperbolic juxtaposition of incompatibles—heifer and girl, laurel tree and girl, rock fountain and matron in Niobe's case—is Ovid's stock in grotesque trade. Among those who write so copiously on boys in Shakespeare plays cast as girls pretending to be boys, I have not encountered anyone who has seen the analogy to Ovidian grotesques of identity. William C. Carroll, writing from the perspective not of feminism but of metamorphosis, is a special case. He sees the implications of Ovidian metamorphosis for gender identity, but misses the point about the grotesque. In his study, the Medea legend figures, but from a perspective quite different from the one in this essay (117–26).

We should add the story of Iphis and Ianthe (*Metamorphoses* 9), in which an infant girl is passed off as a boy to save her from death and then thirteen years later, at the time of marriage with Isis' intervention, actually becomes the boy she has always seemed. The elaborate toying with gender in this story is obviously relevant, with all its attendant Ovidian ironies. No one, I believe, not even Carroll, comments on this myth to throw light on Shakespeare's altered genders and their paradoxes.

In Portia's case there is no fear that she will have the wrong gender at the wrong time. The gender problem does obtrude in *All's Well That Ends Well*, however, where Helena is another Medea figure, a virgin yearning for a husband while at the same time a highly competent professional with quasi-supernal powers; but Helena never "abandons" her gender as Portia does, and the result is a serious resistance by the palace courtiers to her attempt to cure the despaired-of King.

The matter of gender disguise is handled in *The Merchant of Venice* with a special effectiveness that Shakespeare did not incorporate in any of his other girl-as-boy plays. In adding Nerissa's cross-dressing as a mimicking of Portia's, Shakespeare enriches a comic dimension. An implausibility parodied by a lower-level analog is doubly ironic, doubly comic. This parallel plotting works very well for him, so well that one wonders why he did not borrow the device for Rosalind or Viola or Imogen. Carroll notes that Jessica is a third character in the play who adopts male disguise.

Moreover, by making Portia take on her new gender identity at the same time that she takes on her new professional competence, Shakespeare combines two kinds of Ovidian grotesque in one character. One supposes that Ovid would heartily approve.

Notes

1. All quotations are from *The Complete Shakespeare* edited by David Bevington, 1992.

Works Cited

Carroll, William C. *The Metamorphoses of Shakespearean Comedy*. Princeton, NJ: Princeton University Press, 1985.

Ovid. *The Metamorphoses*. Trans. Arthur Golding. Ed. W. H. D. Rouse (London, 1904). Rpt. Carbondale: Southern Illinois University Press, 1961.

———. *The Metamorphoses*. Trans. Rolfe Humphries. Bloomington: Indiana University Press, 1983.

Shakespeare, William. *The Complete Works*. Ed. David Bevington, 4th ed. New York: Harper Collins, 1992.

SHAKSPER ("The Electronic Shakespeare Conference"). May, 1999.

Velz, John W. "The Ovidian Soliloquy in Shakespeare." *Shakespeare Studies* 18 (1986): 1–24.

Does Source Criticism Illuminate the Problems of Interpreting *The Merchant* as a Soured Comedy?

JOHN K. HALE

The value of source-criticism within Shakespeare is ancillary, negative, and indicative. It will help us think about a play or scene. It will tell us how *not* to think about them. And in the absence of other hard evidence as to the genesis or intention of a play, source-criticism—by showing where and how a play began—can indicate directions of imaginative change. In fact, the pattern of what Shakespeare leaves out, picks up, extends, and adds from elsewhere indicates a great deal.

These truisms apply with particular force to *The Merchant of Venice*, for two main reasons. First, the play's storyline keeps very close to its main source, the story of Giannetto from *Il Pecorone*—from the initial borrowing of capital for a wooing journey by the young protégé of the Venetian merchant, through the sex-disguising and trial scene, to the concluding practical joke of the wedding rings. Secondly, source-study has something to put alongside the play's theatre and critical history, in which Shylock dominates. Just as Shylock's original, the "Jew of Mestri," had not even a name, so Shylock appears in a bare five scenes and is absent from the finale: what sort of play did Shakespeare *think* he was writing, even if we know better about the one he did create?

Without expecting to change anyone's mind, and indeed without quite knowing my own mind,[1] I offer as a reality check the following observations about how Shakespeare went to work on the chosen materials. The chief emphasis will fall on *Il Pecorone*, which is a skeleton for the story and characters together—the entire central transaction, of the pound-of-flesh bond and its results.[2] The parties to the transaction will be called the "Beneficiary" of the bond (Giannetto/Bassanio), its "Donor" (Ansaldo/Antonio), the "prize" or "Lady" (the widow of Belmonte/Portia[3]), and the "Bondholder" (the Jew of Mestri/Shylock). Other sources will be acknowledged at the appropriate points of a (mainly) scene-by-scene analysis.[4]

The opening scene shows the young protégé raising the wind from his kinsman.[5] This is exactly as in the source, except that Bassanio is doing it for the first and only time: Shakespeare cunningly alters Giannetto's three attempts at his widow, into Bassanio's being the third of three suitors tackling the moral riddle whose solution brings marriage with Portia. (He shows mental and moral penetration, whereas Giannetto had trouble achieving the physical sort.)

More simply, Shakespeare begins as usual *in medias res*. The emotions of Bassanio on this single occasion are those of Giannetto at the final one— embarrassment, some shame, dependency, and withal a loverlike determination. The emotions of the Donor, and indeed his prominence, have shifted, towards or even past equality. Though we instinctively call the source "Giannetto's story," Shakespeare is launching "the Merchant of Venice," Antonio's story. Antonio is onstage for the entire scene, with emphatic probing of his melancholy. In this, the feelings of a surrogate father (Ansaldo) are extended into a burdensome overplus of grief (which "wearies" Antonio himself, and all of the group [1.1.2] if "you" is plural) for imminent loss, which Antonio cannot express to Bassanio but which all the more clouds the giving.

The second scene is assigned to Portia, Belmont, and the strange conditions of courting her. Since the first two conditions have been introduced already, the new scene concentrates on the third: there is more to this courtship than a cash float and love-glances. Shakespeare of course splices in here his adaptation of the "Caskets" romance,[6] but he dwells equally on her father's mysterious will for Portia. The play has much to say about fathers, and even more about people whose life's fulfillment depends—in the manner of a wager—upon a single choice, made by someone else. Because the scene holds no events, only exposition, jokes, and thematic wonderment, it makes us think around the design; to other fathers (Shylock and old Gobbo, maybe Antonio as father-figure); and to those who depend on choices by others (Antonio, three couples, Shylock, and Jessica). The source said much less about fathers, so Shakespeare's addition of them is intriguing. Risk, however, was embedded in the source, at all its points, in both its locations. The scene also sets going a connection of places (whether to differentiate them, or to align them), by which Belmont will have almost as many scenes as Venice and the action will close there—Shakespeare again giving life to what lay inert in his source.

In his third scene Shakespeare introduces the remaining figure of his source's quadrilateral transaction, the Jewish moneylender. It is striking that when (improbably but necessarily) the Donor can find no lender except the hostile Jew, the latter is not found out as a last resort by Ansaldo himself but by Bassanio, who brings him along to Antonio. Of what is the change indicative? Is it made to involve Bassanio more deeply in responsibility (a character-based explanation)? To build up the Bondholder by giving him further relationships (for enhancement of another character)? To enable him to express motivation through soliloquy, such as no previous character has needed? To strengthen the fateful transaction and its scene by building to the meeting of the play's two mighty opposites? Although one purpose does not preclude another in Shakespeare, a source-approach hints at the last-named possibility. The scene is made stronger by the change, and many other source-changes serve the same end. The previous two scenes having rearranged a mass of good detail to gain strong scenes, this third one seeks a still stronger scene, a scene not of latent tension but outright conflict, and not of things unsaid but palpable rancor, ominously patched up.

This, however, leaves unexplained why Shylock alone of the main four-some needs a soliloquy to launch him. After all, later on he will talk of his motives to any bystander, and Shakespeare will give him Tubal for more inti-mate confidences. In general, soliloquy near the start of action puts emphasis on apartness, aloneness, secrecy, and ill will, if Richard III's or Hamlet's are parallel. But in particular, using the source as guide, the soliloquy is Shake-speare's expansion of *minimal* matter from his source. The Jew of Mestri's intentions are not stated at all at the equivalent point of the novella (Bullough 469), and emerge only later, when after the crash of Ansaldo's fortunes he refuses the offer of repayment from "many merchants joined together . . . for he wished to commit this homicide in order to be able to say that he had put to death the greatest of the Christian merchants" (472). The changes are extremely indicative here, and helpful to Shakespeare's interpreters, includ-ing all three actors of the scene. He wants to establish motivation at once, not by and by. Nor is the motivation that of the novella, a Guinness-Book-of-Records ambition for a twisted glory. The soliloquy expresses contempt and Jewish identity (36), then religious antipathy (37), "but more" it expresses commercial resentment. Then "grudge," against Antonio as commercial and racial enemy: "he hates our sacred nation" and so in return "cursèd be my tribe / If I forgive him." All of these manifold motives, entwined like a snake dance, will be developed into actions later; and albeit extended by new motives such as his loss of Jessica and her looted dowry, they are here already made his guiding principles. It is simply *untrue* that Shylock means his "merry sport" merrily, or as a genuine overture, or that he plans revenge only after later losses, because Shakespeare has written such a strong welter-ing of motives into this explanatory, unsourced, initial soliloquy. In soliloquy, characters do not lie, except sometimes to themselves.

Shakespeare is putting further expansion, that is to say conscious effort, into the argument about Laban's sheep (lines 66–97). Using the Bible now as source, he shows us Shylock raising the subject of Jacob's triumph in that story of patriarchs' wagering. Antonio gives a haughty rebuttal whilst Shylock col-lects the laugh. Which was more Shakespeare's design is still being debated, but from our present standpoint in any case we can see both characters more deeply

as a result—Shylock aggressively identifying with the most tricky of the patriarchs who was nonethelesss to carry the blessing upon Israel, and Antonio self-
righteous in orthodoxy (Bassanio silent, embarrassed and impatient). A wider
significance, perhaps, is that Shakespeare has picked on this precise passage of
the Scripture which their religions share, with its inscrutable sheep genetics and
its awkward (surely *ex post facto*) vindication (Genesis 31.12), in which God in
Jacob's dream had explained his success as divine retaliation against Laban's
exploitations of Jacob. The murky episode, in which Shylock casts himself as
Jacob, makes Antonio an exploitative Laban: this accounts for Antonio's otherwise excessive anger, for he hates losing face in front of Bassanio.

The rest of the scene is all Shakespeare's own, with its excess and hubris
on Antonio's part,[7] Bassanio's fears for his benefactor and dismay at the
terms of the Bond, and Shylock's steady working of the advantage first
gained in the biblical altercation.

The following ten scenes, 2.1 through 3.1, are mainly short ones. Individ-
ually they may seem minor, preparing as they certainly do for the double crisis
of act 3, scene 2. Nonetheless, they are better seen together first, because thus
they reveal Shakespeare's persistent interweaving. The sequence interweaves
the pound-of-flesh motif with the wooing motif, the two strands of the main
plot, and furthermore interweaves both with several further risk-actions
(Gobbo, Gratiano, Jessica). These come from diverse sources. They are not all
interwoven in the same way. They do not all have the like impact. The
manysidedness of this whole is the myriad-mindedness which Coleridge
admired in Shakespeare. And it provides the key to full enjoyment of this play.
Seen in this context, Shylock's refusal to change provides one dark contrast to
the many changes for the better which characterize comedy, though it is not the
sole such contrast. Just the same, comedy normally favors change.[8]

Briefly to substantiate all that, Morocco—another outsider as to race and
religion—is the first to undertake the risk of the caskets test (2.1 and 7). Then
in the longer 2.2, Gobbo tricks his father, only to rue it; together they sue for
him to leave Shylock's service and join Bassanio's. Gratiano, too, "must"
accompany him to Belmont. Jessica, not seen till 2.3, dominates the next four
scenes—not joining Bassanio nor at this juncture going to Belmont, but decisively rejecting her father Shylock, religion and all. In 2.8 Antonio's losses
commence, and with them the threat from Shylock, whose other losses
(daughter and ducats) have enraged him. Antonio was angry and off-balance
in 1.3: now it is Shylock's turn. Losses proliferate as Arragon (an outsider in
religion though not in race) becomes the second to pick a wrong casket, and
Shylock is torn between grief and glee; grief at his own losses, glee at Antonio's. I discern no privileging whatever of Shylock's strand over all the others
within this expert web. Interaction and multiplicity are the guiding principles.

In 3.2, by contrast, hierarchy is pivotal. Bassanio's successful choosing
modulates, absurdly, into Gratiano's noisy jubilation: Bassanio's choosing,

which is not a lucky dip, occasions Gratiano's success, which is, a silly side bet. Then by a further excellent modulation, "Enter Lorenzo, Jessica, and Salerio, a messenger from Venice": Salerio brings news of Antonio's mortal danger, while Jessica's sole speech confirms that danger. The spotlight moves away from the Beneficiary, and from the Lady, too, though to a lesser extent because the plot still keeps her passive, to the Donor and Bondholder. It stays with the last two for the next scene. But then with the sex-disguising of the Lady, and her getting into motion at last, attention shifts to her preparations for meeting—her sole, and incognito meeting—with the Bondholder.

What, then, is 3.5 included for? It is not enough to say it covers the lapse of time while Portia reaches Venice, since that journey can be quick or slow at Shakespeare's own wish (and any other small scene would serve the same purpose). It shows Jessica, with Gobbo again, then with Lorenzo. Jessica, to my mind, is Shakespeare's largest and most significant addition to the Bondholder's role. It is worth mentioning that she has seven scenes, her father five. She shares only one scene with him, in which she speaks to him only when spoken to (receiving several commands and one hot question—2.5.10–55). So what does this large addition contribute?

Contrasting strongly with her passive, innocent prototype Abigail,[9] Jessica is proactive and determined. She throws down her father's money from a window like Abigail, but to her lover, not her father. She is given many of the quintessential attributes of heroines in romance comedy—male disguise, giggling about it, participation in masque, abandoning family for lover like Juliet—but like Desdemona crossing a racial gap, too. Is it her change of religion which alienates current feminist sympathies? If so, this too was taken from Marlowe's Abigail. I find it odd, then, that Jessica attracts a modern odium, for example from many of my students: Shakespeare is empowering her, at least equally with the other two cross-dressing heroines.

He is not empowering her for empowerment's sake, but to represent a strong counterweight to what her father represents. It is done subtly whenever she has a scene, or (more often) part of one. "Our house is hell," she says to Gobbo, "and thou (a merry devil) / Didst rob it of some taste of tediousness" (2.3.2–3, her first speech in the play sings a keynote). At the other end of the play she is "never merry when I hear sweet music," which Lorenzo diagnoses as "attentiveness"—thoughtfulness or intenseness. She has had reason to be both; and yet the two laugh together about dangerous topics like untrustworthy lovers (5.1.1–22).[10] Shakespeare seems eager to qualify her for comic luck, all the more because he writes so many passages which explain that her father is *dis*qualified for it![11]

It is amongst all of this added Jessica material that Shakespeare adds two passages which have most elicited sympathy for Shylock: "Hath not a Jew eyes?" and Jessica's theft of his wife's engagement ring, both in 3.1. The first is said to Solanio and Salerio, after they have concluded their jeering at him;

the second is said to Tubal, whose alternating good and bad news has reduced Shylock to a suffering automaton.

The first is therefore natural anger, strongly expressed, and meant to alarm them. They have deserved all of it. The second is actually the stronger effect, because it swings between absurdity and pathos. The element common to the two passages is reductiveness, in the one case Antonio's flesh as fish bait and the meaning of life narrowed to revenge, in the other case Shylock swung between extremes of *schadenfreude* and self-centered misery. As Shakespeare is inventing all of this,[12] we need to ask for what purpose, or to what discernible authorial effect? So far, I discern the desire to make a strong scene, part of which is the aptness of Shylock's words to his Venetian interlocutors.

But then, next, to Tubal. What is the fellow-Jew up to? Presumably we are not to think, with friends like this who needs enemies? Perhaps Tubal is up to nothing, being an unknown quantity—there for Shylock to react to, and to his news, not himself. So we keep our eyes on Shylock, more than in the previous exchange. This helps explain why Jessica gets the blame. One could just laugh at the idea of wasting a valuable ring on a pet monkey, or relish the idea that the miser's daughter has become one of life's big spenders. Or one could sympathize with Shylock's hurt at his engagement ring being lost to him. Should we? We know nothing about his Leah, nor whether she was Jessica's mother. The passage as a whole is nonetheless showing us a strongly suffering Shylock, who is "tortured" and excessive and absurd, by turns or even all at once. The stronger this scene is, the stronger will be the showdown in 4.1. Source-criticism is alerting us to Shakespeare's extensions and additions, and these alert us to his dramaturgy; here, in the form of that "principle of episodic intensification" which is normal on the Elizabethan stage, but can lead to overinterpretation or misunderstanding. Shakespeare's wealth of specificity and ambivalent empathy in the scene can distort our perception if we do not recognize that they exist in Jessica's scenes too, and others—such as the Trial scene itself, greatest and last for Shylock, yet not for others. (The fact that Jessica is withheld means that counterweight is available later.)[13] Hence, by the principle of episodic intensification once more, in the Trial scene Shakespeare gives his Bondholder the most rousing possible finish, trusting to his own experience and intuition to restore the balance later, by benefitting later scenes similarly. Did he succeed, is the question? And are we prepared to let him, is the question to ourselves.

The Trial scene is the one closest to the novella. The source has the same shape: pleas from "the merchants of Venice one and all" are made to the Jew, who, however, insists on getting Venetian—that is, strict—justice (Bullough 472); he is offered up to ten times the amount of the bond, without avail; the disguised heroine hears the case and urges him to quit while he is so far ahead; and when he refuses, she springs the trap; and a reverse-auction (Dutch auction) ensues. Here we begin to notice divergence in Shakespeare's treatment. In the source the bond is declared null and void, everyone "mocked at the Jew, saying, 'He who lays snares for others is caught himself' " (Bullough 474). The Jew then "took his bond and tore it in pieces in a rage." In the play there is less of a reverse-auction, and nothing explicit about the bond itself,[14] more of mockery, a different *moralitas*. Responses of bystanders differ from one another (this is important and often ignored by critics). Instead of a stormy sudden exit like Malvolio's, Shylock's is prolonged. The delaying of the exit, and its qualities when at last it does come, is the heart of the problem of this play for us all.

My view can already be guessed. It is dramaturgical more than ethical. Shakespeare has seen how to milk the situation for a bewildering variety of effects, now that the hard work is all done and before the comic sequel is reached. And he does milk it.[15] It is episodic intensification with a vengeance, because it creates not just a variety of strong effects but a literally *bewildering* variety. We are left not knowing what to think; and as the debate shows, this is not a contented relinquishing of any need to make judgment, but rather a need to make judgment which is not, and cannot, be satisfied. I take those points of divergence one by one in the same order.

The bond is not declared "null and void" in Shakespeare; rather, it is upheld to the full by Portia ("all justice," "nothing but the penalty" she says), and woe betide Shylock if he deviate by a hair's breadth. This emphasizes the peripeteia, not suddenly, but by a reverse literalism, rubbing in the defeat. What is swift in the source, with "everyone present" mocking the loser when his plot backfires, and with the Jew tearing up his bond, is being made gradual and (among other things) educative. It is by nature hard to distinguish "teaching someone a lesson" (with deterrence and reform uppermost in the punishment) from retribution; and the slower the process, the more like a vengeance.

The case is alike regarding the Bond, the paper document as stage property, whose presence is often implied, and which must end up somewhere once Shylock has lost. Many actors of Shylock have torn it up anyway, as a good dramatic admission of defeat; but Shakespeare does not specify it, and this may well be because the trial is now passing beyond what the bond says, to something else. That something else is not a contest about bonds, but about what is to happen on the other charges to which (Portia reveals) he is liable, conspiracy against the life of a Venetian (345). Shylock is not getting more than he bargained for. Seen one way, this is fitting, being inherent in any act of hubris. Seen in the light of the sequel, his forcible conversion and stripping of assets, it looks more as if he is being punished for what he is, than for what he has done—since in a sense he has done (accomplished) absolutely nothing. Whose will is done, then? The court's? The state's? Portia's? Antonio's? Let us see who says what, in the process by which Shakespeare diversifies what "everyone present" said, into the responses of Gratiano, Bassanio, the Duke, Portia, and Antonio.

Gratiano is very vocal, jeering in the loudmouth way which Bassanio had long before disrelished and which now blossoms into racist jokes. Bassanio simply wants to give the Jew back his principal (333) but is overruled by Portia: since in 1.3 and later in the present scene he is overruled by Antonio, he seems decent, dependent, and accommodating, the sort who finds it hard to say no. The Duke pardons Shylock for two lines, then imposes conditions—as befits a lawcourt, but hardly a comic one.[16] Portia is legalistic now: her celebrated appeal for mercy is absent, or muted into asking Antonio "What mercy can you render him, Antonio?" She is keeping up her role, and testing the Merchant of Venice (whose "mercy" comes last and is made the Duke's decision also). Maybe the whole play tests this merchant. It is Antonio who disposes of Shylock's possessions and insists on the enforced conversion. None of this, to repeat, was in the novella.

It is Antonio again who insists on Bassanio's surrendering his wedding ring, and neither is this in the novella. In an age which respected oaths as binding, and considering that the ring is the emblem of a marriage taken most seriously (and not even yet consummated), Antonio is asking a lot. The fact that Bassanio as Beneficiary owes him so much makes it harder to deny him, and so he ought not to have asked. Portia rightly smells a threat. Far from being misnamed after Antonio, the play is correctly seen as about his ambivalences; not simply here at the end of the trial, when he punishes Shylock not for what he does but for what he is, but at points throughout the sequel. His burdensome love of Bassanio is the last of all the obstacles which stand (like increasingly difficult obstacles in a steeplechase) between the lovers and their joy. I completely agree with Anne Barton's reading of Antonio.[17]

The finale expands on the joking and partying of the source's ending, but has to provide a counterweight to the complexity and intensity and unresolved emotion which Shakespeare added to the trial scene. How does it attempt this, and does it succeed?

It attempts the task, which Shakespeare has just made very hard for himself and unquestionably harder than he found it in his main source, by the following discernible sequences: a night duet for Lorenzo and Jessica (1–23); messengers, from outside the household and inside (Stephano and Gobbo, *eisangelos* and *exangelos* so to speak, 25–53); rhapsody on the music of the spheres and the music of earth (54–88). There is much talk of the time, of lights and whether dawn is come; it does not come, so that at the close it will still be suitable time for the lovers' going to bed.[18] Enter Portia and her company (89), then Bassanio and his, which now includes Antonio (127), whereupon she is at long last introduced to him. Small talk follows till the rings' quarrel erupts (142), and the exploitation of this and then its elucidation fill out the last half of the finale. The first half is added from other sources, while the second expands on the novella.

The litany of lovers, I have argued, mentions instances of the tribulations of lovers, not because they apply, but because they do not. Lorenzo and Jessica can warble (respectively) of the separation of Troilus and of Dido from their faithless lovers because they themselves are *not* separated, hence *not* thinking about betrayal either. When they bring themselves into the litany, they do a crossover, woman naming man and vice versa. Ovid is being appropriated for love-expression, not subpoenaed to help cast a blight.

So these lovers are being authorized, as it were, to give us the play's backward look at the strife now ended. We could say that Jessica, not Shylock, gets the last word, so long as we recognize her exact state of mind. She says nothing at all while Lorenzo interprets the stars as symbols of celestial harmony, a music of the heavenly bodies. But when he moves on to physical music, her answer is edgy, transitional, ambivalent . . . What is the word for it? Maybe just realistic: music, heeded, draws us into itself, and that is the bliss it gives. And denies to "the man that hath no music in himself." Frank Kermode's comment was that the passage "tells the audience how to interpret the action" so that "only by a determined attempt to avoid the obvious can one mistake the theme" (221, 224).

Broadly, I agree. To reinsert the thought of Shylock—except here, where Shakespeare himself does it, and does it moreover by a glancing generalization—is to superimpose one's own play on the very sufficient one the dramatist wrote. Let people do so, by all means, but let them not call it *his* play. His play, though multi-centered and problematical, does center where its title puts the emphasis, on Antonio.

I should have said, it does this when allowed to. If a company's best actor takes the role of Shylock, and his scenes are arranged to suit him, and if further Shylock-allusions are inserted by the director in the finale, then of course he will upstage Antonio and the other parties to the four-way transaction which the play enacts. It is self-fulfilling. But if he does upstage them we will have an unresolved, or soured, comedy—or even a tragedy.[19] And so we will not be watching the play which Shakespeare wrote, nor the design which source-criticism establishes. And similarly with written interpretation: if attention starts or finishes with Shylock, in and beyond his five scenes, the play will emerge less perfect and more skewed than if we keep our attention wheresoever Shakespeare is directing it. This option is more difficult, but more rewarding. The play manifests a tense, shifting balance throughout, the balancing of four principal agents with several love stories, which—let us not forget—he chose to work out. That, and not Shylock alone, is the play's driving force.

Notes

1. I approximate to the view of M. M. Mahood, ed. *The Merchant of Venice*, New Cambridge Shakespeare (Cambridge: Cambridge University Press, 1987), Introduction, pp. 24–25, where she speaks of our "multiple and shifting responses . . ." The text used for quotation and reference is this one, hereafter termed "Mahood."

2. "Plot," in Aristotle's full sense of the term: the what and the who as they merge in causality, hence governing characterization also.

3. The "golden fleece" of 1.1.169 (also 3.2.240, typically vulgarized by Gratiano).

4. The essay owes something to my essay *"The Merchant of Venice and Il Pecorone, or Can Source-Study resolve the Question of Shylock?"* in *AUMLA: Journal of the Australasian Universities Language and Literature Association* 40 (1973), (271–283), and to my book *The Shakespeare of the Comedies. A Multiple Approach* (Berne: Peter Lang, 1996).

5. 1.1.57, the only time kinship is mentioned: a vestige of Giannetto's story, where Ansaldo is Giannetto's godfather?

6. From the medieval *Gesta Romanorum*, Englished in 1577 and revised just before the play (see Mahood 4).

7. Implicit in the source, where Ansaldo "decided to sell everything he had in the world, to equip another ship" (Bullough 469).

8. As Mr. Woodhouse in *Emma* recognizes. He dislikes weddings because they are inseparable from change: the play accumulates changes, of gender-dress, allegiance, status, religion, ownership, matrimony, and most especially of who has the power.

9. Mahood (8) is cautious about accepting Marlowe's *Jew of Malta* as a source at all, speaking instead of its "pervasive presence," and mainly in terms of contrast. Considering the Marlovian language of Morocco, "pervasive presence" seems right. But so does significant contrast as regards Abigail/Barabas and Jessica/Shylock.

10. What with the many other *comedic* features assigned to Jessica, it seems misguided to dwell on the allusions to false love as signs of falsity in their speakers: spoken between lovers they are more a sign of confidence and security than of skating on thin ice. The dangerous stuff can be acknowledged, by lovers who have made a dangerous alliance, without imperilling anything.

11. I understand the off-color jokes in 3.5 similarly: Lorenzo talks of being jealous of Gobbo because he is not jealous, not because he is, though it is open to some humorless or axe-grinding director to play the scene against the grain. See also Hale, *The Shakespeare of the Comedies*, p. 17.

12. Bullough 472: the Jew of Mestri is merely laconically adamant.

13. We never see father and daughter at ease with each other, they never say anything good about each other. She is "ashamed" to be his child, and once he notices her rebellion the feeling is strongly reciprocated. She is "dead" to him.

14. Despite stage tradition, intuitively reinstating the Jew of Mestri's impassioned gesture.

15. As he does elsewhere, to similarly problematic effect: Iago's humiliations to Othello are prolonged too, because they make good theater. Shakespeare's rigor can look like cruelty.

16. He is the harshest of Shakespeare's comedy-dukes in passing judgment.

17. In the Riverside edition. I am reminded of Jonathan Miller's solution of the ending of the *Taming of the Shrew*, another ending unpleasing to modern sensibilites, *until* it is psychologized. Just as Katharina has been exorcised of a

demon by Petruchio's play-acting, so Antonio must stand aside lest he become the demon of Bassanio's married life.

18. Like, but not like, the close of *A Midsummer Night's Dream*: these lovers get to bed late, in the nick of time, whereas the symmetrical puppets of the previous play go at the set time, midnight. The delayed wedding night in the *Merchant* is part of its design, seen very clearly by the contrast with its source where consummation had to *precede* the wedding, the former performance qualifying Giannetto for the latter.

19. The play ended with Shylock's exit in some eighteenth-century versions (Mahood 43)—a curious opposite to the happy ending of Nahum Tate's *Lear*. If the latter is scorned as travesty nowadays, why not the former also? And with it, the intrusion of Shylock where Shakespeare did *not* put him?

Works Cited

Barton, Anne. "Introduction." *The Merchant of Venice*. In *The Riverside Shakespeare*, ed. G. B. Evans. Boston: Houghton, Mifflin, 1974. 250–53.

Bullough, Geoffrey, ed. *Narrative and Dramatic Sources of Shakespeare*. Volume 1. London: Routledge, 1957.

Hale, John K. "*The Merchant of Venice* and *Il Pecorone*, or Can Source-Study Resolve the Question of Shylock?" *AUMLA: Journal of the Australasian Universities Language and Literature Association* 40 (1973): 271–83.

———. *The Shakespeare of the Comedies: A Multiple Approach*. Berne: Peter Lang, 1996.

Kermode, Frank. "The Mature Comedies." *Stratford-upon-Avon Studies 3: Early Shakespeare*. London: Edward Arnold, 1961. 211–27.

Shakespeare, William. *The Merchant of Venice*. Ed. M. M. Mahood. Cambridge: Cambridge University Press, 1987.

Shylock is Content
A Study in Salvation

HUGH SHORT

Late in act 4, scene 1 of Shakespeare's provocative play *The Merchant of Venice*, its most problematic and controversial character, Shylock, the Jewish moneylender, finds himself in a peripety, a reversal of circumstance and fortune. He believes he has successfully conspired against the merchant Antonio's life by demanding the penalty agreed upon in a loan that Antonio has failed to repay in the contracted time period. That penalty is a pound of flesh from the area closest to Antonio's heart. This penalty will surely result in Antonio's death, but Shylock has insisted on that penalty alone, and has refused generous and highly profitable alternatives. When Portia, posing as Balthazar, turns the tables on him, essentially finding him guilty of conspiracy to commit murder, Shylock finds his own life threatened by the state. The state proves less bloodthirsty than Shylock. The Duke pardons his life. Antonio foregoes the monetary penalty he could exact from Shylock, stipulating three conditions: Shylock must let Antonio manage half of his estate on behalf of Jessica and Lorenzo, he must become a Christian, and he must will the rest of his estate to Jessica and Lorenzo upon his death. Shylock agrees to these provisions, stating: "I am content" (4.1.394).[1]

Never have directors, actors, or audiences believed him. In every production of the play that I have seen or about which I have heard or read, Shylock's line has been perceived as constrained, forced out of him. But suppose that perception is mistaken. Suppose Shylock means what he says, and really is content. Suppose the words are freely uttered and reflect Shylock's actual state of mind and soul at the time he speaks them. Is such a reading possible? Does it *work* in the play? I would like to suggest that this reading of the line more thoroughly accounts for and accommodates the other details of the play than any of the readings that have so far prevailed, and makes apparent a depth and richness in the play that is otherwise lost.

199

I concede that the thesis stated above represents not just a minority perspective, but a virtually unique one. Before developing it, it seems only fair to provide a quick summary of the perspectives that have prevailed over the years. The play does not seem to have been very popular in Shakespeare's lifetime, or through the rest of the seventeenth century, and through part of the eighteenth century it was supplanted by a version that made Shylock a stereotypical villain. Even when Shakespeare's text was restored, however, Shylock was seen as the villain. The role seems to have been played by an actor wearing a red wig, thus signaling the audience that Shylock was a stock character, a Vice figure to be mocked and scorned (Alter 29). Since the Romantic era he has increasingly been seen in a more sympathetic light, as a man, to borrow a phrase from *King Lear*, "more sinned against than sinning." Some productions have even presented him as approaching the status of tragic hero. This shift in the perception of Shylock has been amply documented in numerous sources, and textual cases have been made for portrayals at both ends of the spectrum.

One making a case for the portrayal of Shylock as a stock villain would point to his deadly, or at very least malicious, intentions towards Antonio even before Antonio appears on stage: his exaggerated miserliness except when given an opportunity to shed Antonio's blood; his rejection by his daughter, Jessica; his hatred of music; his obvious intention to carry out the penalty of the contract rather than accept far more than the originally contracted price in payment; even his gratuitous cruelty in whetting his knife on the sole of his shoe during the trial scene. These textual details and others testify to Shylock's villainy, and many details indicate murderous intent on his part. So, the view that Shylock is a straightforward villain is capable of defense, and he has frequently been played in this manner down through the years.

At the other end of the spectrum is the more recent and now dominant view that Shylock is to be viewed with at least some degree of sympathy. This perspective does not, by and large, deny Shylock's behavior and intentions. Rather, it views his deeds and intentions as provoked and therefore justified by the treatment he has received over the years by the Christians among whom he has lived. One version of this perspective sees Shakespeare as intending to portray Shylock as vicious only because of the treatment he has received, and therefore credits Shakespeare with writing a dark condemnation of Christian hypocrisy. A more extreme version of this view is that Shakespeare intended to write a play portraying Shylock as a simple and contemptible villain, and unwittingly revealed the prejudice and anti-Semitism present in himself and in his time, thereby producing an even darker condemnation of Christian hypocrisy. These views conclude that, whatever Shakespeare's intentions, the play must now be read and experienced as one in which Shylock has ample grounds for his anger and murderous intent, having been driven to rage by a vicious, cruel society that hypocritically calls itself Christian.

These perspectives, too, have textual justification. Antonio freely admits to having spat upon and kicked Shylock in the past, and admits to a willingness to do so again whether or not Shylock agrees to lend him money. Lorenzo has no compunction about making off with Shylock's wealth as well as with his daughter. Salerio and Solanio take obvious and excessive delight in baiting Shylock, and are pleased at his discomfiture. Shylock is frequently addressed disparagingly as "Jew," and sometimes even as a devil. This perspective gives weight to the argument for Shylock's humanity found in the famous "Hath not a Jew eyes?" speech. Without doubt this perspective can indeed point to a good deal of Christian hypocrisy in the play.

Of course, one's perspective on Shylock's character influences one's views concerning the other characters in the play. If Shylock is a villain, then Antonio must be the opposite, and Portia must be praised for preserving Antonio's life and thwarting Shylock's malevolent scheme. On the other hand, if Shylock is a victim of Christian hypocrisy, then Antonio, the man who has spat upon him, looks like a more malignant force, and Portia begins to look like the archetype of Christian hypocrisy. Naturally the details of the play can be interpreted variously depending on the perspective from which they are viewed.

The recent trend has been to interpret the actions of Portia and the other Christians in a bitterly negative light. Leslie Fiedler sees Portia as carrying out "in a ritual of Jew-baiting not only her own anti-Semitism, but that of all the other characters in the play" (66). He sees her as motivated by hedonism rather than Christian principles (87), claims that "the truth of the play is revenge and retribution," (96), and asserts that "mercy is the weapon with which Shylock is clubbed over the head" (100). Finally, he has this description of Portia's behavior during the trial scene: "Feeling her claws in Shylock's flesh, she drives them deeper and deeper in order to exact her own pound of flesh" (101). In short, Fiedler finds Portia guilty of carrying out on a figurative level the plan that Shylock only hopes to carry out on the physical one.

Fiedler has plenty of company in his condemnation of Portia and the action of the play. Just a few examples will suffice to reveal the general tenor of this vein of critical commentary. A *New York Times* editorial described Portia as "the playgirl of the Western World," and considered her "quality of mercy" speech as "the ultimate hypocrisy" (Danson 4). Another critic contends that in the trial scene "The Christians out-Shylock Shylock as the letter of the law defeats the letter of the law in ways oblivious to its spirit and destructive of the human spirit" (Lyon 107) due to "the cruel hypocrisy of Portia's excessive justice" (Lyon 116). Harold Goddard contends that Portia, during the trial scene, tortures all parties, friend and foe alike, for no better reason than to create "a spectacle, a dramatic triumph with herself at the center" (35), and concludes that "Shylock's conviction that Christianity and revenge are synonyms is confirmed" (35). Thus this view renders a negative judgment of the characters, the action, and the play itself, in reaction against the more traditional view that the play is a comedy that ends in harmony as good triumphs over evil.

Though the traditional and more recent views of the play differ in most respects, both, interestingly enough, find a significant point of agreement: that Shylock is not telling the truth when he says "I am content." Both see these words as forced from his mouth to save his life now that he has been so thoroughly defeated and destroyed. The traditional perspective reads this line as indicative of Shylock's final, well deserved defeat, his surrender, and hence the victory of Portia and company. The more recent perspective hears the line as the final evidence of Shylock's utter destruction at the hands of vicious Christians. Critics have uniformly seen Shylock's conversion as "forced" (Engle 36; Alter 32). Most have seen him as "a broken man" (Cohen). Those who do not see him as absolutely broken tend to claim that the words "I am content" come out of "a profound weariness" (Danson 168). Even critics not particularly inclined to defend Shylock note that an actor playing the role of Shylock is justified in saying the line in question "as despairingly or angrily as he can" (Kerrigan 134). The mildest claim that I have been able to find with respect to Shylock's agreement to Antonio's terms is that he submits only to preserve his wealth (Hamill 241). Virtually no reading sees the words as freely uttered and reflective of Shylock's actual state of mind and soul. Nonetheless, that is precisely my claim. Shylock speaks the truth when he says he is content. The words not only do not signal his destruction, they proclaim his salvation.

As a preliminary step in justifying my reading of the line in question, let us back up a bit to consider some pertinent details of Shylock's behavior and character early in the play, moving as quickly as possible to the trial scene of 4.1. Shylock has certainly been abused in the past; he argues that Antonio has mistreated him, and Antonio makes no attempt to deny Shylock's allegations that Antonio has called "me misbeliever, cutthroat dog, / And spet upon my Jewish gaberdine" (1.3.111–12). In responding, Antonio admits to the truth of all of Shylock's charges. Moreover, he volunteers that he is likely to treat him so again, and warns that Shylock should not misunderstand his request for a loan: Shylock is to consider Antonio his enemy, and to keep this thought in mind as he loans him money. If Antonio does not repay the loan on time, he can "exact the penalty" (1.3.137) with a clear conscience. Antonio holds Shylock in contempt and thinks himself secure in his superiority.

For his part, even before Antonio's entrance Shylock has informed the audience that he hates Antonio and yearns to revenge himself for past wrongs, saying, "If I can catch him once upon the hip, / I will feed fat the ancient grudge I bear him" (1.3.46–47). When Shylock offers to lend Antonio the money without interest, but with the "merry sport" (145) of a "pound of flesh" penalty for lack of payment, Antonio takes the offer as a generous one, and accepts it in that spirit. Antonio is so sure of his financial situation that he does not fear the penalty; rather, he actually sees Shylock as having made a "Christian" gesture by providing a loan without interest. Nevertheless, the reader should not share Antonio's delusion. Whatever it might mean to "feed fat" his grudge (the phrase does take on suggestive overtones when we consider that the "merry sport" Shylock refers to would present Shylock with a pound of Antonio's flesh), Shylock means no good to Antonio, even if it is not certain at this point that he means to take Antonio's life. He has provided himself with a clause that he knows is unlikely to be invoked, but one that, if it does come to be invoked, can at the very least make Antonio squirm.

As the play continues, however, his mood darkens as he suffers at the hands of "Christians." His daughter runs away, taking treasure that belongs to Shylock. Christians, friends of Antonio, aid her. Christians like Salerio and Solanio delight in Shylock's discomfiture and publicly mock his pain. Having lost money through Jessica's flight, he learns that he is in danger of losing even more through Antonio's reverses, and whatever his intention previously, his thoughts toward Antonio certainly become bloody. 3.1, if it does not necessarily show us the moment in which Shylock's intentions turn to bloody revenge, at the very least shows that his intentions are now murderous, and that he justifies these intentions by referring to the treatment he has received.

After mocking and denouncing Shylock, Salerio has the poor judgment to ask whether Shylock knows if Antonio has suffered any reverses at sea. Of course, Shylock has heard stories that would indicate that he will lose not just the money that Jessica has run off with, but also the money he has loaned to Antonio, and he warns, three times, "Let him look to his bond" (3.1.47). Salerio is shocked to hear that Shylock intends to hold Antonio to the bond, noting that the flesh that is forfeit is not "good for" (52) anything, but Shylock responds that it will provide him with revenge. He justifies himself by repeating in essence the charges he lodged against Antonio in 1.3, claiming that all of the offenses against him stem from the fact that he is a Jew. It is possible to argue that the abuse of Shylock has been based instead on his occupation of usurer, and has been aggravated by Shylock's abrasive and bitter character, but we need not resolve that question here. Suffice it to say that Shylock feels a powerful anger not only against Antonio but against the Christians of Venice, that his anger can be justified by the treatment he has received, and that he finds himself in a position to gratify that anger against one particular Venetian, and indeed against the one Venetian he hates most, Antonio.

Shylock argues convincingly that he is a man like other men, feeling all of the same emotions that other men, notably Christians, feel, and claims that he has learned from Christians how to behave. He claims that Christians have taught him the efficacy of revenge, and he vows now to "execute" (3.1.72) the villainy that he has been taught. Shylock's words at the end of this speech are of great importance in understanding the later trial scene, for he makes "Christian" behavior responsible for his own behavior. Having been taught to seek revenge, he does so. Having never been treated with compassion, having never experienced mercy, he has never *learned* to be merciful, and so he is incapable of exhibiting compassion. It is this consciousness that Shylock brings to the trial scene.

Before proceeding to that scene, one final preparatory stipulation must be made about Portia's role in that scene. Though not all audiences and critics have perceived it, it is crucial to understand that Portia enters the trial scene with the knowledge that can save Antonio. The logic of the play completely breaks down if we envision her as rushing to the courtroom without a foolproof plan to save Antonio, simply trusting to her wits. With Bassanio's dearest friend's life at risk, such a cavalier attitude would be inappropriate in the extreme, even within the confines of a comedy. Portia could not have so blithely replaced Bellario in court. Moreover, on this point the textual evidence is clear. Portia comes to court with Bellario's legal expertise, and we can see the proof in the law books that she uses late in the scene to confirm the penalty for directly and indirectly conspiring against the life of Antonio. The books are not simply props, and when Portia takes them up she immediately opens them to the statute that frees Antonio and damns Shylock. She could at any point bring the issue to a close by simply opening those books and pointing to the pertinent law, as she does very late in the scene, giving the Duke grounds to arrest Shylock immediately, preventing him from carrying out the penalty for forfeit of the bond.

The question then arises, why does Portia take so long to bring forth those books? Why does she allow everyone in court to linger so long in the belief that Antonio has no recourse within the law? Goddard has argued that Portia draws out the scene to indulge her ego and to torture Shylock (33). A more justified claim might be that she does so in order that Shylock's intention, directly and indirectly, to take Antonio's life, may be amply demonstrated to the court (Engle 35). While this last claim has real force, the scene unfolds as it does primarily because Portia wishes to provide mercy to Shylock, and wishes to teach him, and the rest of the court, the need for mercy. Furthermore, she succeeds.

The scene takes place in a Venetian court of justice, and justices are indeed present, but from the first moments of the scene the Duke himself presides, and from his first words we see that he is inclined toward Antonio and against Shylock. Before Shylock makes his appearance, the Duke expresses his sorrow for Antonio, and contends that he knows Shylock to be

A stony adversary, an inhuman wretch,
Uncapable of pity, void and empty
From any dram of mercy. (4.1.4–6)

Balthazar

Accurate though the Duke's assessment may be, however, he speaks differ-ently once Shylock is present to hear what he has to say. Having just stated his belief that Shylock is incapable of mercy, he tells him that he and the rest of the city believe that Shylock is only feigning his malice, intending to keep up the act until the last moment, at which point he will demonstrate his mercy. Interest-ingly, though Bassanio is present and ready and willing to pay off the debt at many times its value, the Duke tells Shylock that he expects Shylock not only to "loose the forfeiture" (23), but to "Forgive a moiety of the principal" (26) as well. One can be forgiven if one hears a note of threat in the Duke's closing line: "We all expect a gentle answer, Jew!" (34). The Duke, having made the audi-ence aware of Shylock's lack of pity, addresses him in such a way that he can pretend to believe in Shylock's kindly intentions while pressuring him to relent.

Shylock refuses to be intimidated. He defends the legality of his con-tract, and points out persuasively that if the people of Venice can presume to hold contracts that make human beings their property, then he can surely lay claim to a pound of flesh. What he wants, he maintains, is justice, and much has been made of this claim, but his stated concern for justice is no more hon-est than the Duke's stated belief that Shylock will be merciful. Shylock wants revenge, and he sees the letter of the law as providing him with the opportu-nity to take that revenge with impunity, and revenge not only against Anto-nio, but against all of the Christians of Venice, who have aligned themselves with Antonio and against Shylock. He believes that he can make Antonio's friends and the Duke himself watch helplessly as he publicly torments Anto-nio, as Shylock himself has been publicly tormented.

Into this hotbed of hate steps Portia, disguised as Balthazar, coming to Venice "furnished with" (157) Bellario's learned opinion in the matter. After being introduced to the litigants, Portia asks whether Antonio admits to the bond. When he does so, she turns to Shylock, stating "Then must the Jew be merciful" (182). It is clear in the context, that is, in her subsequent lines, that what she means is that what this situation *needs* is mercy from Shylock. Shy-lock, however, hears her words differently, as kindred in spirit to the Duke's earlier "We all expect a gentle answer, Jew." He thinks she is saying he must be forced to be merciful, but Portia is quick to set him straight, with her famous speech on mercy, which demands close examination.

She turns to him and notes that

> The quality of mercy is not strained.
> It droppeth as the gentle rain from heaven
> Upon the place beneath. It is twice blest:
> It blesseth him that gives and him that takes. (184–87)

Responding to Shylock's misperception, she tells him that mercy cannot be forced, but must be given freely; when it is so given it has healing, restorative

powers both for the one who gives and for the one who receives. It functions
like rain, nurturing, feeding, making things grow, bringing life. Portia steps
entirely outside of the mindset of the men in court, all of whom are interested
in forcing, pushing, constraining to get their will, reminding Shylock and
everyone in court that the very rain that sustains life cannot be constrained,
but is received as a blessing.

She goes on to note that "'Tis mightiest in the mightiest" (188), and
makes reference to the power of the "throned monarch," "his crown," "His
sceptre," "the force of temporal power," and "the dread and fear of kings"
(189–92), but points out that mercy is "above this sceptered sway" (193). She
is talking to Shylock, who seems to wield the power of "justice" in this situation, but her words have a broader application and a larger audience as well.
Her words pertain readily to the Duke, since he is the only "monarch" present.
They can also be applied to the Christians present, since the dominance of
their religion has given them *de facto* power over nonbelievers like Shylock.

Portia tells Shylock and her larger audience that mercy "is an attribute to
God himself" (195), and warns him against his often-asserted claim of justice, because

> . . . in the course of justice none of us
> Should see salvation. We do pray for mercy,
> And that same prayer doth teach us all to render
> The deeds of mercy. (199–202)

Knowing already that Shylock's trust in the law is unwise, she reminds him
that justice is not the best thing, and that all human beings need something
more than justice. What Portia tries to teach him is true Christian charity, but
Shylock's memories of abuse from Christians and the intensity of his thirst
for revenge make him deaf to her plea.

Portia concludes the speech on a less elevated note, reminding Shylock
of the specific case being considered:

> I have spoke thus much
> To mitigate the justice of thy plea,
> Which if thou follow, this strict court of Venice
> Must needs give sentence 'gainst the merchant there. (202–205)

It might be and has been argued that Portia deliberately and cruelly undermines the thrust of her argument by suggesting to Shylock that he will win
his case if he persists in pressing it and rejecting mercy, but that argument
misunderstands the point of the speech, which is that the greatness of mercy
shines most clearly when it is exercised by those with the power to inflict
harm, by those who have justice on their side and reject it for something

higher and better. It is not Portia's intention to overwhelm Shylock with oratorical power that blinds him to the legal strength of his case; rather she wishes him to choose mercy because it is best for everyone. We must remember that Portia can end the trial at any moment because of the legal evidence that she already possesses that can turn Shylock from accuser to accused. She is not trying to save Antonio throughout the scene, or at least she is not trying to save his life; she is trying to save Shylock, and the souls of Antonio and the Christians of Venice. Imagine for a moment what good feeling Shylock would have generated had he been touched by Portia's speech and exercised mercy. Had he done so, the legal case against him would have disappeared, and Portia would have had no occasion to open those books and level her charge against him. How could anyone argue that Shylock conspired against the life of Antonio, when, of his own free will, he granted Antonio his life? Rebuffed in her first attempt, Portia continues her efforts to save Shylock, though for a very long time he is deaf to her pleas. It proves fortunate for Shylock that others in the court do listen to her message of mercy and heed it.

But Shylock, having learned only cruelty and revenge from his encounters with Christians, is untouched by Portia's words, responding "My deeds upon my head!" (206), deliberately and directly rejecting the principle of mercy in favor of a strict and unrelenting justice. Portia, of course, knows that Bassanio is present in court and willing to pay any kind of financial price Shylock might name. He states his willingness to pay ten times the borrowed sum, and pleads that if that price does not suffice, it is clear that "malice bears down truth" (214). Surely malice does bear down mercy and reason at this point, but Bassanio would have the Duke "Wrest once the law to your authority" (215), denying Shylock's pursuit of the penalty for nonpayment of his debt by pure power rather than by justice. Portia quite correctly rejects this alternative, noting that one cannot just play at justice, accepting it when one approves the result, and twisting it when one does not. At the risk of excessive repetition, let us note again that Portia can make her case against Shylock whenever she wants to; if she wanted to catch him and torture him, what better time to break out the law books than this time? "My deeds upon my head!" almost demands the response: "So be it. You have conspired against Antonio's life, and now your life is forfeit. Your deeds demand death." Yet Portia still does not turn to those books.

Instead, she casts about for a better resolution, bidding him to show mercy, twice reminding him that he can profit greatly even on a simple financial level, by relenting. She asks him to "bid me tear the bond" (234), and again we must pause to consider her motivation. What happens if Shylock does tell Portia to tear up the bond? If he does so, again, the case that Portia knows can be made against Shylock disappears. It is precisely that bond and Shylock's insistence that the terms of the bond be carried through that comprise the case against him. Portia is asking Shylock to destroy the case against him, but the desire for revenge still burns too hotly within him, and he cannot hear her.

He makes a maddeningly literalist response to each of her attempts to prod him in the direction of mercy. He insists that he cut Antonio's breast, the area closest to the heart, because the terms of the contract stipulate that it be done so. He rejects Portia's appeal that he provide a doctor, claiming that there is no such provision in the contract. Her comment that it "'Twere good you do so much for charity" (261) is met by rejection because "'tis not in the bond" (262). Shylock's insistence on the strict terms of the bond provides Portia with an opportunity to hammer home a lesson on the nature of justice, that message that she had stated earlier, that in the course of justice no man finds salvation. She shows him that he has erred in placing his faith in justice. She demonstrates that justice can not only strip him of his revenge, prevent him from accepting the threefold payment of the debt previously offered, deny him even the return of the original loan, and prevent him from leaving the site of his defeat, but also put him under sentence of death. The tables turned, she notes that he has placed himself at the mercy of the Duke, whom Shylock scorned as the scene opened.

The Duke demonstrates that if Shylock was not able to respond to the pull of Portia's speech on mercy, the Duke was. Shylock has given the Duke an opportunity to take revenge in his turn upon the man he has described as a "stony adversary, an inhuman wretch" (4), the man who has demeaned his court with his thirst for revenge, insisted that he will answer for his deeds, and claimed that he wants only justice. In an extraordinary display of mercy, the Duke grants Shylock his life before Shylock has even requested it. He even goes so far as to suggest that if Shylock behaves in a humble manner, he will refrain from claiming half of Shylock's wealth, but will settle for a fine instead. Portia points out that the Duke has it within his power to reduce his claims upon Shylock, but that he cannot impose any restrictions on Antonio's claim: Antonio is entitled to half of Shylock's wealth.

Before Antonio gets a chance to speak, Shylock rejects the Duke's proposed mercy, no doubt sure that Antonio, the man who has spat upon him in the past, will not miss this opportunity to torment him. He cries out

> Nay, take my life and all, pardon not that:
> You take my house when you take the prop
> That doth sustain my house; you take my life
> When you do take the means whereby I live. (374–77)

The speech is significant in several respects. First, it shows that a mere seventeen lines before the speech in which he says "I am content," Shylock is unrepentant and unredeemed. He is still defiant after he has received the mercy of the Duke, and he is not at all hesitant to say so. Why should we think, then, that he is lying when he does come to say "I am content"? What justifies us in thinking that Shylock is not content when he claims to be, strange though it may seem to us? But if we accept the possibility of his contentment, what explains it? What happens between the time of his defiant speech daring the Duke to take his life, and his claim of contentment?

Only two things happen: Shylock's enemy Antonio is asked by Portia "What mercy can you render him, Antonio?" (378), and Antonio responds. If Shylock does not perceive Antonio's speech as merciful, why would his tone change so dramatically? Shylock's "I am content" cannot be understood as the final surrender of a beaten man, for nothing in Antonio's speech can be seen as worsening his fate. Yes, a twentieth-century audience can claim that a forced conversion is worse than death, but Shylock has just shown that he is willing to lose his life, so it cannot reasonably be argued that he is now willing to face any humiliation to preserve his life. No, something must happen to Shylock to dampen his defiance. Having told us earlier that Christians have taught him how to behave, and have taught him that revenge is to be sought upon one's enemies, Shylock discovers that he has more learning to do, because perhaps his primary and most profound teacher, Antonio, shows that he has learned a few things himself.

Portia's question to Antonio is pointed and direct: "What mercy can you render him, Antonio?" (378). Antonio has been a man willing to spit upon and kick Shylock because of his occupation, and since he has done so he has been forced to bare his breast to a knife, expecting to die, so what can be expected from him? If we expect him to exact revenge for his suffering, we are just expecting him to behave towards Shylock as he has in the past. Yet Antonio's actual response is not at all what we expect. Perhaps his own closeness to death, his own experience of humiliation at the hands of his enemy, has taught him a lesson. More likely, he too has heard Portia's speech on mercy not only with his ears but with his heart and soul as well, and has been touched by it. After all, both the Duke and Antonio profess to be Christians, and so Portia's speech should speak directly to them. Shylock has told us already that he has learned how to behave from men such as Antonio, and now he sees and hears an Antonio unlike the man he has known.

Antonio takes seriously Portia's question about what mercy he can render Shylock, and provides an answer that Shylock can and does accept as merciful. Before Antonio can respond, Gratiano breaks in with a response along the lines of what Shylock must expect: "A halter gratis! Nothing else, for God sake" (379). We recognize the irony of Gratiano's claim that Shylock should be hanged for God's sake, but surely that is just the kind of response that Shylock's dealings with Christians have led him to expect. This time, however, the Christian who has been his primary enemy responds in a new way.

Before Antonio speaks, Shylock has been granted his life, but one-half of his goods have been awarded to Antonio. The Duke has already conditionally allowed that the other half, in law forfeit to the state, be retained by Shylock, minus a fine, but Shylock has seemingly thought such terms punishing enough that he mocks them and dares the Duke to take his life. In order for Shylock actually to be content with Antonio's mercy, and to agree to accept it, it would seem that he must find something of value in Antonio's words. He must see Antonio's mercy as genuine. With this point in mind, I suggest that when Antonio says

> So please my lord the Duke and all the court
> To quit the fine for one half of his goods, (4.1.380–81)

he is requesting that the Duke release Shylock even from the need to pay a fine. So, Antonio begs that Shylock be allowed to keep *all* of the money forfeit to the state. For his part, Antonio refuses to take *any* of Shylock's property as his own personal wealth, but will instead become trustee of one half of the estate, using it in behalf of Shylock's daughter, Jessica, and her husband Lorenzo. All of this leads Antonio to say, in anticipation of Shylock, "I am content" (382). Critics do not seem to notice the generosity of such an act by a man who still thinks he has lost all of his ships and wealth. What people do notice are the "[t]wo things provided more" (386) that Antonio requires: that Shylock make Jessica and Lorenzo his heirs when he dies, and that Shylock become a Christian.[2]

That last condition has aroused the wrath of contemporary audiences, but it defies logic to contend that this stipulation is one last outrageous bit of hypocrisy meant to further torment Shylock. Granted that conversion is a matter of the soul and cannot be forced; granted that no one in the court is in a position to know whether Shylock's conversion will touch his soul or not; granted that we are right in this day and age to leave religious belief to the individual and his conscience; granted that today such a stipulation must seem wrong. Even so, it is a strange and contrary reading to insist that Antonio's provision amounts to some kind of cruelty against Shylock. Antonio is a Christian himself, and so he is asking Shylock to be like him, to join his community. Certainly a Christian of that age would have seen such a conversion as opening up the possibility of salvation to Shylock, not further torture.

More to the point, though, how would Shylock hear Antonio's words? When all of his experience would lead him to expect the same kind of scorn and torment that he has received from Christians throughout his life, when he has done everything possible to *deserve* hatred and vicious treatment, a miracle takes place. Portia's speech about the quality of mercy has dropped down upon the Venetian court like a gentle rain indeed, like God's grace. It has caused mercy and forgiveness to grow in the hearts of two men whose treatment of Shylock had previously been anything but Christian. It has caused them to take the first step, to be better than they have been. The last thing Shylock could ever have expected from Antonio is what he received; it covers over his wrath and defiance. Quietly, freely, he agrees to Antonio's terms.

And so Shylock speaks the truth when he says he is content. Short moments later, overwhelmed by the experience, he departs, never to be seen again in the play, but he does not depart as Laurence Olivier played him, with a final despairing cry of pain. He leaves in silence. As he says, he is not well, but he is on the road to health. The diseases of anger and lust for revenge have been removed, and tragedy has been averted, not only for Antonio, but also for all present, and Shylock too is included in the greater harmony of the play's message.

The healing force of mercy continues in the grand resolution of act 5. Bassanio, having vowed in 3.2 that he would die before giving up the ring given to him by Portia, having accepted the ring as the very sign of his marriage contract, having agreed that Portia could justly denounce him if he ever parted with the ring, finds himself held accountable for having given that ring away. The vows he made so comfortably and confidently seem to damn him, if the strict letter of the law is observed. But Bassanio is fortunate, for Portia is his judge, and she is not interested in strict justice. Antonio intercedes for Bassanio, begging mercy as Portia begged mercy for Antonio. Earlier in the play Antonio was willing to bind his body for Bassanio; now he is willing to bind his very soul, and it is fitting that he is willing to hold his soul forfeit to Portia, for it was Portia who restored it to him. The ring is given again; the marriage is intact. Harmonious music dominates the scene, for mercy rules.

Shylock's contentment allows the play as a whole to achieve the harmony discussed and displayed in act 5, and that is perhaps the most compelling argument in its favor. If Shylock is not content at the end of the trial scene, then the harmony of act 5 is a lie, and a vicious one at that. When has Shakespeare ever treated his audience in such a manner? Knowing so well the greatness of Shakespeare's soul, demonstrated in play after play, do we not owe him the most charitable reading we can provide? Has not Shakespeare throughout his career shown us how well he understands the worth and weight of mercy? Is it not better, when it is defensible textually, to choose the interpretation most in keeping with the spirit of the body of his work, rather than one which denies that spirit?

Notes

1. All quotations from the play come from *The Riverside Shakespeare*, ed. G. B. Evans (Boston: Houghton, Mifflin, 1974).
2. In the introduction to his edition of the play, W. Moelwyn Merchant notes that Antonio proposes a different disposition for each half of the penalty. The court is first asked "To quit the fine for one half of his goods." "To quit for" is a curious grammatical use: if "quit" retains its meaning of "settling" or "quittance" (in Hamlet's sense a "quietus" or final settlement), it would seem that Shylock has

even the fine remitted. For the second half of Shylock's goods, which might have been awarded Antonio as the aggrieved party, Antonio renounces any claim he might have to possess it himself but asks for it "in use," a legal provision to secure the inheritance for Jessica and Lorenzo. [In a detailed note on line 380, Merchant explains that "in use" is a legal term, "the device of a 'a conveyancer to a user,' whereby an estate intended for inheritance by a second person (Jessica in this instance) is made over to a third person (Antonio) for security of the inheritance. In full legal terms, Antonio would be declared seised of half Shylock's estate to the use of Lorenzo and Jessica after Shylock's death." (202)] These provisions in turn reflect upon the demand that Shylock become a Christian, for Coryat, whose *Crudities* were published in 1611 after his tour in Italy and stay in Venice, describes the sardonic treatment of the baptized Jews: "all their good are confiscated as soon as they embrace Christianity" in order that this renunciation of their wealth may "disclog their souls and consciences." From this material humiliation Shylock is released. (Merchant 30–31)

Merchant also notes that, in claiming that "You take my life / When you do take the means whereby I live," Shylock may be quoting from Ecclesiasticus 34.23: "Who so robbeth his neighbor of his living, doth as great sin as though he slew him to death." (Editors of the play have noted that Portia may also be alluding to Ecclesiasticus [35.20] in her reference to mercy dropping "as the gentle rain from heaven" [185].)

Works Cited

Alter, Robert. "Who Is Shylock?" *Commentary* July 1993: 29–34.

Cohen, Stephen A. "'The Quality of Mercy': Law, Equity and Ideology in *The Merchant of Venice*." *Mosaic* 27.4 (1994): 35–55. 18 December 1997 http://sbweb2.med.iacnet.com/infotrac/session/14/495/5660548/4!xm_37&bkm.

Danson, Lawrence. *The Harmonies of "The Merchant of Venice."* New Haven: Yale University Press, 1978.

Engle, Lars. "'Thrift Is Blessing': Exchange and Explanation in *The Merchant of Venice. Shakespeare Quarterly* 37.1 (1986): 20–37.

Fiedler, Leslie A. "These Be the Christian Husbands." *William Shakespeare's "The Merchant of Venice."* Ed. Harold Bloom. New York: Chelsea House, 1986. 63–90.

Goddard, Harold C. "Portia's Failure." *William Shakespeare's "The Merchant of Venice."* Ed. Harold Bloom. New York: Chelsea House, 1986. 27–36.

Hamill, Monica J. "Poetry, Law, and the Pursuit of Perfection: Portia's Role in *The Merchant of Venice*." *Studies in English Literature* 18 (1978): 229–43.

Kerrigan, William. *Shakespeare's Promises.* Baltimore: The Johns Hopkins University Press, 1999.

Lyon, John. *"The Merchant of Venice": Twayne's New Critical Introduction to Shakespeare.* Boston: Twayne, 1988.

Merchant, W. Moelwyn, ed. *The Merchant of Venice.* Harmondsworth: Penguin, 1967.

Shakespeare, Willliam. *The Riverside Shakespeare.* Ed. G. B. Evans. Boston: Houghton Mifflin, 1974.

Isolation to Communion

A Reading of *The Merchant of Venice*

MARYELLEN KEEFE, O.S.U.

> Come, buy wine and milk without money and without price.
> Why do you spend your money for that which is not bread,
> and your labor for that which does not satisfy?
> Listen carefully to me, and eat what is good,
> and delight yourselves in rich food.
>
> ISAIAH 55: 1–2

In her introduction to *The Merchant of Venice* in *The Norton Shakespeare*, Katherine Maus recognizes the controversy generated by this play's implied questions: "Is it anti-Semitic? Does it criticize anti-Semitism? Does it merely represent anti-Semitism without either condemnation or endorsement?" (1081). Although evidence can be summoned to support any of these views, I would argue that the unusual frequency of alimentary imagery points to the broader context of "human nature," within which Shakespeare acts as God-like judge aware of all his characters' foibles and faults. Too large a person and playwright to focus narrowly on any one stereotype, Shakespeare rather provides, through the lens of Shylock's character, a glimpse at the universal human condition. Like Shylock, all the characters are flawed, as are all the readers and/or spectators.

The alimentary images seasoning Shakespeare's dialogue throughout the play betray a hint of similar Scriptural images that, unlike Portia's direct lesson on the importance of mercy, imply Shakespeare's familiar underlying theme—the impotence of material creatures to satisfy the longings of the human heart. Accordingly, *The Merchant* ends with Jessica and Lorenzo's prepared welcome for Portia, Bassanio, Nerissa, and Gratiano—sinner and sinned against. The festive setting complete with music may seem an appropriate one for the mutual reconciliation represented by the restoration of both couples' wedding rings. A delayed marriage celebration, in effect, the concluding scene may even suggest the heavenly marriage feast to which Christians aspire. Joan Holmer finds the comedic spirit prevailing here as it did in Venice, with Antonio twice blest—having given and received "half of his original wealth"—and responding to Portia's announcement of the return of half his ships by "I am dumb!" (5.1.279).[1] This bewilderment she interprets as "joyful silence replac[ing] the melancholic stillness" of the opening scene (269). But this play's ending, unlike most of Shakespeare's comedies, leaves a bittersweet aftertaste. As Robert Zaslavsky observes in "Which is the merchant heere / and which the Jew?" the reunion at Belmont "neither integrates the offending element nor embodies the health of the secular authority of the Duke" and consequently "cannot be regarded as the full reconciliation which comedy classically requires to achieve its closure" (4). In fact, the alimentary images embedded within *The Merchant of Venice's* Elizabethan religious context are emblematic of its characters' desires and provide clues to this tragicomedy's meaning.

To those familiar with the Bible, as were many Elizabethans in Shakespeare's audiences, Belmont—beautiful mountain—may itself figure heaven and recall several passages in the Book of Isaiah which invite the just to a heavenly banquet. "On this mountain the Lord of hosts will make for all peoples a feast of rich food, a feast of well-aged wines, of rich food filled to the marrow, of well-aged wines strained clear" (Isaiah 25: 6). This passage, like that of the epigraph, illuminates the play's numerous references to food, hunger (desire), and sharing in feasts—or being excluded from them. Analyzing such alimentary references in relation to each character reveals Shakespeare's compassionate view of humanity and may explain Shylock's and Antonio's positions at the play's conclusion.

Appetite, as James W. Brown observes in *Fictional Meals and Their Function in the French Novel*, "signals a real or symbolic emptiness" and "confirms the nothingness separating subjective and objective being . . . [figuring] the conversion of an absence into a presence or, at least . . . the reduction of the space between the desiring subject and the object of his desire" (12). Freud's linking of orality and sexuality takes the act of eating a step further, positing it as an archetype of both social and sexual intercourse. For the Christian there is a further level of meaning. The rite or sacrament of communion, enacted within the parameters of the believing community, takes the symbolic value of eating to the mystical or spiritual level where signifier and signified are consubstantial. The Eucharistic bread, always shared within a community of believers, points to the root meaning of the "bread" itself. *Panis* in Latin, bread also suggests "companion." Appetite/desire, then, by signifying distance, absence, or emptiness, engenders social consciousness, as eating and ingesting suggest proximity/presence/social rapprochement. Eating, like language a communicative act, allows humankind to "appropriate and incorporate the world" (Brown 13). In literature, then, "of all the signs associated with the culinary . . . food serves as one of the prevalent markers of character," and eating coincides with "the more advanced psychological activities—spirituality, metaphysical quest, communion with the divine—which border on transcendence," taking on an aesthetic form when a writer uses food imagery to poeticize a message (Brown 15).

Given this background, one wonders at the *Merchant*'s opening revelation of a melancholy ("weary") Antonio and asks: for what is he hungering? Not material prosperity—he has that—but, having risked his fortune in various seaborne ventures, Antonio becomes aware of something deeper stirring within. "What stuff 'tis made of, whereof it is born" he/we gradually learn through the ensuing action of the drama. This hunger stems not from the potential loss of Bassanio's friendship through marriage, as many critics suggest.[2] Rather, Antonio's undefined yearning may betoken a type of mid-life crisis so vague that he can neither recognize nor resolve it. Perhaps he subconsciously hungers for love, whether platonic, sexual, or spiritual.

In the second scene Portia, though surrounded by plenty, is similarly melancholic, her "little body . . . aweary of this great world" (1.2.1–2). Here the cause is clear: she is in love with someone who may never be hers. Out of sorts, speaking flippantly and sarcastically of her various suitors, she complains understandably of her father's circumscribing will. Yet, deep down she is committed to fulfilling its demands and appears open to Nerissa's counsel: "Your father was ever virtuous, and holy men at their death have good inspirations" (27). The father figure introduced early in the play will reappear in old Gobbo, in Shylock, in the prodigal father of the gospel, and in the Duke. Each one nuances the playwright-creator as well as the Creator-God. For now, Nerissa's perceptive comment on Portia's weariness, "They are as sick that *surfeit* with too much as they that *starve* with nothing" (5–6, italics mine) sets the tone for the play's subtext—the emptiness of creaturely possessions—and its implied question: what, if anything, can satisfy our deepest hunger? When Portia wins her desired Bassanio, it is because he bypasses the "gaudy gold, / Hard *food* for Midas" (3.2.101–102, italics mine) and chooses the lead casket. As though guided by Nerissa's lead (pun intended), Portia manipulates his choice, revealing the intensity of her desire for him in her song's subtly hinting rhymes: "Tell me, where is fancy *bred*, / Or in the heart or in the *head*? / How begot, how *nourished*? Reply, reply" (3.2.63–65, italics mine).

However, Bassanio's desire for Portia is coupled with his desire for the money he deems necessary to woo her. A double hunger, it is fed, ironically, by Antonio's readiness to part with his very life, if required and, with greater irony, echoes in Shylock's alternately lamenting his double loss of ducats and daughter. The contrast of these double hungers, if viewed only as Shylock's, with Antonio's love-inspired pledging of a pound of flesh to Shylock's knife might conjure up medieval stereotypes of the Jew as Christian-killer, thereby introducing an anti-Semitic note. However, the double hunger is also Bassanio's, and some desire on Antonio's part motivates his pledge. The pelican image so prevalent in medieval liturgical art comes to mind. A creature that sheds its own blood to *nurture* its brood, the pelican fittingly symbolizes Christ's sacrificial love and nourishes the faith of believers (see Figure 8 below). While it may obliquely raise the image of the Jew as Christ-killer, it more accurately suggests Antonio's generous, Christ-like love. (Considering the pelican image from another angle, that of allegory, one may find Sir Israel Gollancz's insights of value. Commenting on Shakespeare's use of Biblical names, Gollancz equates Schiloch with Shallach, "the Biblical Hebrew for cormorant," pointing out that in Elizabethan English "cormorant was an expressive synonym for usurer" [41]. In this context, the antithesis between Antonio and Shylock becomes more pronounced.) Nevertheless, Antonio's generosity may also be construed as an "attempt to buy Bassanio's love," given the language of commerce and exchange that characterizes Bassanio's courtship of Portia (Maus 1086). In this latter sense, Antonio's self-serving gesture may constitute a major component of the vague melancholy coloring his general mood and highlight again the futility of relying on wealth for happiness.

Even Portia's willingness to pay Antonio's "petty debt twenty times over" (3.2.307) lest Bassanio lie by her side "with an unquiet soul" heightens the reality that money, whether possessed or sought, rather than bringing peace, causes doubt and worry—a message reinforced by the Jessica-Lorenzo subplot. As their thieving casts a shadow over the masked, eloping pair, so the combined losses of daughter, ducats, and Leah's turquoise ring alarm and outrage Shylock. His prior preoccupation with material goods led him to disparage Launcelot for, among other things, being "a huge *feeder*" (italics mine) whose running away generated a certain vengeful delight—the runaway servant would now waste Bassanio's borrowed purse, becoming Shylock's "gain" and Bassanio's "loss." So too, Shylock's last words to Jessica, "Fast bind, fast find— / A proverb never *stale* in thrifty mind" (2.5.56, italics mine) are ironic in light of her own imminent departure, and emphasize Shylock's absorption with acquiring and hoarding possessions vis-à-vis Antonio's liberal prodigality, as Shylock would have it. In his view, Antonio is "a bankrupt, a prodigal" (3.1.41–42), especially when his richly laden ships become "carcasses" buried in the Goodwin Sands. Is this name a Shakespearean pun? Does the good wind implied in the punned site represent a further commentary on the paradoxical good to be gained from the loss of wealth?

As ruminating on Antonio's largesse in lending money *gratis* arouses in Shylock both hatred and hunger for revenge, the alimentary imagery of his discourse escalates, indicating perhaps a corresponding inner, spiritual emptiness: "I will *feed* fat the grudge I bear him" (1.3.44, italics mine).

This metaphor, inversely repeated in 3.1.50 where Shylock evaluates Antonio's flesh as good only "to bait fish withal . . . it will feed nothing else [but his] revenge," comments obliquely on Antonio as Christ-figure and indicts Shylock as the antithesis. In his unwitting frenzy, Shylock sounds the ominous note that will echo in the trial scene where mounting desire for Antonio's flesh will ironically feed Shylock's revenge, even as Shylock *"crave[s]* the law" (4.1.204 italics mine). Alimentary images also inform Shylock's opinion that Antonio has "squandered" his fortune—a word suggestive of the Scriptural prodigal son who "squandered" his share of his father's fortune. Fallen into desperate poverty, that starving son began to *crave* the very pods his father's pigs were fed—a desire born of the hunger that motivated his homeward journey to paternal forgiveness and restoration to familial communion. When the prodigal Jessica steals Shylock's fortune and wastes her mother's turquoise on a monkey, his response is far different from that of the welcoming, forgiving father of the gospel parable.[3] Though such casting of Shylock in a harsh and negative light may color Shakespeare as anti-Semitic, it moves an objective reader/spectator to question the kind of Christianity represented by Lorenzo and his soon-to-be converted wife, whose mutual theft of her father's possessions violates both Jewish and Christian law. Again, Shakespeare's alimentary images, combined with those of the parable, keep before the reader/spectator's mind the familiar paradox: wealth alone does not suffice and may be the cause of great unhappiness.

Invited to dine with Bassanio and his friends, Shylock had refused initially because he would have to "smell pork" and eat swine. His firm rejection of an opportunity for connection, if not communion, with Christians—"I will not eat with you, drink with you, nor pray with you" (1.3.34)—appears to soften later. Though aware that he is "not bid for love," he will go "in hate to *feed* upon the prodigal Christian" (2.5.16–17, italics mine). His revenge-induced appetite will sate itself at the Christian host's expense despite the "ill-a-brewing toward [his] rest"(19). Had he fasted from revenge, the ensuing elopement/theft might have been averted or at least postponed. As it is, the consequences for Shylock are both foreshadowed and satirized in Gratiano's ironic comments as he awaits Lorenzo's masked arrival at the same feast: "Who riseth from a feast / With that keen appetite that he sits down?" (2.6.9–10) and "All things that are, / Are with more spirit chased than enjoyed" (13–14). These lines, echoed shortly in Gratiano's ironic simile, allude once again to Luke's parable of the prodigal, and acquire here a certain poignancy in connection with Jessica:

> How like a younker or a prodigal
> The scarfed bark puts from her native bay,
> Hugged and embraced by the strumpet wind!

How like the prodigal doth she return,

. . . .

Lean, rent, and beggared by the strumpet wind!" (2.6.16–20)

What little appetite Shylock had for dining with Christians is completely lost when he discovers her elopement and realizes that his dream of money-bags was, indeed, prescient. Interpreted another way, Shylock's "gluttonous" feeding of his revengeful spirit by the deliberate wasting, however slight, of his Christian host's substance provokes a metaphoric vomiting as his own house is evacuated of both ducats and daughter. Nevertheless, the inner emptiness driving Shylock's preoccupation with money and revenge, combined with his ill treatment by Antonio (spitting upon him, calling him "dog" and "devil," laughing at his losses), color his character for the reader, enlisting sympathy while arousing, simultaneously, a growing distancing from Antonio.

In quite a different reading, Kim F. Hall, in "Guess Who's Coming to Dinner? Colonisation and Miscegenation in *The Merchant of Venice*," views the "language of eating" in this play within the context of cannibalism, a concept both fascinating and terrifying to Elizabethans, and regarded as "one of the final lines drawn between the savage Other and the civilized self" (98). Hall sees "fears of erasure . . . embedded within metaphors of eating," and Shylock as "merging images of cannibalism with older accusations of blood libel" (99). In Hall's view, Shylock's "reluctance to eat with Christians displays the fear of 'be[ing] subsumed . . . by a hostile host,' but in terms that ratify the reciprocal Christian fear of being consumed by a guest/alien . . . allowed into the home/country" (99).

Shylock, as noted above, is not alone in desiring material wealth. In fact, his desire for money magnifies the desires of Bassanio, who, though seemingly humble in choosing the lead casket, has from the play's outset been intent on winning a "lady richly left . . . nothing *undervalued* to Cato's daughter . . ." whose "*sunny* locks" remind him of a "*golden* fleece" (1.1.161–70, italics mine). Indeed, Portia's father's words may constitute a necessary corrective to Bassanio's mishandling of wealth prior to the play's beginning,[4] as Bassanio himself implies in approaching Antonio for the loan. The scroll left in the leaden casket by Portia's father warns appropriately, if obliquely, of Bassanio's potential for wasting her inheritance: "Since this fortune [Portia] falls to you / Be content and seek no new" (3.2.133–34). Even Morocco's and Aragon's choices reflect a hunger for wealth and honor not unlike Shylock's and Bassanio's.[5] These several characters, desiring material wealth while suffering its concomitant malaise, temporarily diminish the reader/spectator's sense of Shylock's preoccupation with money by indicating that almost everyone in the play needs to reorder his/her valuing of wealth and recognize its impotence to satisfy the deeper hungers of the human heart. Aragon came close to such a realization, eschewing the golden casket as too obvious a symbol of the barbarous multitude who "choose by show" (2.9.26). However, in selecting the silver casket, he "pries not to th' interior" (2.9.28) but aligns himself with those taught by the "fond eye" to build like a martlet on the "outward wall, / Even in the force and road of casualty" (2.9.29).

Though Shylock's desire for money is shared by many other characters, in the trial scene his appetite for revenge surmounts his love of wealth and momentarily seems to distinguish him. Twice refusing Portia's monetary offers, he unwittingly lays himself open to the "unkindest cut": Portia's revelation of unexpected consequences contained in her interpretation of Venetian law. While Antonio's breast is spared, the vilification, contempt, and insult heaped on Shylock by the Christians attending the trial confront the reader/spectator, revealing a hatred, if not greater than, at least equivalent to Shylock's for Antonio. Are these so-called Christians, one wonders, motivated by revenge as well? Are Portia's remarks on the quality of mercy intended only for Shylock? The Duke's question to Shylock, "How shalt thou hope for mercy, rendering none?" is articulated by one who represents justice, but it recalls a fundamental truth taught by Christ in the context of a lesson on prayer. The "Lord's Prayer" petition "Give us this day our daily bread" is prelude to "and forgive us our trespasses as we forgive those who trespass against us"—a powerful reminder of the necessary relationship between receiving mercy and bestowing mercy on others, in turn.[6] The bread's symbolic allusiveness also serves both to recall the manna provided by God to the Israelites in the desert—a symbol of trust in the Providence of God to satisfy basic human needs—and to typify the Christian Eucharist, symbol of unity and forgiveness. Interpreted by theologians as representing "all that we need for daily living," not luxury or excess, "bread" conflates the prodigal son's hunger with a warning: obsession with wealth or avaricious hoarding signals spiritual emptiness.

In the final scene at Belmont, three couples appear to be happy at last. But are they? Or if they are, for how long will they be so? Ominous allusions lace the seemingly beautiful Jessica/Lorenzo dialogue, each one hinting at infidelity or betrayal (5.1.54ff.). Antonio's solitary presence and Shylock's absence are inconsistent with the expected comic ending. What else is missing? Perhaps Lorenzo's referring to his and Jessica's "inheritance," awarded at Shylock's expense through the combination of Portia's legal expertise and Antonio's generosity, as "manna" dropped "in the way of starved people" (294) contains a clue. The reference may figure for the reader/spectator not only the hunger of Moses and the Israelites in the wilderness, but also Isaiah's heavenly banquet table from which the necessary sustenance has fallen. Can the nourishing God be implicated in the redirecting of Shylock's wealth? If so, is Shylock's loss paradoxically a gain, in the gospel sense?

Such a reading points beyond both the entangled commercial ventures of urban Venice and the apparent bucolic peace of Belmont to the place described by the prophet Isaiah as "the heritage of the servants of the Lord," where everyone who thirsts is invited to come to the waters, even those without money. The Isaiah passage quoted in the epigraph warrants inclusion here in its entirety:

> Why do you spend your money for that which is not bread
> and your labor for that which does not satisfy?
> . . . eat what is good, and delight yourselves in rich food . . .
> You shall call nations that you do not know,
> and nations that you do not know shall run to you,
> Because of the Lord your God, the Holy One of Israel,
> for He has glorified you.
> Let the wicked forsake their way and the unrighteous their
> thoughts . . . and our God will abundantly pardon.
> For my thoughts are not your thoughts,
> nor are your ways my ways, says the Lord. (Isaiah 55: 1–5)

All are invited to buy and eat . . . wine and milk without money and without price—a notion repulsive to Shylock and perhaps to Antonio, the merchant, as well. Though Jessica and Lorenzo may not understand the full burden of the manna image, it signifies for the reader/spectator the deeper, spiritual values that most of the characters in this play seem to have missed, with the possible exception of Portia. She, at least, attempts to teach Shylock about the fullness of God's mercy which not only "blesseth him that gives and him that takes," (4.1.185) but also, when it *seasons* justice, renders earthly power most like God's. Perhaps the strongest argument for the play's not being anti-Semitic lies in Portia's lesson: Shylock and all Christians present are reminded that "although justice be [his] plea . . . in the course of justice none of us / Should see salvation"—a fact impelling all to "pray for mercy" and realize that "that same prayer doth teach *us all* to render / The deeds of mercy" (4.1.196–200, italics mine).

The combination of frequent references to food and meals—Shylock's to dining with Christians, Bassanio's "We'll feast tonight," Lorenzo's "First let us go to dinner" (3.5.83)—as well as the allusions to the parable of the prodigal with its "prodigal" father's concluding banquet in celebration of his son's return, have kept the tropes of mercy, dining, and communion before the reader's imagination. Intertextually read with the bread of the "Our Father," the manna in the desert, and the heavenly table of Isaiah, the play's father-son (Gobbo-Launcelot) and father-daughter relationships (Portia and her father; Jessica and Shylock) figure the Father/Creator/God's relationships with his human creatures and endow *The Merchant of Venice* with a dimension of truth, or a "quality of mercy," which transcends individual differences and human failings. Antonio's melancholy remains at the end, lessened though still unexplained, and not wholly removed. He doesn't partake of the usual happy ending, nor does Shylock. Both are left on the fringe of the banquet, the "community." Worse, for John Gross, Shylock is "consigned to oblivion. . . . He no longer exists" (101). But for this reader, their very marginalization raises questions which suggest connection. Might they, if one were to write *Merchant of Venice II*, be given reflective speeches in which, like Prospero abjuring his magic, each admits to having learned that the antidote to melancholy or a vengeful spirit lies in abjuring the power money formerly had for them? Might they take on new roles—perhaps as transformed grandfather-figures to Bassanio's and Jessica's children?

However, such thinking may be too romantic a dream-wish. Certainly, James Shapiro's *Shakespeare and the Jews* reminds us all too graphically and painfully that our experience of living in our world with our histories and our various cultures is far from achieving Isaiah's vision. His detailing of European, specifically English, attitudes to Jews in the years preceding and following Shakespeare's writing of *Merchant* bursts all romantic bubbles. The interplay of myth, economic concerns, and unenlightened behavior on the part of both Christian and Jew challenges our beliefs about race, nation, sex, and religion. In Shapiro's words:

> To avert our gaze from what the play reveals about the relationship between cultural myths and peoples' identities will not make irrational and exclusionary attitudes disappear. Indeed, these darker impulses remain so elusive, so hard to identify in the normal course of things, that only in instances like productions of this play do we get to glimpse these cultural faultlines. . . .
>
> One thing remains certain: as long as anxieties about racial, national, sexual, and religious differences continue to haunt the way we imagine ourselves and respond to others, Shakespeare's words will remain 'not of an age, but for all time.' (228–29)

So, too, the words of the Scriptures, offering nourishment to both Jew and non-Jew, will, if assimilated, suggest more satisfying ways of interacting on our life journeys and extend a more realistic hope of universal human communion. "Such harmony is in immortal souls; / But whilst this muddy vesture of decay / Doth grossly close it in, we cannot hear it" explains Lorenzo to Jessica, referring to the music of the spheres (5.1.62–64). As Israel Gollancz glossed it, this passage expresses Shakespeare's rounding off the play with harmony and the hope that, divested of "hatred, indignity, narrowness, strife"—humanity may indeed experience "Righteousness . . . meet[ing] Truth from heaven; Mercy and Truth . . . meet[ing] together; Righteousness and Peace . . . kiss[ing]" (68). This, the real music of the play, foreshadowing the real heavenly banquet, is Shakespeare's vision, or as Gollancz would have it, "the burden of Shakespeare's spirit, of Shakespeare the thinker, the myriad-minded, the humane, the wise, the man of understanding, who looked forward hopefully to the allaying of jarring notes that grate on the human soul" (43). Or, more in keeping with the alimentary images noted in this essay, this harmonious music reflects the hopeful vision of humanity sharing the pleasures of good food and drink in harmony and communion at Isaiah's prophetic banquet. Would that this play, in providing a framework for reflecting on issues such as greed's power to engender divisiveness, might, as Zaslavsky suggests, like the inscriptions of Portia's caskets, guide the reader/spectator to proper choices, informed, I would add, by the "mercy-seasoned" justice creative of peace, harmony, and union.

Notes

1. All quotations from Shakespeare come from the *The Merchant of Venice*, ed. David Bevington.

2. See, for example, Lawrence Danson's essay on "Love and Friendship" in *The Merchant of Venice* in his study, *The Harmonies of "The Merchant of Venice,"* pp. 34–35. Danson notes the widespread attribution on the part of critics—notably E. M. Tillyard and Graham Midgely—of Antonio's melancholy to his homosexuality. Danson himself concurs with my view that there is not enough evidence in the play to support such an interpretation. Robert Zaslavsky, on the other hand, reads this play as "focused on the homoerotic (clearly latently homosexual) Christian Antonio, who coldly uses Shylock to defend his relationship with Bassanio against the intrusion of Portia," the cause of his melancholy (2).

3. See *Luke* 15: 11–24. Unlike the forgiving "prodigal" father of the parable, Shylock would have his daughter "dead at my foot and the jewels in her ear! . . . hearsed at my foot and the ducats in her coffin!" (3.1.75–76)

4. Cf. 1.1.122–25: " 'Tis not unknown to you, Antonio, / How much I have disabled mine estate / By something showing a more swelling port / Than my faint means would grant continuance." Katherine Maus's comments on the inevitability of Christians' intermingling of spiritual and economic values are apt. Maus notes that marriage is a "hybrid social relation" which, though associated with love, is "simultaneously a property relation, involving the economic alliance of individuals and families." Ironically, in Maus's view the person "most fitted to be Portia's husband is one who, by Christian standards, knows the limitations and the right use of wealth. This knowledge enables him to value characteristics in his wife—virtue, intelligence, and beauty—that make her precious in more than monetary ways" (1086). In my reading, Portia's wealth appears to be the dominant element in Bassanio's desiring her. See also Frank Whigam's "Ideology and Class Conduct in *The Merchant of Venice*," in *Renaissance Drama as Cultural History*, which addresses Bassanio's unconcern with the apparent tension between "the artful form of his meditation and its moral content" (495), as he contemplates his choice of cas-

    ket. Whigam's treatment of the play's "major themes of sharing and exclusion" (488) points to Bassanio's calculated picking of Portia's locks with the "keys of courtesy" (508) to secure his status within the aristocracy.

5. Norman Rabkin in *Shakespeare and the Problem of Meaning* concurs but also observes: For many critics "the opposition in the play is . . . symbolized by the inscriptions on the caskets: Morocco trusts appearances and puts his faith in gold as Shylock does; Aragon demands what he deserves, insisting like Shylock on rational justice; both are beaten by Bassanio, who gives and hazards all . . . What these critics describe is there and arises from unmistakably personal experiences of the play . . . Yet . . . their writing conveys a sense of uneasy tentativeness . . . [because] they recognize that they have not in fact explained the very things that provoked them to the elucidation of meaning in the first place" (pp. 10–12).

6. Maus notes that "Portia's plea for tolerance and compassion might seem to rest on universal premises, but in fact it neatly excludes the Jew" from her inclusive "we" in "We do pray for mercy. . . ." Her position would strengthen my point that in a real sense the Christians are ironically the ones on trial.

    Furthermore, as Zaslavsky notes, "the treatment of Shylock is so far from the Christian Scriptural exhortation to love even one's enemies that it constitutes an indictment of the hypocrisy of Christian society" (4). He adds that the presentation of Shylock as apparently friendly to Christians and apparently craven in acquiescing to the demand for conversion "constitutes an indictment of Jews whose practice so belies their principles that conversion seems only right and proper."

Works Cited

Brown, James W. *Fictional Meals and Their Function in the French Novel.* Toronto: University of Toronto Press, 1984.

Danson, Lawrence. *The Harmonies of "The Merchant of Venice."* New Haven: Yale University Press, 1978.

Gollancz, Israel. *Allegory and Mysticism in Shakespeare.* Ed. Andrew W. Pollard. London: The Sign of the Dolphin, 1931.

Greenblatt, Stephen, Walter Cohen, Jean E. Howard, and Katherine Eisaman Maus, eds. *The Norton Shakespeare.* New York: W.W. Norton & Co., 1997.

Gross, John. *Shylock: A Legend and Its Legacy.* New York: Simon and Schuster, 1994.

Hall, Kim F. "Guess Who's Coming to Dinner? Colonisation and Miscegenation in *The Merchant of Venice*." *New Casebooks: "The Merchant of Venice."* Ed. Martin Coyle. New York: St. Martin's Press, 1998.

Holmer, Joan Ozark. *"The Merchant of Venice": Choice, Hazard and Consequence.* New York: St. Martin's Press, 1995.

Metzger, Bruce and Roland Murphy, eds. *The New Oxford Annotated Bible.* New York: Oxford University Press, 1991.

Rabkin, Norman. *Shakespeare and the Problem of Meaning.* Chicago: University of Chicago Press, 1981.

Shakespeare, William. *The Merchant of Venice.* Ed. David Bevington. New York: Bantam Books, 1988.

Shapiro, James. *Shakespeare and the Jews.* New York: Columbia University Press, 1996.

Whigham, Frank. "Ideology and Class Conduct in *The Merchant of Venice.*" *Renaissance Drama as Cultural History.* Ed. Mary Beth Rose. Evanston: Northwestern University Press, 1990. 487–509.

Zaslavsky, Robert. "Which is the merchant heere? And which the Jew?: keeping the book and keeping the books in *The Merchant of Venice.*" *Judaism* 44 (Spring 1995): 181–92. *Humanities Full Text.* http://webspirs3.silverplatter.com/cgi-bin/waldo.cgi

The Less into the Greater

Emblem, Analogue, and Deification in *The Merchant of Venice*

JOHN CUNNINGHAM AND STEPHEN SLIMP

> A day in April never came so sweet
> To show how costly[1] summer was at hand.
> (2.9.93–94)

I. Emblem, Analogy, Typology

The Christian analogic and emblematic mode of perception that character-ized Renaissance thought passed, as we know, during the seventeenth century imperceptibly away, leaving Dryden and Dr. Johnson not understanding what to make of Metaphysical Poetry; likewise, by the eighteenth century Shake-speare's plays had begun to present "problems."[2] Austin Warren's brilliant paragraph distilling his researches into the emblematic conceit allows a twentieth-century student to understand as Dryden and Dr. Johnson could not.[3] Something of this same recovery helps one toward humility as one judges Shakespeare's plays. The way of "realism" by which the late twenti-eth century habitually looks at experience is probably not an adequate mode for discerning the being of any of the plays, and *The Merchant of Venice* in particular harries some audiences and critics.

Analogy and emblem[4] belong to the larger category of allegory but are very unlike Bunyan's allegory or the Moral in one of Shakespeare's sources for the play, tale XV of *Gesta Romanorum*, in which the princess is the soul and the emperor's son is Christ. Rather, emblem presents the surface of expe-rience in a manner that urges one through the surface to discern eternal pat-terns shadowed forth in the "realistic" detail.[5] One may not draw an equal sign between the "realistic" detail (A) and the patterns (B) darkly present in it (A = B); the most one may draw is a congruent sign (A $\cong$ B). In trans-forming the material from his source, Shakespeare gives it the indirect man-ner of emblem or analogue. George Wither's emblem of a pelican (1635)

Figure 8. The Pelican, in George Wither, *A Collection of Emblemes* (1635). By Permission of the British Library (C.70.h.5).

shows in the foreground a "realistic" mother pelican in the wilderness opening her breast with her beak to feed her starving young with her blood; in the
background, dimly, one sees the crucifixion with people holding up chalices
to catch Christ's blood (Figure 8). A proper emblem, then, abides both in the
realm of "realistic" detail and also in the realm of the supernal reality that the
detail adumbrates; "symbolism felicitously combines with realism" (Jenkins
545). The "universal system of harmonious correspondences" that Lorenzo
invokes in act 5 as he praises music makes emblem possible and justifies it;
because of these correspondences, objects in one realm point to those in
another realm; and the visible can give insight into the invisible.[6]

The details in an emblem, as in the pelican and her progeny, receive
much clearer and bolder drawing than the shadowy background crucifixion;
therefore, emblem allows for many kinds of reading: psychoanalytic, historicist, feminist. These readings may be illuminating, internally consistent, and
faithful to the work as far as they go. They may be fully adequate, however,
only if they allow themselves to be drawn into the figurative dimension of the
analogue; otherwise, by themselves, they will achieve but incompleteness
and thereby distort.[7]

"Realistic" criticism that lifts characters and their actions out of the
matrix of metaphor in which they exist and which guides one's understanding of them will be no more than the personal speculation of the critic—a
curious procedure for empiricists to follow.[8] Likewise, this kind of criticism
gives almost no attention to the metaphoric structures of the comedy that
carry most of the meanings of the play.[9] Nabokov surely puts it best: "the
verbal poetical texture of Shakespeare is . . . immensely superior to the structure of his plays as plays. With Shakespeare it is the metaphor that is the
thing, not the play" (89–90). One would not think of approaching medieval
religious drama, to which Shakespeare was profoundly indebted (John Cox
324), without attending to its figurative implications.[10] O. B. Hardison
demonstrates that a "sacramental psychology" directs the behavior of the
characters in those plays (289). Yet, while everyone acknowledges the proximity of Renaissance plays to the older drama and their debt to it,[11] few
recent Shakespearean critics look beyond character and action. The radical
change in epistemologies[12] that occurred almost unnoticed in the seventeenth
century does not invalidate the older ways of knowing; it merely makes them
unfashionable.[13] Fashion, Pope told us before he was twenty-one, is one of
the causes of bad criticism. And faction, he said, is another. The allegory of
Shakespeare and Dante is "far more realistic" than "the [kind] we
are . . . familiar with" (Fergusson, *Trope* 5). Its "realism" gives a concrete
particularity to the archetypes behind it (Roth 146–47).

A pervasive archetype of medieval and Renaissance comedy is transformation, and *The Merchant of Venice* dramatizes metamorphosis. Shylock, the
character most in need of such redemption, is figurative of the Old Man, the

Senex,[14] the Geron (Shylock's name in one of Shakespeare's sources);[15] he is the Pauline Old Man full of "wrath, fierceness, maliciousness"—actually potential in Everyman—that must be "put . . . off" (Col. 3:8–9, BB).[16] Our reading does not reduce Shylock to an abstraction; he is as "real" as any character may be. His state as senex does, however, make Shylock an alien in Shakespearean comedy until he accepts the bond of mercy in act 4. The Old Man is the mere natural man, descending from the fallen first, or "old," Adam, who was not a Jew. Christian theology teaches that the condition is put off in baptism. "Race . . . [is] not . . . significant" in this play, Leo Kirschbaum argues well; rather, Shylock is a "symbol" of "hatred and inhumanity" (18, 26).[17] Jessica, though born a Jew, is never seriously treated as such.

Biblical typology gives this "old" nature the name, "Jew." This typology can look at one thing and faintly see another; Old Testament types shadow forth New Testament matters, the fulfillment of the type (or antitype).[18] Thus are Noah, Jonah, David, and many another prefigurement of Christ.[19] By "Jew," however, typology and theology speak not of the race of Jews or of any individual Jew. In the best piece on this play, Lawrence Danson directs attention to the malice in Antonio which "convicts him of being . . . himself spiritually a 'Jew' " (32).[20] Shakespeare uses the typology that he inherited. The Good Friday Reproaches in the liturgy address the congregation of Christians in their crucifying sins as Jews.[21] Those made sacramentally New Men by baptism, having been given "that thing which by nature they cannot have," are also "Jews" of the "new Israel," "thy people Israel" that St. Simeon names them (Luke 2:32 BB). That the inheritance promised to Abraham and descending from him passed from the Old Israel to the New Israel, the Church, is commonplace Christian typology.[22] Discussion of the Old Man and the New necessarily suggests the Old Law and the New; but the interest of this essay is not in the law but in the metamorphosis of one who is merely natural—the less—into one who begins to participate also in the divine nature—the greater. This alchemy usually proceeds slowly, but its result is radical. With the preoccupations of the present generation, the play's use of *Jew* probably can but offend; nevertheless, the "Old Man" must be named *Jew* to call up the typology. Yet the typology need not be anti-Semitic—the bigotry is in Antonio and a few of his associates (Nevo 128), not in the play[23]—to anyone willing to submit oneself to a bit of historical imagination and to abandon, just for the nonce, one's disbelief in an analogic perception of experience.

Emblematic perception resembles biblical typology because each is able to look at one thing and darkly to see another.[24] This essay reads the play with the help of Christian type and emblem;[25] the play is "not a mystery play nor a morality play nor even . . . consistently an allegory. But it has a significance that can be generalized beyond the immediate story. . . . The parabolic intention . . . is a product of Shakespeare's conscious art" (Danson 69).[26] The action is analogical of deification, of the process of bringing humanity into divinity. Transformation from death to life, from what typology names the "Old Man" to the "New Man," even, as the earliest Fathers posit, to theosis or deification,[27] is at least one rhythm of the play. The Eastern Worthies never tire of writing, "God became man that man might become divine"; the Western version occurs in the Athanasian Creed when it speaks of the Incarnation occurring "not by conversion of the Godhead into flesh: but by taking of the manhood into God."[28] Dante used the term "in-godded" to describe the process. Pope's epigram in *An Essay on Criticism* declares the possibility of participating in divinity: "to err is human, to forgive divine"; in *The Merchant of Venice* Portia affirms something of the same, "mercy . . . / Is an attribute to God himself" (4.1.189–91). John Middleton Murray recognizes that mercy is "the spontaneous imitation in the human soul of the love of God" (3); but "imitation" is not participation. Even Danson confuses imitating with participating (57). To forgive is to engage in divinity,[29] to be made "partakers of the divine nature" (2 Pet. 1:4 D–R).[30]

Such a radical metamorphosis is like that effected by the structure of comedy where some of the characters suffer a transformation before the comedy concludes: Duke Frederick and Oliver; Benedick and Beatrice; Claudio and Hero; Leontes; Angelo; Alonso, the King of Naples. It is one of the contours of *The Merchant of Venice*. Some characters, however, choose the nothing of illusion. Don John refuses comic redemption, Malvolio exits in a dudgeon, the condition of Sebastian and Antonio at the end of *The Tempest* is ambiguous. Theosis begins on this side of the grave with baptism. The divine waters of mercy, like rain from heaven, nourish the baptismal grafting and allow increasing participation in the divine nature. Those so fed already live, in part, in the age-to-come, in the eon breaking through in the New Testament miracles and resurrection. Belmont at the end is, among other things, analogic of those whose lives already participate in eternity. Patricia Parker recognizes that Shakespeare's comedies conclude with an "anagogic" state of waiting, occurring between two conditions. One condition is of new marriages (the "one flesh" "signifying . . . the mystical union . . . betwixt Christ and his Church" [Gen. 2:24 BB, Eph. 5:23–32 BB; Booty 290, 297]) figurative of the accomplished Incarnation, of a time when the unions that are achieved remain, nevertheless, still incomplete. The second condition, figured in the circle of eternity of the golden ring, suggests the Apocalypse upon which the complete consummation of union must wait.[31] Theosis is never completed here; only beyond the grave must this mortal "put on" immortality and this corruptible "put on" incorruption (1 Cor. 15:53 BB). Even Shakespeare's metamorphosed characters all have imperfections; even in Belmont they wear the "muddy vesture of decay."[32] Therefore critics need not be unduly troubled by the play's ironies that only reveal Shakespeare's awareness of the frailty and inconsistency of all mortals, even of Christians.

II. Launcelot's *Psychomachia*

With the introduction of the Clown, Shakespeare practices analogue;[33] he gathers the actions, rhythms, themes, and metaphors of the play, inverting them, paralleling them, parodying them, using them straightforwardly. Act 2, scene 2, Launcelot's wonderfully funny *psychomachia*, is a mock epitome of the play.[34] The incidents in this scene develop the plot "very slightly, but they clarify its themes in the medieval analogical manner which Shakespeare had made his own" (Brown, "Mr. Pinter's" 261).

One theme of *Merchant* parodied in 2.2 is the necessity and peril of choice. The battle for Launcelot's soul—the fifteenth-century paradigm is *The Castle of Perseverance*, or more to the point, *Doctor Faustus* and the Henry IV plays or Sonnet 144[35]—would be straightforward: but conscience (following 1 Pet. 2:18) counsels the Clown to remain with his master, Shylock, who is "a kind of devil" (21–22), "the very devil incarnation" (26);[36] a devil, however, advises the Clown, against Scripture, to flee from his master, saying, "For the heavens rouse up a brave mind . . . and run" (2.2.11–12). The devil is right, and St. Peter and conscience are wrong. Launcelot's irruption follows the scene in which Portia warns Morocco of the gravity of choosing a casket. The last words of 2.1 hang over this scene: Morocco's "To make me blest or cursèd'st among men!" (46).

The injunction in St. Matthew's Gospel that one cannot serve two masters is incumbent upon all; no one is allowed not to choose. Some form of the word *choose* occurs forty-four times in this play.[37] Moses charged the Israelites (the "old Jewry"), "I call heaven and earth to record this day against you, that I have set before you, life and death, blessing and cursing: therefore choose life, that both thou and thy seed may live."[38] The Moral of the fifteenth tale in *Gesta Romanorum* cites this same passage. 2.2 gives the Clown names alluding to two other men who underwent a contest for their souls, one with a happy issue out of his affliction and one otherwise. The first is Job. In the early speech headings, Q_1 (1600) and F_1 for Gobbo read *Iobbe*;[39] the compositor of F_3 makes clear that the intention is *Job*. Surely the last scene of the play has its own oblique allusion to Job's restorations. The second significant name is King Arthur's Lancelot, who was tempted, too, but fell; and Camelot unravelled.

All in *The Merchant of Venice* must undergo some kind of *pyschomachia:* the sad Antonio in lending money that he does not have, and later and much worse in suffering the trial scene; Portia in electing to obey her father's will; Jessica, perhaps the bravest of all, in leaving her father and her race for an untried suitor;[40] Nerissa in choosing Gratiano; Morocco, Arragon, and Bassanio in their casket scenes revealing who they are; and Bassanio tried again when the lawyer asks the ring of him, as is Gratiano. Even the Duke must resist the temptation to bend the law. Shylock and his law at the trial scene are tested and both found wanting. Or is he? One knows not what choice he makes when he actually approaches the font. Shylock identifies himself with two Patriarchs, each of whom must undergo his own successful *psychomachiae.* First, Abraham in choosing to accept the call to leave Ur of the Chaldees and to journey in a strange and unknown land (Gen. 11:31, 12:1) and then when he was asked to sacrifice Isaac (Gen. 22). Likewise Jacob wrestled with God all night and prevailed (Gen. 32:24 ff.). Each received a new name; but Shylock refers to them by their old names, not their new.[41] Baptism will confer a new, Christian name on Shylock; its validity will depend on the choice he makes then. Finally, the allusions to the crucifixion in the trial scene point to Christ's *psychomachia* at Gethsemene and on Golgotha. In the mock-serious dilemma of the Clown, metaphor and analogy set the consequences of the grave choices that all must face.

This epitome gives Launcelot typological language:[42] the choice is between "my old master the Jew . . . [and] my new master the Christian" (2.4.17–18).[43] *Old* often governs *Shylock* (2.5.2, 4.3.11); he is "old master" (2.2.146), he is "old carrion" (3.1.31). The Clown admits, "I am a Jew if I serve the Jew any longer" (2.2.107–108). He desires to "serve" Bassanio (135). The word *master* and the related word *serve* ring throughout the first one hundred and fifty lines of the scene. Shakespeare casts the Clown's victory over conscience in the shape of a metamorphosis, of a mimic death and rebirth.[44] Launcelot reports to his old father that he "is indeed deceased" (60–61). After a bit more of the jester's obfuscations, his father asks, "Is my boy . . . alive or dead?" (68–69). When Old Gobbo recovers from the spoof, he says of his son, "Lord, how art thou chang'd!" (95).[45]

In this spoof Shakespeare defines the "old" by humorous metaphors of privation that certainly are not so humorous elsewhere in the play and the "new"—who are, in fact, the young[46]—by metaphors of comic vitality. Because he is "famished" in Shylock's service, Launcelot maladroitly says, "You may tell every finger I have with my ribs" (102–103); Shylock complains that "the patch is . . . a huge feeder" (2.5.45). The metaphor of food becomes darker. Shylock agrees to sup with Bassanio and his retinue only to "feed fat the ancient grudge I bear him" (1.3.42); he goes only "in hate to feed upon / The prodigal Christian" (2.5.14–15). If the forfeit of the bond "will feed nothing else, it will feed [Shylock's] revenge" (3.1.47–48). The festive merriment of supping is perverted into a kind of cannibalism, perhaps into a grotesque parody of the Eucharist. Shylock agrees to go, though he says, "I will not eat with you, drink with you, nor pray with you" (1.3.32–33); here Shylock mentions three features of the communion service.[47]

If one may repair to 2.3 as ending the epitome set forth in 2.2, one hears of further privation. Jessica speaks of the "taste of tediousness" in the "hell" that is her home (2.3.2–3).[48] "Merry" Launcelot at least did "rob" it of some of its severity. From it, old Shylock has banished the sound of "the drum / And the vile squealing of the wry-neck'd fife"; he orders, "Lock up my doors . . . stop my house's ears, I mean my casements; / Let not the sound of shallow fopp'ry enter / My sober house" (2.5.29–36). The "man that hath no music" in him has "affections dark as Erebus" (5.1.83–87).[49] Soberness does not allow of the comic values of mirth, dancing, feasting; it knows not the "skipping spirit" (2.2.178), masking, dining, making-merry, the laughter of friendship, of the "liver . . . heat[ed] with wine" (1.1.81). It cannot allow love of friend, of parent, of child, or amorous love that characterize the young who stand against the Senex.[50] Shylock's only use for "merry" is grimly to modify the bond, and the sport he will have in taking the forfeit of the bond (1.3.144, 169). In his puritanism, he is the "reverse of an Antonio . . . the more Shylock has the less he is; the less [Antonio has] the more [he] become[s]" (Weiss 133).

In 2.2, Shakespeare sets Launcelot's choice of a new master in the context of asking for his father's blessing. By this means, the realities of love and of hatred enter the epitome. Old Gobbo, who is literally "sand-blind," loves his son and can see what his son morally is; Shylock, who has sight, is blind as to who his daughter is and comes to wish Jessica, if not cursed, then "hearsed" (3.1.79) at his foot. Old Gobbo in his literal blindness thinks the man before him cannot be his son, for the man has too much hair.[51] Blind Isaac finally believed the sly Jacob to be his first son because Jacob had affected a goat's skin in pretending to be the hairy Esau. Very like Old Gobbo, Isaac says, "Who art thou, my son?" and "knew him not," giving his blessing, the Abrahamic inheritance, to the wrong son (Gen. 27:18, 23 BB). Old Gobbo soon comes to recognize his "own flesh and blood" (2.2.87), and Shylock comes to despise his. He says of Jessica, "She is damn'd"; he did not discern that his "own flesh and blood [would] rebel" (3.1.29, 31). The question may not be so much, "Hath not a Jew eyes?" as can Shylock not see with his?

By several analogies, Shakespeare mandates that one understand Jessica's "betrayal" in ways more significant than "realism" allows. Both Old Gobbo and Old Shylock are like and unlike Isaac; Launcelot and Jessica like and unlike Jacob. Old Gobbo's blessing is somehow a part of Launcelot's inheritance of a "new master." The inheritance that was rightly Esau's was transferred to Jacob by guile; and Jacob became Israel and received the promise descending from Abraham.[52] According to Christian typology this inheritance passed to the Church, to the "New Israel," who in the *Te Deum* prays to God, "Bless thine inheritance."[53] Jessica herself simply takes the blessing of gold and jewels by Jacobean wiliness without asking for it. By stealth, the women of the Old Israel spoiled the Egyptians of their gold and jewels before the Exodus, taking the treasure along with them.[54] Typology sees in this spoliation a prefigurement of Christ's "spoiling" (Col. 2:15 BB) Hades of the righteous spirits waiting there for liberation at his descent for the Harrowing of Hell, a victory over principalities and powers,[55] leading the Old Man—the old Adam and the old Eve—into the new dispensation.[56] Danson (179–80) associates Jessica's "spoliation" with the richness of the Jews passing to the Gentiles, as St. Paul teaches in Romans 11. Jessica's defection with Shylock's gold and jewels follows hard on 2.2 and 2.3 that treat of Launcelot's "new master." Jessica takes her Egyptian spoils with her to her new Christian master. Shylock understands this transfer when he speaks of his "Christian ducats" (2.8.16).[57] Jessica receives her inheritance at Shylock's conversion; her "mere wealth and jewels . . . , like all the other properties and qualities in the play, . . . will soon be converted," by the alchemy of Belmont, "into something far more rich and fair" (Roth 154). Portia's inheritance, in contrast, depends upon her obedience to her father and passes to Bassanio because of his ability to love Portia.[58]

Preveniently, Bassanio says to Launcelot, "Thou hast obtain'd thy suit" (2.2.137), with a mischievous pun; for the servant's new liveries seem already in the making (111): "rare new liveries" (105), "more guarded than his fellows' " (138). Jessica, too, will have a change of clothing, the "page's suit [that] she hath in readiness" (2.4.32). By her choice she will "end this strife, / Become a Christian and [Lorenzo's] loving wife" (2.3.20–21). "Strife" suggests the separation between what she is by disposition and what Shylock requires of her. Jessica, though born Jew, was never St. Paul's "Old Man," full of "anger, wrath, malice." She says, "But though I am a daughter to his blood, I am not to his manners" (2.3.18–19), that is, not to his demeanor, not to his behavior; therefore, Jessica "is completely accepted by the Christians."[59] As to Jessica's behavior between the time she left her father's house and when one finds her at Belmont, one has only Tubal's report by which he intends to incite Shylock to rage,[60] a studied alternating of Jessica's putative misdoings and Antonio's putative ruin. With Jessica and with Shylock Shakespeare elucidates the difference between a racial Jew and the "Old Man."[61] At his baptism, Shylock, too, will be given new liveries, as the Church, from her beginning has given her new Israelites and as St. Paul's metaphor of baptism presupposes;[62] the Moral to the fifteenth tale of *Gesta Romanorum* speaks of putting off the old life and clothing oneself with the new.

Finally, Old Gobbo's valiant attempt to learn "which is the way to Master Jew's," a "hard way to hit" (2.2.31–32 [also 36–37], 42), humorously introduces into Shakespeare's mock epitome the metaphors of the journey, of "argosies" that are "tossing upon the ocean," "ventures" upon the waters, "vessel[s]," "bottom[s]" (1.1.9, 8, 15, 21, 42, 32, 42). "Argosies" suggests Jason; and Bassanio says of Portia, "Her sunny locks, / Hang upon her temples like a golden fleece, / Which makes her seat of Belmont Colchos' strond, / And many Jasons come in quest of her" (1.1.169–72). Bassanio's quest is a "sweet pilgrimage"[63] (1.1.120) by water to Portia's "shrine" (2.7.40) in Belmont where one sees the eon breaking in. Jessica must make a voyage that "is an analogue of Bassanio's" (Velz 319). Since the time of St. Augustine at the latest, a pilgrimage, especially by sea, to a shrine has been an ancient figure of the parlous course of the Christian life as the Flood Prayer in the Prayer Book baptismal office reflects (Booty 270–71).[64]

These journeys involve hazards such as Salerio mentions to Antonio at the beginning of the play and such as the disasters reported to have come upon Antonio's ventures.[65] These are the risks involved in any *psychomachia*. The moral and ontological norms of this play require that one "give and hazard all" (2.7.9) if one wishes to reach Belmont and, there, win Portia.[66] Instead of risks, hazards, ventures, Shylock chooses "well-won thrift" (1.3.45);[67] to "thrive [is to be] blest; / And thrift is a blessing." This way is that of Shylock's model, the devious Jacob (1.3.84–85, 66–83). Shylock's way is "Fast bind; fast find— / A proverb never stale in thrifty mind" (2.5.53–54). But he has left his house in the charge of Launcelot, "an unthrifty knave" (1.2.172); and his daughter "with an unthrift love did run from Venice" to Belmont (5.1.16).

Launcelot speaks of the "Fates and Destinies and . . . the Sisters Three, and such odd branches of learning" (2.2.59–60) as the forces that govern one's life and one's death; Morocco trusts his proper choice of caskets to "Good fortune" (2.1.45). But Nerissa teaches Portia to trust the comic grace of the play: Portia's father was a virtuous and holy man; such men have "good inspirations" at their death. Nerissa is careful to say that "holy men" *have* (she does not say "may have" or " often have"). Nerissa must be referring to the guidance of a divine afflatus, since the "spirit of hazarding, as opposed to the spirit of calculation" notes Holmer, "is allied with Providence" (*The Merchant* 97); "therefore the lott'ry that he hath devised in these three chests . . . will . . . never be chosen by any rightly but one who you shall rightly love" (1.2.27–32). Bassanio called at Belmont during the time of Portia's father. Did the "inspired" father recognize Bassanio's potential and arrange the will, therefore, as he did? Faith in comic[68] grace is the means by which all who risk and hazard may hope to prosper in their pilgrimages.

Into the mischievously perverse epitome of his play, 2.2, Shakespeare contrives to draw together most of the themes, metaphors, rhythms, structures, and norms of *The Merchant of Venice*. Though the scene is full of mirth and merriment, the choices that it proposes are grave—sight or blindness, reality or mere appearance, hazard or thrift, love or hatred; the rewards are either Belmont or privation, absence, illusion, that is, either life or death. "To make me blest or cursèd'st among men," as Morocco has it.

III. The Norms of the Play

The Less (reality) into the Greater (Reality)

In act 5 Shakespeare opens clearly the nature of emblem and analogue; an adequate understanding of the play depends on an accurate understanding of the emblem and of its relation to its archetype. When Portia returns to Belmont she notices the candle shining in her hall, like "a good deed in a naughty world"; and Nerissa adds that they could not see the candle while the moon was shining. Then Portia introduces three analogies of union, of the way that "the greater glory [doth] dim the less," of the way the less is taken into the greater to be made part of the greater, as human mercy enters divinity: (1) a candle's light taken up into the moon's light—light answers light; (2) the substitute's shining disappearing when the king himself (who is the source of the substitute's light) returns; (3) a brook's emptying itself into the main of waters (5.1.93–97). The less is suitable only until the greater appears. The embodied emblem or analogue is always the less, though it is a true model of the greater; the embodied emblem, however, is always difficult to discern aright in this naughty world. One must be free of illusion to see correctly. Those who mistake gold, silver, or the law for reality are like those who would mistake the candle, the substitute, the brook for the thing itself. As her name indicates, Portia is an adequate door until the real Door comes. She is an ample sun to lighten Italy (5.1.127–28) until the real Sun arises. Belmont in act 5, though perhaps the loveliest scene in Shakespeare,[69] is only an emblem where Jew and Gentile are united in each other's arms, where the eon has begun to break through into time.

Portia's metaphors of the less taken into the greater involve diversity entering union: "All the world desires Portia; / From the four corners of the earth they come / To kiss this shrine" (2.7.39–40). This and other lines suggest a number of Biblical passages describing the heavenly Jerusalem.[70] These passages also allude to the biblical quest for Wisdom, for Sophia,[71] who, when found, comes down from her beautiful mountain[72] to rescue the righteous, and then returns to dwell with all those who love her:[73] "Give me wisdom which is ever sitting about thy seat . . . send her out of thine holy heavens and send her from the throne of thy majesty, that she may be with me and labour with me that I may know what is acceptable in thy sight" (Wis. 9:4, 10, BB). Sophia is a woman in Wisdom and Proverbs,[74] an hypostasis; the Geneva Bible, in its margin, identifies Wisdom with Christ, the Word (Proverbs 8:22, McCombie 115). Portia, a lady of "wondrous virtue," a "mortal breathing saint," an "angel," descends from Belmont to rescue Antonio and to bring him and divers others to Belmont. Shylock is an "alien" (4.1.345) in Venice; but in the trial scene the Duke and Portia report all to be alien to righteousness. Portia defines what is necessary for one to enter Belmont: "I stand for sacrifice" (3.2.57). The truth of Stephano's tale of Portia "stray[ing] about / By holy crosses" before her return to Belmont and kneeling and praying "for happy wedlock hours" (5.1.30–32) may or may not be literal; but these acts of submission before symbols of the supreme example of risk and hazard underline the place of sacrifice in this comedy.

This is a Christian contour in the play: to be willing to give up all, like Job, in order to receive all (Matt. 10:39), to lose in order to gain (Matt. 16:25), to give up in order to receive it all back better.[75] Without intending so to do, Shylock gives and hazards all, but his faith is in the law. This illusion must be banished. He must put off the old, to put on the new—to give and hazard is a kind of death, not unlike baptism, to which Shylock has admitted himself "content." Jewish circumcision is a type in the Hebrew Bible of Christian baptism. As early as Deuteronomy, circumcision—by which one enters the communion of the old Israel and becomes a Jew—begins to have metaphoric significance in the Law and the Prophets. The prophet Jeremiah urges the old Israel to moral reformation, radically to "cut away the foreskins of your heart,"[76] adding to the ancient rite a significance of purification. The cutting of the pound of flesh from around the heart may, therefore, be symbolic of circumcision[77] and, then, of baptism, by which one enters the communion of the new Israel and becomes a Christian. In following his implacable vengeance, Shylock does Antonio a mercy without planning to do so, as this merchant needs metamorphosis also:[78] Shylock gives Antonio the occasion to cleanse his heart with the gentle rain of mercy and to forgive the attempted murder. The ironies of Shakespeare's "comic enterprise" force one "to read salvation in the light of corruption," and to recognize "how necessary the fallen world is" for the success of redemption (Grund 157–61).

An allusion to such a transforming rite appears in act 5 in the sequence of tragic lovers, Troilus and Cressid, Pyramus and Thisbe, Dido and Aeneas; Shakespeare unexpectedly breaks this sequence and abruptly redirects it by the fourth pair, not Jason and Medea, as one would anticipate from the tragic series—not lovers at all[79]—but Medea "renew[ing] old Aeson," her father-in-law, by a potion of "enchanted herbs." This story may have been "Shakespeare's favourite passage of the *Metamorphoses*" (7, 159–293).[80] Jason, through an act of sacrificial love, offers some of his own years to his father; and old Aeson's "leane, pale, hore, and withered corse grew fulsome, faire and fresh"; but the risk, however, loses Jason nothing, as Medea transforms Aeson in another way and gains Jason a young father. She begins with a threefold cleansing, sprinkling Aeson with the purifying agents of water, fire, and sulphur, administered by an olive branch. Much of this account suggests the New Testament rite of baptism. The New Testament speaks of baptisms of water and of fire; an olive branch is part of the story of Noah that prefigures baptism. St. Paul uses the metaphor of an olive tree to describe the effects of baptism (Rom. 11). Baptismal anointing uses olive oil. After the sprinkling, Medea cuts the old man's throat, takes out the "old bloud," and replaces it with her mixture of supernatural herbs boiled up in her cauldron. The physical change causes a like spiritual transmutation: "Even so a lively youthful spright did in his heart renew." In some versions, Aeson suffers Medea's famous pot;[81] and, therefore, his renewal resembles baptism even more closely. The whole action originates in a religious context; Jason acts because his father is too weak to participate in the sacrifice that the elders are offering.

Thus are the three "destabilizing" examples of unhappy love themselves destabilized by a fourth, and then by a fifth, Lorenzo and Jessica; and the ambiguous allusions associating Bassanio with Jason, Portia with the Golden Fleece, and Belmont with Colchis resolve themselves in this comic metaphor of renewal.[82] The tragic pattern gives way to comic restoration by a kind of mysterious rite not unlike baptism, with its waters of supernatural grace. The tragic situation of 4.1 gives way to the comic saving of Shylock from death, the funding of Shylock, and the death of the Old Man by water and the birth of the New Man. To Jewish circumcision, a rite that unites one with the race, the Law and the Prophets added the connotation of purification. Christian baptism, the fulfilling of this prefiguration, further adds the sacramental metamorphosis of the old into the new described by a metaphor of union, namely grafting a branch of the wild olive tree onto the good olive tree (Rom. 11), the less into the greater.

Portia's three emblems of the union of the less with the greater follow hard on Lorenzo's discourse on the union of heaven with earth. The light of the moon shines in the darkness of the night; the heavenly and the earthly are joined "as the moonlight sleeps upon this bank." The divine and human join as "the moon [Diana] sleeps with Endymion." "Immortal souls" sit in celestial light and listen to the earthly analogue of celestial music. The "sweet harmony" describes more than just the music.[83] Lorenzo's vision is upward, of an earthly-celestial correspondence. Music recalls for Lorenzo the music of the orbs. The movement of even the smallest sphere "quir[es] to the young-eyed cherubins" who quire to God. For Pythagoras (at least the Elizabethan Pythagoreans), the mysteries of the harmonies of music figure the mysterious harmonies in the life of God, where even opposites are united and transcended, the less taken into the greater.[84] Even though the ravages of death ("this muddy vesture of decay")[85] keep mortals from hearing it, nevertheless, "such harmony is in [their] immortal souls";[86] and humans can indeed hear earthly concord as it "creeps in our ears" and "change[s our] nature," as it "draw[s Portia] home." Because of the union of heaven and earth, music answers music.[87] The "man that hath no music in him," that is not moved with "concord of sweet sounds" is "stockish, hard, and full of rage," like the Old Man. Lorenzo joins emblems of music with ones of light. The stars which "thick [inlay] . . . the floor of heaven"[88] are called "patens." Patens hold the consecrated bread at communion; this word, in the preferred meaning of the Arden edition notes, alerts one to the sacramental or emblematic nature of creation; creation is like consecrated bread (cf. "manna," l. 295), the body of Christ according to Christian theology. Mercy in the human heart is sacramentally or emblematically an "attribute of God" (4.1.191).

The emblems of music and light take place in the context of young love, "sweet moonlight," the "soft stillness of the night," and, Portia being at hand, of restoration. The christological echoes in Antonio and Portia[89] reveal the eternal music in the human soul. The norms reigning at the end of the play involve human participation in divinity: mercy, love, sacrifice, union. They include music and light, death-by-water, and banqueting (implied in "patens" and "manna"). These norms represent the new, or perhaps one should say the young.[90] These norms manifest Reality in the play.[91]

Reality against Illusion: Giving and Hazarding

Bassanio's meditation before the caskets[92] discovers illusion to be no mere neutral absence of reality but rather insidious, rotten, and deadly. By it "the world is deceived" (3.2.77), as are Morocco and Arragon. It is "evil," "tainted," "corrupt" (3.2.77, 75). Shylock's being participates in this same rottenness; he is like "a goodly apple rotten at the heart. / O what a goodly outside falsehood hath" (1.3.96–97). In law, a "gracious voice"—but without grace—"obscures the show of evil" (3.2.75–77). In religion, "damnèd error" is "bless[ed]" by a "sober brow" and a "text" that hides the "grossness" with "fair ornament" and loses salvation for some hearer (77–80). Any vice, no matter how simple, takes the "mark of virtue" (82): else why would anyone choose vice? It is so with courage, too: those cowards with beard of Hercules and frowning of Mars—"valor's excrement"—may have hearts "as false" and as fatally treacherous as "stairs of sand." Inward they have "livers white as milk" (86–87). So it is, too, with a woman's beauty: purchased by weight, the lightest (that is, fairest) are the heaviest (because of the weight of the cosmetics they wear), a false paradox. Bassanio also puns on a "light," unfaithful, woman. Such a woman's "crispèd snaky golden locks," long, sensuous, but venomous and deadly, are likely to have come from a "skull" already in the "sepulchre" (91, 92, 96). A "beauteous scarf" may veil an "Indian beauty," swarthy, not fair (97, 98). "Ornament is but the guilèd shore" to a "dangerous sea" (96–97); here Bassanio uses a principal metaphor in the play: illusion is deadly to hazarding, to argosies at sea, causing them shipwreck. "Gaudy gold" is deadly food for Midas (101).[93] To be freed of the fatal golden touch, Midas had to wash himself in the River Pactolus.[94] Ornament "entrap[s] the wisest" (3.2.101). The length and thoroughness of Bassanio's meditation on illusion attests to its importance in the play and to his understanding of its deceptive allure.

The song that Portia causes to be sung while Bassanio meditates defines illusion, "Fancy,"[95] as death, advising that "all [should] ring fancy's knell."

The words of the song give wisdom; the music itself modifies the soul of the listener—as it does Benedick, also, in *Much Ado* (2.3.59)—and leads him into "concord," the "sweet harmony" that changes one's "nature," echoing the music of the orbs and the cherubim and the mind of God (5.1.55–63). "Fancy" is infatuation, gotten from "gazing" with the sensuous eyes alone that see not beyond "gilt," "shadow," and "outward shows." "Fancy dies / In the cradle where it lies": it cannot mature. Not being reality, it cannot abide; it can only die and lead to death.

Reality and its riches come only to one prepared to "give and hazard all he hath";[96] Bassanio is capable of redemption because he rejects illusion and its death. He has also a potential for love, honor, and dignity that Antonio and Portia recognize in him and encourage (Sheppard 142). He chooses "meagre lead" which offers no promising ornament but rather "threaten[s]," pointing to the rhythm of risking that is essential to prosperity. Lead cannot lie; its paleness argues its reality and recommends it more than the gaudy colors of "eloquence." Here Bassanio chooses, hoping for "joy [as] the consequence" (3.2.107).[97] Bassanio in his meditation has pierced beneath appearance and illusion to reality. He has chosen properly[98] to hazard. Therefore, love and life result;[99] or, knowing how rightly to love (as old Belmont surely knew he would), he rightly elects.

Living (and loving) require that one choose reality. In this scene, forms of *choose* (2, 11, 24) three times precede *life* (25, 30, 34).[100] Here Bassanio chooses life and not death, not the blindness of Morocco's skull, nor the idiocy of Arragon's casket.[101] Antonio, because he is like Bassanio, is the "semblance of [Portia's] soul" (3.4.20).[102] Shakespeare deals here in emblems. Yet Bassanio must prove this resemblance by his choosing rightly. Determining rightly is a matter not of luck or fortune but of moral disposition;[103] the interlacing of "live" and "life" with "love" argues this rectitude.[104] Portia teaches him "deliverance" because "life" for Bassanio is Portia's "love" of him (38, 34). The egoism of Morocco's gold and Arragon's silver and of Shylock's "thrift" are death. Earlier (1.1.161–76) Bassanio has confessed his desire to mend his fortunes at Belmont.[105] Is there then "treason" (3.2.27) in his love? His eyes have spoken love to Portia: has he been transformed by Portia and she by him? Love answers love.[106] "Confess," "confession," "deliverance" (34, 35, 38) are theological terms. "Deliverance" and "redeem" (l. 65) are also legal terms and financial terms; as such they are metaphors of theological concerns. Love, which is life, is an agent of redemption. By love Bassanio chooses the right casket, chooses Portia, who is his deliverance. Portia instructs him, "If you do love me, you will find me out"; "I am locked in one of them" (41, 40). Likewise, Jessica is locked in Shylock's house; and Lorenzo's love finds her out and delivers her.

Faith in the comic order—which is the order of life and love—is necessary for one who risks and hazards all. Portia will not teach Bassanio how to "choose right" because she would then be "forsworn"; rather, she is obedient to the comic order and trusts in it (10–12).[107] At the beginning of the third casket scene (3.2.4–5), as a kind of prologue to the choosing, Portia says to Bassanio, "Something tells me . . . I would not lose you." Bassanio, in his work, is heroic like Hercules, who played on the lyre and sang, who "redeem[ed]" the virgin tribute, Hesione, from the sea monster. Should Bassanio choose wrongly, Portia would be sacrificed to the "sea monster," namely to life without Bassanio. Therefore, Portia "stand[s] for," symbolizes, "sacrifice." Thus Portia says, "Live thou, I live"; or, fail thou, I die. She sacrifices herself to her father's will: a choice that she has endorsed more than once. The scroll teaches Bassanio that "fortune" and "chance" are a result of rightly "choos[ing] not by view."[108] What Bassanio "see[s will not] be true," however, until Portia has "confirmed, signed, and ratified" it. He thus gives the choice back to Portia. The scroll advises Bassanio to "seek no new" because he has the "new." "New," rhymes with "true," "you," "not view." If Bassanio can be pleased with this fortune, he may "claim [his lady] with a loving kiss." "Kiss" and "bliss" rhyme here as they do in Arragon's scroll: but with a great difference. This scroll mentions bliss, true, fair, kiss, loving, lady, but not by view. The other two scrolls offer but death, idiocy, carrion, blindness, tombs, worms, gilded, old, cold, not gold, glisters, appearance, fool, and shadow.

"Come by note," "to give and to receive," "confirm," "sign," "ratif[y]" (140, 148) point to legal and mercantile concerns transformed by trust into life and love, into the new, into joy. To give and to receive a kiss involves mutuality (as does giving and receiving mercy). Bassanio's speech is full of words like "doubt," "doubtful," "unstable," "giddy in spirit": all must be approved by Portia's acceptance. He relieves Portia of her obligations to her father's will. Then on her own she accepts Bassanio as "lord," "governor," and "king." Portia says to Bassanio: "You see me . . . where I stand, / Such as I am"—sight and reality are the same here. Portia gives herself to Bassanio with the ring, and Bassanio passes the test. And so does Portia.[109]

After he has passed the test and achieved Portia's portrait, Bassanio moves on to consider the relationship between a true image and the reality it copies; Shakespeare here traces the relationships present in emblem. In the casket, Bassanio finds "Fair Portia's counterfeit."[110] In saying that a "demigod" (115) has come "so near creation" (116), Bassanio suggests the figure of God as a creator; the painter is an artisan, a "demi-god," one who imitates (at a great distance) God's work.[111] Because the lesser participates in the greater, Jessica speaks therefore of the "blessing that [Bassanio] has in his lady" and allows that in her "he finds the joys of heaven here on earth" (3.5.69, 70). The purpose of the emblem or analogue—the less—is to teach of the Reality—the greater—that it, in part, reflects.

One may, however, mistake the creation for the Creator; the painter has, like a spider, woven "a golden mesh" (122) not unlike the "snaky golden locks" (92) above "t'entrap the hearts of men / Faster than gnats in cobwebs"

(122–23). Bassanio wonders how the painter has managed to paint the eyes without losing his own to hers. Bassanio's description of the "counterfeit"[112] has much troubling imagery in it: "snaky," "entrap" as a spider entraps a gnat (122);[113] the word *counterfeit* itself carries connotations of fraud, and *shadow* points back to Arragon's scroll ("shadows kiss . . . shadow's bliss" [2.10.66–67]). Bassanio's praise of the painting wrongs the painting by "underprizing" it. Bassanio must later be willing to sacrifice Portia (the ring) to something higher, trust in comic grace; otherwise, she may become a trap. The continuum of emblem or analogue begins in God, proceeds to Portia, then to the portrait; but one who confuses the portrait with the Reality, the creation with the Creator, proceeds further to illusion, nothing, privation, perdition.

Bassanio's praise is only a "shadow" of the painting and "limp[s] behind the substance" (3.2.129) of the painting as the painting "limp[s] behind the substance" of Portia; and, implied, as Portia "limp[s] behind the substance" of which she is an imitation ("image," "likeness")—that which is complete, the Creator. Being made by Christ, Portia is an emblem of him, the Door, the one who comes down from the beautiful mountain to fulfill the law and to substitute mercy for the penalty of the law.[114] St. Paul uses "shadow" in the sense of an emblem (Col. 2:17 and Heb. 8:5). Plato is also relevant here.

IV. Against the Norms

Rejection of Sacrifice: Assuming Desert, Illusion, the Less into Nothing

The appearances of the first two caskets are illusory: gold offers death and blindness, silver offers idiocy. The mottos of the caskets, however, offer reality and judgment: to seek anything other than renunciation brings disaster. In these trials, one deliberately chooses life or death. Selection is a moral act with moral antecedents and moral consequences;[115] what one chooses at any moment shows what one has always been choosing, choices that determine what one will be.[116] The Fall came from choosing illusion rather than reality; and illusion, absence, privation are the traditional attributes of evil and Hell. Shylock, blind, dead, idiotic, chooses "the law" (illusion) and achieves the ruin of all.[117] To be willing to hazard all brings one to reality, to Portia, to the "inheritance."

In the first casket scene, 2.7, Morocco asks, can "lead contain . . . her?" To think so is damnation; it is "too gross" to wrap her in a "cerecloth" of lead for an "obscure grave."[118] Can lead contain gold? The alchemists thought it could; "base" and "gross" are alchemical terms (49–51). Hazard, give, venture, sacrifice in *Merchant* are the elixir that can turn lead to life and love, to gold that does not glister; hazard can transform the less into the greater.[119] Stanton J. Linden traces the alchemical metaphors in the seventeenth century that emphasize themes of moral purification and spiritual transformation;

these figures associate Christ with the philosopher's stone (102–24). Well before the seventeenth century and soon after the Arabic treatises on alchemy were translated into Latin, the mysterious element of that occult learning began to be related to the central Christian mysteries of salvation. The philosopher's stone, thus, is an adumbration of Christ; and the alchemical transformation is analogic of transubstantiation (Grennen 550–51, Reidy 33, Gardner 13, 15). Donne develops "Resurrection, imperfect" on this conceit.[120] The lead in *Merchant* does contain gold, as the alchemist might have thought.

What Morocco takes as "tried gold" has, in fact, not been tried at all; therefore, it merely "glisters," it is "gilded tombs." Rather the caskets try Morocco, Arragon, and Bassanio. Fire is a frequent biblical image for refining the gold and silver of Israel. Speaking for "the Lord," the prophet Zechariah says that a "third part" of Israel will pass the test of fire and prove to be gold; this third "is my people," the remnant of Israel to be redeemed (13:9 BB). One third of the suitors, Bassanio, successfully undergoes the trial of the caskets. The prophet Malachi defines the Messiah as a "purging fire" (3:2 BB). The New Testament continues this imagery: all men's works will be revealed and tried by fire (1 Pet. 1:7, Rev. 3:18; 1 Cor. 3:12–15). Tried gold would be, as Morocco says, a proper setting for the gem that is Portia; hence, Morocco chooses gold. But the gold he elects has not been tried. Shylock's false equation—Jessica = ducats (2.8.20)—would be a true equation if Portia could be set in this kind of gold. But she cannot be; she is set in lead. Lead, rightly chosen, is transmuted by venture into the gold of Belmont.

Morocco chooses gold and hopes to "thrive" as he may (60); in this comedy, thriving ("thrift") stands against hazard, the principle of life, and is, therefore, deadly. Seeing the Death's-head Morocco calls it "hell" (cf. "damnation," 2.7.62). "Gilded tombs [which] worms infold" (2.7.69) hold "carrion" (2.7.63); Shylock (the greatest truster in illusion, blindness, death) is "old carrion" (3.1.32). Bassanio speaks of the skull that bred the illusory false hair of the falsely beautiful lady as being already "in the sepulchre" (3.2.96). Morocco's mentioning the "empty eye" suggests the blindness of those who confuse what only glisters with that which is golden. Morocco "his life hath sold" for this death, for this "outside" (3.7.67, 68); *gilt, gaudy, glisters* all suggest illusion. The scroll associates Morocco with "old," "cold," "frost," and "losers."

The silver casket, chosen by Arragon in 2.9, warns: "who chooseth me shall get as much as he deserves" (36). That one deserves anything at all Portia later defines as illusory (4.1.195–96).[121] One's unredeemed self is nothing, is illusion. Morocco, however, assures himself to the contrary, "If thou be'st rated by thy estimation, / Thou dost deserve enough" (2.7.26). Morocco chooses wealth (illusion) and achieves death and blindness. Arragon assumes "the stamp of merit" (2.9.39); his presumption is, of course, unfounded. This pride is self-love, appearance, idiocy; it is quite unlike hazard and sacrifice.

He knows that the "fool multitude" chooses "by show," by what the "fond [mad] eye" teaches; he knows that the multitude "prises not to th'interior," as the "martlet / Builds . . . on the outward wall" (26, 27, 28–29). He knows that estates, degrees, and offices are often corruptly derived and, therefore, founded on appearances, "undeserved dignity" (2.9.40). Nevertheless, he chooses appearance; he chooses the silver casket and discovers himself with a "blinking [*OED*: 'weak-eyed'] idiot," announcing, "How much unlike . . . deserving." He asks, do "I deserve no more than a fool's head? / . . . Are my deserts no better?" (57–60).

The casket represents illusion, but the scroll tells the truth. The "fire [has] seven times tried" (67) the silver of this casket; the one whose judgment is "seven times tried" does not judge amiss. The real silver, like the "tried" gold, contrasts with the apparent silver of Arragon's judgment. The passage alludes to Ps. 12:7: "the words of the Lord are pure words: even as the silver is tried and purified seven times in the fire." These words, being of the Logos, contain Wisdom; they are tellingly set against Arragon's misjudgment of himself. The Psalmist goes on to lament the vanity, flattery, and dissembling of all about him; but the Lord shall preserve his words from the proud and vain generation that surround the Psalmist who are ignorant of their real state, like Arragon, who "assume[d] desert." These are they who "shadows kiss" and have only "a shadow's bliss" (66, 67). A shadow is illusion, absence of light, nothing—dark like thrift, like the law, like hell. To kiss a shadow is to love illusion; therefore, the misjudging suitors may not wive because they love illusion and not women.[122] Theirs is living death: "there be fools alive (Iwis)" (66).[123] Arragon seems to have learned: "With one fool's head I came to woo, / But I go away with two" (75–76), with what he deserves. Morocco has learned, too, though perhaps not so well. May Shylock possibly also have learned after being "tried"? Morocco and Arragon, like Shylock, go offstage and are seen no more.[124]

V. The Trial Scene: The Testing of the Norms

Exposing illusion and discovering reality, act 4 effects the work of comedy. Literal and moral death are done away; legal and financial disaster give way to redemptions; law pushed to its extreme yields the celestial rain of mercy; inhuman vengeance learns to practice divine humility; Shylock receives a chance to test the waters; and Bassanio successfully makes his final hazard. 3.5, which precedes the trial, is set at Belmont and speaks much of the approaching "dinner" (43, 54, 56, 80), of the comic values of the play which the trial scene will secure as it turns from potential tragedy to comedy. The canons of "realism" cannot hope to account satisfactorily for act 4, driven, in part, like the rest of the play, by the energies of emblem and analogy. As Launcelot's *psychomachia* is a humorous mimic of the grim battle for Shylock's soul, and as the casket

scenes all have an analogical dimension, so the Trial Scene, 4.1, extends figuratively beyond a case in Venetian law and points to the divine economy and
the statutes of the deity before which none is innocent from offense; Everyman
is guilty of transgressing them. All who wish the celestial mercy of forgiveness,
however, may have it.

In this economy, the "letter [of the law] killeth" (2 Cor. 3:6 BB) anyone's
putative righteousness; and then the law may be "our schoolmaster to bring
us" beyond it (Gal. 3:24 GB). When Portia gives Shylock the force of the law
against Antonio, Shakespeare, with exceeding art, introduces into the structure of the dialogue a chiasmus (Elam 206), that is, the form of a cross
shaped by the rhetorical pattern of their speech:

SHY: We trifle time, [A] *I pray thee pursue sentence.*
POR: A pound of that same merchant's flesh is thine,
              [B] *The court awards it*, and [C] *the law doth give it.*
SHY: Most rightful judge!
POR: And you must cut the flesh from off his breast,
              [C] The *law allows it*, and [B] *the court awards it.*
SHY: Most learned judge! a [A] *sentence, come prepare.* (294–300)[125]

This chiasmus prefigures Shylock's quickly approaching agony. At this
point begin in Shylock both the crucifixion of the letter of the deadly law and
also his movement toward the vital dispensation beyond the law. Moreover,
spread across the dialogue of Shylock and Portia, the chiasmus unites them
in the crucifying action just ahead, as Antonio and Shylock are later bound
together through each of them saying, within twelve lines of one another, "I
am content." Venetian law is an analogue of what theology calls "the old
law"; and the mercy and relief given of the Duke to Shylock are analogue of
what theology calls the "new law" of grace. "Most rightful judge" is the center turning point of the chiasmus that comes at a crucial point in the scene.

The scene begins as the trial of Antonio, who is delivered. It ends as the
trial of Shylock, who is also delivered.[126] It proceeds with allusion to the trial
of Christ, who is not delivered, but whose forfeit of blood is a means of
deliverance for all who wish it.[127] The scene is a trial even of the law, that
both convicts and delivers, with the Duke as a distant emblem of divinity,
God the Father as judge,[128] and with Portia as a distant emblem of God the
Son—"the Advocate" (1 John 2:1 BB)—pleading for man before the Father.
In this scene, Portia pushes the law as far as it will go, leading to Shylock's
condemnation to death; she fulfills the law, and she transcends the law. She
defines the new law of mercy and grace. Shylock, who pleads only the law, is
undone by the law; that in which he has put all his faith leads to death, blindness, idiocy, nothing. Having lost all that he has trusted, being left with nothing, perhaps he is ready to begin again.

The imagery of water—the venturing by faith upon the waters,[129] "the gentle rain from heaven" (4.1.181), and the curative powers of the waters upon "old Aeson"—may allow one to suppose that Shylock, too, can learn to trust the waters and to hazard their destructive and restorative powers. This imagery leads to the typology of the "Old Man" and the "New Man." The trial is, literally, between Shylock and Antonio, but figuratively between old and new. With the symbolic defeat of Shylock, the trial brings the rout of the old. This scene asks Shylock to choose reality, life, love, and sacrifice. Like Morocco and Arragon in their Casket Scenes he fails; unlike them, he is given more than the just outcome of a bad choice.[130] Does Shylock, then, have about him that which is worth redeeming? The action tests him as to whether or no he will participate, as Portia says one may, in the divine nature, and be, thereby, united to God. Shylock fails, chooses wrong. Yet in his baptism, if he has faith, his less will be sacramentally grafted into the greater, the body of Christ; and his theosis will begin.

Shylock, as a "stony adversary," however, is metaphoric of death, not life, with a "heart . . . of flint," a "brassy bosom"; "what's harder . . . than his Jewish heart?" (4, 31, 79–80). Ezekiel asks God to take away our "stony heart" and to replace it with a "fleshly heart," a "new spirit" (11:19, 36:26 BB). But Shylock whets his knife on the stone of his "soul" (123). He is an "inhuman wretch" (4), an "unfeeling man" (63), "wolvish, bloody, starved, and ravenous" (138).[131] He has the soul of a wolf that entered his "unhallowed dam [and] / Infus'd itself" in him (136–37);[132] "uncapable of pity" (5), he is not, therefore, human,[133] "void and empty / From any dram of mercy" (5–6). M. C. Bradbrook says that Shakespeare exhibits a man lapsing into beast (174).[134] To be "void and empty" is to be in a state of privation that is emblematic of hell (which theology defines as nothing), the terminus of the Old Man. The play often associates Shylock with the devil.[135] This scene sets "rigorous," "obdurate" (8), "fury," "tyranny" (10–13) against Antonio's "patience" (cf. Rom. 5:1–4). Early the Duke calls Shylock "to stand before our face" (16): thus from early on Shylock is the one on trial (and with him law, hatred, and illusion), though only Portia knows that he is. The Duke expects "human gentleness and love." He expects Shylock to "forgive a moiety," not to be like "Turks and Tartars" untrained in "offices of tender courtesy." He expects "a gentle answer" (26, 32–33, 34). Even though the Duke does not know yet of Shylock's particular crime, he knows all humans are sinful: "How shalt thou hope for mercy, rendering none?" (88).[136] Under "the law" all are dead—"the reward of sin is death" (Rom. 6:23 BB)—and, therefore, all must pray for mercy and, receiving it, thereby, be taught to "render mercy" (197–98).

Shylock, like Arragon, fatally assumes righteousness. He naïvely asks, "What judgment shall I dread, doing no wrong?"[137] Knowing one's own unrighteousness is requisite to understanding the trial scene: for Shylock is

Everyman given a local habitation and a name.[138] In calling Antonio a "fawning publican" (1.3.36), Shylock associates himself with the damned in Christ's parable of the Pharisee and the publican (Luke 18:10–14),[139] told for the benefit of those who trusted in their own righteousness. He "choose[s] to have / A weight of carrion flesh," of rottenness. Shylock compares his desire to kill Antonio to having a rat "baned." For him, Antonio is an animal: a pig, a cat, a serpent. His reason? "No reason," "a lodged hate and a certain loathing"; Antonio's contemptuous use of Shylock has been deadly, like a "serpent['s] sting" that one would not care to suffer twice. To hate is to wish to kill.[140] Shylock does not follow the Jewish law even in its most austere statement, "an eye for an eye . . ." (Exod. 21:24; Lev. 24:20; Deut. 19:21 BB); rather he commits himself to Antonio's death in payment for verbal abuse.[141] Frank McCombie assembles many citations from the Wisdom literature by which Shylock "is condemned, not by the New Testament teachings attributed to his antagonists, but out of the books of the Old Testament" (123). Moreover, in identifying himself with Jacob (2.5.36) in Gen. 32: 10 (BB), Shylock fails to remember that the Patriarch prays to God, "I am not worthy of the least of all [thy] mercies."

Likewise, Portia says, "In the course of justice none of us / Should see salvation" (4.1.195–96).[142] All must ask for mercy, else they, failing of salvation, will see damnation, the absence of all attributes of divinity.[143] Shylock's settled habit of "thrift," of "fast find[ing], fast bind[ing]" of refusing to give and hazard, of refusing to dine, of turning his house into a "hell" (2.3.2)—in short, of refusing to love—has been exacerbated by Antonio's cruelty. This habit has become worse and has given way to malice and vengeance, to a worse death. Shylock wants his "pound of flesh" that "is dearly bought" (4.1.99). Earlier, Portia has said that Bassanio is "dear bought" (3.2.312). Shylock does not know how dearly bought the pound of flesh is: it will cost him not less than everything.

The comic forces of the play—the moral order, cosmic grace—work during the trial scene to undo Shylock, who sets himself against the divinizing rhythm of sacrificing, of loving. No prayers can "pierce" (4.1.126) the stony heart of Shylock; but the law can and does. The introduction of Bellario, "a learned doctor" (144), turns the plot of the play around and begins to effect Shylock's destruction and Antonio's redemption. With nice dramatic irony, Shylock says, "I stand for judgment" (103), "I stand here for law" (142); earlier Portia, in contrast, has said, "I stand for sacrifice" (3.2.57). The Duke, who says, "Let him stand before our face" (16), summons Bellario and from him has the answer to Shylock's question as to what judgment he should dread. Bellario and Portia are "cousin[s]" (3.2.49), the old and the young are not unrelated, "old head" and "young body" (4.1.160–61);[144] St. John Baptist, the last prophet of the old law, and Christ, the new law, are cousins.[145] "Old Bellario" and "old Shylock" are not "old" in the same way.

The name Portia assumes, Balthazar,[146] is the Babylonian name of Daniel, the righteous servant of God. In the book of Daniel, the prophet prays, "We do not present our prayers before thee in our own righteousness, but in thy great mercies" (9:18 BB).[147] Portia affirms that the Venetian law supports Shylock, as does the "old law"; nevertheless, she says, "Must the Jew be merciful" (18). He *must* show mercy, the water of life, if he is not to remain dead as a moral and spiritual agent.

Like much else in *Merchant of Venice*, however, there is no legal "compulsion" (179); life-giving mercy is a matter of choice, of electing the right casket. Mercy is "charity" (257), disinterested love, which "covereth a multitude of sins" (1 Pet. 4:8). One learns to practice mercy from having received mercy. It "droppeth . . . from heaven," like "the gentle rain." It is then a gift, the source of which is God. It is life-giving, like moisture, coming without its being asked for, without one's deserving it—like transforming celestial music creeping as by stealth into one's ears. It falls "on the just, and on the unjust."[148] Mercy is "twice blest": (1) mercy is "blest" in those who receive it, for by taking it into themselves they attain an attribute of divinity; (2) it also blesses the one who gives, waters his spirit with "rain from heaven," divinizing nourishment. Mercy is more than a matter of ethics or even of religious obedience; mercy, being "an attribute to God himself" (182–92) "whose property is always to have mercy" (Booty 263), is a sacramental participation by deeds in the life of God. It involves a mysterious union with God: not a mere likeness or closeness, but a taking up of the less into the greater, the theosis or deification of the Fathers. The image in story XV of *Gesta Romanorum* is not of likeness or closeness or imitation but of marital union. The Moral informs: the King's daughter, the soul, choosing the right casket, may marry the Emperor's son, Christ.[149]

"Thronèd in the hearts of kings," "an attribute of awe and majesty," mercy makes a "thronèd monarch" an analogue of the humility of God,[150] the less revealing the greater. When self-pityingly Antonio says, "I am a tainted wether of the flock, / Meetest for death" (4.1.114–15),[151] and when he says that "he repents not that he pays [Bassanio's] debt" (275), he introduces the image of the merciful *Agnus Dei*,[152] though the Passover lamb was to be without spot or blemish. "Suffice," spoken twice (206, 209) by Bassanio recalls Shylock's statement twice that Antonio "is sufficient" (1.3.14–15, 23); together with "sacrifice . . . to deliver" (282–83), they echo the canon at Communion in the Prayer Book that addresses the heavenly father who, "of [his] tender mercy [did] give [his] only Son Jesus Christ, to suffer death upon the cross for our redemption; who made there . . . a full, perfect, and sufficient sacrifice . . . and satisfaction for the sins of the whole world; and did institute, and . . . command" the perpetual memorial of the Eucharist (Booty 263) that this scene and this play invoke. Portia says, "We do pray for mercy, / And that same prayer doth teach us to render / The deeds of mercy"

(196–98); of course, she refers to the Lord's Prayer: "Forgive us our debts as we forgive our debtors."[153] Mercy answers mercy. This imagery of cash is consistent with the financial metaphor that runs throughout the play.[154] All those who are willing to give and hazard mercy are invited to Belmont,[155] as the redeemed who forgive their enemies may enter heaven.

The "strict [law] court of Venice," however, must give sentence "against the merchant there" (200–201); of course, Portia means Antonio, but, except for "there," she could mean Shylock, a merchant of money, too.[156] Shylock is given chance upon chance to elect a right act. His answer, "My deeds upon my head" (202), alludes to biblical passages from both testaments. The two spies promise Rahab that, after the invasion, her family will be protected, else their "blood shall be on our head" (Jos. 2:19 BB). Shylock associates himself, thereby, with the violation of a vow and with the consequent spilling of blood. He also echoes those at the crucifixion who answer Pilate, "His blood be on us, and on our children" (Matt. 27:25 BB); Shylock thus is here identified with the slaughter of a man all know to be innocent, whose blood theology teaches to be saving. With his forced entrance into the baptismal waters, that same blood will be on Shylock's head. That it will be salvific depends upon another choice—to believe or not—which Shylock must make. Shylock's allusion to Barabbas (292),[157] like Adam a thief and a murderer,[158] alludes also to the crucifixion (296).

Paradoxically, by taking upon himself all the sins of Adam, Christ, the Last Adam, who is a Jew, frees Barabbas and all his tribe from the consequences of murder and theft. Lacking sufficient faith, Bassanio asks the Duke to "wrest once the law . . . / To do a great right," to "curb this cruel devil" (211–13). The devil and Shylock both, one at Calvary and the other at Venice, must be allowed the law; in neither case may it be bent. The effects of the law, however, will in neither case be what either expected or wanted.[159] Bassanio asks for an easy way out that does not allow hazard and venture to have their consequences, Bassanio having learned only part of his lesson at Belmont; but "no power in Venice / Can alter a decree established"—"it cannot be" (214–18). For these words Shylock nominates Portia "a Daniel," a "wise young judge,"[160] an "excellent young man," an "upright judge" (219, 220, 242, 246). The dramatic irony here quite shatters Shylock; for Portia turns out to be, as Gratiano using typological language says, "A second Daniel." In the book of Susanna, Daniel confounded Susanna's accusers who are older Jewish men ("thus the innocent blood was saved the same day" [verse 62]) by upholding the law, as Portia,[161] an analogue of Christ, does Antonio's adversary.[162]

With "tarry a little" (301), Portia begins a steady destruction of the claims of righteousness under the laws of Venice which are analogous of the moral law against which Shylock has set himself.[163] She draws Shylock "deeper into self-condemnation . . . [and] wind[s] the comic springs . . . tight" (Jensen 38). Portia makes the law his "schoolmaster" (Gal. 3:24 BB);[164] for by only one "jot" of Antonio's blood, Shylock loses his lands and goods to the state. "Realistic" criticism will see Portia's victory as merely a trick;[165] but here Shakespeare alludes to Christ's teaching that "one jot . . . of the law shall not scape, till all be fulfilled" (Matt. 5:18 BB) as it is in the Passion. "The Jew," the Old Man, "shall have all justice," shall have "merely justice"; and Shylock, an "alien . . . [who] seek[s] the life of [a] citizen," puts his life at the mercy of the Duke (345–47). Therefore, "the law hath yet another hold on" him (343); yet "the spirit of the law latent in its letter"—against which all offend—finally "yield[s] mercy through rigor" (Danson 63).[166] Once the gentiles were "aliens from the commonwealth of Israel, and were strangers from the covenants of promise"; but Christ "abrogat[ed] through his flesh . . . the Law of Commandments[, . . . making] . . . one new man" in himself so that the gentiles were "no more strangers and foreigners; but [became] . . . citizens . . . of the household of God" (Eph. 2:12, 15, 19 GB). This conversion is effected by baptism[167] that "crucif[ies] the old man" and by which the "new man [is] raised up" (Baptismal office, Booty 275, 274); but to be renewed by the potion of enchanted herbs, "old Aeson" must first have his throat cut. He is a classical prefigurement of the sacramental powers of baptism from that book of transformations, the *Metamorphoses*.

Portia, in asking Shylock to provide surgeons for Antonio, asks him to do "charity" (257). In earlier literature, charity is disinterested love (271, 273), the mode by which God loves man and by which he asks man to love him and other men. The Prayer Book links St. Paul's teachings about charity (1 Cor. 13) with the gospel story of the healing of blind Bartimaeus,[168] thereby defining proper sight as charity. By charity one learns to see more than merely "in part"; by it a mortal may learn to see, not "through a glass darkly, . . . but . . . face to face." By charity one may learn to "know [God] even as [one is] known [by him]" (1 Cor. 13:12 GB). Morocco had a blind skull rather than this sight.

Theosis, begun in baptism, continues by, among other means, the practice of charity that Shylock "cannot find . . . ; 'tis not in the bond" (258).[169] Though he is still wedded to "thrift" and "hatred," he can observe charity in Antonio's willingness to die for Bassanio; and he can learn by having to bend "down . . . and beg mercy of the Duke" (359) who, like God, preveniently pardons before he asks.[170] A stony heart is not easily broken, nor turned to flesh; and Shylock is still not "content" (390), not content with the gift of his life nor with the payment of a mere fine rather than one-half of his estate, should he find "humbleness" (368). Antonio discovers unexpectedly, however, that he has in him a further mercy for Shylock; this mercy brings Shylock, on pain of baptism, to be able to say, "I am content."[171] A dozen lines earlier, Shakespeare gives Antonio the forgiving grace to say, "I am content";

thereby the two antagonists are newly "bound" together by the stylistic repetition, as Portia and Shylock are bound earlier in a chiasmus. Shylock receives the same mercy that the other gives;[172] and their opposition is transcended, the same "mercy bless[ing] him that gives and him that takes." Shylock's bonding to the two characters emblematic of Christ figuratively binds Shylock to Christ and must surely inform how one is to understand Shylock's "content."[173]

The symmetries of the play point toward Shylock's conversion.[174] Shylock has spent the play pursuing the mortal life of Antonio; with the reversal, as Nevill Coghill shows, Antonio offers the "old Jew" the chance of eternal life, to be a "new Jew," Antonio's "own best jewel" (220). Kirschbaum says that as "the Jew wished to kill the goodness which is Antonio, so Antonio wishes to kill the Old Adam which is Shylock" (30).[175] Shylock's conversion is just as real as Jessica's, Irving Ribner maintains; Shylock's punishment is "his reception into the Christian community" (48).[176] The "deed of gift" (390) balances the "merry bond" (1.3.169) that "nooses" (Bradbrook 175) Shylock. This metamorphosis is the thing that by nature alone Shylock cannot have, the union with divinity that gives the hope of Christian eternity. Walter F. Eggers, Jr., points to another symmetry: at the beginning of the play love is based on likeness, the congruence between oneself and one's friend; and Eggers defines the progress of the play as a "transforming of the law of likeness." In the "conversion of Shylock and the marriage of Jessica" unlike characters enter "a complex and difficult kind of love which affirms their essential human likeness" (327–28):[177] in amorous love, male and female; in divine love, of which amorous love is emblematic,[178] creature and Creator. Finally, Danson defines the baptism as the completion of Shakespeare's emblem and typology of the "Old Man," or old Jew. He cites St. Paul's teaching about conversion of the Jews into the New Adam: "if the fall of [the Jews] be the riches of the world, and the diminishing of them the riches of the Gentiles, how much more shall their abundance be? For if the casting away of them be the reconciling of the world, what shall the receiving be but life from the dead?" (Rom. 11:12–15 GB). The restoration of God's ancient Chosen People before the Apocalypse is requisite to fulfillment of the Christian dispensation (164–68).[179] Thus can Marty Roth define the conversion as "the center of the play, and a direct response to Portia's plea for mercy." Roth asks, "How else can we understand the rapid and apparently incoherent sequence that includes Portia's plea, a triple defeat (when any one would have been adequate), and the destruction of the Jew?" In the play, "Christ as mercy and grace has long sat beside the throne in heaven"; but Shylock "stands outside this dispensation, testifying to its incompleteness." The justice "of Christianity is in effect being defined for the first time" as art is a "recurrently definitive gesture, a perpetually renewed 'in the beginning'" (152).

To the fashions peculiar to our era baptism is not an attractive comic resolution—but as Shakespeare does not give us Shylock's mind when at the
last he approaches the baptistry, one does not know that, indeed, it was
merely enforced. Moreover, one must see the resolution in the tradition that
Bradbrook (173) and Coghill (215) assure us was the heritage of sixteen centuries, accepted by Shakespeare and his age as commonplace; the emblematic mode of perception and its typologies are part of this lineage. If one tries
to wrench the play free from the heritage and its analogic way of seeing
experience, one can end with only a distorted and disjointed play and with
interpretations that cannot hope to be coherent.[180] Either this, or Shakespeare
is a dramatist for the Theatre of the Absurd.

Shylock never obliges by saying what others may wish to hear—"I am
not obliged to please thee with my answers" (65); moreover, Shylock could
have chosen a satisfactory but more evasive word had he cared to do so.[181] All
the illusions in which he has trusted have been wholly taken from him. His
world is in collapse.[182] He is "not well."[183] He wearily asks to go home, to
have the deed sent to him. There he will sign it. He has "been forced outside
himself for the first time, reduced to the state of nothing from which all
redemption springs. . . . Portia has put him through the ritual of self-abnegation and surrender that precedes all enlightenment, and his response is at
once bitter and affirmative" (Allman 148). Because he is obliged to begin
again, perhaps, he is, in fact, "content."[184] As other characters in Shakespeare
make a more rapid turnaround than this (Edmund, Laertes, Duke Frederick,
Oliver, for example), one need not be unduly skeptical about Shylock's "conversion." Financial deliverance here is dependent on theological deliverance,[185] of which it is a metaphor throughout the play.

If Antonio is an imperfect analogue of Christ, Shylock is, perhaps, an
analogue of Judas, as Gratiano's "hang thyself," "hanged," "halter" and "gallows" (360, 363, 375, 396) suggest. (Anyone who objects to Gratiano's
raillery might think how bland this patch of the action would be without
it.[186]) But despite Gratiano, Shylock comes not to the gallows but to the font
for "christ'ning." This word means "made into Christ" (cf. *whitening,*
enlightening, and the like), deified or, rather, anointed into the Anointed One,
which the word *Christ* means. The image is of union, like that of husband and
wife. In the word "christ'ning" Shakespeare catches up the themes of venturing upon the waters, of new clothing, of new masters, of the old giving way
to the new. Death gives way to life, justice to mercy, hatred to charity. In
despair, Judas hanged himself; content, Shylock does not. With baptism,
Shylock is invited to the condition of which Belmont is analogue.[187] With
death by water the old may become new, thrift may become hazard, justice
may become mercy, and hatred may become love. If they do, then Shylock
has entered the comic rhythm of the play; and his less may be taken up into a
greater. He will have been joined to Portia and Antonio by something more

ontological than rhetoric. One cannot know if theosis has begun for him, but at the least, one may hope, his imbruting of himself is over.

As yet, however, Bassanio has not fully entered this rhythm. He chose it in his casket scene, but there only began his willingness to risk and hazard. In the trial scene, he offers to sacrifice self, wife, and world to "deliver" (280–83) Antonio. The trial scene cannot end until Bassanio's gold and silver have been "seven times tried," until he does give self, wife, and world away with the ring. Shylock has stood for justice and law, and Portia has stood for sacrifice; Antonio (and Bassanio) now "stand indebted . . . in love and service" to Portia (409–410). Salvation may not be paid for and does not ask for payment; and Portia is "well satisfied" and "well paid" in "delivering" (411, 413) Antonio. As a token "for [Bassanio's] love," however, she will have only the ring which Bassanio "in love shall not deny" her (425–26). He unknowingly has drawn himself into the redeeming pattern of hazarding that he cannot now avoid.[188] To follow his "wife's commandment," the "vow" (447, 438) that she required of him, not to hazard the ring would mean, by the values of the play, moral death for Bassanio (Bryant 45–46). In giving the ring, he follows not the law of "commandment," but the necessity of love, "beset with . . . courtesy" (5.1.217). A new Bassanio understands honor and gratitude as an earlier one may not have.

To Antonio he is "infinitely bound" (5.1.135); Portia confirms Bassanio's obligation twice by the word *bound*. The bond of love is more inescapable than the fleshly bond of the law. Earlier, Portia has confessed a circular bond: Bassanio, her lover, is the "bosom lover" of Antonio, who "must needs be like" Bassanio; therefore, Antonio is "the semblance of [her own] soul" (3.4.17–20). Bassanio is the image and likeness of the two characters who are analogues of Christ. Bradbrook contrasts the gold of this circle of love, "the gold of Belmont," with the gold of Shylock's usury to which Portia and Antonio are "superbly indifferent," and with the gold that Bassanio rejected in his casket scene and that which the "unthrift Lorenzo acquires in so light-fingered a fashion" (177–78). The alchemy of giving and hazarding all has metamorphosed lead into tried gold that does not merely glister and that does not gild tombs.[189] The "hoop of gold" and the "infini[ty]" of Bassanio's debt to Balthazar are metaphors of the eternity of this ring of charity, of the taking of the less into the greater, of theosis.

VI. Conclusion: Belmont at the End

In the commonwealth of mercy, in Belmont, consequences of acts are very often other than what one may fear; antinomies "resolve themselves in a more comprehensive whole" (Danson 21)[190] or, rather, as the Pythagoreans might have said, transcend themselves in the mind of God. Bassanio gave the ring to a man who was male only in appearance.[191] The ring though given away has only in appearance been given away. The quarrel that follows is only mock, as that between Troilus and Cressid is real. Bassanio's reasons for giving the ring away would have been approved by Portia, as indeed they are.[192] Bassanio recognizes that he, like Shylock, requires pardon and asks it; but pardon here requires the intercession of Antonio, who binds this time his "soul upon the forfeit"(253)—a much more "reckless" bond (Bradbrook 177). Bassanio cannot achieve Portia on his own merits.[193] The trial at Venice was real and the stakes deadly; the trial at Belmont is a jest[194] and the stakes comic. If one must draw a contrast between Venice and Belmont, one may speak of those who live only in Venice and those who live in Venice and also in the world-to-come, in Belmont.

By the mysterious workings of the comic order, Gratiano is "amaz'd" (266) and Antonio rendered "dumb" (278) by the "strange accident" (278) revealing that "three of [his] argosies / Are richly come to harbor suddenly" (276–77)—unexpectedly, like the resolution of the trial in Venice, or the trial of Job. The metaphor of proper life as venturing at sea comes to its conclusion. Portia gives "life and living" (286) to Antonio as she did to Shylock.[195] The rings, the rich argosies, the "special deed of gift" (292): all are "manna" that Portia "drop[s] in the way / Of starvèd people" (294–95). Manna, the food divinely provided for the old Israel in the wilderness, is an ancient type of the nourishment of the new Israel in its own wilderness of this world, the communion, itself a type of the marriage supper of the Lamb. Earlier in the scene, the "patens" (59) on the floor of heaven, perhaps, suggest the "celebration [of] a cosmic Eucharist" (Dobbins 118); here manna is appropriate to earthly nuptial festivity. Much earlier in the play, Launcelot, asked "Whither goest thou?" replies, "Marry, sir, to bid my old master the Jew to sup to-night with my new master the Christian" (2.4.16–18). We have shown the references in act 4 to the crucifixion; Gary R. Grund has found a number of allusions following hard on these and completing them in act 5. They invoke formulas in the Easter liturgy and scriptural passages, with their themes and types of passover and redemption, embedded in that rite. The allusions are manifest and persuade of Shakespeare's intent that one see the joy in act 5 as emblematic of Christ's comic resurrection victory (155–62) and of the eon breaking into time.[196]

Reluctantly, Bassanio has acted with some kind of faith that he will not lose Portia and, with her, all. He has now permanently returned to Belmont where Jessica and Lorenzo have preceded him, having already entered upon the saving rhythm. The hellish hatred of the trial scene gives way to the "joys of heaven . . . on earth" (3.5.70), with the union of "the fleshly and the golden ring" (Danson 195) at Belmont.[197] There the less continues its slow ascent into the greater: with the emblem's entering the Reality; with mystery that has teased the play from its first line about Antonio's melancholy and that always teases emblem and analogy; with Portia returning "before the break of day"

(29), with light's replacing darkness; with the dawn of a new beginning. The consummation of the marriages makes them legally and canonically valid. Yet all these glories are attenuated by the muddy vesture of decay.

An emblem, participating as it does in two realities, is a mystery, as is a mortal suffering deification, as is a comedy displaying this alchemy analogically. Of course, such a play will elude the talents of anyone who has only reason by which to interpret its node of mysteries. Though much about *The Merchant of Venice* exceeds discursive wit, we have offered evidence of Shakespeare's interest in emblem and in the transforming of mortal lead into Belmont gold. We have educed a structure of figures and themes that embody Shakespeare's thought in *The Merchant of Venice*, and we have shown how it inheres in character and in contour of plot. Perhaps by suggesting how the several elements of the play cohere, we may have lessened some of the problems that it raises with recent audiences and critics. We cannot, however, regret that Shakespeare's art goes very much beyond our ability to pluck out its mystery and that its mischievous wit remains despite our best effort to defeat it. Bassanio's praise of the portrait limps behind the demi-god's portrait that limps behind Portia who limps behind her Creator. Into the mirror that Shakespeare holds up to nature our optics see but darkly.[198]

Notes

1. *OED*: "costly," "lavish," "rich."
2. For the emblematic way the Elizabethans viewed the world, see Lomax 34.
3. "Both the emblem and the 'conceit' proceed from the wit, the faculty which discerns analogies, and shows itself the more witty as the things analogized are the more separate one from the other. . . . [The] wit . . . may be an instrument of vision. With its discovery of occult couplings, it perhaps penetrates to the center of the universe, where, however dissimilar they appear to the unobservant, all things unite. . . . The wonder which poetry must produce may be not at the wit of its author but at the wit of God, at the fearful and wonderful nature of His creation" (75–76).
4. Judith Dundas distinguishes between a proper device in an "emblem" book and Shakespeare's "emblematic use of imagery" that she describes as "interpreting experience symbolically. . . . things are both themselves and something else." She confesses herself to have no quarrel with the looser meaning that we allow the term *emblem* (47, 55).
5. In "The Crosse," Donne sees emblems of the cross in, among other things, the mast of a ship, in the spread wings of flying birds, in a man who swims, in the network of parallels crossing meridians that holds the earth in a web. Though Duke Senior speaks of "tongues in trees, books in running brooks, / Sermons in stones, and good in every thing" (2.1.16–17), Shakespeare is more inclined to see emblem in the shape, rhythm, and contour of an action or a plot.
6. Elam (143) citing Ernst Gombrich, who alludes to Rom. 1:19–20.

7. "The more definitively partial and selective one's focus is, the less one is likely to see how that part fits into the whole of the play." The chief "deterrent for seeing Shakespeare's overall unity in the play" comes from a "tendency to overemphasise the idea of opposition . . . , whether of plots, settings, ideological dilemmas, or the relationships of characters" (Holmer, *The Merchant* 43, 44).

8. Regarding speculation, productions must not "encourage the audience to assume that the play is closer to realism than to fantasy and to ask the wrong sort of question"; " 'real life' is not the same as drama" (Muir 59). Almost the whole of Anthony Brennan's piece on *Merchant* is hardly more than a congeries of speculation about character without reference to the texture of metaphor in the play (225–45). Yet "Shakespeare's characters frequently manifest the desire to be recognized as something more than they 'seem,' that is, to belie the visible and audible evidence of their presence onstage by suggesting it does not and cannot adequately represent what they are." At its "most powerful drama does not explain too thoroughly; it preserves something of the mystery of human motive and action" (Weller 342, 343).

9. Richard Levin allows that proper "understanding of the characters comes only by appreciating the social context in which they function" (*Love* 32).

10. "Shakespeare sacrificed plausibility, as a romantic and poetic dramatist is bound to do, for the sake of other things." Shakespeare blends "two improbable" tales to "illuminate a number of eternal problems by attaching them to archetypal myths" (Muir 63, 67). David Willbern's intention is "to free the language of the play from its illusory anchors in characters, like prying loose barnacles, so that words can dance and take flight" (10). The Reformation, which took against imagery in liturgy, was "seeking at least in part to do away with wonder"; its efforts "have an obvious bearing on literary interpretation and production" (Platt xiii).

11. Launcelot derives from "the Vice tradition" (Wiles 7). "Even though the critic who prizes irony, subtlety, and realism finds little merit in the late moral drama, these plays did bequeath to the age of Shakespeare solution to various problems" (Dessen 160; see also, 137, 139, 144). See Holmer, *The Merchant*, 6–7.

12. To the epistemological changes that occurred during the seventeenth century, Camille Wells Slights adds the "post-enlightenment separation of moral sentiment from intellect with consequent aversion to intricate moral reasoning" (143).

13. The decline in "the allegorical approach to Shakespeare" is "largely the result of a change in critical fashions rather than of any convincing refutation of the approach" (Levin, "Relation" 1).

14. Shylock is "that cruel, repressive father, which it is the business of comedians from Aristophanes to Ionesco to deceive and to laugh at and to put to scorn" (Holland 91). "No critical card tricks, no juggling of lines" can cloud that Shylock "is a greedy usurer who dreams of money bags and is implacable in his demands for Antonio's pound of flesh," a cantankerous old man who "hates music and parties and speaks to his daughter only to issue orders" (Bronstein 4).

15. Arden, Appendix II, 153–56.; Intro xxxii.

16. The Bishops' Bible (1568). As Shakespeare knew both the Bishops' Bible and the Geneva Bible (1560), cited as GB, we shall make use of each as may be most convenient; once or twice we quote from the Douay-Rheims New Testament (1582), cited as D-R. Six times " 'old' man" refers to Shylock (Holmer, *The Merchant* 193).

17. Shylock is not "meant to be a realistic portrayal of a Jew" (Wertheim 75). "The 'tough' critics are correct in holding that Shylock was malevolent from the beginning" (Tillyard, *Shakespeare's* 191).

18. Shakespeare relies on "the great biblical principle by which the old creation both points toward and rejects the new, while the new both abolishes and fulfills the old," as "nature is perfected by grace." The "dialectic relation" is between "dispensations of saving truth—between the two Testaments and, similarly, between the 'world' as a temporal process and the 'world' to come." "Lesser glories will vanish, but not as things condemned"; their purpose "is described by the metaphor of the 'substitute,' . . . . Like 'types and shadows' passing into the full light of truth with the coming of Christ, the *fabula vitae* is ultimately to be interpreted by love." Portia calls the night just at the coming of dawn as like "the daylight sick . . . a little paler, . . . as . . . day is when the sun is hid"; "it is as though nature itself were about to repeat the symbolism of opening the pale casket to reveal the bright image it secretly promised" (Coolidge 260–61, 263, 261).

19. The Jesse tree, showing the descent of Christ from David's father, Jesse, printed at the beginning of the Bishops' Bible defines "the 'root' of the Christian faith in the faith of Israel. . . . Therefore, Christians honored the role of Israel in biblical salvation history and claimed the ancient patriarchs and prophets as their own" (Holmer, *The Merchant* 15).

20. Danson cites Romans 2.28–29 where St. Paul distinguishes between the one who is only outwardly a Jew because he lacks righteousness, and a righteous man who, lacking circumcision, is yet a Jew inwardly (32). Danson sees clearly that "the play's parabolic aspect does not depend upon a simple polarity of good Christians versus bad Jews" (111).

21. John Gross overlooks this complicated theology when he writes that by tradition "all Jews . . . bore responsibility for the original rejection of Christ's message, and for the Crucifixion" (15). Even Christ's mother?

22. John Cassian reads *Jerusalem* according to fourfold allegory: the city of the Jews, the city of Christ, the city of God, and the human soul (14.8.4). St. Augustine speaks of the "truer Israel of God . . . , the elect from both the Jews and Gentiles" (*Fathers of the Church,* 20, 253). Theodoret of Cyr defines "*All Israel*" as "all those who believe" (*Patrologia Gracae* 82, col 180).

23. Not Shakespeare but his characters endorse such prejudice; he "understands those prejudices fully for what they are." Shylock's willingness "to transgress Jewish dietary laws, the Duke's public appeal for Shylock to live up to Jewish teaching concerning mercy, Portia's understanding of the Lord's Prayer as a Jewish prayer" will not allow one to see the play as "anti-Jewish" (Yaffe 46, 20). Moreover, if Antonio hates the " 'sacred nation' " of the Jews, one never finds evidence of it for any other Jew than Shylock (Holmer, *The Merchant* 61).

Raphaële Costa de Beauregard argues well that Jew and Christian are not necessary antinomies in the play but that greed and pride stand opposite charity and humility and comprise the dialectic of the play (6). Readers and viewers know that "the conflict between Christian and Jew" is not "at the heart of the play"; rather "release from evil bondage to the fullness of life through the power of love" is. The play, "like all comedy, and like the divine comedy of the Christian story itself, is about the salvation of love," about "that felt reference to the larger harmony and that larger love story, once one of the great commonplaces of our civilization."

That Shylock is "held in bondage to money and hatred is more important than his Jewishness," which is an "accident of a particular time and place. . . . Shakespeare expected his audience to associate Judaism, Puritanism, and usury" (Sisk 217, 221, 223).

24. Wither draws his pelican from Psalm 102:6, a messianic psalm, BB and GB.

25. Chew (35–48), Gollancz (27, 40, 50), Coghill (217), and Danson (14, 37, 61, 69) demonstrate persuasively Shakespeare's connection with the emblematic and analogic mode of thinking and writing which characterized Christian European thought for many centuries. Kirschbaum mentions Shakespeare's connection with "the methodology of earlier English drama" and its mixture of "realism *and* the symbolical." The play is a fantasy, "but . . . at bottom, a serious fantasy" (3, 7).

26. "The connections between allegory and religious ideology in the play seem deeply entangled also with a pervasive allusiveness to the Bible" (Grant 191). Richard Halpern observes that, while "it is, of course, Christian readers who have tended to interpret *Merchant* allegorically," the first one to do so seems to have been Sir Israel Gollancz before the Jewish Historical Society in 1916 (219).

27. Sewell (44), Coghill (217), Bradbrook (172) have defined the action of the play as a movement from one kind of law, often designated the Old Law, to another kind, often designated the New Law; we would, however, say that this definition stops too short and needs to go on to the transformation of the "old man" into the "new man." Failure to understand the teachings of theosis or deification causes Gary R. Grund's brilliant essay to go a little out of focus. He argues that those who see "an extended emblem of the Redemption," as an "allegory of salvation . . . symbolically re-enacted in the play," do not account for the continual exposing of "the ironies of the situation," for the fragility of a Christian's virtue, for the sad lapses of every Christian (153). If the play has allegorical intent, that intent points not to a once-and-for-all change in a person's behavior but to a slow and fault-ridden growth into divinity, only accomplished finally on the other side of the grave. The maturation and eventual fullness provide the "hope" and "the comic spirit at the end of the play" (163), not the perfection of virtue on earth for which Grund seems to wish. Turning Venetian lead into Belmont gold, the bringing of the less into the greater, is a very slow process indeed.

28. Appointed by the Prayer Book to be read at matins on designated feasts (Booty 66).

29. "God-like amity" Lorenzo calls it in another context (3.4.3). "As mercy is a
     reflection of the love of God for man," this theme "is woven into the stories
     of the wooing of Portia and the elopement of Jessica." The highest image of
     God's love in human love "is the kind of love reflected in Antonio's sacrifice
     for his friend, of Bassanio's willingness to . . . hazard all, and of Jessica's
     readiness to leave her father and his gold for Christian salvation" (Ribner
     47). Patrick Grant places the mercy "concealed at the centre, in the secret
     heart of things where overarching transcendence and vulnerable interiority
     are presented as mysteriously at one" (204).

30. BB and GB have "godly nature"; the Authorized Version (1611; cited here-
     after as AV) picks up D-R's "divine nature." Weller points to St. Paul's
     teaching in the Epistle to the Ephesians (5:30 GB): "For we are members of
     [Christ's] body, of his flesh and of his bones" and to the gloss on it in the
     Geneva Bible: we "are not only joined to him by nature, but also by the com-
     munion of substance, through the holy Ghost and by faith: the seal and tes-
     timony thereof is the Supper of the Lord" (346). Mercy, however, is a vital
     part of Shylock's own religion. If the opening lines of Portia's "mercy"
     speech "have a single source, it is . . . from Ben Sira, the Jewish sage" cred-
     ited with Ecclesiasticus (Gross 81).

31. The "one flesh," Parker continues, of the marriages points toward "the mys-
     terious joining of the Incarnation as the definitive 'Copula' (which Nicolas
     Udall calls 'The wonderful copulation of the sayd nature unto ours')." But
     this union of two natures also involves "a breaking down . . . through the
     Cross"; for he who "is our peace, who hath made both one, . . . hath broken
     down the middle wall of partition between us" in order "to make in himself
     of twain one new man" (Eph. 2:14–15). "Breaking down the wall of parti-
     tion" between "citizen Jew and 'alien' Gentile' " is like the "rending of the
     veil of the temple . . . a radical crossing or abolition of boundaries; and both
     link the Crucifixion to the analogy it figures, the final apocalyptic" removal
     of every wall (38–39).

32. The balance at the end of the play is "neither perfect justice nor perfect love.
     Still, it is enough to content the imperfect characters in their quotidian lives.
     They have intimations of celestial harmony, but" cannot hear it (Slights
     148).

33. "As he does so frequently in his comedies, Shakespeare has his clown act
     out a foolish and inverted pattern of the more serious and central tensions of
     the play" (Colley 187).

34. Levin sees Launcelot as only a nasty little "touchstone" by which to inter-
     pret the nefarious journeys undertaken by other characters; but Levin's grim
     account of Launcelot and his shameful carryings-on robs the very funny
     scene of any laughter at all (*Love* 32–33). Michael W. Shurgot is much
     closer to the point: the scene is a "microcosm [of] one of the play's major
     themes: the limits and imperfections of human charity." Old Gobbo intends
     to give a dish of doves "to the man whom all the other Gentiles in the play
     consider their enemy." The dove is a traditional emblem of peace; and "one
     senses in Gobbo's giving at least the spirit of Christian tolerance and recon-
     ciliation," of Christ's command to love one's enemies (139–40).

35. The *psychomachia* in this little room of 1609 enjoyed an earlier version in *The Passionate Pilgrim*, published in its second edition in 1599; the sonnet is, therefore, contemporary with our play.

36. "This wonderfully resonant malapropism" alludes to "a very different Jew from Shylock, and to a vastly different vision of Jewishness from the one Launcelot entertains" (Douglas Anderson 120).

37. The play in which it appears next most frequently is *All's Well*, with seven instances.

38. Deut. 30:19 BB. The "beauty and pertinence" of this text "assert themselves . . . again and again in Shakespeare's works where the choice is between life and death, good and evil." It becomes "a central feature of Shakespeare's . . . imagination" (Douglas Anderson 122). See Ecclesiasticus 15:16–17: "He hath set water and fire before thee, reach out thine hand unto which thou wilt. Before man is life and death, good and evil." Shakespeare "intended the caskets to represent the great choices of spiritual life and death" (Lewalski 336).

39. Q_2 (1619) regularizes *Iobbe* to *Gobbo* as it appears later in the scene; F does not follow Q_2's suggestion. *Iobbe* is a frequent sixteenth-century alternative to *Iob*. See, for example, the Marprelate tracts and the answers by Nashe and Lyly.

40. "Jessica's elopement . . . is a Venetian . . . correlative of the Belmontian casket test" (Holmer, *The Merchant* 122).

41. To "Abram" at 1.2.168, 155. To Jacob at 1.3.68, 73, 76, 2.5.32. "Shakespeare is highly conversant with Genesis"; on all other occasions Shakespeare uses the name *Abraham* (Nathan, *Notes* 127). Shakespeare's use of the old names must be deliberate.

42. As the play does Gratiano at 4.1.331: "A second Daniel."

43. Christ made the "transition from the Old Testament" of the "Jewish dispensation" to the "New Testament," the "Christian dispensation"; Launcelot's venture figures Christ's (Holland 107).

44. "The son is metamorphosed from the Launcelot 'that was' to the 'son that is'" (Homan 162).

45. "This satisfying reconciliation" of Launcelot and Old Gobbo is a "pattern . . . [that] enable[s] us to recognize the movement, however tentative and aborted, that Antonio and Shylock make" (Rosenheim 201).

46. See, for example, 2.2.29, 34, 43, 45, 50, 53, 64; 2.5.19; 2.9.87; 3.2.55; 3.5.63; 4.1.144, 153, 244; 5.1.18, 62.

47. See Holmer, *The Merchant* 151. *Feast* "quite natural[ly]" carries a "religious sense . . . in the Bible and in ecclesiastical calendars," referring to the Eucharist; but Bassanio's " 'feasting' will degenerate to [Shylock's] 'feeding' " (2.5.14–15). This eating is a "black parody" of the feasting in the Eucharist (205).

48. Jessica "escape[s] from what are finally inhuman attitudes" (Traversi 192).

49. "The musical metaphor tells us about Antonio, too. Antonio's melancholy shows that he is out of tune" (Danson 33).

50. 1.1.80 ff, 83; 1.2.17 ff.; 1.3.164, 166, 169; 4.2.8, among other passages. Shylock's refusal of these pleasures is the "utter rejection of those Christian

values" of friendship, love, hazarding, charity (Kirschbaum 20); see also Weiss (130) and Ferber (464).

51. The metaphor of seeing, of eyes, sight, blindness, occurs repeatedly in the play: 2.1.36; 2.2.32, 69 ff.; 2.5.1; 2.6.36, 54; 2.7.63; 2.9.26; 3.1.51; 3.2. 67; 3.2.123, 142, 147; 3.6.58; 5.1.113, 242.

52. The biblical importance of the theme of inheritance appears from the frequency of its occurrence, as a concordance will show. The "issue of inheritance and conveyance of the patriarchal blessing" is "basic to [the] play." Abraham's holiness and faith contrast with Shylock's guile and "reliance on himself" (Holmer, *The Merchant* 158–59).

53. This locution occurs also near the end of Lauds in the old Roman Breviary. "The story of the original passing of the birthright and blessing to the younger brother prefigures the coming of Christ and the emergence of the new Church as a replacement for the Old Law and the old religion" (Colley 186). Jacob's stealing the inheritance "foreshadow[s] . . . the way the Jews, who were the older chosen people, would lose their birthright, the blessing of God, to the younger order of Christians" (Holland 107).

54. Rachel stole the images that were her father Laban's when Jacob left Laban (MacCary 166).

55. Egypt is a figure of this sinful world; and of man's state by nature: "the tyranny and captivity of Satan and this sinful world, whereof the captivity of Egypt under Pharaoh was a figure" (Bradford 149). See also, Nowell 121. If Shylock's house is a "hell," then Jessica has spoiled it with sufficient Jewish precedent.

56. The Duke in *Measure for Measure* quotes almost directly from the account of the Harrowing in 1 Pet. 3.19: "I come to visit the afflicted spirits / Here in prison" (2.3.4–5).

57. Old Gobbo's "dish of doves" intended for Shylock reminds of the doves that figure "prominently . . . in pictorial representations of the Presentation in the Temple"; they also recall "the doves that Noah sent forth from the Ark (Genesis 8:8–12)." They therefore are both a reminder of God's original covenant with the Jews and a symbol of the "transfer of that covenant to the Christians"; the "gift intended for Shylock is given to Bassanio instead" (McLean 50).

58. And is transferred back to Portia (3.2.148) and back to Bassanio (3.2.171). Portia uses the word "master" to describe what she was to herself and what was hers before Bassanio won her; then she uses the word "lord," or "new master" to describe Bassanio.

59. Although "Shylock cannot recognize in [Jessica] any difference from himself" (Allman 140), Kirschbaum says of the Christians that their virtues can so "translate the individual that racial distinctions disappear" (19). Theodore Weiss sees love in this comedy as effecting a "maturing and realizing; it releases the best in man." Before Bassanio confronts the caskets, he is already "educated by his lighthearted life, his friendship with Antonio, and most of all his love for Portia." He already knows not to "put his . . . trust in things" (138). Indeed one might say that this life is a Venetian analogue of life at Belmont that is an analogue of the breaking in of the eon. Salerio says

that the difference between Shylock's flesh and blood and Jessica's is as the difference between "jet and ivory" (3.1.33–34). Perhaps love and mercy do redeem Shylock and transmute his fool's gold into real gold.

60. Professor Thomas L. Berger made us aware of Tubal's mischief. Although nearly everyone who writes of Jessica accepts without doubt Tubal's report, Grebanier says that Tubal is "an intimate (we cannot think of [Shylock's] having a true friend, nor does Tubal behave like one)." Tubal "play[s] on Shylock as on an instrument" (204, 208). See Gross (54–55). Moreover, if Leah's ring is greatly important to Shylock, why is he not wearing it, the wearing of rings being of much ado in the play?

61. "Shylock *uses* gold and Portia *is* gold, and *The Merchant of Venice* accommodates the former as it moves toward the latter. This movement requires, therefore, a sense of 'play'—transference, metamorphosis, conversion—with the physical, but not its denial. While one may choose to view Jessica's throwing down moneybags to the courtiers as unfilial theft, it also represents play, as well as being the prelude to the masque or play, a transference from a home where money's value is only literal–where gold is gold is gold—to a new home in Belmont where gold can be a gift of love or friendship" (Homan 162). Hazard as a kind of alchemy and Belmont as gold we discuss below. That Jessica, who is the "main escapee" from Shylock's world, takes the music of Belmont seriously argues "a deeper dimension to her" than her critics allow (Homan 169).

62. St. Paul's metaphor, "put off," "put on" (Rom. 6:6, Eph. 4:22, 24, GB; Col. 3:9, 10, BB and GB. D-R makes the metaphor clear with "stripping"); a change of clothes in Shakespeare's plays, likewise, reveals a change in character.

63. Gollancz associates Bassanio with the medieval everyman figure who in his pilgrimage on earth had to woo "Grace Dieu," a noble and beautiful lady, the daughter of divinity, the Grace of God, represented in *Merchant* by Portia (53).

64. The King's daughter in tale XV of *Gesta Romanorum* came by sea, and her ship was wrecked. She was swallowed by a whale. The story of Jonah is one of the ancient prefigurements both of baptism and of resurrection; and Shakespeare alludes specifically to it in *The Tempest*, 2.1.245: "cast" (Jon. 2:3 BB and GB); "belch" at 3.3.56 seems to allude to the great fish also.

65. Shylock objects to the risks involved in Antonio's shipping that is subject to the "peril[s] of water, wind, and rocks" (1.2.21–22), all scriptural images of the hazards of seeking salvation.

66. Portia's riches "increase in every way but they do so precisely because she gives them away." When she gives the ring back to Bassanio by way of Antonio, she "implicates Antonio in her union with Bassanio." Through giving, Bassanio comes to understand "not just Antonio's and Portia's love for him but love in general." When Lorenzo refers to Shylock's "special deed of gift" as "manna," he associates giving with "mercy, which also falls from heaven" (Sharp 254, 262, 263, 262). Danson also offers a splendid explanation of the place of giving in the ontology of the play (50–55, 189–91).

67. Usury "was condemned," among other reasons, because it "involv[ed] no risk" (Holmer, "Education" 312). Shylock cannot understand the paradoxical nature of giving and hazarding. He "does have the choice of killing Antonio" but at the price of life and property. He "decides *not* to hazard all; instead, merchant-like, he opts for a bargain" (Sharp 254, 263).

68. Shylock "is a perverter of the natural order. But characters like Shylock do not retain the upper hand indefinitely in the world of comedy" (Pearlman 223).

69. "The gayest, happiest, most blessed scene in all Shakespeare" (Wilson 115).

70. Ps. 72:10–11 GB: "The kings of Tarshish and of the Isles shall bring presents: the Kings of Sheba and Seba shall bring gifts," from the lectionary for Epiphany. The Epistle for the feast is: Gentiles shall be inheritors also of the "unsearchable riches of Christ" (Eph. 3); and the Gospel is the marriage at Cana (John 2). See also Matt. 8:11, "Many shall come from the East and West, and shall rest with Abraham, and Isaac, and Jacob, in the kingdom of heaven"; Matt. 24:31: "they shall gather together his chosen, from the four winds." *Belmont*, "beautiful mountain," recalls Mount Sion.

71. "Portia is the wisest character in the play, and her wisdom shines more brightly with each new act" (Holmer, *The Merchant* 99).

72. "The imagery of act 5 . . . seems to be derived from the Gospel of Matthew [5:14–16], which likens the New Law to a city on a hill and to a candle shining its light before men" (Fortin 270).

73. Mahood (187) cites McCombie (113–24). See, especially Wis. 9:1–4, 10; Prov. 3:13–14; 31:18. Francis Fergusson's rather stiff allegorical identification of Portia with Beatrice, who comes from "the top of Mount Purgatory" (actually, in the *Commedia*, she comes from the Celestial Rose in the *Paradiso*), and of Bassanio with Dante is much less satisfactory than McCombie's discussion of Wisdom (*Trope* 119–121).

74. Samuel C. Chew traces the long history in literature prior to Shakespeare of the discussion of Ps. 85:10 regarding the reconciling of "mercy and truth, . . . righteousness and peace," and places *Merchant* in this tradition. Portia is like Sapience; at first she seems to take Shylock's side (Justice) but then pleads for mercy. The parallels between the tradition and *Merchant* are "perhaps too close to be . . . coincidence"; Shakespeare conceived and composed a scene "effective without recourse to esoteric interpretation, yet adding overtones audible to those with ears to hear" (35–48). Gollancz (27, 39) and Coghill (215) cite this same tradition of the four daughters of God. Sir Israel traces the allegory back to an "old Midrash which passed into medieval literature" (27).

75. *"The Tempest* . . . brings to its culmination . . . the comic theme of losing oneself to find oneself." This "pattern has . . . its usual Christian reading" (Van Laan 252).

76. Deut. 10:16; 30:6; Jer. 4.4, BB; see also Rom. 2:29, Col. 2:11. See Shapiro, pp. 126–28.

77. For response to the interpretation as castration, see Pearlman 236 and Roger L. Cox 81–83.

78. "The moral education of Antonio and the attempted moral education of Shylock constitute one of the central concerns" of the play. Shakespeare introduced the enmity between Antonio and Shylock before he established the bond; "the extent to which Antonio can renounce his hatred and practice Christ's commandment 'to love one another' " will be the fruit of his faith and the sign of his redemption (Holmer, "Education" 307, 316).

79. Critics can mention Medea and Aeson and then blindly say, "Hardly a happy couple among the four" (Feldheim 96); but there are not four *couples* in the list, only three. Aeson is, of course, Medea's father-in-law. R. Chris Hassel, Jr., fails to distinguish between "past romantic figures"—Cressid, Thisbe, Dido—in this sequence, on the one hand, and, on the other hand, Medea, who is not linked here with Jason but with Jason's father (69). Austin C. Dobbins and Roy W. Battenhouse actually name "Jason and Medea" as in this list and mention Aeson not at all (117). A. P. Riemer likes to include "Jason and Medea" among "images of cruelty, treachery and death" (146); and Levin mentions "Medea and Jason" under the category of betrayers (*Love* 81). Leonard Tennenhouse contrives to confuse one father with another when he says, "On just such a night . . . Medea was in the act of betraying her father" (64). Others, too, err thus: ". . . and Jason and Medea, all ominous archetypes" (Boose 337); ". . . when Jason abandons her" (Carroll 118, 124); Weisberg (101); Yaffe (67); Belsey (197); Gross (60); alas, the sharp-sighted Grund (157); Coolidge (261).

80. Mahood (154). The comic contours of this play, ending with a situation like the renewal of old Aeson, may offer one reason for Shakespeare's comedic pleasure in this passage from Ovid. In quoting Ovid, we use Arthur Golding's 1567 translation.

81. Swinden (70). Sir James Frazer mentions all sorts and conditions of men and women, Aeson among them, that Medea restored in her pot (1, 181), though some, like Pelius, die there. Jonson's "Epitaph on S. P. a Child of Q. El Chappel" tells of the gods attempting "in bathes to steepe" the boy to give him "new birth." Jonson's first version has the gods trying to give him "new breath" and the second version, closer to Shakespeare's, involves the use of "charms" (8, 77). Ian Donaldson glosses the passage: "as Jupiter restored to life the young Pelops, and as Medea rejuvenated the aged Aeson" (70). In "To his Mistresses," Herrick puts it that "*Ason* had . . . / Baths that made him young againe" (18).

82. "Shakespeare deliberately avoids the darker" side of the Ovidian material regarding Jason (Holmer, *The Merchant* 115).

83. The harmonies of 5.1 offer a "deeper intuition glimpsed if not retained of universal fitness" (Traversi 197).

84. J. T. Sheppard argues that Shakespeare had all this in mind when he allowed Lorenzo to refer to Troilus who experienced the harmonic sounds of heaven as he moved up through the seventh and eighth spheres (134–35).

85. Normally, it is not death but sin that keeps mortals from hearing the celestial music. That the inheritance from Adam is death, not sin, is a notion of Eastern Orthodox theology.

86. The silence to human ears of the beautiful music of the cosmological order, the "unheard music," is like the paleness of lead, the silence which Nerissa says bestows "respect" and perspective; yet it connects with inner reality. It is "intimated at Belmont, where actual music is heard, . . . where the Venetian incompatibilities of gold and love" finally resolve themselves as much in the "golden music as in the golden ring" (Hollander 70, 71, 72, 73).

87. Lorenzo knows that "the whole universe is singing" and "calling for human music"; he also knows, from Orpheus, of the "intimate relationship between music and conversion." Shylock earlier shut his ears against music; "but now, the universe is renewed by his conversion" (Roth 154).

88. In act 5, the "heavens proclaim the glory of God, and the firmament showeth his handiwork." They are witnesses to that law whose seat is "in the bosom of God, and whose voice is the harmony of the world" (Zeeveld 156).

89. We explain this below. For Antonio, see 3.2.263–66, 4.1.114–15. Portia has a christological analogue in the Wisdom literature; moreover, her name means *door*. Christ says, "I am the door" (John 10.9 BB). "Portia, like Beatrice, . . . serves as a figure for Christ" (Fergusson, *Trope* 121). Gollancz agrees in "identifying Antonio with Christ," citing Eph. 5:25 ("husbands love your wives, even as Christ also loved the church, and gave himself for it") and John 15:13 ("Greater love hath no man . . .") (32, 38). Kirschbaum quotes Theodore Reik, who says, "Behind the figure of Antonio . . . is the greater one of Jesus Christ" (17). "Antonio's loving nature contrasts with Shylock's vengefulness; his self-sacrifice with Shylock's ego-centrism; his calmness with Shylock's emotional volatility . . . ; his dispassionate reasonableness with Shylock's unreasonable passion" (Hirsh 133–34). In the play, "the religious element is far from pervasive; at the same time it is unmistakable, and it manifests itself most strongly in two of the central characters, Antonio and Portia" (Gross 78).

90. "The play's close celebrates values that have been advocated throughout its unfolding and in both its major plots: giving, good judgment, life, and love" (Jensen 42).

91. The analogical condition that the Forest of Arden represents, where moral evil may not enter except it be transformed, does not admit of precise definition; nor does the "paradise" (4.1.124) of being in *The Tempest*, nor the kingdom of fairies in *A Midsummer Night's Dream*. Nor would one be judicious in trying to define very specifically the emblematic condition that Belmont suggests. On such occasions the canons of "realism" rather betray one.

92. The caskets, G. Wilson Knight maintains, "are symbolically central to the play's action. At the heart of this play is the idea of riches: false and true wealth. Jesus' parables are suggested. Venice is lost in . . . the false. Portia possesses the true. Not only is love and beauty continually in Shakespeare metaphorically a matter of riches, but Portia is vitally associated with Christianity, and is, moreover, an heiress with an infinite bank-balance" (92).

93. When Shylock invokes the story of Jacob to justify usury, Antonio asks him if his "gold and silver [are] ewes and rams?" (1.2.91). Has Shylock reduced life to death?

94. To be freed of the leprous touch, Naaman had to bathe in the River Jordan (2 Kings 5:14); this story is one of the Old Testament types of baptism.

95. *Fancy*, "originally a contraction of *fantasy*," carried the connotation of " 'illusion,' 'error' " (Wilson 100).

96. "Love is one thing" only, "giving"; "it is above all a giving of the self" (French 104).

97. His first reaction at this successful choice is praise for the beauty of the portrait, not rejoicing at the wealth that he has gained; "critics [who] . . . have called Bassanio a heartless 'fortune-hunter' . . . have failed to see the balance and judgement of the play as a whole" (Brown, *Shakespeare 72).*

98. Professor George W. Williams alerts us to Bassanio's earlier words, "I like not fair terms and a villain's mind" (1.3.175), that vouch for his choice here as licit. One cannot meditate closely upon illusion and also pay attention to faint clues and indirections, nor can one be but a fortune hunter.

99. "Wise love" as the "ideal union of knowing and doing well is symbolized by the choice of the leaden chest. The dominant dramatic symbol in the play is the casket test." In the three "chests lies the heart of the play's dramatic meaning" (Holmer, *The Merchant* 45, 95).

100. "The notion of love is projected beyond sexuality, as a force for harmony, acceptance . . . in general human life" (French 100).

101. Bassanio should be judged in terms of romantic comedy; he is a "Jason" dedicated to love's adventure and disposed to risk for it. He readily chooses "inner reality rather than the deception of outward show" (Traversi 190). Nor is Apollonius' Jason a mere fortune hunter.

102. See Danson's illuminating discussion of the identity of the three: "Portia extends [the] act of giving . . . until it includes Antonio within the circle of mutual exchange" (38, 48–49).

103. In changing the contents of the caskets in his sources from bones, earth and worms, and jewels "to 'heads'—a death's head, a fool's head, and a picture of Portia's head"—Shakespeare "illustrates the emphasis on wisdom that the scrolls make literally clear." The choice of caskets "represents a test of wisdom, proving the internal worthiness of the suitor" (Holmer, "Loving" 56, 59).

104. *The Merchant of Venice* is a "comedy of affirmation whose subject is love"; one must see the play as an "affirmation of ethical values basic to Christian belief" (Ribner 46, 47). Holmer discusses "the pervasive preoccupation in medieval-Renaissance literature with matters of love, both true and false choices." The question is not "solely aesthetic but also profoundly . . . philosophical and theological"; and it involves loving both wisely and well. In Shakespeare's plays the "blessed will be those who rightly love God and all others as God has loved them"; giving and lending freely "are ways of loving." In the play, the "rhythm of Dantean divine comedy" prevails; and those receive blessing who come to an "understanding of 'the love that moves the sun and all the stars' " (*The Merchant* 7, 9, 10, 284).

105. "In Bassanio's relation to Belmont and Venice there is a close approximation of the medieval paradigm. Bassanio, like Proteus and Bertram, is very much a prodigal son; indeed, he refers to himself as one at the outset

(1.1.129), which gives us hope of change in him. Shylock also uses the epithet 'prodigal' for Bassanio (2.5.15), and there are three other allusions in the play to Luke's archetype of waywardness [2.6.14, 17; 3.1.45]. This is a play in which fallibility is ripe for conversion" (Velz 318).

106.   "Antonio . . . is the recipient of the selfless actions to which the power of love has raised both Bassanio and Portia" (Champion 64).

107.   Danson calls the will "numinous" and argues that the "sense of the play as a whole" does not allow for Portia helping Bassanio choose. For her to do so would turn "a romantic comedy [into] a farce" (117).

108.   Bassanio has learned "the truth of platonic love, which places all surface, all materiality, at nought." The formula of risking "is an apt definition of love in the mystical sense in which an individual risks all he . . . has known or believed to seek a higher truth. Love is always a gamble. In marriage, lovers make a leap of faith, . . . risk all they have for the rest of their lives . . . for something that cannot be weighed, measured, or explained" (Dreher 131–32).

109.   "So fully Edenic is this moment that it contains the human history of paradise, its loss and its restoration" (Allman 138).

110.   Arthur Rogers has drawn our attention to Sonnet 53 in which Shakespeare brings together many of the words that Bassanio uses to open the relationships among Portia, the painting of her, and Bassanio's praise of the painting: "substance," "paint," "shadow," "counterfeit." Moreover, Bassanio begins his meditation with another word of the sonnet, "show." In both cases the poet interests himself in the likeness between a reality and the copy or image of it. The line, "And you in every blessed shape we know," appropriately states the way that a lover sees something of the beloved in every other shape that he encounters; but the line even more appropriately describes the way one may see reflected something of the Creator in each creature. The beauteous perfection of the young man is but a dim manifestation of the beauteous perfection of God. As God created man in his own image, male and female, so the young man's excellence is emblematic in the dimmer copies of him, male and female, in both Adonis and Helen. In Bassanio's praise, the Creator is implied in the words "demi-god" and "creation." In both places, Shakespeare deals in emblem and analogy. The darker connotations of "shadow," "shade," and "counterfeit" but supply the qualification that becomes necessary when the unlimited enters the realm of limitation.

111.   Neither Bassanio here nor Portia in 5.1 suggests "an endless series of 'greater glor[ies]' replacing and shading each other" so that "man does not look to Everlasting Glory"; Lorenzo's discourse on music moving hierarchically from earth to eternity renders such a perpetual sequence null. Moreover, though one may know only the "godlike 'earthly power' " of mercy as "an *attribute* to God," rather than God himself (surely unknowable as Christian theology teaches), such ignorance does not, therefore, negate the existence of God as the source of the mercy that Portia asserts. To think that Portia can "seek, prophetically the perfect balance of . . . human attributes in the society of Belmont" (Oz 190) is surely utopian.

112. *OED*: "represented by a picture or image"; "made in imitation of that which is genuine"; "made to a pattern"; "a false or spurious imitation."

113. Anthony J. Lewis rather misses the point when he thinks Bassanio "confuses the golden fleece with the false locks of 'supposed fairness' " and thinks Portia's "beauty turns men into trapped insects" (44). The deadly confusion of the emblem with the Reality takes the creation for the Creator. David Sundelson errs in a like manner (84,86) and Homan (165). Richard Halpern's reading of Bassanio's not-so-complex thought embodied in this nexus of metaphors is really quite bizarre (199–200). See Normand (63).

114. "Portia searches out every jot and tittle [of the law], not in order to wrest or overthrow the law but to fulfill it; and the paradoxical result . . . is to reveal the spirit of the law inherent in its letter, its mercy in its constraints" (Danson 56).

115. "The fundamental purpose of this 'love test' is to prove the inner worthiness of a spouse in a choice between 'good and evil,' spiritual 'life and death' " (Holmer, *The Merchant* 96).

116. Bradbrook recognizes that to ignore the moral significance of the choice of caskets is to ignore "the main counter balance to Shylock" (177).

117. Morocco and Arragon are "analogues" for Shylock (Holmer, *The Merchant* 98, 106).

118. The Arden edition glosses this expression: corpses of the wealthy received a wrapping of lead.

119. In *Measure for Measure*, Shakespeare introduces imagery of minted coins; "the debased metal of mankind" receives a new imprint with Christ in "the womb of the Virgin," the place of "infinite riches." The lead casket, a box with "a portrait of a merciful virgin within" is a "symbol that would be transparently obvious. . . . The virgin within the box is the box (the coffer, the casket) within the virgin." The lead casket is the "new Mint . . . the Wombe of the Blessed Virgin" described in a sermon of Donne's. Bassanio chooses "riches greater than the earth can provide" (Pearlman 234, 235).

120. The Arden edition notices the alchemical pun on *base*.

121. The Lord Hamlet, "Use every man after his desert, and who shall 'scape whipping?" (2.2.516-17).

122. "This severe penalty of barrenness emphasises matters of the heart" (Holmer, *The Merchant* 97).

123. Arragon and Morocco remain "personally infatuated, narcissistically self-obsessed"; they so love themselves that they "could not possibly love another" (Holmer, *The Merchant* 56, 105).

124. Neither Morocco nor Arragon can "hazard all he hath" (2.7.17); like Shylock "they expect a guaranteed return on the expenditure" (Homan 162).

125. The italics mark the terms of this chiasmus. Chiasmus is a rhetorical trope or figure of a cross, deriving from the classical authors, used in various ways and often by Renaissance writers. It has at least two terms that wittily play off one other by inverting the two ([A] "the last shall be [B] first, and [B] the first [A] last"). For Elam, this chiasmus is part of the fun and games of verbal comedy. As regards the meaning of the play, it is most timely.

Chiasmus hardly escapes the notice of Renaissance Christian poets. Donne writes of the Crucifixion itself: "We thinke that [A] *Paradise* and [B] *Calvarie*, / [B] *Christs* Crosse, and [A] *Adams* tree, stood in one place" ("Hymne to God my God, in my sicknesse," 21–22). The italics are Donne's. Of his own renunciation, one of Donne's speakers says, "[A] As the trees sap doth seeke the root below / [B] In winter, in my [B] winter now [A] I goe, / Where none but thee, th'Eternal root / Of true Love I may know" ("Hymne to Christ," 13–16).

126. "How vicious . . . the Christians are to the Jew, say most of the critics"; the test is how they treat Shylock, the "alien" who has sought the life of a "citizen." The Jew has been merciless to a Christian; "now that they have Shylock on the hip," the Duke pardons him and Antonio grants him mercy (Kirschbaum 29).

127. "The play does say a great deal about how we ought to treat our fellow human beings, but it does so in a very particular theological context. . . . These matters are . . . explicitly referred to the unique event of Christ's redemptive sacrifice" (Danson 18).

128. "In her allegorical capacity [Portia] can be seen as a female Daniel, the judgement of God in the trial" (Holmer, *The Merchant* 196).

129. In story XV of *Gesta Romanorum* the princess sets out upon the sea in faith.

130. Portia offers Shylock the choice between life and death, good and evil "very nearly in Moses's own words" (Deut. 32:1–4) at the end of the Pentateuch that "foretells the repeated pattern of anger and forgiveness which will characterize God's relations with Israel" (Douglas Anderson 123).

131. These accusations are "validated by Shylock's own behavior" (Beiner 190); he is "ranting," "obsessional," "hysterical" (Hirsch 132).

132. Murry says that the suffering of the Jews for a thousand years speaks through Shylock "were it not that revenge is stamped as unjust by the eternal law that is written in the human heart" (1).

133. "Whatever degree of sympathy we grant to Shylock, he is clearly guilty of inhumaneness" (Boose 104).

134. Shylock's "Hath not a Jew eyes" turns out not to be a plea for Shylock's "essential humanity," but rather an excuse for revenge. By the end of the scene he and Tubal have given way to "wolfishness." "Wolf," "cur," "dog," words commonly describing Shylock, he here ("feed my revenge" [3.1.46]) in his own mouth calls himself (Schmerl 135–36, Lever 385). "Only eyes so blinded with sentimental tears that they cannot pierce hypocrisy, rationalization, and savagery can read this speech as a plausible justification of Shylock"; modern readers do not see how completely Shylock here condemns himself. To Shakespeare's audience, "sociological determinism was never a valid cause. It was always a villain's excuse" (Kirschbaum 24, 25, 31). Weiss refers to "the beast that Shylock has Ovidianly become in succumbing to the vices of greed and hatred"; "given his potentialities, if man is not more than a wolf . . . he is much less." His wolfish behavior is participation in nature and its inhuman laws (134, 147–48). Danson names the speech "diabolic rhetoric" (108). Shylock uses "personal suffering only as a supposed justification for inflicting suffering on others"; Shylock "may accuse

the Christians of not being as merciful as they ought to be, but the play emphasizes at considerable length that he himself does not possess even a grain of the virtue of mercy. They may be imperfect, he is atrocious" (Beiner 181, 188). "Shylock does not change . . . ; he becomes only more what he always was" (Bloom 4). Shylock "behave[s] not as an outraged Jew or an offended usurer, but as a hypocritical, plotting revenger." In his speech, "Hath not a Jew eyes?" he gives up "his identity both as usurer . . . and as a Jew" (Linda Anderson 60). Shylock invokes "his humanity in order to justify an inhuman purpose" (Gross 54).

135. 1.3.94, 156, 311; 2.2.23; 2.5.2; 3.1.19, 28, 67, 114; 3.2.274; 3.4.21; 4.1.215, 285. At 1.3.156, Shylock disclaims, "O father Abram"; John (8:44 BB) mentions "Your father the devil"; 53: "Our father Abraham"; 56: "Your father Abraham"; 58: "Before Abraham was, I am"; Lorenzo says, "my father Jew" (2.6.25).

136. "If each of us were to be judged by God according to what we deserve, we should all be damned. We, therefore, [Portia] continues, have need of God's mercy, we pray for it, and therefore must show it to our fellow human beings" (Grebanier 284).

137. Even Shylock's "sense of religion has a self-sufficient and narrowly prudent quality: he takes no chances on mercy (although a good Jew should), for he thinks that he can justify himself" (Westlund 27).

138. "The success of a comedy of forgiveness depends on the audience's identification with the sinner" (McLean 61).

139. In *Gesta Romanorum* the gold vessel is "full of dead men's bones," an allusion to Christ's metaphor of the Pharisees (Matt. 28:25), those lawyers who trusted in the deadly illusion of their righteousness. Some might also like to think of the parable of the steward, forgiven of his great debt, who then demands payment of those lesser servants who owe him money (Matt. 18: 23–35); Shylock will not forgive Antonio's debt, though part of that debt Shylock owes to someone else.

140. *The Merchant of Venice* "luxuriates" in "love and friendship." Only Shylock, "a creature who nourishes but hate, is cut off from these tender and ennobling emotions. And when he disappears from the play in the fourth act, the air is never again tainted with the fumes of hatred" (Grebanier 174).

141. Shylock has sworn "by our holy Sabbath"; he has an "oath in heaven" to have the forfeit. Shall he "lay perjury upon [his] soul"? As Shylock's fidelity to the Jewish religion turns out to be suspect, the play allows discount of all this appeal to that same religion. In saying, "The curse never fell on our race till now," Shylock reveals himself an egomaniac, without loyalty to religion or race (Schmerl 136). Shylock is "strict about ritual defilement . . . , but he also violates several important commandments of the Mosaic Law" (Holmer, *The Merchant* 189). Shylock "has never felt hurt before. But any wrong to him is a wrong to all Jews" (Grebanier 204). "Hath not a Jew eyes" reveals Shylock's "renunciation of Jewish principles" (Lever 385). The Old Testament has not "served" Shylock well; he knows nothing of "the splendor and nobility of the prophets or Job" (Weiss 127). In going to eat with the

Christians, Shylock violates the Jewish dietary laws as he also violates Mosaic statutes in seeking the life of Antonio by blood-letting (Feldheim 103–104). If the play is anti-Semitic, "the Old Testament, the 'Bible' of Judaism, itself is revered" though Shylock's "invocations of [it] . . . are either shallow or self-serving" (Homan 161). In 2.5, "we are given occasion to question the steadfastness of Shylock's piety" (Yaffe 4).

142. She refers not just to an individual but to mankind; she means "redemption from the just damnation of man by the mercy of Christ" (Kirschbaum 14).

143. "When Portia lectures Shylock on mercy," the others think of the fate of Antonio; she thinks of Shylock's and "implore[s him] to recognise his own peril and to mind the salvation of his own soul" (Tillyard, *Essays* 32).

144. Danson explains the "Renaissance moral commonplace," the "*puer senex*" or "*paedogeron*," the "young body and the wise old head" (121–22).

145. René Fortin puts this affiliation in terms of fathers and sons. Launcelot offers a "counter-statement to the major allegorical statement of the play," the opposition between "Jewish Law and Christian Love," a "corrective to the . . . reductiveness . . . [of the] naive allegory"; the "point . . . of . . . the father-son relationships" in Launcelot's *psychomachia* is the "indissoluble bond of filial piety . . . between the two traditions" (259, 267).

146. Hebrew for "master of the treasure," one "who lays up treasure in secret."

147. Holmer cites Daniel's reputation for "wisdom" (*The Merchant* 195).

148. Matt. 5:45 BB: in the context of loving one's enemies, of blessing those that curse one, that one may be a child of the "father." Ecclesiasticus 35:19 BB, is also relevant: "Mercy in the time of anguish and trouble . . . is like a cloud of rain . . . in the time of drought"; ver. 17: "the prayer of him that humbleth himself, goeth through the clouds"; ver. 18: the Lord "will . . . [smite] in sunder the backs of the unmerciful."

149. Gollancz uses the metaphor of spouse (39).

150. Portia's linking power and mercy also characterizes Moses' words in Deut. 32:1–4 that summarize God's dealings with his people (Douglas Anderson 123).

151. "Taint" suggests an "awareness of sinfulness appropriate for a Christian who is 'well-prepared' for death" (Holmer, "Education" 309). *Wether* need not suggest emasculation (Holmer, *The Merchant* 254).

152. The "central action" of the play "involves the word made flesh, commercial paper [3.2.365–67] made into the precious pound of Antonio's flesh." The play as an "allegory of God's risking or venturing his only Son is not far-fetched" (Holland 106, 108). By the "sheep metaphor," Antonio "can be seen as a type of sacrificial lamb . . . , here signifying a reenactment of the crucifixion scene" (Holmer, "Education" 310). "The crux of the conflict between friendship and some versions of Christianity lay precisely in Antonio's distinctive act, the extreme expression of classical friendship, standing surety for another. Medieval Christianity generally approved of it, encompassing it under the doctrine of *imitatio Christi*. So Antonio, the 'tainted

wether' . . . becomes the *Agnus Dei*, submitting to sacrifice by the Jew so others may live" (Ferber 439).

153. A prayer in the language of Portia's "fellow Christians" but for Shylock in "the language of universal prayer" (Gross 81). "Debts" in Matt. 6:12 BB, GB, D-R; "sins" in GB, BB; D-R (Lk. 11) reads, "Forgive us our sins, for we also forgive every one that is indebted to us"). The Prayer Book gives "trespasses" (Booty, *passim*).

154. The saving of Shylock recalls the "biblical economics of faith and love" in Christ's payment for the "debt" of sin (Holmer, *The Merchant* 69; see note 152 above).

155. The community of the church is "the most inclusive and enveloping form of fellowship which Shakespeare knew" (Weller 346).

156. Danson notes the "purposeful ambiguity" of the title of the play (32). The trial on stage seems to be of Antonio, "but the audience . . . comes to realize that it is witnessing the trial of Shylock who, by his stubborn search for revenge, exiles himself from community and forfeits the right to any mercy from those whose appeals he has denied" (Brennan 231).

157. The choice of Barabbas over Christ "constitutes a symbolic rejection of the leaden chest, the choice of wise love" (Holmer, *The Merchant* 206).

158. Adam stole the fruit and, thereby, cast murderous death upon his race; Barabbas is of the "tribe" of Adam, being his descendent, as well as of the tribe of Jews.

159. When Shylock says that he will use Antonio's flesh "to bait fish withal," does Shakespeare allude to the patristic figure of Christ's cross as the fish hook that God used to catch the devil? A similar figure, the cross as a mousetrap, must certainly occur in *Hamlet*.

160. Holmer traces the connection between Daniel and wisdom (*The Merchant* 194–95).

161. In saving others, one saves oneself; to love others, "in a theological sense, [is to love] oneself properly" (Kirschbaum 17).

162. We doubt it possible to limit Shakespeare's Daniel either to the "canonical" Daniel of the book by that name or to the Daniel in the apocryphal book of Susanna; Shakespeare seems to conflate the two.

163. John Middleton Murry comes close to the typology and the emblematic perception of the play when he says, "In Portia the new Eve confronts the old Adam" (3).

164. Danson cites St. Paul, "I knew not sin, but by the Law" (Rom. 7:7) and adds, "in making sin appear *as* sin, God's law performs the crucial didactic function that Portia will make Venice's law perform" (76, 77).

165. Modern "separation of moral sentiment from intellect" contrasts with the late-sixteenth-century European conception "of conscience . . . as a part of the practical intellect, at once moral and intellectual and directed towards the judgment of specific cases, a procedure requiring considerable hermeneutic and logical skill. The power that Portia uses to mediate between the harsh Venetian law and Antonio's individual plight is precisely this ability to apply general laws with acute discrimination to the unique circumstances of a specific case. By distinguishing justice from mercy, flesh

from gold, and citizen from alien, she transforms Shylock's vindictive triumph into defeat. As readers and audience, we need similar powers of discrimination" (Slights 143–44). "It will be bad for business . . . if Antonio is let off. . . . Antonio is a good man, a dear friend, and does not deserve to die at Shylock's hands. The conflict is absolute; when Portia arrives from Belmont it simply melts away. The course of law is upheld *and* Antonio is saved" (Bamber 118). Such a legal technicality is often decisive in trials. Portia's strategy may appear as "legal entrapment to the uninformed"; but "more discerning eyes" will see it as "nothing less than Portia's delicate public-spirited attempt to extricate Shylock from his grim predicament" (Yaffe 84). Camille Pierre Laurent cites Max Plowman: " 'A verbal quibble?' Not at all; on the contrary, the turning upon itself of a weapon of logic basely misused in its attack upon life. And Shylock was convinced by the only means that would carry conviction" (23). Criticism of Portia's direction of the trial "overlooks the complex interplay of her pedagogic and judicial functions. . . . Shakespeare ingeniously exploits Paul's metaphor for the Law as a 'Schoolmaster' to 'bring us' to Christ (Gal. 3:24) in his characterization of Portia." Portia's reversal "works legally in this strict court precisely because it is strict construction" (Holmer, *The Merchant* 200, 202).

166.   Danson continues: "The perfect fulfilling of the law, with its issue in mercy, is an ideal that goes beyond ordinary human possibilities into the realm of divine paradox" (64). Christ adds forgiveness to the law and makes "mercy . . . part of the law, rather than an opposing principle" (65). Pushing the law all the way is not an "exposure of judicial deceit but . . . the revelation of truth"; "the spiritual truth"—the necessity of rendering mercy—"is embodied in a secular analogue" (119).

167.   The Prayer Book baptismal office echoes with words of citizenship, admission to the commonwealth: "received into Christ's holy Church," "received into the congregation of Christ's flock," "grafted [by baptism (see Rom. 11:17–24)] into the body of Christ's congregation," made "partakers of his everlasting kingdom," "heirs of everlasting salvation," (Booty 270, 275, 272).

168.   The Propers for Quinquagesima (Booty 106–107).

169.   When "Portia and Nerissa finally move beyond the 'letter' of their 'ring vows' and forgive their husbands for violating those vows, we remember Shylock and his inability to get beyond the letter of the bond" (Hartwig 193).

170.   As soon as Shylock "loses the upper hand, the court in which he stressed justice immediately becomes a court of mercy" (Nathan, "Rejoinder" 387).

171.   Shylock does not object to conversion as he did to judgment (Lewalski 341).

172.   Shakespeare "intends Antonio's anagnoresis to teach Shylock by right Christian example the value of mercy and giving" (Holmer, "Education" 318–19); as Shylock says that he learned revenge from Christian example, so here he may learn mercy from the same source (Holmer, *The Merchant* 231).

173.   Shakespeare lets Shylock "fade quietly from the stage. . . . Morocco exits in grief and Arragon in anger, but neither of their mischoices receives any mercy, only just deserts. Shylock's very silence recalls the proverbial idea in

the play's opening scene that wise men are given to silence" (Holmer, *The Merchant* 244).

174. With Shylock's naming Portia as *Daniel*, "the focus of the courtroom becomes Shylock's conversion." *Daniel* means something like "the Judge of God," or "God is my judge." The secret that Daniel prophesies is the triumph of the Gentiles over Israel and the coming of the Messiah, of Christ, St. Jerome says, "as none other has done so clearly." Ironically, "as a new communicant, Shylock will be admitted to the ritualistic consumption of Jesus's flesh and blood. A new spark of meaning then illuminates the whole myth of the pound of flesh, . . . a repressed desire to share in the Last Supper. . . . [Shylock's] hubristic attack on the very foundations of Christian society could then be seen as an unwitting attempt to have the violence of conversion inflicted on himself" (Laurent 24). Holmer explains how "the conversion trope is integral to the whole play" (*The Merchant*, 226).

175. Robert M. Smith does not find the baptism "compell[ed]" but rather a gift, "not intended as a final insult" (294). Weiss affirms that "however harsh" the requirement "may sound to modern ears, we must remember that, for this society, being Christian could alone save a man's soul" (150). For Elizabethan Christians, baptism "was the only way Shylock could escape eternal damnation"; it is "an additional act of mercy" (Muir 58). Coghill adds that to an Elizabethan, Shylock has no hope of entering Christian eternity except by baptism: "No man cometh to the Father but by me" (219). To maintain that Shylock is a broken victim of "Christian vindictiveness" and anti-Semitism "is to ignore not only the equitable basis on which [the] judgment rests, but the comic structure which supports it" (Zeeveld 155).

176. Jessica, he says, is an "agent in her father's redemption."

177. In the trial scene, Eggers argues, Shylock, an alien, "loses suit and gains salvation"; the love in the two acts of mercy, of the Duke and of Antonio, "triumphs over unlikeness." Shylock's enforced conversion is an "affirmation of common humanity and identity"; love is the "human agent of divine mercy" (331–32).

178. In changing the motto on the leaden casket from the source text, "Who so chooseth mee, shall finde that God hath disposed for him," to "Who chooseth me, must give and hazard all he hath" Shakespeare "implicitly link[s] human love with divine love, since in the Renaissance human love was ideally supposed to be modeled on divine love." Love is "the gift or hazard of oneself" demonstrated in God's gift of his son. Hazarding for amorous love is, therefore, "allied with Providence" (Holmer, "Loving" 56).

179. Patrick Grant writes persuasively of St. Matthew's use of the Greek word *seismos*, "which means a commotion or shaking, and is translated as 'tempest' or 'earthquake.' " The Evangelist employs it seven times, as in his description of Jesus' entering Jerusalem, of the earthquake at the crucifixion, and of the centurion's terror. "Translations obscure the fact that Matthew uses the same word to indicate Christ's renovating power breaking in upon the world, and also the radical upheavals upsetting normal order and expectation"; the Christian "*energia*" uses symmetries, laws, and organizations,

"brilliantly unsettling" them and making "them the mediator of something new and strange." "God's ways remain disconcerting, surprising to our expectations," revealing an expectation, a pattern to fulfil (195–96). Nor would *seismos* be an inappropriate word for the Apocalypse, of which the trial scene in the play is an emblem.

180. *Merchant* is "among the most vexatious of all Shakespeare's plays" (Danson 20; see also 36, 40).

181. The *OED* gives this range of significations for *content* (nouns, verbs, adjectives): *satisfaction, pleasure, acceptance, acquiesence, calm, quiet, not uneasy, pleased, gratified, ready, consenting, agreed.* It also allows "having one's desires bound by what one has (though that may be less than one could have wished)." So far as we can tell, uses of the word in Shakespeare's other plays fall within this range of meanings. Antonio's "content" (1.3.148) seems very like Shylock's in signification.

182. Norman Nathan argues that Shylock in identifying himself with Jacob, and Antonio with Laban, persuades himself that God will bring him, like Jacob, to triumph over his adversary. When God does not so act but rather gives the property to Antonio, Lorenzo, and the Christian state of Venice, Shylock crumbles. He has admitted that Portia is his Daniel, the name *Daniel* meaning "God is my judge." We would argue that Shylock's trust is in the illusion of the law and that when the law betrays him, his world and its norms are in collapse. Nathan also suggests that Shylock's "have [Antonio] on the hip" is a perversion of God's touching Jacob in the hollow of his thigh ("Shylock" 257–59, 256). Roger L. Cox makes a similar use of Shylock's identification with Jacob and finding himself like Laban instead. Jacob went away with Laban's daughters and his gods; therefore, when Shylock recognizes the reversal, he suffers an "internal [change] as well as [an] external [one]" (79–82).

183. Metaphors of sickness (giving place to ones of healing) that characterize the movement of several of Shakespeare's comedies do not obtain in this play; this one of disease is the only remarkable one, other than Antonio's melancholy. Ruth M. Levitsky draws attention to the Christian assumption that, in refusing to receive the New Testament scriptures, the Jews had "cut themselves off from . . . the only medicine that could cure the ills of the soul." Though Levitsky does not cite the imagery of feasting, starving, and cannibalism that Shakespeare introduces early in the play, she says that the Jews cut themselves off in the same way from "the only food that could afford true nourishment for the spirit." Without this, one is merely a "natural man"; regeneration, effected by baptism, is "the remedy offered for this affliction" (58, 60, 61).

184. At 1.3.67–70, Shylock identifies his "thrift" with Jacob's; Jacob and his "wise" mother tricked Isaac so that he gave his blessing to Jacob instead of Esau. *Wise* indicates Shylock's approval. Jacob was "from our holy Abram" (1.3.156), the source of the nation Israel. The new Israel takes Abraham as its source, too. By wrestling with God, Jacob received a new name, *Israel*, which means "the one who struggles with God." Abraham also suffered a change of names. Does Shylock receive a new name, having wrestled with the moral order? If he does, that name will come in his baptism.

185. "Shylock, like all the other Venetians, is offered the opportunity to lose his money and find grace" (Wertheim 85). Shakespeare has "closely entwined the issues of religion and usury"; Antonio "accepts Shylock as a fellow human being who has needs, need of wealth and need of Christ" (Holmer "Education" 321, 322). Judith Rosenheim departs "from the recent critical tendency to define Shylock and Antonio with reference to their economic identities as usurer and merchant. Rather, it seems to [her] that the economic identities of these antagonists subserve their more important identities as Jew and Christian. And this view of their identities leads [her] to address their conflict through the teachings of St. Paul rather than those of Karl Marx." The lack of "precise realism in the play's economics" is due to "its function as the vehicle of a theological tenor," a function that integrates "the play's economic and theological realms of meaning" (158–59).

186. Portia's "control of pace and nuance . . . provide validation in the theatre for both Gratiano's repeated . . . taunting of Shylock and the seeming tendency of audiences to endorse, by their laughter, the young man's outbursts" (Jensen 38).

187. If one feels obliged to worry oneself about Shylock's absence from act 5, John Gross offers much comfort: Belmont is aristocratic. Jessica's "manners" get her a place there. Shylock does not have, or does not yet have, those manners (86). Or rather, perhaps, the others have been long desiring Belmont and long preparing for it; Shylock may have but begun. The manners necessary for entrance upon Belmont, like much else in the play, are emblematic. Entrance into Belmont is not dependent upon class but upon moral quality.

188. To give the ring to the lawyer is entirely fitting; for as lawyer Portia has, analogically speaking, embodied the same values (sacrifice and hazard) in the trial scene (allowing Shylock to have strict justice) as she has during Bassanio's casket scene. If the ring is symbolic of Bassanio's love for Portia, with her moral qualities, he fittingly gives the same ring to the lawyer who embodies exactly the same qualities.

189. We have not the space nor the need—as Danson has done it so very well (11, 19–21, 195)—to discuss the metaphor of the circle and even of its dance.

190. "The movement of the scene is not a descent but an encircling, an inclusion of differences" (Holmer, *The Merchant* 272–73).

191. But this "appearance" is quite other than illusion.

192. "In the strange world of [this play] it becomes possible simultaneously to give and to keep" (Danson 21).

193. "In play[,] each member of the triad has become the other," and whatever conflicts may have existed among them are dissolved (Allman 154).

194. "One of the effects of the sexual references and jokes at the end of the play is precisely to point to human characters rather than to a disembodied allegorical abstraction. Mercy may not indulge in jokes about sex, but women like Portia and Nerissa can do so with their husbands" (Beiner 277). The sexual significance of the ring, with Gratiano boasting about "keeping safe Nerissa's ring," "perfectly blend[s] with ideas of friendship, fidelity, bond, and mutual submission" (Bevington 60).

195. The moral law of this comedy is the same as the "law common to all Shake-
      spearean comedies"; "felicity . . . equitable to superabundant compensation
      await[s] the virtuous"; and "Antonio is no exception." "The nearly univer-
      sal . . . mistaken critical view" that Antonio finishes "excluded and
      unhappy . . . must be imported and imposed by readers" (Pequigney 217,
      218). Nearly all critics suppose that Antonio is left alone at the end; but
      "Bassanio, Antonio, Gratiano, *and their followers*," who are directed to
      enter (SD 126), are never ordered to exit and leave Antonio behind. Anto-
      nio's isolation is created only by a willful director.

196. Grund's real subject is *felix culpa* in the play; but he greatly enhances one's
      understanding of this Augustinian conception by use of the Easter liturgy.
      One is, therefore, baffled that he does not seem aware in his discussion that
      the Easter Vigil's *Exultet* (with its repetition of "This is the night. . . ")
      chronicles the same transformations of man's state as a slave, as lost, as spir-
      itually dead to the state of freedom, salvation, and life that Shakespeare
      makes in his redirection of his sequence (with its repetition of "In such a
      night . . .") that charts the movement from tragic lovers to the renewed
      Aeson.

197. "A physical object, the ring literally surrounds the flesh, encircles it, adorns
      it" (Homan 170).

198. Mrs. Marsha Stevens, Mrs. Madaline Spickard, Messrs. Arthur Rogers and
      William Tootle, Professors Thomas L. Berger, the late Harold Jenkins, Ellen
      Mahon, John Mahon, and George W. Williams have done their kindest best
      to rid this essay of the progeny of Sad Error; the remainder of the unhappy
      spawn is unfortunately our own.

Works Cited

Allman, Eileen Jorge. *Player-King and Adversary: Two Faces of Play in Shakespeare*.
      Baton Rouge: Louisiana State University Press, 1980.

Anderson, Douglas. "The Old Testament Presence in *The Merchant of Venice*." *ELH*
      52 (1985): 119–32.

Anderson, Linda. *A Wild Kind of Justice: Revenge in Shakespeare's Comedies*.
      Newark: University of Delaware Press, 1987.

Bamber, Linda. *Comic Woman, Tragic Man: A Study of Gender and Genre in Shake-
      speare*. Stanford: Stanford University Press, 1982.

Beiner, G. *Shakespeare's Agonistic Comedy: Poetics, Analysis, Criticism*. Rutherford:
      Fairleigh Dickinson University Press, 1993.

Belsey, Catherine. "Love in Venice." *Shakespeare and Gender: A History.* Ed. Debo-
      rah Barker and Ivo Kamps. London: Verso, 1995.

Bevington, David. *Action Is Eloquence: Shakespeare's Language of Gesture*. Cam-
      bridge: Harvard University Press, 1984.

The Bible. Rheims New Testament in *The Precise Parallel New Testament*. Ed. John
      R. Hohlenberger. Oxford: University Press, 1995.

———. Geneva Version. Genève: Rouland Hall, 1560.

———. Bishop's Version. London: R. Jugge, 1568.

Bloom, Harold, ed. *William Shakespeare: Comedies and Romances*. New York: Chelsea House Publishers, 1986.

Boose, Lynda E. "The Father and the Bride in Shakespeare." *PMLA* 97 (1982): 325–47.

Booty, John E., ed. *The Book of Common Prayer 1559: The Elizabethan Prayer Book*. Charlottesville: The University Press of Virginia, 1976.

Bradbrook, M. C. *Shakespeare and Elizabethan Poetry: A Study of his Earlier Work in Relation to the Poetry of the Time*. London: Chatto and Windus, 1951.

Bradford, John. *The Writings of John Bradford*. Ed. Aubrey Townsend. Cambridge: Cambridge University Press, 1848.

Brennan, Anthony. *Onstage and Offstage Worlds in Shakespeare's Plays*. London: Routledge, 1989.

Bronstein, Herbert. "Shakespeare, the Jews, and *The Merchant of Venice*." *Shakespeare Quarterly* 20 (1969): 3–10.

Brown, John Russell. "Mr. Pinter's Shakespeare." *Critical Quarterly* 5 (1963): 251–65.

———. *Shakespeare and His Comedies*. London: Methuen & Co. Ltd., 1957.

Bryant, J. A., Jr. *Hippolyta's View: Some Christian Aspects of Shakespeare's Plays*. Lexington: University of Kentucky Press, 1961.

Burckhardt, Sigurd. *Shakespearean Meanings*. Princeton: Princeton University Press, 1968.

Carroll, William C. *The Metamorphoses of Shakespearean Comedy*. Princeton: Princeton University Press, 1985.

Champion, Larry S. *The Evolution of Shakespeare's Comedies: A Study in Dramatic Perspective*. Cambridge: Harvard University Press, 1970.

Chew, Samuel C. *The Virtues Reconciled: An Iconographic Study*. Toronto: University of Toronto Press, 1947.

Coghill, Nevill. "The Basis of Shakespearian Comedy." *Shakespeare Criticism: 1935–1960*. Ed. Anne Ridler. London: Oxford University Press, 1963.

Colley, John Scott. "Launcelot, Jacob and Esau: Old and New Law in *The Merchant of Venice*." *The Yearbook of English Studies* 10 (1979): 181–89.

Coolidge, John S. "Law and Love in *The Merchant of Venice*." *Shakespeare Quarterly* 27 (1976): 243–63.

Cox, John D. "Renaissance Power and Stuart Dramaturgy: Shakespeare, Milton, Dryden." *Comparative Drama* 22 (1989): 323–58.

Cox, Roger L. *Shakespeare's Comic Changes: The Time-Lapse Metaphor as Plot Device*. Athens: University of Georgia Press, 1991.

Danson, Lawrence. *The Harmonies of "The Merchant of Venice."* New Haven: Yale University Press, 1978.

de Beauregard, Raphaëlle Costa. "Interpreting *The Merchant of Venice*." *Cahiers élisabéthains* 39 (1991): 1–16.

Dessen, Alan C. *Shakespeare and the Late Moral Plays*. Lincoln: University of Nebraska Press, 1986.

Dobbins, Austin C. and Roy W. Battenhouse. "Jessica's Morals: A Theological View." *Shakespeare Studies* 9 (1976): 107–20.

Donaldson, Ian, ed. *Ben Jonson: Poems*. London: Oxford University Press, 1975.

Donne, John. *The Divine Poems*. Ed. Helen Gardner. Oxford: Oxford University Press, 1952.

Dreher, Diane Elizabeth. *Domination and Defiance: Fathers and Daughters in Shake-speare*. Lexington: University Press of Kentucky, 1986.

Dundas, Judith. "Shakespeare's Imagery: Emblem and the Imitation of Nature." *Shakespeare Studies* 16 (1984): 44–56.

Eggers, Walter F., Jr. "Love and Likeness in *The Merchant of Venice*." *Shakespeare Quarterly* 28 (1977): 327–33.

Elam, Keir. *Shakespeare's Universe of Discourse: Language-Games in the Comedies.* Cambridge: Cambridge University Press, 1984.

Ferber, Michael. "The Ideology of *The Merchant of Venice*." *English Literary Renaissance* 20 (1990): 431–64.

Feldheim, Marvin. *"The Merchant of Venice."* *Shakespeare Studies* 4 (1968): 94–109.

Fergusson, Francis. *Shakespeare: The Pattern in His Carpet*. New York: Delacorte Press, 1971.

———. *Trope and Allegory: Themes Common to Dante and Shakespeare*. Athens: University of Georgia Press, 1977.

Fortin, René E. "Launcelot and the Uses of Allegory in *The Merchant of Venice*." *Studies in English Literature* 14 (1974): 259–70.

Frazer, Sir James. *Adonis, Attis, Osiris: Studies in the History of Oriental Religion.* 3rd edition. New York: The Macmillan Company, 1935. 2 vols.

Freeman, Rosemary. *English Emblem Books*. London: Chatto and Windus, 1948.

French, Marilyn. *Shakespeare's Division of Experience*. New York: Summit Books, 1981.

Gardner, John. *"The Canon's Yeoman's Prologue and Tale*: An Interpretation." *Philological Quarterly* 46 (1967): 1–17.

Golding, Arthur. *Shakespeare's Ovid*. Ed. W. H. D. Rouse. New York: Norton, 1966.

Gollancz, Sir Israel. *Allegory and Mysticism in Shakespeare: A Medievalist on "The Merchant of Venice"* [reports of three lectures]. Privately printed, 1931.

Grant, Patrick. *Literature and Personal Values*. London: The Macmillan Press Ltd., 1992.

Grebanier, Bernard. *The Truth about Shylock*. New York: Random House, 1962.

Grennen, Joseph E. "The Canon's Yeoman's Alchemical 'Mass.' " *Studies in Philology* 62 (1965): 546–60.

Gross, John. *Shylock: Four Hundred Years in the Life of a Legend*. London: Chatto & Windus, 1992.

Grund, Gary R. "The Fortunate Fall and Shakespeare's *Merchant of Venice*." *Studia Neophilologica* 55 (1983): 153–65.

Grudin, Robert. *Mighty Opposites: Shakespeare and Renaissance Contrariety.* Berkeley: University of California Press, 1979.

Halpern, Richard. *Shakespeare Among the Moderns*. Ithaca: Cornell University Press, 1997.

Hardison, O. B., Jr. *Christian Rite and Christian Drama in the Middle Ages*. Baltimore: Johns Hopkins University Press, 1965.

Hartwig, Joan. *Shakespeare's Analogical Scene: Parody as Structural Syntax*. Lincoln: University of Nebraska Press, 1983.

Hassel, R. Chris, Jr. "Antonio and the Ironic Festivity of *The Merchant of Venice*." *Shakespeare Studies* 6 (1970): 67–74.

Herrick, Robert. *The Complete Poetry*. Ed. J. Max Patrick. New York: New York University Press, 1963.

Hibbard, G. R. *The Making of Shakespeare's Dramatic Poetry*. Toronto: University of Toronto Press, 1981.

Hirsh, James E. *The Structure of Shakespearean Scenes*. New Haven: Yale University Press, 1981.

Holland, Norman N. *The Shakespearean Imagination*. New York: The Macmillan Company, 1964.

Hollander, John. "*Musica Mundana* and Twelfth Night." *Sound and Poetry*. English Institute Essays for 1956, ed. Northrop Frye. New York: Columbia University Press, 1957.

Holmer, Joan Ozark. "The Education of the Merchant of Venice." *Studies in English Literature: 1500–1900*, 25 (1985): 307–35.

———. "Loving Wisely and the Casket Test: Symbolic and Structural Unity in *The Merchant of Venice*." *Shakespeare Studies* 11 (1978): 53–76.

———. *"The Merchant of Venice": Choice, Hazard and Consequence*. New York: St. Martin's Press: 1995.

Homan, Sidney. *Shakespeare's Theater of Presence: Language, Spectacle, and the Audience*. Lewisburg: Bucknell University Press, 1986.

Horowitz, David. *Shakespeare: An Existential View*. New York: Hill and Wang, 1965.

Jenkins, Harold, ed. *Hamlet*. The Arden Edition. London: Methuen, 1982.

Jensen, Ejner J. *Shakespeare and the Ends of Comedy*. Bloomington: Indiana University Press, 1991.

Johnson, Lonnell E. "Shylock's Daniel: 'Justice More than Thou Desir'st.' " *CLA Journal* 35 (1992): 353–66.

Jonson, Ben. *The Works of Ben Jonson*. Eds. C. H. Herford, Percy and Evelyn Simpson. Oxford: Clarendon Press, 1947. 11 vols.

Kermode, Frank. "Frank Kermode: Some Themes in *The Merchant of Venice*." *Twentieth-Century Interpretations of "The Merchant of Venice*." Ed. Sylvan Barnet. Englewood, NJ: Prentice Hall, Inc., 1970.

Kirschbaum, Leo. *Character and Characterization in Shakespeare*. Detroit: Wayne State University Press, 1962.

Knight, G. Wilson. "The Ideal Production." *Twentieth-Century Interpretations of "The Merchant of Venice."* Ed. Sylvan Barnet. Englewood, NJ: Prentice Hall, Inc., 1970.

Laurent, Camille Pierre. "Dog, Fiend and Christian, or Shylock's Conversion." *Cahiers élisabéthains* 26 (1983): 15–27.

Lever, J. W. "Shylock, Portia and the Values of Shakespearean Comedy." *Shakespeare Quarterly* 3 (1952): 383–86.

Levin, Richard A. *Love and Society in Shakespearean Comedy: A Study of Dramatic Form and Content*. Newark: University of Delaware Press, 1985.

———. "The Relation of External Evidence to the Allegorical and Thematic Interpretation of Shakespeare." *Shakespeare Studies* 13 (1980): 1–29.

Levitsky, Ruth M. "Shylock as Unregenerate Man." *Shakespeare Quarterly* 28 (1977): 58–64.

Lewalski, Barbara K. "Biblical Allusion and Allegory in *The Merchant of Venice*." *Shakespeare Quarterly* 13 (1962): 327–43.

Lewis, Anthony J. *The Love Story in Shakespearean Comedy*. Lexington: University Press of Kentucky, 1992.

Linden, Stanton J. "Alchemy and Eschatology in Seventeenth-Century Poetry." *Ambix: The Journal of the Society for the History of Alchemy and Chemistry* 31 (1984): 102–24.

Lomax, Marion. *Stage Images and Traditions: Shakespeare to Ford*. Cambridge: Cambridge University Press, 1987.

MacCary, W. Thomas. *Friends and Lovers: Phenomenology of Desire in Shakespearean Comedy*. New York: Columbia University Press, 1985.

Mahood, M. M., ed. *The Merchant of Venice*. New Cambridge Shakespeare. Cambridge: Cambridge University Press, 1987.

McCombie, Frank. "Wisdom as Touchstone in *The Merchant of Venice*." *New Blackfriars* 64 (1983): 113–24.

McLean, Susan. "Prodigal Sons and Daughters: Transgression and Forgiveness in *The Merchant of Venice*." *Papers on Language and Literature* 31 (1996): 45–62.

Muir, Kenneth. *Shakespeare's Comic Sequence*. Liverpool: Liverpool University Press, 1979.

Murry, John Middleton. "The Significance of Shylock." *The Adelphi* 22 (1945): 1–5.

Nabokov, Vladimir. *Strong Opinions*. New York: McGraw Hill, 1973.

Nathan, Norman. " 'Abram,' not 'Abraham,' in *The Merchant of Venice*." *Notes and Queries* n. s. 17 (1970): 127–28.

———. "Rejoinder to Mr. Lever's 'Shylock, Portia, and the Values of Shakespearean Comedy.' " *Shakespeare Quarterly* 3 (1952): 386–88.

———. "Shylock, Jacob, and God's Judgment." *Shakespeare Quarterly* 1 (1950): 255–59.

Nevo, Ruth. *Comic Transformations in Shakespeare*. London: Methuen, 1980.

Nicoll, Allardyce. *Shakespeare: An Introduction*. New York: Oxford University Press, 1952.

Normand, Lawrence. "Reading the Body in *The Merchant of Venice*." *Textual Practice* 5 (1991): 55–73.

Nowell, Alexander. *A Catechism Written in Latin: Together. . . .* Ed. G. E. Corrie. Cambridge: Cambridge University Press, 1853.

Oz, Avraham. *The Yoke of Love: Prophetic Riddles in "The Merchant of Venice."* Newark: University of Delaware Press, 1995.

Parker, Patricia. "Anagogic Metaphor: Breaking Down the Wall of Partition." *Centre and Labyrinth: Essays in Honour of Northrop Frye*, eds. Eleanor Cook, Chaviva Hošek, Jay Macpherson, Patricia Parker, and Julian Patrick. Toronto: University of Toronto Press, 1983.

Pearlman, E. "Freud, and the Two Usuries, or Money's a Meddler." *English Literary Renaissance* 2 (1972): 217–36.

Pequigney, Joseph. "The Two Antonios and Same-Sex Love in *Twelfth Night* and *The Merchant of Venice*." *English Literary Renaissance* 22 (1992): 201–21.

Platt, Peter G. *Reason Diminished: Shakespeare and the Marvelous*. Lincoln: University of Nebraska Press, 1997.

Reidy, John. "Chaucer's Canon and the Unity of *The Canon's Yeoman's Tale*." *PMLA* 80 (1965): 31–37.

Ribner, Irving. "Marlowe and Shakespeare." *Shakespeare Quarterly* 15 (1964): 41–53.

Riemer, A. P. *Antic Fables: Patterns of Evasion in Shakespeare's Comedies*. Manchester: University Press, 1980.

Rosenheim, Judith. "Allegorical Commentary in *The Merchant of Venice*." *Shakespeare Studies* 24 (1996): 156–210.

Roth, Marty. " 'The Blood that Fury Breathed': The Shape of Justice in Aeschylus and Shakespeare." *Comparative Literature Studies* 29 (1992): 141–56.

Schmerl, Rudolf B. "Comedy and the Manipulation of Moral Distance: Falstaff and Shylock." *Bucknell Review* 10 (1961): 128–37.

Sewell, Arthur. *Character and Society in Shakespeare*. London: Oxford University Press, 1951.

Shakespeare, William. *The Merchant of Venice*. Ed. John Russell Brown. The Arden Edition. Cambridge, MA: Harvard University Press, 1955.

Shapiro, James. *Shakespeare and the Jews*. New York: Columbia University Press, 1996.

Sharp, Ronald A. "Gift Exchange and the Economics of Spirit in *The Merchant of Venice*." *Modern Philology* 83 (1986): 250–65.

Sheppard, J. T. *Music at Belmont and Other Essays and Addresses*. London: Rupert Hart-Davis, 1951.

Shurgot, Michael W. "Gobbo's Gift and the 'Muddy Vesture of Decay' in *The Merchant of Venice*." *Essays in Literature* 10 (1983): 139–48.

Sisk, John P. "Bondage and Release in *The Merchant of Venice*." *Shakespeare Quarterly* 20 (1969): 217–23.

Slights, Camille Wells. *Shakespeare's Comic Commonwealths*. Toronto: University of Toronto Press, 1993.

Smidt, Kristian. "Unconformities in *The Merchant of Venice*." *Historical and Editorial Studies in Medieval and Early Modern English*. Eds. Mary-Jo Arn and Hanneke Wirtjes. The Netherlands: Wolters-Noordhoff Groningen, 1985.

Smith, Robert M. "Clarence Derwent." *Shakespeare Quarterly* 1 (1950): 293–95.

Sundelson, David. *Shakespeare's Restorations of the Father*. New Brunswick, NJ: Rutgers University Press, 1983.

Swinden, Patrick. *An Introduction to Shakespeare's Comedies*. London: Macmillan, 1973.

Tennenhouse, Leonard. "The Counterfeit Order of *The Merchant of Venice*." *Representing Shakespeare: New Psychoanalytic Essays*. Eds. Murray M. Schwartz and Coppélia Kahn. Baltimore: The Johns Hopkins University Press, 1980.

Tillyard, E. M. W. *Essays Literary and Educational*. London: Chatto and Windus, 1967.

———. *Shakespeare's Early Comedies*. London: Chatto and Windus Press, 1965.

Traversi, Derek. *An Approach to Shakespeare I: "Henry VI" to "Twelfth Night."* London: Hollis and Carter, 1968.

Van Doren, Mark. "*The Merchant of Venice*: An Interpretation." *Shakespeare, The Merchant of Venice: a Casebook*. Ed. John Wilders. London: Macmillan, 1969.

Van Laan, Thomas F. *Role-playing in Shakespeare*. Toronto: University of Toronto Press, 1978.

Velz, John W. "From Jerusalem to Damascus: Bilocal Dramaturgy in Medieval and Shakespearian Conversion Plays." *Comparative Drama* 15 (1981–1982): 311–26.

Warren, Austin. *Richard Crashaw: A Study in Baroque Sensibility*. Baton Rouge: Louisiana State University Press, 1939.

Weatherby, Harold L. *Mirrors of Celestial Grace: Patristic Theology in Spenser's Allegory*. Toronto: University of Toronto Press, 1994.

Weisberg, Richard. *Poethics: And Other Strategies of Law and Literature*. New York: Columbia University Press, 1992.

Weiss, Theodore. *The Breath of Clowns and Kings: Shakespeare's Early Comedies and Histories*. New York: Atheneum, 1971.

Weller, Barry. "Identity and Representation in Shakespeare." *ELH* 49 (1982): 339–62.

Wertheim, Albert. "The Treatment of Shylock and Thematic Integrity in *The Merchant of Venice*." *Shakespeare Studies* 6 (1970): 75–87.

Westlund, Joseph. *Shakespeare's Reparative Comedies: a Psychoanalytic View of the Middle Plays*. Chicago: University of Chicago Press, 1984.

Wheeler, Thomas. *"The Merchant of Venice," An Annotated Bibliography*. New York: Garland Publications, 1985.

Wiles, David. *Shakespeare's Clown: Actor and Text in the Elizabethan Playhouse*. Cambridge: Cambridge University Press, 1987.

Willbern, David. *Poetic Will: Shakespeare and the Play of Language*. Philadelphia: University of Pennsylvania Press, 1997.

Wilson, John Dover. *Shakespeare's Happy Comedies*. Evanston: Northwestern University Press, 1962.

Yaffe, Martin D. *Shylock and the Jewish Question*. Baltimore: The Johns Hopkins University Press, 1997.

Zeeveld, W. Gordon. *The Temper of Shakespeare's Thought*. New Haven: Yale University Press, 1974.

"Nerissa Teaches Me What to Believe"

Portia's Wifely Empowerment in
The Merchant of Venice

CORINNE S. ABATE

In 3.4, Portia proposes to Nerissa that they travel to Venice disguised as men to "see our husbands / Before they think of us" (58–59). Nerissa's famous question, "Why, shall we turn to men?" (78), is answered with a decisive dismissal by Portia: "Fie, what a question's that!" (3.4.79).[1] Clearly, Nerissa is referring to Portia's plan to dress up as men—turning *into* men—but leaving aside that surface meaning, Portia's rather bristling reply should not be unexpected. After all, she has never had the opportunity in her young life to turn to a man. She is the only child to a dead father, and she is sole owner and director of the Belmont estate. Hence, she does not have dependent and submissive inclinations, those traits traditionally associated with women, to turn to men for anything, because she has always already dealt with men directly in the absence of any male figures in her life.

If anything, Portia learns by Nerissa's example throughout the first half of the play that should she need to turn to anyone, it should not necessarily be to a man.[2] As Portia will later explain to Bassanio in 5.1, "Nerissa teaches me what to believe" (207). I suggest that Portia learns from Nerissa the lesson of becoming an empowered wife. The role of wife is one to which both Nerissa and Portia have the most direct access and the one in which they both have the most invested, because whatever happens to Portia directly affects Nerissa as well. Thus, I will argue that the result of the casket test, which is responsible for Portia becoming Bassanio's partner, is a happy outcome carefully orchestrated by her most beloved friend Nerissa, whose partial and biased interest in what happens to her mistress may account for her careful arrangement of Portia's marital future to a man who is most decidedly not Portia's financial equal. Portia learns to negotiate successfully within the confines of the sex/gender system that, like her father's lottery, does not necessarily have her best interests in mind.[3] And it is through the character of Portia, as Karen Newman adduces, that *Merchant*, "far from simply exemplifying the Elizabethan

sex/gender system of exchange," instead "short-circuits the exchange, mocking its authorized social structure and hierarchical gender relations" (126). The
purpose of this essay is to examine how Portia ultimately learns—through
marrying beneath her station, cross-dressing with a difference, accomplishing
in a Venetian court what no man can, and securing her husband's loyalty
through subordinating his male friendships—the invaluable lesson of turning
to herself.

The many scholars who have already written on Portia in *The Merchant of Venice* have often focused only on her role as Antonio's savior or
Shylock's judge. Yet these are parts Portia will perform only for a limited
run; her role as Bassanio's wife is one in which she will be cast for a lifetime, which is why I think it deserves more careful study. Further, Nerissa's
involvement in Portia's most private thoughts and schemes leads me to take
a closer look at 1.2, where she first discusses with Portia both the strictures
of the casket test, and those suitors who are currently vying for a chance to
win Portia and all that her inheritance entails. After Portia declares that
"my little body is aweary of this great world" (1–2), Nerissa defends Portia's late father's lottery and, as if to pass the time, asks for Portia's opinion
of the round of contenders. All of them come up short in Portia's estimation. The Neapolitan prince is overly fond of his horse, Count Palatine
frowns too much, Monsieur Le Bon appears to be too easily distracted,
Baron Falconbridge is not educated enough, the unnamed Scottish lord is
too violent, and the German is a drunk.[4] The common theme, then, of Portia's objections to each potential mate is that he does not seem to offer
assurances that she will secure in her marriage the privileged position of
empowered woman to which she has become accustomed. What they are
lacking is a *need* for Portia's estate because they all appear to come with
their own money. Her assets, while desirable, would only enhance what
they already own, so Portia may not be as important to them as she would
like. They are lords, princes, counts, barons, and dukes; only Bassanio,
described by Nerissa as "a Venetian, a scholar and a soldier" (104)—
listing his affiliation with Venice first is an important detail—is in outright
want of money, having admitted to his friend Antonio in 1.1 that "*I* have
disabled mine estate" (123, emphasis mine). Bassanio could use Portia's
ample coffers to rebuild the capital he himself has squandered.[5] If Portia
were to marry Bassanio, she would be gaining a husband who is dependent
on her estate, and this may help her secure an empowered position in the
marriage.

Though Bassanio reveals in this same exchange with Antonio that he
means to become a suitor, nevertheless he is not yet in contention in 1.2.
When Portia has finished criticizing the candidates, Nerissa reassures her
mistress by saying

> You need not fear, lady, the having any of these
> lords. They have acquainted me with their determina-
> tions, which is indeed to return to their home and to
> trouble you with no more suit. (92–95)

Nerissa's unwavering confidence about the imminent departure of all six suitors is, to me, puzzling. How can she be so confident that Portia will not be forced to marry any of these men? Admittedly, the price of losing the test once it is taken is harsh, for not only does each man walk away empty-handed, but he must swear, as Portia will later warn Morocco, "Never to speak to lady afterward / In way of marriage" (2.1.41–42).[6] Perhaps, then, none of the six men wanted to risk never producing a legitimate heir, and decided to keep their future marital options alive, even if it meant passing on the possibility of marrying an heiress. However, it seems unlikely that all six of these men would voluntarily and simultaneously decide to stop pursuing Portia's fortune.

Then Nerissa offers Portia an alternative, saying that the men are leaving

> unless you may be won
> by some other sort than your father's imposition, de-
> pending on the caskets. (95–97)

Is Nerissa here innocently passing along to Portia what the suitors have said to her, or is there another reason she is making this remark? After all, Portia has bemoaned her state, complaining that

> I
> may neither choose who I would nor refuse who I dis-
> like, so is the will of a living daughter curbed by the will
> of a dead father. (21–24)

But when pressed by Nerissa, Portia is resolute:

> I will die as chaste
> as Diana unless I be obtained by the manner of my
> father's will. (98–100)

It is never explained whose idea it is—the suitors' or Nerissa's—to present Portia with a Plan B. Nor does it matter very much because Portia swiftly rejects it. However, Nerissa has been at every step of these important nuptial proceedings, and has a vested interest in whom Portia marries. If Portia leaves Belmont, then so too must Nerissa. The six suitors, like Morocco and

Arragon who will follow them, are foreigners. And while Portia has been accused by some critics of being, at best, a xenophobe, and, at worst, a racist, my point in mentioning their nationalities here is to suggest that Nerissa, already involved in a secret romance with Gratiano, has a compelling reason to stay near Venice.[7] While it cannot be proven that Nerissa, somehow, persuaded the six suitors to abandon their pursuit of Portia's fortune all at the same time, nevertheless Nerissa would want and need Portia to remain in the vicinity of Venice.

Yet Nerissa is not alone in wanting to stay at Belmont. After all, Portia is sole proprietor of a highly desirable estate that is coveted—it is mentioned several times by various characters—by men throughout the world, and though her protestations against the casket lottery are justified, she does agree to honor her father's will.[8] Portia refuses to violate the terms of his contract, outraged though she may be by its limitations which, by the way, are of concern. Not only can she not choose a man she deems acceptable, but she is also unable to stop any unsuitable man from taking the test. Thus, as a businesswoman with substantial property to manage wisely and protect fervently, her critiques of the suitors seem warranted and are reasonable grounds on which to reject them. Her catalog of complaints is not concerned with matters of the heart; love is not what she seeks. It is Nerissa who continually associates love with marriage. Instead, Portia is looking for an educated man, focused on something other than his horse or alcohol, one whose tendency is not to frown nor throw punches. It should come as no surprise, then, that when Nerissa first mentions Bassanio, he sounds like the first male to have come along (though he has not yet arrived) who has any potential. Nerissa takes care to highlight his attributes as she describes him as being endowed with those qualities Portia has found lacking in the others. Nerissa asks Portia to recall "in your father's time, a Venetian, a scholar and a soldier" (103–104), and it is Portia who instantly supplies Bassanio's name, adding that he was worthy of praise. Monsieur Le Bon merely "pass[es] for a man" (52–53); Bassanio is a soldier, a decidedly masculine profession. Baron Falconbridge "hath neither Latin, French, nor Italian" (64–65); Nerissa calls Bassanio a scholar. And perhaps his most important assets are listed first: not only is he a Venetian, but one whom Nerissa carefully aligns in name with Portia's father. Therefore, Bassanio is a homegrown solution to what has been for both women a foreign problem.[9] With the exotic competition now removed, and Bassanio maneuvered into range, Nerissa has carefully set the stage for Bassanio to play, and win, the casket lottery.

But he cannot and does not go first. In line before him are Morocco and Arragon, both of them, again, foreign and royal, but they are precisely the type of men to fail such a test. Both men explain why they choose the caskets that they do—gold and silver respectively—but their suppositions about how to play the game are erroneous because they both put first their own desires, rather than trying to put themselves in the place of a father who devised this scheme for the protection of his daughter and land. Only a (too) protective father would have the correct casket inscribed with "Who chooseth me must give and hazard all he hath." What father would want a son-in-law who was not willing to risk all on behalf of his daughter? As Nerissa says in 1.2, the winner of the casket test will be the man "who chooses his meaning" (29). It is a dead father's will, therefore, that needs to be satisfied, not Portia's nor even the suitor's.

When Portia first meets Morocco in 2.1, the first line she speaks to him contains the word "led" (13), a homophone for the correct casket, and the last line contains the word "hazard" (45), which is part of the inscription on the lead casket ("Who chooseth me must give and hazard all he hath"). When Arragon arrives (out of nowhere, it seems, for he is not part of the original list of six contenders, nor is he mentioned at any point before he appears in 2.9; is this Nerissa's hand again?) and agrees to the terms of the test, Portia again employs the word "hazard" (17) to describe the risk Arragon is taking. And later when it is Bassanio's turn, Portia will ask him to delay the "hazard" (3.2.2) he is about to take. My reason for mentioning Portia's language is that, though she is clearly partial to Bassanio and behaves differently when it is his turn, she is first and foremost a woman from a privileged landowning class, and she speaks "the language of reckoning and acquisitiveness" (Hopkins 51) in her dealings with the suitors; to break outright the bonds, admittedly unforgiving, that tie her both to her father's game and the sex/gender system at large, therefore, would be unthinkable. Further, given all that rides not on making the correct choice, but the *incorrect* one, Morocco, Arragon, or Bassanio would seem to have other matters on their minds. I question how attentive they can be in listening to what Portia is saying when it is remembered that while she is speaking the men are simultaneously facing three imposing caskets that decide whether they get married now or never. Thus, one "led" here and another "hazard" there do not seem to be sufficient "hints" for even the most astute listener to discern.[10] If anything, Portia's language gestures towards reminding the participants by whom this test was devised because the path to Portia's hand runs through the "wit" (2.1.18) of her father. To associate the various metals with Portia's perceived worth or what the suitors themselves desire leads only to bachelorhood and the presumed end of their family lines.[11] Morocco and Arragon, then, bring this unfortunate outcome upon themselves because, as Joan Ozark Holmer contends, "the casket test illustrates that as a man perceives, so he is; each suitor's choice is a projection of his moral character" (59).[12]

But I am less interested in analyzing how or why Morocco and Arragon lose the test. What is more important is that, at least by the time Bassanio shows up (though she may have known since the beginning), Portia knows that the lead casket is the correct one, which may explain her behavior

Figure 9. Friedrich Brockmann, *Portia and Nerissa* (1849). By Permission of the Folger Shakespeare Library.

throughout 3.2. It is at the end of 2.9 when, after Arragon has chosen the incorrect silver casket, a messenger announces Bassanio's impending arrival. But Bassanio is not referred to by name. It is Nerissa who first names him; such foreknowledge on the part of Nerissa, and *only* Nerissa, suggests to me that Nerissa has again been orchestrating events. She is the only one who had contact with the original six suitors—it is she who informs Portia that they are all leaving; Portia does not appear to have firsthand knowledge of their goings-on—and she is the first to float Bassanio as a possible suitor. And though Bassanio does not need Nerissa to obtain an audience with Portia, Nerissa seems to be the only one expecting his arrival. At the end of this scene Portia is curious to see who this latest suitor is; Nerissa, not Portia, asserts it is "Bassanio, Lord Love" (100).

Arguably, it is Portia's language and actions throughout Bassanio's casket test in 3.2 that have received the most attention, and whether or not she is helping Bassanio cheat to victory continues to be cause for academic debate.[13] If Portia is guilty of cheating, then she breaks her father's will, which means by extension that she goes back on her own word. Throughout the play she has repeatedly said she will abide by her father's decree, and again in this scene declares to Bassanio, "I am forsworn" (11). As mistress of Belmont, which is where she and the caskets reside, her word is her bond, so it makes sense she would not risk making it "a wild of nothing." Yet having said that, does she, perhaps, drop hints that Bassanio could possibly pick up? According to Holmer, even if Portia's language did contain clues, this would not "invalidate the test" because "a clue is but a clue. A clue is not an answer" (99). Portia's use of the word "hazard" (2) with all three suitors has already been mentioned. Later in this same speech, in which she begs Bassanio to delay playing the lottery, she says that should he win, "so all yours" (18), and the inscription on the lead casket, "Who chooseth me must give and hazard all he hath," is the only one that contains the word "all" in reference to the amount that the contender must risk. Because Portia is speaking directly to Bassanio, she very reasonably changes the third person "he" to the second person "you," so that "all he has" easily transmutes into "all yours."

In Portia's next speech, she compares Bassanio's endeavor to the

> young Alcides when he did redeem
> The virgin tribute paid by howling Troy
> To the sea monster. (55–57)

The legend to which Portia refers is of Laomedon, king of Troy, who asks Hercules (or Alcides) to rescue his daughter Hesione from a sea monster that is ravaging Troy. It should be noted that Laomedon is the cause of this disastrous event because he did not fulfill a promise to Apollo and Poseidon, who then retaliated by unleashing the creature and demanding Hesione as a sacrifice. Hercules promises to kill the monster and rescue Hesione only if Laomedon will reward him *not* with his daughter, as might be expected if this were an affair of the heart, but instead Laomedon's prized horses.[14] For Hercules, this is a business deal. Laomedon agrees to Hercules's terms, but once Hesione is safely returned to him, Laomedon again refuses to honor his end of the bargain, so Hercules kills him. In effect, if Bassanio is successful in his Herculean task, he will have rescued Portia by fulfilling her father's will, thus killing his stranglehold over her, and Bassanio's reward, like Hercules's, would be an enhancement of his material holdings. Bassanio, "a scholar," might be familiar with the myth, so perhaps Portia's allusion is none-too-innocent and provides him with a clue. And finally, there is Portia's declaration "I stand for sacrifice" (57) which Harry Berger and others have made much of as a key to Bassanio correctly selecting the lead casket.[15] Yet all of these moments are few and very far between, so it is doubtful that they can be tallied as proof that Portia is a cheater.

The most damning evidence against Portia is the clues in the music that she commands be played while Bassanio makes his choice. There is no denying that the first half of the song contains many words that rhyme with the "ed" in "lead"—bred, head, nourishèd, engend'red, fed—and the second half of the song has words that end in "el"—knell, bell, bell—so this could be a reversal of the two sounds that comprise the word "lead." Further, as Lisa Hopkins notes, even the closing lines which call for a bell to be rung may put Bassanio in mind of lead, for though bell metal "is not the same as lead, it is considerably closer to it than either silver or gold, and the triple rhyme-sound may well seem insistent" (55). Yet I question the ease with which so many scholars assume that Portia is singing. It seems highly unlikely that the mistress of Belmont would unceremoniously break out into song. That is, though Portia does call for a song to be played while Bassanio muses to himself, this then does not make it "Portia's song." Several recent authoritative editions of *Merchant* have taken care to make this distinction as well, and have more correctly attributed the singer to a member of her train.[16] It could be argued, I suppose, that Portia coached her attendants or even the musicians in advance to sing this particular song, emphasizing its leaden rhymes. Yet given her stalwart refusal to break the rules of the test, it seems to me she would not resort to such outright cheating. To do so, according to M. M. Mahood, "belittles Portia's integrity and Bassanio's insight" (115).[17] However, there is one among her train who has already demonstrated that she is not above bending the rules and maneuvering people into whatever circumstances suit her best. If anyone, then, is responsible for the peculiarities of the song, it is Nerissa.[18]

Leaving aside any help he may or may not have received from the women, Bassanio is unique among the suitors who have already tried their hand at the test, and this may also explain why he chooses the correct casket. For one thing he is not a prince, and though he holds the title of lord, as John M. Steadman points out, Bassanio is in no way Portia's *social* equal.[19] He comes to Belmont insolvent, heavily in debt financially to Antonio. Bassanio, without making too fine a point, has been heretofore "lead" by the generosity of his closest male friend. Further, like Morocco and Arragon, Bassanio may covet gold and silver, but he is alone in needing Portia's fortune to settle his debts with Antonio and rebuild the capital he did not take care to protect. As Bassanio himself admits, he has lost his fortune because he overtaxed his resources "By something showing a more swelling port/Than my faint means would grant continuance" (1.1.124–25). That is,

Bassanio was more interested in appearing outwardly wealthy than in subsisting at a more meager level. Thus it is a humbled, even desperate Bassanio, depreciated in value, who is a living embodiment of the caskets' paradox.[20] That the caskets contain a paradox is important, because it provides further evidence that Bassanio would not be influenced by any clues that may or may not be present. In his seminal book *Shakespearean Meanings*, Sigurd Burckhardt cogently argues that "if we think of the rhyme as a clue in the ordinary sense, intentionally placed and consciously interpreted, it would be out of tune with the quality of his [Bassanio's] choice, which lies in the *rejection* of even such clues as are legitimately provided" (217, emphasis mine). Bassanio knows from personal experience the discrepancy between outward appearances and inward worth: "outward shows be least themselves / The world is still deceived with ornament" (73–74). It is no surprise, then, that Bassanio, who has in the past "hazard[ed] all he hath" and who now stands before the caskets with so little, decides upon "meagre lead" (104) as the correct choice.[21]

Portia is delighted with the outcome, and makes a congratulatory speech to Bassanio that may begin in an unexpectedly self-deprecating way—Portia first describes herself as "an unlessoned girl, unschooled, unpractised" (159)—but by the end conveys in no uncertain terms what she expects from Bassanio now that Portia is the person upon whom he will and must rely for all of his needs. As Juliet Dusinberre so elegantly puts it, "submission is a garment she wears as gracefully as her disguise" (85).[22] Portia embodies the economic viability of Antonio, so Bassanio will now turn to her for any future assistance as he once did to his male friends. This position of Bassanio as dependent is one Portia establishes immediately in her first speech act as a woman freed from her father's strictures, while simultaneously fashioning for herself the role of empowered wife. Pointedly employing economic metaphors throughout her speech, Portia calls herself "the lord / Of this fair mansion" (167–68), before she apparently bequeaths the estate and all it entails, including herself, to Bassanio: "This house, these servants, and this same myself / Are yours, my lord's. I give them with this ring" (170–71). This seems to be a gesture of traditional wifely submission and self-marginalization on Portia's part. Instead, she has successfully inverted the subjugation and oppression expected during the nuptial process because she collapses and consolidates Bassanio's access and entitlement to her worth in a ring, a symbol of ownership traditionally bestowed by men upon women. In effect, as Diane Elizabeth Dreher points out, when Portia "seals their marriage contract with a ring," she is playing "the groom's role" (133) having no father to give her away. By proffering a ring in an engagement only moments old, "lord" Portia relinquishes nothing to Bassanio, which means that any enhancement of his own depleted assets to which he may now lay claim can only occur with his wife's permission and blessings.[23]

Bassanio demonstrates his acknowledgment of the terms of his marriage as devised by Portia when Salerio and friends arrive. Bassanio begins to welcome his fellow Venetians to Belmont, but then he checks with Portia to make sure that he is in the right to make such an overture:

> *By your leave,*
> I bid my very friends and countrymen,
> Sweet Portia, welcome. (222–24, emphasis mine)

Portia magnanimously gives him permission to continue: "They are entirely welcome" (225). Portia not only employs this tone of unquestioned and empowered wifely authority throughout the rest of the scene, ordering everyone around (especially Bassanio), but Bassanio too invests Portia with importance because he needs her money to bail out Antonio. Bassanio now admits that he is worse than a "braggart" (258) because his debts have endangered the life of his good friend. Portia is the only one who can save Antonio, and she agrees to provide Bassanio with twenty times the amount of what she deems is a "petty debt" (307). Yet before she will allow Bassanio to return to Venice, Portia reminds him that her needs must now be satisfied before all others: "*First* go with me to church and call me wife / *And then* away to Venice to your friend" (303–304, emphasis mine). After the bond has been cancelled, Portia mandates Bassanio to "bring your true friend along" (308).[24] Bassanio, therefore, may welcome his friends to Belmont and leave with them to attend to Antonio's pressing matters, but only because Portia so chooses.

Bassanio ends the scene by giving thanks again to his fiancée because he has earned her "good leave" (323)—provided they first get married—to return to Venice. Bassanio may have finally laid to rest the man whose lottery has dictated events in Belmont from beyond the grave, but Portia's recent strictures still survive in transmuted form within their marriage. As Vera M. Jiji contends, "Portia's initiative, intelligence, and boldness demonstrate an ability to govern her affairs which make it seem remarkably out of character for her to turn suddenly around and passively submit to another authority, albeit a male one" (8). In her new role of wife, Portia will control the fortunes of men and ships, and this hard-earned position of power, which will now cross over from Belmont to the mercantile world of Venice, signals the emergence of Portia as a dominant character throughout the rest of the play; with the gender-reversal bequeathment of a nuptial ring on her wedding day, Portia has proven that she has heeded well Nerissa's earlier lessons of success through subterfuge, and these are tactics of which Portia will make good use during her time in Venice where, as Leonard Tennenhouse and others have noted, Portia is able to accomplish what no Venetian male can.[25]

But why is Portia compelled to go to Venice in the first place? She is not invited to accompany Bassanio, as Antonio's letter is addressed to "Sweet

Bassanio" only.[26] Further, it does not appear that she is worried about the money she has given to Bassanio because Antonio's debts were, by her own account, trivial. And though she may feel some affinity with Jessica and her recent declaration of independence from a controlling father, Portia's involvement with Jessica and Lorenzo has been indirect at best. I suggest that Portia's impetus to leave Belmont and insert herself into Venetian matters is to spy on Bassanio and, as Lars Engle says, "protect her investment" (34). Bassanio may be her husband, but theirs is a relationship that can be measured in minutes; he has been aligned with Antonio for a much longer, more significant, and more meaningful amount of time, and the wording of Antonio's letter to her husband, according to Marianne Novy, "makes Bassanio's appearance [in Venice] a test of his love" (142).[27] It is to shape, solidify, and claim the primacy of her role as wife, then, that Portia is propelled to Venice.

Throughout the play Bassanio and Antonio have spoken of their mutual love, and while I am not at all suggesting that theirs is a homosexual relationship, their homosocial bond is undeniable and, if you are Portia, perhaps worrisome. Portia, as Olivia Delgado De Torres points out, "is all too conscious of Antonio's grip upon her husband" (349), and Portia acknowledges the men's closeness when she describes Antonio as "the bosom lover of my lord" (3.4.17).[28] Later in 5.1, Portia's order to Antonio to give back to Bassanio the ring she first gave to him, coupled with her seemingly magical restoration of Antonio's ships and his money, can be interpreted as Portia attempting to wrest Bassanio away from Antonio's continued influence by buying off the latter. While Bassanio is in Belmont, removed from his familiar environs and Antonio's presence, he can praise his good fortune and happy marriage with hyperbolic ease, and he can make all the right assurances that his allegiance is now to Portia. Portia's actual challenge to Bassanio, then, is not the ring test. If anything, that is a test within a test.[29] Rather, Portia's will is to see whether the reverse is also true: when Portia's presence is removed, does Bassanio revert to privileging the role of Antonio's best friend? It is not unreasonable for Portia to demand an answer to this question, for throughout the play, as Elizabeth S. Sklar argues, "Bassanio seems thin-blooded and ultimately rather trivial, and his stature is further diminished by the brilliance and panache of Portia" (500). Only in disguise can Portia gauge with any accuracy just where her new husband's loyalties lie. This is why she concocts an unbelievable cover story that she and Nerissa are going to move into a monastery while Bassanio and Gratiano are away (Lorenzo's gullibility on this point is jaw-dropping; how can he believe that an heiress, who still refers to those who are in her employ as "my people" and not Bassanio's, would leave her own estate and attendants in favor of a monastic lifestyle, even if it is only temporarily?) Lorenzo must not know what Portia is planning, because he could contaminate the test conditions by alerting the test subject, Bassanio.

Portia is the sole architect of this scheme as well, which she reveals in 3.4 when she explains in private to her trusted confidante Nerissa that "I have work in hand / That you yet know not of" (57–58).[30] As Lawrence Norman notes, Bassanio must learn from Portia "the lesson of bodily exclusivity that marriage signifies, and as part of this process friendship is subordinated to marriage" (70). Never one to be left out where Portia is involved, Nerissa unhesitatingly follows her mistress, and looks forward to testing her own husband for the same signs of fraternal privileging. And their husbands-cum-guinea pigs fail the test almost immediately.

In 4.1 Portia and Nerissa arrive in court disguised as Balthasar, a doctor of law, and his clerk, respectively. Portia has somehow managed to convince her cousin Bellario not to attend the proceedings and instead allow her, a woman, to render judgment in his place. It is a staple of Shakespeare's comedies (like *Measure for Measure*, it is sometimes difficult to remember that *Merchant* is a comedy) that the female protagonist cross-dresses at some point in the play. But as Jiji importantly suggests, Portia "moves from female to male and back to female not under the pressure of events from outside (as Julia, Viola, Rosalind, and Imogene do), but by her own choice of time and circumstance" (8).[31] She does not dress up, then, as Keith Geary points out, to explore "the psychological consequences of a sexual disguise" (58); she dons hose and doublet to make sure Bassanio—and perhaps Antonio too—does not forget he is a husband, financially and socially tied to Belmont and her mistress. Indeed, they do not. When bidding farewell to Bassanio, Antonio asks his good friend to "Commend me to your honorable wife" (271) and to tell her "how I loved you" (273).[32] Bassanio also refers to his beautiful wife, but only to say that he would sacrifice his relationship with her if it meant saving Antonio's life, because "my wife, and all the world / Are not with me esteemed above thy life" (282–83). Portia's riposte is legendary: "Your wife would give you little thanks for that / If she were by to hear you make the offer" (286–87). Clearly, Portia has witnessed that Bassanio is still allied with Antonio rather than herself. Not to be outdone, Gratiano unhesitatingly wishes aloud that his wife Nerissa were dead "so she could / Entreat some power to change this currish Jew" (289–90). Nerissa, too, has learned something about the man who pined away for her love.

Bassanio's outbursts throughout the rest of the scene are also indicative of his unwavering loyalty to Antonio. While Portia-as-lawyer attempts to hoist Shylock by his own petard, Bassanio continually interrupts, begging Shylock to take Portia's money and cancel the bond. Bassanio is very free in offering money that is not his own, and is willing to disrupt juridical proceedings and attract the wrath of the court, all to save Antonio's life. Bassanio's fealty to Antonio may be commendable, but it signals to Portia that her reasons for coming to Venice—to check on her husband and test his loyalty to her—were justified. Portia's wrath, therefore, is directed towards the one target to which she has access, Shylock, and despite her speech acts, there is little "quality of mercy" in the verdicts she renders. Not only does she strip Shylock of everything, forcing him to give half of his wealth to Antonio and the other half to the state (which later gets passed on to Lorenzo at Antonio's behest), but she saves her own money and Antonio's life in the process. It has been suggested that Portia single-mindedly targets Shylock and does not relent until he has been left with nothing because he symbolizes a father figure whose destiny she can control. Perhaps Portia is enjoying the power she now owns to effect such a role reversal, which is why Portia's methods throughout 4.1 are, as Robert Hapgood and others have described them, "highhanded" (21). But it results in more than Shylock's demise; Antonio now joins Bassanio in being indebted to her. The Duke recognizes the debt when he mandates Antonio to "gratify this gentleman [Portia] / For in my mind you are much *bound* to him" (404–405, emphasis mine). Shylock, then, is merely a tragic pawn in Portia's larger scheme to extricate Bassanio from Antonio's influence.

Yet Portia provides Bassanio one more opportunity to assert the primacy of his marriage. After she refuses to accept her money back from her unsuspecting husband, she instead asks for Bassanio's ring, the very symbol of their marriage and her power contained therein that she established, once the casket test was completed. Bassanio first describes it as "a trifle" beneath Balthasar's consideration, and despite Portia's attempts to goad Bassanio into giving up the ring, he remains resolute and will not part with it. But once Portia exits, leaving Bassanio again solely in the company of Antonio, he quickly succumbs to his friend's wishes that "my love withal / Be valued 'gainst your wife's commandèment" (448–49). Bassanio unhesitatingly complies and orders Gratiano to overtake the departing lawyer and give him Portia's ring. Portia and Nerissa have watched as their husbands, in open court, offered to sacrifice their wives and relationships in exchange for Antonio's life. The women's spirits and confidence in the men must have been buoyed, then, when Bassanio refused to relinquish the symbol of his marriage. But any progress Portia felt she was making in shifting Bassanio's allegiance to her is quickly nullified when Gratiano explains in 4.2 that Bassanio, "upon more advice" (6), has sent along his ring. If Portia (and Nerissa too, who is also regrettably successful in getting her own ring back from Gratiano) was gaining confidence that her husband was finally beginning to turn to her and their marriage even in Antonio's presence, the unwelcome delivery of her own ring in 4.2 must have shaken that hope to her wifely core. Portia needs a new plan to remind her husband, as Dreher says, that he should no longer be "subordinating conjugal love to male friendship" (135) because he should now be turning to Portia. Though Nerissa was previously successful in making other unwelcome men disappear from Portia's life, Antonio's "excessive friendship" (369), to use Alice N. Benston's apt description, has not been curbed. Thus, Portia cannot rely on Nerissa for assistance. Instead, Portia very cleverly uses Antonio himself as the means by which he will be removed from Bassanio's consideration, as Portia skillfully adapts an old adage to her advantage: she has been unable to beat Antonio; therefore, she will make him joined to her.

Both Portia and Nerissa have learned that, at least in Venice, they are still not privileged by their new mates who, as Leonard Tennenhouse describes, have by their actions declared that "the patronage bond is stronger than even the marriage vow" (59). Once back in her own environs, Portia wastes no time in telling Nerissa to go in and "Give order to *my* servants" (119, emphasis mine) while she awaits the impending arrival of Bassanio, in front of whom she deliberately mends her speech and welcomes Antonio to "*our* house" (139, emphasis mine). Almost immediately, Gratiano and Bassanio are challenged to produce their rings. Gratiano admits to what he did, but Bassanio's first instinct is to lie to Portia, saying to himself "I were best to cut my left hand off / And swear I lost the ring defending it" (177–78). Gratiano does not afford Bassanio that luxury for he tells the women what happened. Bassanio still does not recognize that he has done anything wrong, and attempts to explain that though he first denied Balthasar the ring, eventually "I was enforced to send it after him" (216). With this admission—that Bassanio was acting on Antonio's mandates rather than heeding her own desires—Portia drops her magnanimous facade, reverts to calling Belmont "*my* house" not once but twice in this scene, and puts her unconventional plan into action.

Until this point, Portia has been unsuccessful in separating the two friends because her focus was on dictating Bassanio's actions. Portia now alters course and targets Antonio, whose influence upon Bassanio continues seemingly unabated. She begins by giving to Antonio the ring, and mandates that he give it to Bassanio this time. She then reveals the true identities of Balthasar and his law clerk, and concludes by restoring to Antonio, who has been conspicuously silenced throughout this scene of double marital discord, the ships and fortune lost at sea. Because Antonio both confers the wedding ring upon Bassanio and at the same time learns that Portia has acted as his savior not once but twice, Antonio becomes wholly bound to her, and thus can no longer be cast in the role of Bassanio's patron. Portia finally succeeds in rendering kinship relations as being stronger than the bond of patronage. As Engle notes, Portia has also established "absolute mastery of the systems of exchange in the play which have routed all blessings economic, erotic, and theological, toward Belmont" (37). Antonio's response in the face of Portia's domination, "I am dumb!" (279), could not be more appropriate, as he understands the woman, not the man, to whom he is indebted for life. Portia has won and, as Anne Parten says, it is in "constantly demonstrating her ability to beat men at their own games [that] Shakespeare allows Portia to emerge as a more potent character than any of her masculine companions" (147).

Portia has now set the stage for Bassanio to reenter his own marriage, having maneuvered him into taking his cues of indebtedness from Antonio. In his final words, as Mahood points out, "Bassanio must now plead and Portia must remain obdurate until the battle of the sexes ends with a graceful capitulation of her power" (40).[33] Bassanio does just this and calls Portia "Sweet Doctor" (284), which consolidates Antonio's earlier epistolary address of Bassanio, as well as Portia's decidedly unwifely behavior in Venice.[34] Bassanio may be Portia's husband, but there is no mistaking that she remains lord of Belmont and the sole director not only of his future, but Antonio's as well. In a role traditionally reserved for high ranking male characters, Portia has tied up all of the plots' loose ends, and though she is not the last character to speak, she outlasts Antonio and Bassanio when she calls for everyone to enter *her* house, where she and Nerissa "will answer all things faithfully" (299). Portia has played and won her father's casket test, attained a problematic but nonetheless valid court ruling in Venice, and subsumed Bassanio and Antonio into a marital arrangement of her own design, agency intact. As a result, Portia emerges by the end as the dominant character of the play, for despite its title, *The Merchant of Venice* has centered on events created by and advantageous to Portia.[35] Though in the beginning she needed Nerissa's help to create a desirable marriage, and in the end drafted Antonio to assist in securing that marriage, Portia eventually wins for herself an empowered role in her marriage, all without ever having broken any rules of the game. Indeed, Nerissa has taught her friend well.

Notes

1. *The Merchant of Venice*, ed. Brents Stirling. All quotations of *Merchant* will refer to this edition, incorporated into *The Complete Pelican Shakespeare*, ed. Alfred Harbage.
2. As Marc Berley concludes, "there is something peculiarly wrong with all the male characters in *Merchant*. Portia shows herself to be superior to all the men in the play" (201). Richard P. Wheeler agrees, asserting that Portia demonstrates, "playfully and virtually effortlessly, resources of strength and insight that dwarf those of the play's men" (197).
3. This term, an alternative to the monolithic "patriarchal system," comes from Gayle Rubin, who explains that "patriarchy" is an insufficient label as opposed to a sex/gender system, which maintains "a distinction between the human capacity and necessity to create a sexual world, and the empirically oppressive ways in which sexual worlds have been organized. Patriarchy subsumes both meanings into the same term. Sex/gender system, on the other hand, is a neutral term which refers to the domain and indicates that oppression is not inevitable in that domain, but is the product of the specific social relations which organize it" (168).
4. In their article "Portia's Suitors," Richard Kuhns and Barbara Tovey attempt to identify the historical counterparts to Shakespeare's six fictional suitors.

5. Alessandra Marzola says that "hers is an inheritance whose never questioned feudal-born wealth is expected to invigorate a gentleman's scanty financial resources" (296). I am indebted to John Drakakis for bringing Marzola's article to my attention, for Marzola is one of the few scholars to note that by being a lord, Bassanio is dependent upon money to finance his title. Unlike Portia, he is no member of the landowning aristocracy.

6. In their book *The Law of Property in Shakespeare and the Elizabethan Drama*, Paul S. Clarkson and Clyde T. Warren point out that "such a condition was clearly illegal, even if there had been any way of forcing the unlucky contestant to abide by his oath" (277) but, they quickly add, such legal analysis of a will that would have been "pronounced illegal, unenforceable, and void" (278) misses the point of the heightened drama Shakespeare was attempting to create.

7. Frank Whigman asserts that in her dealings with Morocco, "Portia is not a rebel against her culture; she is its judgmental representative" (98). Similar conclusions are reached by Richard A. Levin and Marianne L. Novy. For disagreement, see Joan Ozark Holmer's book, *"The Merchant of Venice": Choice, Hazard and Consequence*, in which she takes Portia's objection to Morocco's "complexion" as a reference to his temperament or "disposition" (102).

8. Keith Geary importantly reminds us that Portia is on her own in Belmont, and that the casket scenes "emphasize Portia's superiority to her suitors and her ability to deal with them directly, without the aid of other men; there is no Boyet or Lafew or even Touchstone in Belmont" (57).

9. But this is not to say that Bassanio is a better or unblemished choice for a mate, only a more convenient one. Indeed, several critics have rightfully questioned why Portia is attracted to Bassanio in the first place. Clara Claiborne Park describes Bassanio as "one of the most firmly nonmemorable of Shakespeare's characters, but Portia is nonetheless delighted with him" (109). Robert Hapgood similarly concludes that Bassanio is "precisely the kind of man her father most wanted to eliminate" (24) with the casket test, and Diane Elizabeth Dreher suggests that "all that Bassanio has to recommend him is his friendship with Antonio, and even that is suspect, gilded by many loans" (130).

10. John Lyon agrees, and points out that if Bassanio actually picks up on any clues that may or may not be imbedded throughout 3.2, "then it does incredible wonders for Bassanio's intellectual and aural acuity" (93).

11. Carol Leventen astutely notes that "although we are told precisely what will happen to her suitors if they fail to choose the proper casket (they are to be confined to a celibate life), we do not know what would happen to Portia were she simply to take matters into her own hands and decide not to abide by her father's system, because the question is never asked—very much in contrast to what Shakespeare takes pains to spell out for us of the coercive pressures applied to heroines like Hermia and Isabella, for example" (69–70).

12. Sigurd Burckhardt makes a similar point: for Morocco and Arragon, "it is this intrusion of their selves and their purposes that misleads them; they are enmeshed in their reckonings" (217).

13. For those scholars who suggest Portia deliberately helps Bassanio to cheat, see, for example, Bruce Erlich, S. F. Johnson, Michael Zuckert, Samuel

Ajzenstat, and Ming-Kae Wang. In her essay, Joan Ozark Holmer further discusses apparent clues throughout Portia's conversations with all three suitors. However, I agree with Robert Hapgood who argues that Bassanio, who "comments on the caskets to himself" (s.d. 229) while the song is being played, would not necessarily hear any supposed clues which "belong at most to the realm of subliminal suggestion" (25). See, among others, Lawrence Danson and Diane Elizabeth Dreher.

14. Only a handful of scholars have bothered to discuss the significance of this myth at any length, and of those, Harry Berger is one of the few who importantly points out that Hercules asks for Trojan horses, and not Hesione, as his reward. Yet even Berger does not make reference to the fact that Laomedon's own missteps are responsible for endangering the life of his daughter.

15. See Berger, as well as David Lucking.

16. *The Oxford Shakespeare*, and Katharine Eisaman Maus's edition for *The Norton Shakespeare*, which is based upon the Oxford edition, say that it is "one from Portia's train" who sings the song. M. M. Mahood's edition for Cambridge has one of the musicians singing the song, while the 1623 First Folio, Stirling's *Penguin* edition, John Russell Brown's *Arden* edition, and G. Blakemore Evans's *Riverside Shakespeare* make no distinction as to who is singing. While there is no consensus as to the identity of the singer (or singers), no edition suggests that it is Portia.

17. Susan McLean also points out that "one does not offer one riddle as the solution to another" (46). For a comprehensive discussion of the various riddles present throughout the play, see Catherine Belsey.

18. David Lucking importantly notes that in *Il Pecorone*, one of the main sources of *Merchant*, the maid helps the hero to cheat in order to win his suit. Therefore, in this play, "since it is Nerissa who appears to stage-manage the ceremonial (II.ix.103) there is nothing improbable in the hypothesis that it is she who has contrived this as a device for acquainting Bassanio with the secret" (365).

19. Steadman goes on to say that Bassanio, like Sebastian and Duke Orsino, should be regarded as "exceptionally lucky—fortunate beyond normal expectations—if not beyond their own deserts" (84).

20. Hapgood correctly describes the casket choice as an "aptitude test" (25). Richard Horwich also argues that it is not intuition but calculation that explains Bassanio's success with the casket test.

21. See also Hugh Maclean, who suggests that Bassanio's name is derived from the word "base," which may account for why Bassanio chooses the casket made from the base metal lead, as opposed to gold or silver.

22. Lisa Jardine makes a similar point: "Portia is not 'unschool'd,' 'unlesson'd' (the plot hinges on her learning); she does not commit her 'gentle spirit' to Bassanio's direction (she continues to act with authority, and without his knowledge or permission); and as her accounting imagery reminds us, she retains full control of her financial affairs (even the servants continue to answer to her)" (17).

23. As David Sundelson reminds us, "with little more than a certain tact and Antonio's love to distinguish him from Gratiano or Lorenzo, this charming young social adventurer will never be master except in name" (250).

24. For a thorough explication of Portia's speech, see Lynda E. Boose, who concludes that "in the space of sixteen lines [298–314], she uses thirteen imperative verbs and four times subjugates male options to the control of her authoritative 'shall' " (248).

25. Leonard Tennenhouse elegantly writes, "As a man without a penis, as a dutiful daughter released from the will of her father, as a source of paternal wealth and maternal love, as a married woman who is still a virgin, Portia can come into Venice, where the males are helpless to act, and can free Antonio" (59).

26. See Leonard Tennenhouse's seminal book *Power on Display: The Politics of Shakespeare's Genres*, in which he discusses the privileging of writing throughout the play. As Tennenhouse says, although Venice and Belmont seem to be two opposing sites, "they concur on the fundamental point that authority resides in and operates through writing" (53). This is seen in Venice, where Antonio's contract to Shylock is "a type of writing so powerful not even the duke can modify it" (53); in Belmont, where Portia's father's will must be satisfied; and in Antonio's letter to Bassanio, which acts as a point where the two varied arenas of Venice and Belmont meet. Similarly, Boose points out that "Antonio's letter is only one of the play's onstage written signifiers of male-male bonds that Portia intercepts and effectively rewrites. By the end of the play, the banking system has been moved to Belmont, for Portia controls and dispenses all bonds and all script" (248).

27. For an enlightening discussion of Antonio and Bassanio's relationship, see Alan Sinfield.

28. For further discussion of the rivalry between Portia and Antonio for Bassanio's attentions, see Lawrence Hyman and Michael Zuckert.

29. For a discussion of the manifold meanings of the ring plot throughout the play, see Coppélia Kahn.

30. For an insightful discussion of the importance of private female conversations in Shakespeare, see Carole McKewin, who says, "Private conversations between women in Shakespeare's plays provide opportunities for self-expression, adjustment to social codes, release, relief, rebellion, and transformation" (129), all of which seem to be present in the women's exchange in 3.4. Lori Schroeder Haslem also discusses the importance of private female conversations and calls them "catechetical."

31. See also Clara Claiborne Park, who correctly notes that Portia is alone among Shakespeare's heroines because she "is allowed to confront a man over matters outside a woman's sphere, and to win" (109).

32. Barbara Tovey intriguingly concludes that "subtly, Antonio suggests that his love is superior to Portia's. It is he who is laying down his life for Bassanio. Greater love hath no man than this" (229).

33. As Jiji points out, "the drive for power seems to be one of Portia's most persistent traits throughout the play" (7).

34. Ralph Berry asserts that "there is no surer sign of personal uncertainty than variation in mode of address, and in the final scene Bassanio, incredibly, addresses Portia in six different ways: 'Madam,' 'sweet Portia,' 'sweet lady,' 'good lady,' 'Portia,' 'sweet Doctor.' That is the measure of Bassanio's unease, as it is the measure of Portia's patrician dominance" (16).

35. Herbert S. Donow has carefully documented Portia's centrality, pointing out that of the play's 2,580 lines, Portia is "present for 1,281 lines and Bassanio for 1,351" (87). Donow concludes, therefore, that "Portia and Bassanio are unquestionably the principal characters," with Portia seeming even more prominent, "for while Bassanio appears in several scenes in which he plays only a minor role, Portia never does" (87).

Works Cited

Ajzenstat, Samuel. "Contract in *The Merchant of Venice*." *Philosophy and Literature* 21.2 (1997): 262–78.

Belsey, Catherine. "Love in Venice." *The Merchant of Venice: New Casebooks*. Ed. Martin Coyle. New York: St. Martin's Press, 1998. 139–60.

Benston, Alice N. "Portia, the Law, and the Tripartite Structure of *The Merchant of Venice*." *Shakespeare Quarterly* 30 (1979): 367–85.

Berger, Harry. "Marriage and Mercifixion in *The Merchant of Venice*: The Casket Scene Revisited." *Shakespeare Quarterly* 32 (1981): 155–62.

Berley, Marc. "Jessica's Belmont Blues: Music and Merriment in *The Merchant of Venice*." *Opening the Borders: Inclusivity in Early Modern Studies*. Ed. Peter C. Herman. Newark: University of Delaware Press, 1999. 185–205.

Berry, Ralph. "Discomfort in *The Merchant of Venice*." *Thalia* 1.3 (1978–1979): 9–16.

Boose, Lynda E. "The Comic Contract and Portia's Golden Ring." *Shakespeare Studies* 20 (1988): 241–54.

Burckhardt, Sigurd. *Shakespearean Meanings*. Princeton: Princeton University Press, 1968.

Clarkson, Paul S., and Clyde T. Warren. *The Law of Property in Shakespeare and the Elizabethan Drama*. Baltimore: The Johns Hopkins Press, 1942.

Coyle, Martin, ed. *The Merchant of Venice: New Casebooks*. New York: St. Martin's Press, 1998.

Danson, Lawrence. *The Harmonies of "The Merchant of Venice."* New Haven: Yale University Press, 1978.

De Torres, Olivia Delgado. "Reflections on Patriarchy and the Rebellion of Daughters in Shakespeare's *Merchant of Venice* and *Othello*." *Interpretation* 21.3 (1994): 333–51.

Donow, Herbert S. "Shakespeare's Caskets: Unity in *The Merchant of Venice*." *Shakespeare Studies* 4 (1968): 86–93.

Dreher, Diane Elizabeth. *Domination and Defiance: Fathers and Daughters in Shakespeare*. Lexington: University Press of Kentucky, 1986.

Dusinberre, Juliet. *Shakespeare and the Nature of Women*. London: Macmillan Press Ltd., 1975.

Engle, Lars. " 'Thrift is Blessing': Exchange and Explanation in *The Merchant of Venice*." *Shakespeare Quarterly* 37 (1986): 20–37.

Erlich, Bruce. "Queenly Shadows: Mediation in Two Comedies." *Shakespeare Survey* 35 (1982): 65–77.

Geary, Keith. "The Nature of Portia's Victory: Turning to Men in *The Merchant of Venice*." *Shakespeare Survey* 37 (1984): 55–68.

Hapgood, Robert. "Portia and *The Merchant of Venice*: The Gentle Bond." *Modern Language Quarterly* 28.1 (1967): 19–32.

Haslem, Lori Schroeder. " 'O Me, the Word Choose!': Female Voice and Catechetical Ritual in *The Two Gentlemen of Verona* and *The Merchant of Venice*." *Shakespeare Studies* 22 (1994): 122–40.

Holmer, Joan Ozark. *"The Merchant of Venice": Choice, Hazard and Consequence*. New York: St. Martin's Press, 1995.

———. "Loving Wisely and the Casket Test: Symbolic and Structural Unity in *The Merchant of Venice*." *Shakespeare Studies* 11 (1978): 53–76.

Hopkins, Lisa. *The Shakespearean Marriage: Merry Wives and Heavy Husbands*. New York: St. Martin's Press, 1998.

Horwich, Richard. "Riddle and Dilemma in *The Merchant of Venice*." *Studies in English Literature, 1500–1900* 17 (1977): 191–200.

Hyman, Lawrence. "The Rival Lovers in *The Merchant of Venice*." *Shakespeare Quarterly* 21 (1970): 109–16.

Jardine, Lisa. "Cultural Confusion and Shakespeare's Learned Heroines: 'These are old paradoxes.' " *Shakespeare Quarterly* 38 (1987): 1–18.

Jiji, Vera M. "Portia Revisited: The Influence of Unconscious Factors Upon Theme and Characterization in *The Merchant of Venice*." *Literature and Psychology* 26.1 (1976): 5–15.

Johnson, S. F. "How Many Ways Portia Informs Bassanio's Choice." *Shakespeare's Universe: Renaissance Ideas and Conventions*. Ed. John M. Mucciolo. Aldershot: Scolar Press, 1996. 144–47.

Kahn, Coppélia. "The Cuckoo's Note: Male Friendship and Cuckoldry in *The Merchant of Venice*." *Shakespeare's "Rough Magic": Renaissance Essays in Honor of C. L. Barber*. Eds. Peter Erickson and Coppélia Kahn. Newark: University of Delaware Press, 1985. 104–12.

Kuhns, Richard, and Barbara Tovey. "Portia's Suitors." *Philosophy and Literature* 13.2 (1989): 325–31.

Leventen, Carol. "Patrimony and Patriarchy in *The Merchant of Venice*." *The Matter of Difference: Materialist Feminist Criticism of Shakespeare*. Ed. Valerie Wayne. Ithaca: Cornell University Press, 1991. 59–79.

Levin, Richard A. *"Twelfth Night, The Merchant of Venice*, and Two Alternate Approaches to Shakespearean Comedy." *English Studies* 59 (1978): 336–43.

Lucking, David. "Standing for Sacrifice: The Casket and Trial Scenes in *The Merchant of Venice*." *University of Toronto Quarterly* 58 (1989): 355–75.

Lyon, John. *Twayne's New Critical Introductions to Shakespeare: "The Merchant of Venice."* Boston: Twayne Publishers, 1988.

Maclean, Hugh. "Bassanio's Name and Nature." *Names* 25.2 (1977): 55–62.

Marzola, Alessandra. "Which is the Woman Here, and Which the Man?: Economy and Gender in *The Merchant of Venice*." *European Journal of English Studies* 1.3 (1997): 291–309.

McKewin, Carole. "Counsels of Gall and Grace: Intimate Conversations between Women in Shakespeare's Plays." *The Woman's Part: Feminist Criticism of Shakespeare*. Eds. Carolyn Lenz, Gayle Greene, and Carol Thomas Neely. Urbana: University of Illinois Press, 1980. 117–32.

McLean, Susan. "Prodigal Sons and Daughters: Transgression and Forgiveness in *The Merchant of Venice." Papers on Language and Literature* 32.1 (1996): 45–62.

Newman, Karen. "Portia's Ring: Unruly Women and Structures of Exchange in *The Merchant of Venice." The Merchant of Venice: New Casebooks*. Ed. Martin Coyle. New York: St. Martin's Press, 1998. 117–38.

Norman, Lawrence. "Reading the Body in *The Merchant of Venice." Textual Practice* 5.1 (1991): 55–73.

Novy, Marianne L. "Giving, Taking, and the Role of Portia in *The Merchant of Venice." Philological Quarterly* 58 (1979): 137–54.

Park, Clara Claiborne. "As We Like It: How a Girl Can Be Smart and Still Popular." *The Woman's Part: Feminist Criticism of Shakespeare*. Eds. Carolyn Lenz, Gayle Greene, and Carol Thomas Neely. Urbana: University of Illinois Press, 1980. 100–116.

Parten, Anne. "Re-establishing Sexual Order: The Ring Episode in *The Merchant of Venice." Women's Studies* 9.2 (1982): 145–55.

Rubin, Gayle. "The Traffic in Women: Notes on the 'Political Economy' of Sex." *Toward an Anthropology of Women*. Ed. Rayna R. Reiter. New York: Monthly Review Press, 1975. 157–210.

Shakespeare, William. *The Complete Pelican Shakespeare*. Ed. Alfred Harbage. New York: Viking Penguin Inc., 1977.

———. *The Merchant of Venice*. Ed. John Russell Brown. London: Methuen, 1998.

———. *The Merchant of Venice*. Ed. M. M. Mahood. Cambridge: Cambridge University Press, 1987.

———. *The Norton Shakespeare*. Ed. Stephen Greenblatt. New York: W.W. Norton & Company, 1997.

———. *The Oxford Shakespeare*. Ed. Jay L. Halio. Oxford: Clarendon Press, 1993.

———. *The Riverside Shakespeare*. Ed. G. Blakemore Evans. Boston: Houghton Mifflin, 1974.

Sinfield, Alan. "How to Read *The Merchant of Venice* Without Being Heterosexist." *The Merchant of Venice: New Casebooks*. Ed. Martin Coyle. New York: St. Martin's Press, 1998. 161–80.

Sklar, Elizabeth S. "Bassanio's Golden Fleece." *Texas Studies in Literature and Language* 18 (1976): 500–09.

Steadman, John M. " 'Respects of Fortune': Dowries and Inheritances in Shakespeare, Spenser and Marvell—an Overview." *Shakespeare's Universe: Renaissance Ideas and Conventions*. Ed. John M. Mucciolo. Aldershot: Scolar Press, 1996. 71–94.

Sundelson, David. "The Dynamics of Marriage in *The Merchant of Venice." Humanities in Society* 4.2–3 (1981): 245–62.

Tennenhouse, Leonard. "The Counterfeit Order of *The Merchant of Venice." Representing Shakespeare: New Psychoanalytic Essays*. Eds. Murray M. Schwartz and Coppélia Kahn. Baltimore: The Johns Hopkins University Press, 1980. 54–69.

———. *Power on Display: The Politics of Shakespeare's Genres*. New York: Methuen, 1986.

Tovey, Barbara. "The Golden Casket: An Interpretation of *The Merchant of Venice." Shakespeare as Political Thinker*. Eds. John Alvis and Thomas G. West. Durham: Carolina Academic Press, 1981. 215–37.

Wang, Ming-Kae. "A Legal and Moral Discourse on the Roles of Shylock and Portia in *The Merchant of Venice.*" *Tamkang Review* 25.3–4 (1995): 311–29.

Wheeler, Richard P. " '. . . And my loud crying still': The *Sonnets*, *The Merchant of Venice*, and *Othello.*" *Shakespeare's "Rough Magic": Renaissance Essays in Honor of C. L. Barber.* Eds. Peter Erickson and Coppélia Kahn. Newark: University of Delaware Press, 1985. 193–209.

Whigman, Frank. "Ideology and Class Conduct in *The Merchant of Venice.*" *Renaissance Drama* 10 (1979): 93–115.

Zuckert, Michael. "The New Medea: On Portia's Comic Triumph in *The Merchant of Venice.*" *Shakespeare's Political Pageant: Essays in Literature and Politics.* Eds. Joseph Aluis and Vickie Sullivan. Lanham, MD: Rowman and Littlefield Publishers Inc., 1996. 3–36.

"Mislike Me Not for My Complexion"

Whose Mislike? Portia's? Shakespeare's? Or That of His Age?

R.W. DESAI

The most significant issue in *The Merchant of Venice* is of course the fate of Shylock. But this concern has assumed the proportions it has during the past fifty years on account of the Holocaust, the culminating horror in the long history of the persecution of the Jewish race in Europe. Shakespeare, ahead of his times, adumbrated in the play a racial conflict that in the twentieth century displayed in full measure what was still embryonic when the play was written at the close of the sixteenth century. History has unlocked the play's secret. Hitherto, understandably, the bulk of criticism has concentrated on this aspect, almost to the exclusion of the strands that the title of my essay indicates.[1]

For, besides Shylock as the Other, there are other Others like the first two suitors who make a bid for the hand of Portia and have, in general, been eclipsed by Shylock. I propose to show that beneath the apparent surface of the happy union of Portia and Bassanio, following the dismissal of the suitors, lies a troubled text that encapsulates what might well be Shakespeare's own unfashionable predilection for "black" that would run counter to the taste of his times. The contradictions that this gives rise to, in what is "express'd, and not express'd" (3.2.183),[2] set off ripples that implicate even a country as remote from Morocco as India, the complexion of whose native women invites a quite unexpected, dual perspective within the play, each one cancelling out the other thereby creating obscurity. Further, I shall argue that paradoxically Portia herself is the Other with reference to the six European suitors whose very absence is a defining presence, and whose ungallant treatment of her, as seen in their having unanimously declined to make a bid for her hand, is endorsed at the play's end in her subjugation and appropriation of her wealth by her own countryman while she, at the same time, becomes the threatening wife.

I

It is all too easy unconsciously to substitute London for Venice, but the specificity of the play's geographical locale in its title should alert us to the importance of its situation, Venice being approximately equidistant from Morocco
and Aragon in the southwest, and from England and northern Europe in the
northwest. Hitherto recognized in critical opinion on the play as being one of
the most prominent trade and financial centers of Renaissance Europe,
Venice has not, however, been looked at for its geographical location in
southern Europe that Shakespeare invests with sociocultural significance,
contextualized by race and color, in *The Merchant of Venice*. Of the eight
suitors, six come from northern Europe, inclusive of the English suitor Falconbridge whom Portia anatomizes: though she approves of his looks ("he is
a proper man's picture" 1.2.69), a concession that Shakespeare makes to his
English audience, no communication between her and the Englishman is
possible because "he hath neither Latin, French, nor Italian," while her
knowledge of English, she confesses, is but "a poor pennyworth" (66ff).
Understandably, Shakespeare makes Portia let him off lightly, but her remark
must give us pause: the text self-consciously and pointedly disowns its own
linguistic identity, English, and asks the audience to imagine its medium to
be Italian—a transposition unique in the canon—to which I will return in the
last section of this essay. Of the six suitors only the Englishman and the
Frenchman have names, though neither of them becomes Portia's husband—
another point that will assume importance in my argument.

Further, though she dismisses each of her European suitors disdainfully
while discussing with Nerissa their national traits, ironically *they* have
already rejected her, not regarding either her beauty or her wealth as sufficient inducements to offset the risk of being doomed to celibacy should their
choice of the right casket miscarry. When she expresses her revulsion at the
prospect of being married to a "sponge" (the German suitor), Nerissa assures
her that all six of them have backed off:

> You need not fear lady the having any of these lords, they have acquainted
> me with their determinations, which is indeed to return to their home, and
> to trouble you with no more suit, unless you may be won by some other sort
> than your father's imposition, depending on the caskets. (1.2.96–100)

Surprisingly, this inversion of choice, or rather, of no choice, has not
been commented upon, as far as I am aware. Rejected by the Europeans in
humiliating fashion, Portia nevertheless tries to maintain a brave front before
Nerissa by replying,

> I am glad this parcel of wooers are so reasonable, for there is not one among
> them but I dote on his very absence: and I pray God grant them a fair depar-
> ture. (1.2.104ff)

The six northern suitors have refused to submit to the patriarchal authority exercised by Portia's "dead father" (1.2.25), while the three southern suitors—Morocco, Arragon, and Bassanio—tamely accept the penalty of castration[3] for making the wrong choice; after all, this is what the prohibition amounts to:

> . . . if you choose wrong
> Never to speak to lady afterward
> In way of marriage . . . (2.1.40–43)

True, Morocco makes a show of preferring a duel for the winning of Portia, but he submits to the terms laid down:

> Mislike me not for my complexion,
> The shadowed livery of the burnish'd sun,
> To whom I am a neighbour, and near bred,
> Bring me the fairest creature northward born,
> Where Phoebus' fire scarce thaws the icicles,
> And let us make incision for your love,
> To prove whose blood is reddest, his or mine. (2.1.1–7)

Morocco's identification of Portia with Scandinavia in the extreme north, as his reference to "icicles" suggests, is, of course, erroneous, though understandable, and would have amused the Elizabethan audience. To Morocco anyone belonging to regions beyond the Mediterranean would be "northward born." In *Merchant* geographical distinctions give rise to distinctive phenomenological perceptions, and it seems reasonable to assume that the ears of Shakespeare's audience were more sensitive to such nuances than are those of today's, belonging as we do to a time when even the distinctiveness of various currencies merges into the all-embracing Eurodollar.

Thus at the very outset the play establishes a dichotomy between north and south: the former assertive, preserving selfhood; the latter submissive, yielding to the effacement of self-identity. While Portia's southern suitors idolize her, the northern suitors reject her, thereby undermining her putative supremacy as a universally desirable object of appropriation. Whereas Morocco rapturously exclaims, "From the four corners of the earth they come / To kiss this shrine, this mortal breathing saint" (2.7.39ff), we know that this is an overstatement from an African suitor who, Othello-like, desires a fair-skinned wife, even as in *Titus Andronicus* the Italian male's preference for the Nordic over the Mediterranean may be seen: Saturninus, after proposing to Lavinia, Titus' daughter, summarily rejects her and chooses Tamora, queen of the Goths, despite her being old enough to be his mother, as Tamora herself observes (1.1.331–32). Saturninus frankly spells out his reason for

this sudden transfer of his affections: "A goodly lady, trust me, of the hue /
That I would choose, were I to choose anew" (262ff). And a few lines later he
declares her to be more attractive than "the gallant'st dames of Rome" (371).

The question of complexion was, and still is, a powerful factor in sexual
relationships. As recently as 1972, when a referendum on joining the European Union was held in Norway, the Opposition's blunt question to the vot-
ers was, "Would you want your daughter to marry a Sicilian?" Portia of
course belongs to southern Europe, then as now regarded generally by northern Europe as racially and physically inferior. The French geographer Jean
Bodin (1530–96), whose works were highly influential and very well-known
during his lifetime, gives a series of sharply contrasting physical and tem-
peramental characteristics of the inhabitants of these two regions from which
there can be little doubt that superiority, in his eyes, rests with the northerners. The inhabitants of southern Europe, he informs his readers, are

> of a contrarie humour and disposition to them of the north: these are great
> and strong, they are little and weake; they of the north, hot and moyst, the
> others cold and dry; the one hath a big voyce and greene eyes; the other
> hath a weake voyce and black eyes; the one hath a flaxen haire and a faire
> skin, the other hath both haire and skin black. (279)

The text of *Merchant* seems to be imbricated with anxieties resulting
from Shakespeare's endeavor to give Portia the traits of the northerners in
contradiction to her actual southern origin. A strange unease may be detected
in Bassanio's reflections as he contemplates the caskets. An Italian himself,
he is conscious that the women of his country are in general dark-haired and,
therefore, looking at the gold casket he is not unexpectedly reminded of
golden-haired wigs that belie the reality lying beneath:

> Look on beauty,
> And you shall see 'tis purchas'd by the weight,
> Which therein works a miracle in nature,
> Making them lightest that wear most of it:
> So are those crisped snaky golden locks
> Which make such wanton gambols with the wind
> Upon supposed fairness, often known
> To be the dowry of a second head,
> The skull that bred them in the sepulcher. (3.2.88ff)

And enumerating instances from classical literature of the power that
golden hair exercises, Robert Burton (1577–1640) concludes his catalog with
an ironically whimsical mention of the use of golden-haired wigs by (especially) "Venetian ladies" so as "to catch all comers":

flaxen hair: golden hair was even in great account, for which Virgil commends Dido, *Nondum sustulerat flavum Proserpinina crinem* (not yet had Proserpine put up her golden hair), *Et crines nodantur in aurum* (the hair is tied in a golden knot). Apollonius will have Jason's golden hair to be the main cause of Medea's dotage on him. . . . Homer so commends Helen, makes Patroclus and Achilles both yellow-haired, *in aurum coruscante et crispante capillo* (with bright curly golden locks). . . . Leland commends Guithera, King Arthur's wife, for a fair flaxen hair . . . Which belike makes our Venetian ladies at this day to counterfeit yellow hair so much, great women to calamistrate and curl it up. . . . In a word, "the hairs are Cupid's nets, to catch all comers, a bushy wood, in which Cupid builds his nest." (Pt. 3, Sec. 2, Mem. 2, Subs. 2, p. 81)

The Anatomy of Melancholy was not published until 1621, but as Barthelemy notes, it "codifies opinions that were in currency long before its publication" (155n). Bassanio's reflections come close to Burton's, or the other way round. Bassanio deplores "those crisped snaky golden locks" that turn brunettes into blondes "to entrap the wisest" (92–101) and, twenty lines later, on discovering Portia's picture in the lead casket, describes her hair in the portrait as "a golden mesh to entrap the hearts of men / Faster than gnats in cobwebs"—a dubious compliment in the light of his earlier animadversion.[4] A peculiar oppositional current is in evidence here which, I think, must be attributed not so much to Bassanio as to his creator. If this suggestion is rejected, then it seems to me that we are compelled to conclude that Bassanio suspects Portia of wearing a golden-haired wig, both in reality as well as in her portrait. Here we should recall that Julia of *The Two Gentlemen of Verona*, studying the picture of her rival in love, Silvia, wishes she had Silvia's auburn locks—an interesting chiasmus in terms of hair color—so that Proteus might love her instead: "Her hair is auburn, mine is perfect yellow. / If that be all the difference in his love, / I'll get me such a colored periwig" (4.4.194–96), she resolves, while noting, "And yet the painter flattered her a little" (192). And Shakespeare's audience knew of course that after her execution when the decapitated head of Mary, Queen of Scots, was held up by the hair for the viewing of the spectators, it was seen that she had worn a wig for the occasion, while Queen Elizabeth herself, it was discovered after her death, had no less than eighty wigs in her wardrobe. It is not only in Shylock that multiple perspectives emerge, ranging from a broadly farcical character to a martyred Old Testament prophet, but problematics of race, complexion, and culture permeate the entire play.

The message of the lead casket is congratulatory of those who "choose not by the view" (131), yet Bassanio sees the beauty of Portia's hair as a snare. True, he himself is masquerading under false colors insofar as his "wealth" is all Antonio's, but to suppose that Shakespeare intended Portia also to be implicated in the practice of deception by using artificial aids to

her beauty would be, perhaps, too farfetched for dramatic credibility—
despite the clear message of the text. Perhaps, then, a happier alternative
would be to turn from semantics to biographical criticism, namely, Shakespeare's mind and art, to borrow the phrase from the title of Edward Dowden's book, one of the great milestones in nineteenth-century Shakespeare
criticism. "In such a study as this," Dowden writes in his introduction, "we
endeavour to pass through the creation of the artist to the mind of the creator:
but it by no means prevents our returning to view the work of art simply as
such, apart from the artist, and as such to receive delight from it" (3).

II

Besides golden-haired wigs and the entrapment of men's hearts in Portia's
hair like gnats in cobwebs, what is it that causes Bassanio's thoughts, while
contemplating the gold casket, to travel to distant India? One of Antonio's
ships, according to Shylock, is bound for "the Indies" (1.3.16), but this can
hardly account for Bassanio's thought process. Deprecating "ornament" for
being deceptive, he describes it as

>   the guiled shore
> To a most dangerous sea: the beauteous scarf
> Veiling an Indian beauty. (3.2.97–99)

The Arden editor, Brown, rightly points out that the lack of contrast between
"beauteous scarf" and the "Indian beauty" it veils is deficient, but his explanation—"the Elizabethan aversion to dark skins gives sufficient meaning to
the passage. The emphasis is on 'Indian' " (82)—is inadequate: while the
first part of his statement is most probably correct, being, as we shall soon
see, substantiated by Shakespeare himself in his sonnets, the second is
unconvincing. G. B. Harrison offers the same explanation—"dark, which
was not considered beautiful: see sonnet 127" (599). For Arthur Quiller-
Couch and Dover Wilson the passage is "much annotated and possibly corrupt; but if emphasis be laid on the word 'Indian,' and the Elizabethan horror
of dusky skins be borne in mind, does the passage present any real difficulty?" (151). Likewise John Munro: "Indian beauty means a dusky beauty,
beautiful in Indian eyes but not to Western" (I, 465). Other ingenious emen-
dations offered by various editors as substitutes for "beauty" are "dowdy,"
"deformity," "idol," "gipsy," "favour," "beldam," "bosom," "visage," and
even "suttee."

    This raises the question of the construction of "India" in Shakespeare.
Does the reference denote a specific region, or is it a generic term for all that
lies east of Arabia? As I have argued elsewhere, in *A Midsummer Night's
Dream* the "lovely boy, stol'n from an Indian king" (2.1.22), whose mother,

dying in childbirth, was Titania's companion and sat by her side "in the spiced Indian air" (2.1.123–25), becomes the bone of contention between Oberon and Titania, the boy's very absence from the play being an overruling presence, and the locale suggestive of a specific region on the west coast of India—the modern state of Kerala—famous then (as now) for its export of spices, particularly pepper and cardamom, to all parts of the known world ("England" 4; see also Margo Hendricks). *Dream* was written shortly before *Merchant* and, given the importance attached to the "lovely boy" and his Indian parents, should be sufficient to disabuse our minds of the pejorative meanings attributed to "an Indian beauty" by the numerous editors mentioned earlier. Neither Shakespeare, nor Burton, would have agreed with them. Burton praises "the Indians of old" for practicing selective breeding, the basis of the caste system so greatly admired by Yeats, "the caste system that has saved Indian intellect" (15–16). "An husbandman," Burton observes,

> will sow none but the best and choicest seed upon his land, he will not rear a bull or a horse, except he be right shapen in all parts. . . . In former times some countries have been so chary in this behalf, so stern, that if a child were crooked or deformed in body or mind, they made him away: so did the Indians of old. (Pt. I, Sec. 2, Mem. 1, Subs. 6, p. 215)

Did Shakespeare know of this practice, inducing him to use the adjective "lovely" for the Indian boy? Thomas Bowrey, fifty years after the publication of Burton's work, explored the Coromandel coast of India and pronounced the natives of that region as "for the most part very Streight handsome featured and a well limbed people" (14).

But my aim here is not to offer an explanation for the lack of contrast in lines 97 to 99, but rather to draw attention to the problem as indicative of the trouble the playwright seems to have had in a scene dealing with appearance and reality in the context of skin color, hair color, golden-haired wigs, Indian beauties, and the general Elizabethan attitude to race. In 1596, the year in which *Merchant* was most probably written, the Queen issued a proclamation for the expulsion of "Negars and Blackamoors" from "Her Majesty's dominions" (Jones 20–21; Fryer 10–12), an order consistent with the opening line of sonnet 127, "In the old days black was not counted fair," which posits the general attitude of Europe to the complexion of the Other, but contradicted by Shakespeare's personal attitude: "Thy black is fairest in my judgement's place" (sonnet 131), and, "Then will I swear beauty herself is black, / And all they foul that thy complexion lack" (sonnet 132). Is the celebration of Portia's putative blonde beauty a concession to "the million," as Hamlet might have said, while contradicting Shakespeare's own predilection? Was he going against the grain of his age by expressing his own personal preference for the dark complexion?

For, as we recall, at least two of his most engaging European heroines are not blondes. Beatrice is dark complexioned and therefore unlikely to attract a husband: "Thus goes every one to the world but I," she whimsically laments, "and I am sun-burnt. I may sit in a corner and cry 'heigh-ho' for a husband" (2.1.332), and Perdita, daughter of a Russian mother and a Sicilian father, has her mother's features (5.1.224–26) and her father's complexion, which makes Florizel's assertion that "she came from Libya" (5.1.156), though an untruth, plausible.[5] If in these plays the heroines are presented as unabashedly dark-complexioned, in *Merchant*, an earlier play, the heroine's complexion has ambiguous connotations, the subversion of conventional attitudes seeming to surface whenever the question of complexion is addressed.[6] Thus, Portia confides in Nerissa twice: first regarding her apprehension about Morocco's bid for her hand, and then her relief at his discomfiture. For Shakespeare's audience this, presumably, would have been the 'correct' reaction to Morocco's presence. Her first statement, "If he have the condition of a saint, and the complexion of a devil, I had rather he should shrive me than wive me" (1.2.123–25); and her second, "A gentle riddance,—draw the curtains, go,— / Let all of his complexion choose me so" (2.7.76–77) are both, however, contradicted by her categorical assurance to Morocco himself:

> Your self (renowned prince) then stood as fair
> As any comer I have look'd on yet
> For my affection. (2.1.20–22)

We are left with two choices: either to regard Portia as a hypocrite and a dissembler, or to believe that the last quoted utterance is expressive of Shakespeare's feelings, projected onto Portia, or, to put it differently, that the negative capability Keats attributed to Shakespeare does break down occasionally. My colleague, Professor Urmilla Khanna, tells me of a production of *Merchant* that she saw at Stratford over ten years ago in which, at the first appearance of Morocco, tall, coal-black, strikingly handsome, magnificent in his loosely flowing garments, there was a long pause as he and Portia stared at each other. Portia was surprised and dazzled. Consequent upon this silent exchange, and based on its unspoken implications, I would like to suggest that at the end of 2.7, after Morocco's departure, Nerissa knows that her mistress has fallen hard for him. With Portia's oxymoron, "A gentle riddance,— draw the curtain," Nerissa looks at Portia for a long moment quizzically, without moving. Portia knows that Nerissa knows: "go," Portia orders sharply, her tone a whiplash. And as Nerissa goes, Portia reassures Nerissa, and the audience, and herself (?) that all is well with her sinking back into conventionality: "Let all of his complexion choose me so."

For Morocco, of course, should be depicted onstage as uncompromisingly black, not brown (Figure 10). As is well known, in many nineteenth-century productions of *Othello*, the Moor was shown in the latter coloration despite his describing himself as "black" (3.3.263; 3.3.387; also 1.1.88; 2.3.29). Likewise, the Arden editor of *Merchant*—and he is not the only one—suggests reassuringly for his light-skinned readers that the stage direction for Morocco being "Enter Morocco (a tawny Moor all in white)," his complexion is, "possibly, in contrast to a 'black' Moor," tawny (p. 32). But from Aaron's unambiguous statement in *Titus Andronicus* regarding his son's complexion, it is clear that for Shakespeare "tawny" meant "coal-black." Aaron addresses the boy as "tawny slave," and four lines later sarcastically observes, "But where the bull and calf are both milk-white, / They never do beget a coal-black calf" (5.1.27–32). Strenuous efforts to mitigate Morocco's complexion from black to brown in order to suit European notions of acceptability are misplaced, for Morocco is proud of his complexion: "I would not

Figure 10. Morocco (Tyrone Wilson) in the Oregon Shakespeare Festival production, 2001. Photograph by David Cooper. Courtesy of the Oregon Shakespeare Festival.

change this hue," he declares to Portia, "Except to steal your thoughts, my gentle queen" (3.1.11–12), and Aaron asks belligerently, "Is black so base a hue?" (4.2.71).

III

A curious little scene (3.5) at Belmont that has puzzled readers is clearly a reversal of conventional attitudes in the play to the black skin. In an under-cutting and dethroning of the white monopoly on sexual attractiveness, Launcelot—the Englishness of whose name is not without significance as I suggest in note nine below—has made pregnant a "negro" woman who, per-haps, belonged to Morocco's retinue since she is called "the Moor." The scene has been dismissed by editors as problematic,[7] but in a recent, percep-tive essay Kim Hall shows "that this pregnant, unheard, unnamed, and unseen black woman is a silent symbol for the economic and racial politics of *The Merchant of Venice*" (94). I would like to divert her argument at this point into a parallel channel and suggest that this woman is once again an expression of Shakespeare's personal challenging of the stereotypical belief that gentlemen prefer blondes. The scene, a vignette, needs to be looked at in its entirety before such an interpretation can claim validity.

Replete with sexual innuendo, it begins with Launcelot questioning Jes-sica's paternity, then Lorenzo suspecting Launcelot of trying to seduce Jes-sica, followed by his accusing Launcelot of "getting up of the negro's belly," and concludes with a dialogue between the two men in which food/dinner becomes a metaphor for sexual appetite: "stomachs" = desire; "cover" = intercourse; "meat" = the flesh trade (Partridge 88, 147, 192). Launcelot rounds off the exchange by saying, "for your coming in to dinner, sir, why let it be as humours and conceits shall govern": in other words, every man to his own taste, as was Launcelot's for the Moor. Thus, the scene is a corrective to Portia's dismissal of Morocco for his "complexion," for, as Professor Hall drily notes, Launcelot and the Moor "are the only immediately fertile couple presented in the play . . . in threatening contrast to the other Venetians' seeming sterility" (108).

Besides this "unheard, unnamed, and unseen black woman," a suitor who has attracted little or no critical attention is the Prince of Arragon. It is all too easy to consider him simply as the second suitor who will, inevitably, choose the silver casket so that we (as well as Portia) might know the secret of the third casket before Bassanio has his turn. But perhaps there is more to him than just this. If Morocco is represented onstage as "tawny" = black, I suggest that Arragon be represented as dark brown, not white. The reason for this is historical. Aragon was under Roman rule till the fifth century, after which it came under the control of the Goths, until the Arabs conquered the kingdom in the early part of the eighth century: Tamora, queen of the Goths,

and her liaison with Aaron, the Moor, in *Titus Andronicus*, reflect this conflu-
ence. Consequently there was a large exodus of the European-Christian population and an influx of Arabs which went on until around the beginning of
the thirteenth century when Aragon, Castile, Navarre, and Portugal were
reconquered by the Europeans from the Arabs, and this process continued up
to the end of the fifteenth century, when the last Islamic strongholds in Spain
were recovered. In 1516, when Charles I of Spain ascended the throne,
Aragon became part of a unified Spain while preserving its regional systems
of justice, taxation, military service, and currency (Barraclough 124, 143,
150). At the same time, it should not be forgotten that Ottoman power,
though losing its grip in the far west, was steadily advancing throughout the
Levant, and especially in Syria, Egypt, Tripoli, Algeria, and Tunisia. Accordingly, at the time that Shakespeare was writing *The Merchant of Venice* in the
final decade of the sixteenth century, neither the Europeans nor the Arabs
could claim ethnic purity, as has been pointed out by Marjorie Raley in her
study of *The Tempest* (95–119).

Shakespeare's introduction of the princes of Morocco and Arragon as
suitors indicates a carefully crafted ethnic and racial semiotics without which
Merchant is an emasculated text. Readers of this collection of essays on the
play are no doubt aware that unlike the other major themes—the caskets, the
money-lending Jew, and the legal legerdemain—all of which Shakespeare
derived from his sources *Il Pecorone* and the *Gesta Romanorum*—the roles
of Morocco and Arragon feature in none of his known sources and are, therefore, unless some other source comes to light, entirely his own invention.
Modern productions of the play that elide differences in complexion among
the characters, reducing all—except Morocco—to a common denominator,
are as insensitive to the play's message as were eighteenth-century productions in which these two roles were often omitted.

Thus, both Morocco and Arragon are the marginalized Other as far as
Portia is concerned, while she, in turn, is, ironically, the Other to the six
northern European suitors who have not esteemed her worth the hazard, and
have departed unscathed. The "wiser sort" in Shakespeare's audience who
knew their history would have seen in Arragon's complexion his hybrid origin, while noting his ouster as well as that of Morocco's from the matrimonial arena as the counterpart of the Jew's ouster from the mercantile arena. If
Shylock is prevented from "thriv"[ing] through "the work of generation" and
"breed"[ing] of his ducats by the Venetians (1.3.77–84), Morocco and
Arragon are literally prevented from breeding "in way of marriage" (2.1.42
and 2.9.13).

Accordingly, a pattern emerges as to the differing complexions of Portia's suitors, a detail that directors of the play ought to consider: the six
absent northern European suitors, presumably white; Morocco, black;
Arragon, swarthy; and Bassanio, tan. To the extent that Portia is finally

matched with the suitor of her choice, and for other reasons, the closure of the last act may seem satisfying, as effecting a reconciliation of one set of values with another in terms of its treatment of law, commerce, friendship, and love, as Danson argues persuasively, but without any consideration of racial difference. As has often been pointed out in contemporary critical studies of the play, some disturbing questions remain unanswered (Drakakis 52; Lyon 131–40).

IV

If, as I have tried to demonstrate, whenever the question of color comes up the play spills onto two levels—the "proper" one ensuring the rejection and dismissal of the threatening alien, the Other, and the "sympathetic" one which seems to partly negate the former, this oppositional presence giving rise to difficulties in interpretation—then such a tendency may also be discerned in the play's last scene, in particular the ring episode, which, as everyone knows, has received abundant critical attention, though not quite from the angle adopted in this paper. Going back to the trial scene, we recall that there Portia's eloquent appeal was for mercy; when this was not forthcoming she applied the letter of the law and scrutinized the terms of the contract with absolute legal exactitude, rendering Shylock's bond infructuous because impossible of implementation. The ring episode likewise polarizes into two possible lines of interpretation: viewed through Portia's legal lenses Bassanio (and Gratiano) stand condemned for having broken their bond with Portia (and Nerissa) by parting with the rings, but viewed in terms of the common humanity that Portia had herself advocated they are justified in what they did, and their wives' anger is unfair. "I was enforced to send it after him, / I was beset with shame and courtesy" (5.1.214–15), Bassanio pleads.

In retaliation, Portia threatens, "If I be left alone, / Now by mine honour (which is yet my own), / I'll have that doctor for my bedfellow" (252–34). Derived from *Il Pecorone*, the ring episode has a significant input from Genesis 38, hitherto unnoticed as far as I know, where Judah believes his daughter-in-law, while in disguise, to have played "the whore." "Bring ye her forthe and let her be burnt," he commands, realizing his own complicity in the deed when she produces his "signet," "cloke," and "staffe" that she had demanded as a "pledge" (Geneva Bible); traces of this episode are present in Portia's ring which first implicates her in illicit sexual activity, as just noted, and then exonerates her ("Were you the doctor, and I knew you not?" 280). Her brinksmanship is of course a joke because we know the truth, which the husbands don't—but it is, nevertheless, a blueprint of Iago's assurance to Othello that "in Venice they do let God see the pranks / They dare not show their husbands" (3.3.206–207)—and at this point Antonio offers his soul as the forfeit for Bassanio's integrity:

> I once did lend my body for his wealth,
> Which but for him that had your husband's ring
> Had quite miscarried. I dare be bound again,
> My soul upon the forfeit, that your lord
> Will never more break faith advisedly. (5.1.249–53)

The symbolic "death" of Antonio, "the merchant of Venice," and the actual death of Desdemona, "that cunning whore of Venice" (4.2.91), as the by now thoroughly deluded Othello describes her, suggest the displacement of Venice on both counts. Thus, in *Merchant*, after the elimination of Morocco and Arragon, the two alien suitors, what follows is the subjugation of the two Venetian suitors/husbands, Bassanio and Gratiano, by their wives. If, on the one hand, Portia is the docile wife who submits herself to "her lord, her governor, her king" (3.2.165), on the other she is the intransigent female who with her body holds out the threat of making her husband a "cuckold" (5.1.265, 281). Newman perceptively traces the path traversed by Portia's ring—initially signifying the faithfulness and chastity of a Renaissance lady—from Bassanio to Balthazar to Antonio and back to Bassanio, picking up in its journey murky associations with "cuckoldry and female unruliness, female genitalia, woman's changeable nature and so-called animal temperament, her deceptiveness and potential subversion of the rules of possession and fidelity that ensure the male line" (130–131), and Belsey argues that the ring episode captures "a specific cultural moment when the meaning of marriage is unstable, contested, and open to radical reconstruction" (48). The body, and in particular the female body, "this muddy vesture of decay" (5.1.64), as Lorenzo describes it, is the site of cuckoldry, of deception, of spurious "crisped snaky golden locks," a contrast to the "floor of heaven . . . thick inlaid with patens of bright gold" (5.1.59) in the night sky, which transcends the vagaries of the body, including its "complexion." But as I shall argue in the next and last section of this essay, this is not all: the play adumbrates an additional dimension in its racial and cultural definition of the heroine.

V

I'd like to conclude by going back to the point I made at the beginning of this essay: that our perspective on the play should be conditioned by what we know concerning the views of Shakespeare's English audience on race and culture, and that we should not superimpose London upon Venice—something we might do inadvertently. Keeping in mind that the English suitor Falconbridge, along with the other European suitors, has escaped entanglement in the "crisped snaky golden locks" that the Italian *femme fatale* displays, we might usefully consider at least one—perhaps representative—opinion stated by a northern European on the sexual machinations of—specifically—Italy's females. In *The Schoolmaster* Roger Ascham (1515–68), an Englishman and the Queen's tutor, cautions his countrymen who must "needs send their sons into Italy" that

> [they] shall sometimes fall either into the hands of some cruel Cyclops or into the lap of some wanton and dallying Dame Calypso, and so suffer the danger of many a deadly den. . . . Some siren shall sing him a song, sweet in tune, but sounding in the end to his utter destruction. If Scylla drown him not, Charybdis may fortune to swallow him. Some Circes shall make him of a plain Englishman a right Italian. (831)[8]

The tacit, underlying assumption here is, of course, that the English as a race are honest, straightforward, "plain," while the Italians, particularly the women, are devious, dangerous, "wanton." *The Schoolmaster*, published posthumously (1570) and then reprinted in 1571 and again in 1589, was a highly influential work, being one of the earliest educational treatises to be written not in Latin but in English, offering a spirited defense of English as a vehicle for thought and literature. In this context it is possible to see the author's warning against the wiles of Italian women as consistent with his wider aim to establish the English tongue as a worthy substitute for the Latin. At the present time when postcolonial studies have proliferated as a consequence of the great wave of what were former colonies in Asia and Africa becoming free in the wake of India's independence in 1947, it is appropriate that we recognize the parallel between the attitude of these erstwhile colonized peoples to their colonizers, and, correspondingly, the attitude of the Britons to the Roman empire which ruled for nearly 600 years, from 54 B.C. to A.D. 577.[9] Political freedom is seldom accompanied by cultural freedom.

The preoccupation, almost obsessive, even ten centuries later, of Elizabethan dramatists including Shakespeare with Italian (Roman) plots has its parallel in modern India: for example, Satyajit Ray being given a national award only after he had won an Oscar, or some of the most successful contemporary India-born novelists like Salman Rushdie, Arundhati Roy, and Vikram Seth being lionized in the home country only after they had been granted recognition in the west. The opposite, the "hate" side of this love-hate relationship is to be seen, or, rather, heard, in terms of the shrill denunciation of certain carefully selected items of western culture like beauty pageants, fashion shows, or the observance of St. Valentine's day coming from the self-proclaimed guardians of the old traditions who, however, see nothing contradictory in sending their children to the best English-medium schools, or encouraging them to pursue computer studies with a view to emigrating to the west. I'd like to suggest that *Merchant* encapsulates similar contradictions.

The English*men* watching *Merchant* may, vicariously, through Falconbridge, the unseen and unheard English suitor, have congratulated themselves for having escaped the clutches of the Italian community which emasculates its men, including Shylock who is stripped of his possessions not only by the Italian state but by his own daughter, an Italian-Jewess. To them, the entrapment of Bassanio, an impecunious Italian, by Portia might have seemed as unenviable and entirely appropriate as was his reciprocal appropriation of her, an heiress, true, but not worth the risk of enforced celibacy. The global vision of Portia's father in which his daughter's "worth" and "sunny locks" attract suitors from all over the world—"For the four winds blow in from every coast / Renowned suitors" (1.1.167–69)—paralleled and reinforced by Venice's international mercantilism covering Tripolis, the Indies, Mexico, and England (1.3.16–18), remains unrealized, for Portia finally gets a husband from nearby Venice: she marries the boy next door. The play seems deliberately to undercut its own large agenda with which it opened. As noted earlier, Shakespeare does not make the English suitor Falconbridge the winner of Portia's hand—something he could easily have done—but faithfully follows his sources whereas, as is well known, in many other plays he made changes with the source material to suit his dramatic purpose.[10] The significance of what he did *not* do in *Merchant* may well be as important as what he did do in his other plays.

To the Elizabethan audience watching the play, the ending would have seemed to stress the divide between play and audience, not just in terms of the unreality of drama or the distinction between fiction and fact ("The best in this kind are but shadows," as Theseus says in *A Midsummer Night's Dream* while watching the enactment of *Pyramus and Thisbe*: 5.1.208–209), but more vitally in *Merchant* than in any other play of Shakespeare's, in terms of an enactment dealing with characters from another country, another culture, another code of values, even another language, in other words, an *Elizabethan* audience watching an *Italian* play. As noted at the commencement of this paper, Portia's admission to her poor knowledge of English is a reminder to the Globe audience that the play is really in Italian, the play that they are witnessing on the stage—Shakespeare's play—being merely a translation. This Otherness that the play emphasizes places the action—the reconciliation and restoration at the play's ending—on a detached plane, a spectacle which the audience is intended to admire but not necessarily empathize with.[11] So complete is this divide that even the miracle of Portia possessing secret knowledge of the safe return of three of Antonio's ships becomes acceptable within the play's picture frame:

Antonio you are welcome,
And I have better news in store for you
Than you expect: unseal this letter soon,

> There you shall find three of your argosies
> Are richly come to harbour suddenly.
> You shall not know by what strange accident
> I chanced on this letter.
> *Ant.*   I am dumb! (5.1.273–279)

All the men in the play are subjugated by Women on Top:[12] Portia and her minions. Antonio is rendered "dumb"; Bassanio and Gratiano are afraid of being made "cuckolds ere we have deserved it" (265); Lorenzo is suspicious of his wife's fidelity on account of Launcelot getting her "in corners" (3.5.26); and Shylock has been completely routed.

If the perspective I have outlined on the play merits plausibility, then though it be true that *Merchant*'s movement from Venice to Belmont is celebratory of matrimony, of identities restored, of synthesis and integration, it is also celebratory of an escape, not only by the six European suitors but the two non-white ones as well, from a possibly disastrous union with an Italian "siren"—to employ Ascham's descriptive term. After all, in the play that Shakespeare wrote just six years later, which also begins in Venice and then moves to Cyprus, miscegenation (narrowly averted in *Merchant*) takes place, and then ends in disaster.[13]

Notes

1. For example, in his recent book-length study of the play, Graham Holderness mentions the Prince of Morocco only in passing (12, 13, 56).
2. Quotations from *The Merchant of Venice* are from the Arden edition, ed. John Russell Brown (London: Methuen, 1967).
3. For a well documented uncovering of trace elements of castration/circumcision/cannibalism in Shylock's design on Antonio's life, see Shapiro (73–91).
4. For a startling analysis of hair as "excrement"—Bassanio's term: 1.87—see Wilson (152).
5. As far as I am aware, stage and screen versions of these plays have missed this point. For a detailed examination of this issue, see Desai "What means?" (311–24). Cleopatra, an Egyptian, is of course dark complexioned, as she herself says: "that am with Phoebus' amorous pinches black" (1.5.28).
6. Interestingly enough, Shylock's complexion (and Jessica's) in stage and screen productions of the play are shown as "white" which, Biblically speaking, is incorrect. The Jews are the descendants of Shem, Noah's second son, while the Europeans claim descent from Japheth, his eldest son. Metaphorically, and perhaps literally, this distinction is hinted at in Salerio's reference to Shylock's flesh being "jet" (3.1.35). For some excellent insights into these and other related racial issues, see Kaul (1–19).
7. Brown: "This passage has not been explained; it might be an outcrop of a lost source, or a topical allusion" (99); Harrison: "The scandal is obviously topical but cannot be explained" (603); Quiller-Couch and Wilson: "We are

      inclined to interpret the reference as a topical one" (158); Munro quotes Furness: "An overlooked fragment of the Old Play which Sh. rewrote" (478).

8.   For Freud, it will be recalled, Portia is the Goddess of Death in the guise of the Goddess of Love (67), and for Goddard she falls short of becoming "the leaden casket with the spiritual gold within" (vol. 1, 112).

9.   That Shakespeare named Hamlet's "mighty opposite" after the Roman emperor Claudius under whom the actual conquest of Britain took place is surely not by accident.

10.   The most drastic change of course being the ending of *King Lear*, but also, equally significant, in *The Winter's Tale* where the jealous husband is Sicilian, not Bohemian. For an examination of this change, see Desai "What means?" (312).

11.   In *Merchant* the names of all the characters are Italian—Portia's identity being pointedly associated with her Roman namesake and predecessor (1.2.165–66)—except, remarkably enough, for that of Launcelot Gobbo whose first name is very English, linking him to his predecessor, Malory's Lancelot, also sexually involved with the forbidden woman. In *Hamlet*, written most probably two or three years after *Merchant*, not all of the names are Scandinavian: Claudius, Horatio, Marcellus, Barnardo, Francisco, and Reynaldo are Roman names. That this period was important for Shakespeare is indicated by his making it the historical setting for *Cymbeline*. *Merchant*, we are entitled to speculate, unlike *Hamlet*, was not intended to have an international ambience but to be quintessentially Italian.

12.   A phrase taken from Natalie Zemon Davis' chapter "Women on Top."

13.   The most powerful modern evocation of Venice as destructive is, of course, Thomas Mann's *Death in Venice*.

Works Cited

Ascham, Roger. *The Schoolmaster* (1570). *The Renaissance in England*, eds. Hyder E. Rollins and Herschel Baker. Boston: D. C. Heath and Co., 1954.

Barthelemy, Anthony Gerard. *Black Face, Maligned Race: The Representation of Blacks in English Drama from Shakespeare to Southerne*. Baton Rouge and London: Louisiana State University Press, 1987.

Barraclough, Geoffrey, ed. *The Times Atlas of World History*. London: Times Books, 1978.

Belsey, Catherine. "Love in Venice." *Shakespeare Survey* 44 (1991): 41–53.

Bodin, Jean. *The Six Bookes of a Commonweale*. Trans. R. Knolles. London: 1606. Quoted in Margaret T. Hodgen, *Early Anthropology in the Sixteenth and Seventeenth Centuries*. Philadelphia: University of Pennsylvania Press, 1964.

Brown, John Russell, ed. *The Merchant of Venice*. The Arden Shakespeare. London: Methuen, 1967.

Bowrey, Thomas. *A Geographical Account of Countries Round the Bay of Bengal 1669–1679*. Ed. Lt. Col. Sir Richard Carnac Temple. 1905; rpt. Nendeln/Liechtenstein: Hakluyt Society, 1967. Vol. 12, series II.

Burton, Robert. *The Anatomy of Melancholy*. Ed. Holbrook Jackson. New York: Random House, 1977.

Danson, Lawrence. *The Harmonies of "The Merchant of Venice."* New Haven: Yale University Press, 1978.

Davis, Natalie Zemon. *Society and Culture in Early Modern France.* Stanford: Stanford University Press, 1965.

Desai, R. W. "England, the Indian Boy, and the Spice Trade in *A Midsummer Night's Dream.*" *The Shakespeare Newsletter*, 48 (1998): 3–4, 26, 39–40, 42.

———. " 'What means Sicilia? He something seems unsettled': Sicily, Russia, and Bohemia in *The Winter's Tale.*" *Comparative Drama* 30:3 (Fall 1996): 311–24.

Dowden, Edward. *Shakespeare: A Critical Study of His Mind and Art.* 1875: rpt. London: Routledge and Kegan Paul, 1953.

Drakakis, John. "Historical Difference and Venetian Patriarchy in *The Merchant of Venice.*" *The Merchant of Venice.* Ed. Nigel Wood, Theory and Practice Series. Buckingham: Open University Press, 1996. 22–53.

Freud, Sigmund. "The Theme of the Three Caskets." 1913: rpt. *Shakespeare: The Merchant of Venice.* Ed. John Wilders. Houndsville: Macmillan, Casebook Series, 1960. 59–68.

Fryer, Peter. *Staying Power: The History of Black People in Britain.* Atlantic Highlands: Humanities Press, 1984.

Goddard, Harold C. *The Meaning of Shakespeare.* Chicago: The University of Chicago Press, 1951.

Hall, Kim F. "Guess Who's Coming to Dinner? Colonization and Miscegenation in *The Merchant of Venice.*" *The Merchant of Venice.* Ed. Martin Coyle. New York: St. Martin's Press, New Casebooks, 1998. 73–91.

Harrison, G. B., ed. *Shakespeare: The Complete Works.* New York: Harcourt, Brace and World, 1968.

Hendricks, Margo. " 'Obscured by dreams': Race, Empire, and Shakespeare's *A Midsummer Night's Dream.*" *Shakespeare Quarterly* 47 (1996): 37–60.

Hodgen, Margaret T. *Early Anthropology in the Sixteenth and Seventeenth Centuries.* Philadelphia: University of Pennsylvania Press, 1964.

Holderness, Graham. *William Shakespeare: The Merchant of Venice.* Harmondsworth: Penguin Critical Studies, 1993.

Jones, Eldred D. *The Elizabethan Image of Africa.* Charlottesville: University of Virginia Press, 1970.

Kahn, Coppélia. "The Cuckoo's Note: Male Friendship and Cuckoldry in *The Merchant of Venice.*" *Shakespeare's Rough Magic: Renaissance Essays in Honor of C. L. Barber.* Eds. Peter Erickson and Coppélia Kahn. Newark: University of Delaware Press, 1985. 104–12.

Kaul, Mythili. "Background: Black or Tawny? Stage Representations of *Othello* from 1604 to the Present." *Othello: New Essays by Black Writers.* Ed. Mythili Kaul. Washington DC: Howard University Press, 1997. 1–19.

Lyon, John. "Afterword: Prejudice and Interpretation." *The Merchant of Venice.* By John Lyon. Boston: Twayne Publishers, 1988. 131–40.

Mann, Thomas. *Death in Venice.* New York: Viking, 1998.

Munro, John, ed. *Shakespeare: The Complete Works.* New York: Simon and Schuster, 1957. Vol. I.

Newman, Karen. "Portia's Ring: Unruly Women and Structures of Exchange in *The Merchant of Venice*." *The Merchant of Venice*. Ed. Martin Coyle. New York: St. Martin's Press, New Casebooks, 1998. 117–38.

Partridge, Eric. *Shakespeare's Bawdy*. London: Routledge and Kegan Paul, 1968.

Quiller-Couch, Sir Arthur and John Dover Wilson, eds. *The Merchant of Venice*. 1926; rpt. Cambridge: Cambridge University Press, 1969.

Raley, Marjorie. "Claribel's Husband." *Race, Ethnicity, and Power in the Renaissance*. Ed. Joyce Green MacDonald. Cranbury: Associated University Presses, 1997. 95–119.

Shakespeare, William. *The Merchant of Venice*. Ed. John Russell Brown. London: Methuen, Arden edition, 1967.

Shapiro, James. "Shakespeare and the Jews." *The Merchant of Venice*. Ed. Martin Coyle. New York: St. Martin's Press, New Casebooks, 1998. 73–91.

Wilson, Scott. "Heterology in *The Merchant of Venice*." *The Merchant of Venice*. Ed. Nigel Wood. Buckingham: Open University Press, Theory in Practice Series, 1996. 124–63.

Yeats, W. B. *On the Boiler*. Dublin: The Cuala Press, 1938.

The Merchant of Venice and the Politics of Commerce

KAROLINE SZATEK

Belmont serves as a locale characterized by all the capitalist abuses normally attributed to Venice. Granted, Belmont does appear a neutral greenworld, especially when juxtaposed against Venice.[1] Belmont's gardens, music, liberality, and levity indeed suggest a fertile environment that captivates characters, audience, and readers. Consequently many critics have underscored Belmont as "a fairy-tale"; "one of those enchanted places where time stands still" (Salingar 177; Auden 234). Nevertheless, this far-too-obvious "greenery" must not continue to mislead this play's critics. Approaching Shakespeare, a healthy dose of skepticism is required. That is, in this play Shakespeare configures the passive greenworld into a dynamic territory where he strategically aligns, resists, and/or challenges divergent socioeconomic and political assumptions that the early modern hegemony traditionally espoused and put into play. Simply put, Belmont is not "the stuff of fairy tales" (Levin 16–17), or the *locus amoenus* that wholeheartedly welcomes strangers, provides a safe environment for runaways, and supplies untold sums of ducats to virtual strangers, in addition to "resolv[ing] the story of Venice" (Holmer 46). Moreover, Portia does not operate as a greenworld *dea ex machina*. Rather, Belmont functions as a borderland contact zone, in all its greenworld finery.[2]

A pastoral borderland may be defined as "an environment or psychological meeting ground where cultural and ideological similarities and differences come in contact. In this bucolic arena, pastoral authors" from Theocritus through to the early modern period "locate both dominant viewpoints and alternative perspectives on a variety of issues" (Szatek 347–48). By mingling the different with the traditional, these writers prompt their audiences to reconsider their own and their culture's positions on a number of controversial issues, from cross-dressing to witch burnings to female authority. The woods of *A Midsummer Night's Dream*, the forest of Arden in

325

As You Like It, the Bohemian meadows in *The Winter's Tale*, the mysterious island of *The Tempest*, and the mountain estate of Belmont are all borderland contact zones.

With the exception of Belmont, each of the borderlands places only two conditions upon the foreigners who enter. First, foreigners must abide by unwritten, but practiced, pastoral law—equality, equanimity, and amicability. In a number of pastorals, such as Anthony Munday's *The Downfall of the Earl of Huntington* and Jonson's *The Sad Shepherd*, an egalitarian form of government endures.[3] Second, any individual who desires permanent residency in the edenic space must recant, repent, convert, and completely readjust his or her attitude and behavior to fit into the idyllic setting to keep it unscarred. The only discontent permitted in this landscape is the conventional pining over unrequited love or a loved one's death.

In part, Belmont accepts both alternative philosophies and foreign peoples within its boundaries. Belmont, though, is far more aggressive and ambitious than its borderland contact zone counterparts. Belmont requires each of its guests and potential inhabitants to pay a high price to stay within its borders. Moreover, Belmont embraces the commercialism Venice introduced to it, and Belmont exploits this merchandizing to such a degree that its own capitalist ethos and commercial practices far outmeasure those of the larger place nearby. As this different kind of borderland contact zone, Belmont reveals the deleterious effects of commerce on Early Modern Britain.

In the Early Modern period, *commerce* meant the buying and selling of products, everything from open-air market transactions to international trade. In 1537, *commerce* signified dealings that occurred in everyday life, as in conversation: "He is now in some commerce with my Ladie" (Maria in *Twelfth Night* 3.4.73–75); or as in writing: "Here is a true natural commerce of senses . . . The lame man lends his eyes to the blind; the blind man lends his legs to the lame" (Hall *Meditation[s] OED*). Sixty-one years later, Florio noted that *intercourse* and *commerce* were synonymous (78). And by 1624 the early moderns linked the pleasures of the flesh with both commerce and *commodity*, as Heywood illustrates in *Captives*:

> Where lust and all uncleanes are commerst
> As freely as comodityes are vended. (1.1. no lines)

Through the years of the English Renaissance, "mercantilism," "merchantry," and "merchandizing" were also associated with "commerce," with "the earlier term [for 'commerce'] being 'merchandise' " (*OED*), defined as the trading of numerous goods and services.

Several Early Modern English tracts and pamphlets depict the often contemptuous sixteenth-century attitudes toward Renaissance Venice, specifically against Venetian commerce and its subsequent wickedness. In *Crudities*,

Thomas Coryat launches a vitriolic diatribe against Venice when he accuses its citizens of vigorously deriding his own people. Coryat states, the Venetians

> brand the English-man with a notable marke, . . . by painting him starke naked with a paire of shears in his hand, making his fashion of attire according to vaine inuention of his braine-sicke head, not to comeliness and decourum. (260)

Coryat also describes Venice as vice-ridden and nefarious, as evidenced by the fashions among Venetian women who, like wives and widows,

> walke abroad with their breastes all naked, and many of them haue their backes also naked euen almost to the middle . . . a fashion me thinkes very vuciuill and vnseemely. (261)

Coryat considered, however, female public exposure less abhorrent than both Venetian commercial support and praise of the "licentious wantons," those infamous courtesans whom the Venetians lift up in "so glorious, so potent, so renowned a City" (264). Outraged by their effrontery and audacity, Coryat asserts the Venetians

> should be dailie affraid least their winking at such vncleannesse should be an occasion to draw downe vpon them Gods curses and vengeance from heauen, and to consume their city with fire and brimstone, as in times past he did Sodome and Gomorrah. (264)

After such vivid, passionate descriptions as these, no wonder William Harrison, among others, speaks out against the "wickedness of such as dwell therin it may be called the sinke and draine of hell: . . . the dwellers therein farre off from anie vertue or goodness" (132; Bk. I, chap. xviii).

On the one hand, these early views substantiate any modern claims regarding Venice's commercial power in the Renaissance; on the other hand, however, Coryat's, Harrison's, and others' assertions help to affirm modern scholars' many derogatory, critical remarks about the city and its mercantile dealings as regards *The Merchant of Venice.* Too often these critics direct their attention mainly to the city and its urban problems. In large part these analyses result from the fact that merchantry "make[s] up the bulk of the" tale (Palmer 54). Belmont frequently escapes this kind of scrutiny. At first Belmont emerges as Venice's contrary, that is, free of commercial and political machination and consequence.

Rather than "an aristocratic retreat from a mercantile center" like its greenworld counterparts, however, Belmont equally engages in risky ventures, commercial enterprise, and the selling of commodities (Hodge 155). Furthermore, a commercial, merchandizing ideology and a strong, self-serving, material culture that depends on contractual arrangement and on the politics of credit (including usury) reflect a corrupt, capitalist state that oddly aligns Belmont with Venice; only Belmont dresses in green.

The affinity between Belmont and Venice emerges linguistically, in the commercial language the two locales share. At the start of act 1, scene 1, Salerio and Solanio wrongly conjecture that a misbegotten merchandizing venture, with the subsequent devaluation of Antonio's worth, has caused Antonio's misery: according to Solanio:

> had I such venture forth,
> The better part of my affections would
> Be with my hopes abroad. I should be still
> Piring the maps for ports and piers and roads;
> Plucking the grass to know where sits the wind,
> And every object that might make me fear
> Misfortune to my ventures, out of doubt
> Would make me sad. (1.1.15–22)[4]

Salerio echoes Solanio's pessimistic and self-reflexive language:

> Should I go to church
> And see the holy edifice of stone,
> And not bethink me straight of dangerous rocks,
> Which touching but my gentle vessel's side
> Would scatter all her spices on the stream,
> Enrobe the roaring waters with my silks,
> And in a word, but even now worth this,
> And now worth nothing? Shall I have the thought
> To think on this, and shall I lack the thought
> That such a thing bechanc'd would make me sad?
> But tell me not; I know Antonio
> Is sad to think upon his merchandise. (29–40)

When comparing Antonio's thinking processes to Antonio's merchant ships' rocking violently on ocean seas, Salerio and Solanio employ Venetian commercial rhetoric: "ventures," "hazarding," "merchandise," "petty traffickers," and "worth," even the "worth nothing[ness]" of a sunken cargo vessel (1.1.40, 12, 35, 36). A few lines later, Salerio and Antonio accentuate the concept of "value" by repeating "worth" and its variation, "worthier" (ll. 61–62). In this way, Antonio's friends theorize that his sadness results from his tying up all his money in merchant vessels that could easily be lost at sea. This loss would realistically devalue Antonio's worth. But, Solanio and Salerio conjecture, once Antonio's ships dock safely in Venice again, Antonio will cheer up. Importantly, Salerio and Solanio suggest that whether earned from engaging in commercial risk or other capital ventures, money is the only route to Venetian self-worth, public value, and happiness.

This early dialogue clearly identifies Antonio as a merchant, most likely a "sedentary merchant," or one who remains on land to conduct business and hires out captains to man his vessels rather than sail himself (Willan 3). Moreover, the mercantile discourse of Salerio and Solanio, which Antonio reiterates later in lines 42 and 45, foreshadows the lamentable consequences of relying too confidently on both unpredictable mercantile enterprise and money. Antonio's friends also underscore the kinds of repercussions that can result from both bad deals and risk-taking, especially when one lacks sufficient monetary resources. In such cases, an individual must often rely on subsequent, sometimes questionable, litigious practice to repay debts, to avoid incarceration, or even to stay alive. In act 4 Antonio faces the court to settle Shylock's bond with him. The trial precipitates Antonio's near execution and causes Shylock's disenfranchisement. The act 1, scene 1 foreshadowing of the Antonio-Shylock plot reveals an urbanized Venice whose commodifiable self-interest depends on malleable laws and, later, inhuman cruelty. More importantly, though, the language discloses not only Venice's commercial (pre)occupations but also Belmont's. Last, the method of exchange the Venetian characters employ in scene 1 grounds the often less overt, subtextual commercial references expressed in Belmont in the immediately following scene.

Textually, geographically, and, in theory, ideologically juxtaposed against Venetian court, trade, and rule, lies Belmont. As mentioned above, Belmont appears to function mainly as a typical *locus amoenus* and *hortus conclusus*. Presumably, Belmont is an expansive, beautiful mountain estate that most likely overlooks both the land surrounding it and the sea that meets its port. This greenworld setting contains Portia's happy home, a walled garden, a waiting woman, Nerissa, and other attendants. Like other greenworlds, sanctuary for the alien, social solidarity, and community seem to be Belmont's greatest resources. Portia, Belmont's only heir, operates as leader, apparently temporarily. Portia's father names no other to replace her, not even her cousin, Dr. Bellario, whose existence Shakespeare does not reveal until act 4. Also, Shakespeare does not indicate whether, in addition to her inheritance, Portia is a landlady who collects rent from her tenants to maintain her solvency; or, as Belmont herself, she enlarges her financial potential by trading with other cities, such as Venice (a point to be explored later). At this early juncture in the play, Shakespeare only insinuates that, as Belmont's only heir, Portia has plenty of money with which she will supposedly be liberal.

Shakespeare does establish, though, that Portia's father expects her to carry out his will by marrying the suitor who selects the right lottery casket. One assumes that then, and only then, will his daughter be assured happiness, for Portia will have turned over the exhaustive management of the estate to a husband supposedly capable of supervising it more wisely than she. In theory, when a wife placed her legacy into her spouse's hands, she would be relieved from additional taxing duties, and this, in turn, would not only ensure her own contentment but also her husband's and the entire household's. According to Alice Clark and Park Honan, this kind of marital relationship operated like a partnership that secured family and community harmony (41; 234). Old Belmont's will seems, then, to coincide with Early Modern patriarchal ideology and economic demand. As did his peers, Portia's father aimed at doubling or even tripling the family's wealth.

According to Bassanio, Portia is a rare commodity indeed:

> nothing undervalu'd
> To Cato's daughter, Brutus' Portia.
> Nor is the wide world ignorant of her worth,
> For the four winds blow in from every coast
> Renowned suitors . . . (1.1.165–69)

Sharing views similar to Bassanio's, Belmont exploits his daughter as a high-quality product whose "wares" are, like Antonio's merchant goods, strong capital investments. Belmont, therefore, markets her in a clever, entrepreneurial strategy that differs from conventional marriage brokering. Basically, Old Belmont devises the casket lottery and raffles her off, like a carnival prize.

Through this shrewd merchandizing scheme, Portia's father hopes to sell his daughter in an open market of prosperous suitors. Furthermore, just as Antonio risks his capital gains whenever one of his ships sails, so, of course, does Belmont. Portia objects to her father's method of investing in a husband for her; nonetheless, she hazards her emotional, psychological, and economic solvency to lotteries and riddles. Like Antonio, Portia is both sad and weary because of potential economic distress. She bemoans the fact that she will be expected to relinquish her money to a preordained marriage partner, and with it, any power she might have had. As with Antonio, at least according to Salerio and Solanio, Portia views money as powerful currency socially, legally, and politically. To be happy means independently holding and controlling the assets.

Belmont's having been influenced by Venetian commercialism occurs in the first exchange between Nerissa and Portia about Portia's melancholy in 1. 2. The words "abundance," "good fortunes," and "superfluity" lace Nerissa's syntax in the first lines of this scene when she attempts to lift Portia's spirits. Portia exploits such phrases as "poor pennyworth," "surety and sealed," "parcel of wooers," and "worthy of praise" when responding to Nerissa (1.2.71, 83, 108, 121). Skillfully, both Portia and Nerissa banter with both the language and the gloomy sentiment expressed by capitalists Antonio, Salerio, and Solanio in scene 1.

The extent to which Belmont employs the Venetian language of commerce—and politics—appears unquestionably in act 3, scene 2. Here, Portia and Bassanio construct a premarital contract after Bassanio selects the lead casket. Initially, Portia adopts a discourse the early moderns would have perceived as appropriate for a young woman, modest in delivery and submissive in tone and demeanor. To appear timid and self-effacing, Portia deftly employs litotes, sweetly claiming to Bassanio that she wishes herself "much better." She states,

> [I] would be trebled twenty times myself
> A thousand times more fair, ten thousand times more rich
> That only to stand high in your account,
> I might in virtues, beauties, livings, friends,
> Exceed account. But the full sum of me
> Is sum of something—which, to term in gross,
> Is an unlessoned girl, unschooled, unpracticed;
> Happy in this, she is not yet so old
> But she may learn. . . . (3.2.153–61)

Without faltering, Portia expresses herself in a form of Venetian merchandizing, political discourse with which Bassanio can identify. Not only does she speak Bassanio's language of commerce but she also plays "the patriarchal view of marriage" game that she comprehends very well (Oldrieve 91).

By appearing to commit, convert, and submit herself and her future to Bassanio, Portia flatters Bassanio into believing that he, not Portia, will play the dominant role in the marriage. Perhaps out of courtesy, or to allow Portia's "desires . . . to be articulated" (Spinoza 390), Bassanio graciously refuses to wed Portia "until" the nuptial pact is "confirmed, signed, and ratified," not by him, but by Portia (148). Bassanio thus assumes the less-dominant, more humble position (390). Portia skillfully takes advantage of this weakness. Both as executrix of her father's will and as current ruler of Belmont, Portia nimbly uses Venetian commercial rhetoric to strike one of her many successful bargains in the play: a marriage to a young man who rather unknowingly relinquishes his control to her. An economic strategist like her father, Portia intends to clutch fast to Belmont and the commercial power it will afford her.

From the onset of their discussion, Portia establishes the ground rules, not Bassanio. She, not Bassanio, manipulates the lottery's outcome by providing Bassanio with hints to which casket he should choose. Bassanio goes to her, not vice-versa. *She* betrothes *him* with *her* ring (173–74; italics mine). Although Portia may indeed love Bassanio, her conferring her ring on him signifies her possession of him—and all the money, property, and power in their relationship.[5] Considering that he lacks the capital interest and material experience of Portia, he has nothing but borrowed money and himself to offer her. Bassanio must assume the weaker position, so he stands silent, "bereft . . . of all words" (175). Portia knows Bassanio must acquiesce to her. And so he does. Portia knows well, too, that had Morocco, Arragon, or her other suitors won her instead of Bassanio, she would not have succeeded in manipulating her father's marketing scheme for her own personal and financial benefit. Not the silly, unlessoned schoolgirl she feigns being, Portia fully understands the "newly contractual world" in which the "Venetians dwell" and in which she successfully operates (Spinoza 386). And she, alone, will wield Belmont's power.

Portia's marital and commercial independence is not without precedents, however. Many an Early Modern housewife handled her own estate's matters, particularly if her husband was away on business, or if he died before his wife. If not trained by her father or her husband, she often taught herself about household commerce. Rather than her husband, Lucy Hutchinson petitioned the House of Commons to prevent the passing of a bill proposed by Lord Lexington (Clark 23–24). Lady Mansell determined the wages of the laborers whom she and her husband employed. In addition, some Early Modern capitalist women ventured out as self-made entrepreneurs, while others conducted business with the existing merchantry and became merchants themselves. Women produced, marketed, and sold numerous commodities, from textiles to fish, and from homemade pastries and breads to twigs.[6] Collet Price helped expose the reality, and the impracticality, behind the patriarchal fictions concerning wifely duty and acquiescence by maintaining her husband's books and managing his property. English businesswomen thus influenced social, cultural, national, and even legal enterprise.[7] According to Clark, independence was capitalism's "first fruit," especially in wives (301).[8] Perhaps for the first time in England's history, late Tudor and early Stuart capitalism empowered many women both personally and economically, and Shakespeare foregrounds this matriarchal, financial authority and independence in Belmont.

Shakespeare does not disparage capitalism—he largely benefitted from it. Rather, he critiques the nascent corruption of capitalism that infected Renaissance Venice and which, he seems to suggest, could adversely plague Belmont's analogue, England, for years to come. To reinforce his position, Shakespeare reveals Portia by act 5 as a female Machiavel, whose business interests seem to consume her. As I will soon illustrate, Portia manipulates, deceives, and commodifies life, values, and the sense of well-being. With Nerissa as her deputy, Portia, Belmont's agent, negotiates in incontestable rates of exchange, unmerciful deals, and even usury. By employing these commercial methods, Portia jealously protects and ensures Belmont's politics of commerce. As Hodge rightly points out, Belmont "allows an exploration of power" (155). Unfortunately, though, Portia's exploration blemishes Belmont. By the end of the play, Belmont clearly materializes as even more tainted by capitalism than perhaps Venice ever was, specifically because Shakespeare initially depicts Belmont as Venice's contrary—an uninfected, pastoral borderland.

One hint toward discovering Belmont's and its inhabitants' schooling in the fine art of merchandizing lies in the character Bassanio, the play's catalyst. Bassanio had visited Belmont when Portia's father, the patriarch, lived, Bassanio informs Antionio in act 1, scene 1. In scene 2, Nerissa mentions Bassanio's visit to Belmont, describing him as "a Venetian, a scholar and a soldier" who "came hither in company of the Marquis of Montferrat" (113–14). Here, Nerissa recalls Bassanio's earlier conversation with Antonio; then she directly testifies to Bassanio's character, saying, "of all the men that ever my foolish eyes looked upon, [he] was the best deserving of a fair lady" (117–19). Portia agrees that Bassanio is "worthy of" Nerissa's "praise" (121). Furthermore, Bassanio's comparing Portia to Cato's daughter and his using commercial rhetoric further links Belmont with Venice. The conversation that takes place between Antonio and Bassanio therefore punctuates the role Bassanio plays in the Venetian-Belmont association.

Though an aristocrat, Bassanio is a spendthrift and thus penniless. He confesses to Antonio his interest in returning to Belmont to court Portia, but he must appear financially worthy of her. Once again, Bassanio therefore appeals to Antonio to foot his bill. Antonio agrees, but he has tied up every ducat in merchant vessels, so he secures money from the usurer, Shylock. Even though Bassanio attempts to dissuade Antonio from taking a loan from the moneylender, Bassanio still instigates the Antonio-Shylock plot of 1.3. In addition, Bassanio precipitates the connection between Shylockian action and the Belmontian marriage plot. Bassanio's request for money from Antonio foreshadows both his petitioning Portia for help on Antonio's behalf and Portia's traveling to Venice to aid Bassanio, to defend Antonio, to exact justice on Shylock, and, especially, to protect her own pecuniary interests.

Bassanio thus operates as the play's mercantilist, ready-to-risk-his-companion's fortune, prognosticator. More significantly, though, Bassanio directly connects Venice with Belmont, which in turn strongly signifies the probability that Venetian capitalism and Belmontian greenworld space have many more similarities than simple love matches. Indeed, in part because of Bassanio, Belmont and Venice are more symbiotic than they might at first appear, especially when pertaining to commerce and trade, as the third clue reveals.

If at one time Belmont had not been compromised by the outside world, as are most greenworlds, it no longer was edenic, at least not since Portia's father lived. Trade at Belmont's port, especially with Venice, seems too resolutely established for it to have materialized suddenly under Portia's short governance. When Portia departs from Belmont for Venice in 3.4 to help Antonio, she does so by

> the [traject], . . . the common ferry
> Which trades to Venice. (53–54, brackets by editor)

Evidently, at least one pier at Belmont's shore stands ready to accommodate Bassanio and the other suitors. Furthermore, the dock is prepared for the unloading of merchandise portside. Ferries were also equipped to hoist anchor with their own Belmontian cargo at a moment's notice. Given the evidence—the commercial rhetoric, the negotiating tactics, the manipulating marketing schemes Belmont and Venice share—Venetian capitalism had been influencing Belmont probably since Portia's father began trading with Venice during its likely transition between its own feudal and capitalist period, long before the play opens. Ever since, Belmont, like Venice, has been occupied with commercial enterprise.

In terms of the visual arts, Venice operated as a direct "field" of influence; that is, an area or space that has the greatest shaping influence on another, more seemingly vulnerable, area, known as the "ground." As a pastoral borderland, Belmont functions as that ground. To state this in another way, Venice at first functions tropically as a dark, spatial field that, when juxtaposed against Belmont, causes Belmont to appear in contrast as a light, airy, idyllic ground. Consequently, Belmont freely seems to accept into its arcadian bosom woeful members of the Venetian metropolis and their divergent beliefs and practices. By welcoming urbanites Lorenzo, Jessica, Gratiano, Antonio, and Bassanio, Belmont seems to inspire its new inhabitants with beauty and cheer that, according to traditional pastoral criticism, should shelter exiles from that other, uncomfortable, bleak, urban world. As soon as Belmont tastes Venetian commerce, it adopts Venice's mercantile way of using language, conducting business, and ensuring power. What occurs is a shift in the field/ground position of Venice and Belmont. When Portia gives Bassanio money to help Antonio, Venice comes under the direct influence of Belmont, so by the end of the play Venice clearly operates as Belmont's ground, with Portia supervising the transactions.

In 3.2, Lorenzo, Jessica, and Salerio confirm Portia's, and therefore Belmont's, superior position. These Venetians enter together immediately after Portia and Bassanio's engagement. Although Bassanio takes the lead and greets them when they arrive, he soon assumes the subordinate position once again by petitioning Portia: "By your leave, / I bid my very friends and countrymen, / Sweet Portia, welcome" (222). Portia, who only moments earlier seemingly objectified herself and appeared to surrender her position and power to Bassanio (168–71), now forswears her initial marital contract. She overtly seizes the subject position and grants Bassanio permission: "They are entirely welcome"(225). In recognition of her authority, Lorenzo directs his gratitude directly toward her, rather than toward Bassanio.

Then, only moments after Salerio delivers Antonio's urgent message to Bassanio, Portia generously offers him 36,000 of her ducats to "deface the bond" between Antonio and Shylock (299), and later "gold / To pay the petty debt twenty times over" (306–307). Being the vigorous tradeswoman she is, though, Portia publicly orders Bassanio to wed her either before bedding her or taking the ferry to Venice. Furthermore, when in scene 4 Lorenzo praises Portia for helping Bassanio and Antonio, Portia diplomatically, yet authoritatively, retorts, "How little is the cost I have bestowed / In purchasing the semblance of my soul" (19–20).

In placing herself in the subject position, Portia asserts her dominance, even if from time-to-time she feigns being Bassanio's subordinate. She does so to capitalize on her continued role as Belmont's mistress to whom Bassanio is simply one more commodity she has purchased in a carefully designed, commercializing, political deal, as act 4 also reveals.

The moment Bassanio, one of Venice's representatives, enters Belmont, the site subsumes him. He transfers any agency he might have possessed to Portia, who pretends to be what she is not—submissive and subservient. Ultimately, Bassanio empowers Portia to persist in her role as agent, one who is surely powerful enough to extend her reach beyond Belmont's green gates.[9] With the Belmont house located probably at the mountain's peak, Portia has easy access to, and financial influence over, not only the surrounding community but also the harbor that docks Venetian ferries and trades Belmont's goods. Herself as Belmont, Portia employs the commercial tools with which Venice had so early on shaped it.

One of Belmont's economic concerns is the Venetian Jew, as depicted by Shakespeare. Renaissance Venice, and Shakespeare's rendition of it, tolerated the subaltern, even Jews, more than any other European country. Upon his visit to the Venetian Ghetto, Thomas Coryat estimated that approximately four to five thousand Jews resided in Venice, a testament to the Jews' success and survival there. Even though Venetian law restricted them from dwelling outside the Ghetto, Jews played an integral part in the capitalist economy as usurers or pawnbrokers, two of the only types of employment available to them. Even though Christians claimed usurers were sinful blasphemers (Exodus 22: 25–27, Deuteronomy 23: 19–21, Leviticus 25: 35–37), Jews like Shylock provided Christian Venetian merchants and entrepreneurs the monetary means by which to manage business.

Furthermore, according to Coryat, if Jews converted to Christianity either by choice or by law, "all their goodes" were "confiscated as soone as they embrace[d] Christianity" (234). Understandably, many Venetian Jews refused to convert to Christianity. The reason: "many of them doe raise their fortunes by vsury" (234), or pawnbrokering. Since the Jews seem to have fleeced "many a poore Christians estate," the Pope

> and other free Princes in whose territories they liue, [ordered] that they shall make restitution of all their ill gotten goods, and so disclogge their soules and consciences, when they are admitted by holy baptism into the bosome of Christs Church. (234)

Coryat asserts that fewer Jews bargained with their religion in this way than "in any country of Christendome" (234).

Jews had emigrated to England shortly after the Norman invasion. The Crown benefited from Jewish income by levying taxes on Jews or by borrowing their money. By 1290, Edward I expelled the English Jews because they had slowly lost their financial significance to the Crown. Prior to their reentry in the seventeenth century, a few Jews had continued to reside in England; in the main, the only Jews dwelling there were Marranos, individuals who nominally converted to Christianity but who secretly practiced Judaism. None of the few remaining Jews dealt in moneylending. Usury, however, had been a consistent ingredient in the English economy.[10] Many English citizens, non-Jewish, lent money for an exorbitant profit. Concerned by lender exploitation, Queen Elizabeth attempted to regulate creditor abuse by authorizing the Proclamation of 1571. According to the declaration, and in the absence of banks as we know them, those who lent money could only impose an interest rate of up to ten percent. Rather than eliminate usury altogether as Elizabeth had hoped, the proclamation merely induced eager businessmen to continue money brokering.

Even as we experience it today, the commercial lending of money for profit participates in a national and political system that controls the manufacturing, production, consumption, marketing, profiting, and taxing of goods. In other words, what we engage in is an economic structure similar to that which played an integral part in Early Modern society. That system of checks and balances, loans and interest fees, defines "capitalism." By issuing the proclamation, Elizabeth ultimately sought to regulate her nation's economy. She attempted to evade inflation, to arrest additional poverty and an increase in vagrancy, to control London's increasing population, and to hinder the eventual increase in disease and invasion, commercial or otherwise, by foreign nations.

Usury played a large role in London's economic and political future. To Shakespeare, ironically, the Shylockian form of usury is not, in itself, of primary concern. What Shakespeare addresses in *The Merchant of Venice* is a method of capitalist and political exchange that disguises itself as something else, but which is, nonetheless, usury. To Shakespeare, this type of commercial exploitation is far riskier and unjust because, like the Venetian characters during the Carnival, usury masks its abusive, victimizing economic power. Belmont participates in this camouflaging form of usury—Portia being the most offensive with it, particularly with Shylock and his daughter Jessica.

Although she enters the play as late as the middle of act 2, Jessica demonstrates the conditions under which a usurer might be allowed to inhabit Belmont. During this act, Jessica flees her father's house to elope to Genoa with Lorenzo, then when returning to Venice, she and Lorenzo encounter Salerio, who convinces them to travel with him to Belmont to deliver Antonio's message to Bassanio.

Regardless of financial position, gender, race, creed, or religion, Belmont, like Venice, accepts travelers and potential residents, but only if they pay some kind of excessive, usurious interest for the privilege of living in what merely seems a fully accommodating environment. No less than any other lender of currency, this contact zone expects to gain substantially from its ostensible benevolence, whether that payment come in cash, favor, or duty. To state this in another way, Belmont, like Venice and England, enlarges its domain by exploiting both its native and foreign citizenry, suggests Shakespeare.

> In exchange for sanctuary, Jessica engages in the "most fatal" form of usury: first, keeping the exchangers ignorant of the exchange value of articles; and secondly, on taking advantage of the buyer's need and the seller's poverty. It is, therefore, . . . the most fatal [form] of usury; for usury means merely taking an exorbitant sum for the use of anything; and it is no matter whether the exorbitance is on loan or exchange, or rent or on price—The essence of the usury being that it is obtained by advantage of opportunity or necessity, and not as a due reward for labor. (Ruskin 172)

The "sum" ordinarily refers to a pecuniary amount, but Jessica's rate of exchange is priceless—for her and for Lorenzo. As one of this play's pawns, Jessica demonstrates the extent to which one will go in order to reside in Belmont, even if the stay might only be temporary. In addition, Jessica signifies both Belmont's shallowness and its Machiavellian, means-to-an-end, capitalistic compulsion to exploit significantly the less commercially savvy.

Jessica's first step in paying back Belmont ironically begins even before she learns she will be relocating there. To enter Belmont, Jessica must become a Christian, as it appears non-Christians are not allowed. To convert from Judaism, though, Jessica must marry a Christian, and for this to occur, Jessica must run away from her father's house. So as not to be recognized, Jessica must risk her gender and sexual preference by transforming herself into the "lovely garnish of a boy" (2.6.39, 45) whom Lorenzo heartily admires.

When Lorenzo helps Jessica sneak out of Shylock's house, Jessica wants to avoid shining the light on her face, because her venture otherwise would be "an office of discovery" (2.6.43). Jessica admits to Lorenzo that she plays an unworthy role in this elopement business: "I am glad 'tis night, you do not look on me, / For I am much asham'd of my exchange" (34–35). She may feel this twinge of guilt, but her behavior and actions do not merit Lorenzo's praise as being wise, fair, and true (2.6.53–56). Knowing the risk, but desiring her freedom from her father more, she runs off with Lorenzo to Genoa, where they squander Shylock's money and her only memory of her mother— a ring—on a monkey. In one critical moment, Jessica lies to her father, steals from him, and tosses his money to Lorenzo because "it is worth the pains" (2.6.33). Like a common thief, Jessica sneaks away in the dark from her father's house and trades his parental guidance and protection, her filial duty, her gender, and particularly her faith, all in adolescent spite against her father.

Jessica may choose to believe she will be safer with Lorenzo, or that love has driven her to take such drastic action, but Jessica's own thoughts indicate otherwise: "If thou [Lorenzo] keep promise, I shall end this strife" (2.3.20). By "strife," Jessica may in fact be referring to Shylock's oppressiveness and to his natural, "blood" claim on her as her biological father. She may also simply wish to run away from what to her seems an intolerant parent. To my knowledge no textual evidence exists to claim that Shylock abused Jessica physically, emotionally, or even psychologically, so when Jessica clearly states that she will "become a Christian and [Lorenzo's] loving wife" (21), she does so out of spite. To end the strife, she may sound convincing—that the blood she and her father share has no link whatsoever with her manners. She may also appear to love Lorenzo; after all, she agreed to be his wife. But Jessica's sense of urgency seems more childishly prompted out of anger toward her father. And the tone she uses as she leaves her father's house is no better in manner than Shylock himself might utter. Abruptly and cynically behind his back Jessica states: "Farewell, and if my fortune be not cross'd, / I have a father, you a daughter, lost" (56–57).

Jessica's risky venture with Lorenzo, her ticket to freedom, cost her her father's house, her gender, her religion, and her inheritance for Lorenzo, whom she may not even love. According to Julia Briggs, "usury is linked with trade" (42). In effect, Jessica trades herself. No less than her father Shylock, therefore, Jessica is a usurer. Like her father, Jessica expects due payment with exorbitant interest for striking such an expensive bargain with Lorenzo. She binds Lorenzo to her, a young woman whom he blindly adores and for whom he promises to care. Unfortunately, once the money is spent, Lorenzo, no wealthier than Bassanio, seems to lose in this marriage deal. Jessica does not return his love. For Jessica, the marriage is merely a convenience, one that releases her from her father's grasp and eventually takes her to Belmont. Eventually, Lorenzo acknowledges his marriage is a fraud.

Again like her father whom she appears to detest, Jessica pays dearly for her brand of usury. After Jessica settles in Belmont, she is miserable. Act 5, scene 1 reveals Jessica's distress, as well as the reality of her marriage to Lorenzo. In this scene Jessica and Lorenzo's conversation about lovers from classical myth transforms quickly into an argument about their own doomed marriage. Lorenzo accuses Jessica of stealing

> from the wealthy Jew,
> And with an unthrift love did run from Venice,
> As far as Belmont. (5.1.15–17)

Jessica curtly informs Lorenzo that he swore "he lov'd her well," while Lorenzo responds with a backhanded compliment that she is "pretty . . . (like a little shrew)" (18–20). She abruptly states he stole "her soul with many vows of faith, / And ne'er a true one," and he points out that she did "slander her love, and he forgave it her" (19–22). Although they may appear to jest, the young couple, especially Jessica, laments the actions they took.

However readers choose to perceive her, again, Jessica is her father's offspring. She may say she is "ashamed to be" her "father's child!" as well as "daughter to his blood," but she nonetheless reflects "his manners" (2.6.17–19). She deceives herself and others. She will also have her way, even if it means converting to Christianity and hurting those who loved her. She has also beguiled herself at an exorbitant cost. Thinking she understood the risks, she has traded—in effect, sold—herself to Lorenzo, her best speculation, merely to live with less freedom than she possibly could ever have imagined. Another reality Jessica faces is that her spouse appears penniless, not having worked a day in his life it seems; and he shows no qualms either about wasting her money, or accepting her conversion to Christianity. Belmont's "sweet music" does not even cheer her; it merely draws her into melancholy, she regretfully admits to Lorenzo who quickly condemns her as one "fit for treasons, stratagems, and spoils" (5.1.69, 85). Lorenzo scolds Jessica for what she is; he also indicates to her where his true loyalties lie, with Portia and Belmont.

Were Belmont a typical borderland contact zone, Jessica would have been exiled almost immediately, and Morocco and Arragon would have been encouraged to leave. In order to stay, Morocco and Arragon must agree to Belmont's rules: surrender to the matriarch, meet her commercial demands, and help her remain independent. Neither Morocco nor Arragon would have labored for Portia, and the contracts and investments made with these two would have set Belmont back to the patriarchal demands of feudalism. As Belmont's proprietor and custodian, Portia, alone, accepts or rejects those who wish to join her. She, alone, rules Belmont. A clear hierarchy, similar to that of both Early Modern London and the literal and fictional Venice, persists in Belmont. Those like Portia who possess more capital interest, who have undergone more life experience, and/or who claim the better end of a bargain, carry more weight and wield more power, just as occurred among the citizens of London, and of both Shakespeare's and the literal Venice.

In Belmont, Lorenzo orders Launcelot to do his bidding; Lorenzo also rules over Jessica, who obediently but reluctantly obeys, just as she once did her father. Gratiano eventually remains dutiful to Nerissa, who yields to Portia, even imitates her in word and deed. Portia keeps her thumb on each of them, including Bassanio and Antonio. Apparently, since Portia appears generous, wise, and judicious, and thus, the namesake of Brutus' wife, Cato's daughter (1.1.166), none of the Belmontians questions or defies her. But Portia calculates her every move—one of the many traits she has in common with Jessica. Perhaps this is the reason Jessica speaks so highly of her, saying that Bassanio should appreciate the "joys of heaven here on earth" that Portia represents (3.5.76). As true corporate wheeler-dealers, both Portia and Jessica expect payment for their so-called generosity. Jessica mistakenly envisioned Lorenzo's recompensing her fully; Portia requires each character to follow her mandates, for something akin to bondage and servitude exists in Belmont—strange, considering Belmont is supposed to be a borderland contact zone.

Among the first whom Portia seems to accept without the remotest consternation are Lorenzo and Jessica. The text also suggests that Portia supplies Jessica and Lorenzo with what they need to live—housing, food, entertainment, and undoubtedly, money, considering that the couple probably spent at least a good portion of Shylock's. In other words, Lorenzo and Jessica freely leech off Portia when they arrive, as Antonio and Gratiano eventually do. Ultimately, of course, Portia's victory over Shylock provides Jessica and Lorenzo with a permanent source of income. Bassanio, too, will pay: but like a merchant usurer, Portia expects a very profitable gain in exchange for granting permission to pass into Belmont. No less than any other lender of currency, space, or food, Belmontian politics expects payment for its benevolence, whether that be in the form of cash, favor, or duty.

Into Belmont, then, enter Lorenzo and Jessica. With them come Venetian modes of commerce, along with their labor. As remuneration, Portia puts them both to work as Belmont's overseers when she travels to Venice. Had Jessica not already been as calculating as Portia or known about one type of merchandizing valued in Belmont, usury, Jessica might not have been permitted entrance. Another part of Jessica's payment is her depression resulting from the loss of her identity from the beginning of act 2. Her ethnicity and her religion were first to be shed; then her sexuality; then her feminine power. Jessica is the only female in Belmont whom a male rules. Had she not already converted to Christianity, Portia would not have countenanced her entrance. No other Jews or other outsiders with foreign religious, sociopolitical, and economic ideologies and practices exist in Belmont.

In act 3, Launcelot readily reminds Jessica of her losses when he intentionally gibes at her about turning her back on her Jewish heritage and both her father and her mother. He tells her that since she and her father have disowned each other, Jessica now has to take on her mother's sins, she now being her mother's bastard. During the Renaissance bastardy did not carry with it most of the same implications as it did only a few years ago. What Launcelot alludes to, then, is that Shylock, by law, is not bound to contract Jessica an inheritance. Furthermore, Jessica faces material consequences since she switched from Judaism to Christianity:

> We were Christians enow before, e'en as many as could well live one by another. This making of Christians will raise the price of hogs. If we grow all to be pork-eaters, we shall not shortly have a rasher on the coals for money. (3.5.21–26)

The clown's jests strike deep: Launcelot blames Jessica and other converts with affecting national economy and inflation. Jessica's irresponsibility, Launcelot asserts, can unequivocally affect Belmont's market, labor, productivity, wages, and the value of the ducat. Belmont, like Venice, engages in trade; but like England, Belmont must also supply its citizens with homegrown and commercially produced goods. Since Launcelot and Jessica dwell in Belmont, Launcelot talks strictly of the capitalist system Portia governs and of Belmont's commercial vitality.

Although jesting in *non sequiturs* and hyperbole, Launcelot's comments to Jessica about pork quite clearly indicate to her that if the supply and demand of the Belmontian market were drastically to change, so would job opportunities. Numerous people who labor from hand-to-mouth would then be unable to find suitable employment, which not only would damage the economy but also would cause a rise in vagrancy, hunger, and disease, three very common conditions in Early Modern, capitalist England.

Launcelot's deriding Jessica merely accents the gravity of Belmont's own economic state. Launcelot also nods to England, for England—and Belmont—might be on a path as destructive as the one Venice took. Again ironic, considering it is supposed to be a borderland contact zone, that Belmont harbors such considerations, but remains rather unaffected by them. Although Launcelot uses Jessica merely as his scapegoat, he reinforces the fact that being welcomed in Belmont means sacrificing oneself, no matter what the cost, in order to comply with Belmont's *quid pro quo* demands. Regardless of whether the lottery was a game of chance, neither Morocco nor Arragon provided an acceptable rate of exchange: their money and power for residency and Portia's leading hand. Commercially, they were worthless to Portia. For capitalism's wealthiest, like Portia, that certain sacred offshoot of capitalism is independence, individualism, and power.

As perhaps with Jessica and Lorenzo, the indigent Bassanio also makes Belmont his home. Similarly, the young Bassanio must rely on Portia, who retains control of her capital and her power. To state this in another way, Bassanio must freeload off Portia as he did off Antonio numerous times. An intelligent, cunning businesswoman, Portia therefore expects good returns on her loans to Bassanio; that is, of herself as wife; of Bassanio's permanently dwelling in Belmont; of the money Bassanio uses to save Antonio's life; and of her own venturing to Venice to help Antonio further. Bassanio does finally render the interest due during the exchange of rings in acts 4 and 5, and in the trial scene of act 4.

Before and during the trial Shylock directly advertises who he is, and for what he stands. He does not misrepresent either himself or his case, nor does he twist legal precedents. Above all, Shylock trusts the Venetian legal system. Distinct from any other Venetian character, Shylock, a formidable adversary, wields a great deal of power that alters people's lives. In the fourth act, he even holds the key to the existence of each of the main characters, not just Antonio's. In contrast, Portia often operates under pretense and nearly always with a hidden agenda. Despite her well-valued reputation, Portia disguises herself while in Venice as Balthazar, a young Doctor of Laws, associated with her cousin, Dr. Bellario. In all likelihood, Portia's reason for her masquerade would not have been that the court would not have heard her. After all, she is Belmont's leader, and Belmont conducts business with Venetian merchants. No, Portia conceals her gender to hide her true purpose: to keep Bassanio from recognizing her as she protects her property and her position. In addition, she endeavors to test Bassanio's loyalty to her, first, and then to Belmont. She informs Nerissa,

> And twenty of these puny lies I'll tell,
> That men shall swear I have discontinued school
> Above a twelvemonth. I have within my mind
> A thousand raw tricks of these bragging Jacks,
> Which I shall practice. (3.4.74–77)

Oddly, it is Shylock whom the Venetian Christians accuse of being a trickster, but even when sealing the bond between Antonio and himself, Shylock never falsifies his identity or his intent with regard to the audience. In act 1 Antonio is too self-absorbed, too full of self-worth, to hear Shylock's bargain as explicitly as he states it.

When juxtaposed against Shylock, Portia's true identity is disclosed; that is, less an idyllic pastoral nymph and more akin to a Venetian entrepreneurial male. A product of the economic material conditions that inhabited her borderland, Portia is a successful merchant. She not only decisively accepts the contemporary market forces, but also exploits them as she freely engages in trade, exchange, and capital investments, especially in Venice. Some critics argue that Portia's attitude and behavior merely protect her interests; indeed, they certainly do. Oldrieve rightly contends, for instance, that "in the privacy of Belmont, Portia again takes control of her estate and her life, and ensures that her marriage to Bassanio will be conducted upon hers and not Antonio's terms or the terms of the patriarchal system under which she was wed" (99). More accurately, Portia might in fact be labeled a greenworld charlatan and a commercial politician, rather than the leader of a borderland contact zone.

Even prior to that last scene, however, Portia fully expects her reach to extend far beyond Belmont into the patrilineal world beyond her mountain where young men like Bassanio brag about their sexual exploits like perky peacocks, and where husbands parade their spousal dominance, as well as to demonstrate more loyalty to their entrusted friends than to their own wives. Clearly comprehending the way of the Early Modern world, Portia chooses to shame Shylock and to disenfranchise him of his money and his religion. Rather than honestly impersonate a lawyer throughout the trial, though, she plays the trickster.

When she enters the Venetian court, Shylock is in the midst of impugning Antonio and supplying ample evidence. The characters attending the proceedings represent Venice, its political and economic ideologies and practices. The court, the Doge, and two of the trial's participants, Antonio and Bassanio, take Portia from the onset to be whom she claims. None suspects otherwise. In stark contrast with Shylock who blatantly presents his accusations, arguments, and defense to a court filled with concerned Venetians, Portia leads the court and the accused to believe that Shylock's claims on Antonio's debt, and his life, are irrefutable. Cleverly, Portia exploits a loophole in Venetian law regarding moneylending. Methodically, Portia begins her counterarguments by rhetorically juggling the legal statutes in order to bend them in her direction. In effect, however, she beguiles the whole court, entangles the Venetians in her snare, and subsequently mocks its system. She also ambushes Shylock.

Portia enables the court to try Shylock for the attempted murder of Antonio. To add insult to injury, Portia leaves the floor open for Antonio's revenge on Shylock. Antonio demands that Shylock convert to Christianity, and he overrides Shylock's parental rights to disown his own flesh and blood. Furthermore, Antonio commands Shylock to leave Jessica and Lorenzo all of his commodities, meaning his home, money, and jewels, upon his death. Successfully, Portia made claim to Shylock's personal, social, economic, and political life. More, Shylock must convert to a religion he detests because of the hypocrisy of its followers. In the Early Modern period, for a Jew to convert to Christianity was a fate probably worse than death, as Shylock's reaction to it demonstrates. Portia, indeed, awards Shylock his wish—"all justice" (4.1.321).

Although his persistence and his inhumanity toward Antonio when he endeavors to collect on his bond may disturb a new millennium audience,

Shylock merely puts into play Venetian law as it was literally drafted. When Portia adroitly maneuvers Shylock right into her hands and the court's and turns the whole trial against Shylock, he becomes her legal victim. No longer at issue is the debt Antonio owes Shylock, as gruesome as it was, but the manner in which Early Modern England practiced law.

Thomas Wilson asserts in his discussion on legal practice in Early Modern England that "none doe more openly offende in thys behalfe than do these counterfeite professours of thys pure religion" (178). Wilson may refer here to "the wilfull Romanist," but he clearly disparages any individual who asserts one position, but then practices another. He alludes to self-proclaimed Christian lawyers who profess leniency, clemency, and benevolence, particularly toward others who need rehabilitation, but who do not, in fact, practice what they preach. "Clemencie," argues Wilson,

> is good, I deny not, but that is to bee used to good men, or else towardes suche as of whome there is hope of theire better behavioure hereafter. But where clemencie is altogether abused, and maketh as it were an open waye to all lowsenes in maners and carnall libertie of lyfe, there severitie must needes stryke a stroke. For to what ende are good lawes made, yf there bee no execucion of them? As good pyke strawes, as make lawes that want a magistrate to see them well kepte obeyed and fulfilled. For the lawe it selfe is a dumme magistrate to al men, whereas magistrates are a speakyinge lawe to al people.
>
> Neither are governours private persons, to lyve honestly to themselves onelye, but they are publique officers to doe good unto many, and by wise advise to have care over them that neyther will, nor can, have care of themselves. . . . For the magistrate abusing hys office deserveth more punishmente than doth the private personne. For as hee abuseth hys charge, so doth hee deceave hys trust, and by example geevethe great cause of muche evill. (179)

By the close of the play, Portia and the other Christians are among those whom Wilson would admonish. They reveal they are little more than hypocrites and more villainous and merciless than Shylock, as many other commentators have also contended. Against a court that agrees to argue so arbitrarily for its own gain, especially when a young, intelligent, but cunning lawyer presents a legal precedent that sounds better than their own, Shylock cannot but fail.

Shakespeare does not design Portia as a solicitor for Venice's and Antonio's cause alone, however. Nor does he shape her to humiliate Shylock, alone, or to represent Belmont's approach to legal and commercial matters. Shakespeare creates Portia as a means to indict English lawyers. Since Shakespeare's father was sued often enough, especially for usury, Shakespeare would know well of courts and of law (Honan). Portia thus imitates those legal techniques executed by some of England's own lawyers, whom Harrison reproaches in 1587 when he points out that current English "lawes that we haue are . . . alwaies so variable, & subiect to alteration and change" (200; Bk. II. chap. ix). In the marginalia on the same page Harrison remarks that "Lawiers of England not alwaies constant in iudgment." As England's lawyers had often done, Portia manipulates the legal statutes. In doing so, she unabashedly tricks Shylock. Unlike Jessica, however, Portia does not feel her decisions and behavior shame her.

As alluded to earlier, Portia is also a bond maker who capitalizes on interest paid, but who manages her business more ruthlessly than Shylock. After the court sentences Shylock, Portia initially accepts no fee—her time and effort, merely a gesture of good faith on her part. Shortly after, however, she demands collateral and interest for her legal maneuvering. Portia thus flatly and directly remarks to Antonio, "Give me your gloves: I'll wear them for your sake"(4.1.426). The unwitting, but always overconfident, Antonio removes his gloves and exposes his hands. Since Bassanio politely told Portia to take two items as a tribute for her legal services, "some remembrance of *us*" (422, emphasis mine), Portia orders that he compensate her with the same ring she had given him in 3.2: "And for your love I'll take this ring from you" (427). She actually prefers nothing else. At this precise moment, Portia begins her injudicious trial of Antonio and the easily beguiled Bassanio.

When Portia arrogantly reaches for the ring, Bassanio withdraws his hand. This ordeal he passes. When Antonio tells Bassanio to give Portia the ring, however, Bassanio obeys, as usual. Portia leaves Venice, stripping Bassanio of the symbol of his patriarchal status and of his marital bond. The ring, in fact, symbolizes Bassanio's offering of his life to Portia (Holmer 39). For Portia to ensure Bassanio will neither risk her nor trade her in any other contract, she exacts suitable compensation from him, plus much more: Bassanio's inevitable and final submission to her. Furthermore, Portia will remind Bassanio that he is indebted to her, and that it is she who collects interest in this one-sided enterprise in which she gambles. In the end, Bassanio will simply lose in Portia's trial and Portia will have commodified and objectified their marriage and Bassanio's love.

After her return to Belmont in 5.1, Portia reestablishes her supremacy over Bassanio, while continuing the ruse she began before leaving Belmont for Venice. The only exception is that Portia has discarded the attire she wore when masquerading as Balthazar. Portia will remain in power, even if in front of all of Belmont she pretends to have cuckolded her husband:

> Let not that doctor e'er come near my house.
> Since he hath got the jewel that I loved,
> And that which you did swear to keep for me,
> I will become as liberal as you. (5.1.223–26)

Eventually, Portia astonishes Antonio and especially Bassanio by revealing to them her role as Balthazar. Bassanio and Antonio soon realize they both owe Portia. For rescuing him from the bond with Shylock, Antonio vowed to Balthazar that he stands "indebted, over and above, / In love and service to you evermore" (4.1.413–14). And in act 5, Antonio swears that he "dare be bound again"—not simply his body, but his "soul upon the forfeit." Furthermore, Antonio vows that Bassanio "will never break faith advisedly" (251–53). Portia saved Antonio's life, so he owes her for the entire life of her marriage to Bassanio. Antonio must surrender to her, Belmont's only ruler and a matriarch, and release Bassanio from any indebtedness due him. According to Spinoza,

> bonds speak out the mute world of customary debt. . . . Bacon himself argued that if one were to give words to a bargain and sale and then seal those words, one would have a bond, not a covenant (a written *assumpsit*). In law, a bond simply signified that a debt already existed, presumably one contracted in a customary way, and that the person who sealed the bond agreed to pay the debt. (391)

Not only Antonio, but Bassanio also is doubly bonded to Portia. His first debt regards his disloyalty to her as husband; he renounced his spousal vow to Portia when he gave Balthazar her ring. Bassanio's second debt concerns Portia's acting as Antonio's savior, both through the money she lent Bassanio to clear Antonio, and by turning the tables on Shylock. In fact, Venice itself owes Portia for not letting Shylock win, and by defying—even overturning—patriarchal expectations.

The final ring exchange among Portia, Bassanio, and Antonio in act 5 finally cements the marriage bond between Portia and Bassanio. Before Portia hands the ring over to Bassanio again, however, she vehemently rebukes him as to its significance:

> If you had known the virtue of the ring,
> Or half her worthiness that gave the ring,
> Or your own honor to contain the ring,
> You would not then have parted with the ring.
> What man is there so much unreasonable,
> If you had pleas'd to have defended it
> With any terms of zeal, wanted the modesty
> To urge the thing held as a ceremony? (5.1.199–206)

Firmly, and inexorably, Portia publicly berates Bassanio. As Antonio and the court do with Shylock, Bassanio pleads for mercy from her when he attempts to defend himself. Antonio's pleas failed, Shylock's pleas failed, so do Bassanio's. Without any other recourse, Bassanio then publicly swears to Portia his enduring faithfulness. By openly calling Bassanio to task, Portia demonstrates to all her citizens her authority over Belmont—and Bassanio. Bassanio ultimately bows down to this mistress of Belmont. Portia insists on singly maintaining power, rather than sharing it equally. To remain in control, she employs such weapons as usury, manipulation, and deceit.

A brilliant tactician, Portia capitalizes on the oaths Bassanio and Antonio just made to her. She extracts Bassanio's ring that she probably hid in a dress pocket. Although the ring symbolizes unbroken union between husband and wife, it also connotes harmony between the married couple. Antonio has some unconventional association with the ring Portia holds, but husband swapping is not in Portia's best interest. Since Portia especially acknowledges the relationship between her husband and his friend, she must steer that relationship in a direction that best suits her. On the stage, Portia would probably direct the other two characters to form a scalene triangle. Because unequal sides shape this type of triangle, the spatial boundaries among the characters differ. Portia would situate herself downstage, but at the triangle point that best suggests her authority. Located nearest to Portia upstage would be Bassanio, with Antonio farther upstage, and therefore separated from Bassanio who would be angled between the two. Of course, all of the characters would be within arm's length, since the ring will be passed among them.

Slowly and deliberately Portia hands the ring first to Antonio. Apparently, Antonio cannot identify the ring, illustrating not only his indifference to detail, but also his blatant disregard for Bassanio's attempting to remain loyal to his wife. Antonio emotionally manipulated Bassanio into paying Balthazar with Portia's ring. Bassanio's deferring to Antonio instead of his marital vow indicates Antonio's power over the younger man.

Portia thoroughly comprehends Antonio's hold on Bassanio. When Portia renders the ring to Antonio, she definitively asserts to him that he, alone, "shall be" Bassanio's "surety." Portia also orders Antonio to see that Bassanio truly upholds his contract with her (5.1.254). In this way, Portia uses the ring as collateral toward Antonio's debt to her while simultaneously holding Antonio accountable for Bassanio's brief infidelity. Antonio continues Portia's negotiations by presenting the ring to Bassanio. Amazed, Bassanio accepts the ring, exclaiming that it is the same one with which he had invested himself in marriage with Portia. Portia reveals how she came by it— defrauding Bassanio. Bassanio, guilty of fraud himself, cannot lay blame. In this scene, Portia uses the ring, lent to Antonio and Bassanio both on credit, to establish her dominance. In one line, Antonio guarantees his credibility and ratifies the contractual bond among the three of them by declaring to Portia, not Bassanio, "You have given me life and living" (286).

Though constructed of smooth, straight lines, the triangle's shape affirms the friction and the complexity of the relationship among Bassanio,

Antonio, and Portia. Moreover, the triangle clarifies for the two men Portia's unwavering position on debt, bonds, contracts, merchantry, oaths, and swearing. The triangle also validates for the men, yet once more, Portia's resolute power that will not, under any circumstances, shift to either Bassanio or Antonio. Portia ensures her role as an independent friend, wife, and sovereign. While Portia merits such praise that describes her—intelligent, generous, selfless, witty, and even charming—she, like Machiavelli, will employ any means necessary to suit her end. The play evidences some of her tools to capitalize on her endeavors: manipulation, conspiracy, craftiness, humiliation, lies, fraud, disenfranchisement, and assuredly, that offshoot of capitalistic mercantilism, usury. That Nerissa mimics the ring switch with Gratiano in a silly display of their own merely endorses the worth of a bond and testifies to Portia's skillful mastery of people, circumstances, law, Belmont, and Venice. Nerissa and Gratiano serve, then, as a backdrop to the power of Belmont.

As a child of Venetian capitalism and currently the dominant field of influence, Belmont's politics of commerce emerge as even more corrupt than Venice's. Shylock might have thought he contrived well enough to outsmart the Christians, but Portia had not yet confronted him. A more virulent field, Portia overrides Shylock's ground and shapes him into another of her submissive puppets. Under the command of the Duke whom Portia impressed with her convenient legal twists, Antonio is permanently grounded by Portia. More powerful than Venice, Portia recasts it, too, to the point where it might, were the play not fictional, actually become a commercial satellite of Belmont. After all, the Early Modern age was rapidly developing economically, and more economic power, and subsequently more countries, fell into England's capitalistic hands, particularly when Venetian merchantry began to wane and English colonialism ensued, a situation which would not have escaped Shakespeare's notice.

By the time Portia returns to Belmont, she has firmly established the greenworld's position as a borderland contact zone. Belmont takes on a problematic cast as a borderland when other pastoral borderlands are scrutinized. *A Knack to Know an Honest Man*, *The Queen's Arcadia*, *Mucedorus*, Theocritus' *Idylls*, and Virgil's *Bucolics* are but a few of many pastoral works, where pastoral characters usually stay in the borderland; rarely, if ever, do they venture to the outside world. If they return, they do so repentant. Next, urbanites who visit the borderland zone do not stay permanently, as Bassanio, Lorenzo, Gratiano, and Jessica seem to do. Traditionally, the pastoral borderland reshapes the temporary guests into worthy citizens comprised of enough *virtù* to affect positive change in the urban locale to which they all eventually return. Moreover, the conventional pastoral borderland contact zone accepts dominant and alternative beliefs and practices, even if only to critique, resist, and challenge them, not to endorse them as an alternative to pastoral living. None of these cases occurs with Belmont, however. Belmont accepted the "Other" freely, but never released it. Instead, Belmont endorsed, and then perverted, the economic system Venice introduced to it.

By the close of *The Merchant of Venice*, Belmont clearly reveals itself as a different type of contact zone. Belmont might very well resemble something analogous to both the anti-pastoral and the post-pastoral of which Terry Gifford speaks in *Pastoral*. Belmont is at once neither what it once was nor what it pretended to be—an idyllic retreat, or a repudiation "of the idealisation of the English countryside," or even an environment that attempts to address "the problems of human accommodation with nature" (120; 149). Rather, Shakespeare may be introducing "an awareness of both nature as culture and of culture as nature." Through Belmont he "points towards" the notion that "with consciousness comes conscience" (156–57; 162; 163).

Still, Shakespeare's Belmont deviates from even these current notions of the interplay between the natural and the human, for Shakespeare designs Belmont as an aberration. Like Frankenstein's creature, Belmont at once "fits in" because of the qualities it possesses, and does not fit in for the very same reasons. In actuality, Belmont stands outside the repertoire of pastorals, yet inside it, too. Belmont functions more along Bakhtinian lines, as dialogical and carnivalesque, but to assign even a postmodern term to Shakespeare's Belmont would restrict its scope of influence. In any case, because of its inclusivity—and its exclusivity—Shakespeare uses Belmont to critique the capitalistic form of commerce and politics that thrived in Early Modern England and in Venice.

Specifically, Shakespeare yet again seems to forecast that England was headed in a Belmont direction: corruption, prejudice, fraudulence, usury, treachery, infidelity, religious mockery, and disregard for human rights all existed and seemed to be getting worse. Shakespeare also emphasizes that sovereigns ought not manipulate commerce to correspond with their own economic and political ends, such as Elizabeth I's crafty authorization of piracy and of the slave trade, along with the increased number of patent contracts and monopolies she endorsed. Shakespeare instead stresses an equitable, legal distribution and merchandizing of goods. The middling sort and the lower classes would then benefit commercially. Shakespeare challenges the government to rethink and to renew mercantile policies and strategies that engage people in a positive manner.

To the extent that Shakespeare may or may not have been a prophet, he warns against Early Modern capitalism and its persistent undermining of proper business tactics, family unity, and spiritual and moral values. As he does with Belmont, Shakespeare suggests lifting the veil that covers England's contemporary and future modes of capitalist commerce and commodification. Ironically, Shakespeare proclaims through Bassanio that "the world is still deceiv'd with ornament" (3.2.74).

Notes

1. When juxtaposed against the "real city" of Venice, Belmont initially appears "symbolic [of] a community in a state of grace," according to Auden (234). It also seems to function as the "conventional critical *other* of Venice" as Salingar and Belsey point out (177; 41).

2. Although multiculturalists generally employ them more than Renaissance scholars, the terms "borderland" and "contact zone" and the theories behind them have been used to comment on pastoral writers from Theocritus through Milton, including Shakespeare. See Gloria Anzaldúa in *Borderlands/La Frontera: The New Mestiza* and Mary Louis Pratt in "Arts of the Contact Zone." See also the following pastoral critics: Sir Philip Sidney's *An Apology for Poetry or The Defense of Poesy*; J. E. Congleton's *Theories of Pastoral Poetry in England, 1684–1717*; Peter Marinelli's *Pastoral*; Thomas Rosenmeyer's *The Green Cabinet: Theocritus and the European Pastoral Lyric*; Helen Cooper's *Pastoral: Medieval into Renaissance*; Louis Frederick Garber's "Pastoral Spaces"; Sukanta Chaudhuri's *Renaissance Pastoral and Its English Developments*; and Terry Gifford's *Pastoral*. See esp. Annabel Patterson, Louis Montrose, and Alan Sinfield, who view the pastoral as a site of contestation rather than a fairy tale.

    See Szatek's "Engendering Spaces: A Study of Sexuality in Pastoral Borderlands" in *Classical and Modern Literature*.

3. See Szatek in *The Discourse of Space and Perception in the English Renaissance Pastoral Dramas*.

4. This and all other citations from *The Merchant of Venice* are from the second edition of *The Riverside Shakespeare*.

5. See Spinoza and Karen Newman in "Portia's Ring: Unruly Women and Structures of Exchange in *The Merchant of Venice*."

6. Anthony Fletcher in *Gender, Sex and Subordination in England 1500–1800*. See also Honan.

7. Joan Thynne, Lady Margaret Hoby, and Anne Southwell are among the many women who cared for their household's financial matters.

8. Clark speaks disparagingly against capitalism here. She believes that women at work threaten the sanctity of the family. Those women not forced to work simply became ladies of leisure; or, lazy, as Clark would put it. But capitalism did benefit women, even though, as Joan Kelly argues, they did not really experience a true Renaissance.

9. See Harry Levin and Catherine Belsey regarding the feminization of Belmont and the masculinization of Venice.

10. See Norman Jones in "Shakespeare's England."

Works Cited

Anzaldúa, Gloria. *Borderlands/La Frontera: The New Mestiza*. San Francisco: Spinsters/Aunt Lute, 1987.

Auden, W. H. "Brothers and Others." *The Dyer's Hand and Other Essays*. 1948. New York: Random House, 1968. 218–37.

Belsey, Catherine. "Love in Venice." *Shakespeare Survey*. Ed. Stanley Wells. Vol. 44. Cambridge: Cambridge University Press, 1992. 41–53.

Briggs, Julia. *This Stage-Play World: Texts and Contexts, 1580–1625*. 2nd ed. Oxford: Oxford University Press, 1997.

Chaudhuri, Sukanta. *Renaissance Pastoral and Its English Developments*. 1989. Oxford: Clarendon Press, 1991.

Clark, Alice. *Working Life of Women in the Seventeenth Century*. 1919. Introduction by Miranda Chaytor and Jane Lewis. Routledge & Kegan Paul, 1982.

Congleton, J. E. *Theories of Pastoral Poetry in England, 1684–1717*. Chapel Hill: University of North Carolina Press, 1944.

Cooper, Helen. *Pastoral: Medieval into Renaissance*. 1977. Totowa, New Jersey: Rowman & Littlefield, 1978.

Coryat, Thomas. *Coryat's Crudities*. London, 1611.

Evans, G. B., ed. *The Riverside Shakespeare: The Complete Works*. 2nd ed. Boston: Houghton Mifflin, 1997.

Fletcher, Anthony. *Gender, Sex and Subordination in England 1500–1800*. New Haven: Yale University Press, 1995.

Florio, John. "Comercio." *A Worlde of Wordes or Most copious, and exact Dictionarie in Italian and English*. Anglistica & Americana 114. Hildesheim: Georg Olms Verlag, 1972.

Garber, Frederick. "Pastoral Spaces." *Texas Studies in Literature and Language* 30 (1988): 431–60.

Gifford, Terry. *Pastoral*. London: Routledge, 1999.

Harrison, William. *A Description of England, or a briefe rehersall of the nature and qualities of the people of England. . . .* 1st ed. 1577. 2nd ed. 1587. *Harrison's Description of England in Shakspere's Youth. . . .* Ed. Frederick J. Furnivall. The New Shakespere Society. Ser. 6. 3 vols. London: N. Trübner, 1878.

Heywood, Thomas. *Captives; or, The Lost Recovered* (1624) in *A Collection of Old English Plays*. Ed. A. H. Bullen. New York: B. Blom, 1964. 4:103–217.

Hodge, Nancy Elizabeth. "Making Places at Belmont: 'You are welcome notwith-standing.' " *Shakespeare Studies* 21 (1993): 155–75.

Holmer, Joan Ozark. *"The Merchant of Venice": Choice, Hazard and Consequence*. New York: St. Martin's Press, 1995.

Honan, Park. *Shakespeare: A Life*. 1998. Oxford: Oxford University Press, 1999.

Jones, Norman. "Shakespeare's England." Kastan 25–42.

Kastan, David Scott, ed. *A Companion to Shakespeare*. Oxford: Blackwell, 1999.

Kelly, Joan. "Did Women Have a Renaissance?" *Becoming Visible: Women in European History*. Boston : Houghton Mifflin, 1977. 137–64.

Levin, Harry. "A Garden in Belmont: *The Merchant of Venice*, 5.1" in *Shakespeare and Dramatic Tradition: Essays in Honor of S. F. Johnson*. Ed. W. R. Elton and William B. Long . Newark: University of Delaware Press, 1989. 13–31.

Lodge, Thomas and Robert Greene. *A Looking Glasse for London and England*. 1594. *The Life and Complete Works in Prose and Verse of Robert Greene*. 15 Vols. Ed. Alexander B. Grosart. 1881–86. New York: Russell & Russell, 1964. Vol. 14. 1–113.

Marinelli, Peter V. *Pastoral*. The Critical Idiom 15. London: Methuen, 1971.

Montrose, Louis Adrian. "Of Gentlemen and Shepherds: The Politics of Elizabethan Pastoral Form." *Journal of Literary History* 50 (1983): 415–59.

Newman, Karen. "Portia's Ring: Unruly Women and Structures of Exchange in *The Merchant of Venice.*" *Shakespeare Quarterly SQ* 38 (1987): 19–32.

Oldrieve, Susan. "Marginalized Voices in *The Merchant of Venice.*" *Cardozo Studies in Literature and Law* 5 (1993): 87–105.

Palmer, Daryl W. "Merchants and Miscegenation: *The Three Ladies of London, The Jew of Malta*, and *The Merchant of Venice*" in *Race, Ethnicity, and Power in the Renaissance*. Ed. Joyce Green MacDonald. Madison, NJ: Fairleigh Dickinson University Press, 1997. 36–65.

Patterson, Annabel. *Pastoral and Ideology: Virgil to Valéry*. Berkeley: University of California Press, 1987.

Pratt, Mary Louise. "Arts of the Contact Zone." *Profession* (1991): 33–40.

Rosenmeyer, Thomas G. *The Green Cabinet: Theocritus and the European Pastoral Lyric*. Berkeley: University of California Press, 1969.

Ruskin, John. *Munera Pulveris*. In *The Crown of Wild Olive*. Boston: Dana Estes, [1890].

Salingar, Leo. "The Idea of Venice in Shakespeare and Ben Jonson" in *Shakespeare's Italy: Functions of Italian Locations in Renaissance Drama*. Eds. Michele Marrapodi *et al.* Manchester: Manchester University Press, 1993. 171–84.

Shakespeare, William. *The Riverside Shakespeare*. Ed. G. B. Evans. Boston: Houghton Mifflin, 1997.

Sidney, Sir Philip. *An Apology for Poetry or The Defense of Poesy*. 1595. Ed. Geoffrey Shepherd. 1965. Manchester: Manchester University Press, 1967.

Sinfield, Alan. "Power and Ideology: An Outline Theory and Sidney's *Arcadia.*" *Journal of Literary History* 52 (1985): 259–77.

Spinoza, Charles. "The Transformation of Intentionality: Debt and Contract in *The Merchant of Venice.*" *English Literary Renaissance* 24 (1994): 307–409.

Szatek, Karoline. *The Discourse of Space and Perception in The English Renaissance Pastoral Dramas*. Diss. Indiana University of Pennsylvania. Ann Arbor: UMI, 1995.

———. "Engendering Spaces: A Study of Sexuality in Pastoral Borderlands." *Classical and Modern Literature* 18 (1998): 345–59.

Willan, T. S. *Studies in Foreign Trade*. 1959. New York: Augustus M. Kelly, 1968.

Wilson, Thomas. *A Discourse Upon Usury . . . Treatise*. 1572. Introduction by R. H. Tawney. 1925. New York: Augustus M. Kelly, 1965.

Names in *The Merchant of Venice*

GRACE TIFFANY

What Marvin Spevack calls Shakespeare's "passion for names" (388) is manifest in *The Merchant of Venice*. In *Merchant* Shakespeare creates an interlocking pattern of character names which, when closely attended to, deepens our understanding of the play's personae and their relationships. To examine this pattern I will begin, as does *The Merchant of Venice* itself, with its eponymous hero, Antonio.

I. Antonio, Flowing Water, and Tragic Homoeroticism

Murray Levith has proposed that Shakespeare named *Merchant*'s protagonist for Antonio da Ponte, the builder of Venice's Rialto bridge, which was completed in 1592, several years before Shakespeare wrote his play (78). Levith also reminds us that the name "Antonio" would to an Elizabethan audience have suggested Saint Anthony, an "ascetic" who was "remembered for showing great patience when faced with many trials," who was the "patron of the poor," and who was also the "patron of swineherds" (79). Antonio's relative sobriety in comparison to his gay young Venetian friends (1.1),[1] his acceptance of near-certain death during the trial scene (4.1), and his known charity—"he lends out money gratis" (1.3.44)—indeed invoke the qualities of Saint Anthony, as does (more comically) his status as the chief of the pork-eating Christians (1.3.32–33).

More recently, Leah Scragg and Joseph Pequigney have (in separate articles) discussed Antonio's likeness to other Shakespearean Antonios, particularly with regard to those Antonios' positions of relative isolation and/or their implied homosexuality. The central comparison Scragg and Pequigney both draw is between *Merchant*'s Antonio and *Twelfth Night*'s sea captain Antonio, young Sebastian's older and most devoted friend. Scragg sees each Antonio playing "a quasi-parental role . . . towards a member of the younger generation," a role which, Scragg asserts without irony, "may carry homosexual overtones" (19). Pequigney argues, in contrast, that Shakespeare meant to distinguish the Antonio-Bassanio relationship in *The Merchant of Venice* from the homoerotic liaison of *Twelfth Night*'s Antonio and Sebastian. Pequigney finds "almost nothing to suggest a sexual dimension in the amity of Antonio and Bassanio," and asserts that "This Antonio is not, then, like the other, 'in love,' and his love for his friend is philia instead of eros" (187). Pequigney implies that the name Antonio is given the merchant of Venice in order to stress the contrast rather than the likeness between the friendships in *The Merchant of Venice* and *Twelfth Night*.

Although I disagree with Pequigney on this last particular, my reading of Antonio's name does not essentially depart from but builds on those of Levith, Scragg, and Pequigney. "Antonio" is variously allusive, invoking both the reputations of genuine historical figures (including the saint), and the associations which would eventually accrue to the Antonios scripted later by Shakespeare—not only the Antonio of *Twelfth Night*, but the Antonio of *The Tempest*, and *Antony and Cleopatra*'s Antony as well.

The historical Antonio da Ponte and the fictional Antonios of *The Merchant of Venice*, *Twelfth Night*, *Antony and Cleopatra*, and *The Tempest* have in common a link to waterways. Da Ponte is significant for Shakespeare not only because he built a structure for the Rialto, the mercantile center where *Merchant*'s Antonio does business, but in that that structure spanned water. *Twelfth Night*'s Antonio is, as mentioned, a sea captain; Mark Antony fights the sea-battle of Actium; and *The Tempest*'s Antonio, Prospero's brother, is storm-tossed at sea and dunked in the brine. While it is not until late in his play that *Merchant*'s Antonio makes a significant maritime journey—I refer to his fifth-act voyage to Belmont—he is, from the play's first scene, likewise associated with water. His generosity (to Christians, anyway) is free-flowing, and he earns his living from cross-ocean trading. He also possesses a darker link with seafaring. His very mind, when we meet him, is, "tossing on the ocean" (1.1.8), or so Salerio charges. Antonio is emotionally tempest-tossed throughout the play, even before Shylock brings his murderous case against him; "Why, look you how you storm!" Shylock chides Antonio during their initial interview (1.3.137).

The reasons for Antonio's characteristic unrest are never explicitly stated, but the play gradually reveals that his disturbance has to do with Bassanio. When, in *Merchant*'s first scene, Solanio suggests that Antonio's unrest results from his being in love, Antonio says "Fie, fie!" (l. 46), a reply that Pequigney interprets as a proof that Antonio has no interest in either hetero- or homoerotic liaisons (185). Along with Scragg and many others, I disagree with Pequigney, and read "Fie, fie!" as a distinctly different response from the calm "Believe me, no" (l. 41) with which Antonio has just denied any worry about his seaborne merchandise. "Fie, fie!" suggests Antonio's sense of shame at the thought of an amorous liaison whose name he finds difficult to speak, but that additional hints in the play suggest is his attachment to Bassanio. Antonio's single solitude at play's end, Solanio's "I think [Antonio] only loves the world for [Bassanio]" (2.8.50), and Antonio's courtroom insistence that in him Bassanio "had . . . once a love" (4.1.277) suggest the erotic nature of Antonio's feelings, as others have argued.[2]

The more strongly stressed homoeroticism of Antonio and Sebastian in *Twelfth Night* casts a backward light on the friendship of Antonio and Bassanio in *Merchant*, as Pequigney has argued. The "openly amorous language habitual to [*Twelfth Night*'s Antonio] whenever he speaks to or about Sebastian" (Pequigney 179) encourages us to view *Twelfth Night*'s Antonio as a frustrated lover, left as lonely by Sebastian's ultimate marriage to Olivia as *Merchant*'s Antonio is by Bassanio's union with Portia, when we see Antonio alone amidst the couples of Belmont (5.1). "My desire, / (More sharp than filed steel) did spur me forth," *Twelfth Night*'s Antonio says to explain his hurried search for Sebastian in Illyria (3.3.4–5). *Twelfth Night*'s Antonio also calls his passion for Sebastian a "love without . . . restraint" (5.1.81), and speaks of having done "devotion" to Sebastian's "image" (3.4.363, 362). The lines run parallel to Solanio's speculation that *Merchant*'s Antonio "only loves the world" for Bassanio. Taken together, the lines in both plays suggest that Shakespeare at times associated the name "Antonio" with a particular kind of tempestuous turbulence: a frustrated homoerotic passion which left its sufferer emotionally at sea.

The examples of *The Tempest*'s Antonio and *Antony and Cleopatra*'s Antony cast additional light on the meanings Shakespeare associated with "Antonio." *Twelfth Night*'s Antonio-Sebastian pairing is curiously revived in *The Tempest*, although *The Tempest*'s Antonio and Sebastian share a political (and criminal) rather than an amorous tie. In *The Tempest*'s second act, Prospero's brother Antonio attempts to seduce Alonso's brother Sebastian into a regicide plot, and frames his argument in terms which revisit the watery associations of earlier Antonios: "Well, I am standing water," says Sebastian. "I'll teach you how to flow," Antonio replies (2.1.221–22). Ariel's thwarting of their planned crime leaves both the unrepentant Antonio and Sebastian out of sorts with the joyful reunions that close *The Tempest*; like *Twelfth Night*'s and *Merchant*'s Antonios, they are at play's end isolated and at clear cross-purposes with the comic conclusion. Like the homoerotic desirings of the earlier comic Antonios, *The Tempest*'s criminals' "flow" has been disrupted by competing comic countercurrents.

All these "comic" Antonios are, in fact, oddly placed tragic figures, prevented by their tabooed homoeroticism or their unrepentant criminality from full accommodation to their communities. Cleopatra's Antony, Shakespeare's only Antonio in a formal tragedy, fares better in terms of such an accommodation. First, unlike the "comic" Antonios, Antony is central to his play's tragic conclusion, in his sustained death scene in 4.14 and in Cleopatra's extended paean to him in 5.2 (78–92, 280–98). Second, Antony is permitted by *Antony and Cleopatra* the full expression of his free-flowing, gender-transgressive eros, while the Antonios of *The Merchant of Venice* and *Twelfth Night* are barred by their unconventional erotic desires from full inclusion in their comic commonwealths. In *Antony and Cleopatra*, the transgressing of gender (if not sexual) boundaries characterizes Egypt, the locale in which the play begins and ends. Gender transgression is celebrated in Cleopatra's gleeful recounting of a night when she and Antony indulged in transvestism: when Antony, albeit unconsciously, lent her his "sword Philippan" and wore her "tires and mantles" at the end of a drunken revel (2.5.21–23). Her recollection invokes the myth of Hercules and Omphale, in which Hercules' love for Omphale constrained him to dress—at her behest—in her clothes; Hercules is in fact Antony's divine patron, who departs from him late in the play (4.3). In *The Merchant of Venice*, Hercules is associated not with Antonio but with Bassanio as he embarks on the successful wooing game which will ultimately leave Antonio high, dry, and alone; "Go, Hercules," Portia exhorts Bassanio as he begins the wooing contest (3.2.60). Portia's self-disguise as a doctor of laws to defeat Shylock in court, and her fifth-act joke that Bassanio's gift of her ring to the "male" doctor constituted a sexual betrayal (5.1.208), flirts with a homoeroticism that seems superficially to validate Antonio's erotic bent. But Portia is as female as Cleopatra, and her transvestism, like Cleopatra's, ultimately puts gender transgression at the service of heterosexual relationship. So Antonio's eros remains uncelebrated, unlike that of Antony—even Caesar speaks in praise of Antony the lover, decreeing that Cleopatra shall be buried near her Antony and acknowledging the pair's fame (5.2.358–60). Thus, and ironically, while the Antonios of *Twelfth Night* and *The Merchant of Venice* and the Antony of *Antony and Cleopatra* are all substantially characterized by erotic desire, it is the Antonio of tragedy (Antony) alone whose eros is welcomed and valorized by his world and made central to his dramatic triumph. Ironically, the deviant eroticism of the "comic" Antonios cuts them adrift from their heterosexual communities, rendering them tragically isolated figures in comic worlds.

II. Bassanio: Weight, Music, and Moral Failure

Bassanio's name first suggests lowness and weight: the musical register of the bass, or the heaviness of the lead casket which he will correctly pick to win Portia's wooing test. "Look on beauty, / And you shall see it purchas'd by the weight," he says as he chooses (3.2.88–89). He is initially paired with Gratiano, whose name complements and underscores the significance of

Bassanio's own. For "Gratiano" signifies lightness, a grace note, a comic leavening influence, all of which Gratiano self-consciously provides: "Let me play the fool, / With mirth and laughter," he demands in the play's first scene (79–80). But Gratiano, as numerous critics have noted, is *too* thoughtlessly free of speech; as Levith points out, he matches Florio's definition of a *gratiano,* "a gull, a foole or clownish fellowe in a play or comedie" (quoted in Levith, 79). He is, as D. M. Cohen notes, "a character who talks too much" (62). Against his lightness Bassanio, though no sad Antonio, counterpoises a needed gravity, telling Antonio that Gratiano speaks "an infinite deal of nothing" (1.1.114) and warning Gratiano that he is "something too liberal" of his tongue (2.2.185).

The note of sobriety with which Bassanio complements Gratiano's wild, foolish discourse is like the bass of a melodic line contrasted with the line's superfluous grace note; therefore Harley Granville-Barker can speak of the "keynote to the true Bassanio" (42).[3] Appropriately, then, Bassanio is given a musical tribute at Belmont, as Portia guides him toward the winning casket that contains her image. "Let music sound while he doth make his choice," she commands (3.2.43), and it does. As Lori Schroeder Haslem writes, "It is hard to miss Shakespeare's great emphasis on musical harmony" in *Merchant* (134), and although it is Lorenzo who speaks most famously about music in the play (5.1.70–88), it is Bassanio whose very name brings musical harmony to mind. Shakespeare might have associated the name "Bassanio" with actual musicians whom he knew: Norman Nathan ("Bassanio" 130) and Nancy Elizabeth Hodge (158) both record that a noted family of musicians, the Bassanos, lived in London during the time Shakespeare was writing *The Merchant of Venice*—though neither notes that Emilia Lanier, the Italian Jewish immigrant thought possibly to have been Shakespeare's "Dark Lady," was a member of this family (see Levi, 106).

Yet a Shakespearean name which includes the word "bass" cannot evade the implication of moral baseness, however intermingled the name's possessor's dark strain may be with higher, musical qualities. In his last play featuring an Antonio, *The Tempest*, Shakespeare reveals the link his imagination readily forged between bass notes and base actions. Alonso, shamed by Ariel for his crimes against Prospero, laments, "The thunder, / That deep and dreadful organ pipe, pronounc'd / The name of Prosper; it did *base* my trespass" (3.3.97–100, my emphasis).[4]

Wherein is Bassanio base? We may easily locate his defects in his prodigality, his thoughtless exploitation of Antonio's love for him, his fortune-hunting search for a wife who is "richly left" (1.1.161)—however true his love for Portia may be, and his complicity in Antonio's rudeness to Shylock (especially in 1.3) and Lorenzo's theft of Shylock's jewels and money. While Hugh MacLean's statement that Bassanio " 'hath no music in himself' "

(56) is too extreme, Bassanio, like all *Merchant*'s characters, is a complex mixture of charity and moral failure. He bears out Anne Barton's claim that the "immutable harmony" of pure virtue is in *Merchant* "fundamentally inaudible" (253). As Lorenzo says, "Such harmony is in immortal souls, / But whilst this muddy vesture of decay / Doth grossly close it in, we cannot hear it" (5.1.63–65).

III. Shylock, Sealing, and Namelessness

"These are my keys," Shylock tells Jessica as he prepares to leave his house for the evening. "Lock up my doors . . . / stop my house's ears . . . / Let not the sound of shallow fopp'ry enter" (2.5.29, 34–36). As the "lock" in his name implies, Shylock is compulsively guarded, proprietary toward his goods, and fearful of penetration by the surrounding Gentile culture. His radical guardedness is evident not only in his hoarding of money, "sealed bags of ducats" (2.8.18), but in his treatment of Jessica, whom he likewise tries to keep from theft and penetration by his Christian enemies. "[S]hut doors after you;" he warns Jessica as he leaves the house. "Fast bind, fast find" (2.5.53–54).[5] When Jessica elopes with the Christian Lorenzo, he wishes her not only returned to him, but entirely sealed in a casket: "Would she were hears'd at my foot, and the ducats in her coffin!" (3.1.89–90).

To the Gentiles, Shylock himself seems locked tight. An "impenetrable cur" whom "no prayers" can "pierce" (3.3.18, 4.1.126), Shylock contrasts with the penetrable Antonio, who "lends out money gratis" and whose purse lies "unlock'd" to all of Bassanio's "occasions" (1.1.139). Set, eventually, on vengeance against Antonio, Shylock will not "yield / to Christian intercessors" (3.3.15–16). Preferring closings to openings, he will not even speak in a "bondman's key" (1.3.123). Like his bond, Shylock is "sealed" (4.1.139), "closed up tight inside himself," to quote C. L. Barber (180).

Shylock's very manner of speech helps construct him as a figure of guardedness. His language in 1.3 presents the greatest possible contrast to Gratiano's free-flowing, "nothing" discourse, heard in 1.1 as well as to the running flow of Portia's and Nerissa's witty exchange in 1.2. Unlike those of the Christians, Shylock's words are carefully and slowly delivered, weighed, and parceled. Here they are used to slow and stop the conversation with Bassanio, when Bassanio requests his loan:

SHY.:   Three thousand ducats, well.
BASS.:   Ay, sir, for three months.
SHY.:   For three months, well.
BASS.:   For the which, as I told you, Antonio shall become bound.
SHY.:   Antonio shall become bound, well.

BASS.:   May you stead me? Will you pleasure me? Shall I know your
         answer?
SHY.:   Three thousand ducats for three months, and Antonio bound.
BASS.:   Your answer to that. (1.3.1–11)

In Mark Van Doren's uncharitable term, Shylock's phrases are "hoarse from
their hoarding" (84).

   Yet Shylock's character is only partly communicated to us by the
"locks" in his name and in—and on—his conversation. The verbal associations between Shylock and hoarding suggest his lack of generosity, even his
spiritual deadness. But in the context of his uncharitable treatment by the
Gentile community, his self-protective reserve seems, if not justified, understandable, and in contrast with Bassanio's prodigality and Lorenzo's outright
thieving, his careful stewardship of his property seems relatively wise. Also,
in the above-cited passage, Bassanio's rude, hasty interruptions of Shylock's
deliberations encourage us to sympathize with Shylock's attempt to slow the
pace of their dialogue. (As I tell students, the immediate contemporary association is with an impatient teenager demanding car keys from a cautious
parent on a Saturday night.)

   In various ways Shylock confirms his separateness from the Gentiles,
and his name, in addition to "lock," suggests that self-separation. Shakespeare's actors may have pronounced "Shylock" as "Shillock"—with an initial vowel like the short *i* in "Phyllida"—evoking the word "shill," which
meant, in the 1590s, not "gull" but "[to] separate" (*OED*).[6] Again, however,
the Christians' harsh treatment of Shylock prevents us from blaming him
entirely for his separateness, or anti-comic marginality. For the Gentiles do
not extend friendship to Shylock at any point in the play. Antonio, most
famously, admits to having "spet" on Shylock in the Rialto, and to being
ready to repeat the insult (1.3.131), while Bassanio's dinner invitation to
Shylock demonstrates either willful ignorance of or lack of concern for Jewish dietary restrictions; Shylock, who would "talk" and "walk" with the Gentiles, cannot "eat" or "drink" with them (1.3.35, 37), though he seems in 2.5
to have suspended this restriction. But the most chilling reminder of the Gentiles' customary alienation of Shylock is their continual substitution of the
insulting epithet "Jew" for his real name. As Levin observes, the word "Jew"
or one of its derivatives is used sixty-nine times in *Merchant* (24), frequently
in place of "Shylock" (e.g., at 3.2.273; 3.5.11; and 3.4.34, 70). "We all expect
a gentle answer, Jew!" the Duke tells Shylock in court (4.1.34), with a pun on
"gentile answer." Shylock is called "harsh Jew" by Gratiano (4.1.123) and
"Jew" by Portia (4.1.197). As D. M. Cohen writes, the epithet "Jew" is "used
as a blunt instrument" (62) to batter Shylock and "set [him] apart from the
other characters" (55). The Gentiles' failure to recognize Shylock as a named

person, as much as Shylock's own habitual insistence on "lock"ing up his goods, his daughter, and his charity, leads to Shylock's anti-comic exclusion from the friendships that surround him.

IV. Portia, the Doorway, and Qualified Welcome

Although *The Merchant of Venice* is famously a play with two divergent plots, the drama forges a subtle connection between Portia's three sealed caskets, the elements of her wooing game, and the locked spaces of Shylock's house and heart. In Belmont as well as in Venice, sealed objects are associated with death. The golden casket approximates a coffin, having sealed inside it a "carrion death," or death's-head, which we see when the Moroccan prince opens the gold box (2.7.63); Portia has earlier joked about being "married to a death's head with a bone in its mouth" (1.2.51–52). Later Bassanio, rejecting the golden casket (and punning on the word "lock"), likens the box's gold outside to the "crisped snaky golden locks, / . . . often known to be the dowry of a second head, / The skull that bred them in the sepulchre" (3.2.92–96). In its composition, the leaden casket may most directly remind us of death in Venice: of the (presumably) lead-lined coffin in which Shylock wants to see his traitorous daughter "hears'd."

Yet in Belmont, Shylock's deathly enclosing of his goods and his—as well as the Gentiles'—obstructions of charity are answered and overcome by an unlocking of things, a generosity which revives rather than deadens. The lead casket wherein Portia's picture lies is not really a coffin but a "cradle," as suggested by the song Portia and others sing while Bassanio unlocks the casket. The open box delivers to the wooer not only the bride but her "livings, friends," and "virtues" (3.2.156), a complex gift which will ultimately redeem Antonio from death at Shylock's hands. Thus, while Shylock's name rightfully suggests his locked house, Portia's name appropriately suggests a portal, or doorway. An open door, Portia yields access to goods and charity, and provides the means by which the threat of death is converted to the promise of life.[7]

Portia is, of course, the second Shakespearean Portia, and is explicitly compared to the first in *Merchant*'s first scene. Bassanio calls her "Portia, nothing undervalu'd / To Cato's daughter, Brutus' Portia" (1.1.165–66). The nominal association between the Portias reinforces our sense of *Merchant*'s Portia as a deliverer from death. The tragic Portia of *Julius Caesar* might have dissuaded her husband from the plot that results in his death and that of his best friend, Cassius; she cannot influence him, only because he keeps his affairs secret from her. In contrast, the comic Portia of *Merchant*, self-disguising as a lawyer, engineers her own participation in masculine affairs in Venice, and the result is not only a legal triumph for her but, as noted, the redemption of her husband's dearest friend from death.

Portia, the open "door" who permits Antonio's "soul" to escape "the state of hellish cruelty" (3.4.20–21), who shows "godlike amity" (3.4.3), and who bears the "yoke of love" (3.4.13), possesses a link to Christ himself (recall John 10:9, wherein Christ says "I am the dore" [Geneva]). In the Venetian courtroom, Portia's dramatic halting of Shylock's knife when it is inches from Antonio's chest suggests God's intervention in Abraham's intended sacrifice of Isaac in Genesis 22; the Old Testament story, of course, prefigures God's redemption of sinners from death by the substitution of his son. These associations between Portia and Christ, taken at face value, would seem to characterize her as Shylock's moral opposite: the "doorway" of charity opposed to the locked room of hoarding and self-love.

But Portia, of course, is as complicated as Shylock in her mixture of virtues and flaws. No Christ, but a human being, her worthy qualities and virtuous actions only cast in bolder relief her moral shortcomings, as numerous scholars have noted.[8] As guilty as Gratiano, Antonio, and Bassanio of brutality toward Shylock, she mars her eloquent plea that Shylock show mercy by harshly punctuating it with the dehumanizing epithet "Jew" (4.1.197). Her charitable halting of Shylock's knife at the very moment when it is about to pierce Antonio's breast may be interpreted as Portia's way of giving Shylock every last chance to relent before she intervenes—thus (it is to be hoped) God tested Abraham. Yet her eleventh-hour intervention might alternatively be seen as part of a callous game, one indifferent to Antonio's fear of dying and the sensibilities of Antonio's friends, by which she may prove her ingenuity and worth in the most spectacular fashion. Her immediately subsequent argument for the unnecessary inflicting of the harsh Venetian anti-alien law against Shylock, as well as her command that Shylock, like a dog, get "down" and "beg mercy of the Duke" (4.1.346–63) both illuminate a strain of unChristlike vindictiveness in Portia's character, and suggest that the "door" she represents is only partially open.

The same is suggested by Portia's treatment of certain marginalized others at Belmont. Unlike Shylock's locked house, Belmont is predominantly a place of hospitality and welcome, where wooers knock at a readily opened "door" (1.2.134) and where Jessica finds refuge, Lorenzo the guardianship of the estate during Portia's absence, and Bassanio a "fair mansion" and "servants" (3.2.168, 170). Yet it is also a place where Portia happily shuts the gate on undesirable wooers, most notably the black, Islamic Morocco, whose exit, following his losing gamble in the wooing game, she seals with a remark of chilling bigotry: "A gentle [gentile?] riddance . . . / Let all of his complexion choose me so" (2.7.78–79). Portia treats Antonio, her subtle rival for Bassanio's love, with similar coldness when he arrives in Belmont in the play's last scene.[9] She has shown Antonio that she could do more for Bassanio than he, and has upbraided Bassanio for giving away her ring—which Bassanio has done at Antonio's request that Bassanio value [Antonio's] "love" higher than Bassanio's "wife's commandement" (4.1.450–51). Now she bids Antonio "welcome notwithstanding" (5.1.238–39)—notwithstanding his guilt for being the cause of a quarrel between Portia and Bassanio, but also *not with standing*, or status, in the household. Thus Portia, for all the charitable hospitality that her name implies and that she sometimes bestows, emerges finally as a person of qualified openness—in short, a woman as vulnerable to moral failure as the closed Shylock or as anyone else in the play.

V. Jessica: "the bird was flidge"

As Levith has suggested (81), Jessica's name seems related to that of Iscah, Abraham's niece, who is mentioned in Genesis 11:29, and whose name means "she who looks out" or "spy."[10] Levith is probably right. Certainly Jessica is one who "looks out" of the window for her lover Lorenzo, in act 2, defying her father's grim command that she "Clamber not . . . up to the casements . . . / Nor thrust [her] head into the public street / To gaze on Christian fools" (2.5.31–33).

I would, however, like to offer an additional interpretation of Jessica's name, one which demonstrates her likeness to other Shakespearean women who wrestle with their ties to male authority figures. In several plays Shakespeare uses the image of a trained (or unruly) falcon to illuminate a female character's relationship to a man who would guide her (or whom she would be guided by or, in one instance, would guide). *The Merchant of Venice*, by virtue of Jessica's name, is another such play. For Jessica's name is in fact most centrally derived from the word "jess," which was in Shakespeare's time the common word for the leather or silk strap that bound a falcon to its master's leash.[11]

Shakespeare's use of the falcon metaphor for Jessica may be illuminated by our brief glance at his more famous uses of the image in connection with other female characters. The most well known and extended instance of the man-woman/master-falcon metaphor occurs in *The Taming of the Shrew*. In *Shrew*'s act 4 Petruchio calls his wife, Kate, his "falcon" and shares with the audience his careful plan for training her:

> till she stoop, she must not be full-gorg'd,
> For then she never looks upon her lure.
> Another way I have to man my haggard [bird],
> To make her come, and know her keeper's call. . . .
>   (4.1.191–94)

In act 5, Kate visually enacts the role of tamed and trained falcon as Petruchio releases her to capture the two disobedient "bird[s]" (5.2.46), Bianca and the new-married widow, and return them to the husbands whom they have defied. Shakespeare uses the falcon image in a way reminiscent of *Shrew* in *Much Ado about Nothing*, when Beatrice, earlier likened to a "lap-wing" (3.1.24), claims that she will return Benedick's love, "Taming [her] wild heart to [his] loving hand" (3.1.112). In *Romeo and Juliet* the falcon image is also heard, charmingly inverted so that Romeo becomes a "tassel-gentle," or male falcon, whom Juliet would summon back to her balcony with a "falc'ner's voice" (2.2.159, 158). She "would have [Romeo] gone,"

> And yet no farther than a wanton's bird,
> That lets it hop a little from his hand,
> Like a poor prisoner in his twisted gyves,
> And with a silken-thread plucks it back again
> (2.2.176–80)

Romeo, who "would [he] were [her] bird" (182), yet simultaneously imag-ines her as the hawk (and himself, presumably, as her owner), calling her "My [niesse]" (167) "nestling hawk."[12]

In all three of the above plays, Shakespeare uses the image of falcon and trainer in a positive sense to suggest a harmonious and, ultimately, desired state of marriage, wherein the wife, capable of free flight, is so "tamed" by the "loving hand" of her husband that she abides voluntarily by his benevo-lent rule; indeed, *Romeo and Juliet* goes so far as to suggest the lovers' free interchange of roles, so that both woman and man may experience them-selves alternately as submissive falcon and loving falconer. However, and conversely, in *Othello* Shakespeare uses the falcon trainer image to represent a marriage characterized by suspicion and disobedience. Tragically, the jeal-ous Othello describes the trusting tie between trainer (husband) and hawk (wife) as lost or unattainable, vowing that "If [he] . . . prove [Desdemona] haggard" (i.e., wild, like a badly trained bird), "Though that her jesses were [his] dear heart-strings," he'd "whistle her off, and let her down the wind / To prey at fortune" (3.3.260–63).

Although *Othello* was written nearly a decade after *The Merchant of Venice*, our noting of the negative use of the falcon image, and of the word "jess," in *Othello* assists us in perceiving the image's tragic application to Jessica in *The Merchant of Venice*. Jessica, whose jesses are her father's "heart-strings," flies "down the wind" to "prey at fortune," to use Othello's words. After her elopement with Lorenzo, Shylock speaks bitterly of her "flight" (3.1.25), and behind his back is mocked by Salerio and Salanio in terms which associate Jessica with an escaped bird:

SAL.:   I for my part knew the tailor that made the wings she flew withal.

SOL.:   And Shylock for his own part knew the bird was fledge. (3.1.28–29)

In *Othello*, Desdemona's tie to Othello becomes an unequal one in which she is dominated and abused by a husband who perceives her as "haggard," or wild. Similarly, Jessica's "jesses" bind her not to a loving but to a grim trainer, a domineering father who cages her. "He is her jailer," notes Granville-Barker (57) and, forbidding her even to gaze out windows, denies her the most qualified freedom to use her wings. As her name suggests, Jessica is defined by her initial bondage to and eventual escape from her harsh falconer, Shylock.

Yet Jessica's "flight" from Shylock takes a form that encourages us, despite our compassion for her, to commiserate with Shylock, too. She not only flees, but robs Shylock's house, gleefully appropriating bags of ducats (2.6) which she squanders on a honeymoon spree, spending with the prodigality of a Bassanio. "Your daughter spent in Genoa, as I heard, one night fourscore ducats," Tubal tells the thrifty Shylock, to Shylock's great dismay (3.1.108–109). Shylock grieves, most poignantly, upon hearing of his lost wedding or betrothal ring which Jessica has also stolen and then traded for a monkey (3.1.118–19): "Thou torturest me, Tubal. It was my turkis [turquoise], I had it of Leah when I was a bachelor. I would not have given it for a wilderness of monkeys" (3.1.120–23). Jessica's connection to and parting from the turquoise ring completes the image of the haggard breaking free from its master; a falcon's jess bore "on its free end a small ring . . . to which the swivel of the leash [was] attached" (*OED*). As the ring attached to the jess links the falcon to its master, so the marriage ring of Leah and Shylock connected their daughter, Jessica, to her family. Jessica's break from the ring, symbol of her mother and thus of her Jewish heritage (derived through the mother's line), impairs our sympathy for her as shackled bird. Jessica's casual exchange of the ring for a monkey (a Gentile husband?) proves her to be, as self-described, "too too light" (2.6.42), heedless of family obligations and devoid of filial piety.

VI. Conclusion

Thus the names of major characters in *The Merchant of Venice* illuminate each character's moral ambiguity. The generosity of Antonio is prompted, like *Twelfth Night*'s Antonio's kindness to Sebastian, by a homoerotic attachment, and this fact undermines our judgment of his character. His extravagant lendings to the free-spending Bassanio are excessive, as Shylock knows (3.1.17–21), and our seeing those loans as motivated by passion rather than simple kindness completes our understanding of the partialness of Antonio's charity. Antonio's beloved Bassanio, who balances Gratiano's "grace note" superfluity with the needed low weight of social decorum, is yet "base" in his thoughtless exploitation of Antonio's love and in his fortune-hunting bent. Shylock, Antonio's and Bassanio's antagonist, is the "locked" man who hoards his daughter like inanimate treasure, and who "shills," or separates, himself from the community. Yet that community's rejection of him, implicit in their habitual reduction of him to a nameless entity, reminds us that Shylock's separation is not only chosen but thrust upon him. In addition, the Christians' harsh lampooning of Shylock's Jewishness tempts us to view his "locked" guardedness as a necessary detachment and reserve.

The play's major female characters' names suggest a like moral complexity. Portia, the "door" who vainly urges Shylock himself to open, is herself only partially ajar. She welcomes Bassanio, Lorenzo, Jessica, and even the servant Launcelot Gobbo to Belmont, and with "godlike amity" rolls the stone away from Antonio's closing tomb. Yet she makes sure that Antonio—like Morocco, her dark-complected suitor—is not fully at home at Belmont. Portia also chillingly tempers her "amity" toward Shylock; to her, as to the other Gentiles, Shylock is less a person meriting sympathy than that harsh non-name, "Jew." Finally, Jessica earns our compassion as the imprisoned bird, tied with "jesses" to her grim father's leash. But her dishonest escape from his house and her thoughtless discarding of her father's ring limit our sympathy for her, prompting us to see her as unbearably light, and criminally devoid of filial feeling.

I do not, of course, think any of these judgments of *The Merchant of Venice*'s characters are new. I do, however, hope that, in newly demonstrating how Shakespeare has matched names to characters in this play, I have enhanced our understanding both of the characters themselves and of the depth of Shakespeare's own interest in symbolic naming. Names in *The Merchant of Venice* advance the play's representation of the characters' moral complexity, helping to create figures who are neither fully tragic nor fully comic, good nor bad, but, to adapt Samuel Ajzenstat's term, "double-minded" (257). *Merchant*'s names remind us that the play's characters actively combine virtues and vices: generosity that is partial, firmness that is intransigent, humble suffering that is indifferent to the suffering of others. In short, *Merchant*'s names contribute to the formation of personae as like human beings as dramatic characters can be.

Notes

1. This and all other references to Shakespeare are to *The Riverside Shakespeare*.
2. See Adelman, Barton, Kahn, MacCary, and Tennenhouse.
3. Hugh MacLean also suggests that Shakespeare chose Bassanio's name "for its association with music (in social as well as linguistic contexts)" (55).
4. We might also recall the joke about a bad musician in *The Taming of the Shrew*, "The base [note] is right, 'tis the base knave that jars" (3.1.47).
5. Harry Levin also points to the phrase "fast bind" as a key (no pun intended) to Shylock's "household wisdom" (26).

6. For alternative discussions of the origin of Shylock's name, see Fleissner, Levith (82), and Roth (149). Avraham Oz calls "Shylock" "a name of obscure origin and without analogues" (160). At the World Shakespeare Conference in Valencia in 2001, Stephen Orgel argued that Shylock's name might have reminded Elizabethan audiences of "Whitlock," an old Saxon name meaning "white-haired."

7. John Ruskin associated the name Portia with "portion," finding in her character "fortune's lady" (quoted in Levith, 81, and expanded upon in Nathan, 427). Karen Newman also notes the link between "Portia" and "portion" (in an essay which focuses on the connection between *Merchant*'s and Cato's Portias). Marianne Novy finds Portia's ability to give even more complete and wholesome than Antonio's.

8. For examples see Ajzenstat, Hassel 187–88, and MacCary 160–70.

9. As Nancy Hodge says, "Antonio is not a creature of Belmont, is not a participant in the repartee which the Belmontians toss about" (166).

10. For other analogies between "Jessica" and Hebrew names, see Nathan, "Portia."

11. "A short strap of leather, silk, or other material, fastened round each of the legs of a hawk used in falconry" (*OED*). Levith has also noted the homonymic likeness between the "jess" of Jessica's name and the sound in the word "*iesses*," meaning "reins attached to a captive falcon" (82), although he does not elaborate on the significance of the echo.

12. The brackets are in the text. See also the footnote explaining this line in the text.

Works Cited

Adelman, Janet. "Male Bonding in Shakespeare's Comedies." *Shakespeare's 'Rough Magic': Renaissance Essays in Honor of C. L. Barber.* Ed. Peter Erickson and Coppélia Kahn. Newark: University of Delaware Press, 1985. 73–103.

Ajzenstat, Samuel. "Contract in *The Merchant of Venice.*" *Philosophy and Literature* 21 (1997): 262–78.

Barber, C. L. *Shakespeare's Festive Comedy.* Princeton: Princeton University Press, 1959.

Barton, Anne. Introduction to *The Merchant of Venice. The Riverside Shakespeare.* Ed. G. Blakemore Evans. Boston: Houghton Mifflin, 1974. 250–53.

Cohen, D. M. "The Jew and Shylock." *Shakespeare Quarterly* 31 (1980): 53–63.

The Geneva Bible, a facsimile of the 1560 edition. Introduction by Lloyd E. Berry. Madison: University of Wisconsin Press, 1969.

Granville-Barker, Harley. "*The Merchant of Venice.*" *Shakespeare: Modern Essays in Criticism.* Ed. Leonard F. Dean. NY: Oxford University Press, 1967. 37–71.

Haslem, Lori Schroeder. " 'O me, the word choose!' Female Voice and Catechetical Ritual in *The Two Gentlemen of Verona* and *The Merchant of Venice.*" *Shakespeare Studies* 22 (1994): 122–40.

Hassel, R. Chris, Jr. *Faith and Folly in Shakespeare's Romantic Comedies.* Athens: University of Georgia Press, 1980.

Hodge, Nancy Elizabeth. "Making Places at Belmont: 'You Are Welcome Notwith-standing.' " *Shakespeare Studies* 21 (1993): 155–74.

Fleissner, Robert F. "A Key to the Name of Shylock." *American Notes and Queries* 5:4 (Dec. 1966): 52–54.

Kahn, Coppélia. "The Cuckoo's Note: Male Friendship and Cuckoldry in *The Merchant of Venice.*" *Shakespeareare's 'Rough Magic': Renaissance Essays in Honor of C. L. Barber*. Ed. Peter Erickson and Coppélia Kahn. Newark: University of Delaware Press, 1985. 104–12.

Levi, Peter. *The Life and Times of William Shakespeare*. NY: Henry Holt & Co., 1988.

Levin, Harry. "A Garden in Belmont: *The Merchant of Venice*, 5.1." *Shakespeare and Dramatic Tradition: Essays in Honor of S. F. Johnson*. Eds. W. R. Elton and William B. Long. Newark: University of Delaware Press, 1989. 13–31.

Levith, Murray J. *What's in Shakespeare's Names?* Hamden, CT.: Shoestring Press, 1978.

MacCary, W. Thomas. *Friends and Lovers: The Phenomenology of Desire in Shakespearean Comedy*. NY: Columbia University Press, 1987.

MacLean, Hugh. "Bassanio's Name and Nature." *Names: A Journal of Onomastics* 25:2 (June 1977): 57–79.

Nathan, Norman. "Bassanio's Name." *American Notes and Queries* 24:9–10 (May–June 1986): 129–31.

———. "Portia, Nerissa, Jessica: Their Names." *Names: A Journal of Onomastics* 34:4 (Dec. 1986): 425–29.

Newman, Karen. "Portia's Ring: Unruly Women and Structures of Exchange in *The Merchant of Venice.*" *Shakespeare Quarterly* 38 (1987): 19–33.

Novy, Marianne. "Giving, Taking, and the Role of Portia in *The Merchant of Venice.*" *Philological Quarterly* 58:2 (Spring 1979): 137–54.

Oz, Avraham. " 'Which is the Merchant Here? And which the Jew?' Riddles of Identity in *The Merchant of Venice.*" *Shakespeare and Cultural Traditions*. Eds. Tetsuo Kishi, Roger Pringle, and Stanley Wells. Newark: University of Delaware Press, 1991. 155–73.

Pequigney, Joseph. "The Two Antonios and Same-Sex Love in *Twelfth Night* and *The Merchant of Venice.*" *Shakespeare and Gender: A History*. Eds. Deborah Barker and Ivo Kamps. NY: Verso, 1995. 178–95.

Roth, Cecil. "The Background of Shylock." *Review of English Studies* 9 (1993): 148–56.

Scragg, Leah. "The Shakespearean Antonio." *English Language Notes* 22:1 (September 1985): 8–19.

Shakespeare, William. *The Riverside Shakespeare*. Ed. G. Blakemore Evans. Boston: Houghton Mifflin, 1974.

Spevack, Marvin. "Beyond Individualism: Names and Namelessness in Shakespeare." *Huntington Library Quarterly* 56:4 (Autumn, 1993): 383–98.

Tennenhouse, Leonard. "The Counterfeit Order of *The Merchant of Venice.*" *Representing Shakespeare: New Psychoanalytic Essays*. Eds. Murray M. Schwartz and Coppélia Kahn. Baltimore: 1980. 54–69.

Van Doren, Mark. *Shakespeare*. NY: Doubleday, 1939.

Singing Chords

Performing Shylock and Other Characters in *The Merchant of Venice*

JAY L. HALIO

Thirty years ago at the first World Shakespeare Congress in Vancouver, BC, Norman Rabkin delivered a paper that began: "Shakespeare criticism is in trouble."[1] Calling for a more comprehensive kind of criticism as against the kinds of reductivism that tended to dominate journal articles and books, interested mainly in thematic approaches, Rabkin drew most of his examples from *The Merchant of Venice*. He noted that while the themes that various commentators identified were surely in the play, and the analyses were in themselves useful, still they left out as much as—or more than—they included about what was in the play, what the play *is*.

Rabkin's admonitions were directed towards literary criticism, and only indirectly towards performance criticism, which at that time was just working up a head of steam (the Vancouver congress did much to stoke the furnace, I'm happy to report). Nevertheless, the main thrust of Rabkin's paper—the need for a more comprehensive approach, one that fully recognizes and responds to the complexities of Shakespeare's characters and a play as a whole—is highly relevant to those interested in Shakespeare's plays as performed.

Twenty years later, as I was working on a new edition of *The Merchant of Venice*, and I included as part of the introduction a brief stage history of the play, I reviewed many productions down the centuries, though by no means all of them (*The Merchant* is second only to *Hamlet* in number of performances). Productions have tended to oscillate between those that present Shylock as a sympathetic character and those that present him otherwise, either as a comic villain or a heinous monster. This is hardly news to anyone, nor is it news that the contradictions and inconsistencies Shakespeare built into his play, which Rabkin emphasized in his paper, lend authority to these various interpretations. Actors, or directors, apparently have to decide which way to go. Or do they? Can't they go both ways? Or is that like asking a baritone to sing chords instead of single notes? Can we ask an actor to be more like a violin or a piano rather than a singer or any univocal instrument? To press the analogy further, can we ask an actor not only to sing chords but to switch from major to minor chords as the script, considered as a score, demands?

That's the problem I pose for an actor playing Shylock: to reveal all sides of his character, the good and the bad, the tragic and the comic, the repulsive and the endearing. And the same for Portia, who too often is either the poor little rich heiress, or the sprightly, sophisticated headgirl. Why not both? Why not combine those traits? After all, most people are a mass of similar contradictions and inconsistencies. Why not Shylock? Why not Portia? Why not Bassanio and others in *The Merchant*? And if it can be made to work for this play, perhaps it can for others.

Shakespeare has given ample warrant for such presentation. The question then may be not why, but how: how to represent fully on stage the inherent contradictions of characters, that is, without risking terrible confusion or blurring of roles.

I submit that the problem is not an impossible one and can be solved. It does require first of all that actors and directors give full credit to the audience, playing up to their adult understanding of complexities rather than down to the inclination toward simplification—a good rousing plot, but not too much of your damn poetry, as Archy's friend in Don Marquis' story puts it. Playing for complexity, however, may be less difficult than we suspect.

Though he appears in only five scenes (six if we include Henry Irving's interpolated one), Shylock dominates the play, leading some to suppose wrongly that it is he, not Antonio, who is the merchant of the title. Endowing him with powerful language and a strong presence, Shakespeare did not need him in any more scenes and could dispense with him altogether in a sometimes problematical fifth act. He appears for the first time in 1.3, completely unheralded (unlike Portia in 1.2, of whom we hear much in the first scene). It is precisely here that the complexities of his character—its contradictions and inconsistencies—must be seized and then realized on stage. Resisting the temptation to cut Shylock's long aside (1.3.33–44) and keeping the text intact, an actor or director must decide how Shylock can remain at one and the same time sympathetic and forbidding.

The forbidding aspect is easy, of course—it's all in the long aside in which he confesses his hatred for Antonio. If he can once get him "on the hip," he'll feed his "ancient grudge," he says (1.3.43–44).[2] Yes, but is the bond, as initially conceived, part of a diabolical plot to do just that? Those who believe it is read the play backwards, it seems to me. They know what happens later and assume therefore it is all part of what Shylock is up to from the start. But if we read the play forwards, that assumption vanishes. In its place we find a Shylock thoroughly inconsistent, but understandably so, given his conflicting feelings. He hates Antonio and all his Christian ilk who have treated him shabbily; but he would be friends with them, turning their repugnance toward him into something positive. This is why Olivier played Shylock as he did in 1970.

Shakespeare makes the point clearly in the ensuing dialogue, when the discussion turns to lending money at interest. Showing no remorse for his scornful attitude, Antonio tells Shylock to lend him money as if to an enemy, not a friend; whereupon Shylock makes an extraordinary gesture:

> Why look you how you storm!
> I would be friends with you and have your love,
> Forget the shames that you have stained me with,
> Supply your present wants, and take no doit
> Of usance for my monies, and you'll not hear me.
> This is kind I offer. (1.3.130–37)

He is improvising, of course, hoping by offering an *interest-free* loan to overcome the historical antagonisms that have divided Jews and Christians, merchants and moneylenders. In his next scene, when in an apparent inconsistency (see 1.3.27–30) he goes off to dinner at Bassanio's, Shylock again confesses his ill-feelings towards the "prodigal Christian"; but he goes anyway. He knows they flatter him; he is not "bid for love," yet he will go in hate, he says. So he goes, and no matter how much he consumes at the banquet he can hardly bankrupt his Gentile host thereby. As Jimmy Durante once sang, he has feelings both to go and stay: classic ambivalence.

This ambivalence, engendered by grudging admiration for the beautiful people of Venice, as well as by deep-seated resentment for their ill treatment of him as a Jew and a moneylender, can and must be communicated, I believe, to be consistent with Shakespeare's text and the inconsistencies of Shakespeare's Jew. Shakespeare gives all the necessary cues, not only in the speech about becoming friends just quoted, but elsewhere, both directly and indirectly. How can Shylock suspect that Antonio will forfeit? The merchant's assurances to Bassanio, made in Shylock's hearing, are perfectly reasonable. Antonio, moreover, is a man of good credit, a "royal merchant" (3.2.238). Even if one or two of his ventures abroad fail, he will make enough on the others to pay back his debt easily. The bond he contracts with Shylock "in a merry sport" may be taken as proposed. (Olivier's hesitation as he tries to think of the forfeit at 1.3.142 beautifully suggested the improvisation and the humor.)

Even toward Lancelot Gobbo Shylock reveals ambivalence: "The patch is kind enough—but a huge feeder," he says to Jessica (2.5.44). Putting a good face on things, he appears willing to let his man go, but he does not initiate the switch; up to then he has been willing to endure Lancelot's laziness, however "snail-slow in profit" he may be. If the brief dialogue between them smacks of sour grapes (2.5.1–5), Shylock also jokes by playing on Lancelot's malapropism (19–21).

That is really all we have, but it's enough. Not until after Jessica's elopement and theft does Shylock really turn nasty. As several commentators and actors have pointed out, it is just then, in his third scene, as Salarino and Solanio taunt him, that the idea of exacting revenge against Antonio first seriously occurs to Shylock.[3] The juxtaposition of Jessica's humiliating behavior with news of Antonio's losses at sea precipitates his murderous desire. For some actors (e.g. Patrick Stewart, David Suchet), the precise moment comes when he laments the loss of Leah's ring, though for others it comes a little earlier, when Salarino foolishly mentions Antonio's misfortunes immediately after mocking Shylock regarding Jessica (3.1.31–34).

From there on it is a straight-line development to the climax in the so-called trial scene, notwithstanding Shylock's alternating emotions in the dialogue with Tubal at the end of 3.1. Shylock has only one other scene before 4.1, a brief one with Antonio and the jailor, in which his hardened heart is fully revealed (3.3). No ambivalence then or later when Portia appeals for mercy, giving him his chance to relent. Only at the end, when he is forced to convert, does Shakespeare suggest another sort of ambivalence. In Shylock's muted responses we detect the truth of "I am not well" (4.1.392).

What is true of Shylock is also true, *mutatis mutandis*, of other characters—Portia, Antonio, Bassanio, even Lancelot Gobbo. All of them suffer conflicts of one kind or another that complicate their characters and their lives. Portia, for example, chafes at the terms of her father's will, but swears to abide by them. She loves Bassanio and wants to help him choose aright, but she is afraid of becoming forsworn. She offers Shylock every chance to show compassion and be merciful, then rigidly upholds the letter of the law, just as he has tried to do. She is bright, queenly, rich, and beautiful—but also an "unlessoned girl, unschooled, unpracticed" (3.2.159), hopelessly in love with her most attractive and suitable suitor. In this she resembles Rosalind in *As You Like It*, in love with Orlando but steadfastly refusing to become sentimental. At the end, to teach Bassanio a lesson about married love, this "unpracticed" girl teases him about the ring he has sworn never to part from and threatens to make him pay dearly for breaking his vow. But she quickly restores concord and, miraculously, Antonio's fortunes, too. She is, in short, a composite of various attributes and qualities hardly consistent with one another, but quite human nonetheless, and she should be played accordingly.

Antonio also reveals incompatible feelings, feelings he says at first he does not understand: "In sooth I know not why I am so sad." Caught between his love for his friend and a desire to see him prosper, he gladly furnishes Bassanio with a loan so he can woo Portia in Belmont. His parting, as described by Salarino (2.8.37–50), brings out all the ambivalence of his feelings, as does his curious letter suggesting Bassanio's return from Belmont to see him die (3.2.314–19). On his part, Bassanio is at several points torn between love for his friend and love for his wife. For example, he exclaims in the trial scene that he would willingly sacrifice his life, his wife, and all the world to save Antonio (4.1.278–83). Later, however reluctantly, he allows Antonio to persuade him to give up his ring to repay "Balthazar" for his good offices. At the beginning of the play, he appears at least as interested in Portia's legacy as in her self; but since the two are one, he does not experience a serious conflict there.

Even Lancelot goes through a tortuous debate over whether to leave the Jew, his master, or not. In a little morality-like scene (2.2), he imagines his good angel and bad angel disputing with him over the rightness of his course. He seems also to have ambivalent feelings about his father, with whom he at first tries "confusions" and then, relenting, becomes embroiled with him in a contest over how to sue for Bassanio's favor. Jessica's feelings toward her father reveal less ambivalence, of course ("Our house is hell," 2.3.2), though she recognizes the sin in being ashamed of her parentage, and later on she may have second thoughts about her defection, if like Jonathan Miller we read too much into—or out of—her last line ("I am never merry when I hear sweet music," 5.1.69).

Given all this ambiguity and ambivalence, how can one adopt a simplistic reading or performance of *The Merchant of Venice*? The play cries out for complex interpretation, and good actors and directors should be able to render it.

Notes

1. "Shakespeare and Meaning" in *Shakespeare 1971*, ed. Clifford Leech and J. M. W. Margeson (Toronto, 1972); reprinted in *Shakespeare and the Problem of Meaning* (Chicago: University of Chicago Press, 1981).
2. All quotations are from my edition in the Oxford World Classics (Oxford University Press, 1993).
3. Jessica's statement later—that she heard Shylock say he'd rather have Antonio's flesh "Than twenty times the value of the sum / That he did owe him" (3.2.285–86)—is sometimes taken as evidence to the contrary. But note its dramatic position—after the turning point in 3.1. Shakespeare supplies this information chiefly to emphasize the seriousness of the threat to Antonio at this point in the play. Jessica's veracity need not be questioned, though she is obviously suing for warmer acceptance among the Christians she has joined.

Making *The Merchant of Venice* Palatable for U.S. Audiences

GAYLE GASKILL

Though still widely performed, *The Merchant of Venice* no longer holds the supremely popular place in the Shakespeare canon that it held in the late nineteenth and early twentieth centuries. From the late Victorian period through the First World War it regularly broke box office records and was recommended by educators as "a child's induction into the serious study of literature" (Rozmovits 2–3). In those years it seemed a sunny commentary on the evolving roles of women and Jews in English and American social politics. Now some find it so anti-Semitic as to be only barely palatable.

The English director Jonathan Miller, whose televised production of the play is still widely available in video, says flatly, "in many respects *The Merchant of Venice* is an unavoidably offensive play" (155). The international theater critic John Gross calmly links the play to anti-Semitic atrocities of the Second World War:

> I personally think it is absurd to suppose that there is a direct line of descent from Antonio to Hitler, or from Portia to the SS, but that is because I do not believe that the Holocaust was in any way inevitable. I *do* believe, on the other hand, that the ground for the Holocaust was well prepared, and to that extent the play can never seem quite the same again. It is still a masterpiece; but there is a permanent chill in the air, even in the gardens of Belmont. (352)

The play that has been sometimes viewed as a plea for tolerance was also used as anti-Semitic propaganda in Nazi territory, from a broadcast shortly after *Kristalnacht* in 1938 through a performance in Vienna in 1943 (Shapiro 90). Harold Bloom, who focuses his mortification on Shylock's forced conversion to Christianity in act 4 writes, "it would have been better for the last four centuries of the Jewish people had Shakespeare never written this play. So shadowed and equivocal is *The Merchant of Venice*, though, that I cannot be certain that there is any way to perform it now and recover Shakespeare's own art of representing Shylock" (190–91). In a brief performance history of the play, one commentator explains, "Whatever the play's intention, there is little doubt that much of the history of the figure of Shylock belongs to the history of anti-Semitism, throughout which he has been cast as the mean, bloodthirsty and vengeful Jewish stereotype" (Smith 6). Like Miller and unlike Bloom, Smith concludes affirmatively that "it is through different productions and adaptations of the play that we can approach the contextual complexities of Shakespeare's representation" (Smith 9). Her intellectual hope for performances as opportunities for discussion, however, offers but a faint promise of the required box office successes that keep theaters operating. Directors face a daunting challenge when they attempt to make *The Merchant of Venice* palatable in performances to new audiences.

In 1999, when Michael Kahn directed the well beloved American stage and television star Hal Holbrook as Shylock in *The Merchant of Venice* at The Shakespeare Theater in Washington, D.C., his successful production harmonized two contradictory but renowned American approaches to the script, one sentimental, the other didactic. The first approach had emigrated from England in 1883 in the theatrical baggage of the actor-manager Henry Irving, who had envisioned a noble, sympathetic, and tragic portrayal of Shylock and played the role himself against gorgeously opulent Venetian sets. Irving first played Shylock in 1879 at London's Lyceum, and as he toured his production his own " 'picturesque . . . but . . . stately' " characterization of the Jew soon supplanted a more traditional "villainous reading" of the part by the American actor Edwin Booth (Hughes with quotation from Irving 226–29). He reprised the role for a quarter century, giving his final American performance in 1903 at the age of sixty-five (Erdman 27–31). In the same production Ellen Terry gave a very attractive portrayal of Portia as a Pre-Raphaelite beauty in Venetian robes of satin and gold brocade. Drawing upon contemporary reviews, James Bulman describes Terry's Portia as "a young, impulsive, blithe spirit . . . an enchantress of gold mixed with virginal beauty" (42–43). Nonetheless, it was Irving who managed the company, and Irving's quiet, "heroic saint" of a Shylock who dominated the performance (Bulman quoting Terry's *Memoirs* published in 1932, 47). Moreover, Irving's performance outlived the actor who created it.

In 1970, in Jonathan Miller's elaborate production at London's National Theatre, the sixty-three year-old stage and screen star Laurence Olivier portrayed Shylock heroically, though the production's nineteenth-century setting restrained him, Miller insists, from the "barnstorming, Irvingish performance of what he thought the traditional Shylock should be like" (Miller 104). His yarmulke concealed by an elegant top hat, Olivier's performance became a definitive influence on subsequent American productions after it was televised in 1973. Without naming him, Miller invoked the spirit of Irving by setting his production squarely in the time period in which Irving had conceived his role, and by giving Shylock the dignified manner of Irving's powerful contemporaries, Rothschild and Disraeli. Miller's Portia, meanwhile, the mature Joan Plowright, emphasized the snobbishness of her wealthy character rather than promoting the romantic disposition, sexual allure, good humor, or generosity that Terry had found in her role. Thus Plowright delivered the audience's sympathies squarely to Olivier's suffering Shylock.

Like Irving before him, Miller believed that Shylock, the suffering Jew, was the center of the play. Furthermore, he believed that for a mid-twentieth-century audience, placing Shylock in the late Victorian setting where an elegantly dressed Jewish businessman was "scarcely distinguishable" from his Christian counterpart "highlights and emphasizes the absurdity of the racial prejudice" (Miller 155–56). Between 1879 and 1970 the director's confrontation with his script's portraits of anti-Semitism had grown from Irving's opportunity to make a tragedian's star vehicle out of Shakespeare's comedy into Miller's perceived public duty to stir and enlighten his audience. As Bulman comments,

> Updating the play thus served Miller's agenda as readily as an anthropologically "correct" production served Irving's; both directors sought thereby to discover the origins of their own culture's attitudes towards Jews, and both suppressed the play's comic potential in order to present the "real"—that is, the tragically verisimilar—Shylock as a representative of his whole persecuted race. (77)

Especially as it was updated by Miller, the Irving legacy conveyed a gravely earnest endorsement of social justice while it displayed the talents of a popular actor who dominated the whole production from the mere five scenes in which he appeared.

By embracing that now famous and conservative legacy and by casting Holbrook as Shylock, Kahn pleased his audience without much surprising them. An attentive critic called the production "powerful theater," and the play was sold out for its seven-week run (Mahon 24). Kahn's production achieved both artistic and financial success, and it upheld the solid reputation of The Shakespeare Theater in the U.S. capital.

In addition to his considerable indebtedness to Irving and Miller, however, Kahn also drew upon two newer approaches to the play that had originated as the controversial inventions of distinctly American directors. Each of these directors had envisioned the play less as a star vehicle than as a contemporary condemnation of the violent excesses of American capitalism. In 1973 Ellis Raab made the understated but tragic homosexual love of Antonio and Bassanio a central point of his production at New York City's Lincoln

Center. Sydney Walker, who played Shylock, according to the *New York Times*, "as a tightly buttoned, dour businessman" (Barnes 23), was a sympathetic performer, but the headliner of the ensemble cast was Rosemary Harris. Her Portia was a notably mature woman won by a Bassanio who in her presence was, according to *The New Yorker*, "unaccountably wooden and inept" (Gill 102). Harris's Portia saw through the transparent designs upon her fortune by all of her wooers, but she remained self-possessed. Jessica, on the other hand, younger and the more deceived, was assaulted by masked revelers as she eloped with Lorenzo and her father's jewels (Novick B:1). "What this play is about," said Raab in an interview shortly before his production opened, "is the corruption of love by money" (quoted in Funke, B:1). While he clearly recognized that anti-Semitism was a facet of *The Merchant*, Raab's early 1970s U.S. production stressed the economic contexts of all the play's relationships. An elegant but cheerless production, Raab's *Merchant*, like Miller's, traded the play's fairy tale romance for dearly bought worldly wisdom and a public warning against the excesses of greed.

In 1994 Los Angeles Festival director Peter Sellars expanded Raab's emphasis on the social ramifications of the play's economic issues. Sellars initiated an international tour of *The Merchant* at Chicago's Goodman Theater with a reworking of the play's portrait of racism. In Sellars's production, African-American actors played the Jews, Asian-Americans the Belmontese, Latinos the Venetians, and Caucasians the Gobbos and a "conservative establishment" Duke of Venice (Weiss, "Shakespeare" S10). By "his dangerous replacing of Shakespeare's controversial stereotypes with controversial modern ones," according to one critic, Sellars produced the play so as to define modern racism as the inevitable extension of economic exploitation (Swed F:1). In the trial scene, while Shylock demanded justice, ubiquitous television monitors played recognizable video tapes of Rodney King being beaten by Los Angeles policemen and of the rioting that occurred when a jury subsequently acquitted those policemen of wrongdoing.

Shunning Irving's elaborate evocations of medieval Venice, as well as Miller's equally elaborate Victorian sets, both Sellars and Raab used minimal staging, screen projections, and modern dress. At the same time, both emphasized the substitution of material wealth for human love as the tragedy of modern American society. Raab set the play in what one reviewer described as "an idealized modern Venice [of] cocktail bars, beach chairs, bikinis, . . . charged with languorous hedonism, decadence and voluptuous money lust" (Kroll 86). Twenty years later, Sellars found southern California a timely multicultural illustration of economic exploitation and flatly transformed Venice to Venice Beach and Belmont to Bel-Air, which some recognized as "the exclusive southern California enclave that [was] home to former president Ronald Reagan" (Weiss, "Peter" 1). To stress the modern substitution of technology for communication, Raab partly concealed his actors behind sunglasses and flash cameras. Similarly, Sellars, who evoked Raab's production by giving Portia "nifty green sunglasses" (Kellaway 15), updated the technological distance between stage characterization and audience empathy by teaching his actors to speak into microphones while looking into camcorders as television monitors projected their faces in close-up from the stage and throughout the house. One critic commented on Sellars's production, "Antonio's friends and Portia's suitors are image-conscious, forever addressing video monitors. . . . Sellars is, presumably, making points here about the terrible way in which modern living is indeed being geared for perpetual broadcast" (Macaulay 15). If heavy-handed, the use of television was nonetheless provocative, not only by challenging a society that makes moral decisions based on sound bites, but also by presenting the actors' faces in close-up to audience members seated in the cheapest seats farthest from the stage.

Both productions skillfully manipulated the familiar, unfeeling news media formats that they deplored. Determined to present a *Merchant* even more somber than Miller's or Irving's, both Raab and Sellars expunged the romance from the Belmont scenes, leaving a Portia who was businesslike and calculating. Sellars's Antonio and Bassanio publicly demonstrated their homoerotic passion more openly than had Raab's characters two decades earlier. Unconsciously acknowledging that the romance of Ellen Terry's Portia had vanished from the current American milieu, one perplexed British reviewer wondered whether Sellars's Portia "has unknowingly married a bisexual. No wonder she acts in court as if she would rather slice bits off Antonio herself than save him from the knife" (Nightingale, par. 5). Both productions presented the lonely merchant's masochistic infatuation with an exploitative playboy as the predominant expression of human love in a grasping world of commerce. In so doing, each director condemned the insatiable American craving for material wealth that he perceived as the root cause of racial and sexual exploitation. To illustrate the point in his stark set design, Sellars left the "three coffin-shaped caskets" perpetually in view (Kellaway 15). By pursuing mere greed, each character wooed and won his or her own moral death.

By comparison, Kahn's 1999 Washington *Merchant* was far more conservative than these two earlier, more sensational American experiments. Its detailed sets by the well established designer Ming Cho Lee conveyed a Venice of the late medieval period, visually appealing and safely remote from current headlines. Nonetheless, Kahn established "money as the primary focus of the Christians' concern" (Mahon 15) at least as clearly as had Sellars and Raab. Furthermore, he brought black actors onto the stage to emphasize the racism that was perceived to grow from a compulsive preoccupation with material wealth, and he portrayed Shylock as one among many victims of not only anti-Semitism but nearly universal racism. Like Raab, Sellars, and

Miller, Kahn diminished the comic scenes, and with them the romance of Belmont. His male characters, who displayed "a sophisticated homoeroticism . . . see women strictly as their meal-tickets" (Mahon 15). Thus while Kahn drew upon Irving's crowd-pleasing exoticism and sentimentality, he also nodded admiringly at Sellars's and Raab's harangues against the moral decay that appeared simultaneously to evolve from and undermine the growth of U.S. capitalism.

Interviewed at the time he was preparing this production of *Merchant* Kahn asked,

> What happens to a society or what goes on in a society when money becomes tremendously important and people begin to be equal with commodities? In this play the suitors pay homage to caskets; they equate Portia with gold, and Shylock equates his daughter with his ducats. (Kahn 22)

Kahn illustrated his first two points in his production as vividly as Raab and Sellars had done in theirs. First Kahn's Portia, like Sellars's, had stage-managed her wooer's choice of the lead casket. Then Bassanio, according to a reviewer astounded at the wooer's "caddishness," turns, "*not* to Portia but to *Gratiano*, and reads the scroll to his friend, embraces him, and only then turns to Portia" (Mahon 24). Kahn had already prepared his audience to experience this materialistic scorn for romantic love in the way he portrayed Jessica's departure with Lorenzo. In a "cartoonish" and heavily didactic piece of stage business, after Jessica throws "her father's jewel-chest down to him, Lorenzo and his fellows immediately open it and empty its contents onto the pavement, so that together they can rejoice in Lorenzo's successful catch. He virtually ignores Jessica" (Mahon 15). Kahn had lifted that action directly from Raab's production of 1973, then coldly removed the sexuality that Raab had added as his "revelers leap at [Jessica] and tear her blouse off" in what one reviewer described as "a phantasmagorical, sacrilegious orgy" (Novick B:1). According to these productions, Jessica's unpalatable mixed marriage to Lorenzo begins in violence, and evidently no late-twentieth-century director can project their eventual happiness.

In Miller's production, Jessica had turned to Lorenzo in the false hope of assimilation into the comfortable Christian majority. In Raab's she was the victim of her false lover's greed and her own inexperienced sexual vulnerability. For Kahn, as for Sellars, Jessica's sordid little story was simply one more dreary expression of modern human acquisitiveness defeating human love. Nonetheless, he was more gracious to Jessica's character than was Irving, whose romantic Jessica had eloped with her lover in a practicable stage gondola and desolated the family home moments before her father's return. In a famous piece of interpolated stage business lifted from Verdi's *Rigoletto* (Bulman 38), Irving allowed the curtain to drop upon the laughter of Jessica's elopement amid merry masqueraders. Then the curtain rose upon the same scene in silence and darkness as Shylock, holding a lantern, crossed a practicable canal bridge toward his house, ironically still ignorant of the silence that awaited him. Ellen Terry described the device with professional admiration: "For absolute pathos, achieved by absolute simplicity of means . . . I never saw anything in the theatre to compare with [it]." An early reviewer was more passionately interpretative: to him, Jessica in her very absence was "an odious, immodest, dishonest creature, than whom Shakespeare drew no more unpleasant character. . . . Lorenzo was at best the receiver of stolen goods" (Hughes 232 quoting Ellen Terry and the *Spectator* of 11 August 1879). More than Irving's Lorenzo, Kahn's was concerned solely with his stolen goods. Consistent in his capitalistic enterprise, he danced joyfully in the last scene upon receiving Shylock's deed of gift. Then he abandoned his "mournful, dismayed" (Mahon 15), and newly enlightened Jessica on stage with an equally regretful Antonio.

Though in its treatment of suitors, caskets, and golden Portia, Kahn's 1999 production supported and illustrated the first two points of his earlier statement about the U.S. commodification of people, it cautiously excused Shylock's apparent commodification of Jessica in the daughter-ducats lament. In an interview, Kahn explained his original intentions to take Shylock's offstage lament, "My daughter! O, my ducats!" (2.8.15), which the script offers only in Solanio's hostile report, and restore it to Shylock himself. At this preliminary stage of preparing for performance, Kahn viewed Shylock's balance of familial and mercantile woes as a reflection of the realistic contradictions Shakespeare had developed in his character and of Shylock's place in the intensely mercantile city of Venice.

> Shylock is worried about his daughter *and* his ducats. Does this mean that *The Merchant of Venice* is an anti-Semitic play? No. It means that a man who is completely and openly interested in money, Shylock, also has the greatest and most humanizing speech about tolerance in the play: "Hath not a Jew eyes, etc." [3.1.49–61]. And this man lives in a society that is devoted to the gathering of wealth. (Kahn 22).

At this point in the interview, Kahn began to describe the Early Modern development of capitalism and colonialism in a way that echoed Peter Sellars's remarks five years earlier, shortly before his *Merchant* opened in Chicago. An interviewer quotes Sellars:

> "In looking at the very beginning of capitalism and colonial imperialism as it was taking shape in his time, Shakespeare made the connection between systematic racism, economic oppression and personal corruption. . . . It is no accident that the East India Company, that extraordinary marriage of political and economic interests, was established within a few years of the

The Merchant of Venice

creation of this play, or that throughout the story there is talk of ships coming from Africa, Asia and Mexico, carrying the products of slave labour. Already in place was the very same relationship with the Third World that now supplies me with my Gap T-shirt and enables an American company to profit from a sweatshop labourer somewhere in south Asia who will never see the value of his or her work." (Weiss, "Shakespeare" S10)

Though he was clearly impressed by Sellars's doctrinaire approach to the script, and though he had evidently discovered an original application of that theory to illuminate the complexities of Shylock's devotion to his investments, Kahn nonetheless reconsidered his original intentions at some point in the development of his production. Perhaps he was simply attempting to please his formidable leading actor, or perhaps he felt his U.S. audience, schooled for a century in Irving's and Miller's simpler, sentimental characterizations of Shylock, would find this complex, bereft but nonetheless frankly acquisitive man unsympathetic or simply unpalatable.

Instead of giving his Shylock the lines reported of him, Kahn retained the speech as Solanio's mockery and then savagely underscored Solanio's verbal abuse of Shylock with a Christian gang's physical assault upon the grieving father. When two Jewish youths rescued Shylock, the gang, in their confused excitement, turned arbitrarily upon one of Antonio's black slaves. Kahn's invented stage business eliminated the complexity he had earlier hoped to reveal in Shylock's character, while it memorably emphasized the racist tensions portrayed in the production. Kahn then abruptly changed the mood with a piece of invented business borrowed from Miller, Shylock's singing Kaddish for his lost child. This interpolation, like Irving's dark and deserted house, brought on the intermission.

Though in production, Kahn sometimes fell back upon Irving's and Miller's successful sentimentality, his stated intentions resembled those of Sellars, who commented,

"This play is about what happens when market values overtake a society completely. Shakespeare titles his play about racism and about the moral, spiritual and romantic collapse of people *The Merchant of Venice* because it's about what happens when making a climate that's good for business is our only concern." (quoted by Billington, "Venice" T6)

Surprisingly, however, in light of the lengthy theoretical explanations Sellars had given to the press, in production Kahn's sympathetic treatment of Shylock resembled Sellars's equally sympathetic treatment. Both Sellars and Kahn were more successful in illustrating and condemning the egregious capitalism of their Christian characters, including the converted Jessica, than in portraying its poisonous effects on Shylock. In Kahn's production, as in Miller's, Shylock pursued his bloodthirsty revenge upon Antonio in order to satisfy a hate caused not by countless financial and personal humiliations but purely by paternal grief. Sellars's Shylock was perceived as only fractionally less heroic. Like Raab, Sellars relied on an acting ensemble rather than a star system and so cast Paul Butler, an actor less famous than Olivier or Holbrook, in the role of Shylock. Furthermore, his reliance on news media technology distanced the audience from all the characterizations. Nonetheless, most reviewers took pains to comment sympathetically on Butler's characterization and to understand Shylock's cry for revenge as a father's justifiable grief.

It appears that only one critic saw the loss of property as a cause for Butler's Shylock to become unhinged, and even that writer paused to admire the actor's restrained performance. According to Michael Billington, "Paul Butler's dignified black Shylock is doomed from the moment he breaks down on hearing of the sale of his turquoise ring: loss of property fuses with dislike of Antonio to drive him into a hopeless court case" (Billington, "Love" T17). Butler's characterization appears to be a milder Shylock than the one Kahn had later envisioned as the cheated moneylender who equated his daughter with his ducats. Billington's critical observation, however, was actually one of the few readings of Butler's performance to allude even casually to Shylock's otherwise reasonable regret for his extraordinary financial losses. At least one critic compared Butler's Shylock to Martin Luther King (Macaulay 15), and another found him "big-hearted" and admired "the gentle gravity with which he voices rage" (Kellaway 15). A third confessed "Shylock is not a Jew, he is a black who is perceived as a Jew. And through him and the others in a production that turns a multiracial cast into a tight ensemble, we see just how deep our racism is, how troubled as a society we are" (Swed F:1). Even a critic who condemned Sellars's "zaniness" and labeled his revised racial designations matters of "mystification rather than enlightenment" admitted, "it makes sense to have a black Shylock, impressively played here by Paul Butler as a fruitily chuckling fat-cat businessman whose world collapses with the flight of his sulky daughter Jessica" (Spencer 25). Despite his professed emphasis on the evils of capitalistic exploitation, and perhaps because he substituted contemporary American anti-black racism for Elizabethan anti-Semitic racism, in 1994 Sellars ultimately refused to tamper with his audience's palatable traditional perception of Shylock. The man who publicly demands the right to cut a leading citizen to the heart remains a figure of sympathy.

The young critic W. B. Worthen has expressed his frustration with the disparity between Sellars's critical designs for *The Merchant of Venice* and Sellars's production of the play. Though Worthen readily accepts the director's insistent reading of the play as a commentary on late-twentieth-century capitalistic excesses, he objects to Sellars's corresponding insistence that he can and must justify that contemporary reading through close reading of Shakespeare's script:

> Sellars stages the play in an explicit relation to the ways that contemporary culture reproduces itself, and reproduces its institutions, its values, its ideologies. At the same time, both the press and Sellars himself represent the work of the production as succeeding or failing to the extent that the director has been able to recapture authentically Shakespearean meanings. (Worthen 93)

Worthen finds Sellars's transformation of Shakespeare's comedy into a sharp rebuke of U.S. racism, capitalistic exploitation, and economic inequities perfectly palatable. As a postmodernist, however, he points out the absurdity of the central premise Sellars shares with his critics, that this social critique must be discovered as latent in Shakespeare's intentions. Theater audiences, however, will not easily dismiss the premise but prefer to cling to the idea that a production must teach what Shakespeare actually meant, and confirm the playwright's universal meaning for his current audience.

The U.S. production history of *The Merchant* has for over a century presented Shylock as a tragic hero, the victim of casual racism. To represent him as a foiled perpetrator of violence against non-Jews would be unpalatable to a U.S. audience. To condemn racism in performance, some other characters must be brought forward. Starting with Miller's production, directors have found their culprit in Portia. Asserting that he was simply acting Shakespeare's intentions, Holbrook summed up the idea at a conversation offered by Washington's Shakespeare Guild at the National Press Club early in his successful run: "Since it is obvious that Shakespeare meant us to take Shylock's suffering seriously, it follows that the romantic plot has to be darkened" (quoted by Mahon 15). Holbrook's statement endorsed the thinking of his director.

While preparing his production, Kahn recalled "the idyllic picture of Ellen Terry" as Portia, only to dismiss it. She was "blond, sometimes with a lawyer's hat on, a sort of angelic and smart 'perfect' person." Then her uninvited soldier-suitor, the Prince of Morocco, sought her picture in the wrong casket and departed forever. Following his exit Portia uttered what for Kahn and several other directors became a telling couplet:

> A gentle riddance. Draw the curtains, go.
> Let all of his complexion choose me so. (2.7.78–79)

For Kahn, Portia's remark was a surprising "racial slur." When he saw the line delivered by a white Portia to a black Nerissa, who "quickly and sharply looked back, [it] brought into the production a fleeting awareness of the complex implications of race" (Kahn 20–21). He used the pointed stage business in his Washington production, where "Portia's casual racism clearly upsets the black maid," and he expanded it.

From the first scene, Salerio, Solanio, Lorenzo, and Gratiano all "shamelessly" fawned upon the wealthy Antonio, while "the two black servants (clever visual anticipations of the slaves Shylock will accuse the Christians of later) are treated carelessly and (by Gratiano) even nastily" (Mahon 15). Kahn made his point skillfully, while his audience and his leading actor accepted the tarnishing of a Portia who was historically once the play's ideal.

The stage history of *The Merchant of Venice* in the United States is always evolving. Perhaps Portia's character will one day be reconsidered. As new directors invent new subtexts and disguise them as Shakespeare's intentions, some new Portia may dismiss Morocco not for his skin color but for his obvious militarism. He wants her money to wage wars, and consequently presents his manliness in terms of military potency, not domestic tenderness. Already one or two critics of Raab's and Sellars's productions commented on Portia's frustrations with the patriarchal control asserted through her dead father's manipulation of the law, and Kahn kept the old man's crepe-draped portrait on display among the caskets.

Perhaps a future production will display an intense sexual attraction between Portia and Morocco, thus reading his militant boasting not as braggadocio or heroic self-assertion but as a strong hint of the sexual potency that Portia has already experienced or that she has eagerly imagined. Such a production could read her couplet as a bitter rebuke of her own desires. Perhaps Lorenzo and Jessica will one day be portrayed as happy in their love. Their moonlight speeches of 5.1 could be recovered from the scarcely suppressed rage of Raab's production or the deliberate boredom of Miller's. A director's speculations about new interpretations of *The Merchant of Venice* negotiate meanings from the script and the audience's powers of perception. In 1999 Michael Kahn's *Merchant*, an extension of the work by both successful and daring predecessors, was an exciting, richly visual, sentimental, and heavily didactic work in which a renowned actor kept the audience's attention on a grieving, dignified Shylock. A future production may dare to rekindle the fires of Portia's humor and romance, or may discover some new subtext altogether, but at the end of the twentieth century, Kahn's work was perfectly palatable to a U.S. audience.

Works Cited

Barnes, Clive. "Stage: Modern 'Venice.' " Rev. of *The Merchant of Venice*, dir. Ellis Raab. *New York Times* 5 Mar. 1973: 23.

Billington, Michael. "Love and Loot in LA." Rev. of *The Merchant of Venice*, dir. Peter Sellars. *The Guardian* 18 Nov. 1994: Features T6.

———. "Venice Champion." Rev. of *The Merchant of Venice*, dir. Peter Sellars. *The Guardian* 16 Nov. 1994: Features T6.

Bloom, Harold. *Shakespeare: The Invention of the Human*. New York: Riverhead, 1998.

Bulman, James C. *"The Merchant of Venice." Shakespeare in Performance*. Manchester: Manchester University Press, 1991.

Erdman, Harley. *Staging the Jew: The Performance of an American Ethnicity, 1860–1920*. New Brunswick NJ: Rutgers University Press, 1997.

Funke, Lewis. "Shylock—Has the Storm Subsided?" *New York Times* 25 Feb. 1973: B1, 3.

Gill, Brendan. "And Still Champion." Rev. of *The Merchant of Venice*, dir. Ellis Raab. *The New Yorker* 10 Mar. 1973: 102–103.

Gross, John. *Shylock: A Legend and its Legacy*. New York: Simon and Schuster, 1992.

Hughes, Alan. *Henry Irving, Shakespearean*. Cambridge: Cambridge University Press, 1981.

Kahn, Michael. "Prologue." Interview by Robert P. Brink. *Teaching Shakespeare Through Performance*. Ed. Milla Cozart Riggio. Modern Language Association of America Options for Teaching. New York: Modern Language Association, 1999.

Kellaway, Kate. "Theatre: Merchant of Menace." Rev. of *The Merchant of Venice*, dir. Peter Sellars. *The Observer* 20 Nov. 1994: 15.

Kroll, Jack. "Money Lust in Venice." Rev. of *The Merchant of Venice*, dir. Ellis Raab. *Newsweek* 19 Mar. 1973: 86.

Macaulay, Alastair. "Peter Sellars's 'Merchant of Venice.' " Rev. of *The Merchant of Venice*, dir. Peter Sellars. *Financial Times* (London) 18 Nov. 1994: Arts, 15.

Mahon, John W. "Holbrook Triumphs as Shylock." Rev. of *The Merchant of Venice*, dir. Michael Kahn. *The Shakespeare Newsletter* 49 (1999): 15, 24.

Miller, Jonathan. *Subsequent Performances*. New York: Viking Penguin, 1986.

Nightingale, Benedict. "The Bard and the Bully-Boy." Rev. of *The Merchant of Venice*, dir. Peter Sellars. *The Times* (London) 18 Nov. 1994. http://web.lexis-nexis.com/universe/docu...zV&_md5fb369d85c4cb9ae24475/.

Novick, Julius. "New Look for Shakespeare?" Rev. of *The Merchant of Venice*, dir. Ellis Raab. *New York Times* 11 Mar. 1973: B1, 5.

Rozmovits, Linda. *Shakespeare and the Politics of Culture in Late Victorian England*. Baltimore: Johns Hopkins University Press, 1998.

Shapiro, James. "Shakespeare and the Jews." *The Merchant of Venice*. Ed. Martin Coyle. New Casebooks. New York: St. Martin's, 1998. 73–91.

Smith, Emma. "*The Merchant of Venice:* Prejudice and Performance." *The English Review* 8 (1997): 6–9.

Spencer, Charles. "The Arts: Bard Hurt in the Riots." Rev. of *The Merchant of Venice*, dir. Peter Sellars. *The Daily Telegraph* 18 Nov. 1994: 25.

Swed, Mark. " 'Merchant of Venice' Beach?: Peter Sellars Strikes Again." Rev. of *The Merchant of Venice*, dir. Peter Sellars. *Los Angeles Times* 12 Oct. 1994: Calendar: F1, 2.

Weiss, Hedy. "Peter Sellars' 'Merchant' of Venice Beach." Rev. of *The Merchant of Venice*, dir. Peter Sellars. *Chicago Sun-Times* 9 Oct. 1994: 1.

———. "Shakespeare: Race Riots and Rollerblades." Rev. of *The Merchant of Venice*, dir. Peter Sellars. *The Observer* 9 Oct. 1994: S10.

Worthen, W. B. *Shakespeare and the Authority of Performance*. Cambridge: Cambridge University Press, 1997.

Shylock in Performance

JOHN O'CONNOR

Introducing an article on Arnold Wesker's *The Merchant*, Iska Alter wrote:

> If *The Merchant of Venice* is not the most problematic of Shakespeare's
> plays, it certainly has become one of the most provocative, not to say pro-
> voking, for the contemporary sensibility, schooled by history to the horrific
> outcome of anti-Jewish prejudice in the twentieth century. A tentative hint
> suggesting the possibility of a production is often enough to generate a
> cause célèbre, prompting attacks on the playwright, cries of outrage against
> the theatre, and the inevitable demands for censorship among those who
> view the play as an antisemitic desecration. Once a production has been
> mounted, unless Shylock has been interpreted as an appropriately heroic if
> frequently sentimentalized figure, attacks often recur. (536)[1]

Such are the controversies which potentially arise from any new production
of *The Merchant of Venice* that no director or actor can prepare for a fresh
interpretation of the character of Shylock without an overshadowing awareness of the implications of getting it wrong; and for actors and directors, the
key question becomes: how sympathetically do we play Shylock? Four factors have been influential in encouraging a history of increasingly sympathetic portrayal. The first is that, from Kean's coruscating performance
onwards, Shylock has almost consistently been a "star" role, since it preemi-
nently offers the actor the opportunity to display his full emotional range—
from humor to bitterness, tyranny to pathos: "The star actors who from the
eighteenth century onwards have chosen to play the role have not done so out
of a sense of moral duty in order to combat anti-Semitism, but because their
theatrical instinct told them that the part, played seriously, not comically,
offered them great possibilities" (Auden 223).

The resulting villain, moreover, seen in a complex and ambiguous social
context, is always likely to elicit more audience sympathy than an unalloyedly

wicked one. Secondly, the role has frequently tended to attract actors more usually associated with tragedy, who have, albeit sometimes involuntarily, brought to the role the sympathy normally attached to tragic figures. Related to that is the fact that, uniquely among Shakespeare's villains, Shylock's argument is one that speaks with conviction and eloquence to the audience's sense of injustice. While condemning the extremity of his planned revenge, we are tempted to endorse the reaction of the woman who, having watched Kean's dignified and intelligent Jew collapse under the force of Christian justice, remarked in Heine's hearing: "the poor man is wronged" (Mahood 44).

Fourthly, and quite simply, Shylock is a Jew. Audiences at least as early as the 1770s were beginning to see Shylock's treatment as part of a wider picture of anti-Semitic[2] prejudice, and by the 1830s were linking his defeat with the whole history of Jewish maltreatment and suffering. If the context of growing nineteenth-century liberalism was enough to encourage Irving's sympathetic portrayal, how much greater are the influences upon actors and directors of the post-war generation who live and work in the shadow of the Nazi Holocaust?

From prompt books and contemporary audience reports, it is possible to see what actors such as Kean, Booth, and Irving made of Shakespeare's Jew; but of the earliest interpretations we know nothing at all, not even the name of the actor who first played the character. There are three reasonably plausible candidates for the creator of the role of Shylock, the most widely supported of whom was for a long time Richard Burbage. As the most celebrated of the Chamberlain's Men, Burbage seems a likely choice, and for a while it looked as though the tradition that he had indeed played the part—and in a red wig—had been borne out by the discovery by the Victorian scholar, J. Payne Collier, of a funeral elegy to the great actor in which his roles, Shylock among them, were lovingly lauded in convincing doggerel.[3] The fact that the manuscript in which the elegy appeared turned out to be a forgery does not, of course, invalidate the Burbage claim, but the volume in which Collier published his "find" contains an interesting piece of surrounding text which goes some way to suggesting why the Victorians in particular might have seen Burbage as the obvious first Shylock, and why they might have been led astray by their preconceptions of the role. Collier writes: "To the list of characters in plays by Shakespeare sustained by Burbadge [*sic*] we still have to add Lear and Shylock, so that we may safely decide that he was the chosen representative of all, or nearly all, the *serious* parts in the productions of our great dramatist" [my italics] (22).

The significance lies in the categorizing of Shylock as a "serious" part. Collier is writing at a time when the two great interpreters of Shylock to date had been Macklin and Kean, both of whom had played the part with utmost seriousness, while the Shylock of William Charles Macready, revived at Drury Lane only five years before the publication of Collier's book, had been "abject, sordid, irritable, argumentative" (Lewes 115). Collier took it for granted that Shylock would always have been played by a "serious" actor; had he lived in the time of the comic Shylock Thomas Dogget, he would presumably not have assigned the role to the Chamberlain's Men's leading tragic actor, but to one of their clowns.

The two outstanding comic actors in Shakespeare's company at the time when *The Merchant of Venice*[4] was first performed were Will Kempe and Thomas Pope. Kempe is known to have played, among other roles, Peter in *Romeo and Juliet*, and Dogberry in *Much Ado About Nothing*, and might also have played Pistol (Gurr 291). Pope, like Kempe, was a senior member of the company—a "payee" with Heminges in 1595, one of the seven sharers in the Globe building costs four years later, and also a sharer in the Curtain. It has been speculated that he played Sir Toby Belch (Baldwin 228–29). That either of these actors might have played the original Shylock, the other taking the role of Lancelot Gobbo (perhaps with Burbage as Bassanio) is, I would suggest, plausible speculation. It is certainly unwise to associate Burbage with Shylock on the Victorian presumption that the role demands tragic weight.

There are no records of a production of *The Merchant of Venice* in the seventeenth century. For the first interpretation after Shakespeare's death we have to turn to George Granville's 1701 version, retitled *The Jew of Venice*, at best a mutilation of the original, an adaptation of Shakespeare's, rather than an independent creation. The comedian Thomas Doggett played Shylock. Despite its box office success, the first real Shylock of the post-Restoration period was Charles Macklin.

When Charles Macklin prepared for his performance of Shylock at Drury Lane in 1741, it was in an atmosphere of hostility and suspicion. There were serious doubts about reviving a play that had not been performed in its original form in living memory (Appleton 44), and this animosity was no doubt fuelled by the fact that ". . . at every rehearsal, whilst he enjoined the rest of the performers to do their best, he himself played both under his voice and general powers, carefully reserving his fire till the night of representation" (Cooke 91).

As Appleton suggests, Macklin did not wish to alarm his fellow actors by "the novelty of his interpretation" (47). Macklin's Shylock was an outrageous success, however, and he went on to play the part for the next forty-eight years. For details of Macklin's Shylock we are indebted to a contemporary visitor from abroad, Georg Lichtenberg, who writes in 1775: "He is heavy and silent in his unfathomable cunning, and when the law is on his side, just to the point of malice" (40). This portrayal seems to have been rooted in Macklin's innovative acting style, which eschewed the then customary forced gesture and sing-song delivery in favor of something which was at least a step towards more naturalistic speech and movement.[5]

I earlier identified several reasons why an actor might wish to endow Shylock with some sympathetic qualities, not the least important of which was the awareness that Shylock's story is indissolubly linked with that of the suffering and persecution of the Jewish people as a whole. This consciousness, and the accompanying fear that the play can be seen as anti-Semitic, can be traced back at least as far as Macklin; and there are two elements of his performance which point to an embryonic sensitivity concerning the ways in which Jews should be played upon the stage.

The first lies in the care with which Macklin researched the role, visiting the Exchange and "adjacent coffee-houses; that by a frequent intercourse and conversation with 'the unforeskinned race' he might habituate himself to their air and deportment."[6] This does not, of course, imply a favorable stage portrayal: most of the contemporary evidence shows that it was not; but it does at least indicate an unwillingness merely to replicate a stale comic stereotype or deny the character individuality.

The second piece of evidence which might be said to demonstrate some unease over the ramifications of portraying an evil Jew is found in the Lichtenberg letter. He writes: "It cannot be denied that the sight of this Jew is more than sufficient to arouse once again in the mature man all the prejudices of his childhood against this race" (40). What I find interesting in Lichtenberg's comment is his reference to the susceptibility of "the mature man" to prejudice and hostility if Shylock is played in certain ways; and the fact that such feelings are inculcated in childhood. This brief statement demonstrates not only the deep-seated hatred which permitted generations of parents to use the figure of the Jew as bogeyman; but also, conversely, the awakening sensibility in thinking men and women that this was fundamentally wrong. Moreover there is something in Lichtenberg's careful phrasing ("It cannot be denied that") which hints that this is not merely a personal confession, but the beginnings of a serious debate upon the implications of restating and reinforcing this racial and cultural stereotype on the popular stage.

Macklin's Shylock was a close ancestor of both Edmund Kean's and Edwin Booth's. Kean's interpretation is notable for two further landmarks in the performance history of Shakespeare's Jew: the endowment of the figure with a degree of tragic grandeur; and the apparent response in the actor's portrayal to the changing moral sensibilities of the age. Booth's Shylock is of particular interest because it did not conform to the "revisionist" interpretation of the semi-tragic and sympathetic Shylock, established by Kean and perpetuated by, among others, William Charles Macready. In a letter to William Winter in 1884, Booth writes:

> I sent you a paper from Baltimore—not for what is said of my performance of Shylock but for what I regard as the true Shakespearian portrait of the Jew. I believe you hold a different estimate of the character, as many do, but

> I have searched in vain for the slightest hint of anything resembling dignity
> or worthiness in the part. (Watermeier 256)

Booth is an unusual Shylock because, although he showed vividly in his famous portrayals of Hamlet, Iago, and Brutus that he found ambiguity interesting, he seems largely to have eschewed it in the case of the Jew. In adopting this stance, Booth denied himself an opportunity which most leading actors since Kean have enthusiastically embraced: to present audiences with an absorbing and many-faceted villain who makes so many demands upon our sympathy that he departs from the stage with the stature of a tragic hero.

Preeminent among these was Henry Irving. In considering probably the most influential Shylock in performance history, I shall follow the lead of many stage historians[7] who have considered it important to introduce their comments on Irving's interpretation with a prefatory account of the actor's encounter with a Levantine Jew on a brief visit to Tunis in the summer of 1879, a meeting which seems to have influenced his later interpretation in a number of important ways. Joseph Hatton recalls a conversation with Irving in which he described the encounter in this way:

> I saw a Jew once, in Tunis, tear his hair and raiment, fling himself in the sand, and writhe in a rage, about a question of money,—beside himself with passion. I saw him again, self-possessed and fawning; and again, expressing real gratitude for a trifling money courtesy. He was never undignified until he tore at his hair and flung himself down, and then he was picturesque; he was old, but erect, even stately, and full of resource. As he walked behind his team of mules he carried himself with the lofty air of a king. He was a Spanish Jew,—Shylock probably was of Frankfort; but Shakespeare's Jew was a type, not a mere individual: he was a type of the great, grand race,—not a mere Houndsditch usurer. He was a man famous on the Rialto; probably a foremost man in his synagogue—proud of his descent—conscious of his moral superiority to many of the Christians who scoffed at him, and fanatic enough, as a religionist, to believe that his vengeance had in it the element of a godlike justice. . . . (269)

It is possible to see in this the seeds of the shifting moods of Irving's subsequent creation, a man who can veer from being "beside himself with passion" to "self-possessed," from "fawning" to "stately."[8] Equally it reveals not merely an awareness of *the other*, but, more than this, a specific range of attitudes towards the Jew's exoticism, at once both admiring ("He was never undignified") and patronizing ("and then he was picturesque").

A particularly interesting detail of Irving's conversation with Hatton is his description of Shakespeare's Jew as "a type of the great, grand race." It is easy to see how this romanticized perception could become the bedrock of a stage interpretation which would move A. B. Walkley to write in 1892: "To say that his was 'the Jew that Shakespeare drew' would be to quote Pope's doggerel inopportunely. It was the Jew idealized in the light of the modern Occidental reaction against the *Judenhetze*, a Jew already conscious of the Spinozas, the Sidonias, the Disraelis, who were to issue from his loins" (159–60).

Irving's portrayal of the Jew as a prosperous and civilized gentleman of his times, and his use of scenery and costume, were both powerfully instrumental in elevating Shylock to the status of near-tragic hero. This, according to Hatton's recollections, is how Irving seems to have seen the character: "I look on Shylock as the type of a persecuted race; almost the only gentleman in the play, and most ill-used" (265).

Presenting Shylock as a representative of an abused and oppressed race, as Irving clearly set out to do, was one major route by which he could expect to get the audience on his side. Another was to portray him as a family man, a patriarch, but with all the vulnerabilities and anxieties that a widower with a single daughter might be expected to possess. There are two notable features of Shylock's implied domestic life which can be exploited by an actor if it suits his designs. They derive, firstly, from his relationship with Jessica; and, secondly, from a single sentence spoken to Tubal. William Winter, writing in 1885 about Irving's performance, referred to both: "His denotement of Shylock's domestic affections, which are passionate and pathetic, was clear and thrilling—especially in the frantic lamentation over his fugitive daughter, and the heart-broken words about Leah and the turquoise ring" (35).

The major source of sympathy from the domestic quarter was, for Irving—and, as will be seen, remains for many actors—the grieving for the loss of Leah's ring. Talking to Hatton, Irving referred to Shylock's "tender recollection of Leah" (272); and, reviewing the moment in performance, the enthusiastic *Spectator* critic felt that "his one pathetic mention of his 'Leah' was as beautiful a touch as ever has been laid on the many-stringed lyre of human feeling" (Hiatt 178). This particular reviewer might seem excessive in his praise and enthusiasm; but, as Alun Hughes observes, "a host of other critics agreed"(258).[9]

The religious and domestic facets of Shylock's life were therefore central to Irving's aim of presenting a Shylock who could be seen as a pathetic and tragic victim rather than an embittered villain. In order to achieve this aim, however, Irving made widespread cuts. According to Hughes, "Irving's text was really little better than that used by Charles Macklin in 1741" (258). Edward Moore writes:

> The cutting of the play was typically Irvingesque. There was actually less of Shakespeare's text than in either of the two most scenically lavish and textually spare productions before him, Charles Kean's in 1858 and the Bancrofts' in 1875. Passages—indeed whole scenes—which tended to dis-

credit Shylock were simply cut out, such as Jessica's conversation with Launcelot (II, iii) and the scene between Jessica, Lorenzo, and Launcelot after Portia leaves Belmont (III, v). (203)

Of particular importance, however, in enhancing the presentation of Shylock as an "affectionate, while austere" family man, was the fact that "he also cut most of Shylock's ravings about the loss of his ducats, though not, of course, of his daughter" (202).

The cuts made by Irving were obviously crucial in helping to create the kind of Shylock he wanted. Equally important, though, and having a much greater impact upon the audience, were his additions in the form of stage business and newly created scenes, the most famous of which came after the flight of Jessica. William Winter gives an eyewitness account (though written seven years after Irving's death) of the moments following the masque :

> there was a lull in the music, and the grim figure of Shylock, his staff in one hand, his lantern in the other, appeared on the bridge, where for an instant he paused, his seamed, cruel face, visible in a gleam of ruddy light, contorted by a sneer, as he listened to the sound of revelry dying away in the distance. Then he descended the steps, crossed to his dwelling, raised his right hand, struck twice upon the door with the iron knocker, and stood like a statue, waiting—while a slow—descending curtain closed in one of the most expressive pictures that any stage has ever presented. (186–87)

Many contemporary observers (including Brereton 307–308 and Robert Hichens [Saintsbury 168]) noted the pathos of the moment: as a piece of stage business designed to convey all Shylock's loneliness, humanity and—looking forward—feelings of deep betrayal, it could hardly have been bettered. Recent productions, as will be seen, have not been reluctant to attempt comparable tours de force, designed to exploit the sensibilities of their modern audiences.

There are one or two concluding remarks to make about Irving's Shylock. The first relates to a comment made by Irving to William Winter, who recalls their conversation in this way: " 'Shylock,' he said, in my presence, 'is a bloody-minded monster,—but you mustn't play him so, if you wish to succeed; you must get some sympathy with him' " (175).

This seems to me to be a candid—and certainly illuminating—admission of an actor's motives and methods. But it does raise the question—perhaps the most important question with which any study of Shylock in performance ought to be concerned—of how far a performance can go in "getting some sympathy for him" before it moves into the area of willful distortion of the text. Hichens was of the opinion that Irving was "far too much of an artist to play for illegitimate sympathy" (Saintsbury 167)[10]; and most would probably agree that there is nothing illegitimate in playing up the

Jew's dignity; or emphasizing the harsh treatment he has received in the past; or exacting every ounce of pathos from his courtroom exit. But other elements of interpretation can be open to harsher judgment. For example, assertions by Irving that Shylock is "almost the only gentleman in the play," or—even more oddly—that Jessica "is the friend of Portia" might encourage us to call in question the care of his reading or even his understanding of the kind of world Jessica and Portia inhabit. Equally Shylock's "Hath not a Jew . . .?" speech can indeed be in some senses a "defense of his race" (Hatton 265–66); but we might well consider it a limitation to play it as though it were only that. Moore believes that "Irving's Shylock was hardly Shakespeare's" and observes that the actor's "attitude led him to play . . . directly against the text . . ." (201).[11] In this he echoes Shaw, who felt that Irving "was simply not Shylock at all" (163). Even more damningly, because it precisely identifies the motive that can lie behind willful misreadings, as well as their potential consequences, was Shaw's comment that Irving's "huge and enduring success as Shylock was due to his absolutely refusing to allow Shylock to be the discomfited villain of the piece. *The Merchant of Venice* became the *Martyrdom of Irving*, which was, it must be confessed, far finer than the *Tricking of Shylock*" (Wilson 252).[12] This "refusal" has been, to one degree or another, a significant trend in many recent interpretations.

Much has been written about Theodore Komisarjevsky's 1932 version of the play as a revolutionary interpretation which once and for all marked a break with the enduring legacy of Irving's noble Jew.[13] In fact, Irving's influence was certainly not universally felt either in London or "the provinces" during the three decades following his death. Nonetheless, many of the key Shylocks from that period were in the Irving tradition, and it had been most strikingly kept alive at Stratford by the remarkable endurance of Frank Benson. Benson had himself acted with Irving and, although his Shylock was fiercer and more aggressive than Irving's, his acknowledgement to the master was apparent in a number of performance features, not least the business of returning to the empty house, the tender relationship with Jessica, the reaction to the loss of Leah's ring, and his final departure from the trial. It was fitting, then, that the production of the play which immediately preceded Komisarjevsky's arrival on the Stratford stage in July 1932 should be the farewell performance given by Sir Frank Benson and the "Old Bensonians."[14] The passage from the old era to the new could not have been more symbolically marked.

Despite that, Richard E. Mennen's assertion that Komisarjevsky's was "the first new interpretation of *The Merchant of Venice* in over fifty years" (386) warrants qualification when we come to focus on the portrayal of Shylock. While it is certainly true that no one before Komisarjevsky had hitherto set out to reject pictorial realism quite so single-mindedly, and, through his technique of "internal eclecticism" (389), restore what Mennen terms "some of the play's complex, interpretive potential" (397), the director's demand for a malicious and comic Shylock was not in itself new. Several notable Shylocks—among others, those of Arthur Bourchier (first performance 1905), Oscar Asche (1915), Louis Bouwmeester (1919), and Maurice Moscovitch (1919)—had rejected Irving's semi-tragic approach for one which emphasized the Jew's malice and vengefulness, and at least one—Moscovitch's—was, in respect of its grotesque comedy, even closer to Komisarjevsky's ideal than his own Shylock, Randle Ayrton.

One of the things that made Komisarjevsky's interpretation distinctive, however, was that, in ways that bring to mind David Thacker's "yuppie" production of 1993 (see below), the Russian director judged that his interpretation might be enhanced by a dimension of topicality. And this is important inasmuch as it demonstrates that productions of the play from the mid-thirties to the late-forties had the option of topical reference if they chose to take it. That no major production during that period did choose to take it—by presenting unambiguous parallels between the treatment of Shylock and the persecution of the Jews under Hitler—is one of the more perplexing features of this challenging play's stage history. In fact, many of the major productions of *The Merchant of Venice* during the thirties and forties could hardly have been less topical in their presentation of the conflict between the Jews and the Christians had they tried. Gielgud, for example, directing the play at the Old Vic in the same year as Komisarjevsky's Stratford production, deliberately shifted the emphasis of the plot away from Shylock (played by Malcolm Keen), making Portia the center of a play which was studiedly unrealistic in design (*Spectator*, 16 December 1932).

Many later productions sound merely bland, such as that at the New Theatre (with Frederick Valk as Shylock) in 1943: "Here . . . is a treatment which in style gives the public what it has never ceased to want—a chance to enjoy the story as a story, with its fairy-tale romance" (*The Times*, 17 February 1943).

Others, such as Wolfit's in 1938, seem in retrospect quite remarkable for the savagery of their interpretation at a time when they might have been expected to be wary of charges of—at the least—insensitivity, and possibly anti-Semitism: "[Wolfit's] Shylock is then the kind of Jew whose humiliation an Elizabethan audience would probably have revelled in, the very Jew the bare plot seems to require, one who, as he leaves the court, spits in the face of Antonio" (*The Times*, 4 October 1938).

In many ways even more extraordinary, when we consider the political context from which they arose, are portrayals which emphasized Shylock's physical repulsiveness. Most striking in this respect are Mark Dignam's Shylock, in a 1935 production "purged of its Irvingesque sentiment and Shakespearean humanity" (*Times*, 3 December 1935), and Gielgud's, performed in the year preceding the outbreak of war. Both of these recall vividly those

Nazi propaganda posters which sought to represent Jews as skulking rats: "[Dignam's] Shylock, a dirty, down-at-heel moneylender in a bowler hat several sizes too big for him, has no shred of dignity left, and whether bewailing the loss of his ducats and his daughter or pleading the cause of a common humanity he is never more than a grotesque little man in a temper" (*Times*). And "[Gielgud's] Shylock: puling, remorseless, toothless—utterly revolting in the remnants of a ginger wig" (*Daily Express*, 22 April 1938). The *New Statesman* (7 May 1938) observed that "[Gielgud's] appearance throughout was extraordinary—gummy, blinking eyes, that suggested some nasty creature of the dark." John Gross's observation upon the theatre's bewildering silence seems, therefore, to me to be overgenerous:

> In retrospect, responses to Hitler during the 1930s are bound to seem slow and inadequate (as indeed most of them were), and it would be absurd to single out the theatre in this regard, let alone the Shakespearean theatre. Ideally, it is true, one might have hoped for a shift in emphasis in productions of *The Merchant of Venice*, an oblique recognition that contemporary events had given the play frightening new overtones. But while such a thing was always possible, it was never very likely; and in the event, it was not to be. (178)

As Gross himself acknowledges (181–82), it was not unknown for newspaper critics to allude to Jewish persecution when reviewing the play. In fact, the allusions are less rare than he implies. For example, the phrases "Jew-baiters" and "Jew-baiting" appear frequently to describe the Christians when they are portrayed as tormentors of Shylock.[15] Moreover, review comments such as the following make it perfectly clear that theater critics could see the topicality of Shylock's persecution, even if the productions themselves were determined to ignore it: "At a time when Jews are being driven to mass-suicide by unsurpassed brutalities, the spectacle of Shylock's baiting becomes almost unbearable" (*New Statesman*, 7 May 1938).[16]

I would furthermore like to suggest that scrutiny of the British national newspapers during the thirties and forties brings to light an additional factor to which Gross does not refer, but which renders the theatrical silence concerning the Jews in Europe even harder to comprehend. This is the regular and prominent publication of articles throughout that period which drew the public's attention to the link between Shakespeare's play and the plight of the Jews in Germany. These articles were of three kinds. The first catalogued the Nazis' determination to establish and define their relationship to Britain's greatest dramatist; the second expressed the growing unease among the Jews in Britain concerning the study of *The Merchant of Venice* in schools; the third took the form of a series of forceful reminders in the newspapers, by journalists and correspondents alike, of the obvious link between Shylock's "Hath not a Jew . . .?" and the persecution of his people by the Nazis.

Typical of the first group are articles commonly to be found in the British press throughout the 1930s. From the *Evening Standard* (26 April 1934) comes this example:

Wilhelm Shakespeare
Not for the first time, Germany has acclaimed Shakespeare as 'a true German.' He appears to be, if anything, rather truer than before. Professor Hecht pointed out yesterday that 'the more heroic ideals' of Nazi Germany make it possible to view the poet's personality in quite a new light. I would give a lot to see a production of *The Merchant of Venice* in Berlin today.[17]

In many respects the last sentence is the most interesting, one of many comments which show that, even if the theater itself were not acknowledging the obvious links between the behavior of the Nazis and Shylock's tormentors, journalists in the popular newspapers were. The German obsession with Shakespeare was, in fact, frequently reported upon. In February of 1936 the *Manchester Guardian* commented that Dr. Goebbels was to make a decision concerning the "Proper Translation" of Shakespeare, the choice to be made between Schlegel's eighteenth-century version and a modern one by Hans Rothe (8 February 1936). The year before, the *Daily Express* had informed its readers that twenty-one theaters in Germany were currently staging Shakespeare's works and that no fewer than forty-six productions of his plays were to be presented in the 1935–36 season (23 September 1935). Moreover, as Nazi oppression becomes more widely reported, so the perspective of *The Merchant of Venice* is more commonly invoked: under the headline "Shakespeare Verboten," the *Evening Standard* notes that "The latest restriction is that Jewish booksellers must not sell Shakespeare. . . . If the Nazis want to be true to their quaint principles, they should compel Jews to sell copies of *The Merchant of Venice* as an additional humiliation" (19 August 1937—in a related item on the same day, the *Daily Telegraph* reported that, from 1 August, "Jewish booksellers may only sell books by Jewish authors and serve only Jewish customers").

While the Nazis were busy accommodating Shakespeare to their philosophies and reshaping him for their own particular ends, British Jews were similarly, but more painfully, coming to the conclusion that *The Merchant of Venice* did not and could not exist in a political and social vacuum. The absence of debate on the stage seems even more remarkable when we read reports about the British Board of Jews' concern that "the character of Shylock should be 'interpreted' by the teacher in such a way that the dignity and nobility of the Jew should not be obscured by the less pleasant traits of his character" (*Daily Telegraph*, 2 August 1934). When seen in the context of the reports which were at this time coming out of Germany, it is not difficult to appreciate the Board's anxiety. It is impossible to know how individual teachers were handling the play in schools; but what is certain is that the

British newspaper-reading public was repeatedly made aware of the connection between Jewish persecution and Shylock's famous plea, especially in popular and patriotic publications such as the *Daily Express*: "This renewed attack on Jews in Germany, not because of any individual offence but in blind antagonism to a race, is merely bestial. 'I am a Jew. Hath not a Jew eyes . . . [etc.]'—*The Merchant of Venice*" (17 September 1935; see accounts in the same newspaper on 11 April 1933 and 22 October 1935).

The story of *The Merchant of Venice* and the British theater's response to Hitler's persecution of the Jews is like that of Conan Doyle's dog that did not bark in the night. And it has more than one ironic coda. The first is that, although, as we have seen, Shakespeare's plays were widely performed in the Third Reich, *The Merchant of Venice* was not:

> During the Nazi period there was a sharp drop in the number of performances [of *The Merchant of Venice*]. Whereas previously it had averaged twenty to thirty productions every year with about two hundred performances, after 1933 the average dropped to less than a third, in 1939 to an all-time low of three productions totalling twenty-three performances. The most flattering explanation is that a sense of shame stopped most theatre managements from adding insult to injury, and it is worth noting that there does not seem to have been more than a single production of the play in Berlin during the whole period. (Hortmann 134–35)

A related irony is that, while the Folk House in Stepney was celebrating the end of the war with a Yiddish production of the play, it was being banned in Frankfurt "as a result of threats and protests from Jewish and Communist quarters, who claimed that 'Shylock cannot be portrayed on the stage without re-awakening anti-Semitism' " (*Sunday* Express, 29 December 1946). The Stepney production, by virtue of its Yiddishness, must have contained at least some implicit allusion to recent history. But, for the mainstream theater, it was as though nothing had happened. Reviewing a production at Stratford, *The Times* commented: "The Jew of Mr. John Ruddock is like some blandly smiling archimandrite showing a party of foreign visitors over his monastery . . . and when he ventures to ask if a Jew has not passions like other men, we can only suppose that he has not" (14 July 1947).

Moreover it was not as though there had been some tacit agreement to keep Shakespeare free from the taint of politicization. In 1944 Olivier's film of *Henry V* had been prefaced by a dedication to "the commandoes and airborne forces" and was, two years later, being shown in Berlin to 1800 students and school children. It seems strange that a version of *Henry V* could have been made as virtually an institutionalized part of the war effort, while productions of *The Merchant of Venice*, even after pictures of the concentration camps had appeared on cinema screens throughout the land, remained doggedly silent about the greatest atrocity in the history of the twentieth century. This is a bewildering dent in the reputation of actors as "the abstract and brief chronicles of the time."

Grotesque and repellent Shylocks remained the norm throughout the 1950s. Peter O'Toole—despite playing the part with what the *Daily* Express called "a foolish, inaccurate, unnecessary, obtrusive, vulgar, distasteful, mock-Yiddish accent" (13 April 1960)—was the first to change the tide (see Figure 13 below); and the unusual quality of his interpretation is reflected in a notable feature of the reviews. After a quarter of a century in which the Holocaust was barely alluded to by theater critics—presumably because performances of grotesque Shylocks seemed to make it an irrelevance—the reviewers writing about Michael Langham's 1960 Royal Shakespeare Theatre production were hard put to keep off the subject. However, O'Toole's attractive Shylock attempted to draw upon the audience's understanding of his suffering, rather than engage their sympathy; and, in the same way, the play as a whole served to remind the audience of contemporary anti-Semitism, only, like York in *Richard II*, to "remain as neuter": "The play remains, of course, a furiously anti-Semitic blast. However, Peter O'Toole's Shylock, disgraced but not disgusting [turns] it into weak propaganda, more worthy theatre, and lighter comedy" (*Glasgow Herald*, 13 April 1960). This neutrality was made possible because Shylock was played "not as the representative of a race but as an individual Jew whose actions make him detestable" (*The Times*, 13 April 1960). In this respect, just as O'Toole's interpretation looks back to Edmund Kean rather than Henry Irving, so it looks forward—as will be seen—to Patrick Stewart rather than to Laurence Olivier.

Jonathan Miller's National Theatre production of *The Merchant of Venice* in 1970 (adapted for television in 1973) has been much discussed and continues to excite a diversity of critical opinion. Of the more recent retrospectives, Bulman's is—with reservations—admiring: "By calling into question what the play traditionally was thought to be about, Miller discovered a new way of looking at *The Merchant* that made Shakespeare—at least for the moment—our contemporary" (100).

Marion Perret is less happy about the production's balance: "The emphasis . . . on commerce and anti-Semitism leads to a slightly cynical de-emphasizing of romance: except for the last, the scenes at Belmont are played for laughs" (Perret 162). Gross takes an even more critical view, complaining that the Christians were "travestied," and that the theme of assimilation and rejection "was something which the production tried to graft on to the play from the outside, and the result was a high degree of incoherence" (302–303).

Tot homines, tot sententiae—a wide variation in responses was indeed apparent from the first performances. Richard Foulkes effusively compared Olivier's Shylock with Irving's, alluding to "the realism which both actors gave to Shylock" and concluding that "They saw him as a human being, worthy of their sympathy and understanding, and with the sensibility and artistry found only in the higher reaches of their calling, they presented that man on the stage" (35). Patrick J. Sullivan, while showing more restraint, nonetheless called it a "highly original interpretation" which

> takes the Shakespearian back to the play and the audience back to them-selves and their deepest intuitions about life. . . . I am also certain that stu-dents of Shakespeare and the theatre must take it seriously as an effort at discovering and dramatizing the essential moral energy of *The Merchant of Venice.* (44)

For Peter Ansorge, writing in *Plays and Players*, however, this was "a production which in theory [Miller] has conceived compellingly but, at best, put very uncertainly into practice" (June 1970, 39). And Ansorge concluded that "the rehearsals for *The Merchant of Venice* may well have been more engaging to watch than the actual performance which, to my mind, reveals just a few pale flickers of meaning borrowed from an original luminous con-ception" (43). In a climate of such extreme views, it is hardly surprising that the body of commentary on the performance has been unparalleled in its multiplicity of approaches.

One of the commonest features of Olivier's performance to excite com-ments in contemporary newspaper reviews was his manner of speech, and particularly his accent. It was a feature, however, which proved difficult to describe. Irving Wardle heard in the accent "a ghastly compound of speech tricks picked up from the Christian rich: posh vowels and the slipshod termi-nations of the hunting counties" (*The Times*, 29 April 1970). This impression was supported both by the critic of the *Daily Telegraph*, for whom the voice was "a contemptuously drawled imitation of upper-class speech" (29 April 1970), and by J. C. Trewin, who felt that Shylock was "probably aware that his carefully nurtured accent [could] slip into plebeian vowel sounds" (*Illus-trated London News*, 9 May 1970).

All reviewers were disappointingly imprecise, however, when it came to describing the constituent sounds that made up the accent. Trewin described one feature of Olivier's speech as a tendency to clip words like "meanin' " and "speakin' "; and Wardle attempted a similar transcription with: "I am debatin' of my present state." These transcriptions of verb endings were accurate enough, but critics got into all sorts of trouble when they attempted to replicate the vowel sounds, the *Daily Telegraph* reviewer's "Ai am a Joo!" being typically crude. But it was the vowel sounds which established the accent with the greatest subtlety, and they are correspondingly the hardest to describe. Three played a major part: those heard in the pronouns *me* and *you* and in the possessive *our*.

Consistently, words such as *memory*—Received Pronunciation ['memrI:] or ['memri:] (memri or memry)—would be pronounced ['memre] (memreh), a mannerism most noticeable in terminal positions of the sound (for example, in ". . . you'll not hear me."). *You* (RP [juː]) was always [jɒ] (yoh), so that "What should I say to you?" became [hwɒt ʃʊd ɑi sɛi tɒ jɒ] (what should ai seh toh yoh: wh— sounds being fairly consistently aspirated [hw]). Finally, the sound in *our*—RP [ɑʊə] became beautifully mutilated to something more closely approaching [æːə]—the first sound of the diphthong is something like the vowel in *cat*. This, for me, was the key sound. It is a vowel frequently heard in speakers of London or Home Counties English when they are striving—without total success—to conform to RP. As such it was the perfect phonetic indicator of a man desperately anxious to be accepted by the merchant class, but always likely to betray his alien origins. Its visual equivalent was the moment when Shylock, confidently waving his silver-tipped cane and holding the financial newspaper under his arm, lifted his glossy top hat in salute, only to reveal the yarmulke beneath.

In addition to using these constituent sounds, Olivier also engaged in the hyper-corrected pronunciation of unusual or impressive vocabulary. Thus we hear [ˈmehɪkoʊ] (mehico) for *Mexico* and [ˈeŋglənd] (eng-gland) for the more usual [ˈɪŋglənd]—pronunciations that Antonio and his friends would die rather than perpetrate—and the over-precise [sʌpoʊˈzɪʃɒn] (sup-position) for [sʌpəˈzɪʃən], [kʌnˈdʒuːəd] (cun-joored) for [ˈkʌndʒəd], and [ˈfɒːfɪtʃuːə] (forfit-yoor) for [ˈfɒːfɪtʃə]). Finally, this studied display of quasi-RP is thrown into relief when, in a glorious moment of defensive self-parody, Olivier descends into the stage-Jewish that the anti-Semites no doubt expect from him, imitating the "bondman's key, / With bated breath and whisp'ring humbleness": "Fair sir, you spat on me on Wednesday last" (1.3.120–22)— [fɛə θɜː juː θpet] . . . (fair thir, you thpet . . .) etc.

Given that the best that other Shylocks from this period could manage were accents lazily—and sometimes offensively—borrowed from the music hall, Olivier's was a masterly creation. Even more than his clothing (Shylock had clearly bought the best that money could buy), or his mannerisms (such as the studiedly casual, one-handed flicking open of the Rialto newspaper), his accent marked him out as a man on the periphery of Venetian society who, however hard he tried (and, with the accent, he tried too hard), would always remain an alien.

In contrast to Olivier's Shylock—a Jew desperately imitating the Christians' manners in a bid for acceptance—Warren Mitchell's BBC portrayal (1980) offered "an ethnic Jew . . . resolutely unassimilated, antagonistic to the proprieties of bourgeois Venetian behavior" (Bulman 102). Secure in the fact that actor, director, and producer were all Jews (or, in Miller's case, a former Jew), the intention was to portray Shylock as authentically Jewish. The result, however, was a performance which, for many, bordered on caricature: "[a] squat, domestic, garrulous little man, [a] comic figure with a plaintive face" (Bulman 103).

Perret and Bulman, themselves drawing on other commentators, testify to the importance of these two television versions in forming images of Shylock which were both memorable and influential. There is, however, one interesting feature of these two productions of central interest to the performance history of this role: the choice of the moment when Shylock appears to decide that the bond can actually be enforced.

For both productions, this moment came in 3.1, but at different points and in different ways. Mitchell's Shylock, intent upon offering his jocular friendship to the Christians until it is absolutely certain that they will reject it, even joins in with Salerio's and Solanio's laughter at his misfortunes. Bill Overton comments on the key moments in the encounter:

> Trading on [Shylock's earlier bid for friendship], they jostle him with unpleasant, intimidating familiarity. At his obscene pun, "Rebels it at these years?", Solanio goes so far as to grasp Shylock by the crotch and heave him up. On his words, "I am a Jew," they sardonically fake getting an obvious point and they supply crude horseplay gestures for most of the following speech, pointing to eyes, presenting hands, offering fingers, prodding and tickling him. (51–52)

For Perret, "the scene becomes almost unbearable" (164). For me, it is somewhat contrived: the Christians' laughter goes on too long, their mocking actions lack conviction; it is one of the few sequences in this production which betray the heavy hand of the director, Jack Gold, whose touch is in most respects a light one.

It is Overton's opinion that the moment of decision comes when Shylock says, "Go, Tubal, fee me an officer" (118–119). I can see no evidence for that. No perceptible change comes over Shylock at that point, neither does Tubal react in any significant way. Surely, unless the actor playing Shylock himself signals the moment when the "merry bond" evolves into a serious threat to Antonio's life, then we the audience have to be guided by the reactions of the characters around him and the visual cues provided by the camera. And in the BBC version that moment is cued very deliberately when Salerio and Solanio freeze in the middle of their mocking laughter on the question, "And if you wrong us, shall we not revenge?" (62–63). At this point the camera, which has held the same three-shot throughout the speech, narrows its focus slightly, and maintains that closer attention to Shylock until the end of his speech. Panning left when Antonio's man enters, the camera then frames the servant and Salerio. The servant is clearly anxious when he delivers what is usually a fairly uninteresting line ("Gentlemen, my master Antonio is at his house and desires to speak with you both" [70–71]), and Salerio's response shows us that he is palpably shaken: having played the character up to this point as a Welsh prop-forward, the actor John Rhys-Davies even prefaces his reply to the servant with a hesitant "Er . . .": a stark contrast to his massive confidence hitherto. The Christians are no longer laughing; and we, the audience, should take our cue from them.

Olivier's moment of decision is both more obviously signalled than Mitchell's, and more theatrical in its execution. The scene takes place outside Shylock's house and the Jew emerges, as though having overheard Salerio and Solanio talking. Upstage are the steps to a bridge and Olivier's Shylock ascends these, turning his back at Salerio's slur upon his and his daughter's "bloods" (38), the camera following him. He reaches the top as Salerio asks him about Antonio's losses and prefaces his reply with a shouted (and interpolated) "Yes!", turning on "a beggar" (43) to make a mocking gesture in parody of Antonio's erstwhile smugness on "the mart." Then he leans on the rail of the bridge overlooking the canal and two things happen. One is that the camera angle changes so that we have a rear view which accentuates his stooped, defeated posture and the depressed costume now revealing bankclerk sleeve-protectors; the other is that we become aware of a bell tolling ominously in the silence. Its slowness suggests that it might be a funeral knell, and after three chimes, we sense Shylock's body stiffening, as though with shock, and, as he slowly turns to camera, his face expresses the appalled realization that he has it in his power to make the Christian suffer. He slowly turns his head to the left and the camera angle changes to capture one of the most evocative shots in screen Shakespeare.

Shylock stares at the camera, the fingers of his left hand touching the lower lip of his slightly open mouth, the whole of the left-hand half of the frame empty. His hand clenches slightly and then slowly drops as he voices the awful thought that has dawned upon him: "Let him look to his bond" (44). He descends the steps, accelerating the remainder of the speech as his excitement mounts, and the camera retreats before him until Salerio comes into frame. The moment when the Christians take in the full import of Shylock's statement is clearly signalled. Salerio laughs through his question, "Why, I am sure, if he forfeit, thou wilt not take his flesh" (48–49), seemingly assured of the preposterous nature of the proposition. But all selfassurance ebbs away as he looks into Shylock's eyes and the conclusion of his speech, "What's that good for?", is deeply troubled and hesitant. This is the point at which the Christians are convinced that Shylock means business; for the television audience, that moment came a few seconds earlier with the change of camera angle as Olivier stood with his back towards us on the bridge, silent except for the tolling of the bell.

Writing of Miller's televised version, Bulman said: "His interpretation often challenged what generations of playgoers had taken the play to mean, but in doing so it *seldom* worked against the text" (83, my italics). Even allowing for the qualifier *seldom*, this is an opinion that many people would be inclined to dispute. To be fair to Bulman, however, it has to be said that he does tackle, in the concluding paragraph of his chapter on this production, the central question of how far an interpretation can go before it ceases to be an interpretation and actually becomes a different play. Quoting Benedict Nightingale's comment that Miller's *Merchant of Venice* looked like "the play Shakespeare ought to have written" (*New Statesman*, 8 May 1970), Bulman asks whether "by accommodating the play to a social and political context in many ways different from Shakespeare's, Miller essentially fashioned a play of his own" (99). Bulman continues:

> He appropriated Shakespeare's text, and with it his cultural authority, to advance an ideological agenda peculiar to his own time. Was Miller's *Merchant* Shakespeare's? This question, of course, can only be answered with another: whose Shakespeare? Miller did what any director of Shakespeare does: he tailored the play to suit his cast, his venue and his audience. Invariably, in the process of staging a Shakespeare play, a director will adapt and revise the text in light of current cultural assumptions and values: such revision is sometimes conscious, sometimes not. (100)

Perhaps the most obvious textual feature of the "conscious" revisions made by Miller in shaping the text to suit his particular lines of interpretation were the cuts. The most significant of these was the aside which accompanies the arrival of Antonio in 1.3: "How like a fawning publican he looks" (38–49). As other interpreters of the play have found, cutting these lines permits the actor playing Shylock to hide several things: that he has a longstanding hatred of Antonio; that this antagonism is not nobly motivated, but is partly fuelled by the Christian's sabotage of the Jew's usury; and—perhaps most importantly for a production that wants to present a sympathetic Shylock—that he is looking out for the moment when he has the Christian at his mercy and can exact his revenge ("feed fat" is the expression he uses) to the full. Cutting the speech also, of course, allows the actor to offer the bond genuinely "in a merry sport," the sole motive of which is to gain the Christians' friendship, and concomitantly to defer the moment at which he decides to exact the forfeit, playing it as a sudden realization rather than a preconceived plan. This crucial cut thereby helps to create a character whose desire for revenge is activated some time into the play, and then only by the loss of his daughter and his realization of the Christians' complicity in her flight. Our sympathy for such a Shylock is engaged from the outset when we hear of his ill-treatment at the hands of Antonio and, if reinforced by other measures such as those which Miller and Olivier took—the business with Jessica's and Leah's photographs, for example, or the portrayal of a set of distinctly unappealing Christians—that sympathy is never completely lost.

Between 1978 and 1981, two actors were to play Shylock with the Royal Shakespeare Company, both under the direction of John Barton—Patrick Stewart and David Suchet.[18] Discussing the role with Barton some years later, Suchet, himself a Jew, said:

It's a terrifying thing studying such a famous part because of the history of how it's been played. Mostly black, as you say, or white. I was desperate to try to look at that play without preconceptions and to look into each scene for exactly what it was, for what it said to me, and to play that. Also to play the inconsistencies throughout the role, and to see what happened if I just went with each scene without overlaying them with something that I had worked out before. (Barton 174)

Stewart shared this determination to "play the inconsistencies"; in fact, it might be said to have become the keynote of their two interpretations. This was certainly recognized in performance by the critic of the *Morning Star*, who admired the production's re-examination of "a play built on unresolved contradictions" (16 May 1978).

For Stewart, moreover, such an interpretation was underpinned by a powerful conviction that Shylock should not be seen narrowly as a racial symbol, but rather a figure who represented "all victims who turn on their persecutors" (Brockbank 19). In rehearsals, this concept of Shylock as a representative of all oppressed people led the actor to hold the view that "the Jewishness which is so often emphasized in *The Merchant* is . . . a distraction" and that "to concentrate on Jewishness can lead to missing the great potential in the character which is its universality." He went on:

I think that whenever I've seen a very ethnic, a very Jewish Shylock, I've felt that something's been missing. Shylock is essentially an alien, an outsider. I think if you see him as a Jew, first and foremost, then he's in danger of becoming only a symbol. Shylock is an outsider who happens to be a Jew. (Barton 171)[19]

A major feature of Stewart's interpretation to excite interest was his "picture . . . of a man in whose life there is an imbalance, an obsession with the retention and acquisition of wealth" (Brockbank 16). This obsession would cause Shylock always to give priority to material possessions whenever he was faced with a choice, whether between his ducats and his daughter or—most noticeably—his fortune and his religion: "I found one dominant motivation, one dominant objective for the whole play: money, finance and possessions. Whenever Shylock is given the choice between race and religion on the one hand, and financial security, commerce and business on the other, he always makes the commercial choice" (Barton 173).

Integral to this all-embracing obsession was a small-scale meanness, cleverly signaled on stage through habits and dress: "Shylock was shabby, almost miserly, carefully preserving the stubs of the home-rolled cigarettes which constantly drooped from the side of his mouth." Accentuating Shylock's distance from his fellow-Jews, "He contrasted sharply with Tubal, who dressed impeccably and smoked cigars, like the smart Venetians-about-town" (Warren 204).[20] The meanness was carried over into Shylock's personal hygiene—he had "a very large bushy beard and a lot of long, dirty, tangly hair" (Barton 172), while his dress—"which showed an almost studied contempt for neatness or even cleanliness"—consisted of "a shabby black frock coat, torn at the hem and stained, a waistcoat dusted with cigarette ash, baggy black trousers, short in the leg, exposing down-at-heel old boots, and a collarless shirt yellowing with age" (Brockbank 18). Looking like "a shabby back-street usurer," in Michael Billington's words (*Guardian,* 4 May 1979), the actor's rationale was that "if [Shylock] was obsessed with money, he would not waste it on how he appeared." Despite this Shylock's unappealing materialism and a distinctly unprepossessing appearance, audiences and critics alike found something strangely attractive in the character. For one thing, Stewart emphasized Shylock's wit (having accommodated Barton's requirement that the character should be a monster by playing him as "a witty monster" [Brockbank 14]) and played down the urge for revenge in order to display cooler, more restrained characteristics.

Stewart's Shylock was attractive for his wit, his control, and his irony; there might even be a sneaking admiration for a man who was determined to survive as an alien in a hostile world. But could audiences actually sympathize with such a character, in the way that they did to a large extent with O'Toole's Shylock or Olivier's? In some respects they could. The actor saw "a bleak and terrible loneliness" in Shylock, the cause of much of his anger and bitterness, and this sense of isolation—and the ways in which Shylock attempts to cope with it—were made evident to the audience in complementary features of behavior: "Of course, it is not loneliness that the actor shows, but its compensating aspects: false gregariousness, ingratiating humour, violence and arrogance" (Brockbank 14).

Shylock's isolation seems therefore to have engendered sympathy of a certain kind during the first two acts. But something more tangible is required if that sympathy is to endure when he turns the full force of his hatred upon Antonio (Figure 11). In this respect a key moment for Shylock is his final exit; and Stewart's was as remarkable for its impact as for its originality. Concerning the moments leading up to it, Stewart wrote:

> In the past I had been puzzled by the speed at which Shylock slams into reverse from "A sentence, come, prepare" to "I take this offer then." If the interpretation is heroic or sentimental I don't know how the actor does it. If it's pragmatic, then it's easy. Shylock is told he will lose his lands and his goods. Portia plays the blood card. Shylock immediately sees the (expected) trap he has walked into, considers for a moment that he will lose, checks the law, and knows at once that he must back off . . . and when the word "alien" hits his ears he knows he is to be finished off. Once again he is an outsider, without rights and utterly vulnerable. This is no place for pride

Figure 11. Shylock (Patrick Stewart) in the 1978 Royal Shakespeare Company production. Joe Cocks, The Shakespeare Centre Library, Stratford-upon-Avon.

> or heroics. Shylock knows if he wants to survive he must get down in the dirt and grovel. (Brockbank 26–27)

The grovelling was of a memorable kind. While remaining impassioned on "Nay, take my life," it was consistent with a Shylock who placed possessions above all else that he should undergo a transformation when Antonio offers a better deal than he could have expected. He listens intently to Antonio's demands concerning his money and the requirement that he must become a Christian; and, when Portia asks, "Art thou contented, Jew? What dost thou say?" he rises from a kneeling position and looks at her. Amazingly—and for many in the audience, quite shockingly—he deftly flicks the yarmulke from his head, smiles broadly, and says, "I am content," holding his arms out in submission. This smile flickers a little only when Portia tells Nerissa to draw up the deed of gift; it is back in full force as he summons all his self-possession and requests leave to go:

> They want him to become a Christian and bequeath his estate to Lorenzo and Jessica and he is content because he has saved something when moments before he had nothing. Now he must get away before they change their minds or think up further punishment. Illness is a good excuse and he leaves them with the assurance that the deed will be signed. (Brockbank 27)

He pats his stomach, explaining confidentially that he is not well, as a man might do who has some embarrassing tummy disorder that can be laughed at but is awkward to discuss in public. Politely and very earnestly requesting that the deed be sent after him, he places the heaviest of stresses on "I *will* sign it." Then, during the Duke's "Get thee gone, but do it," he bows three or four times to the court, still smiling, and makes to leave. Gratiano's bitter jeers have often been used as the final indignity which sends Shylock from the court a broken man. Stewart used them very differently:

> Every actor playing Shylock looks for an effective way to "get off." Here Gratiano provided the clue. He makes a cruel joke out of Shylock's christening, and the person who must laugh most is, of course, Shylock. And so he leaves. (Brockbank 27)

Stewart's Jew pays polite attention to Gratiano, pauses briefly when he has finished, thinks about the jibe, and then, as though beginning to see the joke, he chuckles appreciatively. This grows to laughter, which is wholehearted as he exits.[21] Stewart wrote: "It saddened me that people were upset by the squalor of Shylock's ending" (Brockbank 27).

The groveling self-abasement undoubtedly is squalid. The impression we are left with, however, is that Shylock considers himself to have been let off lightly, and is quite willing to play the Christians' games if it will get him off the hook. He will undoubtedly be back. Among their many achievements, these two interpretations directed by John Barton demonstrated for the first time that it was perfectly possible to engender a healthy disgust at anti-Semitism without having to play Shylock as a tragic hero and martyr.

When Bill Alexander began rehearsals for a production with the Royal Shakespeare Company in 1987 (first performance, in the main house at Stratford, on 23 April), it was decided that Antony Sher's Shylock should in many respects be a stereotype Jew in the traditional, pre-O'Toole sense; and it is revealing to consider which choices were made in realizing an interpretation of that kind. Physically, Sher's Shylock was as unattractive as he could make him: a "lip-smacking, liquid-eyed Levantine bargain hunter" (*Jewish Chronicle*, 8 May 1987), first seen seated, "a gypsy Jew in a canopied lair" (*Financial Times,* 30 April 1987), as if asserting his power over Bassanio, until leaping up on "Rest you fair" (56). And making the offer of the bond, chillingly imitating with flailing arms the action of cutting off the flesh, accompanying the clause "In what part of your body pleaseth me" (148) with a flourish down the length of Antonio's torso, culminating ominously around his genitals. Of all the actor's telling gestures, this is the one which might be said to have been designed to play most powerfully upon the audience's collective subconscious fears about Jews and, at an early stage, draw upon the stereotype which Alexander wished to conjure up. As James Shapiro points out,

> Those watching or reading *The Merchant of Venice* are often curious about what part of Antonio's body Shylock has in mind when they learn of Shylock's desire to exact "an equal pound" of Antonio's "fair flesh, to be cut off and taken" in that "part" of his body that "pleaseth" the Jew. Those all too familiar with the plot may forget that it is not until the trial scene in act 4 that this riddle is solved and we learn that Shylock intends to cut from Antonio's "breast" near his heart. Or partially solved. . . . Why don't we learn of this crucial detail until Shylock's final appearance in the play? (121)

Sher's gesture was, to me, clearly understood by the "tainted wether," Antonio; and went some way to explain the knowing laughter with which the Christian readily accepted the terms of the bond. In a footnote to his account of Christian fears of circumcision, Shapiro quotes Freud's observation that "here we may also trace one of the roots of the anti-semitism which appears with such elemental force and finds such irrational explanation among the nations of the west" (259, ftn.2), and points out that, for Freud, "circumcision is unconsciously equated with castration." Audience aversion to Sher's Shylock might then be said to have operated on a number of levels, many of them unconscious, but all bound up with the cultural stereotyping that Alexander sought to confront (see Figure 7 above, with Jessica).

From my own recollection of the performance, however, it was with his presentation of a more than usually unattractive bunch of Christians that Alexander made a more successful challenge to our liberal attitudes. John Peter observed the central point that Alexander was anxious to convey through his presentation of the male Christians:

> It is not that Antonio and his friends are nasty in themselves. No, Alexander drives home the most appalling thing about racism: namely, that agreeable

people, bluff companions, loyal friends, ordinary decent, likeable men, can be transformed into baying, spitting, racist hounds. No other production has brought out for me this fatal schizophrenia of Western civilization. (*Sunday Times,* 3 May 1987)

There was one feature of the Christians' behavior, however, which was designed to elicit a particularly ambivalent audience response, and this was the clear strand of homoeroticism running through the production:

it was soon to be made clear that [Antonio's] melancholy stemmed from frustrated desire for Nicholas Farrell's Bassanio. Antonio reeled as Bassanio spoke praise of Portia, and kissed him with despairing passion but little response as they parted. Antonio was obviously to be understood as a depressive homosexual, and Bassanio's reciprocation of his affection did not preclude the thought that their relationship might have been physical as well as emotional. (Wells, 1989 164–65)

Among the many reviewers who commented upon Antonio's homosexuality (Bulman [126] counts 15), Michael Billington saw John Carlisle's merchant as "a tormented closet-gay," who "in such a rabidly conformist world would actually prefer death to restricted life; and [who] greets his salvation with sullen, angry resentment." Most interestingly, David Nathan, writing in the *Jewish Chronicle* (8 May 1987), made a connection between homosexuality and racism, in that the "self-hatred" Antonio experiences because of his homosexual longing for Bassanio "adds to the depth of his anti-Semitism." Other characters were clearly shown to share Antonio's sexuality:

By making [Salerio and the (younger) Solanio] lovers we paralleled the central relationship and pointed up the way the two follow its vagaries, hang upon its changes of mood, and thereby fuel the cold embers of their own affair. At one point we had the sentimental Salerio attempt to kiss his young toy-boy. It seemed a valuable moment, neither gratuitous nor provocative—but it was hell on schools' matinées. (Doran 72–74)

Gregory Doran's amusing punch line contains a serious point. It is often the case that children respond unaffectedly to things that adults will force themselves to accept lest they should be considered unsophisticated. The Stratford adult audience might be expected to be as determinedly liberal in its attitudes to homosexuals as it was to Jews; but the reviewer who remarked that Carlisle's Antonio was "distinctly creepy" (Terry Grimley in the *Birmingham Evening Mail,* 30 April 1987) no doubt unwittingly gave voice to feelings of unease that many of the audience experienced but were unwilling to admit to.

Comments such as these, taken with the many objections voiced by members of the Stratford audience (Bulman 126), suggest that the portrayal of Christian homosexuality had awakened prejudices in ways that Shylock's presentation as an unsavory alien had not. If that were indeed the case, then Alexander might be said to have achieved only the lesser half of his aims. While audiences had indeed been goaded with stereotypes designed to test their liberal attitudes, these stereotypes had, in my opinion, only been effective in the realm of sexuality. If I am right, the difference in response can perhaps be attributed to the fact that, since the Holocaust, a Stratford audience is likely to know where it stands with regard to anti-Semitism. This is not to say that the audience will be free of racists; rather that the presentation of a normally "civilized" Shylock engaging in barbaric vengefulness these days has fewer dark areas of the bourgeois audience's subconscious to tap into, than the vision of an otherwise "masculine" Antonio kissing a young Bassanio passionately on the lips. If Shylock's meaningful gesture towards "what part of your body pleaseth me" conjures up any image at all, therefore, it is more likely to be one of the tainted wether's emasculation than of the Jew as legendary castrator. Contemporary anti-Semitism tends to be religious, economic, and social ("they keep to themselves, look after their own, get to the top"); homophobia is an altogether murkier prejudice, difficult for its proponents to articulate because it lacks even the vestiges of (albeit perverted) rationalism attached to racism. This is why Alexander's testing of the audience's prejudices failed with Shylock's unappealing foreignness, but worked spectacularly well with Antonio's sexuality.[22]

Perhaps, in fact, Sher's portrayal was finally—despite its alien exoticism and crude, unappealing physicality—too conventional to stir up the kinds of visceral reaction that Alexander wanted, and such as he did achieve in arousing with his gay Christians. For all his toad-like squatting, wailing voice, and a general demeanor which "offend[ed] all patrician sense of propriety and decorum" (John Peter in *Sunday Times*), Sher's Jew remained an entertaining and essentially sympathetic figure.[23] In keeping with so many other post-1960 Shylocks, he offered the bond playfully, in genuine "merry sport," became crazed with revenge-lust only after the loss of Jessica (whom he had formerly treated with affection), and realized only during his maltreatment at the hands of Salerio and Solanio, in 3.1, that the bond could be for real.[24] Add the fact that he was being played by one of the most attractive and exciting actors of his decade, and a Jew into the bargain, and it is easy to see why Alexander's aim that our liberal notions should be challenged by gut aversion to a grotesque stereotype had the odds stacked heavily against it.

Where Alexander's production addressed the issue of anti-Semitism quite openly, the London West End production which followed soon after was notable for its apparent absence of a distinctive ideological agenda. One of the most interesting things historically about Sir Peter Hall's production in 1989 (first performance, 1 June 1989 at the Phoenix Theatre—see Figure 2 above) is that it brought out into the open two distinct camps: those who liked to see the darker and grittier aspects of *The Merchant of Venice* given expression in performances which clearly displayed a particular ideological stance; and those who preferred issues such as anti-Semitism to be explored less overtly, if at all. In this debate about the degrees to which such issues should be made explicit onstage, it was interesting to see how often Alexander's 1987 RSC production was raised as the standard around which the "more explicit" camp rallied. Its supporters clearly found Hall's directorial approach to this production somewhat anodyne:

> Peter Hall's finely crafted production of *The Merchant of Venice* never really allows us to take the play seriously. Although it works very well as a comedy, the deeper significance is never satisfyingly brought out. . . . If you like your Shakespeare straight, no cuts, no ruffles, and little depth then this will surely please. If, however, you are after something more stimulating, prepare for disappointment.[25]

Those in the opposing camp took the line that Alexander's version had lacked subtlety and had overstated the play's themes, while Hall's was creditable for its restraint and apparent willingness to "let the text speak for itself."

Hall's Shylock was Dustin Hoffman. Given the many and varied comments that might be made about an actor's interpretation of the role of Shylock, one curious phenomenon in the reviews of this production was the frequency of allusion to Hoffman's stature.[26] Almost without exception, the references were disparaging, the following being typical of the tone and content: "Dustin Hoffman is at a considerable disadvantage in undertaking Shylock in London because he is American and short" (*London Evening Standard*, 2 June 1989).

Even those who made neutral references to the actor's stature linked it with the observation that the performance was low-key, small-scale or light-weight, qualities which in turn were said to befit the interpretation's key-note mode, irony: "Hoffman, a ferrety little figure, bearded and with long hair curling in ringlets over his ears, gave a light-weight performance, stronger on irony than on passion" (Wells, *Production* 187).

Several critics made a connection between the character's "sardonic humour and . . . ironic detachment" (*Daily Express,* 2 June 1989) and his wary dislike of the Christians, but not all made the same connection. It was seen variously as deriving from contempt:

> With a half-smile playing around his lips as he cringes before the insults of his tormentors, this Shylock's yearning for revenge is a product of his contempt for them. (*Standard*, 2 June);

as a form of defensive self-parody:

> Hoffman's Shylock is more full of quick sardonic wit than any burning desire for revenge on the "Christian" Antonio. It is almost as if he were

responding to the bullying Venetians' expectations of how a villainous Jew ought to behave. (*Spectator*, 10 June);

as insecurity:

there is little dignity in Hoffman's smothered Brooklynese. His outrage is undercut by a querulous self-mockery. This is a man who knows how to position himself only in the company of his compatriot Tubal. (*Tribune*, 16 June);

as an assertion of superiority:

Dustin Hoffman plays Shylock for his comic potential, displaying an impish grin which raises him above even the basest of insults and the perpetual stream of spit hurled venomously in his direction. . . . Shylock wipes it off his face as if it were pigeon droppings, unpleasant but of no real consequence;[27]

or as an aspect of his determination to survive:

Hoffman and Hall stress not so much Shylock's villainy or his tragedy as his resilience. Hoffman characterizes him with wit, daring, sly irony. (Bernice Kliman, *Shakespeare Bulletin*, Spring 1990, 12)

Christopher Edwards was among several critics to perceive the effect of Hoffman's non-starry, ironic, and jocular interpretation on the trial scene and its closure: "Shylock certainly carries a sense of ironic vindictiveness with him into the trial scene. Hoffman flashes smiles at the Venetian judges as he insists on the letter of his bond—see, I'm acting the heartless Jew, he seems to be saying" (*Spectator,* 10 June). Here, the low-key closure is offered as a natural outcome of Hoffman's sardonic interpretation and one to be valued alongside more dramatic performances. Most, however, were less happy with the result, finding the interpretation "consistent but . . . theatrically unsatisfying."[28] Rhoda Koenig (in *Punch*) interestingly felt a coldness in Hoffman's interpretation, and it was this, rather than exclusively its irony and sardonic detachment, which most strongly influenced her response.

While the act 4 closure was regarded by most as having been a disappointment, there were compensations elsewhere in the shape of a scene which frequently causes difficulties: Shylock's leave-taking of Jessica in act 2. For this scene, Hoffman seemed to have found quite a different mode of delivery, throwing off the otherwise pervasive irony to produce what more than one reviewer considered "one of the most moving scenes in the play."[29] It was also notable for its originality in more than one respect. To begin with, the exchange between Shylock and Lancelot Gobbo was unusual for its good-natured banter.

Some of the actors who have been attracted to the role of Shylock because it offers the opportunity to play villainy tinged with victimization (a mixture most evident in 4.1—a scene which most critics felt Hoffman failed to carry off) have nonetheless expressed dissatisfaction with their performance of 2.5. David Suchet, for example, felt that this was a scene which he never got right; and Philip Voss expressed concern that the scene was too short for him to demonstrate to the audience how much Shylock loved his daughter. Hoffman, however, succeeded with it, possibly because his style of acting was best suited to the intimate and domestic, rather than the expansive and semi-tragic. Significantly, he was also much praised for the scene with Tubal, which Wells rated as his best, in that "his quick alternations of mood created a complex comedy" (Wells, *Production* 188) and which Irving Wardle called "his most expressive scene" (*The Times,* 2 June 1989).

It is indicative of the essentially small-scale, low-key nature of Hoffman's Shylock (adjectives which need not be pejorative) that he succeeded in these scenes while falling short of a truly memorable performance elsewhere.

While Hoffman's interpretation might be termed broadly sympathetic, David Thacker's RSC production of 1993 (first performance 27 May 1993 at the Royal Shakespeare Theatre) went further than any previous Stratford interpretation had done in attempting to present Shylock as a wronged victim whose recourse to villainy has nothing whatever to do with his being a Jew. Thacker's plan for accomplishing these aims was three-fold. First, he directed the audience's attention in the opening acts not especially to religious or cultural differences, but to the unifying agency of money; second, he worked with David Calder to produce a highly sympathetic Shylock; and third, he encouraged the audience to draw the conclusion that, while we might condemn Shylock for the extremity of his response, his behavior is in no way to be seen as representative of all Jews.

Peter Holland's account of the production both identifies its analogical dimensions and pinpoints the real success of Thacker's approach:

> Played in modern dress in a context of the yuppie explosion of business-dealing in the modern City of London, *The Merchant*'s attitude towards exploitative capitalism risked nonsense . . . Yet Thacker found, through the analogy of setting, a means to reveal much else about the social organisation of the play, its exploration of both belonging and being an alien within a tightly controlled community. (163)

David Calder's interpretation of Shylock was central to the success of this exploration, characterized by a variety of commentators as "dignified, erect, urbane"; "humorous"; "genial, shrewd and totally lacking in Hebraic trademarks"; "a substantial and credible human being, well set, at ease with himself when he [was] alone, watchful and sardonic in his dealings with the outside world." In the early scenes he appeared, writes Holland, "a man desperate for assimilation (no skullcap for him), his voice cultured and angli- cized" (164), a picture established from the opening moments of 1.3, as the lights went up on a preoccupied and successful businessman, sitting behind an expensive desk, his busy-ness signaled by the fact that he had removed his jacket to reveal his suspenders and was intently interrogating a computer ter- minal, while Bassanio sat, a little removed, uncomfortably sipping coffee in embarrassment and unease.[30] Shylock was clearly in charge and light- heartedly joked with his guest, expressing mild incomprehension that Antonio should have "a fourth for England," and giving the lightest of touches to "Yes, to smell pork . . .", a response almost completely devoid of sarcasm, but interestingly wary.[31] The subsequent reference to eating "of the habitation" was delivered with little if any seriousness, the word *conjured* accompanied by stage magician's gestures, as if to imply that such supersti- tious nonsense was beneath intelligent and sophisticated business people like "us." Even when he delivered his aside, "How like a fawning publican," it was low-key, importing little resentment and certainly no real conviction of hatred. Unusually "for he is a Christian" raised a laugh from the audience, delivered as it was with a fussy gesture which suggested that Christians were rather some irritating little sect, than the persecutors of his "sacred nation." All of this was to establish that Shylock's attitude towards Antonio, far from being one of murderous intent, was only marginally on the negative side of neutral: Antonio might occasionally be troublesome, but there were no really hard feelings.

There are, of course, lines in this aside (as it appears in the text) which make such a genial interpretation hard to follow through: "Cursed be my tribe / If I forgive him" has to be delivered with quite extraordinary lightness if the audience is not to be left with the otherwise unavoidable impression that Shylock is harboring a bitter grudge. Even more damning in this respect are the lines which many directors have taken to be an unambiguous expres- sion of intent: "If I can catch him once upon the hip / I will feed fat the ancient grudge I bear him."

So difficult were these words to fit into Thacker's conception of Shylock as an essentially urbane and well-balanced businessman with no strong feel- ings of animosity towards his Christian rival, that they became one of many strategic cuts (or "slight adjustments," as the RSC Production Pack described them) made by the director:

> By cutting . . . ['If I can catch him'] there is an initial equality between the two men which as David Calder explains allows the bond to be an overt thing of nonsense, the extremity of which exposes its absurdity . . . David Calder . . . explains: 'You can't do the play that is on the page. It has atti- tudes of its time which are not acceptable today.' (Production Pack 11–12)

Important though cuts to the text were in helping to portray the kind of Shylock that Thacker and Calder wanted, they inevitably made less obvious an impact on the audience than did the added business. Typical of the additions was a memorable moment at the beginning of 2.5, when the lights went up on an expensively comfortable armchair, coffee table and hi-fi system. Shylock entered in a dark red velvet smoking jacket, inserted a CD in the player (something "classical" but not too popular) and, as it began, picked up the photograph of his dead wife, which he stared at longingly until interrupted by Lancelot Gobbo. Peter Holland summed up the effect of this moment:

> seen at home in 2.5, listening to Schubert on his CD player and hugging a photograph of Leah, this cultured man did not deserve his treatment. It made Jessica's betrayal both something incomprehensible and something far more culpable, a commitment to the triviality of the yuppie culture, all champagne and mobile phones. (165)[32]

The most interesting feature of 3.1 was Thacker's decision to insert the second half of the scene (with Tubal) immediately after the opening conversation between Salerio and Solanio.[33] This permitted Shylock to demonstrate (again in the footsteps of Irving) that his distress was occasioned by the loss of Jessica, rather than by the theft of his ducats.

3.3 was notable for the role played by Nick Simons's Tubal. To begin with, instead of playing the opening line as an *in medias res* response to Antonio, Calder's Shylock directed it at his friend (for good measure, adding his name): "Tell me not of mercy, *Tubal*" (3.3.1; my italics). Thus Tubal the Jew was shown to have been pleading for mercy, a quality normally in this play the preserve of Portia and the Duke. Furthermore, sitting by Shylock's side behind his office desk, Nick Simons's Tubal signaled increasing discomfort at his fellow Jew's determined refusal to be moved by Antonio's pleadings; displayed shock at Shylock's placing of his hand on a holy book to accompany "I have sworn an oath"; listened with dismay as Shylock directed at him (again, rather than at Antonio) the assertion that "The Duke shall grant me justice"; and then finally, unable to take any more of Shylock's irreligious intransigence, stormed out, leaving his friend to shout after him, in self-justification,

> I'll not be made a soft and dull-eyed fool
> To shake the head, relent, and sigh, and yield
> To Christian intercessors. (14–16)

Tubal's final contribution might be said to have been made in 4.1, when his absence from the trial strikingly conveyed Shylock's isolation, not only from humanity generally, but from the Jewish community in particular.

In this scene, Calder's Shylock was notable for his quiet restraint and total lack of triumphalism when it appeared from Portia's pronouncements that things were going in his favor. When he said "I crave the law" (203), it came across as an appeal to our sense of fair play; when he cried "I have an oath"(225), he seemed to mean it quite genuinely; and in the middle of "'I have a daughter" (292–94), he broke down, a powerful reminder of the loss that had driven him to this position. Although plainly baffled and defeated when Portia threw in the blood clause, he was only really rocked when she referred to him as an alien (345). Penny Downie's Portia seemed fully aware of the power that this word would have in the now studied destruction of the Jew; she paused before uttering it, and then did so as if to imply: "you will realize the full import of what I am saying." Accordingly it was at this point that Calder's physical collapse began, to culminate in what appeared to be a stroke or heart attack after he begged leave to go, uttering "I am not well" (392) in a surprised tone, as though he could not work out what had happened to him. The rest of the court dispersed, and Shylock was left alone in a spot-light. Then, as he struggled up on to a chair, Gratiano's final taunting words—"far from jubilant" (Jackson 342)—were heard coming out of the darkness. Shylock nodded, struggled to his feet and then turned and glared out defiantly and challengingly at the audience as the lights dimmed. Although the scene—as represented in the text—had not ended, the moment was reminiscent to some degree of many of Irving's productions, which ended at this point, leaving the great man to take his curtain call. Calder's performance regularly drew enthusiastic applause as the lights dimmed on the defeated Jew, and then the scene re-started on the upper floor of the set; but, such had been the tragic dimension to Shylock's fall that there was a sense in which the real business of the play was completed.

In concluding his review of the Goodman Theater production of *The Merchant of Venice*, which visited London in November, 1994,[34] Michael Shapiro referred to director Peter Sellars's view that the play exposed the urge in people to exploit others, adding: "One wonders if straitjacketing actors in a thesis-ridden, media-besotted production, tapping into Rodney King's pain, and rewriting the Jessica-plot also count as acts of exploitation."[35]

Shapiro's conclusion contains most of the major criticisms which were subsequently to be leveled at the production during its four days at the Barbi-can:[36] it was ideologically overbearing; it used technology distractingly and untheatrically (characters filmed the action, which was shown on monitors in the auditorium) ; it inappropriately exploited emotions stirred up by the then recent Los Angeles race riots; and it distorted the text.

The one element of Sellars's production to remain immune from wide-spread criticism, however, was Paul Butler's Shylock, a performance which drew almost universal praise. Played, according to one commentator, "with Robesonesque weight," and recalling Martin Luther King, Butler's "excep-tionally fine Shylock . . . [writes another] [was] sardonic, cautious, full of impassive power"; "laconic and abrupt"; "dignified"; behaving throughout with a "gentle gravity." Undoubtedly one of the most sympathetic of all Shylocks, his stillness was often imposed by the need to remain in frame while the cameras were on him, or to use one of the standing microphones (given that, as an underclass Jew, he did not have a remote mike of his own).

In a performance which recalled Calder's, and was later to be echoed in Kentrup's (see below), Butler's demeanor throughout the trial scene was notable for a complete absence of triumphalism—there was no gloating in his praise of the young lawyer's judgements—and he seemed sincere in declaring that his pursuit of justice was motivated by "an oath in heaven" (225). A moment which recalled Sher, but which here had a different cutting edge, was his delivery of the speech "You have among you many a purchased slave" (89–99) direct to camera. With Butler's four interpolated repetitions of "Let them be free!", it was one of the few moments in the production that made the audience feel genuinely uncomfortable.[37]

One particular piece of business stands out as representative of the way in which the interpretation went as far as any production can in protecting Shylock from charges of personal vindictiveness against Antonio. Many Shylocks, even those presented as having a real and understandable grievance, have nonetheless forfeited audience sympathy when they approach the merchant with intent to take their pound of flesh. Even David Calder, one of the most sympathetic Shylocks since Olivier's, seemed to relish the moment, delineating the flesh to be removed, by drawing an outline with a marker pen on the hapless Antonio's bare chest. Butler's Shylock eschewed all such personal satisfaction: in a stance that recalled Othello's insistence that the killing of Desdemona should be a sacrifice and not a murder (5.2.67–68), he remained seated behind his desk—as he had been throughout the trial— while two courtroom guards made ready to perform the operation. As though presiding over a lawful execution, Butler's Shylock barely looked up until Portia was heard to stay the guards' hands.

If the aim were to give us a sympathetic Shylock, Paul Butler had the dice loaded more heavily in his favor than any actor since Irving: with a director anxious to atone for white guilt; the casting of blacks as Jews; the back-drop of the Los Angeles riots; a deserting Lancelot Gobbo played as a physically repulsive lecher; a Lorenzo who was clearly about to abandon Jessica for Portia; a Bassanio whose affections were plainly going to be transferred back to Antonio as soon as he had secured his wife's fortune; and a merchant who seemed to have fabricated the whole story of the lost ships in order to prove his love, Butler's Shylock was always going to show up rather well. In terms of his performance, perhaps Benedict Nightingale summed up the majority view when he said: "I only wish he was in someone else's *Merchant*" (*The Times,* 18 November 1994).

Philip Voss had the advantage of being part of a coherent and convincing production, which opened at the Shakespeare Theatre in Stratford on 4

December 1997. In an interview which took place four weeks into rehearsals, Voss had been passionate in his assertion that Shylock should not be played as a seedy, cringing usurer, but as a wealthy and prosperously attired businessman. In such a representation, Voss felt, "it would be more telling to be spat upon and kicked, looking good and respectable, than otherwise."[38] This image was powerfully realized in performance, not least when Shylock arrived in the impressive surroundings of the Doge's palace. He entered a little like an expensively dressed Renaissance Willie Loman, clutching his case and looking around uncertainly, a traveling salesman arriving at an unfamiliar, and surprisingly sumptuous, department store. Placing his case down right, he sat upon it to whet his knife and would return to it as a secure base throughout the scene. Tired of hearing the Christian arguments, maintaining a resilience which manifested itself as "a sort of pedantry,"[39] he wearily covered his eyes when Portia asked him to be merciful and, in an unusual and suddenly impressive reaction, broke free of his accustomed restraint to sneer at the Christian lovers: "Would any of the stock of Barabas / Had been her husband rather . . . [pausing to look with obvious disgust at the embracing Antonio and Bassanio] . . . than a Christian!" (4.1.293–94)[40]

When interviewed, Voss had said that his super-objective as Shylock was "to win." It was clear that, with such an ambition, the Jew's defeat would be devastating; and so it proved. Almost unable for a long time to accept that he had lost, he kept hold of the legal book which had been his undoing, and glanced down at it when told "Take thy forfeiture" (331). On "To be so taken at thy peril, Jew" (340), he even approached Antonio for a second time, and it was possible to believe that, despite the capital penalty hanging over him, he would actually kill the Christian, until, groaning painfully at his inability to proceed, he finally admitted defeat. His "I am content" (389) was cold and bitter, and, in a spectacular coup de théâtre, he scrabbled on the floor in a pool of golden ducats, unable to get a foothold, before finally scrambling to his feet and instructing that the deed should be sent after him. In a final act of cruelty, Bassanio and Gratiano brutally snatched the yarmulke from Shylock's head—"in other words, the stereotype of Jew and money was followed by the pain of the Jew being denied his religious identity."[41] Voss's Shylock was thoughtfully conceived and skillfully executed. Many commentators concurred with Alastair Macaulay's opinion that "Voss returns us to many aspects of the essence of Shylock more truly than any other recent interpreter" (*Financial Times,* 15 December 1997).

The acclaim was less widespread for the first ever production of *The Merchant of Venice* at the new Globe Theatre on Bankside the following year. Directed by Richard Olivier, the production's first performance was on 20 May 1998. This play was always going to be something of a test case for a theatre which, as part of a policy to replicate what they considered to be the actor-audience dynamic of Shakespeare's own time, had in its first full season encouraged audiences to boo the French in *Henry V*. After nearly four decades of productions which had either inadvertently laid themselves open to charges of anti-Semitism, or had offered highly sympathetic Shylocks in an attempt to make the play acceptable, it seemed unthinkable that the Globe would encourage audiences to hiss a villainous Jew. At the same time, they would be open to charges of inconsistency and anachronism were Shylock to be presented in the kind of sympathetic and even semi-heroic light that we have come to think of as being distinctly post-Irving, and latterly, post-O'Toole.

In the event, Richard Olivier opted for anachronism, while retaining the hissing, a combination of choices which seems to me to have offered him the worst of both worlds.[42] Norbert Kentrup's bear of a Shylock was humorous, genial, and impossible to hate. With his native German accent augmented by "Jewish" modulations, he contrived to make us understand that, while he had good cause to hate Antonio for the shames that he had stained him with, he was absolutely sincere in offering the bond as an act of friendship, and clearly thought up the flesh clause as a genuinely merry absurdity which was the occasion for considerable mirth from both him and the merchant. In keeping with many notable recent Shylocks, he expressed great affection for his daughter—it was extremely difficult to see in what ways the house could conceivably be considered "hell"—stroking her cheek affectionately on "Say I will come" (2.5.39) and, in a manner reminiscent of Dustin Hoffman, chuckled indulgently about Lancelot's supposed shortcomings (45–47), his only flash of oppressiveness being sparked at the mention of masques (28 ff.). When he appeared in 3.1, it was obviously the loss of Jessica which had destroyed him and not the stolen ducats. Audiences who had enjoyed booing Oliver in *As You Like It* a few hours earlier (the two plays alternated) were given no grounds for indulging that pleasure on Shylock's entrance, but they did so all the same.

Watching Kentrup's Shylock as it were undermining the theory underlying Globe performance offered a powerful support for Anthony Dawson's belief that theater is "inescapably practical, concrete, anti-theoretical," and that "the very contingency of performance in whatever venue generates uncontrolled interpretations" (310). It was very difficult to see Kentrup's performance as that of an authentically Elizabethan Shylock (even allowing for the serious doubts over how the character might have been played at that time): everything about it, from the care taken to avoid negative stereotyping to the stress placed upon paternal grief, was redolent of post-Holocaust sensibility. Hissing, in such a context, was totally inappropriate and led Michael Billington to wonder "whether one effect of this new theatre is to morally simplify Shakespeare's plays and turn them into a form of Victorian melodrama . . . simple contests between heroes and villains." He went on: "I would argue that *The Merchant* is still morally complex. It is the Globe style that simplifies it . . . when you come away from a production of *The Mer-*

chant in which Gratiano has been cheered and Shylock hissed, something disturbing has occurred" (*Guardian,* 1 June 1998).

Billington was absolutely right. The first *Merchant* at the new Globe offered an unusual and effective Shylock, but the performance sat very uneasily in front of a groundling audience who had been whipped up to hysteria by Marcello Magni's entr'acte antics[43] and who were discouraged from dealing in the kind of moral ambivalence that this play almost uniquely demands. As an experiment in replicating the actor-audience dynamics of the Elizabethan playhouse, it proved only that we should think very carefully indeed before concluding that Shakespeare's actors and audiences engaged in the kind of crude pantomime behavior that the Globe seemed to be encouraging. To me it rendered extremely implausible the notion that an age which demanded the kind of sensitive and attentive looking and listening required for the appreciation of works of the subtlety of Hilliard's miniatures and Byrd's masses might have performed one of their foremost dramatic poet's more ambiguous creations in a red wig and a funny nose.

There could be no more fitting an interpretation with which to conclude the twentieth century and open the twenty-first than Henry Goodman's at the Royal National Theatre, first performed in the Cottesloe Theatre on 17 June 1999. The play later transferred to the Olivier Theatre. Goodman's Shylock, which won him the Olivier Award for Best Actor, and which was variously described as "overwhelming"; "superb"; "magnificent"; "magnificently perceptive"; "brilliantly conceived, superlatively detailed"; "penetrating, complex, and . . . moving," was rooted in a production founded on the premise that *The Merchant of Venice* should be reinvestigated as a naturalistic play about worth and value, in which the two cultures of Venetian Christian and alien Jew had to be presented with utmost clarity. Speaking during rehearsals, Goodman said, "The great challenge of this play is to make sure that there's a real sense of a culture and a life off-stage."[44] This challenge was met triumphantly, not least because of Hildegard Bechtler's harsh design for the intimate Cottesloe traverse staging and director Trevor Nunn's decision to set the play in the 1930s. Such scenography permitted the ensemble to invoke a world in which anti-Jewish sentiments could be expressed as unthinkingly as observations on the weather; but which also reminded us continuously that this was the fertile ground of hostility and ignorance out of which the Holocaust was to grow. To reinforce the picture of a society in which anti-Semitism was casual and matter-of-fact, Nunn had deliberately eschewed graffiti, swastikas, and outward acts of insult and violence (such as the spitting embraced so wholeheartedly by Bill Alexander and others). In other words, he resisted the kind of polarization which can render the dialogue on this play's issues crude and obvious.

This setting, in which the two cultures were presented with striking clarity, was the bedrock on which Goodman developed the psychology of his Shylock:

Figure12. Shylock (Henry Goodman) in the 1999 Royal National Theatre production. Photo by John Haynes.

a religious, conservative Jew, tired of the old animosity between himself and Antonio, who offers the bond as a genuine attempt to break down the barriers; but nonetheless feels profoundly that the hedonistic Christian society of the louche Bassanio and his friends has irredeemably lost its way.

Trevor Nunn's approach in the early rehearsals had reinforced Goodman's instinct, as he put it in an interview (14 July 1999), to "just get inside the man" (Figure 12). Himself a Jew, Goodman had said, "I want to get the sense of a man who reads Hebrew all day long, who speaks Yiddish at home, for whom English is a second language" (July interview). More than this, there was the powerfully evoked sense of Shylock's devotion to and pride in his religion and culture, a dedication which was at the heart of every single aspect of his daily life. It was easy to see why such a man, mourning the recently dead Leah,[45] would impose intolerable burdens upon his daughter. Many actors have bemoaned the few lines given to them in which to portray Shylock's relationship with his child. But, such was the dramatic power of the scenes we were able to observe—Jessica being chastised and slapped one minute, caressed and sung to the next—that it was possible to imagine the whole daily existence in the Jew's household.[46] For this Jessica (sensitively portrayed by Gabrielle Jourdain, with what the *Observer* critic called "the air of a refugee child, bewildered by the two worlds to which she belongs"), the house was "hell," not because of specific ill-treatment, but because of the incessant demands upon her to be both wife and daughter to Shylock, preparing his food according to strict dietary laws and participating in the regular highly emotional services for the dead Leah.

It was natural, therefore, that Goodman's Shylock should have been utterly destroyed by the loss of Jessica; and, of course, that the audience should have been prepared for his desolation as he returned alone to his empty house only to find the front door left open. From that moment, everything Goodman's Shylock did could be traced back to "the emotional state that he's in and the circumstances of his home life" (July interview). Unusually the first steps in his decision to enforce the bond were taken before his entrance in 3.1; his meeting with Salerio and Solanio served as an affirmation of that decision; and it was during his conversation with Tubal that it became irreversible. By the time he arrived at the Duke's court, he had "made a pact with God" and entered the room "cold, committed" (July interview). Of this scene, John Peter wrote: "I have never seen a more morally harrowing trial scene. Shylock listens to Portia intently, for a good Jew . . . wants to believe in due process; and you sense that he has always wanted to be spoken to, and reasoned with, like this, by Christians" (*Sunday Times,* 27 June 1999).

Goodman's Shylock seemed almost visibly shaken and moved by Derbhle Crotty's intense and persuasive Portia. Not only did she speak this religious man's language, but "[he sees his] wife sitting next to [him], saying 'Be reasonable' " (July interview). For an instant you felt that he was capable of change; but the moment passed; and, when the loyal Tubal made a dignified and disapproving exit, and Shylock cried "I have a daughter," you knew that it was too late.

Defeated, in a moment of terrible denial, Goodman's Shylock threw his yarmulke into the empty pan of the scales. There was no physical collapse or harrowing offstage scream; in fact, the actor was himself uncertain about what fate awaited his character. But he did feel that Shylock leaves the court "thinking it's my fault and God has taught me a lesson and if Leah had been here it would have been different" (July interview). The *Sunday Times*'s John Peter commented that Shylock "knows too that he will now be what he, the outsider, worked so hard not to be: an outcast. This is when you realise that perhaps the play is, after all, a tragedy: of value and of values." Goodman himself thought that the play asked us the question, "What must we value in life?" (17 May 1999 interview).

For the characters who remained, however, things would never be the same and the play ended with a rumble of thunder as Jessica sang the lament taught to her by her now broken father.

Two unusual textual transpositions are worthy of note. The first was Nunn's decision to move a crucial part of Shylock's 1.3 aside to the end of 3.1:

> If I can catch him once upon the hip,
> I will feed fat the ancient grudge I bear him . . .
>   Cursèd be my tribe
> If I forgive him. (1.3.43–44 and 48–49)

Goodman explained Nunn's decision in this way: "If you leave it where it is, the audience locks on that he is driven by that; and you only hear everything after as trickery and guile . . . By 3.1 the audience has experienced the loss of Jessica" (May interview). This is undoubtedly true; but the transposition represented to me a failure of nerve and the sole retreat from an otherwise unflinching treatment of Shylock's less palatable characteristics. Goodman is an actor of consummate skill and would have relished the challenge to retain audience sympathy even with that early aside intact.

The second transposition involved moving a customarily unnoticed and innocuous speech of Portia's to the moment following Gratiano's bawdy couplet (5.1.306–307), thereby serving to herald a closure which was to be characterized by melancholy, regret, and foreboding:

> This night methinks is but the daylight sick.
> It looks a little paler. 'Tis a day
> Such as the day is when the sun is hid. (5.1.124–26)

While still only four weeks into rehearsals, Goodman was asked about Patrick Stewart's point concerning "playing the inconsistencies" in Shylock. He replied, "That's what I'm in the middle of . . . If the audience can love him and hate him, understand him, then not understand him . . . then you've got him" (May interview). Goodman got him.

Judging from the last ten years, it is difficult to see how the interpretation of Shylock will develop in the early decades of the twenty-first century. Possibly, after its initial foray, the Globe will attempt a bolder interpretation, less obviously influenced by modern sensibilities. Two certainties are that reinterpreting Shylock will continue to be one of the most formidable challenges in the classical theatre; and that there will be no shortage of major actors waiting for the opportunity to play him.

Notes

1. Alter cites Joseph Papp's 1962 production of Shakespeare's play in Central Park (George C. Scott as Shylock) and Paul Berry's in 1984 for the New Jersey Shakespeare Festival as examples of productions in the United States which have given rise to attacks upon the play for its alleged anti-Semitism.

2. Strictly speaking, the term "anti-Semitic" is an anachronism if applied to the earliest Shylocks, since the phenomenon of despising Jews as a race (as distinct from despising them for their religion) did not appear until the nineteenth century. Hostility to Jews up to that time should, therefore, more correctly be termed "anti-Judaism." The more familiar term will be retained throughout this essay, however, since the greater part of it is concerned with interpretations from Sir Henry Irving's onwards.

3. Collier (53) quotes "A Funeral Elegy on the Death of the Famous Actor, R. Burbadge [*sic*], who died on Saturday in Lent, the 13th of March, 1618":

> Heart-broken Philaster, and Amintas too,
> Are lost for ever; with the red-haired Jew,
> Which sought the bankrupt merchant's flesh,
> By woman-lawyer caught in his own mesh . . .

4. I am following most current thinking, including that of Jay L. Halio in the Oxford edition, in assuming a date of composition between summer 1596 and summer 1598.

5. Macklin's biographer James Kirkman quotes from John Hill's *The Actor, A Treatise on the Art of Playing* . . . (1750): "[Macklin] would bid his pupil first to speak the passage as he would in common life, if he had the occasion to speak the same words, and then give them more force, but preserving the same accent, to deliver them on stage" (quoted in Stone and Kahrl).

6. Appleton (46) quotes George Colman and Bonnell Thornton, "The Connoisseur," 1 (31 January 1754).

7. Notably Toby Lelyveld, James C. Bulman, and John Gross.

8. H. A. Saintsbury to some extent echoes this chameleon portrayal when he recalls that Irving's Shylock reminded him of some Moroccan Jews he had once seen: "impudent and cringing, insolent, cunning, and prone to self-pity" (166).

9. In a footnote, Hughes cites the following newspapers as having carried equally enthusiastic reviews: *Glasgow North British Daily Mail*, 8 September 1893; *Liverpool Daily Post* 3 October 1883; *Boston Daily Evening Traveller*, 13 December 1883; *Edinburgh Scottish Leader*, 3 September 1887; *Edinburgh Evening News*, 3 September 1887; *New York Daily Tribune*, 7 November 1883.

10. Hichens does not explain why he believes artistry to be an infallible guard against theatrical "illegitimacy."

11. As evidence, Moore cites Irving's actions after he has said "I would my daughter were dead at my foot" etc.: "Irving paused, hid his face in his hands and murmured an anguished "No, no, no, no, no!" and in the subsequent self-pitying lines on his losses, he opened his robe and smote himself continually, slowly, and heavily on his bare breast" (201–202).

12. Shaw's comments, however, always have to be read in the light of his lifelong championing of Barry Sullivan over Irving, for whom he rarely had a good word.

13. Notably by Richard E. Mennen and by James C. Bulman.

14. Benson's company had performed the annual repertoire of plays at the Memorial Theatre, Stratford-upon-Avon, every year from 1886 to the theatre's closure during the Great War in 1916. The farewell performance by the "Old Bensonians" was on 16 May 1932. Komisarjevsky's production opened two months later, on 25 July.

15. See, for example, *The Times* for 26 July 1932, 15 April 1936, and 17 February 1944.

16. See also the *Daily Express*, 15 March 1934, and the *Birmingham Gazette*, 16 April 1936.

17. Similar articles appeared in the *Evening Standard* (27 April 1936), the *Daily Telegraph* (26 April 1934), and the *Morning Post* (27 April 1934), which reported Professor Hecht as having claimed that Shakespeare—the "greatest poet of the Germanic race"—was "In the realm of the theatre . . . as German as the German classic dramatists themselves."

18. The first production opened with Patrick Stewart as Shylock in The Other Place, Stratford-upon-Avon, on 11 May 1978, and subsequently transferred to the Theatre Royal, Newcastle (from February 1979), and the Donmar Warehouse, London (from May 1979). The production featuring David Suchet opened in the main house at Stratford on 21 April 1981 and transferred to the Aldwych Theatre in London in July, 1981.

19. Stewart later wrote: "Jewishness could become a smoke screen which might conceal both the particular and the universal in the role" (Brockbank 18).

20. Of particular interest to semioticians, "Antonio smoked cheroots, Tubal a Havana, and Shylock his mean little hand-rolled cigarettes" (Brockbank 19). Ian McKellen was to gain a similar effect with hand-rolled cigarettes when playing Iago with the RSC in 1990.

21. David Suchet had not seen Stewart's Shylock when it was first performed. As the audience applaud the performance of this scene on *Playing Shakespeare*, Suchet is heard to remark, "That was amazing!"

22. A similar experiment along these lines had been conducted by Peter Zadek in Germany in 1972; he provoked "embarrassment to the point of physical revulsion as the result of 'revealing what in our society is not allowed to be revealed' " (Hortmann 257).

23. On the video recording in the Shakespeare Centre library, the audience are heard to laugh throughout 1.3, not only on Shylock's jokes about pirates, or making gold and silver "breed as fast," but on unusual lines such as his comment that Antonio "brings down the rate of usance."

24. In a moment highly reminiscent of Olivier's performance, Sher's Shylock suddenly falls silent as he hears the distant tolling of a bell. In Olivier's case, it was a funeral knell; in Sher's , a ship's bell (Doran 74, and the prompt book held in the Shakespeare Centre, Stratford-upon-Avon).

25. Lydia Conway, *What's On*, 14 June 1989. Carl Miller called the production "as sturdy, starry and full of life as Madame Tussaud's" (*City Limits*, 8 June 1989).

26. Twelve of the reviews published in the *London Theatre Record* (21 May–3 June 1989) made some allusion to the actor's height, Martin Dodsworth notably describing him as "notoriously not tall" (*Times Literary Supplement*, 8 June 1989, 666).

27. Conway (see note 25). Almost all reviewers referred to the incessant spitting, Rhoda Koenig memorably describing Hoffman's Shylock as "a perambulating spittoon for any velvet-robed Christians who want to relieve themselves of phlegm and contempt" (*Punch,* 16 June 1989). The fullest account of the spitting is given by Irene G. Dash, who describes the patient deliberation with which Hoffman's Shylock wiped the spit from his face with a handkerchief "specifically designed for the purpose" (*Shakespeare Bulletin,* Spring 1990, 10).

28. David Nathan, *Jewish Chronicle,* 9 June 1989. Shulman (in the *Evening Standard*) also noticed that Shylock showed "surprisingly . . . little resentment to the demand that he become a Christian." Michael Billington adds that Hoffman's Shylock shows "strangely little sense of horror at the injunction that he turn Christian" (*Guardian,* 2 June 1989).

29. Conway (see note 25). Paul Taylor felt that "without in any way sentimentalising Shylock, Hall . . . included touches evoking the human side to him which years of being treated as inhuman by the Christians [had] warped" (*Independent,* 3 June 1989).

30. Description based on the video recording of the production made by the Royal Shakespeare Company and held in the Shakespeare Centre, Stratford (recorded 13 January 1994).

31. Russell Jackson wrote: "When he remarked that he would refuse to eat pork, he was clearly disturbed not so much by the prospect of an affront to his religion's dietary laws as by the threat to his self-respect in accepting an invitation to eat where he could not yet be sure he was respected" (341–42).

32. Peter Smith felt that the scene made Shylock "humane and empathic" and "alluded to the civilized intelligence and loneliness of Inspector Morse" (*Cahiers Élisabéthains,* October 1993). Nearly sixty years earlier, Arthur Phillips's Shylock had engaged in a similar piece of theatre: *The Times* of 1 October 1935 referred to "a wordless scene showing Shylock at home with the daughter who is about to steal his ducats and jewels."

33. The section from "How now, Tubal!" (usually lines 75–123), was inserted after lines 19–20 ("lest the devil cross my prayer"), cutting "For here he comes in the likeness of a Jew." (Prompt book held in the Shakespeare Centre, Stratford)

34. Directed by Peter Sellars, the production opened in Chicago on 10 October 1994, and then played from 16 to 19 November at the Barbican Theatre, London. Performances also followed in France and Germany.

35. *Shakespeare Bulletin,* Fall 1994, 33. The video recording of Rodney King's beating by the Los Angeles police was one of the sequences shown to the audience on television monitors.

36. He also condemned the performance for its "funereal pacing and lugubrious line delivery," continuing, in the vein of several other critics, "At the performance I saw, spectators wanted to laugh, but, given no encouragement, stopped trying. Many left at the interval" (32).

37. Michael Billington wrote: "The court-room drama, pitched halfway between Welles's *The Trial* and Shakespeare's trial scene, is played in creepy silhouette and becomes a display both of judicial corruption—the Duke has

already decided that Shylock is 'an inhuman wretch'—and private angst"
(*Guardian,* 18 November 1994).

38.   Interview with John O'Connor, 25 October 1997. Voss later wrote:

> From the play I had come to the conclusion that Shylock should look
> presentable. So often Shylock is cringing and browbeaten but he's
> referred to as a rich Jew all the time. The key line is when Portia comes
> in and asks, "Which is the merchant here? And which the Jew?" This can
> often get a laugh and I thought, "No, Shylock goes to the Rialto, he
> trades, he has to be a respectable business man." (Education Pack for
> *Merchant*, RSC, 14)

39.   According to Helen Schlesinger, who played Portia (RSC Education Pack, 15).

40.   I must, incidentally, take issue with Nicholas de Jongh, who saw "no frisson
      of sexual strain" between Bassanio and a "paternal" Antonio (*Evening Stan-
      dard,* 1 December 1997): the delicate and subtle way in which Julian Curry's
      repressed Antonio gently but purposefully rejected any physical approach
      from Bassanio was the clearest of indications that he dared not permit it.

41.   Peter Holland in correspondence with John O'Connor, 15 October 1998.

42.   It is possible that Mark Rylance's injunction to the audience, "Have no con-
      cern if you don't know how good the actors are or how *authentic*" (program
      note; my italics), indicated a shift away from claims for "authenticity" which,
      the previous season, had been supported by the much-vaunted fact that the
      actors in *Henry V* were sporting Elizabethan underwear. While this is not the
      place for a continuation of the debate, it should be said that a drive for authen-
      ticity seemed not to extend to readings of lines such as "he had a kind of
      taste" (2.2.16–17), which were given a distinctly twentieth-century meaning.

43.   Magni played Lancelot Gobbo, but also fulfilled the role of audience-inciter
      between acts, whipping the younger members of the audience into a frenzy.
      In the three performances that I attended, he showered people with water,
      and, at one point, dragged a teenaged boy on to the stage and engaged in
      some kind of parody of simulated sex.

44.   Interview with John O'Connor, 17 May 1999.

45.   Goodman decided that Leah had died within the past year. Early rehearsals
      "completely affirmed my sense that he's living on his own without his
      wife . . . and I just built up a whole picture of his personal life which I found
      liberating" (July interview).

46.   Paul Taylor refers to the slapping as "a shocking but pathetic expression of
      his anxious love" (*Independent,* 21 June 1999). Talking about Shylock's dis-
      approval of Lancelot Gobbo, Goodman said, "In this house, people have to
      work. . . . It's a moral house" (May interview).

Works Cited

Alter, Iska. " 'Barbaric Laws, Barbaric Bonds': Arnold Wesker's *The Merchant.*"
      Modern Drama 31 (1988): 536–47.

Appleton, William W. *Charles Macklin: An Actor's Life.* Cambridge, MA: Harvard University Press, 1961.

Auden, W. H. "Brothers and Others." *The Dyer's Hand and Other Essays.* London: Faber, 1962. 218–37.

Baldwin, T. W. *The Organization and Personnel of the Shakespearean Company.* Princeton, NJ: Princeton University Press, 1927.

Barton, John. *Playing Shakespeare.* London: Methuen, 1984.

Brereton, Austin. *The Life of Henry Irving.* 2 vols. London: Longmans, Green, 1908.

Brockbank, Philip, ed. *Players of Shakespeare 1.* Cambridge: Cambridge University Press, 1985.

Bulman, James C. *Shakespeare in Performance: "The Merchant of Venice."* Manchester: Manchester University Press, 1991.

Bulman, James and H. R. Coursen, eds. *Shakespeare on Television.* University Press of New England, 1988.

Collier, J. Payne. *Memoirs of the Principal Actors in the Plays of Shakespeare.* London: Shakespeare Society, 1846.

Cooke, William. *Memoirs of Charles Macklin, Comedian.* London, 1804. New York: Benjamin Blom, 1972.

Dawson, Anthony. "The Impasse Over the Stage." *English Literary Renaissance* 21 (1991): 300–310.

Doran, Gregory. "Solanio in *The Merchant of Venice.*" *Players of Shakespeare 3.* Jackson and Smallwood, eds. 68–76.

Foulkes, Richard. "Henry Irving and Laurence Olivier as Shylock." *Theatre Notes* 27 (1972): 26–35.

Granville, George. *The Jew of Venice.* London, 1701. London: Cornmarket, 1969.

Gross, John. *Shylock: Four Hundred Years in the Life of a Legend.* London: Chatto and Windus, 1992.

Gurr, Andrew. *The Shakespearian Playing Companies.* Oxford: Oxford University Press, 1996.

Halio, Jay L., ed. *The Merchant of Venice.* Oxford: Oxford University Press, 1994.

Hatton, Joseph. *Henry Irving's Impressions of America.* Vol. 1. London, 1884.

Hiatt, Charles. *Henry Irving: A Record and Review.* London: George Bell, 1899.

Holland, Peter. *English Shakespeares: Shakespeare on the English Stage in the 1990s.* Cambridge: Cambridge University Press, 1997.

Hortmann, Wilhelm. *Shakespeare on the German Stage: The Twentieth Century.* Cambridge: Cambridge University Press, 1998.

Hughes, Alun. "Henry Irving's Tragedy of Shylock." *Educational Theatre Journal* 24 (1972): 249–68.

Jackson, Russell and Robert Smallwood, eds. *Players of Shakespeare 3.* Cambridge: Cambridge University Press, 1993.

Lewes, G. H. *Dramatic Essays Reprinted from the "Examiner."* Eds. William Archer and R.W. Lowe. London, 1894.

Lelyveld, Toby. *Shylock on the Stage.* Cleveland, OH: Case Western Reserve University Press, 1960.

Lichtenberg, Georg Christoph. *Vermischte Schriften.* III, 226. Gottingen, 1867. Trans. Margaret L. Mare and W. H. Quarrell. *Lichtenberg's Visits to England.* New York: Benjamin Blom, 1938, revised 1969.

Mahood, M. M., ed. *The Merchant of Venice*. Cambridge: Cambridge University Press, 1987.

Mennen, Richard E. "Theodore Komisarjevsky's Production of *The Merchant of Venice*." *Theatre Journal* 31 (1979): 386–97.

Moore, Edward M. "Henry Irving's Shakespearean Productions." *Theatre Survey* 17 (2): 349–51.

Overton, Bill. *"The Merchant of Venice": Text and Performance*. Basingstoke: Macmillan, 1987.

Perret, Marion D. "Shakespeare and Anti-Semitism: Two Versions of *The Merchant of Venice*." Bulman and Coursen, eds. 156–68.

Saintsbury, H. A. and Cecil Palmer, eds. *We Saw Him Act: A Symposium on the Art of Sir Henry Irving*. London, 1939.

Shapiro, James. *Shakespeare and the Jews*. New York: Columbia University Press, 1996.

Shaw, George B. *Pen Portraits and Reviews*. London: Constable, 1931.

Stone, George Winchester, Jr., and George M. Kahrl. *David Garrick: A Critical Biography*. Carbondale: Southern Illinois University Press, 1979.

Sullivan, Patrick J. " 'Strumpet Wind': The National Theatre's *Merchant of Venice*." *Educational Theatre Journal*, 26(1974): 31–44.

Walkley, A. B. *Playhouse Impressions*. London: T. Fisher Unwin, 1892.

Warren, Roger. "A Year of Comedies: Stratford 1978." *Shakespeare Survey* 32 (1982): 201–202.

Watermeier, Daniel D. *Between Actor and Critic: Selected Letters of Edwin Booth and William Winter*. Princeton, NJ: Princeton University Press, 1971.

Wells, Stanley. "Shakespearean Performances in London and Stratford, 1986–87." *Shakespeare Survey* 41 (1989): 162–65.

———. "Shakespeare Production in England in 1989." *Shakespeare Survey* 43 (1991): 186–88.

Wesker, Arnold. *Plays*. Vol.4. London: Penguin, 1980.

Wilson, Edwin, ed. *Shaw on Shakespeare*. London: Cassell, 1961.

Winter, William. *Shakespeare on the Stage*. London: T. Fisher Unwin, 1912.

Portia Performs

Playing the Role in the Twentieth-Century English Theater

PENNY GAY

I. Portia's Eloquence

When the actress playing Portia launches into the play's most famous speech, "The quality of mercy is not strained," is her character delivering a prepared speech, or is it an impromptu argument? By the same token, is her last-minute legal quibble that saves Antonio's life a well-prepared piece of court-room histrionics, or a genuine flash of desperate inspiration? In general, how does the character feel about playing a "boy"—anxious, empowered, embar-rassed, liberated?—and where does the experience leave her? These are some of the questions that actresses preparing the role of Portia must resolve, with or without the help of their directors.

Portia is one of the most sociologically complex of Shakespeare's women. We meet her in a specifically defined and constraining social class and financial milieu, subject to her father's disposal of her (even from beyond the grave). We also watch her venture into autonomous action in the real world outside Belmont's gilded cage; but she can only act effectively in this world by disguising herself as a clever boy. We see her at the end of the play return to Belmont as the confident woman and ruler of the household, which includes, now, her husband and his friends. She is the only one of Shake-speare's comic heroines, apart from the socially superior Princess of France in *Love's Labour's Lost*, not to be silenced by male resumption of power at the end of the play. No other of Shakespeare's plays leaves us with the image of such a powerful and self-determined woman: in the course of the play she has developed, before our eyes, from somewhat petulant girl to young woman blissfully in love, and thence to authoritative married woman; her husband—supposed master of his wife and her household—humiliated and metaphorically cuckolded. The "detour" of her experience as the apparently male young lawyer is a vital aspect of this development, for it is in this episode that Portia experiences the masculine power of authoritative

Figure13. Portia (Dorothy Tutin) and Shylock (Peter O'Toole) in the 1960 Shakespeare
Memorial Theatre production. Angus McBean, The Shakespeare Centre Library, Stratford-
upon-Avon.

speech—that is, speech that a representative sector of (male-defined) society
will listen to with respect.

Portia's accession to the right of public eloquence is carefully set up. Her
first scene (1.2) shows her speaking freely in the company of her waiting
woman and friend, in a private, domestic situation.[1] In a parallel to 1.1's
scene of male camaraderie (and Antonio's melancholy), we see Portia to be
not only "aweary of this great world," but a woman of sparkling wit and
irreverence concerning her hopeful suitors. In the following scenes with the
suitors Morocco and Aragon, she is blandly decorous in blank verse. All the
more surprising, then, is her passionate eloquence in 3.2's scene of Bassanio's choice of the caskets. Portia has 115 lines in this scene, most of them
in four big speeches: "I pray you tarry, pause a day or two" (1–24), "Away
then! I am locked in one of them" (40–63), "You see me, Lord Bassanio,
where I stand" (149–74), "What, no more? Pay him six thousand, and deface
the bond" (297–313). These four speeches (as is evident from their opening
lines) map Portia's personal development in this crucial scene. Each of them
is a piece of masterly rhetoric—that is, a speech designed to persuade a particular audience in a specific situation. In the play, of course, the audience is
dual—that on stage (Bassanio), and that in the theatre auditorium. What we

see (or rather, hear) is a rapid development from the speech of an almost flustered young woman in the first flush of love ("One half of me is yours, the other half yours — / Mine own, I would say. . . ." (16–17)) to the richly metaphorical and syntactically complex language of a woman who has reserves of intellect and dignity which will protect her from anything that the patriarchy and chance combined may impose on her. Portia's speech giving herself "and what is mine" to Bassanio is an elegantly formal acquiescence in the conventions of patriarchal society, an eloquent elaboration of the marriage vows from one who clearly has words at her command. And, that being so, she is not slow to resume actual command—it clearly comes as naturally to her as eloquent speech. Only one of the nine sentences in this final speech is in the indicative mood ("My maid Nerissa and myself meantime / Will live as maids and widows"); the rest are all imperatives reflecting the decisions of a quick-thinking tactician: "First go with me to church, and call me wife, / And then away to Venice to your friend."

What Bassanio makes of Portia's linguistic brilliance is never clear: his great speech of contemplation and choice is, although long, less fresh in figure and less fluid in syntax than Portia's remarkably varied four major speeches. The audience gains little sense of Bassanio's personal development during this momentous choice (e.g. the clichéd blazon with which he addresses "fair Portia's counterfeit"—always a trial for an actor to make in any way convincing). It seems appropriate that his most eloquent and personal speech in the scene should begin "Madam, you have bereft me of all words"; he finds a metaphor to describe the effect of Portia's speech which indicates that even in her apparent ceding of authority she is naturally, effortlessly, authoritative:

> . . . there is such confusion in my powers
> As after some oration fairly spoke
> By a beloved prince . . . (3.2.177–79)

In the courtroom scene, Portia's great piece of rhetoric, the "quality of mercy" speech, is, ironically, a complete failure in its main aim of persuasion. Its underlying cultural assumption is that the audience is Christian— which is "true" of everyone else on the stage and in the original theatre audience. But Shylock, intent on revenge (as he has already informed us in 3.1), is in no state to be persuaded by an argument that concludes

> . . . Therefore, Jew,
> Though justice be thy plea, consider this:
> That in the course of justice, none of us
> Should see salvation. We do pray for mercy,
> And that same prayer doth teach us all to render
> The deeds of mercy. (4.1.193–98)

The prayer is, of course, the "Lord's Prayer" (Matthew 6: 9–13).[2] Portia's lack of experience of the masculine Venetian world is embodied in the collision of her eloquent idealism with the reality of one man's life driven to an extreme position by the unchristian behavior of his neighbors. (This is further demonstrated by the reactions of the Christians as they scent victory in the court scene.)

Whether or not Portia knows the quibbling technicality that can save Antonio when she enters the courtroom will affect the actress's performance of the mercy speech and ultimately the whole scene.[3] But whatever her state of preparedness, her powerful intellectual grasp of the legal issues is demonstrated in the speeches that follow the mercy appeal. These reveal a wholly new aspect of Portia, not evident in the various Belmont scenes, where as I have argued she is eloquent and rhetorically elegant, but lacks the intellectual toughness here on show in the masculine world. She does not lose this on her return to Belmont.

In fact her first speech as she returns carries strong suggestions that she is a symbolic bringer of light (a spiritual and intellectual metaphor) to this still-dark world:

> That light we see is burning in my hall.
> How far that little candle throws his beams!
> So shines a good deed in a naughty world. (5.1.89–91)

Portia has, after all, achieved what none of the powerful and rich men of Venice seemed able to do, saving an innocent man from being violently murdered while the law stood by, helpless. She continues to demonstrate her abilities in forensic debate as she humbles the hapless Bassanio ("If you had known the virtue of the ring . . ." 5.1.199ff.), and issues a series of imperatives based on his apparent failure of marital fidelity:

> Let not that doctor e'er come near my house.
> Since he hath got the jewel that I loved
> And that which you did swear to keep for me,
> I will become as liberal as you.
> I'll not deny him anything I have,
> No, not my body, nor my husband's bed;
> Know him I shall, I am well sure of it.
> Lie not a night from home. Watch me like Argus. (5.1.224–30)

The final demonstration of the heroine's complex power confirms the play's return to romantic comedy, as Portia takes over the author's role and blithely dispenses unlikely final twists to the story.[4] In her production of the letters which clear up all uncertainties, and particularly that which restores to

Antonio his "life and living" with the news that "three of [your] argosies /Are richly come to harbour suddenly," she hints that she is in touch with mysterious forces, which must remain secret—"You shall not know by what strange accident / I chancèd on this letter" (5.1.276–79). Despite her official entry into the status of wife to Bassanio, which implies his possession of all her worldly goods, Portia does not relinquish the intellectual and spiritual power which she displayed in the courtroom scene (nor, for that matter, the seigneurial power—she still speaks of "my house" and welcomes Antonio to it). She here signals that she will *always* be more knowledgeable, and wiser, than the mere males who have got themselves into such a mess in the course of the play, and whom it has been her business to rescue. Portia's last speech, with its pointed use of legal jargon, is a reminder both to the men onstage and to the audience that their patriarchal culture—the "great world"—cannot, in fact, finally control the power of an enterprising and intelligent woman. Seizing the opportunity for action has relieved the "weariness" that she admitted to in her opening lines, and released an energy that is powerfully embodied in effectual speech, an impressive development from the gossipy wit of 1.2.

II. Portia Onstage

Questions and complaints from theater critics about the presence or lack of "femininity" in any *performance* of Portia ignore the play's developmental structure in regard to this character. A tendency to simplify Portia, to assimilate her into a stereotype (whether of fairy-tale imprisoned daughter or modern-day brattish financial princess)[5] is to be observed alike in criticism and in theatrical productions which, in the hands of male directors, channel most of their analytic energy to interpreting the unique and fascinating figure of Shylock, and to a lesser degree to explicating the precise nature of the love between Antonio and Bassanio.

It is only in more recent years that Portia has been admitted to have a "voice" that may in fact oppose the vision of the play's director, if that functionary unthinkingly accepts the play's patriarchal politics. The admirable series of essays by the Royal Shakespeare Company's actors, *Players of Shakespeare,* features essays by actresses in which they reflect from a clearly feminist perspective on the problems of playing Shakespeare's women; Portia is, so far, twice represented as being a role fraught with difficulties for a woman in the latter part of the twentieth century (just as the role of Shylock is now seen as an extraordinary intellectual and emotional challenge in a post-Holocaust world). Later in this essay I will look in detail at Deborah Findlay's and Sinead Cusack's discussions of their experiences of this role, both of them remarkable for taking Portia seriously as a complex woman to whom modern audiences can relate: a far cry from the fairy-tale romantic heroine of the earlier twentieth century.

In fact Portia only became a notable role—and role-model—in the Victorian period. A light comic heroine in the eighteenth century, she matched the comic stage villain of Shylock. For the Victorians, Portia made a 180-degree swerve, to become the embodiment of noble womanhood. Anna Jameson's influential book, *Characteristics of Women, Moral, Poetical, and Historical* (1832), also later published as *Shakespeare's Heroines*, opened with Portia, "a gracious, happy, beloved, and loving creature . . . all the noblest and most lovable qualities that ever met together in a woman . . . this heavenly compound of talent, feeling, wisdom, beauty, gentleness" (67–68).[6] But Jameson was forced to admit that Portia, "placed in this age, and in the actual state of society, would find society arm'd against her . . . firmness would become pride and self-assurance; and the soft, sweet, feminine texture of her mind, settle into rigidity" (95–96).

In performance, as Richard Foulkes has shown, "the two pre-eminent actresses of the Victorian period, Helen Faucit and Ellen Terry," offered contrasting embodiments of this ambivalent figure of the ideal woman. Lesser actresses tended to opt for an unattractive "mannish" performance in the courtroom scene,[7] but Faucit's "mercy" speech found a way of being womanly: performed "with eyes uplifted . . . [she] raised the covering from her head as if in very deed she stood in the divine presence of Him whose attribute of mercy she extolled."[8] Faucit played the whole courtroom scene "as a youth who never for one instant lost her tone of high breeding and earnest sense of the serious nature of the work in hand"; she entered the scene fully apprised of the legal technicality that would save Antonio, but not wishing to discomfit Shylock "until she had found that every appeal to his heart or his avarice was of no avail" (*Blackwood's* in Foulkes 31–32). Faucit was reportedly much less effective in the comic scenes, her witty speeches sounding forced.

Ellen Terry added an end-of-the-century touch of the New Woman to Portia, particularly in her amorousness and humor, while still fulfilling the Victorian role of ideal woman figured as Beauty: wearing a dress of shimmering brocaded gold, she was "A lady gracious and graceful, handsome, witty, loving and wise."[9] In the courtroom scene, she was striking in rose-colored robes, but the disguise was barely sustained: she acted "a woman in love, a woman knowing herself to be loved, and radiant with happiness because of that knowledge."[10] M. M. Mahood comments that "when [Terry] played opposite Irving her conviction that Shylock was a martyr undermined her own performance; she saw Portia's mercy speech as a mere baiting of the trap, and delivered it to charm the stage and house audience rather than to move Shylock" (50–51)—though for her the quibble was a last-minute inspiration after "a series of increasingly desperate appeals to the Jew" (Foulkes 33). Terry herself wrote:

I had considered, and am still of the same mind, that Portia in the trial scene ought to be very *quiet*. I saw an extraordinary effect in this quietness. But as Henry's Shylock was quiet, I had to give it up. His heroic saint was splendid, but it wasn't good for Portia. (Terry 163)

That is, Irving as actor-manager—de facto director—imposed his reading of Portia on an actress who nevertheless managed to make this the role with which she was most identified in the public mind. What might she have done with the role if she had been allowed to do something other than play second fiddle to Irving's tragic hero?[11]

Analysis of the performance of a Shakespearean role in one cultural center can give us an image of how perceptions of the role have changed in response to changes in the society at large. This essay will now focus on performances of Portia in England in the second half of the twentieth century, the period after the massive disruptions of World War Two and the Nazi Holocaust. In 1931, Peggy Ashcroft's combination of nobility, charm, and a decorous wit had set a benchmark for Portia thought of as a romantic heroine—that is, one who inhabits the gender-transgressive and chance-controlled world of Shakepearean comedy, rather than being an accessory to the quasi-tragedy of those productions, like Irving's, that focussed largely on Shylock. Nevertheless a return to eighteenth-century "light comedy" was no longer the way to provide satisfying readings of the play, and particularly of Portia, in a post-Holocaust world.

The first post-war production of *The Merchant of Venice* at Stratford-upon-Avon's Shakespeare Memorial Theatre was Michael Benthall's of 1947–48. Consciously anti-realistic, it seemed determined to ignore the massive changes in the image of Jews and of women brought about by the cataclysmic six years of the war—the advance publicity quoted Benthall's view of the play as a "balletic fantasy." Notwithstanding this decorative impulse (reinforced by designer Sophie Fedorovitch's vivid color schemes), Benthall's first Shylock and Portia were cast unconventionally. John Ruddock was admired for a dignified, unmelodramatic Shylock, although rather lightweight; but Beatrix Lehmann's casting puzzled people. A deep-voiced woman in her forties, with a "strong" stage presence, she gave a brisk, cool Portia which, though obviously intelligent, failed to move audiences. In 1948 Benthall bowed to tradition and recast the roles, with Robert Helpmann as Shylock and the young and beautiful Diana Wynyard making her Shakespearean debut as Portia. Wynyard's Portia was a delightful fulfillment of the fairy-tale fantasy (as was Helpmann's ogre-like Jew). "Enchantingly lovely," "bewitching," "serene," and beautifully matched with a young, romantic, assured Bassanio in Paul Scofield, Wynyard conquered even the hardened critics of the London newspapers. Only the anonymous reviewer of the

Leamington Spa Courier showed some interest in an unconventional and more historical reading: Wynyard was "scarcely the Renaissance great lady whose wit and insight found a way out of the complicated problems in which the mere males had involved themselves" (23 April 1948).

This inkling of a change in the audience's expectations of Portia was developed further in Peggy Ashcroft's 1953 return to Portia, playing opposite Michael Redgrave's greasy, slobbering Jew in a production by Denis Carey. For most critics, drawing on their nostalgia for pre-war glories, Ashcroft was "the quintessence of graciousness," or of "innocence" and transparent sincerity. Even Kenneth Tynan looked no further into Portia's possibilities:

> The jewel of the evening is Peggy Ashcroft's Portia, a creature of exquisite breeding and uncommon sense. She speaks the poetry with the air of a woman who would never commit the social gaffe of reciting in public, with the result that the lines flow out newly minted, as unstrained as the quality of mercy itself. Her handling of the tiresome princelings who come to woo her is an object lesson in wit and good manners; later, in the court-room, we wept at her compassion; and the last act, invariably an anticlimax, bloomed golden at her touch.
> (*Evening Standard*, 20 March 1953)

Nevertheless, in the courtroom there were some daring touches which suggest that Ashcroft might have done more with the image of Portia under the encouragement of a more exploratory director. She was placed in a strong position, on the plinth at the center of a symmetrical semicircle, as her "judgement" began;[12] but as the scene raced to its climax, she became passionately involved in it. W. A. Darlington noted her

> subtle emphasis . . . on the feeling of revulsion with which Shylock filled her. Most Portias are content to turn the tables on Shylock with the triumphantly detached air of a schoolmistress telling the bad boy of his class that he is not going to get away with his nonsense this time. Miss Ashcroft is much too indignant for this to content her. She hurries across and interposes herself, bodily, arms outstretched, between the Jew's knife and the Merchant's breast. (*Daily Telegraph*, 18 March 1953)

This seems a curiously unthinking ("passionate," yes, but stereotypically melodramatic) appropriation of the anti-Semitism which had so recently caused grief and anguish to millions. The English stage, it seems, was still in 1953 a privileged space separate from the concerns of the real world—it was, after all, the Coronation year; romantic fantasy, after the strains of the war, provided welcome relief.

The Shakespeare Memorial Theatre's next production, by Margaret Webster in 1956, continued the deliberate visual prettiness of a "fairy-tale" production: a picture-frame set presenting delicate images of Venice and Belmont, the women costumed in frothy, vaguely Renaissance dresses, the men, according to one critic, looking like "striped sticks of peppermint rock" in their doublets and hose (Alan Dent, *News Chronicle*, 18 April 1956). Webster's production was not feminist, but "feminine," and welcomed as such by the reviewers who noted her gender. Her Portia, the young Australian actress Margaret Johnston making her Shakespearean debut, was pretty, charming, and unexpectedly forceful in the court scene and her masculine dress. The *Sunday Times* reviewer approved her freshness (a reflection perhaps on her colonial origin?), especially in the mercy speech: "She does not treat this effusion as a piece of familiar rhetoric, but as a legal argument new-minted in the brain by a remark of Shylock's. This gives it an unexpected dramatic force" (21 April 1956).

By setting the play clearly in the eighteenth century, Michael Langham, in 1960, was the first director to insist on a precise social context for the whole story. The tide had at last turned for *The Merchant of Venice;* it was now acknowledged as a "problem play," its twin foci being anti-Semitism and money. Desmond Heely's design, variations on an eighteenth-century *capriccio*—lit superbly by Maurice Daniels so that Venice had the air of dark decay, Belmont that of golden light—created a world in which money was paramount. It was a deliberate re-vision of the play, in tune with the new Royal Shakespeare Company's left-liberal agenda.

Against this background walked the characters of eighteenth-century rationalism, in their tight wigs and frock coats (see Figure 13 above). "Poetry" was given short shrift—there were some diehard complaints about Portia's (Dorothy Tutin's) "cleverness" and playing for comedy. A notable moment in the production came when, in the courtroom scene, Shylock finally collapsed: it was Portia who went quietly to his rescue despite the pack of baying Venetians—thus *demonstrating* for the first time the quality of mercy. In spite of her lack of inches, Tutin commanded both at Belmont and in the court, by her energy, humor, and intelligence: an "urchin Portia," the *Observer* (17 April 1960) called her: "sharp-witted and sunny, [who] missed out on the great lady and the submissive virgin"—a loss few regretted. Langham used his eighteenth-century setting to emphasize the play's wit, working with the assumption that this was a culture which expected women of the upper class to be clever.

Something of a backlash meant that there was little that was new in Clifford Williams's production of 1965—his refusal to take a strong directorial interpretative line, and his decision to keep the play's design in the Renaissance period meant that the players tended to fall back on the "fairy-tale" tradition—with two exceptions: Janet Suzman's Portia and the depiction of the relationship between Antonio and Bassanio, overtly homosexual for the first time in an English production.

Portia was Suzman's first major role for the RSC, and she brought to it the strong contemporary woman's presence which her later career capitalized on. According to Milton Shulman (*Evening Standard,* 17 April 1965), her Portia had "an easy intelligent maturity about it which reduces the men she is defending to even more negative ciphers than Shakespeare had already made them." B. A. Young found her lacking in seductiveness, but admitted, "She is, I suppose, just the kind of hard society girl such a Bassanio would fall for, but she is seldom loveable" (*Financial Times,* 17 April 1965). The *Tribune* (23 April 1965), from the opposite political perspective, applauded in Suzman's Portia

> the first appearance in drama of the Shaw heroine, the girl who is both brainy and sexy. Here is an intelligent and strong-minded young woman; Miss Suzman is that all right, and I've never been so near forgetting the absurdity of the imposture at the trial.

This reviewer also found her a witty comedian and a "radiant" lover. The contrast between these two critics suggests that what constitutes the image of an admirable young woman depends on the observer's political position.

In 1970 Jonathan Miller's radical version of *The Merchant,* with Laurence Olivier and Joan Plowright, was produced by London's National Theatre at the Old Vic. Setting the play in late-nineteenth-century Venice, Miller emphasized that both Venice and Belmont were constructions of a plutocracy; the actors, both male and female, swaddled in heavy Victorian costumes, embodied an anally retentive, money dominated society. Romantic love—either between Bassanio and Portia or between Bassanio and Antonio—was well-nigh impossible: Bassanio was simply a charming fortune-hunter, willing to enter into a relationship with anyone for financial gain. For most audiences and reviewers Miller's was a valid and disturbing re–vision of Shakespeare's play, showing the roots of the twentieth-century Holocaust in nineteenth-century capitalism.

Of the trial scene, played in a judge's chambers rather than open court, Miller said,

> I recoiled from the sentimental radiance that actresses bring to Portia's famous mercy speech. I could imagine the speech being delivered in a much more argumentative and impatient way, in response to the apparent stupidity of Shylock's enquiry. . . . In my mind's eye I saw Portia leaning impatiently across the table . . . as if having laboriously to explain what should have been self-evident to someone too stupid to understand. (Miller 107)

Fortunately the television version of this production, made in 1973, allows a later generation to see the effectiveness of Joan Plowright's radical performance of this moment in the play. Neither radiant nor sentimental,

Plowright's Portia belongs to a realistically-represented world—the late nineteenth century—in which it will soon be possible for women to display just such forensic and rhetorical skills in a public court.

However, for the young Terry Hands at the RSC in 1971, Miller's production was an intolerably weighty precursor, and he retreated to a romantic view of the comedy. This at least was an intellectual, structuralist reading of the fairy tale: Venice and Belmont were contrasted, according to the program's quotation from John Russell Brown: "the wealthy, generous, and prosperous transactions of love's wealth are compared and contrasted with Shylock's wholly commercial transactions in which gain is the object, enforcement the method, and even human beings are merely things to be possessed." The caskets were huge: a gold sarcophagus, a silver box, a leaden coffin containing a life-size effigy of Portia. Timothy O'Brien's set contrasted the reflecting gold of Venice with a Belmont all hazy blues, and showered in gold leaves. Audiences were delighted by the production, in particular enjoying the ardent romantic playing of the newly-married Judi Dench and Michael Williams as Portia and Bassanio (Figure 14). Despite her stated dislike of the role, Dench managed to invent a tender and moving Portia: "when disguised as the young lawyer her pale strained face and pure diction suddenly command and receive both awe and respect" (John Barber, *Daily Telegraph*, 31 March 1971). Others commented on the comic ability she brought to the Belmont scenes, especially with Polly James as Nerissa; but there was a general feeling that the "two Portias" were not connected.[13] Susan Fleetwood took over the role when the production moved to London in 1972, and according to John Barber, she

> found a link between the ardent lady of Belmont and the stern lawyer at the trial. It is, simply, passion. In love, her heart heaves to her mouth and she seems vulnerable and exposed. The "quality of mercy" speech is not the usual sermon but a blaze of angry feeling. She ends by cutting through all the clichés and showing a Portia who can match the Jew in venom and give him lessons in cruelty. (*Daily Telegraph*, 23 June 1972)

Tension was further increased by the fact that Portia did not discover the flaw in the bond until Shylock was (it seemed) actually beginning to slice Antonio's flesh, allowing the audience a glimpse of the dark impulses behind comedy's daylight. The "games" that followed the courtroom scene had the air of joyous, perhaps somewhat hysterical liberation from an intolerable threat. Like the romanticism of the post-war productions, this was perhaps a subliminal sign of the ever-present anxieties produced by the Cold War.

III. Portia in the Later Twentieth Century

In 1978 John Barton undertook a small-scale production of *The Merchant* in The Other Place at Stratford: its admired experiments were to blossom in his

Figure 14. Bassanio (Michael Williams) and Portia (Judi Dench) in the 1971 Royal Shakespeare
Company production. John Brooke, The Shakespeare Centre Library, Stratford-upon-Avon.

main-stage production three years later. Following Miller's cue, he set the
play in the nineteenth century, though with considerably less realistic detail,
which some found confusing. Why the nineteenth century? The answer is
partly that this period setting provided an easily recognizable image (as with
Miller) of bourgeois wealth in an overtly patriarchal society, in which daughters are marketable possessions. This was made particularly pointed in the
1981 production, which revealed Portia (Sinead Cusack) in 1.2 huddled mis-
erably in front of the caskets, wrapped in her father's old coat; for the actual
casket scenes, she was ritually "tied" with a rope of gold, silver, and lead.
Barton was concerned to "re-balance" the play, in response to new feminist
criticism, in favor of Portia. According to Anne Barton's program essay, "it is
only Portia . . . who can rescue Venice from its dilemma. She does so by
demonstrating the inadequacy of Shylock's attitudes to protect even the man
who believes in them."

Cusack played a serious Portia (she herself thought in retrospect that she
"wasn't quite witty enough, nor sure nor light enough in touch in [the] last
scenes" [40]); greater weight was thus placed on Portia's oppressed situation—"the behaviour of her comic suitors puts her through a purgatorial
ordeal of silent, painful waiting which tends to hold laughter at bay" (John

Barber, *Daily Telegraph*, 22 April 1981). If this was a fairy-tale lady, she inhabited Grimm's proto-Freudian world rather than the Perrault-prettiness of Stratford's earlier productions. Cusack played her as one "unschooled in the social ways of men and the world, and awkward in her relationship with Bassanio" (Cusack 34); her other suitors were repellently phallic males who pawed at her. Emphasizing her isolation, she herself sang "Tell me where is fancy bred" as an unaccompanied folk song (the song, signalling Portia's spiritual authority, was repeated by the whole cast in chorus at the end of the play); and as Bassanio chose the right casket, she "breaks out of the terrible prison her father's love has built for her" (36): "I pick up those wretched boxes, which have threatened me for so long, and I fling them violently across the room" (37). At last, Michael Coveney commented,

> this Portia comes alive, dropping her inhibitions with her grey cloak and, turning on Bassanio, blossoming as an ecstatic vision in primrose. The liberation of Portia continues through the court scene, where Miss Cusack's lawyer is less an impersonation than a revelation of her true crop-haired self. In the exchanging of the rings she asserts her independence, for Bassanio now sees he is married to a woman of wit, steadfastness and resource. (*Financial Times*, 22 April 1981)

Cusack's Portia played the courtroom scene as one who was confident in her forensic skills, not a girl with a sudden instinctive flash of inspiration:

> I decided that when I entered the courtroom I knew exactly how to save Antonio; my cousin had shown me that loophole in the law which would save him from his bond. A lot of people ask why then does she play cat-and-mouse with Shylock. The reason is that she doesn't go into the courtroom to save Antonio (that's easy) but to save Shylock, to redeem him—she is passionate to do that. She gives him opportunity after opportunity to relent and to exercise his humanity. She proposes mercy and charity but he still craves the law. She offers him thrice his money but he sticks to his oath. It is only when he shows himself totally ruthless and intractable (refusing even to allow a surgeon to stand by) that she offers him more justice than he deserves. (39)

Irving Wardle was relieved to report (*Times*, 22 April 1981) that "There is no trace of the bitch or the boss lady" (terminology which offensively replicates Victorian critics' anti-feminism) in Cusack's consistently-developed Portia. This was an accusation which Barton's previous Portia, Marjorie Bland, did not escape, nor did Frances Tomelty's Portia for John Caird's 1984 RSC production. Tomelty's Portia was a strong, severe, not particularly young woman, clearly chafing at her father's postmortem rule; "She comes into her own at the trial scene, which she handles with cold, fearsome efficiency. [Ian McDiarmid's] Shylock is hardly a match for her" (Irving Wardle, *Times*, 11 April 1984). Wardle found her "a confident insensitive bachelor girl who finally takes vengeful pleasure in making Bassanio squirm over the lost ring. Anything less like a woman in love or a girl reluctantly bound to the will of a dead father it would be hard to imagine."

Jack Tinker, heading his review with the catch-cry of the early 1980s, "Monetarism rules in Venice—OK," commented,

> suddenly I recognised everyone in sight . . . We are right here and now. Monetarism is obviously the order of the day. Bassanio is surely Mark Thatcher getting rich. If I had to choose a performance which sets the tone of this faithful and rich production it would be Frances Tomelty's high-handed Portia. A cross between the intellectual adroitness of Germaine Greer and the female instincts of Christina Onassis, Miss Tomelty dominates the stage from first to last. . . . A child of her time in a production of this era. (*Daily Mail*, 11 April 1984)

No other critic recognized these allusions, however; they were distracted no doubt by the production's nightmarish Victorian Gothic version of the Renaissance: an overdetermined "design solution" to the perceived ideological problems of the play.

This was not the case with Bill Alexander's production for the RSC in 1987, which presented a play about racism in a society which considers itself composed of an elite and its outsiders. It was set in the Shakespearean period. Despite Alexander's argument that "All the themes of the play—justice, mercy, the law, revenge, money, love and how they relate to all those things—are thrown off centre if you try to find an analogical social context" (Alexander in Berry 181), Kit Surrey's single set evoked not Jacobean London or Venice, but a crumbling city of any period in the last millennium of Western civilization; on the back wall, next to a Christian icon of the Madonna, was a daubed yellow Star of David. The association of this image with twentieth-century anti-Semitism was unavoidable: we might have been in Hamburg, or Warsaw, or Lyon.

All the reviewers commented on the striking recuperation of the play, the seriousness with which Alexander treated it as an exploration of the driving forces of our "civilization." Complaints from those who yearned for poetry or romance were very few. Both Antony Sher's Shylock and Deborah Findlay's Portia were implicated in the play's discourse of racism—there was no separation between Venice and Belmont. The whole of Venetian Christian elitist society was shown to be thus tainted. Deborah Findlay as Portia casually but maliciously hit her servant, and listened to Nerissa's xenophobic description of the suitors with obvious distaste for them; John Peter noted that "she visibly shudders when Morocco touches her" (*Sunday Times*, 3 May 1987). Findlay's acting of the erstwhile romantic heroine astonished some critics, even while they acknowledged the coherence of her performance within Alexander's production. John Peter thought her "bossy, dully energetic and determined . . . [she] misses the ironical treatment of romantic feeling"—that which would still allow Portia some charm; but other critics realized that charm was not a necessary part of this Portia's armory. Michael Coveney found her

> a stuck-up daddy's girl, the first really I have seen, whose pious application of the law as the disguised Balthasar is even more insufferable than the banality and smut she articulates elsewhere. I salute Ms Findlay in rendering Portia as nasty as she ought to be but so rarely is. (*Financial Times*, 30 April 1987)

"Would such a tough Portia know much about the quality of mercy?" asked another critic. In fact she delivered the speech with reason and passion, as though it were an ideal to be evoked when appropriate, but as the scene built up to a hysterical pitch led by Shylock, Portia's reason was overtaken by the prevailing ugly passion, and her interruption "Tarry a little" was violently excited—the prospect of victory. Bill Alexander commented:

> Some people objected to the way I saw Portia, feeling she should be shown as just beautiful, gracious, poetic and brave, but I felt that was sentimentality. People want heroines out of Mills and Boon rather than real people and I really liked the Portia in my production. She was part of that corrupt world of Venetian society, and even if she did live out in the country it didn't make her a paragon of virtue. She's brave but also a nuisance. Brave people are often quite unpleasant in real life and nice people are not at all brave. (Alexander in Cook 67)

Here we can see the final shift in category for the play, post-Miller, from the "fairy-tale" concept of the fifties to a naturalistic model explaining the behavior of all the characters. Deborah Findlay, however, "came to feel that [she] was in a production which ultimately misplaced and undervalued her role in the play":

> It was my ambition to catch some of this [Elizabethan] full-bloodedness and for us all to embrace characters who could hate and love, and feel joy and sorrow, passionately. It takes great generosity of spirit to do this and I fear too often we slipped into violence and harshness in the attempt. (Findlay 52–53)

Findlay's perception of the role was, simply, at odds with the stern critique of racism that was Alexander's agenda. As an experienced actress she felt that she had a right to the part, that it had an essence which she had intuited:

> Portia . . . is never mean. Any choice you make about motivation for this
> character has to be made with all the generosity of spirit that you can
> muster. She is as loving, as intelligent, as witty, as brave, as compassionate,
> as everything as you can make her. (56)

Who is right here? The actress who with all her talent, training, and
experience undertakes the part and inhabits it as it makes sense to her, or the
director whose vision of the whole play necessitates a re-vision of the heroine? There is of course no simple answer, though the problem is peculiar to
the twentieth century and the age of the director. Findlay eventually worked
out an accommodation of her conception of the role with Alexander's
fiercely critical reading of the play:

> [In court] she sees the violent world of men from a different angle and as a
> man can teach these men how they should behave. So my judge was not a
> shrouded clerk but a confident raunchy boy. Because her life has turned to
> happiness she believes in the power of mercy and that people do behave
> decently towards each other. The mercy speech is thus an act of faith. How
> prepared is she when she comes into court? This was an area that I changed
> completely in performance and is the most telling example of underselling
> Portia in rehearsal. . . .
>
>   I thought at first that she got drawn into the violence of the scene and
> proved to be more vindictive than any of them. . . . as I got to know Portia
> better I realized that this was to undervalue her. I think now that she *does*
> have all the alternatives when she comes into the trial. Rather than being fed
> the solution by Shylock *she* runs the scene. . . . (62–64)

On the mercy speech, Findlay comments, with a revealing metaphor ("not
man enough"),

> Hers is an act of strict impartiality, explaining the law to everyone present.
> If you reject human mercy then there is only the implacable face of justice
> to fall back on. . . . I had to shout the first line and deliver the speech in a
> more aggressive fashion than I think it merits, but the company was hooked
> on the dramatic tension and I was not man enough to cut this away. What I
> tried to do was to portray that notion of teaching and impartiality as much
> as I could within the existing structure.
>
>   I felt increasingly that the outcome saddened her. It isn't a pleasant
> victory. (64)

Alexander's stern revision of the play's romance towards realism
undoubtedly influenced RSC orthodoxy. The company's next production, by
David Thacker in 1993, took the play into the modern corporate world—the
RSC's first ever modern-dress production of the play.[14] The set was a two-
level high-tech office, complete with computers, faxes, and mobile phones,

gleaming glass, and chrome. "Belmont" was established by dropping in front of this a large Japanese-style screen wall of opaque glass barred with rectangular panes which at times created the effect of a prison rather than a place of Zen-like calm (though Gary Yershon's music insisted on a contrast between the two places: techno-disco for Venice, "heavenly harmony" for Belmont). The effect was to suggest that (as with Alexander) Belmont's gracious luxury could not be detached from the rapacious world of the stock exchange on which it depended. Traditionalists among the critics did not care for the design (by Shelagh Kegan), claiming that the "poetry" and folktale quality of the play were lost, and, perhaps more pertinently, that the conditions of modern business life and law would never have allowed Antonio's ships to venture uninsured or Shylock to demand his pound of flesh (the fact that the latter condition would have been equally unacceptable in the world of sixteenth-century commerce in which the play is traditionally set is conveniently ignored in this complaint).

David Calder's assimilated and sympathetic Jew for many critics dominated Thacker's production, but Penny Downie's Portia drew favorable comment also. She was a woman in her thirties, impatient at her imprisonment, leaning wearily against the lead casket at the end of Aragon's scene. She was polite and compassionate to the elegant and civilized Morocco ("Let all of his complexion" was cut), and, in the scenes of Bassanio's wooing, passionate and excited with Owen Teale's Bassanio. Some rearrangements of speeches in 3.2 and 3.4 gave Portia a commanding position once she was released from her father's posthumous constraint: she ended 3.2 with the energetically-spoken lines

> My maid Nerissa and myself meantime
> Will live as maids and widows. Come away,
> For you shall hence upon your wedding day!

The impression of Portia's determination and abundant energy increased in 3.4: Lorenzo's opening lines and much of the pious speech "I never did repent for doing good" were cut, and the emphasis was on activity. Nerissa was haled into action with a loud "Come on Nerissa! I have work in hand" as Portia, in red business suit, grabbed her briefcase—her new identity and sense of autonomy strongly evident.

Downie carried this energy, both vocal and physical, through into the courtroom scene, which consequently seemed anything but a foregone conclusion. Her "mercy" speech began as an intimate address to Shylock, then rose to a passionate exhortation to all hearers; "*None* of us should see salvation," with an expansive gesture, did not discriminate between Christian and Jew. "*You*! Merchant! have you anything to say?" put Antonio as much on trial as Shylock before this intense young judge. But as he dissolved into panic (the realistic modern man rather than the Renaissance paragon his speech suggests), Portia remained still and distant, clearly expecting Shylock to respect the moral authority she embodied. She seemed impatient with his refusal to show mercy, and spent the time of Antonio's speech checking the bond document to ratify her next move. "Tarry a little" was low, fast, and authoritative, rising to a crescendo. Every time Portia spoke the word "mercy" from here until the end of the scene it was emphasized, almost pedantically. In keeping with her image of moral authority, she never addressed Shylock with the contemptuous sobriquet "Jew" of the script. Distressed by his final "I am content," she left the room at that point, and her gravity was maintained when Bassanio's ring was forced upon her. The final scene, consequently, had an undercurrent of toughness as Portia directed the comic resolution—a reading which was taken considerably further with the two more recent modern-dress productions which I discuss below.

Downie's Portia was characterized by a recognizably modern feminist intelligence which was able to speak with authority and confidence in a world hitherto ruled by men. The play became, in this production, as much Portia's discovery of her own potential to direct affairs (signified by the brief-case and business dress of her arrival home), as it remained a modern Jew's tragedy. Critics commented on Downie's "intense and watchful Portia" (Maureen Paton, *Daily Express*, 9 April 1994); her "sense of wit and breeding" (Robert Hanks, *Independent*, 11 April 1994). But audiences were left with a sense of discomfort rather than triumphant reconciliation at the play's end. Thacker's production, undercutting Portia's romantic charisma, offered a reading of the play that reminded audiences of the power of money in the modern world and showed a young woman who, for all her passion and energy, found it difficult to escape the tentacles of this global monster.

Following her modern-dress production of *The Taming of the Shrew* at the West Yorkshire Playhouse in 1993, Jude Kelly directed her Katherine, Nichola McAuliffe, as Portia in a similarly radical *Merchant of Venice* in 1994. An older Portia than most, McAuliffe had a stage presence and authority that insisted that Portia's story be attended to. The production was set in the early twentieth century, thus enabling a nuancing of the play towards, on the one hand, nascent fascist anti-Semitism, and on the other, the issues faced by the New Woman of the turn of the century.

McAuliffe's Portia opened her first scene as a version of a deeply world-weary Hedda Gabler, playing Russian roulette with a pistol before shooting it at the portrait of her father the judge which dominated the stage. "[S]he is filled with disdain for lesser mortals and for herself. . . . She has the same ruthless streak as her adversary, the same grim determination" (Richard Wilcocks, *Plays & Players*, April 1994). "She can still be Portia the great lady and Portia the dangerous wit . . . but she achieves that poise only on the brink of despair. And she learns that her father is not the only man whose wishes will confront hers" (Alastair Macaulay, *Financial Times*, 26 March 1994). McAuliffe's own perception of the role matched this:

> a woman with a certain arrogance, the daughter of a lawyer . . . an efficient organiser of her household, who is seldom challenged. . . . One of the images that came to me is of Christina Onassis, who in some ways was incredibly gauche and naive and in others incredibly astute. She was her father's daughter, like Portia.
>
> (McAuliffe interviewed by Lynne Greenwood, *Daily Telegraph*, 11 March 1994)

Reviewer Timothy Ramsden commented, "Her need to shape up to him is seen just before the interval as she holds out the marriage contract [to her father's portrait], as if saying 'Will this do you?' " (*Times Educational Supplement*, 15 April 1994).

Jude Kelly saw the play as dealing with "the tragedy of Portia" as well as the issues of racism, revenge, and mercy centering on Shylock:

> Portia's journey is crucial—she is wooed as an heiress by a young man who needs the cash; turns up in a courtroom to discover that the man she's affianced to is saying that although he has a wife he'd rather give her up for a man; is witness to a shocking degree of anti-Semitism from other characters; and finally administers justice with no mercy having pleaded for it as a quality that is higher than all others. It's a rude awakening for her about what the real world is like and who she is within it. I think she regrets her cruelty to Shylock. There are lots of references in the play before the fifth act to Portia roaming about, praying by holy crosses for a happy marriage accompanied by no-one save her maid and a holy hermit. She's in a state of grieving for what she has experienced. (Interview, program)

During the courtroom scene, she had dragged the "sobbing and raving" Antonio from Bassanio's "lingering embrace" (Richard Wilcocks, *Plays & Players*, April 1994) and then shown "a spasm of malice" against Antonio, urging Shylock "Prepare thee to cut off the flesh," even after Antonio had thought himself saved. This critic found her "quality of mercy" speech to be "just formal and clever: she is merciless in this place where the winner takes all, and yet is made more thoughtful, perhaps more humane, by her experiences." Aghast and on the edge of despair when Bassanio sends the ring to the young judge ("as if to initiate her into their gay mafia"), in the fifth act, as Alastair Macaulay recorded (*Financial Times*, 26 March 1994), "she confronts Bassanio . . . with real rage and heartbreak at his perfidy." Moments earlier she had coldly greeted Antonio, and placed herself between him and her husband, wrapping Bassanio's arms around her. Thus her final welcoming of Antonio into her home in the last minutes of the play was a hard-won defeat of her own intransigence. "The fifth act," said Jude Kelly, "is all about the tragedy of Portia revealing to Bassanio what she knows. In the end it's 'We'll discuss it,' but can they move forward or not? Because they have destroyed *so much*" (Schafer 122).

Several critics commented that the production, which also featured a complex and sympathetic Shylock from Gary Waldhorn and a cast of extras from the Leeds Jewish community creating a powerful image of the ghetto, put Jude Kelly in the front rank of Shakespearean directors. This is an unusual achievement still for a woman in British theater, and one might hazard that her decision consciously to use a feminist perspective contributed to the power and freshness of her vision of the play: "as a woman director," she says, "I am likely to be reading a piece of material and considering how the women in that material are dealing with the world and I will judge whether the playwright has understood how women may have felt about the world" (Kelly in Schafer 45).

It is arguable that Kelly's re-vision of the play, especially her reemphasizing of Portia's story, had a significant influence on Trevor Nunn's equally praised production for the Royal National Theatre in 1999. The period setting was similar, though more precisely placed in the late 1920s to mid-1930s. This was a decadent Venetian society with more than a whiff of Berlin: the masquing scene, for example, took place in an Isherwood-like cabaret, in which Launcelot Gobbo's Conscience and the Devil monologue became an anti-Semitic stand-up piece. Derbhle Crotty's Portia was no self-destructive Hedda Gabler, however, but a bored socialite who discovered her true métier in the course of her adventure into this seedy world.

For the casket scenes Portia, in black evening dress, knelt on a hassock center stage like a sacrificial victim—or at the very least an expensive commodity on show, utterly at the mercy of the suitors' choice. She was clearly attracted to the charming Morocco, and upset when he failed. Before he left they embraced, and her line "Let all of his complexion choose me so" was delivered as a face-saving throwaway as she struggled to regain her composure. With Bassanio (Alexander Hanson) she was even more emotional, begging him not to choose yet on "I pray you tarry," and wringing her hands in prayer as he surveyed the caskets. When at last they embraced and kissed it was clear that Portia had fallen profoundly in love; Bassanio, boyishly, seemed unable to believe his luck.

The courtroom scene then developed as a series of emotional shocks for Crotty's Portia. Beginning confidently, she took a chair and sat close to Shylock to reason with him on the quality of mercy. Shylock (Henry Goodman) seemed on the verge of being convinced by her eloquence: there was a long, tense silence before he declared "My deeds upon my head!" Portia appeared to have played her one card and lost; during the next sequence of events she was staring at the bond with obvious increasing distress and anxiety. Bassanio's offer to sacrifice his wife added to her dismay (neither his line nor Portia's "Your wife would give you little thanks for that" was played for comedy). As Antonio's death seemed inevitable, Crotty's sudden "Tarry a little" exploded into the palpable tension in both court and theater. Having discovered the last-minute quibble, she became very authoritative as she instructed Shylock to "beg mercy of the Duke." But this dominance was not to last: as the triumphant men began their punitive revenge on Shylock, Portia became increasingly horrified. She knelt solicitously before him on "Art thou contented?" (dropping the "Jew"); and was clearly shaken by Shylock's gesture of placing his yarmulke and tallith in the scales. She spoke coldly to Antonio, and was still obviously distressed in the next scene. Bassanio's sending the ring to the "young judge" was the last straw—"It cannot be!" she cried, trying to refuse it, as Gratiano forced it into her pocket.

The return to Belmont was far from a comic resolution: Jessica (Gabrielle Jourdan) was weeping as Beethoven's "Moonlight" Sonata reminded her of what she and, by metonymy, all her race, had lost: unfettered access to a civilized life. When Portia and Nerissa arrived, they gently danced together to the music, happy to have left what Portia called the "naughty world" of male society. Bassanio and Antonio's arrival brought back all her anxiety and tension, and her "If you did know the virtue of the ring" was angry and hurt. In the play's final moments Crotty and Hanson remained separate, he downstage with his friends, she center stage, judgmental. They looked at each other warily as Nerissa and Gratiano spoke their bantering lines and left the stage. As Jessica sadly sang the Hebrew song she had earlier practiced with her father, Portia and Bassanio moved closer together, soberly realizing that they had to face a far from romantic life together. Portia's lines from the earlier part of the scene were moved here to give her a last speech, one that reasserted her moral authority but also indicated her sense of its ineffectuality in the face of the coming Holocaust:

> This night methinks is but the daylight sick,
> It looks a little paler; 'tis a day
> Such as the day is when the sun is hid.

After a pause, she added "It is almost morning," cueing birdsong and then a rumble of thunder, and the lights went down to end this twentieth-century tale of man's inhumanity to man, and the inability of women—even highly intelligent and determined women—to do anything to prevent it.

A feminist critic has observed that "[d]irectors and their male stars wrestle with the problem of Shylock for a whole host of politically laudable reasons, but they often still do so within structures that make it all too easy to forget who has the most lines."[15] The history of the twentieth century has forced all intellectually honest directors to reassess the role of Shylock, and some, like Barton, Nunn, and Kelly, to reexamine Portia's story. The question now remains whether directors will be able to avoid the temptation to return to a simplistic image of Portia that has no connection with the reality of women's lives in the western world on the cusp of the twenty-first century. The performers of Portia are certainly ready to seize the power that her lines offer.[16]

Notes

1. "Portia and Nerissa's talk apparently helps to resolve the heroine's ambivalent feelings towards the role she as a woman can play in the patriarchal society of the play. . . . [B]ecause Nerissa takes up the defense of Portia's dead father's edict . . . the waiting-woman does become a kind of antagonist against whom Portia can realize her frustrations" (Haslam 130–31).

2. "Portia is unable to guarantee that his offer of mercy to Antonio will elicit any favor from the Christians: all that Shylock's granting of mercy will do is bless him (4.1.183), prove him to be mighty (184), and potentially grant him salvation in a heaven not his own (196)." I am grateful to William Brilliant for this observation and other close readings of the rhetoric in this scene (Honors dissertation 1999, Sydney University, 43).

3. If Portia is aware of the technicality, and therefore deliberately "choreographing" the whole scene, "then the 'quality of mercy' speech is no longer a critical persuasive plea, but rather becomes an offer to Shylock, granting him the choice to save himself. . . . Portia is offering him a chance of escape, even if she does not persuade him of its virtues or forewarn him of the dangers that lie in rejecting her offer" (Brilliant 44).

4. Considered by the criteria of realistic drama, this moment is absurd: "Like Antonio, we are dumb, and can only admire Shakespeare's impertinence. We 'shall not know,' either, what easy morality overtook Portia, prompting her to read a letter not addressed to her (and then to seal it again), let alone how she came to pick it up, or why Antonio's fortunes should be so opportunely mended" (Slater 179–80). Such authorial "impertinence" is typical of the genre of romance.

5. Even actresses succumb to the temptation to register dislike or irritation with various of these stereotypes of Portia. Judi Dench: "How dare she behave so churlishly over that ring at the end? That's so petty—and boring." Janet Suzman, despite her own strong feminism (which was probably less conscious when she played Portia), thought herself "a very bad Portia. But then I can't stand Portia. . . . She's so po-faced—that awful recognition-scene and the casket-scenes. Awful to play. But it begins to pick up when she goes to Venice" (Pitt 205, 218).

6. Julie Hankey, in an important revisionist article, argues that "Portia upset the crystallizing categories of gender" for Victorians through being perceived as "mannish" (i.e. unashamedly intellectual): "Women writers needed to tread carefully . . . they had internalized the feminine ideal, at least in part, and needed some subterfuge to do justice, as they saw it, to Portia without disturbing that ideal" (433–34).

7. Hankey (433) quotes William Winter's dislike of Portia played by "heavy formidable females, unlovely, unromantic, hard, cold, practical, matter-of-fact,

some of them provided with the stalwart legs of a piano and the booming voice of a trombone" (*Shakespeare on the Stage* [1911]).

8. Hankey (447) quoting *Blackwood's Magazine* (Dec. 1885, 741–60).

9. F. J. Furnivall, quoted in Gross (135). Henry James's critique was somewhat less enchanted: "Miss Terry's Lady of Belmont giggles too much, plays too much with her fingers, is too free and familiar, too osculatory, in her relations with Bassanio. . . . When Bassanio has chosen the casket which contains the key of her heart, she approaches him, and begins to pat and stroke him . . ." (quoted in Richards, 119).

10. Winter, *Shakespeare on the Stage*, quoted in Hankey (445); he thoroughly approved Terry's breaking with the tradition of "masculinity and declamation."

11. Further discussion of the Victorian ideological dilemma regarding Portia can be found in Linda Rozmovits, "Portia: the White Woman's Burden" (*Shakespeare and the Politics of Culture*, 31–58). Rozmovits makes the important point that "it was not Portia's proverbial appeal to 'the quality of mercy' but her betrothal speech to Bassanio which conveyed a sense of the heroine's exemplary femininity" (48)—"In short, here was a woman who had it all and was, nevertheless, willing to give it up once she had found the right man" (51). Thus, 3.2 was "the moral center of the play . . . [but] the surety with which people pointed to the betrothal speech was more than matched by the anxieties they betrayed about other aspects of the text" (51–52).

12. Mahood (51) notes that Ashcroft's Portia "had studied her case."

13. See note 5 for Dench's antipathy to the role.

14. Other companies had made the connection between sixteenth-century Venice and the modern world of high finance before this: the Bell Shakespeare Company of Australia, for example, in 1991–92 presented a designer-clad Portia, quite at home in Venice; Nerissa took notes in the court on a laptop computer.

15. Rosemary Gaby, "Performing Portia: Company Politics and the Comic Heroine," unpublished paper presented at the Australia and New Zealand Shakespeare Association conference, Brisbane, 1998. I am indebted to Gaby's paper for drawing my attention to the central significance of this issue in assessing the stage history of Portia.

16. Richard Olivier's production of *The Merchant of Venice* for the new Globe in Southwark in 1998 is dealt with elsewhere in this volume. However, it is worth commenting that Kathryn Pogson's Portia was considered by many to be the outstanding performance in this Renaissance-costumed production. Critics spoke of the tall Pogson's presence, her authority in every scene, and her excellent verse-speaking. The epithet "slightly old-fashioned" was also used of her performance—the implied contrast being with the productions I have described that moved the play into a more modern era.

Works Cited

Berry, Ralph. *On Directing Shakespeare*. London: Hamish Hamilton, 1989.

Cook, Judith. *Director's Theatre*. London: Hodder and Stoughton, 1989.

Cusack, Sinead. "Portia in *The Merchant of Venice*." *Players of Shakespeare*. Ed. Philip Brockbank. Cambridge: Cambridge University Press, 1985. 29–40.

Findlay, Deborah. "Portia in *The Merchant of Venice*." *Players of Shakespeare 3*. Eds. Russell Jackson and Robert Smallwood. Cambridge: Cambridge University Press, 1993. 52–67.

Foulkes, Richard. "Helen Faucit and Ellen Terry as Portia." *Theatre Notebook*, 31 (1977): 27–37.

Gross, John. *Shylock: Four Hundred Years in the Life of a Legend*. London: Chatto & Windus, 1993.

Hankey, Julie. "Victorian Portias: Shakespeare's Borderline Heroine." *Shakespeare Quarterly*, 45 (1994): 426–48.

Haslam, Lori Schroeder. " 'O Me, the Word Choose!': Female Voice and Catechetical Ritual in *The Two Gentlemen of Verona* and *The Merchant of Venice*." *Shakespeare Studies*, XXII (1994): 122–40.

Jameson, Anna. *Characteristics of Women, Moral, Poetical, and Historical*. London: George Routledge and Sons, 1870 (1832).

Miller, Jonathan. *Subsequent Performances*. London: Faber and Faber, 1986.

Pitt, Angela. *Shakespeare's Women*. Newton Abbott: David & Charles, 1981.

Richards, Sandra. *The Rise of the English Actress*. London: Macmillan, 1993.

Rozmovits, Linda. *Shakespeare and the Politics of Culture in Late Victorian England*. Baltimore and London: Johns Hopkins University Press, 1998.

Schafer, Elizabeth. *Ms-Directing Shakespeare*. London: The Women's Press, 1998.

Shakespeare, William. *The Merchant of Venice*. Ed. M. M. Mahood. Cambridge: Cambridge University Press, 1984.

Slater, Ann Pasternak. *Shakespeare the Director*. Brighton: Harvester Press, 1982.

Terry, Ellen. *The Story of My Life*. London: Hutchinson & Co., 1908.

Notes on the Contributors

Corinne S. Abate has published articles on *Henry V, Paradise Lost,* and John Ford's *Perkin Warbeck*. She holds a doctorate from New York University and teaches at The Morristown-Beard School in New Jersey.

John F. Andrews, former editor of *Shakespeare Quarterly*, is President of the Shakespeare Guild. Among his many publications, he has edited the plays, including *The Merchant of Venice,* for the Everyman Shakespeare.

John Cunningham is Professor of English at Hollins College in Roanoke, VA. In addition to articles on subjects ranging from *King Lear* to *A Handful of Dust*, he has published *The Poetics of Byron's Comedy in "Don Juan."*

R. W. Desai, author of *Yeats's Shakespeare* and editor of *Hamlet Studies,* is a retired Professor of English from the University of Delhi, India.

John Drakakis is Professor of English Studies at the University of Stirling in Scotland. He is currently completing an edition of *The Merchant of Venice* for the Arden 3 Series, and is the general editor of the Routledge New Critical Idiom Series.

Gayle Gaskill is Professor and Chair of the English Department at the College of St. Catherine in St. Paul, MN. Her recent publications include essays on *A Midsummer Night's Dream* and *Much Ado About Nothing*. Gaskill has been a frequent lecturer at the McMaster University Seminars in Shakespeare and Theater in Stratford, Ontario.

Penny Gay is Head of Department and Associate Professor of English at the University of Sydney, Australia. Her published work includes *As She Likes It: Shakespeare's Unruly Women* and *Shakespeare's "As You Like It."*

John K. Hale teaches English at the University of Otago, New Zealand. His books include *The Shakespeare of the Comedies: A Multiple Approach*.

Jay L. Halio is Professor of English at the University of Delaware. He is the editor of *The Merchant of Venice* for Oxford University Press, and completed a casebook on historical contexts of the play for Greenwood Press.

Joan Ozark Holmer, Professor of English at Georgetown University in Washington, D.C., includes among her publications *"The Merchant of Venice": Choice, Hazard, and Consequence,* as well as articles on Shakespeare, Milton, Nashe, and others.

Maryellen Keefe, O.S.U., teaches English at Iona College and is completing a doctoral dissertation at the University of Delaware.

Murray J. Levith is Professor of English at Skidmore College in Saratoga Springs, NY. His books on Shakespeare include *What's In Shakespeare's Names* and *Shakespeare's Italian Settings and Plays.*

Ellen Macleod Mahon, who has published articles on modern literature as well as Shakespeare, is Connecticut Director of EPS, an adult education program sponsored by Trinity College, Washington, D.C. She is also Adjunct Associate Professor of English at Iona College.

John W. Mahon, co-editor of *The Shakespeare Newsletter,* is Professor of English at Iona College. He edited, with Thomas Pendleton, *"Fanned and Winnowed Opinions": Shakespearean Essays Presented to Harold Jenkins.*

John O'Connor, a freelance writer who prepares editions of various texts, including Shakespeare's plays, for students in secondary schools, is also a part-time tutor for the Oxford University Department for Continuing Education in Oxford, England.

Hugh Short is Associate Professor of English at Iona College.

Stephen Slimp is an Associate Professor of English at the University of West Alabama in Livingston, AL.

Karoline Szatek earned her Ph.D. at Indiana University of Pennsylvania and currently teaches English at the University of Massachusetts, Dartmouth. She is an Associate Editor of *The Shakespeare Newsletter.*

Grace Tiffany, who has published *Erotic Beasts and Social Monsters: Shakespeare, Jonson, and Comic Androgyny,* is Associate Professor of English at Western Michigan University in Kalamazoo, MI.

John W. Velz, Professor Emeritus of English at the University of Texas, Austin, has published widely on Shakespeare's background in the classics, including two recent articles on Shakespeare and Ovid. His *Shakespeare and the Classical Tradition: A Critical Guide to Commentary, 1660–1960* (1968) has recently been republished on the Internet Shakespeare Editions website.